# Horses

# A PRACTICAL AND
# SCIENTIFIC APPROACH

# A PRACTICAL AND SCIENTIFIC APPROACH

MELVIN BRADLEY, Ph.D.

*State Extension Horse Specialist*
*College of Agriculture*
*University of Missouri, Columbia*

## McGRAW-HILL BOOK COMPANY

*New York   St. Louis   San Francisco   Auckland   Bogotá*
*Hamburg   Johannesburg   London   Madrid   Mexico*
*Montreal   New Delhi   Panama   Paris   São Paulo*
*Singapore   Sydney   Tokyo   Toronto*

This book was set in Baskerville by Automated Composition Service, Inc.
The editors were James E. Vastyan and Carol Napier;
the designer was Joan E. O'Connor;
the production supervisor was John Mancia.
The cover illustrations were drawn by Ivan Powell.
R. R. Donnelley & Sons Company was printer and binder.

Horses: A Practical and Scientific Approach

2 3 4 5 6 7 8 9 0    DODO    8 9 8 7 6 5 4 3 2 1


Library of Congress Cataloging in Publication Data

Bradley, Melvin.
    Horses: a practical and scientific approach.

    Includes index.
    1. Horses.   I. Title.
SF285.B729        636.1        79-22553
ISBN 0-07-007065-2

# CONTENTS

# PREFACE

he horse has always played a unique role in the history of many civilizations. Yet in the United States, in this century, the horse was almost replaced by the machine during the middle decades. However, in the 1980s horses are once again very much a part of the American life style.

This book was written primarily as a college text, but it is also useful as a source book for a much broader audience. New horse owners of all ages, members of 4-H clubs, and those interested in the various aspects of horse feeding, management, shows, and judging will find this text invaluable.

Chapters 1 through 3 cover a brief history of the horse, their primary uses and economic impact, and the various breeds and their origins. Chapter 4 addresses horse judging and selection with emphasis on the relationship of form to function (of particular interest to members of 4-H and other agriculturally oriented groups).

Chapters 5 and 6 present horse and horse handler psychologies and safe handling procedures; and Chapter 7, Horsemanship, is a discussion of proper equipment and preparation for showing.

Chapters 8 through 10 cover managing horses of various ages and temperaments and controlling breeding herds; while Chapters 11 through 13 present nutritional requirements, rationing preparation and ratios, feeding considerations, basic health care, and proper foot maintenance.

Chapter 14 covers basic health care, including trade names of wormers and when to use them while Chapter 15 discusses the anatomy of the foot and a simple shoeing procedure.

Finally Chapter 16 covers zoning and legal problems, stable construction and materials, and budgeting considerations for the horse owner.

The organization of the book imitates the correct sequence of horse ownership; for example, the chapter on managing the adult, well-trained horse is followed by the chapter on how to handle the young horse, which is in turn followed by the genetics and breeding chapter. In addition, the text is heavily illustrated. In the interest of accuracy, hundreds of photographs have been included, depicting all aspects of horsemanship.

This text generally uses generic masculine pronouns to refer to individuals whose gender is not otherwise established. The author wishes to emphasize, however, that this is done solely for succinctness of expression and that such references do apply equally to men and women.

No one has all the solutions to horse problems or correct answers to all horse questions. However, if this information, gleaned from a lifetime of horse experience and academic endeavor, results in an extension of your enjoyment and enrichment in the horse experience, the objective of the book will have been realized.

*Melvin Bradley*

# A PRACTICAL AND
# SCIENTIFIC APPROACH

# THE COMEBACK
# OF THE HORSE

The horse in this country is galloping out of near-oblivion back into the limelight in dozens of individual and family activities. No longer a necessity, the horse has become a prestigious vehicle of pleasure. While television and the cinema have glamorized horse and rider without much concern for authenticity, undoubtedly they have also contributed to the horse's newfound popularity by emphasizing its recreational potential.

The affluence and greater leisure time of the populous middle class are probably the main reasons for the comeback of the horse. While horse ownership is undoubtedly still something of an economic burden for the average family, it is a burden less reluctantly shouldered by a modern affluent society which is eager to increase its recreational variety. For those who would rather "do" than watch in this day of television spectator sports, there are genuine physical advantages to the riding and care of horses. Good roads and safe means of horse transportation bring many activities within reach of the average horseowner. Horse shows, trail rides, rodeos, fox and coyote hunts, dressage shows, polo, and horse packing are found in many states. Horse auctions and vacation tour packages compete for the horse-

FIGURE 1-1   Horse activities do more to draw family members together than al-most any other activity. [*Photograph by the author.*]

man's time and money. Further, horse activities lend themselves to the participation of the entire family. They do more to draw family members together than almost any other activity (Figure 1-1).

The horse industry in the United States is a gigantic and dynamic one. It generates billions of dollars per year, employs tens of thousands, and gives pleasure to millions of horse fanciers. According to an October 1977 Gallup survey sponsored by the American Quarter Horse Association, an estimated 39 million people now own or have owned horses and another 30 million hope to become horse owners.[1]

## THE HORSE POPULATION IN THE UNITED STATES

According to the United States Department of Agriculture (USDA) statis-tics, the horse and mule population peaked in 1915 at about 25.5 million.[2] Most of these were farm and ranch horses, and those 2 or 3 million kept in cities were not included in the count. Today, horses are kept almost exclu-sively for riding, and there are more riding horses now than there were in

[1]"Gallup Survey Shows Horse Ownership Popular," *Horseman's Gazette,* March 1978, p. 19.
[2]U.S. Department of Agriculture, *Agricultural Statistics,* 1952, p. 445.

TABLE 1-1   ESTIMATED HORSE
POPULATION IN TEN LEADING STATES

| State | Population estimate |
| --- | --- |
| Texas | 624,778 |
| California | 604,000 |
| Oklahoma | 226,738 |
| Tennessee | 250,000 |
| Ohio | 205,000 |
| Kentucky* | 204,000 |
| Mississippi | 200,000 |
| Michigan | 169,000 |
| Missouri | 167,154 |
| Minnesota | 157,000 |

*Kentucky Equine Survey, Kentucky Horse
Council, Lexington, Ky. (P.O. Box 11992, Iron
Works Pike), 1978, p. 30.
SOURCE: From "Agricultural Situation," The
Crop Reporter's Magazine, USDA, July 1972.

1915. In 1976, Lloyd Davis, retired USDA Extension director, estimated
that the number of horses in the United States ranged from 8.5 to 10 million
head.[3] The American Horse Council conservatively estimates 8.5 million
head, and most authorities agree with this figure.

Texas leads the nation in the number of horses, and the American Quarter Horse leads all other breeds in popularity.[4] Table 1-1 ranks the ten states
leading in horse population; the ranking is based on 1972 USDA estimates
and a 1978 Kentucky survey.

## ECONOMIC IMPLICATIONS

Congress has been pressured by the American Horse Council and other concerned groups to fund a horse census, and is now considering legislation
that would appropriate funds for that purpose. Until completion of an official horse census, business leaders and producers can only guess at the economic impact of the vast industry from scattered data.

Basing its figures on the 1968 Spindletop Research Project, the American Horse Council estimates that $13 billion is generated annually by the
nation's horse industry.

[3]Lloyd H. Davis, Keeping a Horse in the Suburbs, The Stephen Green Press, Brattleboro, Vermont, 1976, p. 26.
[4]Jack Hopper, "The Impact of Horses on the Economy of the U.S. in 1968," Spindletop Research, Lexington, Ky. (P.O. Box 481, Iron Works Pike), 1970.

One of the greatest single sources of revenue is the vast amount of taxes collected in the thirty states permitting pari-mutuel betting. Horse racing is the nation's leading spectator sport, without a close second. In 1975, 76.5 million people attended the races and wagered $7.8 billion, from which $5.8 million was taken directly by the states in taxes.[5]

The economic impact of breeding and showing is also significant. The feed and transportation industries are directly affected by fluctuations in the horse industry. The salaries of those both directly and indirectly involved with horses, such as trainers, grooms, farriers, saddlemakers, and pari-mutuel clerks, rise with the good fortune of the horse. Less obvious, but no less important, is the economic contribution of backyard or pleasure horses, for over half the horses in the United States are pleasure horses, that is, nonracing, nonshow animals.

## Jobs, Education, and Money

The National Horse and Pony Youth Activities Council (NHPYAC) recently classified 195 jobs within the United States horse industry according to level of education required (Table 1-2) and type of job (Table 1-3). This classification is a comprehensive one, covering jobs connected with racing, showing, and pleasure-horse activities from the least-skilled position (e.g., hotwalker or jump crewman) to that of the specialist (e.g., veterinarian or geneticist).

[5]*Pari-Mutuel Racing*, National Association of State Racing Commissioners, Lexington, Ky. (P.O. Box 4216, 1736 Alexandria Drive), 1975.

TABLE 1-2   GENERAL LEVEL OF EDUCATION FOUND IN THE HORSE INDUSTRY*

| Education level | Number of positions |
|---|---|
| 1. High school or less (unskilled) | 20 |
| 2. High school or less (semiskilled) | 33 |
| 3. High school (skilled) | 41 |
| 4. One year of college | 15 |
| 5. Two years of college | 15 |
| 6. Baccalaureate degree | 44 |
| 7. Baccalaureate degree plus substantial additional training and experience | 11 |
| 8. Master's degree | 6 |
| 9. Ph.D. or professional degree | 10 |

*Entries selected from 195 possible positions.
SOURCE: NHPYAC Committee on Education and Employment, "Employment and Educational Opportunities for Youth in the Horse Industry," in *Proceedings: Second Annual Youth Horse Symposium*, University of Missouri Extension Division, 1978.

TABLE 1-3  TYPES OF JOBS IN THE HORSE
INDUSTRY*

| Type of job | Number of jobs |
| --- | --- |
| Administrative | 26 |
| Government regulatory | 13 |
| Training horses | 4 |
| Training personnel | 8 |
| Design, manufacturing | 9 |
| Research and laboratory work | 5 |
| Sales | 18 |
| Services | 112 |

*Entries selected from 195 possible positions.
SOURCE: NHPYAC Committee on Education and Employment, "Employment and Educational Opportunities for Youth in the Horse Industry," in *Proceedings: Second Annual Youth Horse Symposium*, University of Missouri Extension Division, 1978.

From about 1960 until 1976 employment within the United States horse industry grew at a phenomenal rate—more than five times the rate of the human population. Employment statistics show that there are nearly a quarter of a million full-time job equivalents in the horse industry, or about one job for every thirty-seven horses.

Table 1-4 lists the type and number of jobs in the United States horse industry and the average annual salaries for those jobs. Although salaries within the industry vary widely—sometimes by as much as a factor of 5—depending on geographic area of employment and type of activity, the figures given are representative.

## NATURE OF THE HORSE INDUSTRY

A 1976 study included the following observations of the Michigan horse industry:[6]

> This study estimates that the Michigan commercial horse industry represents $12.5 million in goods and services purchased directly by the industry in 1971. Total investment in horses and facilities for the state exceeded $275 million spread out over 450 separate places of business. . . . This research concludes that: (1) the commercial horse industry in Michigan is dominated by small, part-time, family-operated enterprises; (2) it is a relatively immature, steadily

[6]*Michigan's Commercial Horse Industry*, Agriculture Business Research Report 323, Michigan State University, December 1976, p. 2.

TABLE 1-4  NUMBER OF JOBS AND AVERAGE ANNUAL SALARY IN THE U.S. HORSE INDUSTRY*

| Position | Number of jobs (× 100) | Average salary per annum (× $100) |
|---|---|---|
| Hotwalker (1)† | 32 | 65 |
| Pony boy/girl (1) | 16 | 73 |
| Grounds maintenance (1) | 20 | 80 |
| Starter (2) | 1 | 174 |
| Rodeo cowboy (2) | 38 | 129 |
| Packer/guide (2) | 5 | 161 |
| Groom (2) | 74 | 80 |
| Trainer (3) | 29 | 159 |
| Stable manager (3) | 20 | 145 |
| Riding instructor (3) | 50 | 112 |
| Jockey (3) | 10 | 221 |
| Saddlemaker (3) | 6 | 161 |
| Veterinary assistant (3) | 22 | 98 |
| Bookkeeper (3) | 17 | 113 |
| Breeder (3) | 83 | 175 |
| Farrier (3) | 6 | 221 |
| Veterinary technician (4) | 8 | 103 |
| Transportation specialist (4) | 6 | 190 |
| Horse show manager (5) | 7 | 118 |
| Drugging inspector (5) | 2 | 170 |
| Racing steward (6) | 2 | 149 |
| Bloodstock agent (6) | 1 | 199 |
| Horse feed distributor (6) | 22 | 167 |
| Farm or ranch manager (6) | 34 | 143 |
| Racing chemist (7) | 1 | 227 |
| County agricultural agent (7) | 68 | 151 |
| College professor (agricultural science) (8) | 46 | 231 |
| Pedigree analyst (8) | 2 | 200 |
| Extension horse specialist (9) | 1 | 275 |
| Veterinarian (9) | 58 | 333 |

*Entries selected from 195 possible positions.
†Numbers in parentheses refer to general level of education attained. (See Table 1-2.)
SOURCE: NHPYAC Committee on Education and Employment, "Employment and Educational Opportunities for Youth in the Horse Industry," in *Proceedings: Second Annual Youth Horse Symposium*, University of Missouri Extension Division, 1978.

expanding industry led by sophisticated, corporate-type enterprises; (3) most enterprises offer at least three income-producing activities, the choice of which is critical to an operation's ultimate success; and (4) the industry is characterized by a relatively high investment–low return nature for most of the enterprises, especially in the smaller size class.

This characterization of the Michigan industry is a generally accurate model for the United States industry as a whole.


## PRIMARY USES

Even in Kentucky, where the number of Thoroughbreds is double its closest rival, the major use of horses is for pleasure riding.[7] Percentages by use are: pleasure, 46.1; breeding, 18.6; work, 11.8; showing, 9.8; racing, 9.6; "other," 3.5; and youth, 0.6. Georgia's horse industry differs in that more horses are used for pleasure and fewer used for racing and work.[8]

Modern uses of the horse will be examined in greater detail in Chapter 3.

[7]*Kentucky Equine Survey*, Kentucky Horse Council, Lexington, Ky. (P.O. Box 11992, Iron Works Pike), 1978, p. 30.
[8]*Georgia Horse and Pony Survey*, Georgia Department of Agriculture, 1978.

# A BRIEF HISTORY
# AND ROMANCE OF
# THE HORSE

orth America, the land where the horse originated some
50 million years ago, abounded at one time in prehistoric horses, but there
were no horses on the continent when Columbus arrived in 1492. The horse
had disappeared about 8000 years earlier, before the arrival of the native
Indians. However, it left ample evidence of its sojourn here; its fossilized
remains are well preserved in the riverbed clays and the sandy, arid regions
of the western United States. The story of the evolution of the family
Equidae[1] is, therefore, an exceptionally well-documented one, and certain
distinct physical and mental characteristics of the modern horse can be
traced back to its early ancestors.

[1]Equidae is the mammalian family comprising the single genus *Equus*, consisting of all domestic and feral horses, donkeys, zebras, and onagers.

FIGURE 2-1   Prehistoric horses were about the size of a terrier; they had four padded toes in front and three behind. Survival depended upon running and hiding. Horses still panic into flight without much consideration for the consequences of such a decision. [*Courtesy of Doug Ross, Columbia, Mo.*]

## PREHISTORY

### Eohippus

The earliest known ancestor of modern horse, *Eohippus* ("dawn horse"), was no larger than 15 inches at the withers.[2] Although *Eohippus* bears a certain resemblance to modern *Equus*, its arched back, rodentlike skull (and correspondingly tiny brain), and relatively short neck prompted its first discoverers to misclassify it (Figure 2-1).

*Eohippus* was physically different from modern *Equus* in other respects as well. Its legs—long and thin, and clearly meant for running—ended in four hoofed toes in front and three behind. The foot was raised foxlike on a small pad at the base of each toe, and so the hooves scrabbled in the dirt as grippers. The teeth were the wrong shape, and too soft, to be useful for grass eating. The teeth, as well as the short neck, indicate that *Eohippus*

[2]See Figure 4-2 for a pictorial representation of the various points of the horse discussed in this section.

fed on the succulent leaves that flourished in the subtropical climate of 60 to 40 million years B.C. Tapirlike *Eohippus*, then, was a browser, who depended on leaping and bursts of brief speed to escape from enemies—and its enemies were many and large compared with the delicate little dawn horse.

## Mesohippus

Fifteen million years or so passed, and with them *Eohippus*. *Mesohippus*, at 20 inches only slightly taller than *Eohippus*, nevertheless presented striking adaptive changes. It had only three toes on each foot. Moreover, the middle toe was the largest of the three, although all the toes still touched the ground. Its spinal column was more nearly horizontal, compared to its predecessor's highly arched one. Its legs were longer and thinner, with muscles concentrated in the upper parts, close to the body, indicating that *Mesohippus* depended on running long distances rather than merely leaping and dashing undercover to flee enemies. Within its more elongated, horselike skull resided a larger brain, which received visual stimuli from eyes placed farther apart from each other. *Mesohippus*'s neck was longer than *Eohippus*'s, but its low-ridged, soft teeth indicated that *Mesohippus* had not yet made the switch from browser to grazer.

## Merychippus

Toward the end of the Oligocene Epoch, during which *Mesohippus*, *Miohippus*, and other strains of horses developed and migrated from North America to Europe, persistent flooding occurred. Lush jungle habitats gave way gradually to grassy plains. In response to such adaptive pressure, the horse's ancestors underwent increasingly dramatic changes.

The teeth of *Merychippus* were suitable for grinding the abundant but tough grasses of the rolling plains. These new, enamel-reinforced teeth continued to grow throughout the life of the horse, and were not worn down by the abrasive action of the harsh forage.

*Merychippus* was some 35 inches tall at the withers. The withers were distinctly humped, indicating corresponding spinal column changes which finally raised the forehand higher than the quarters, as is true in the modern horse.

The legs were further modified for speed. Sacrificing sideways movement of the joint at the radius and ulna in the front of the leg and tibia and fibula behind, the successful ancestors of the modern horse evolved with high speed in one direction for escape (forward or reverse). Although *Merychippus* still possessed three toes, only the large middle toe touched the ground.

## Pliohippus

The elongation of the spine, the forward shift of the center of gravity, and the restriction of joint movement to one direction were evolutionary adaptations given increasingly successful expression in succeeding generations of horses over millions of years.

The most horselike creature of all these prehistoric ancestors was *Pliohippus*, who appeared about 7 million years ago. Often mistakenly referred to as the first monodactylic equine, *Pliohippus* still had three visible toes. However, the two smaller side toes were beginning their retreat up the leg. In modern horse, evidence of these toes is still present as the vestigial but trouble-causing splint bones on either side of the cannon bones. *Pliohippus* was about 44 inches high at the withers, the size of a small pony. *Pliohippus* and its cousins were fleet and nomadic. Possessed of great stamina, they were able to wander far from water to graze.

## Equus Caballus

Roughly 2.5 million years ago the horse appeared in pretty much its present form. Aside from a greater height (up to 53 inches at the withers) and more complicated tooth structure, *Equus caballus* was not too different from its immediate ancestors.

This era, the Pleistocene, was marked by dramatic climatic changes, with successive freezes and thaws. The horse migrated via the ever-changing land and ice bridges between continents to South America and Europe. And it met man. *Equus* was the subject of the early cave paintings. Indeed, much of the life of many tribes of man revolved around this tough but timid creature. Before man learned to control the wandering herds, he followed the horse, eating its flesh and sometimes worshipping it.

It was the horse's interaction with man, who began selective breeding and feeding for special work purposes, that ultimately produced the great differences in type, from Shetland to Shire, that we see today. Since the extinction of the tarpan horse at the end of the nineteenth century, there has been only one herd of truly wild, unmodified horse left today—*Equus przewalskii.*

For unknown reasons the horse became extinct in North and South America some 8000 years ago, although climatic changes, devastating diseases, and/or mass migrations probably played some role.

## EQUITATION HISTORY

The early history of man's attempts to tame the horse is obscure. The Chinese, Mongolians, or Scythians were probably the first to truly dominate the horse—as opposed to merely managing it in herds for food. Chinese chariots dating to 3500 B.C. have been unearthed, but it still cannot be proved which came first, breaking to drive or riding astride.

It was undoubtedly the successful use of the horse in war that led to the first serious studies of equitation. Xenophon's was one of the first written treatises, dating to the early fourth century B.C. Systematic "school" equitation seems to have been practiced by the Persians and their imitators, the Byzantines, but unfortunately no written account has survived. Federico Grisone published the first systematic account of schooling in Italy in 1550 A.D. Since that time, treatises on the schooling and handling of horses have been produced with regularity by some of the best minds of the centuries.

Books on the development of the bit and the saddle alone provide fascinating accounts of human ingenuity (and sometimes cruelty) and the seemingly infinite patience of the horse. A bibliography is offered at the end of this chapter for those wishing to acquaint themselves with some of this history in more detail.

## THE HORSE IN THE UNITED STATES

The repopulation of the New World with horses started with Columbus's voyage to the West Indies in 1493. By 1525 large horse herds had been established in the West Indies from Spanish importations. So great was the demand for the best horses of Spain that the Crown restricted their exportation.[3]

From the West Indies, horses were taken to the mainland of South America and Mexico by conquistadors, and from there they spread northwest into the Southwestern United States. Cortez used horses in the conquest of Mexico in 1519. De Soto brought 237 horses to the United States in 1539 and explored the Southeastern part of the country with them.

Many historians claim that some animals escaped from coastal shipwrecks to create the vast wild horse herds of the Southwest. However, Crowell considered this factor to be insignificant, and asserted that foundational stock was continually added from Mexico and the West Indies because these horses were better acclimated to this hemisphere than those coming directly from Europe.[4] Denhardt's comprehensive study on horses of the Americas gives no credit to de Soto's expeditions as a source of seed stock for horse herds.[5] Rather, he cites the seventy-nine missions in the southeast, established by 1650, from which English and Indian pilferage spread horses of Spanish stock northward, as the primary source. These Spanish horses were small, rather plain animals, but they represented thousands of years of crude but selective breeding.

[3]Robert M. Denhardt, *Horses of the Americas*, The University of Oklahoma Press, Norman, Okla., 1975, p. 39.
[4]Pers Crowell, *Cavalcade of American Horses*, McGraw-Hill, New York, 1951.
[5]Denhardt, op. cit., p. 193.

FIGURE 2-2 Until the turn of this century man's food supply, prestige, and in some cases his life depended upon his competence in horse handling and the speed, strength, and competence of his horse. [*Courtesy of Doug Ross, Columbia, Mo.*]

## The Horse and the Plains Indian

The most spectacular changes in behavior of the Plains Indians came in the 1600s when the tribes became mounted. They quickly developed into superb horse handlers and vastly increased their range of hunting, fishing, and food-gathering activities (Figure 2-2). Unfortunately, the new mobility also encouraged raids and tribal wars. Their hardy Indian or Mustang ponies flourished on native grass and under extreme climatic conditions, and could outdistance better-fed U.S. Cavalry mounts in almost any situation.[6]

## Work Stock

> Look back at our struggle for freedom,
> Trace our present day's strength to its source;
> And you'll find that man's pathway to glory
> Is strewn with the bones of a horse.
>
> ANON.

Work stock are the unsung heroes in the development of our country. They labored faithfully under packs and in harness day after day, often shabbily

[6]John C. Ewers, *The Horse in Blackfoot Indian Culture*, US. Government Printing Office, 1955.

FIGURE 2-3    Work stock are the unsung heroes in the development of our country. Without their contribution, conditions today would be drastically different for all of us. [*Courtesy of the University of Missouri.*]

treated and poorly fed, until mechanization replaced them (Figure 2-3). Of course, there were good teamsters wherever horses were worked, but they were in the minority.

The colorful Conestoga wagon drivers hauled freight from Philadelphia to Pittsburgh between 1750 and 1850. George Shumway describes these men as devoutly religious, heavy-drinking, and hardy individuals who fed and cared for their horses well.[7] They bred a particularly large horse to pull the huge freight wagons in four- to six-horse hitches. These men rode the near (left) wheel horse, controlling the team with voice commands and a "jerk-line"—a single line to the near horse's bit.

It is assumed that they rode the near horse to free the whip hand (the right), although they seldom touched a horse with a whip. This practice necessitated driving on the right side of the narrow roads for better visibility when meeting other vehicles or passing them. It was also a more strategic position for voice and whip when the drivers were passed by snobbish stagecoach teamsters, who sometimes had unkind remarks for lowly freighters. The practice of driving on the right side of the road was originated by these teamsters.

[7]George Shumway and Edward Durrell, *Conestoga Wagon 1750–1850*, Early American Industries and George Shumway, Pennsylvania, 1964, pp. 81, 84, 132, 152.

One teamster overtaking another mired in the mud could replace the stalled team with his own. If his team pulled the load out, the victorious teamster won the other team's coveted bells—harmonious, musical bells attached to the harness of each horse. The saying "I'll be there with bells on" originated in this friendly rivalry. Tavernkeepers sold whiskey at cost to the teamsters at the end of each day's drive. A mark was placed beside each customer's name on a slate—P for pint and Q for quart. When the carefree teamster began imbibing beyond his means (at 3 cents a pint and 5 cents a quart) it was the tavernkeeper's responsibility to remind him to watch his "Ps and Qs."

Most cigars shipped inland traveled by Conestoga wagon to water transportation at Pittsburgh—hence the name "stogie."

## Cavalry Horses

United States history is replete with glowing accounts of the horse's contribution in war. Cavalry mounts led hard lives. They suffered more from lack of food and water, perennial sore backs, and overwork than from war wounds.

Perhaps the best-known cavalry horse is Comanche, sole survivor of General George Custer's last stand at Little Bighorn River. Comanche was found suffering from multiple wounds, nursed back to health, and shipped to Fort Riley, Kansas, for retirement, where he lived to an advanced age. His mounted hide may still be seen, scars and all, at the University of Kansas at Lawrence.

There were still thousands of horses and pack mules in the employ of the U.S. Army at the beginning of World War II (Figure 2-4). The Fort Riley Cavalry Training Center in Kansas was teeming with troopers and horses soon after the declaration of war, although part of the post had converted to mechanized cavalry training prior to that time. Soon after mobilization, the decision was made to mechanize all units, abolishing horses because "mounted units are impractical under present conditions of heavy fire power."[8] In late 1942, the order came to deliver about half of the least valuable horses to a killing plant near camp and to send the others to Fort Robinson, Nebraska, for resale. Few military decisions were more controversial than this one. Many high-ranking officers, including Gen. George S. Patton, a former cavalryman, disagreed with it. Some old troopers were reported to have committed suicide at the prospect of losing their horses. In the end, however, most traded saddle, spurs, and horse equipment for a gas can and grease rag.

Nevertheless, pack animals and horse cavalry were used extensively on many fronts in World War II. Some United States mule pack units were used

[8]Major V. Dunskai, "Mounted Attack," *The Cavalry Journal*, vol. 53, no. 6, 1944, p. 50.

FIGURE 2-4    Troop C, 115th U.S. Cavalry, during field-training exercises in Oregon, 1942. They were among the last of the mounted troops to be mechanized. The era of the U.S. Horse Cavalry has passed, but its history will live on and be appreciated by each passing generation of horse lovers. [*Photograph by the author.*]

in Sicily and Italy, and a cavalry troop was recruited from members of the Third Infantry and outfitted for mounted combat.

The *Cavalry Journals of 1942–1945*, albeit a little biased, are replete with success stories of mounted units. Most glowing are those by our then-allies, the Russians. Undoubtedly, the Russians did use cavalry and tank units effectively in defending their homeland. The Russians used horses to outmaneuver infantry, and today horses can be used for the same purpose and will probably always be used in conflict under certain terrain conditions.

The best known U.S. Cavalry combat unit was probably the First Cavalry. Its troopers relinquished their horses before going to the South Pacific and Japan and performed with distinction as infantry and reconnaissance units. They were allowed the high privilege of being the first military unit to enter Tokyo, Japan. They did so to the tune of "The Old Gray Mare She Ain't What She Used to Be," played by a Marine Corps band.

## The Pony Express

Pony Express horses and their rugged riders traveled the 10 to 12 miles between way stations at top speed relaying mail from St. Joseph, Missouri, to Sacramento, California. Much of the route crossed hostile Indian territory, and not a few riders paid bounty with their scalp. Most of the horses used from Salt Lake City and farther west were native mustangs from California.

FIGURE 2-5 Working stock horses were a necessary part of the production of beef for food in the development of our nation. [*Courtesy of the University of Missouri.*]

### The Cow Pony (Figure 2-5)

With the taming of the West and the development and expansion of cattle ranching, a cow pony deluxe emerged as a result of the necessity to expedite ranch chores and to work cattle. The cow pony's contribution to the beef-production industry was enormous. It was indispensible for trailing cattle to railheads. These western stock horses have been refined, separated into breeds, and redirected to other activities, but horses with cow sense are as essential today for cattle work on some ranches as were their ancestors generations ago. Rodeo activities could not take place without them.

The cow pony, with its docile disposition, has tolerated a whole new generation of inexperienced horse people during the last three decades. The cow pony has come of age in the sport of kings, horse racing, and is gaining popularity in English jumping and dressage riding.

### Fire and Circus Horses

The heyday of fire and circus horses was at the turn of the nineteenth century. In the 1800s cities depended on men on foot and handpumps for fire fighting. A colorful and effective innovation was the horse-drawn steam-water pump, first used in San Francisco in October 1863. This steam machine was pulled—whistles screaming and bells clanging—at full gallop by three fire-horses to the scene of the fire. In the firehouse, firecrews suspended the harness with pulleys. The horses, when released from their stalls at the sound of the alarm, dashed to position beneath the harness for quick hitch-up. According to Natlee Kenyor, some crews in San Francisco could be on their way in less than 10 seconds after the alarm sounded.[9] The firehorses of fire-prone San Francisco so endeared themselves to the city's inhabitants that the horses were voted better retirement benefits than their drivers.

European horses still have many uses, but labor, transportation, and feed costs have reduced their numbers in circuses in this country. The daring performances of riders on bareback horses and high school and liberty acts enrich the memories of those lucky enough to see a live circus (Figure 2-6). In the old days, even the baggage horses, which positioned equipment in big hitches on the circus lot, drew crowds in circus parades, because many

[9]Natlee Kenyor, *The Firehorses of San Francisco*, Westernlore Press, Los Angeles, Cal., 1970, p. 15.

FIGURE 2-6    Trained horses have thrilled audiences for centuries. Mr. Rythm, trained and shown by Darrel Wallen, does more than fifty tricks and dances to the delight of his audiences. [*Courtesy of Darrel Wallen, Sedalia, Mo.; photograph by George Laur.*]

spectators were experienced drivers themselves and admired good pulling hitches.[10]

BIBLIOGRAPHY

Gianoli, Luigi: *Horses and Horsemanship through the Ages*, Crown, New York, 1969.
Herr, John K., and Maj. Gen. Edward S. Wallace: *The Story of the U.S. Cavalry, 1775–1942*, Little, Brown, Boston, 1953.
Littauer, V. S.: *Horseman's Progress*, Van Nostrand, 1961.
Trench, Charles Chevenix: *A History of Horsemanship*, Doubleday, New York, 1970.

[10]Charles Philip Fox, *A Pictorial History of Performing Horses*, Bramhall House, New York, 1960.

# Three

## BREEDS OF
## HORSES

*breed* of horses is a group of animals sharing certain distinguishing characteristics, called *breed character*, that often result from generations of selection for a specific trait. The head, ears, and other body features, as well as performance end results, are used as reference points. For example, Arabian horses are distinguished by dished faces, elevated tail carriages, and short bodies (Figure 3-1). In some breeds, the defining characteristic is almost exclusively color. The distinguishing characteristics of thoroughbreds, which were bred to run, are long legs, lean bodies, and great competitive spirit. They inevitably outrun Percherons, with their typically short legs, thick bodies, and docile dispositions.

The purity of a breed is the responsibility of the Horse Registry Association. The Registry records individuals born into each breed and keeps records of the ancestry, or *bloodlines*, of its members. Obviously, purity or records of ancestry extend further back in old breeds than new ones, and some breed registries place more emphasis on ancestry than others. Thoroughbreds have extended pedigrees of recorded, unmixed ancestry for hundreds

FIGURE 3-1 The blood of the majestic Arabian flows through the veins of all domestic light horse breeds. The horse shown is Donna Fernava, owned by P. A. Norris, Fort Worth, Texas. [*The International Arabian Horse Association, Photograph by Johnny Johnston.*]

of years. A Quarter Horse with one Thoroughbred parent may be registered as a Quarter Horse.

Regardless of recorded ancestry, there are good horses both in pure breeds and in *grade horses*, which are unregistered horses, usually of mixed parentage, and which outnumber purebreds.

## Specific Breed for Specific Function

Most horsemen confine their activities to one breed. Some may be so prejudiced against other breeds that the mere mention of another breed "turns them off." Breed associations turn this bias to advantage by diversifying show classes and activities, and then claiming that their breed "does it all." Larger breeds do have some ability to diversify, but none in fact does it all.

Versatile individuals may be found in most breeds, but most breeders stress *specialization* in their breeding programs. For example, concentration on speed over generations in a breed is probably not conducive to producing a high percentage of "all-around" horses. Conversely, if speed is required, the probability of getting it is greater if individuals are selected from a breed noted for speed. If the purposes for which a horse will be used are known before purchase, selectivity by breed, as well as by individual, can be exercised.

## A Breed for Every Need

Breeds were created out of necessity, usually for a more or less specific purpose, resulting in the development of horses with differing conformation, disposition, and other characteristics. A combination family riding-and-driving horse and a yoke of oxen (later replaced by draft horses) fulfilled the needs of most Americans very well during the early development of the United States. Then, as roads and streets were built in and around cities, coach horses from Europe were imported and bred in large numbers. Soon a need arose for horses to help with ranching and cattle work, and the western stock horse was born. Gaited horses were developed to negotiate trails between villages and trading posts, and for use on plantations.

## WESTERN STOCK HORSES

Stock horses have cow sense that is bred in: they are born to watch, follow, head, cut out, and drive cattle. Such work requires bursts of speed, quick turns, hard stops, and quiet dispositions (Figure 3-2). Centuries of breeding under ranch conditions fixed these traits in western stock horses through careful selection of those animals that performed the best. Although old in vintage, western types have only recently been registered; the oldest stock horse breed association was founded in 1938. At that time, performance was used as the criterion for propagation, and some outstanding families emerged even before registration programs were initiated (see *Quarter Horse*).

Stock horses have good canters, or lopes. They can canter slowly in good rhythm and balance without undue stress on either themselves or their riders. However, by gaited horse standards they walk slowly and trot or jog joltingly. Because of their role in working cattle, stock horses are the only type of horse that is really economically essential in this mechanized era. There has always been a special appreciation for those horses that could run fast for short distances in matched races, and much of the emphasis of stock horse breeders today is directed toward developing speed. The stockhorse's great burst of speed upon leaving a starting gate allows it to dominate short-distance (quarter-mile) racing.

Two or three decades ago a good disposition was a major characteristic of the western stock horse. Indeed, many fledgling riders are eternally indebted to the old-fashioned Quarter Horse for tolerating them during their learning years. Recently, however, the great infusion of Thoroughbred blood into stock horse breeding lines has produced a more hot-blooded disposition.

While a number of breeds participate effectively in stock horse activi-

**FIGURE 3-2**   Western stock horses have bred-in cow sense. Their work requires quick turns, hard stops, bursts of speed, and totally obedient dispositions. Pictured is Crickets Dollye, 1976 Honor Roll Champion Cutting Horse, owned by L. M. Pearce, Jr., Houston, and trained by Sonny Rice. [*The American Quarter Horse Association, photograph by Dalco.*]

ties, only those whose associations claim this activity as their major purpose are discussed here—the Appaloosa, Dun, Buckskin, and Grulla, Paint, and Quarter Horse. (These versatile stock horses, however, are often used for other purposes; these will be covered briefly in this chapter.)

## Appaloosa

ORIGINS   Horses of Appaloosa color patterns are found in French cave drawings believed to predate 500 B.C. Spotted horses, which appear in the Chinese art of 400 to 500 B.C., were revered as the "heavenly horses of Emperor Wu Ti."

An Appaloosa-colored stallion of unknown breeding sired the good mare Bay Bloody Buttocks in 1729 in England. Man O'War the famous American Thoroughbred racehorse, distantly traces to that stallion through this mare.

Historians believe that Appaloosa-colored horses were imported to Mexico from the Near East or Spain at the beginning of the seventeenth century. As the horses spread northward, the Nez Percé tribe, in the territory of Idaho, Oregon, and along the Palouse River in Washington, acquired them about 1750. During the following hundred-odd years the Nez Percé developed them into a distinct type by trading inferior horses to other tribes and castrating undesirable stallions.

Racing, war, and hunting were the main pursuits of this tribe. Races from a few hundred yards to 12 to 15 miles identified horses with speed. Buffalo hunts of long duration identified horses with stamina and good disposition. War identified horses with speed, stamina, and maneuverability over rough terrain. The rigid culling program gave the Indians good results in the development of these desirable traits.

The Nez Percé were said to be the best-mounted of all the tribes. During the Nez Percé War, Chief Joseph made a daring 1350-mile dash to Canada over some of the roughest terrain, outdistancing five U.S. army units while transporting women, children, and belongings. With the decline of the Nez Percé, the breakup of their herd, and the settling of the area by homesteaders, draft blood was introduced into many bands of Appaloosas. Their numbers declined sharply until the last four decades. Appaloosas now rank fifth in popularity in the United States.

CHARACTERISTICS   Appaloosa color patterns include:

1  Blanket pattern—darker body with white, often spotted blanket over croup and hindquarters (Figure 3-3).
2  Leopard—diamond, squaw, or teardrop spots, varying from mere specks to 4 inches in size, splashed over entire white body (Figure 3-4).
3  Frost—white hairs intermingled in dark coat, especially over croup.

These body color patterns may have many variations. However, all Appaloosas *must* possess the following additional characteristics: the iris of Appaloosa eyes must be encircled in white, like the human iris; the hooves must be vertically striped in alternating black and white; the skin itself must be mottled in black and white, especially around the muzzle. The mane and tail of the Appaloosa are unusually thin.

Generally, the Appaloosa should present a compact, functional appearance, ranging from no smaller than 14 hands to 15-3 hands in size.[1] Muscling should be adequate, but not as extreme as the stock Quarter Horse's. Excessive evidence of draft blood, shown usually in head, neck, and rump

---

[1] A hand is equal to 4 inches. Height is expressed in hands and inches; i.e., 15-3 is fifteen hands, three inches. The horse is measured from withers to ground.

FIGURE 3-3 Malibu Apache Joe, blanket-colored, high-point colt at fair in Pomona, California, owned by B. Buritus. [*The Appaloosa Horse Club, Inc., photograph by Gail Bliss.*]

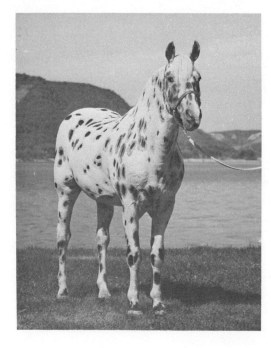

FIGURE 3-4 Money Creek's Rockledge, leopard-colored Appaloosa stallion owned by Money Creek Ranch, Houston. [*The Appaloosa Horse Club, Inc., photograph by Alf.*]

area, is reason for refusal of registry. Nevertheless, variation in type is not uncommon because of the youth of the registration association, and achieving a specific color pattern from a mating is still uncertain. However, recent infusion of Quarter Horse and Arabian blood has improved conformation and quality in many Appaloosa lines.

FUNCTIONS    Although the modern Appaloosa is adapted to a variety of tasks, it is best classified as a western stock horse. Because of its stamina, it has excelled in open endurance rides of 50 to 100 miles. Its feet are tough and its legs straight and sound, and yet it has sufficient speed to do reasonably well in short-distance racing. Some ranchers in rough country have given the Appaloosa preference over all other breeds as stock horses. Because of its unusual coloration, the Appaloosa is frequently seen in parades.

THE REGISTRY    The Appaloosa Horse Club was organized in 1938, with Claude Thompson elected president. It barely survived World War II. In 1946, only sixty-five horses qualified for registration. In 1956, there were 666 new Appaloosas registered; in 1966, 12,700. By 1976 over 200,000 Appaloosas had been registered (in total), 20,000 of these in 1976 alone.

The association has over 225 active regional clubs that sponsor activities and support the national association. The club has a well-balanced activity program based on halter and performance, showing, racing, and distance riding.

## Dun, Buckskin, and Grulla

ORIGINS    Dun, Buckskin, and Grulla horses represent a colorbreed which, because of its advantages in sun reflection and heat tolerance, has adapted well to the work of the stock horse (Figure 3-5). Dun and buckskin colors appear naturally in many breeds due to various inheritance (dilution) factors; however most breeds forbid registration of foals with these colors.[2]

Not all inheritance factors producing buckskin color will breed true— that is, they will not consistently produce buckskin-colored horses, which, when bred together, also produce buckskins. The Dun and Buckskin Registry traces a 700-year history of the colors to apparently true-breeding Spanish and Norwegian stock. By the early 1600s these animals were being crossed with Arab stock—as was happening to many other breeds at this time—for the characteristic refinement and soundness of the Arabs' horses.

CHARACTERISTICS    *Dun* is a yellowish-gray shade of black, bay, and brown. The brown dun is responsible for the creamier, lighter yellow tints usually

[2]The following explanation of dun and buckskin inheritance is adapted from Hetty M-S. Abeles, "A Coat of Many Colors," *Equus*, vol. 17, pp. 37-38.

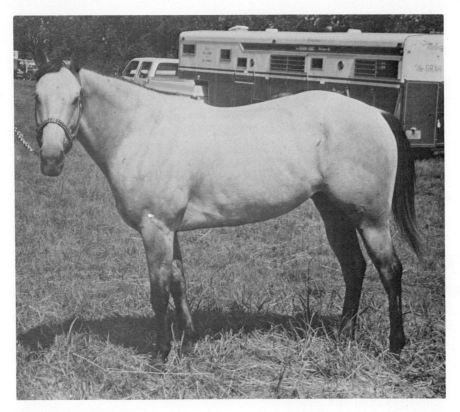

FIGURE 3-5 Buckskin and Dun horses are of the stock horse type. [*Photograph by the author.*]

called plain dun. The black dun is usually called *grulla*, *mouse*, or *blue dun*, the overriding bluish tint being very distinctive. The bay dun, ranging in tint from gold to brownish cream, is called *buckskin*. There is also a *red dun*, ranging in tint from reddish yellow to flesh color. All varieties of Dun horses also exhibit black *points*—mane, tail, and legs—except the red Dun, whose points are red. Inherited independently of basic coat color is the prized *dorsal stripe* (also called *dorsal list*, *eel stripe*, or *lineback*), which is a line of darker color running along the spine to the tail. While the Buckskin is not required to show a dorsal stripe to be eligible for registration, the grulla, red dun, and lighter dun tints must have one. Some Dun and Buckskin horses may also exhibit *leg barring* with a darker color and *shoulder striping*, which is an irregular patch of darker color running from the withers forward and down for a distance along the shoulder. White markings are allowed on all varieties on the face and lower legs up to the knees and hocks, but never on the body.

Constant crossbreeding with grade cow ponies and with the Quarter Horse has produced the stock-horse type of Buckskin and Dun, a handy-sized (up to about 15-2 hands) horse of pleasing appearance.

FUNCTION   Buckskin and Dun horses have been popular for years in the range country for their endurance, stamina, disposition, soundness, and cow sense. They are very much in demand under rugged ranching conditions, for example, in Argentina.

THE REGISTRY   The American Buckskin Registry Association (organized in 1947 as the Dun and Buckskin Registry) and the International Buckskin Horse Association are very active in the study, selection, and registration of these specially colored horses. Both organizations contribute to research to establish sound genetic laws for the production of better, true-breeding Dun, Buckskin, and Grulla horses.

## Paint Horses

ORIGINS   The appearance of spotted horses predates recorded history; such horses are pictured even in cave paintings. The word "Pinto" derives from a Spanish root meaning painted or spotted, and therefore those terms are sometimes interchangeable. However, the establishment of three different registries for the Pinto horse in the United States leads to practical distinctions based on lineage and avowed end purpose.

The American Paint Horse Association (APHA) registers only horses sired by a stallion registered in the APHA, the American Quarter Horse Association, or the Jockey Club (Thoroughbred). Appaloosa-colored or Appaloosa-bred horses, ponies, and draft types are *not* eligible. The main purpose of the APHA is to develop spotted horses of the *stock horse type*.

CHARACTERISTICS   The British use two words to describe spotted horses: *piebald*, which is a black horse having white spots, and *skewbald*, which is a horse with white spots on a field of any color other than black.

There are two basic spotting patterns in Paints and Pinto horses, *overo* and *tobiano*. (Extreme variations of these two patterns as well as "cropouts" make their classification difficult.) The terms "overo" and "tobiano" refer to type and location of markings on the horse's body.

Generally speaking, the white areas of the overo originate on the underside of the horse and appear to have been splashed upward in an irregular pattern (Figure 3-6). White seldom crosses the back, and the head is almost always splashed with a bald, aproned, or blazed face. In contrast, the tobiano's white coloring starts on the back and spreads downward with a white area extending over the withers. Many tobianos have dark heads and

FIGURE 3-6 Yellow Mount, winner at halter, performance, and racing, and the first American Paint Horse Champion. The dun overo stallion is owned by Mr. and Mrs. Stanley Williamson, Iowa Park, Texas. [*Photograph courtesy of the owner.*]

necks and white front legs below the knees (Figure 3-7). These complex color patterns are explained in detail and well illustrated by Haynes and Green.[3,4]

Genetically speaking, the tobiano gene seems dominant. The ratio of foals registered each year is about four tobianos to one overo. When two excessively white overos are bred together, they may produce a foal with little body pigment and atresia coli (blockage of the colon), which can result in death if surgery is not performed.[5] The problem is easily avoided by not breeding such overos together.

The American Paint Horse Association places its emphasis on a stock

[3]Glynn W. Haynes, *The American Paint Horse*, University of Oklahoma Press, Norman, Okla., 1976, p. 70.
[4]Roxanne D. Green, *Breeding Pinto Horses*, Animals for Education, Pinto Horse Association of America, Inc., San Diego, Ca. (910 W. Washington Ave.), 1973, pp. 9-95.
[5]William E. Jones and Ralph Bogart, *Genetics of the Horse*, Caballus Publishers, East Lansing, Mich., p. 26.

FIGURE 3-7 Cherokee   War Chief, Supreme Champion No. 8. Good stock horse conformation characterizes this tobiano stallion. [*The American Paint Horse Association.*]

horse type similar to the Quarter Horse (see *Quarter Horse*). Horses must stand at least 14 hands high, and those ranging up to a convenient 15-2 hands are preferred. Stallions weigh 1100 to 1200 pounds; mares and geldings are somewhat lighter. A sturdy individual of adequate bone and muscle is desired, with attractive markings. Other paint horse characteristics are glass, blue, or watch eyes and a two-colored mane (and sometimes tail).

FUNCTION   Cowboys and ranchers have held Paint horses in high esteem for decades. Paints were represented in most remudas and brood mare bands for general ranch use, with color receiving secondary emphasis. Will Rogers, horseman and roper supreme, was fond of Paint horses. One of his best polo ponies was a Paint, and he used them extensively for his children.

Painted Joe outran some of the fastest horses in short races a few years ago and Little Nip, a small Paint mare from Texas, became famous racing at 220 yards in the 1940s.

Present demand is largely for a working stock horse for ranch, rodeo, show, race, and parade.

THE REGISTRY   With the advent of registration associations for other western breeds, especially the Quarter Horse, many spotted horses found themselves without a home. The extensive drought of the 1950s in the range country necessitated a drastic reduction in the number of horses, and registered horses received preference. However, the rigid culling of unregistered horses may have ultimately improved the spotted horse, for in many cases only the best ones survived.

A group of interested Paint horse owners met in Texas in 1962 to form an association of Paints "of the stock horse type." In 1965 the American Paint Stock Horse Association and the American Paint Quarter Horse Association merged into a new organization called the American Paint Horse Association. In 1967, 2170 horses were registered. In recent years there has been a 25 percent increase in registration. Racing is well underway, and new efforts in publicity and education, and a well-rounded activities program, have renewed interest in Paint horses.

## Quarter Horse

ORIGINS   It is remarkable that a type so well-established and valued as the Quarter Horse could develop for nearly 300 years without the formation of a breed registry. It is for this reason that much of the early history of the breed is cloudy.

Quarter Horse types have been present in the United States since colonial days. Match racing at short distances—usually a quarter mile—was popular in sparsely settled Virginia and North Carolina. Most probably these horses represented a mixture of the Arab, Barb, and Turk lines, brought to North America by the Spanish, with English coldbloods. Soon, however, the appearance of the Thoroughbred, with its great stamina and speed over longer distances, coupled with the clearing of more stretches of land, popularized distance racing and steeplechasing. The quarter-running horse then began to move westward with the new pioneers. In the West, the early Quarter Horse types lent themselves well to ranch work.

Most Quarter Horse foundation sire lines trace to Janus, an English Thoroughbred imported to Virginia in 1752. Although this grandson of Godolphin Barb (see the section on Thoroughbreds, below) himself won races of 4-mile heats, he was outstanding as a sire of speedy quarter-mile sprinters. Little Janus, so-called because of his small 14-hand, ¾-inch stature, also sired many exceptional Thoroughbreds, and lived until the advanced age of thirty-four. In the last 40 years, Quarter Horse breeders have again returned to Thoroughbred blood in their search for increased speed and stamina (Figure 3-8).

Early western Quarter Horses, still without organization or registration, were nevertheless so "typey" that breeding "families" arose from certain prepotent sires. In 1846, Steeldust was sent to stud in Texas as a 3-year-old. This horse stamped his get so strongly that for nearly a century all Quarter Horse types were called "steeldusts." Similarly, other spontaneous family lines arose from Copper Bottom, the favorite horse of San Houston, and Old Shiloh.

The most famous Quarter Horse sire was Peter McCue, foaled in 1895, whose influence on the tail-male of Quarter Horses registered before 1948 was without parallel. His grandson, Old Sorrel (foaled in 1915) became the foundation sire of the King Ranch Quarter Horses, and a rigid linebreeding program was based on this blood.

Traveler, foaled in 1889, was also a distinguished sire, though less influential than Peter McCue. When a 2-year-old, Traveler was shipped by rail

FIGURE 3-8   The immortal Three Bars, first of the Thoroughbred stallions to greatly increase speed in running Quarter Horses. He was leading sire of racing Quarter Horses from 1949 to 1968. [*The American Quarter Horse Association.*]

to Texas with a load of work stock for use in road building. The value of this horse was recognized by a breeder who rescued him from working on a slip scraper with a mule.

A revival of interest in racing has led to a great infusion of Thoroughbred blood. The Thoroughbred, Three Bars, was the leading racing sire of running Quarter Horses from 1949 to 1968. Go Man Go, whose progeny have won over $5.5 million, is the Quarter Horse son of the Thoroughbred, Top Deck.

CHARACTERISTICS    The Quarter Horse is most notable for heavy muscling in the hindquarters (Figure 3-9). The impression given by its muscling and heavy frame is one of strength and ruggedness. The head is short and wide between the eyes, with a prominent jaw, small muzzle, firm mouth, and short ears. The cannon bones are short, the knees and hocks low-set, the legs set squarely under the corners of the body. The chest is deep and broad, the back short, the quarters broad, deep, heavy, and well-muscled. (Somewhat longer, smoother muscling is becoming preferred over the formerly characteristic bunchy muscles.) The feet are small and tough-textured, but are well-formed at the heel. The heavy muscling and rather short legs dictate a low, short stride at the walk, a lively jog, and a tremendous burst of speed into the gallop from a standstill. The stock-type Quarter Horse ranges from 14-2 to 15-1 hands at 1100 to 1300 pounds.

FIGURE 3-9   Snippers   Sarah, 1976 AJQHA World Champion Aged Mare and Honor Role Halter Horse, owned and shown by Chris Marting, Britt, Iowa. This great show mare accumulated 561 halter and western pleasure points in her career. [*Courtesy of Chris Marting.*]

Years of show ring selection for small feet, coupled with an increasingly heavy body, led many Quarter Horses to a predisposition to navicular disease.[6] A heavy horse working vigorously on hard surfaces is likely to develop this condition, because there simply is not enough surface area to dissipate the concussion generated by such a weight-surface ratio.

Selection for the racing-type Quarter Horse, with its high percentage of Thoroughbred blood, has led to more height at the withers, greater length of leg, increased foot size, and longer muscling. Today, many racing Quarter Horses are nearly indistinguishable physically from the Thoroughbred. Racing heights are 15 to 16 hands, weights up to 1300 pounds.

Any color without spots is registerable.

FUNCTION   Quarter Horse numbers lead all other breeds without a close second. The Quarter Horse virtually dominates the fields of cattle work, short racing, rodeo, and western pleasure riding. Recently the Quarter Horse has been used increasingly as a hunter-jumper. Its good disposition and ability to thrive without pampering has put it in the forefront in growth of breeds.

THE REGISTRY   The American Quarter Horse Association (AQHA) was formally organized in 1940; Bob Denhardt was elected secretary. It set about registering horses by having an inspector evaluate the breeding and conformation of each horse. "Doing" ability, as well as attractiveness, was stressed. Sixty thousand Quarter Horses were registered in 1967. That number had increased to almost 100,000 in 1976 alone. A total of over 2 million horses are expected to be registered by the association by 1980. Presently the registry is partially closed; that is, only purebred Quarter Horses and Thoroughbred-Quarter Horse crosses are admitted.

The entire horse industry has benefited from the imaginative leadership, innovative programs, and research support the AQHA has fostered. It is second only to the United States government in horse research funding and second to none in programs offered to membership.

## BREEDS USED FOR SPEED AND SPORT

The difference between horses used for sport and horses used for other purposes is speed—speed at the gallop, trot, or pace or speed of reflexes and execution of movement in turns, stops, rollbacks, and bends. Speed elevated the horse from the role of food to the role of servant in prehistoric man's life. If it has speed, the horse is given a good life.

[6]An inflammation of the surfaces of the navicular bone and the deep flexor tendon (see Chapter 14).

The Greeks had developed chariot racing to a high degree by 1200 years B.C., and they devoted the entire island of Chios to it.

Racing horses without chariots was a later development. Although horse races were an important part of the first Olympic games in 776 B.C., credit must be given to the nobility of England for developing racing as a popular sport. Henry II promoted the Smithfield races in the twelfth century, and soon racing had England firmly in its grip.

Henry VIII required his dukes and archbishops to keep seven racehorses, each over 14 hands high. He caused a furor in England by having smaller horses killed.

Horses from the East streamed into England from 1649 to 1685 during the reigns of James I and his son, Charles I, who was titled "father of the turf" because of his intense promotion and breeding programs. Because of the support they received from the nobility, Thoroughbreds acquired the nickname "blood horses."

Trotting and pacing races were widely popular in America because of a need for transportation and a desire to make an impression with a fast horse. At the turn of the century "drag" strips were common in New England and on the east side of Manhattan, where young men of wealthy families met to establish their reputations in harness racing.

The classic sport breeds are Thoroughbreds, used for distance and steeplechase racing, Quarter Horses used for short-distance racing, and Standardbreds used for trotting and pacing races. But the popularity of racing and the economic benefits associated with it are attracting many other breeds. Purses for Appaloosas, Paints, and Arabs racing at short distances have greatly increased.

The Thoroughbred excels at distance racing, hunting, polo, and jumping. Its great courage, competitive energy, and inbred speed make it well suited for these activities. The Thoroughbred of today differs little from its ancestors of a century ago except that it has more speed at sprint distances of approximately 1 mile and is seldom required to show its stamina over distances of 4 or more miles.

Western horses dominate quarter-mile racing and the sport of rodeo, with the Quarter Horse leading the way. The Quarter Horse explodes from the starting gate and burns down the short track to the finish line when racing.

The Standardbred is valued almost exclusively for speed on a mile racetrack at the trot or pace. It replaced Morgans in harness racing at the turn of the century. Stamina is the trademark of this breed. A Standardbred might trot or pace a mile track eight to twelve times while preparing for a day's race, and then compete in up to four heats in the race, to determine the winner of the two fastest heats.

Competitive racehorses command enormous prices and have seemingly unlimited earning potential. Stallions are often syndicated for millions of dollars, stock being sold to people with high hopes for the horses' breeding potential. Racing indeed is a "sport of kings"; it requires great skill and knowledge for success in breeding, training, and campaigning on the racing circuit.

### The Standardbred

ORIGINS   No breed of horse is more typically American than the Standardbred. Its bone and fiber were cast in the mold of necessity in our young country. It was the "motor" of most of the business and pleasure vehicles of its day. The meek, as well as those made bold from wealth, thrilled to this fast-stepper.

It was only natural that its services, so necessary in commerce, would be enlisted in an activity as unnecessary but as compelling as racing (Figure 3-10).

So popular was the Standardbred and so serious were the breeders about producing ever-faster horses that by 1871 a registry system based on performance developed. Horses that could trot or pace (see Chapter 4) the mile within a set or "standard" time were registered as Standardbreds. The competitive nature of this registry led to an influx of a great variety of bloodlines in the establishment of a strong trot-and-pace gene pool: Morgan, Barb, Thoroughbred, Norfolk Trotter, and Narragansett pacer lines all contributed to the making of the Standardbred.

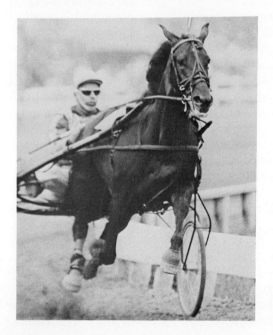

FIGURE 3-10   Nevele Pride, former world's fastest trotter on a mile track (1:54 4/5), soars through the air in the able hands of his driver, Stanley Dancer. He won 57 races in 67 starts and established 16 world records. Diagonal legs (right front–left rear) are paired in the trot. [*The United States Trotting Association.*]

Influential in the establishment of the breed was the gray Thorough-bred Messenger, a running horse imported from England in 1788. His great-grandson Hambletonian (in whose pedigree Messenger appears three times) is regarded as the true foundation sire. An exceptionally prepotent and successful sire, Hambletonian covered thousands of mares in his time at stud, establishing four separate families of harness horses, two trotting and two pacing. The "derby" of harness racing, the Hambletonian, is named in honor of this stallion; it is now held at DuQuoin, Illinois.

Early races were under saddle, usually between Narragansett pacers—the type ridden by Paul Revere on his famous midnight ride. Harness races were launched in an official capacity on a regulation course on Long Island, New York in 1823. The New York Trotting Club was organized in 1826 and immediately opened a second racetrack on Long Island where harness racing was introduced to large crowds as a fill-in between running races.

Morgan horses often carried the day. Races ranged from 4 to 16 miles, with varying heats. (Earlier races were much longer, with establishment of the 30-mile record of 2 hours, 10 minutes in 1793.)

As speeds at the mile increased, a standard of 2 minutes, 30 seconds (2:30) for trotters and 2:25 for pacers was first established as a requirement for registration in the National Association of Trotting Horses.

Standard speeds were made to be broken. Dan Patch, a brown stallion foaled in 1896, paced a mile in 1:55¼ at Lexington, Kentucky, in 1905 (Figure 3-11). He was a widely traveled and greatly admired horse in his day, performing before audiences exceeding 100,000 people—quite a tribute to his greatness given the traveling conditions of the day. Greyhound, a big, gawky gelding foaled in 1932, was sold at auction when a yearling for $900 and later established five trotting records. Billy Direct, foaled in 1934, set the world pacing record of 1:55 on Sept. 28, 1938, the day before Greyhound established his trotting record of 1:55¼.

Some families tend to produce pacers and others, trotters, although both types may be equally distributed within a family. Few individuals both pace and trot. However, Calumet Evelyn, half sister to Greyhound, trotted a mile in 1:59½ and paced the distance in 1:59¼, and Steamin' Demon paced the mile in 1:58⅘ and trotted it in 1:59¼ a week later.

Since the long reigns of Greyhound and Billy Direct, trotting and pacing records have been felled with increasing frequency. Nevele Pride is current holder of the mile trotting record of 1:544/5, and Steady Star holds the pacing record of 1:50 flat.

CHARACTERISTICS    A stopwatch is the major criterion for selection of Standardbreds. If the horse has speed it will be selected for breeding; if not, it will be passed up because of the great expense of breeding, training, and racing.

Standardbreds tend to be shorter-legged and longer in body than Thoroughbreds, with heights ranging from 15 to 16-2 hands and weights from

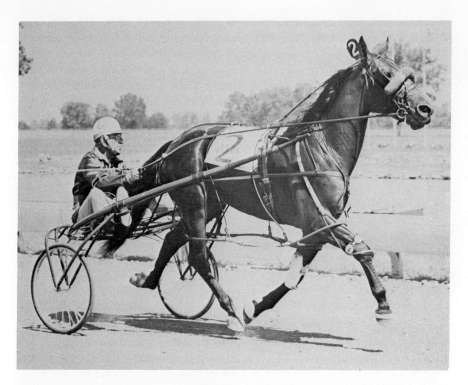

**FIGURE 3-11**    Bret Hanover (1:53 3/5), former world champion harness horse of the 1960's, paces in good form for his driver, Frank Ervin. The pace is a lateral gait with both legs on the same side moving forward and backward together. [*The United States Trotting Association.*]

850 to 1200 pounds. The neck is medium in length; throat and head are less refined than in the Thoroughbred. The hindquarters are powerful, with long, smooth muscling.

The Standardbred is unparalleled in racing endurance. Soundness is important because of stress from racing at young ages. The stride is low and very long, and appears effortless. Shoeing the Standardbred has become almost an art form, because under the stress of racing in extended strides the breed is afflicted with many and serious interferences (see Chapter 15).

Bay is the most common color, but chestnut, brown, black, and gray are also seen.

FUNCTION    Unlike Thoroughbreds, Standardbreds that do not race well or are not of adequate conformation to show as roadsters in society shows do not find a ready market. Some are used by certain religious groups, but not very many. Promising racing prospects or well-bred broodmare prospects sell quite well. Night racing, legalized betting, and the recent development of the mobilized starting gate have given the breed a boost.

THE REGISTRY    For many years the U.S. Trotting Association permitted the registry of horses whose pacing or trotting performance fell within the set standard. Today, however, the stud book is essentially closed to all except the offspring of already registered animals. Over 10,000 foals have been registered each year since 1973.

## Thoroughbred

ORIGINS    Thoroughbreds have been bred exclusively for stamina and speed at the gallop for hundreds of years.

Their bloodlines have been judiciously guarded by the English *General Stud Book* since 1791, and *The American Stud Book* since 1873.

Three stallions were the founding sires of the breed. Godolphin Barb was foaled in Barbary in about 1724 and entered England through France, where he was presented to Lord Godolphin. Byerly Turk was brought to England in about 1689. Darley Arabian, purchased in Syria, was imported to England in 1706. Bred to English cold-blooded mares, these three stallions stamped their get with speed, refinement, and uniformity. Three outstanding stallions established three male lines of descent through which almost all Thoroughbreds trace: Herod (Byerly Turk), foaled in 1758; Matchem (Godolphin Barb), 1748; and Eclipse (Darley Arabian), 1764. Eclipse was the greatest racehorse of his time, and close to 90 percent of all Thoroughbreds trace to this champion.

Unlike any other breed, Thoroughbreds continue to be cosmopolitan; the good ones, stallions as well as mares, move freely from one country to another for both breeding and racing purposes. England and the United States continue to exercise dominance in Thoroughbred bloodlines, with Italy not far behind, followed by Ireland and France.

The major countries have developed a system of classic races for the selection of outstanding individuals. In England, there is the classic series for 3-year-olds: the Derby (1½ miles); the Oaks (1½ miles), the St. Leger (1¾ miles), the 1000-Guineas (fillies only, 1 mile); and the 2000-Guineas (1 mile). In the United States there is the Triple Crown for 3-year-olds: the Kentucky Derby (1¼ mile); the Preakness (1³⁄₁₆ mile); and the Belmont (1½ miles), followed by the classic distance stakes races for 3-year-olds and upward such as the Woodward, the Marlboro Cup, and the Jockey Club Gold Cup. The Prix de l'Arc de Triomphe (1½ miles), held in France, is the supreme European championship test.

The first Thoroughbred—Bulle Rock, sired in England by Darley Arabian—was brought to America in 1730. But it was Diomed, imported from England in 1799, who established the premier male line in America comprising such outstanding individuals as Sir Archie, Henry, and Boston. Diomed was, interestingly, also the first winner of the English Derby in 1780.

Lexington, a son of Boston, was foaled in 1853; he headed the list of Thoroughbred sires for 16 (nonconsecutive) years, and was also instrumental in founding the American Saddle Horse and Standardbred breeds. The illustrious Man O'War was descended from Lexington.

Man O'War (1917-1947), the greatest American Thoroughbred of his time, won twenty of the twenty-one races he ran and established numerous track records. Man O'War exerted great influence on subsequent generations of Thoroughbreds.

French imports—Sir Gallahad III, sire of Triple Crown winner Gallant Fox, and Bull Dog, sire of Bull Lea, exerted great influence on twentieth-century American breeding. But the influence of the Italian sire Nearco is unparalleled. Nearco's son, Nasrullah, was imported to the United States from England, and was leading sire five times. Nasrullah's son, Bold Ruler (1954-1969), may well prove to be the premier American Thoroughbred sire. Bold Ruler was leading sire for seven consecutive seasons, an unsurpassed feat. Ranked by lifetime cumulative average earnings of progeny, he was still leading sire through 1977—eight years after his death! Among Bold Ruler's last crop was Secretariat, first Triple Crown winner in 25 years.

CHARACTERISTICS   Thoroughbreds represent the supreme speed type. Their appearance is one of strength and refinement. The skin is thin and shows many veins. The head is very refined, with fine, expressive eyes, small, active ears, and clean muzzles. The throatlatch (the attachment of head to neck) is well defined; the neck itself is usually long and slender. Shoulders are long and sloping, and the arm is upright to facilitate extreme extension of stride (Figure 3-12). The forearm and gaskin are long, the cannon bones short. The withers are high and well shaped. The ribcage is deep and well sprung. The croup is long, the back relatively short, and the length from hip to hock long—all factors tending to increase the power of the hind legs to come up under the horse and drive. Feet are usually proportionate to the horse's size and weight. Thoroughbreds tend to be tall, usually ranging from 15 to 17 hands or more, and weigh 1000 to 1300 pounds. The Jockey Club carefully records the colors and markings of all Thoroughbred foals. Registerable colors are black, brown, bay, chestnut, gray, and roan (the latter being defined as a nonblack gray).

The stride of the Thoroughbred at all natural gaits is characteristically low, smooth, and ground-covering. Thoroughbreds tend to be more sensitive to stimuli than other breeds.

FUNCTION   Although bred to race, Thoroughbreds have distinguished themselves in other areas. The Thoroughbred is second only to the Arab in

FIGURE 3-12 Secretariat, Triple Crown winner in 1973, widens his lead to 31 lengths in the Belmont Stakes in setting a track record of 2:24 in the 1½-mile race. He was bred by Meadow Stables of Virginia, and is now syndicated. [*The New York Racing Association, photograph by Bob Coglianese.*]

influencing the development of other breeds with which it is crossed to gain speed and staying qualities.

Hunters, jumpers, steeplechasers, and cross-country horses are usually Thoroughbreds. Great Heart established the record high jump of 8 feet $^{13}/_{16}$ inches in 1923. The U.S. Olympic Equestrian teams rely on Thoroughbreds and Thoroughbred crosses to achieve their great successes.

The U.S. Remount Service made services of Thoroughbred stallions available for public use for years and used the get of these sires for military purposes, both under saddle and on light field artillery.

Many Thoroughbred stallions have been used by ranchers to improve ranch horses for use as stock horses.

The modern Thoroughbred, of course, is basically bred to run. If it runs well, it is difficult to overprice its worth for racing or for stud. If the Thoroughbred does not run well, its value is somewhat reduced, but there is nevertheless a steady demand for Thoroughbred horses for other competitive and pleasure purposes.

THE REGISTRY The first volumes of *The American Stud Book* were published in 1873. The Jockey Club took over this registry in 1894, and now publishes the *Stud Book* annually. The registry is closed, which means that only those horses whose parents are registered in *The American Stud Book* or in the registry of another country recognized by The Jockey Club can be registered as Thoroughbreds. Approximately 750,000 Thoroughbreds have been registered through 1978.

## BREEDS OF GAITED HORSES

American Saddlebreds, Tennessee Walkers, Missouri Fox Trotters, Peruvian Pacers, and Paso Fino horses are classified as gaited horses.

Gaited horses ride softly and cover distances well, allowing their riders to maintain a good physical and mental condition so that they enjoy the riding experience. Many gaited horses require no special training, shoeing, or feeding for pleasure activities.

Trail riders are increasingly choosing gaited horses. On one large trail ride, the ratio of western to gaited horses has changed from 9:1 to 3:7 over the past 20 years.

"Society shows" are for gaited horses. Great style, fine features, and a flashy way of going (action) make them crowd pleasers. However, the society show image has probably reduced lay demand for gaited horses in many activities where they could do well.

By western horse standards, gaited horses are less surefooted, more likely to shy at objects, and canter with less precision and composure. They do react nervously to sudden noises and movement, but they seldom buck seriously or prance and charge when in a group.

The running walk of the Tennessee Walker, the fox trot of the Missouri Fox Trotter, and the Paso Fino gaits of Peruvian Pacers and Paso Fino horses are mostly inherited and are rather easy to develop in elemental form. The slow pace and rack of the American Saddlebred Horse is mostly "man-made" and more difficult to teach. All of the gaits are difficult to perfect for show competition. A complete description of gaits will be found in Chapter 4.

Tennessee Walkers have an extremely soft gait over flat terrain. The Paso Fino gait is equally soft. Saddlebreds learn to blend a form of the slow gait with a modified rack, which gives a soft ride at various speeds. Missouri Fox Trotters were developed for transportation in rough country and perform this function well. Most, but not all, have soft gaits and kind dispositions.

All gaited horses walk fast, sustain speed well in their gaits, and have dispositions quiet enough for most amateur riders.

### American Saddlebred

ORIGINS   This breed was developed during the last half of the eighteenth Century in Kentucky, Tennessee, Missouri, and Virginia to meet a need for transportation. Thoroughbred, Standardbred, Morgan, and Arabian blood was used in crossing with native ambling mares, resulting in a rather coarse animal found on many farms for both harness and saddle use. The foundation sire was Denmark, a Thoroughbred, foaled in 1839. The Denmark and Chief families contributed greatly to the breed's early development, through Gaines's Denmark 61 and Mambrino Chief, a trotter tracing to the Thoroughbred Messenger. Rex McDonald, famous show horse and sire, was a notable early contributor (Figure 3-13). Rex McDonald, Rex Peavine (Rex McDonald's son), Bourbon King, and Edna May's King were voted by prominent breeders and exhibitors to be the four greatest sires in the breed's history.

As the need for horse transportation diminished with the coming of the auto, breeders redirected their efforts toward developing a model breed for showing and pleasure riding.

Two recent great horses, as measured by the yardstick of show ring per-

FIGURE 3-13    The late Rex McDonald, voted one of four foundation sires of American Saddlebreds, slow-gaits (stepping pace) in championship form. In the slow-gait, lateral feet rise together (or almost together), but the front foot arches higher, hesitates, and then reaches the ground much later than the hind foot. [*The University of Missouri, Columbia.*]

formance, are the stallion Wing Commander and the mare My My, both of
Kentucky. Wing Commander was undefeated at the major shows from
1948 through 1954, and My My reigned equally supreme for a 5-year period
until her untimely death.

CHARACTERISTICS    Some writers have described the American Saddlebred as
"the most beautiful horse in the world," while others call it the "peacock of
the horse world." Certainly the Saddlebred has no equal in refinement of
head and longness of neck. The withers are well formed, the shoulders sloping, the back short, the croup flat, and tail set is high. The hindquarters are
well muscled through the gaskin. The straight legs end in long, sloping
pasterns for springiness. The feet are sound, and the toes are allowed to grow
excessively long to accentuate lifting.

The Saddlebred moves with greater flexion and animation and struts
in the show ring with more style than any other breed. The beauty of conformation and balance of form give the better specimens of this breed much
class.

American Saddlers are bred and trained almost exclusively to be shown
under saddle at either three or five gaits or to be shown in fine harness.

*Three-gaited horses* (Figure 3-14) are shown with clipped mane and
trimmed tail at the walk, trot, and canter. They are usually smaller and more

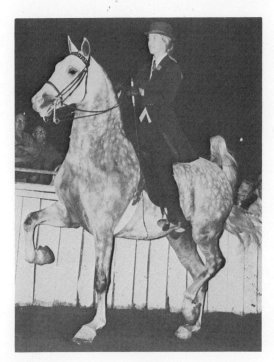

FIGURE 3-14    Sword Play, three-
gaited    American    Saddlebred
horse, trots in good form for
his    rider,    Cathy    Ethredge
Henderson. Note the clipped
mane and tail of three-gaited
Saddlebreds. Owned by Stephens
College. [*Stephens College, photograph by Morris.*]

compact and are shown at less speed and boldness than five-gaited horses. Three-gaited horses should do a four-cornered trot at moderate speed, folding their knees and flexing their hocks in a collected, balanced manner. Their canter should be slow, but not lazy or listless. Weight is shifted to the haunches with the front feet always on the correct lead striking the ground lightly.

*Five-gaited horses* are shown in full mane and tail at the walk, trot, slow gait, rack, and canter (Figure 3-15). Both five-gaited and three-gaited horses should show a flat-footed, animated walk. A horse should not prance and

**FIGURE 3-15**    The late Wing Commander at the trot. Undefeated American Saddlebred show stallion and leading sire, and six-time winner of the $10,000 Kentucky State Fair five-gaited championship stakes class. Five-gaited horses are shown in full mane and tail. Owned by Dodge Stables, Lexington, Kentucky, trained and ridden by Earl Teater. [*The American Saddle Horse Breeders Association, photograph by John H. Hors.*]

dance at the walk or toss its head from bit pressure. Five-gaited horses trot with more speed and reach than three-gaited horses, but they must maintain form and height of action. The stepping pace or slow gait allows a stylish horse much opportunity to "strut." It is one of the most attractive learned gaits. The rack is flashy, fast, and crowd-pleasing. It challenges the horse more than any other gait. Few horses can maintain form at great speed. When they do, they are winners.

Horses used in *fine harness* are especially refined in form, elegant in style and quality, and airy in motion. Since speed is not required, emphasis is placed on beauty, manners, and motion.

Modern American Saddlebred horses are of good size, standing 15 to 16 hands and weighing 1000 to 1200 pounds or more. Chestnut, bay, brown, and black are the preferred colors, with grays and roans not infrequently seen. Spotted colors are not allowed.

FUNCTION    Development of a finished American Saddlebred requires a schooling process handled by a skilled trainer. This is beyond the skills of many horse enthusiasts, but it does not prevent a novice from enjoying a comfortable ride on a horse bred especially for riding.

Recent efforts of the American Saddle Horse Breeders Association have been directed toward promoting saddlebred horses for uses other than show, such as pleasure riding and jumping. The American Saddlebred Pleasure Horse Association was established some years ago, and movies and slide cassettes showing various uses of Saddlebreds in daily horse activities have recently become available.

THE REGISTRY    The first record association was established in 1891 in Louisville, Kentucky. Called the American Saddle Horse Breeders Association, it has registered approximately 175,000 horses since then. The book is closed; all breeding stock must be descended from a registered sire and a registered dam.

## Missouri Fox Trotting Horse

ORIGINS    A need for sure-footed, tough, easy-traveling horses was recognized by pioneers of the Ozarks more than a century and a half ago. Country doctors, ministers, vendors, cattle traders, lawmen, and politicians sought horses that could travel at a comfortable speed of 5 to 8 miles an hour for long distances. To produce these, breeders drew upon horses brought from Kentucky, Tennessee, and Virginia of Arabian, Morgan, and Thoroughbred breeding to cross with native stock. Later, American Saddlers, Tennessee Walkers, and Standardbreds were used in developing the Missouri Fox Trotting horse. Recently, Tennessee Walking Horse crosses have been used in many breeding programs. The first registry was organized in 1948.

CHARACTERISTICS    As in any new breed, extremes in type are common. Sufficient time has not passed to permit a consensus among breeders and leaders on which objectives to formulate and emphasize. Variations among horses in performing the gait are not uncommon. Even so, it is a fast-growing breed, and horses that perform well are in great demand.

Adult horses should be 14 to 15-2 hands tall and of sufficient body conformation to carry weight. The back should be reasonably short and strong, the body deep and well-ribbed, the shoulders muscular and properly sloped, and the legs straight and well-placed. A neat, clean, well-shaped head with pointed ears is desirable. Colors vary, with bays, chestnuts, blue and red roans, blacks, browns, and palominos common. White markings are also seen frequently.

The distinguishing characteristic of Fox Trotting horses is a broken gait—the animals walk with their front feet and trot with the back feet. Formerly it was required that the back foot disfigure the front track by stepping directly on the track made by the front foot, but now simple overreaching is allowed (Figure 3-16). The Fox Trotting horse is not a high-stepping horse, but an extremely sure-footed one; and because of the sliding action of the rear feet, rather than the hard step of other breeds, the rider experiences little jarring action and is quite comfortable in the saddle for long periods of time.

One is reminded of a running walk when viewing the Fox Trotting

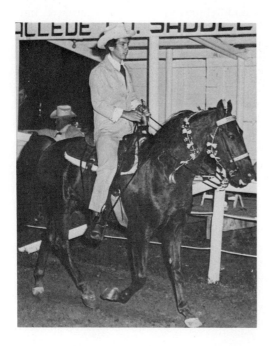

FIGURE 3-16    Zane's Play Boy exhibits the Missouri fox trotting gait well. The left front foot has just reached the ground to be closely followed by the right hind. These horses walk in front with a good nod of the head and trot behind. He is ridden by Clyde Connelly and owned by Helen Edge, Stockton, Missouri. [*Photograph courtesy of the owner.*]

horse, except that the gliding motion of the running walk is in the hind legs rather than in the forelegs.

Since the gait appears to be inherited, training of most Fox Trotters is not considered difficult. Once learned, the fox trot is easy for the horse to maintain, even if requested only intermittently. For this and other reasons, Fox Trotters have been described as "the common man's pleasure horse."

FUNCTIONS   The greatest demand for the Fox Trotting horse is for trail riding and shows, and as a family pleasure horse. The U.S. Forest Service has taken many to the Pacific Northwest for use by their rangers.

Fox Trotters are shown in model classes and under saddle at the walk, fox trot, and canter without artificial appliances such as tie-downs, set tails, switches, or braces.

THE REGISTRY   The Missouri Fox Trotting Horse Breeders Association, Inc., was formed in 1948, but was not very active until 1958. Recently, extensive promotion through shows, sales, and advertisement has stimulated interest and growth of the breed. The annual celebration in September at Ava, Missouri, where the world champion is named, has received wide acclaim and attracts fans from many states.

The American Fox Trotting Horse Breed Association, organized in 1970, is another national registry. Horses are now often double-registered in both associations.

## The Paso Fino and Peruvian Paso

ORIGINS   "Paso Fino" is a Spanish phrase meaning "fine step," "fine gait," or "walk fine." The Paso Fino (imported from Puerto Rico, Cuba, Colombia, and the Caribbean) and the Peruvian Paso have been bred for about 400 years. Both Pasos descend from the Andalusian-, Barb-, and Friesian-blooded Spanish horses left in Santa Domingo in 1493. Bred solely for transportation, the Pasos evolved into small, tough, gentle horses with remarkably easy gaits (Figure 3-17).

CHARACTERISTICS   Heights are usually 14 to 14-2 hands, with ranges of 13 to 15-2. Paso Finos are refined in bone and build, showing great style in motion. They are broad-chested and short of neck and body, with reasonably light hindquarters.

Typical colors are bay, chestnut, palamino, gray, roan, black, and albino. Spotting does occur, but solid colors, grays, and roans are sought.

The Paso Fino gait is a lateral, four-beat gait—legs on the same side move together but the hind foot strikes the ground a fraction of a second ahead of the front foot on the same side, thus breaking up the jarring jolt

FIGURE 3-17 Hercules, a United States National Champion of Champions, by Hecianda de la Salana. [*The Peruvian Paso Horse Registry of North America. Photograph by Foucher.*]

of a true pace. The head does not nod, and the body does not move up and down or from side to side. "Termino" (winging) of the front feet is exaggerated and encouraged. Horses are often judged while riders carry a glass of water in one hand without spilling it (Figure 3-18). The paso gait is capable of great variation. The three most used forms are:

1  *Paso Fino* (fine walk) A highly collected, delicate, soft walk; a show gait
2  *Paso Corto* (short walk) Less collected and stylish, but faster and more relaxed
3  *Paso Largo*  A long, extended, high-stepping, speed gait

All Paso Finos exhibit the paso gait naturally, and some individuals can also trot and canter.

FUNCTION  The Paso Fino and Peruvian Paso were originally developed for practical light riding and farm purposes, which heightened the value of their easy-to-ride gait. They are now bred almost exclusively for the show ring, and are valued for the flashy curiosity of their unusual gait.

FIGURE 3-18 The Paso Fino gait is a lateral, four-beat gait. The two legs on the same side move together, but the hind foot strikes the ground slightly ahead of the front foot, resulting in a very soft gait easy on both horse and rider. [*Courtesy of John Campbell.*]

THE REGISTRY   There are only a few thousand Pasos of either type now in the United States, but there are at least six different groups promoting and registering them (see Appendix 3-1). As breed numbers increase, these groups will undoubtedly coalesce to strengthen their voice. Despite the scattered Paso population, owners and breeders enthusiastically organize many shows, especially in the Midwest and far West.

## Tennessee Walking Horse

ORIGINS   Tennessee Walking Horses originated in about fourteen counties in Tennessee over a century ago. Early breeders were not concerned about establishing a breed but were attempting to fill a need for transportation, for saddle, and for driving, as well as for tilling the fields. As the breed developed, more selection pressure was applied for an easy-riding horse for plantation supervision—hence the nickname "plantation horse."

Breeds used extensively in the development of the Tennessee Walker were: the Thoroughbred for speed, the Standardbred for endurance, the Morgan for docility and strength, and the American Saddlebred for style, finish, and quality. The breed came into its own with the discovery of a small, handsome black horse foaled in 1886 and registered as a trotter. As a racing trotter, Allen F-1 was a failure because of a peculiar loose gait not speedy enough for racing. As a result, Allan F-1 changed owners repeatedly, each time lessening in value until he was relegated to the lowly service of mare teaser in a mule-breeding establishment. His potential as a Tennessee Walking Horse was recognized by James R. Brantley, who purchased Allen for a small sum in 1903 at age 17. Allan F-1 exceeded all expectations as a performer in the hands of a good trainer and as a sire in Mr. Brantley's band of good mares. The crosses between Allan F-1 and these mares produced outstanding sons so true to type that, when the registry was opened in 1935. Allan was proclaimed the foundation sire. Although some top-line (male) outcrossing continued, particularly with descendants of

Tom Hall F-20, linebreeding has been used more in this breed than in any other for fixing type and establishing gait.

CHARACTERISTICS    Modern Tennessee Walkers are about 15 or 16 hands high and weigh around 1100 to 1200 pounds (Figure 3-19). The appearance is

FIGURE 3-19    Shades of Carbon, 1976 World Champion Tennessee Walking Horse, owned by Glen Loe, Tullos, Louisiana, and trained and shown by Joe and Judy Martin. [*The Tennessee Walking Horse Breeders' and Exhibitors' Association of America, photograph by Larry Lowman.*]

rugged without coarseness. The neck is shorter than the American Saddle-bred, the back short, the croup sufficiently long and level, and the shoulders and quarters strong. They may appear bold about the head, with some tending toward Roman noses. Most will be even-tempered with kind dispositions.

Not all Tennessee Walkers are as smooth and refined as they could be. Tolerance of sickle hocks has caused this condition to plague some lines. Variation in type is not unknown. Some stumble in rough terrain and may refuse to negotiate obstacles.

The running walk is the major inherited characteristic of this breed. The gliding, level motion is easy on both horse and rider. Few gaits are more comfortable to the rider or easier on the horse than this one. The association's slogan is "If you ride one today, you'll own one tomorrow." Speed

FIGURE 3-20    Shades of Carbon. The running walk must have a "big lick." The front feet must rise high, fold well, and reach far without pointing. The back feet glide with great length and overreach without trotting. Head nodding is exaggerated. The gait is very smooth and is easy on both horse and rider. [*The Tennessee Walking Horse Breeders' and Exhibitors' Association of America, photograph by Jim Dixon.*]

is about 7 or 8 miles per hour, with some horses traveling up to 10 miles per hour for short periods in the show ring. However, form should not be sacrificed for speed, as it sometimes is. A ring of well-trained horses at the running walk presents a picture of uniformity and boldness of gait (often in contrast to the riding styles of their handlers).

The walk is bold, fast, even, and comfortable, but less springy and animated than that of American Saddlebreds. The canter is slow and collected, and characterized by height and exaggerated roll, like a rocking chair. It is more artificial than the canter of any other breed.

Tennessee Walkers are shown in full manes and tails with long hooves in front extensively weighted to increase action (Figure 3-20). All solid colors, grays, and roans are registrable, and extensive white markings on face and legs are common.

FUNCTION    Since the gaits of Tennessee Walkers are natural, many persons with a reasonable amount of horse experience can train them satisfactorily for their own use, especially for pleasure and trail riding. However, competition at major shows is fierce and is not likely to be seriously challenged by amateurs.

Recently, some have competed well on endurance rides. Crossing with Missouri Fox Trotting strains to produce trail horses has become widespread in southern Missouri and northern Arkansas.

THE REGISTRY    The Tennessee Walking Horse did not come to national attention until the Tennessee Walking Horse Breeders, and Exhibitors, Association of America was established at Lewisburg, Tennessee, in 1935. The next decade witnessed an explosion in registrations because of the breed's popularity and the association's open registration policy. By 1978 some 200,000 Walkers had been registered in the United States.


## BREEDS OF GENERAL PURPOSE HORSES

General purpose horses find favor with owners who demand a variety of tasks from their mounts. During our country's early years, many horses were used by different members of the family for field work, riding, and light driving. Even temperament, adaptability, and durability, and a willingness to perform a variety of tasks at the hands of various individuals characterized these horses. Many owners today prefer horses that do a variety of tasks well to those that are specialized.

### Arabians

ORIGINS    It is difficult to omit sentiment from a discussion of Arabs. Through the centuries they have been gifts of kings, championed by artists, and sub-

jects of romantic and imaginative legends. Cave drawings of 3000 years
B.C. offer evidence that Arab horses existed in Asia, North Africa, Asia
Minor, and Arabia in much the same form as we know them now. They are
conceded to be the progenitors of all light horse breeds as well as most draft
breeds. The Darley Arabian, Godolphin Bark, and Byerly Turk were instrumental in founding the Thoroughbred breed, from which most light
breeds have descended. Extreme refinement, speed, endurance, intelligence,
and beauty of form standardized over thousands of years accounted for their
popularity for crossing.

Arab, Barb, and Turkmene horses all arose in the Mideast (the "Fertile
Crescent") and Northern Africa, and exhibit similar characteristics. However, which of these three horses came first and is therefore the true "first
ancestor" is not known.

Importations to this country have extended over a long period of time,
but have been limited in number. George Washington's gray charger,
Magnolia, was sired by Ranger, the first known imported Arabian.

However, from before 1908, when the breed registry was established in
this country, until 1943, the Jockey Club handled Arab and Anglo (Thoroughbred)-Arab cross-registrations.

CHARACTERISTICS   The Arab is characterized by a finely chiseled head (Figure 3-1) with a dished face, small ears, and large, dark eyes. The neck is
highly arched and set high on sloping shoulders. The withers are well-
shaped and not too high, the forearm is long, and the cannon bone is short,
with well-defined and strong tendons. The croup is rather flat, with the tail
carried high and gaily away from the body (Figure 3-21). The Arab is a "big
little horse," with heights ranging from 14-2 to 15-2 hands and weights from
850 to 1100 pounds. (Strains of the Egyptian Arab, currently popular, may
be slightly larger.) Extreme quality of head, hair coat, and bone make the
Arab attractive. Arab hooves are flint-hard, extraordinarily durable, and
free from unsoundness. Trained groups of Arabs have shown unusual
adeptness at learning.

The Arab is distinctively short backed. For many years it was commonly thought that the Arab had one vertebra less than other horse breeds,
but recent autopsies have shown that this is not the usual case. Nevertheless, the short back enables the Arab to carry more weight than would be
thought possible for its size. Some strains exhibit poor conformation of the
hind legs.

The Arab has a flat-footed (daisy-cutting) walk, a rather uncomfortable
jog-trot, and a smooth, easy canter. A well-developed respiratory system,
as exhibited by wide flaring nostrils, a clean throatlatch, and well-sprung
ribs, enables the Arab to continue the canter untiringly over long distances.

The colors registered are bay, gray, black, brown, and chestnut. The
grays turn to white with age. Although for many years the association and

FIGURE 3-21  Farlito, owned by Fidel D. Villasenor, Escondido, California. Arabs do a variety of things well, ranging from cattle work to costume classes and dressage to endurance riding. [*The International Arabian Horse Association.*]

breeders have strenuously weeded out spotted horses and Duns, which they claimed were throwbacks to non-Arab blood, it is becoming generally understood that such anomalies of coat color are actually proofs of antiquity of blood.[7]

FUNCTION   One of the Arab's greatest contributions has been in providing seed stock in the formation and improvement of other breeds. But the Arab has been handicapped by its small size and by competition from the breeds it founded.

Pound for pound the Arab has no peer in stamina, courage, durability, and willingness. The Arab performs a variety of tasks very well (Figure 3-22). It has done extremely well in endurance rides, when carrying more weight relative to size than its competitors. Many show classes are available to Arabs, including native costume classes. Some Quarter Horse tracks have recently included Arab races in their schedules.

THE REGISTRY   The Kellog Arabian Horse Ranch of Pomona, California, was instrumental in preserving records and breeding fine strains of Arabs

[7]Gladys B. Edwards, *Know the Arabian Horse*, The Farnam Horse Library, Nebraska, 1971.

**FIGURE 3-22**   Prince Faff, 7-year-old Arabian gelding ridden by Kathy Creighton of Glendale, Arizona, was National Champion Endurance Ride Horse of 1973. Arabs are tough and durable, and are very competitive in endurance events. [*The International Arabian Horse Association, photograph by Charles Barieau.*]

during the decline of the horse in this country. The Arabian Horse Club of America was founded in 1908 and is still the official registry for the breed. By 1978 there had been approximately 150,000 Arabians registered in this country.

## Morgan

ORIGINS   Justin Morgan was born near Springfield, Massachusetts, in 1789. Considered in retrospect, the Morgan's contribution to American horseflesh is unparalleled by any other horse, because it founded the first American breed. Its blood has influenced other breeds that have developed in this country since that time. Justin Morgan is the only horse to have had a breed named in his honor.

An impoverished schoolteacher from Vermont walked 150 miles to Massachusetts to collect a debt. He returned with no money, but leading a three-year-old gelding followed by a bay stallion named Figure—a name later changed to Justin Morgan, after the teacher himself.

The lineage of Justin Morgan is unknown, but the stallion is credited with being a son of the fine Thoroughbred Beautiful Bay and is supposed to have been from Arabian breeding on the dam's side. Some geneticists consider Justin Morgan a "sport" or genetic mutant. Justin Morgan was 14-1 hands tall and of unusually heavy build, with extra heavy muscling in the hindquarters. Claims linger that this horse could outpull and outrun any horse he ever met in short races. He proved to have unusual prepotency, and his outstanding traits of type and docile disposition were passed on to his offspring and their offspring in succeeding generations.

The life of Justin Morgan was a hard one, consisting of menial work at logging, freight hauling, farming, and racing in the hands of no less than eleven masters. At age 29 the horse, unsheltered, died of infection from an unattended flank wound during the hard winter of 1821 near Chelsea, Vermont.

The three most famous sons of Justin Morgan were Bulrush, Sherman Morgan, and Woodbury. They sired the versatile utility horses of the New England farm and village. In the mid 1800s the Morgans became the leading breed of harness-racing horses and were instrumental in the development of the Standardbred. Colonel Battell of Middlebury, Vermont, published volume I of the American Morgan Horse Registry in 1894, beginning the registration association that is still active today.

CHARACTERISTICS    The Morgan head may be straight or slightly dished, with prominent, wide-set eyes and small, wide-set ears. The muzzle is small and firm, the jaw prominent. The neck is slightly crested in both mares and stallions, giving a heavy appearance from the view of the casual observer; however, the throatlatch should be clean and well-defined. The shoulder is very sloping and has great depth and muscling. The back is short, the hindquarters relatively well-defined.

Morgans are rather small, standing 14-1 to 15-1 hands and weighing from 900 to 1100 pounds. Most are smoothly turned, stylish, and clean-headed, with sufficient body, bone, and muscle to give them the appearance of ruggedness (Figure 3-23). Most are straight-legged—true movers at the walk, trot, and canter. All colors except white, spotted, and Appaloosa-coloration are registrable. White is permitted only on the face and the legs below knee and hock. Bay, brown, chestnut, and black are common colors, with liver-chestnut particularly abundant.

Although extremely rugged for their size, many Morgans are too small to meet the current demand for larger saddle horses. Although recent efforts to breed longer necks, bodies, and legs have been successful, many Morgans are too heavy in the neck and chunky in type for some buyers. Furthermore, many breeders prefer to remain true to the historical type.

FIGURE 3-23  Official drawing of a Morgan stallion. Morgans are even-tempered and adaptable, and they are tolerant of individuals with different levels of handling skills. [*The American Morgan Horse Association, Inc.*]

Nevertheless, as an all-around horse with a docile disposition, the Morgan has few peers (Figure 3-24).

FUNCTION   Morgans played a prominent role as ranch horses in the opening of the West, the offspring of Morgan crosses with Thoroughbreds were held in high esteem as U.S. Cavalry mounts.

Endurance rides have been won by Morgans repeatedly under rigid conditions supervised by the U.S. Department of Agriculture and recently in open competition.

The modern Morgan is still one of the country's most versatile breeds. Their dispositions cannot be beat. They are excellent driving animals for the greatly revived carriage activities. They are the choice of many schools and riding establishments from coast to coast.

THE REGISTRY   The Morgan registry was begun in 1894, and today is known as the American Morgan Horse Association. The University of Vermont

FIGURE 3-24 Benfield's Ace, a modern Grand Champion Morgan stallion. The trend in type is toward more length of leg, body, and neck without loss of Morgan "character." [*The American Morgan Horse Association, Inc.*]

operates a large Morgan breeding establishment near Middlebury for the preservation of this breed, the first truly American one. By 1978, approximately 60,000 Morgans had been registered.

## COLOR BREEDS

Breeds of colored horses are of two types—those bred mostly for utility and those bred mostly for color. Appaloosas, Buckskins, and Paints, while outstanding for their unusual color, are bred for purpose first and color second. Albinos, Palominos, and Pintos are bred first for color, and may have wide variations among them.

Colored horses are used in parades, on drill teams, and for circus acts, and to attract attention in crowds. Large groups of matched colored horses can be seen on television each New Year's Day in the Rose Bowl Parade in

Pasadena, California. Some are Palominos, dappled greys, and various assortments of spotted colors. Spots are arranged in various combinations and produce unique and beautiful color patterns. Loud-colored horses of good conformation command high prices.

A certain amount of symmetry, style, and animation is desirable in addition to color if a horse is intended to be conspicuous. Individuals of any breed that have coarse, rough, faulty conformation are seldom satisfactory, regardless of color.

## American Albino

ORIGINS   The breed of American Albinos originated on the White Horse Ranch in Naper, Nebraska, and was developed and promoted by owners Caleb and Ruth Thompson (Figure 3-25).

The foundation sire was Old King, foaled in 1906, a milk-white stallion with pinkish skin and brown eyes. The sire and dam of this stallion were thought to be mostly Morgan and Arabian. Old King was crossed

FIGURE 3-25   Albino white horses on the range. [*Courtesy of Ruth Thompson, Crabtree, Ore.*]

mainly with mares of Morgan blood to produce white sons for use on mares of mixed breeding, including some pony mares.

The American Albino is born white; other breeds showing white (e.g., the Lippizzaner) are born black or gray and turn white with age.

When two American Albinos are bred together, 25 percent of the resulting fetuses will die in utero, 50 percent will be white, and 25 percent will be colored. Crosses of the American Albino on colored horses will produce 50 percent white foals.

CHARACTERISTICS    Color is the major requisite for registration, in addition to pink skin and blue, brown, or hazel eyes. Type and size vary widely in both horses and ponies of any recognized breed, including light draft horses eligible for registration.

In addition to the American Albino, four other types (and combinations of these four) were added to the Albino registry in a subsection in 1970 and designated American Creme Horses. Varying in color from cream to pale ivory, these color types are referred to genetically as cremello and perlino, and crop out in Dun, Buckskin, and Palomino breeding.[8]

The American Albino has style, good disposition, and learning ability.

FUNCTION    Albinos have always been popular as circus horses. They are also used as parade mounts, trick horses, and general riding horses. Perhaps the two best-known Albinos are Silver of the "Lone Ranger" television series and Fubuki, an American-reared Albino used by the late Hirohito, Emperor of Japan, during World War II.

THE REGISTRY    The American Albino Association, begun in 1937 by the Thompsons, has registered approximately 3200 horses.

## Palomino

ORIGINS    A poem written about the eighth century B.C. describes the hero Achilles as mounted in battle on Balios and Xanthos, both palomino-colored horses with golden bodies and silver manes. This special color has been treasured over the centuries. In Spain, the color was called Golden Isabella, after that country's beloved queen.

Palomino-colored horses occur naturally in many breeds, although they may not always be registrable. Palomino-registrable bloodlines are limited to horses which have at least one parent registered with the Palomino Horse Breeders of America (PHBA), and to horses of the desired color with one registered Arab, Quarter Horse, American Saddlebred, Thoroughbred, Morgan, Tennessee Walker, or Standardbred parent.

---

[8]The approach to cremello and perlino inheritance is adapted from Abeles, op. cit.

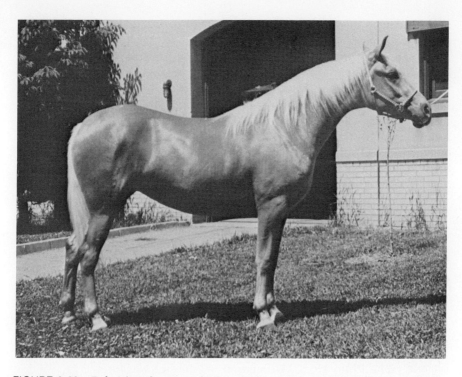

FIGURE 3-26 *Palomino* denotes a body color as golden as "a newly minted gold coin." They must have white manes and tails. They have long been popular as parade mounts. [*The National 4-H Service Council.*]

CHARACTERISTICS The term *Palomino* denotes a color as golden as "a newly minted gold coin" (Figure 3-26). In practice, five slight variations from the gold coin color are allowed. Since the desired color depends on a genetic dilution factor from a chestnut gene, breeding two Palominos together will result in 50 percent Palomino, 25 percent cremello, and 25 percent chestnut offspring. Palmomino crosses chestnut horses produce 50 percent Palominos.[9] A survey of the top show winners in 1963 revealed that only 30 percent were from two Palomino parents, but 70 percent were sired by Palominos.

There are two registries for Palominos in the United States, the PHBA (1941) mentioned above and the Palomino Horse Association. The main difference between the two is that the PHBA registers only horses having dark skin, whereas the PHA accepts both dark- and light-skinned horses. A limited amount of white is allowed on the face, hocks, and legs below the knees, but never on the body. No leg barring, shoulder striping, or dorsal

[9]G. W. Salisbury and J. W. Birtton, "The Inheritance of Equine Coat Color, II," *Journal of Heredity*, vol. 32, p. 225.

lists (evidences of dun background) are permitted. Mane and tail must be at least 85 percent white.

Before registration each horse must undergo a color and a conformation inspection. The conformation inspection makes reference to the individual's breed ancestry. Signs of draft and pony blood are disallowed. Minimum weight and height are 900 pounds and 14 hands. Popular heights are 15 to 16 hands, with stallions weighing 1000 to 1200 pounds. The Palomino should stand and move correctly and should represent the breed of its parentage in quality and refinement. For example, if from Quarter Horse stock, the Palomino will be more rugged than if from American Saddlebred ancestry.

FUNCTION   Although bred for beauty of coat color for use in parades and gala events, the Palomino may be seen performing many different tasks because of the different bloodlines. Ropers, barrel racers, jumpers, and gaited horses are all found in this breed. Many Palominos are double-registered.

THE REGISTRY   Approximately 50,000 Palominos, concentrated mainly in the Midwest and far West, have been registered in both associations.

## Pinto

ORIGINS   The Pinto Horse Association of America was formed in 1956 for the purpose of registering spotted horses. Spotted patterning is the major requirement. Unlike Paint horses, which are selected from stock horses only, Pintos have been bred from a variety of breeds, with color pattern receiving primary emphasis. As a result, all sizes and shapes were produced, from large horses to small ponies. Although color is still the major requirement for registry, breeders are encouraged to breed the same, recognized breeds together rather than crossing dissimilar breeds (Figures 3-27 to 3-29). The pony division was recently eliminated with the establishment of a height requirement of 14 hands.

FUNCTION   Today's Pinto horses show more style and quality. Use of American Saddlebred and other hot-blooded lines lends animation and beauty of conformation, which, when combined with the flashy coloring, make the versatile Pinto truly stand out in a crowd.

Hidalgo, an 8-year-old Pinto from Wyoming, won one of the world's most grueling races in 1890. The annual 1000-year old race started at Aden, Arabia, and extended over 3000 miles of heat, sand, and desert. He finished in 68 days, some 33 hours ahead of the horse that finished second in the field of over 100 Arabian horses. Hidalgo's grandmother was a spotted Indian pony for which the rider, Frank J. Hopkins, paid $3.

The only major continental ride in history was the 2½-year, 10,000-mile ride by A. F. Tschiffely from Buenos Aires to Washington, D.C., from 1925 to

FIGURE 3-27 Spee-D-Bar Boy, stock-Quarter-type horse, one of three Pinto types. [*Photograph by Johnny Johnston, courtesy of Roxanne Green.*]

FIGURE 3-28 Raffiana, Arabian pleasure-type Pinto mare. [*Courtesy of Roxanne Green.*]

FIGURE 3-29 Witch's Brew, Saddlebred-type Pinto mare. Because of style and high action, this type competes well in parade classes. [*Courtesy of Roxanne Green.*]

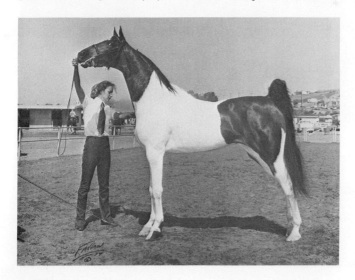

1927. Mancho, an 18-year-old Pinto, and Gato, a 16-year-old dun, both under 14 hands and of native stock, carried the rider and his equipment over the extremely difficult terrain. They were thwarted by war, malaria, and injury, but the final obstacle that terminated the journey in Washington, D.C., instead of New York City as planned, was automobile traffic.

THE REGISTRY   Each horse is subject to inspection before registration. Approximately 35,000 Pintos had been registered by the PHAA by 1978.

## BREEDS OF PONIES

Just as the size of young riders varies, so does the size of the ponies they ride (Figure 3-30). However, pony breeders (with exception of breeders of miniature ponies) are under the same pressure as horse breeders to increase size. This is because ponies large enough to be trained by an adult are usually better trained and more dependable than those trained by children.

Breeders of Gotlands emphatically classify them as horses. However, their size does not distinguish them from most of the larger breeds of ponies,

FIGURE 3-30   Ponies and children go together well. Ownership and care develop responsibility, character, and self-sufficiency early in the life of a youngster. [*Photograph by Bob Fleming.*]

and hence they are included here. Some pony breeds are shown primarily in English events, but most ponies are used and shown in a variety of events by adults and children. Recently pony harness racing, with pari-mutuel betting, has become popular. Pony-pulling contests are also received with great enthusiasm.

The American Horse Shows Association defines a pony as being under 14 hands, 2 inches. The large pony ranges from any fraction above 13 hands up to 14-2 hands. The small pony is 13 hands and below. In reality, however, many breed registries define a pony as being under 14 hands.

## Connemara

ORIGINS    The rugged, windswept hills of Western Ireland have tested the mettle of Connemaras for centuries. Rugged living favored survival of the fittest (Figure 3-31).

The Connemara was originally a mix of cold-blooded native ponies with ancient Spanish Barb, Andalusian, Jennet, and Arab blood. Later there was also extensive crossbreeding with Welsh Cobs.

Importations of the Connemara to America began less than 3 decades ago.

FIGURE 3-31    Connemaras on the Mavis Connemara Farm, Rochester, Ill. Originally from the rugged, windswept hills of western Ireland, these animals thrive well in this country. [*The Mavis Connemara Farm, photograph by Galloway.*]

CHARACTERISTICS    Average height is about 14 hands, but regimens of management and nutrition under conditions in the United States cause many to exceed this. A new section for those over 14-2 hands has been added to the registration association.

Connemaras have long, true strides resulting from long, sloping shoulders. They are deep of body and rib with sufficient strength to carry weight well. They have good refinement and quality of head, bone, and hair coat, and tough, sound feet and legs. All solid colors are registrable, with grey seen often.

FUNCTION    The Connemara is used by children and lightweight adults alike for a variety of events, but is particularly adept at hunting and jumping.

THE REGISTRY    The American Connemara Pony Society was founded in 1956. It had registered approximately 5000 Connemaras by 1978.

## Gotland Horse

ORIGINS    Gotland is a Swedish Island in the Baltic Sea. Gotland horses have occupied this island for centuries. The Gotland was used as a cavalry mount by the Goths, Swedes, and Vikings, who introduced the use of stirrups as an aid in outmaneuvering their mounted enemies in battle. Rome fell to cavalrymen mounted on Gotlands in the year 410 and again in 493. King Gustavus Adolphus, the great pre-Napoleonic cavalry warrior, is said to have defeated 4000 dismounted Russians with 800 Swedish horsemen in 1632.

CHARACTERISTICS    Gotlands are 12 to 14 hands tall; they have great depth of body and rather short legs. The neck is of moderate length, muscular, and slightly arched. The withers are of sufficient height to hold a saddle, the back is short and strong, and the croup is rounded with a well-carried tail. Winter hair coats are dense, but shed in the summer to become short and glossy. Bays and charcoal duns are common colors, with most other solid colors represented (Figure 3-32).

Gotlands are strong for their size and carry medium-sized adults with dispatch. Good dispositions make them popular with children.

FUNCTION    The Gotland Horse is used in Sweden in a variety of show events, such as jumping, hunting, pleasure riding, and driving. It is raced in both running and trotting events at distances of approximately 1½ miles.

The breed was introduced to this country around 1957. The Gotland is shown largely in western pony classes in pleasure, conformation, and games. The Gotland competes well in endurance rides.

FIGURE 3-32 Netta Raketen No. 26, imported Gotland mare, side-passes in a trail class exhibition with rider Chris Lee. Because of versatility and weight-carrying ability, the American Gotland Horse Association emphasizes that Gotlands are small horses, not ponies. [*Courtesy of Pepper Lee, Leeward Farms, Elkland, Mo.*]

THE REGISTRY  The American Gotland Horse Association has organized a closed registry. By 1978 about 500 Gotlands had been registered. Numbers continue to increase as rapidly as possible given the limited availability of breeding stock.

## The Hackney Pony

ORIGINS  The Hackney breed of harness horses epitomized the ultimate in transportation in England before the advent of railroads. Ancestors of the Hackney Horse were developed in Norfolk in the eighteenth century. Some attained heights of 17 hands.

The nineteenth century in Britain, the "golden century," brought into being a class of people appropriately titled "the newly rich." Fine high-stepping carriage horses, the envy of many, attracted the attention of this group. Breeders set to work in earnest to fulfill a lucrative demand. With the help of the Norfolk Trotter stallion, Marshland Shales, foaled in 1802, the high-stepping Hackneys known today developed in remarkably short time. These Hackney Horses are smaller than their ancestors—from 14-2 to 15-2 hands.

Christopher Wilson then selected small stallions and mares in a successful effort to develop a pony type of Hackney. Sir George was the foundation sire, with Little Wonder crossed with his daughters. Years of linebreeding fixed the type and accomplished the objective of breeding small Hackneys of excellent symmetry and extreme action.

CHARACTERISTICS  The modern Hackney is rich in quality and refinement, yet has substantial width and depth of body and is abundantly endowed with hard muscle (Fig. 3-33). The blend of body parts is excellent, indicating great smoothness and symmetry. Much of the high-stepping ability of the Hackney comes from the extreme length and slope of the shoulder, the short back, and the long underline. The neck is naturally arched, comes out of the

FIGURE 3-33  May Day Elise, many times Junior Champion Hackney mare, driven by Mrs. Eugene Kennedy, Taylorville, Il. Haughty high-stepping Hackneys are favorites in many horse shows. [*The American Hackney Horse Society, photograph by Jack Holvoet.*]

shoulders high, and is surmounted with a beautifully expressive head and eyes. Show classes based on height are usually divided into 11-2 to 12-2 hands, 12-2 to 13-2 hands, and 13-2 to 14-2 hands.

FUNCTION    Today Hackney Horses are seldom seen in society shows, but Hackney Pony classes are included in many programs because audiences love them. Indeed, the Hackney Pony is the pride of harness show horses. For brilliance of motion, precision and height of action, grace of movement, and symmetry of form, the Hackney Pony has no close competitor.

THE REGISTRY    The registration association was established in 1891 and remained open to fillies until 1949; that is, fillies from registered sires and nonregistered dams were entered in the "half-registry" upon passing inspection. Their offspring from registered sires were eligible for full registry.

Both Hackney Horses and Hackney Ponies are registered in the same association. Over 20,000 have been registered through 1978, 95 percent of which are ponies.

## Pony of the Americas

ORIGINS    The Pony of the Americas (POA), a western-type "using" pony, was developed for children who had outgrown Shetland ponies. According to the association, A Pony of the Americas is a happy medium of the Arabian and Quarter Horse in miniature, ranging in height from 11-2 to 13-2 hands with Appaloosa coloring in order to give the breed distinction, flash, and color (Figure 3-34).

Leslie L. Boomhower, an attorney in Mason City, Iowa, acquired an Appaloosa mare and a foal sired by a Shetland Pony stallion. The colt, born in 1954, was named Black Hand No. 1.

From this colt, through crosses with Appaloosas, Quarter Horses, and Arabians, and Mexican and South American imports of the desired size and coloring, there developed this distinctive pony breed in a rather short time. The registry was closed in 1970.

CHARACTERISTICS    The POA should show style, substance, beauty, and symmetry. The neck should be slightly arched with a clear-cut throatlatch. The head should be well-proportioned in size and may be slightly dished to accentuate the Arab lineage. Maximum height is 13-2 hands.

Feet should be well-shaped and well-proportioned, and surmounted by straight legs. The body should be full-ribbed, and intermediate in muscling between the Quarter Horse and Arabian. The action should be straight and long, and of medium height.

The six acceptable color patterns are:

1    *Snowflake.*    White spots in varying degrees over a solid colored body

FIGURE 3-34 The Pony of the Americas (POA) is of stock horse type with Appaloosa coloring. It is 46 to 54 inches tall. Young in years, the breed has **expanded** rapidly, and POA owners have many association-sponsored activities they can engage in. [*The Pony of the Americas Club, Inc.*]

2 *Frost.* White hair intermingled in coat; white usually concentrated on croup, which often forms a blanket as pony matures
3 *Blanket.* Dark body with white blanket over croup and hindquarters with a variation of spots
4 *Leopard.* Diamond, squaw, or teardrop spots over entire white body
5 *White body with black spots over croup, loin, and back, with diamond or feather spots.* This is the color pattern of Black Hand No. 1, the foundation sire of the POA.
6 *Marbelized roan.* Roan body with varnish marks on head, elbows, and stifles, with strong Appaloosa characteristics

In addition to these colors the pony must have white or partially white sclera around the eye and some mottled skin. Striped hooves are desirable but not a requirement.

FUNCTION The POA is a handy, versatile performer, often shown in halter and western performance and costume classes.

THE REGISTRY The Pony of the Americas Club, organized in 1955, had registered over 25,000 ponies by 1978—tremendous growth considering its short history.

## Shetland

ORIGINS    Shetland ponies have occupied the Shetland Islands of Scotland since the sixteenth century. Rough, rocky terrain, sparse feed, and a cold, damp climate created extremely unfavorable conditions that resulted in development of a small but hardy pony with proportions like those of a draft horse. Shetland ponies were used on the islands as pack animals, and some were imported to England in the nineteenth century for work in mines. Some breeders on the islands began systematic breed improvement

FIGURE 3-35    Twinkles, 1967 All Star and All-American three-year-old Shetland stallion. When gelded, Twinkles won first nationally in Ladies and Amateur Harness (or both) four different years. Shetlands used for show are attractive, stylish, refined, show and abundance of quality and have good action. He is owned and shown by Mrs. Virgil L. Cagle, Columbia, MO. [*Courtesy of Mrs. Cagle, photography by Bobbie.*]

at about this time. Importations began to flow into the United States and Britain to fulfill the demand for a child's pony.

CHARACTERISTICS   Until World War I, little effort was made to change type from the thick-bodied, shaggy, roly-poly pony on stubby legs that had characterized the breed (Figure 3-30). Since World War II, Shetlands of extreme quality and refinement have evolved to emulate American Saddlebred horses on a miniature scale, both in type and style (Figure 3-35).

Modern Shetlands have substance, muscle, and bone, but are not coarse. Quality and refinement of feet, legs, and joints are stressed, with refinement of head, ears, and neck demanded.

With current emphasis on showing and pony harness racing, demands have increased for length and slope of shoulders, freedom and style of action, and correctness of leg set. Maximum height is 12-2 hands at the withers. Any color is permissible.

While some Shetlands have dispositions which make them unsafe for children, many are merely spoiled because of improper treatment.

FUNCTION   Like American Saddlers, the more refined Shetland is shown in fine harness mostly by adults, and under saddle in English tack mostly by children in many society shows.

The major use of Shetlands is for children's mounts. Since they are likely to be the first horse with which the child has experience, they should be well trained for inexperienced children. (For some reason people often purchase a green pony at a low price, wrongly expecting that the pony and the child will "learn together.")

The amount of use a family can get from a Shetland may depend upon how young the child is when he or she starts riding and how many children there are in the family to use the pony, as children tend to outgrow them rather rapidly.

THE REGISTRY   The Shetland enjoys wide distribution in the United States in both rural and urban areas. The American Shetland Pony Club was organized in 1888 to promote the popular little animal. Some 140,000 had been registered by 1978.

### Welsh Pony

ORIGINS   The Welsh Mountain Pony has been in the hills and valleys of Wales for a very long time. Even Henry VIII's edict which ordered all horses under 15 hands to be destroyed did not eliminate it. Arab, Thoroughbred, and Hackney crosses resulted in a larger pony called a Welsh Cob, but a selection program was established to develop saddle ponies suitable for children's mounts for domestic and export demand. The first importation was to Aurora, Illinois, around 1884.

CHARACTERISTICS  The modern Welsh Pony is refined, with a small head, large, bright eyes, and adequate spirit for fine harness and saddle show events (Figure 3-36). The Welsh is larger than the Shetland. Class A division of the Stud Book limits height to 12-2 hands, whereas class B ponies may not exceed 14-2 hands. Years of living close to nature gave the Welsh Mountain Pony stamina and soundness of limb and body which are useful for a variety of tasks.

Welsh Mountain Pony breeders strive to maintain the *natural* refinement of the breed, and therefore no artificial aids are enlisted to heighten action or spirit in showing. The hardy soundness and good nature of the Welsh is frequently drawn upon by other ponybreeds, so a Welsh Halfbred and Welsh Crossbred registry has been established.

FUNCTION  In addition to pleasure riding and showing under saddle, the Welsh Pony is raced in harness, shown in fine harness, and used in jumping, hunting, and western riding events.

Distribution in this country has been widespread, but larger numbers are found in the east.

FIGURE 3-36  Three-year-old chestnut-roan Welsh mare owned by Mrs. Karl Butler, Ithaca, N.Y. Many Welsh ponies are white. They are used extensively by teenagers in the New England states in pleasure and English show classes. [*Courtesy of Harold A. Willman, Ithaca, N.Y.*]

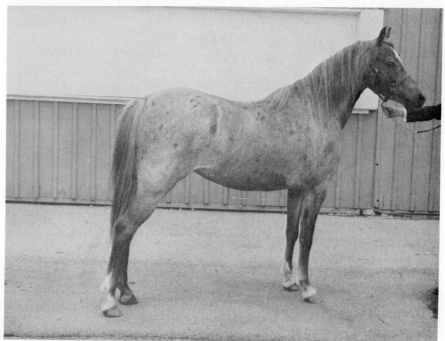

THE REGISTRY    The Welsh Pony and Cob Society of America was established in 1906. In 1946 its name was changed to the Welsh Pony Society of America. Some 40,000 Welsh Ponies had been registered by 1978.


## MINIATURE HORSES

Numerous breeders have assembled small ponies in an attempt to breed miniature horses. Some have succeeded in developing attractive, tiny horses. The American Miniature Horse Registry, a division of the Shetland Pony Club, maintains a recording service for them.

Height of a miniature horse is 32 inches at the withers or less. Some are under 20 inches tall. The smaller they are, the more valuable.

Many are kept as pets (some even as house pets), and others are hitched to tiny vehicles in parades, shows, and pleasure driving.

Miniature horses are neither *dwarf horses*, as was Tom Thumb, the noted sideshow horse, nor are they *Fallabellas*, from Argentina. Fallabellas originated from small Shetlands, but have been selected for small size for over a century. One is only 15 inches tall and weighs under 30 pounds. Many Fallabellas are well-formed horses of extremely small size.

Miniature horses of small size are expensive, but the offspring they bear sell well. Demand is good and supply limited, a condition not likely to change in the immediate future. They are healthy animals, but not very competitive when raised with other animals, even dogs. The offspring of some become too large to be of much value.


## DRAFT HORSES

Tremendously diminished in number only a few years ago, purebred draft horses are presently enjoying a renaissance. The ecologically minded small farmer is responsible in a great part for the draft horse revival. Although draft horses will never compete with the tractor on large farms, they are particularly well suited to the small farm. Unfazed by rolling, hilly terrain and tight corners, draft horses, despite their large size, are handy (Figure 3-37). Their use in food production is not limited to mechanical service, for farmers use the horses' waste as fertilizer. Certain religious groups in this country have never abandoned the draft horse. However, for these horses the hours are long and the work hard.

The annual draft horse sale at Waverly, Iowa, averages approximately $2000 each on over 100 head at their mixed breed consignment sale. Matched pairs of good geldings ready to pull a show rig in a parade or a hay wagon in deep snow or mud often sell from $3000 to $5000. Revived interest in heavy pulling contests and logging has also pushed up prices.

FIGURE 3-37    Combines pulled by thirty-three horses and/or mules harvesting wheat in eastern Washington at the turn of the century. [*Washington State Historical Society, Tacoma, Wash.*]

The five major draft breeds in the United States are *Shire*, *Belgian*, *Percheron*, *Clydesdale*, and *Suffolk*, in order of decreasing size. The Percheron was the most popular breed around the turn of the century, but many Belgians were also used. The "feather" breeds (those with long hair below their knees and hocks), Shires, and Clydesdales, were leaders in their native countries but never gained much favor in the United States. The sanitation problems caused by mud and filth in the heavy hair on their legs caused most farmers to pass them by.

Most drafters are found in Canada and the north central United States, although they are widely distributed in both countries.

## The Belgian

ORIGINS    As the name implies, this breed originated in Belgium from large horses which evolved there centuries before Caesar invaded the area.

The characteristic coloration and docility of the Belgian made it popular for use in crossing with native American drafters. Gradually however, the pure Belgian came to be considered as too slow-moving and coarse. Guided by the American Association of Importers and Breeders of Belgian Draft Horses, breeders began to make progress in breeding for more action, quality, and refinement. Jay Farceur, international grand champion in 1938, 1939, and 1940 combined these traits well with typical Belgian size, muscling, and strength. The progeny of this champion were equally prepotent in the expression of quality and size in their offspring. Today the pedigrees of many modern Belgians trace to Jay Farceur.

CHARACTERISTICS    The Belgian is the second largest draft breed; many Belgians weigh more than a ton. Compared to Percherons, the Belgian is rather coarse, short-necked, and sluggish. The Belgian does not take well to hot climates or rough footing. However, it is docile and dependable, and easy to break and train. The Belgian is muscular and strong, and especially suited for heavy draft work on farms at moderate working speed.

The modern Belgian is still large, but has more style, quality, and refinement than its predecessors (Figure 3-38). Many weigh more than a ton and stand 17 hands tall. The Belgian is almost always docile—a trait especially valuable for new drivers in parades and crowds. Like the Percheron, the Belgian has good feet and legs and a deep, sturdy body and is a willing worker and competitive puller.

The Belgian has been selected mostly for sorrel color. Blond sorrel (white mane and tail) is highly valued for crossing by draft mule breeders. There are also many roans and some bays, blacks, and other colors.

FUNCTION    The Belgian is used for pulling in contests, as a logger and farm horse, and increasingly in parade hitches.

Currently, the most spectacular draft horse exhibition in the world may be the giant circus wagon and forty-horse hitch of Belgians owned

FIGURE 3-38    This "ton" Belgian team pulled a covered wagon on the Bicentennial Wagon Train from southwestern Missouri to Valley Forge, Pa. Belgians are the second largest of the draft breeds. They are docile, dependable, willing workers, and good pullers. They lead all draft breeds in registration. [*Photograph by the author.*]

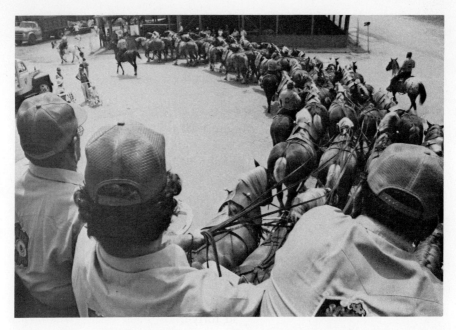

FIGURE 3-39  The famous forty-horse hitch of Belgians owned and driven by Dick Sparrow of Zearing, Iowa. For each hand full of lines, there are four out-riders and a "pit" crew to brake and keep the lines straight, Sparrow guides lead horses 120 feet from his seat on the wagon around a 90-degree turn. [*Courtesy of Frank D. Lessiter.*]

and driven by Dick Sparrow of Zearing, Iowa (Figure 3-39). These ten teams, four abreast, and their 22-foot wagon occupy more than 125 feet of space on the streets over which they parade. Outriders are necessary in the crowded streets because the front team is often out of sight of the driver on a ninety-degree turn.

THE REGISTRY    The Belgian Draft Horse Corporation of America was begun in 1887. A few Belgian breeders kept the registry alive during the lean years by conducting its meager business in their homes. When the demand for draft horses increased, enough registered Belgians were available to start small breeding herds. About 80,000 had been registered by 1978. In 1978 alone, 1000 Belgians were registered—four times the number of Percherons registered during the year.

## Percheron

ORIGINS    The Percheron originated many centuries ago in the tiny LaPerche district of Northwestern France. From 1850 to 1920 importations to the

United States were numerous, and the population of this breed exceeded that of all other draft breeds combined.

CHARACTERISTICS    Stallions stand at least 16-3 hands high, with mares and geldings somewhat shorter. The Percheron averages from 1600 to 2000 pounds (Figure 3-40).

The head is characterized by wide-set eyes and a deep cheek. The neck is powerful and deeply crested. The chest is wide, the back short. Legs are medium in length, with big knees and strong hocks. Pasterns should be free from coarse feathering.

The Percheron is noted for its alert disposition, fast walk and strong trot, and willingness to work hard.

The two basic coat colors are black and gray, making it easy to assemble matched hitches. Other solid colors and white markings are not unknown, however.

FUNCTION    An excellent worker, the Percheron is used in circus hitches, in parades, for shows, and in pulling contests. Increasingly it is being used as a farm horse.

FIGURE 3-40    Donald Laet, many times champion stallion in Canada, is typical of the modern Percheron horse. Percherons dominated all other breeds when draft horses were at peak numbers. [*The Draft Horse Journal*.]

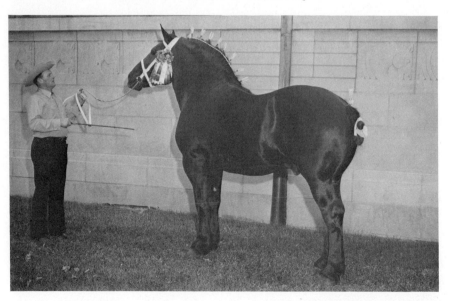

THE REGISTRY   The progressive farm and firm owners of Percherons were quick to use tractors and trucks in their businesses, and this great draft breed began to feel the effects of such competition soon after the turn of the century. Its breeders did not sustain faith in the "comeback" of draft horses as did Belgian breeders and were short of breeding stock in the late 1960s and 1970s when demand revived.

The Percheron Horse Association of America was organized in 1876. By 1978, approximately 250,000 Percherons had been registered. However, recent growth has been small, with only a few hundred foals registered each year.

## Clydesdale

ORIGINS   The Clydesdale originated in the fertile valley of the Clyde River in Southwestern Scotland. This distinctive breed arose from crosses of Flemish stallions on smaller Scottish native stock during the mid-1800s.

CHARACTERISTICS   Great style, flashy coat, and high action are the hallmarks of this breed. However, although the Clydesdale may be the aristocrat of the drafters, not all look like those in the Anheuser-Busch hitches. Indeed, it takes a band of forty mares and five or six stallions to keep the Anheuser-Busch hitches supplied because of stringent requirements for size, color, quality, and disposition.

The modern Clydesdale stands tall—17 to 18 hands—and weighs 1600 to 1800 pounds, with some individuals exceeding a ton (Figure 3-41). The Clydesdale has a proud carriage with a high head and more spirit than other draft breeds. (Early breeders exaggerated their horses' spirit by not trailing them with a whip in halter classes, as was customary by handlers of other drafters.)

The Clydesdale is basically bay or brown, with some roan and chestnut appearing occasionally. Most have extensive white markings on the head, the legs, and, to a lesser extent, on the body. In an effort to interest farmers in the horse, early United States breeders attempted to reduce feathering. Today, however, the Clydesdale is bred for extensive feather to emphasize its high, true action and stylish way of going.

The Clydesdale tends to be more nervous than other drafters. However, when compared with light horse breeds they are models of docility. Stallions are often worked among mares in pasture without incident.

The Clydesdale was never well received by farmers in the United States because of the feathering on the legs and other conformation problems. Many Clydesdales are leggy, narrow-chested, and shallow-bodied, and are hard keepers. Although their feet are large and round, they also tend to be shallow and therefore hard to shoe.

**FIGURE 3-41** One of the Clydesdale stallions at Grant's Farm used in the breeding program to produce geldings for the Budweiser (Anheuser-Busch) hitches. [*Photograph by the author.*]

FUNCTION The Clydesdale is mainly used as a parade horse. There has been recent interest in crossing Thoroughbreds with Clydesdales to achieve a large, strong horse well-suited to jumping.

THE REGISTRY Only a few thousand Clydesdales have been registered by the Clydesdale Breeders Association. About 125 foals have been registered each year for the past 5 years.

### Shire

ORIGINS The Shire originated in east central England in a very fertile area of abundant feed supply. The Shire is said to have developed from the Great Horse of the medieval knights.

Extensive promotion by an English firm, Truman's Pioneer Stud Farm of Bushnell, Illinois, resulted in many importations from 1880 to 1890. However, in this country, Shires were overwhelmed by competition from Percherons and Belgians, and never became popular.

CHARACTERISTICS   The Shire is a massive horse in every dimension (Figure 3-42). The Shire is taller, longer, and heavier than the Belgian, usually weighing over a ton. While similar in coloration and feathering to its cousin the Clydesdale, the Shire is heavier-boned and heavier-muscled, and is less active. The Shire stallion is often 17 to 18 hands, with mares averaging around 16+ hands. The Shire is quite docile.

The traditional color is black, although bay, brown, and gray are also common. White markings are extensive, as in the Clydesdale.

FUNCTION   In England many breweries still use Shires for short-distance hauls. In the United States, the Shire is still mainly a curiosity, but with the renewed interest in pulling contests, this attitude is bound to change.

THE REGISTRY   The record books of Shire registrations were salvaged from a roofless farm building in 1975 for the reorganized American Shire Horse

FIGURE 3-42   Grange Wood William, a recent champion at the Shire Horse Show in Peterborough, England. Shires are the largest of the draft breeds. Some weigh 2500 pounds and stand taller than most adult males. [*The Draft Horse Journal.*]

Association of Pingree, Idaho. Sue Wilson, secretary of this organization, is recording registrations and promoting the breed. She imported some Shires from England recently and has a herd of approximately fifty head. Two breeders in Maryland, Herbert Behrendt of Highland and Howard Streaker, Jr., of West Friendship, have also imported some Shires and established breeding herds.

## Suffolk

ORIGINS    Known originally as the Suffolk Punch, the Suffolk hails from East Anglia in England. Tradition has it that the breed traces to Norman stallion crosses on ancient native Suffolk mares. Some authorities claim that every Suffolk traces to a stallion called *Crisp's Horse of Ufford*, foaled in 1768.

CHARACTERISTICS    The Suffolk is short (relative to other draft breeds) and compactly powerful in appearance—it is 16 hands tall and weighs from 1400 to 1500 pounds (Figure 3-43).

The Suffolk is a true-breeding chestnut horse which may have small

FIGURE 3-43    Happy Valley Jason, many times champion Suffolk stallion in England, shows the modern type of this breed. They are smaller, more rotund, and more "punched" in appearance than other draft breeds. [*The Draft Horse Journal, photograph by Harold Cline.*]

white markings on the face and legs. The neck is highly crested, the shoulders and quarters massively muscled, the legs unfeathered and sturdy, and the feet hard. The Suffolk is an attractive if not flashy mover, and has a docile and willing disposition. Suffolks are extremely long-lived—one mare of 37 was shown with foal at side.

FUNCTION   The Suffolk is bred and used in England for farming and dray pulling. In the United States it is mainly used in show hitches.

THE REGISTRY   Frank Lassiter suggests there may be only 200 Suffolks in the world, shared equally by breeders in England and the United States.[10] However, it is known that some Suffolks have been exported to Africa, Australia, and the Soviet Union. The American Suffolk Horse Association has registered only about ten foals each year for the past decade.

## Mules

A mule is a hybrid resulting from a cross between two species of the Equidae family—the *Equus caballus* or mare and the *asinus* or jack. The cross of a jennet (female ass) with a stallion produces a hinny, which cannot be distinguished from a mule.

Mules are almost always sterile. Mare mules have regular heat cycles; however, they do not settle. Uncastrated mules are aggressive breeders, but are likewise sterile.

Modern usage of mules justifies classifying them into three size and use categories:

1  Draft mules for show and work
2  Riding mules for pleasure and competition
3  Miniature mules for driving, riding, showing, hunting, and jumping

*Draft mule* production is essentially static; riding mules and miniature mules are in greater demand. *Riding mules* can be seen more frequently on endurance and trail rides—activities formerly relegated to horses. The *miniature and hunting mule* (Figure 3-44) industries are less than 2 decades old and are growing rapidly.

Mule shows to accommodate all types of mule activities have sprung up around the country. Perhaps the largest mule show and exhibition is the annual mule festival in Bishop, California.

Most mules are good workers, some are excellent jumpers, and a few are superb riding animals. All are clever and patient, and willing to pay a small price to achieve their objectives—which may conflict with those of

[10]Frank Lassiter, *Horse Power*, Reiman Publication, Milwaukee, Wisconsin, 1977.

**FIGURE 3-44**  A boy and his miniature mule. Randy Conklin, Columbia, Mo., and the mule size each other up. A number of young people find pleasure with miniature mules. They make good 4-H projects. [*Courtesy of Duane Dailey.*]

their owners. Mule tenders find these characteristics easy to cope with and are saddened by the written and spoken abuses heaped on mules.

The nature of the mule is different from that of the horse. The mule is wiser when it comes to its own welfare than a horse. When frustrated or uncertain, the mule stops and thinks it over. We call it stubborn for this. Unlike a horse, the mule almost never will overeat or founder and will seldom run into obstacles when running off.

Mules are surefooted in rough terrain. Their intuition about what is unsafe footing is quite good, and they will negotiate danger areas, such as slick spots and quagmires, only after careful appraisal.

The disposition of mare mules is considered to be more desirable than that of horse mules. Horse mules play with great vigor. They sometimes get injured in the process, playing with such enthusiasm that they keep getting spots of hide and hair knocked off. Chasing calves is sometimes a problem when cattle are kept with them. However, not all horse mules are this active.

Mules are hardier than horses. They can withstand more heat and stress, carry and pull heavier loads, and live longer than horses. They take care of themselves better than horses under conditions of hardship and probably do so with less feed. However, this difference is not great, and overwork and stress should not be imposed upon mules merely because they can be expected to survive it.

## Draft Mules

ORIGINS Draft mules are expensive to breed, maintain, and show. Sorrel is about the only acceptable color, and Belgian mares are bred to Mammoth jacks to produce it. Feed costs per mule produced, especially in herds of low fertility, are high (Figure 3-45).

CHARACTERISTICS Winning draft show mules must have attractive heads with long, pointed ears. While many weigh 1400 pounds or more, they must show refinement and quality in the neck, head, and legs. Although shown in very high (fat) condition, their necks must not show heavy crests or "pones" of fat. Mules are longer-backed and shorter in the croup than horses; however, short backs and long croups are very desirable. Smoothness and reasonably straight legs are sought.

FIGURE 3-45 Draft mule show scene at a recent Missouri State Fair. The excitement of a mule show is in a class by itself, and large crowds gather to see the gyrations of mule handlers in an attempt to "get their ears up" when the judge approaches. [*Courtesy of Duane Dailey.*]

FUNCTION   Draft mules are shown in hand by age and sex as singles, pairs, and groups of five. Adult mules are shown in two- and four-mule hitches in decorated harness, pulling attractive wagons.

It is rare to see mules doing farm or field work even in states sponsoring large shows for draft mules. Most mules are purchased for show or sale and are hitched only to wagons for practice, parade, or show. However, numerous mules of various quality may be seen doing field work in the southeastern United States. Farm teams as well as show prospects sell well at the annual mule sale in Memphis, Tennessee.

## Riding Mules

ORIGINS AND CHARACTERISTICS   A trim, 14-hand jack crossed with Quarter Horse or Thoroughbred-type mares produces a good riding mule prospect. However, many leisure riders prefer a smaller mule and select those in the 54- or 56-inch height range.

Gaited riding mules, rare but popular, make excellent mounts. They are obtained by breeding Tennessee Walking mares or Fox Trotting mares to small jacks. About half of the offspring from these crosses inherit, to

FIGURE 3-46 Virl Norton of San Jose, California, and his good traveling mule, Lady Louise, winner of the Bicentennial Great American Horse Race from Frankfort, New York, to Sacramento, California. Starting the race were 152 contestants; 52 finished. Good mules are very competitive in distance riding events. [*Photograph by Dennis Underwood, courtesy of Curtis L. Lewis.*]

some degree, the natural gait of their mothers. Weanling or yearling mules with a "shuffle"—a tendency to gait—sell for high prices.

FUNCTION   Since Virl Norton of San Jose, California, won the Bicentennial Great Horse Race riding a mule from Frankfort, New York, to Sacramento, California, demand for riding mules has been brisk (Figure 3-46). During the 1970s they have appeared on distance and trail rides with increasing frequency and with substantial success. Because of the mule's characteristic toughness, it is likely that the number of mules in endurance riding events will increase. Mules have always surpassed horses in tests of hardship and endurance.

## Miniature, Hunting, and Jumping Mules

ORIGINS   Size is the only visible difference between these three types of mules, for they are bred alike and perform in similar activities. Mares of the

FIGURE 3-47   Julie, a 48-inch jumping mule, clears a 65-inch jump for her handler, Roger Conklin, Columbia, Mo. A standing jump is required, and hind legs below the hocks must not touch the top board. [*Photograph by Duane Dailey.*]

Shetland pony type are usually crossed with a small jack to produce these mules.

CHARACTERISTICS  Miniature mules are 48 inches at the withers or less. Hunting and jumping mules have several height divisions: 48 inches and under; 50 inches and under; 52 inches and under; and over 52 inches.

Mules tend to have low, wide, round withers, and do not hold a saddle well. A medium-wide gullet in the saddle helps somewhat. Mules are generally harder-mouthed than horses and require more control.

FUNCTION  Miniature mules are broken to ride and drive and also are shown for conformation. Coon-hunting mules follow hounds over wire fences by the simple expedient of the rider dismounting and placing a coat over the wire so the mule could see it. Today, most hunting mules are used primarily in show jumping, as the mule has amazing ability to stand flat-footed and jump a solid wall 12 to 16 inches higher than the withers (Figure 3-47). Some hunting mules never show-jump, but can jump over a tailgate into a pickup or over a farm fence easily. Because of their toughness, miniature and hunting mules are used in rough terrain for trail riding.

## APPENDIX 3-1  BREED AND HORSE ASSOCIATION ADDRESSES

### Light Horses

*Albino*

American Albino Association
Box 79
Crabtree, OR 97335

*Andalusian*

American Andalusian Horse Association
c/o Sweet Life Farm
P.O. Box 809
Warrenton, VA 22186

*Appaloosa*

Appaloosa Horse Club, Inc.
Box 8403
Moscow, IL 83843

Appaloosa Horse Club of Canada
Box 3036 Station "B"
Calgary, Alta. T2M 4L6

*Arabian*

Arabian Horse Club Registry of America, Inc.
3435 S. Yosemite Street
Denver, CO 80231

Half-Arab & Anglo-Arab Registries
P.O. Box 4502
Burbank, CA 91503

International Arabian Horse Association
P.O. Box 4502
Burbank, CA 91503

*Bashkir*

American Bashkir Curley Registry
Box 453
Ely, NV 89301

*Bay*

American Bay Horse Association
P.O. Box 884F
Wheeling, IL 60090

*Buckskin*

International Buckskin Horse Association, Inc.
P.O. Box 357
St. John, IN 46373

*Cleveland Bay*
Cleveland Bay Society of America
Middleburg, VA 22117

*Easy Rider*
Easy Rider Gaited Horse Association
Box 365
Herrin, IL 62948
Paul D. Short, President

*Fox Trotting Horse*

American Fox Trotting Horse Breed Assn., Inc.
100½ South Crittenden
Marshfield, MO 65706

Missouri Fox Trotting Horse Breed Assn., Inc.
P.O. Box 637
Ava, MO 65068

*Galiceño*

Galiceño Horse Breeder's Association, Inc.
111 East Elm Street
Tyler, TX 75701

*Morab*

Morab Horse Registry of America
P.O. Box 143
Clovis, CA 93612

*Morgan*

American Morgan Horse Association, Inc.
Oneida County Airport Industrial Park
P.O. Box 1
Westmoreland, NY 13490

Half-Morgan Horse Register
P.O. Box 341
Leavenworth, WA 98826

*Mustang*

American Mustang Association, Inc.
P.O. Box 338
Yucaipa, CA 92399

Spanish Mustang Registry, Inc.
Route 4, Box 64
Council Bluffs, IA 51501

*Paint*

American Paint Horse Association
P.O. Box 13486
Fort Worth, TX 76118

*Palomino*

Palomino Horse Breeders of America
Box 249
Mineral Wells, TX 76067

Palomino Horse Association, Inc.
P.O. Box 324
Jefferson City, MO 65101

*Part-Blooded*

American Part-Blooded Horse Registry
4120 SE River Drive
Portland, OR 97222
J. C. Abbett, Registrar

*Paso Fino*

American Paso Fino Horse Association, Inc.
Mellon Bank Building, Room 3018
525 William Penn Place
Pittsburgh, PA 15219

American Association of Owners and Breeders of Peruvian Paso Horses
P.O. Box 2035
California City, CA 93505

Paso Fino Owners and Breeders Association, Inc.
P.O. Box 1579
Tryon, NC 28782

Peruvian Paso Horse Registry of North America
P.O. Box 816
Guerneville, CA 95446

International Peruvian Paso Horse Assn., Inc.
P.O. Box 157
Lancaster, TX 75146

Peruvian Paso Half-Blood Association
43058 N. 42nd Street West
Lancaster, CA 93534

*Pinto*

Pinto Horse Association of America, Inc.
910 W. Washington Avenue
San Diego, CA 92103

*Quarter Horse*

American Quarter Horse Association
Amarillo, TX 79168

National Quarter Horse Registry, Inc.
P.O. Box 235
Raywood, TX 77582

Original Half-Quarter Horse Registry
Hubbard, OR 97032

Standard Quarter Horse Association
4390 Fenton Street
Denver, CO 80212

*Racking Horse*

Racking Horse Breeders Association of America
Helena, AL 35080
Susan M. Derocher, Editor

*Rangerbred*

Colorado Ranger Horse Association, Inc.
7023 Eden Mill Road
Woodbine, MD 21797

*Saddle Horse*

American Saddle Horse Breeder's Assn., Inc.
929 South 4th Street
Louisville, KY 40203

American Saddlebred Pleasure Horse Association
801 South Court Street
Scott City, KS 67871

Half-Saddlebred Registry of America
660 Poplar Street
Coshocton, OH 43812

*Spanish-Barb*

Spanish-Barb Breeder's Association
P.O. Box 7479
Colorado Springs, CO 80907

*Tennessee Walking Horse*

Tennessee Walking Horse Breeders' and Exhibitors
Association of America
P.O. Box 286
Lewisburg, TN 37091

*Thoroughbred*

 The Jockey Club
 300 Park Avenue
 New York, NY 10022

 American Remount Association, Inc.
 Thoroughbred Half-Bred Registry
 P.O. Box 1066
 Perris, CA 92370

*Trotting Horse (Standardbreds)*

 United States Trotting Association
 750 Michigan Avenue
 Columbus, OH 43215

## Draft Horses

*Belgian*

 Belgian Draft Horse Corporation of America
 P.O. Box 335
 Wabash, IN 46992

*Clydesdale*

 Clydesdale Breeders of the United States
 Route 1, Box 131
 Pecatonica, IL 61063

*Percheron*

 Percheron Horse Association of America
 RFD #1
 Belmont, OH 43718

*Shire*

 The American Shire Horse Association
 Box 19
 Pingree, ID 83262

*Suffolk*

 American Suffolk Horse Association
 672 Polk Blvd
 Des Moines, IA 50312

## Ponies

*Appaloosa*

> National Appaloosa Pony, Inc.
> P.O. Box 206
> Gaston, IN 47342

*Connemara*

> American Connemara Pony Society
> RFD #1
> Hoshiekon Farm
> Goshen, CT 06756

*Gliding*

> Gliding Pony and Horse Registries
> 19100 Bear Creek Road
> Los Gatos, CA 95030

*Gotland*

> American Gotland Horse Association
> RFD #2, Box 181
> Elkland, MO 65644

*Hackney*

> American Hackney Horse Society
> P.O. Box 174
> Pittsfield, IL 62363
>
> Pony of the Americas Club, Inc. (POA)
> P.O. Box 1447
> Mason City, IA 50401

*Pony*

> Kanata Pony Association
> 35388 Hallert Avenue
> Matsqui, B.C.

*Quarter Pony*

> American Quarter Pony Association
> RFD #1
> New Sharon, IA 50207

*Shetland*

> American Shetland Pony Club
> P.O. Box 468
> Fowler, IN 47944

*Trotting Pony*

> National Trotting Pony Association, Inc.
> 575 Broadway
> Hanover, PA 17331

> U.S. Trotting Pony Association
> P.O. Box 468
> Fowler, IN 47944

*Walking Pony*

> American Walking Pony Association
> RFD #5, Box 88
> Upper River Road
> Macon, GA 31201

*Welsh*

> Welsh Pony Society of America, Inc.
> P.O. Drawer A
> White Post, VA 22663

## Donkeys and Mules

*Donkey*

> American Donkey & Mule Society, Inc.
> 2410 Executive Drive
> Indianapolis, IN 46241

*Miniature Donkey*

> Miniature Donkey Registry of United States
> 1108 Jackson Street
> Omaha, NB 68102

*Jack and Jennet*

> Standard Jack & Jennet Registry of America
> RFD #7, Todds Road
> Lexington, KY 40502

*Miniature Mule*

Missouri Miniature Mule Association, Inc.
801 Logan
Harrisonville, MO 64701

## Associations

American Horse Council
1700 K Street, NW
Washington, D.C. 20006

American Horse Shows Association
527 Madison Avenue
New York, NY 10022

American Stock Horse Association, Inc.
P.O. Box 56
Omaha, AR 72662

National Cutting Horse Association
P.O. Box 12155
Fort Worth, TX 76116
[Zack T. Wood, Secretary]

National Reining Horse Association
R.R. #3
Coshocton, OH 43812
Kay Potts

National Trotting and Paceing Association, Inc.
575 Broadway
Hanover, PA 17331
Donald R. Moul, Exec. Sec.

Thoroughbred Racing Associations
5 Dakota Dr., Lake Success
Hyde Park, NY 12538

Thoroughbred Owners and Breeders Association
P.O. Box 4038
Lexington, KY 40504

## BIBLIOGRAPHY

Ensminger, M. E.: *Horses and Horsemanship*, Interstate, Danville, Ill., 1969.
Evans, J. W., A. Borton, H. Hintz, and L. Dale Van Vleck: *The Horse*, Freeman, San Francisco, 1977.

Gianoli, Luigi: *Horses and Horsemanship through the Ages*, Crown, New York, 1969.

Kays, John M.: *The Horse*, Barnes, New York, 1969.

Lassiter, Frank: *Horse Power*, Reiman Publications, Wisconsin, 1977.

Mills, Frank C.: *History of American Jacks and Mules—Recollections*, Hutch-Line, Inc., Kansas, 1977.

Stoneridge, M. A.: *A Horse of Your Own*, Doubleday, New York, 1968.

Thompson, Diana: "Resurrection of the Draft—Is the Draft Horse Coming Back over the Horizon?" *Equus*, vol. 13, p. 42.

Welsh, Peter C.: *Track and Road—The American Trotting Horse*, Smithsonian Institution Press, Washington, D.C., 1967.

Willett, Peter: *The Thoroughbred*, Putnam, New York, 1970.

# FORM FOLLOWS FUNCTION

## JUDGING CONFORMATION

t is difficult to overstress conformation when appraising the worth of a horse. Except for breeding stock, the horse is useful only when in motion, for in a very real sense, the horse is an athlete. Any physical handicap that causes the horse to be clumsy, use excessive energy to perform a task, be hard-riding, lack strength or speed, or wear excessively decreases its potential usefulness.

The breeder or prospective buyer can save much time and expense by avoiding horses whose potentials are limited by physical handicaps.

Some physical handicaps are acquired through faulty diet or injury, but probably far more of these are claimed than actually exist. In most cases, the condition is genetic and must be ascribed to the sire and/or dam. For this reason, breeding animals, especially stallions, should be free of major defects in conformation.

Certain characteristics of conformation are prerequisites for good performance, no matter what breed or end use is contemplated. Soundness is essential for any kind of performance. A good disposition increases the likelihood of satisfaction in all horse activities.

THEME PRIZE

FIGURE 4-1   Nowhere was "accurate appraisal and total recall" more essential in horse judging than in assembling the famous Anheuser-Busch Clydesdale hitches before establishment of the breeding herd at Grants Farm, St. Louis, Missouri, that now produces them. [*Courtesy of Anheuser-Busch, Inc., St. Louis, Mo.*]

Judging is not guessing; it is sound reasoning, based on accurate observation and evaluation of what is seen. Buying horses requires prompt accurate appraisal with total recall (Figure 4-1).

## The Judging Procedure

To develop a procedure for observing a horse that brings into good view all component parts, a firm foundation of knowledge is necessary. First, know what the points of the horse are (Figure 4-2); second, carry in mind the *ideal* horse of the specific breed or type with which to compare the parts and the individual you are observing.

There are two parts to a good judging procedure. The first is a *brief but systematic overview*. Any horse passing muster in this first observation deserves the time it takes for the second part of the judging procedure, a *careful, point-by-point analysis*.

SYSTEMATIC OVERVIEW   First look at the horse from the side from a distance of 15 or more feet. This is a rough sorting out into "haves" and "have-nots." Look for overall balance, size, breed type, attractiveness or style, and for major faults. Smoothness, balance, and symmetry result when all parts blend together, are of proportionate size, and contribute equally to the whole of a symmetrical individual. These, combined with refinement, alertness, and a proud carriage, contribute to style (Figure 4-3) in every breed.

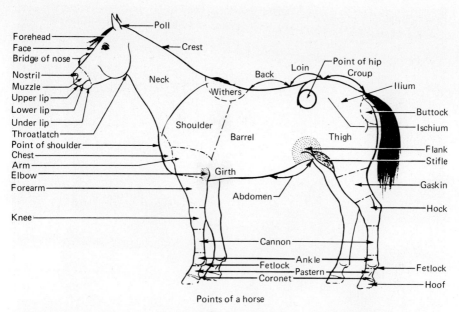

Points of a horse

FIGURE 4-2   Points of a horse. These must be learned before developing a procedure for observing and judging a horse. [*Courtesy of the American Quarter Horse Association.*]

Move in front of the horse to look at its head, chest, and front legs (Figure 4-4). Does the horse have a good head, good eyes, alert ears? Does the neck blend into the shoulders well? Pay particular attention to the front legs and feet for few horses are perfect here. Do the legs come out of the corners of the body with the correct width of chest? Are the knees, ankles, and the center of the feet straight under the corners of the upper leg and body? Are the feet dark? Do they appear to be dense and tough?

Move three or four steps to the left at a 45° angle to the horse's body. Are the hips smooth? Are the coupling and back short and strong? Are the legs straight with reasonably large, round, deep-heeled feet? How do the parts of the horse blend?

What about refinement? Does the horse have trim legs with flat bone and clearly visible arteries and veins on them rather than coarse, thick, meaty legs which denote poor circulation? Are the shoulders long and sloping and the pasterns of appropriate length and slope?

Move straight behind the horse (Figure 4-5). Are the legs straight and well-muscled, the cannons short, and the hips smooth? Looking over the back, do you see a blending of parts, high withers that will hold a saddle, and a fine, nicely arched neck?

Move back to the far side for another overall view for balance and final deliberation.

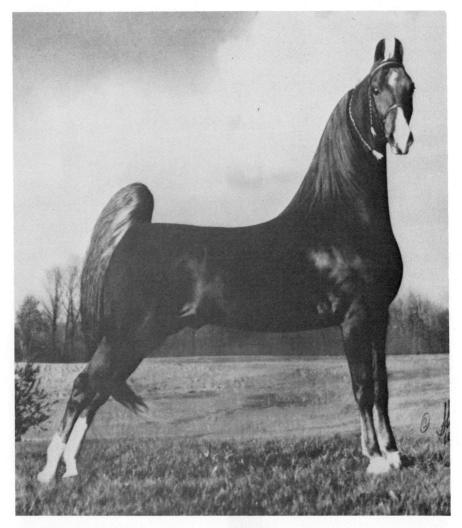

FIGURE 4-3   Smoothness and blending of parts combined with refinement, alertness, and proud carriage contribute to style, as shown by Mr. Magic Man. [*Photograph by Shirley, courtesy of Mr. and Mrs. Alvin C. Ruxer, Jasper, In.*]

A thorough overall examination of a standing horse need not take more than 2 or 3 minutes, with 1 or 2 more minutes spent in deep thought comparing the horse to the ideal. After the initial examination, if you are still impressed, examine in more detail for conformation, soundness, and way of going.

CAREFUL, POINT-BY-POINT ANALYSIS   The practiced horseman begins his analysis at the *foot*—because "no foot, no horse." Feet should be neither too

FIGURE 4-4    Look for a good head, blending of parts, straight legs, alertness, and style when evaluating a horse from a front view. [*From Bradley and Slemp, 1976.*]

FIGURE 4-5    Stand directly behind a horse and evaluate him for straight legs, muscling, height of tail-set, and blending of parts. [*From Bradley and Slemp, 1976.*]

large, too small, nor too narrow. The heels should not be high enough to give an upright position to the foot. The soles should not be too flat; well-shod horses generally leave a faint impression of the frog on a well-raked surface. The bulbs of the heel should be elastic. The feet should be free from scratches and pathological conditions such as thrush (see Chapter 14).

The *pastern* should be clean-cut and wide from front to rear, thick and wide when viewed from the side. Tendons and ligaments should be well-defined and developed. The best pastern is medium in length—a long pastern strains tendons, a short pastern lacks the spring necessary to absorb shock.

The *cannon* bone should be relatively short as compared with the forearm. Good bone is in evidence if the cannon looks wide when viewed from front to rear and is clean-cut, well-defined, and vertical when seen from any direction. Tendons running down the cannon should also be well-defined.

The horse's knee is equivalent to the human wrist. It should be clean and well-defined, the covering skin thin and relatively delicate. When viewed from the front, the knee should be thick and flat, from the side, wide. A wide surface at the knee indicates good articulation, strength, and stability in movement. The knee-cannon connection line should be as nearly vertical as is reasonable.

The *forearm* is composed of two bones, the radius and the ulna. Taken as a whole the forearm must be long, wide, thick, and muscularly well-defined.

The ulna, or *elbow*, uniting the arm or humerus to the radius, should be prominent and stand well away from the sides of the chest, but parallel to the body.

The *arm*, or humerus, connects the shoulder to the forearm. It is extremely important, but often overlooked because it is well-hidden by muscles. Length of stride is directly affected by the arm; a long arm will describe a large arc which will increase amplitude in the gallop and jump.

The scapula, or shoulder bone (Figure 4-6), is not attached directly to the backbone. Instead, it is connected by muscles and ligaments to the neck, withers, and ribs. It is an oblique bone, and should be long and flat.

The point of the shoulder should be well-defined, with legs set on at proper intervals.

A plumb line dropped from the point of the shoulder should bisect the knee, cannon, ankle, and foot. One dropped from the arm should bisect the forearm, knee, cannon, and fetlock, and pass behind the heel (Figure 4-7).

Splayed feet and pigeon toes are quite common and affect action in proportion to their degree. Knock knees, bowed knees, and base-narrow defects are less common but affect action and predispose the horse to unsoundness.

Short, straight pasterns increase concussion to the horse and rider, seriously predisposing the horse to unsoundness and inducing fatigue in

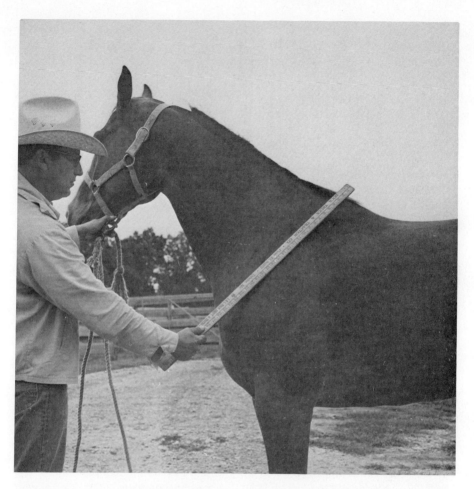

**FIGURE 4-6**   Long, sloping shoulders (at an angle of about 45°) indicate an easier ride, less shock and wear on the feet and legs, and more extension of stride in walking and running. Also observe the withers; they should be high and sharp, and extend well back under the saddle. [*From Bradley and Slemp, 1976.*]

both the horse and rider. Long, weak pasterns allow an easy ride but affect action and are undesirable for good stops with roping horses (Figure 4-8).

Calf knees are common and detract from appearance; buck knees are uncommon except with jumpers. A "tied-in" condition below the knee indicates tendon and ligament development that are inadequate for long trouble-free service.

The *hock* corresponds to the ankle in humans. It acts as a powerful spring to furnish impulsion, and also absorbs the shock of locomotion. It

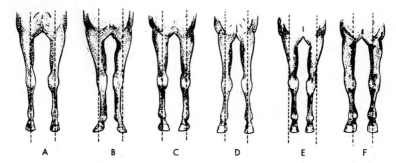

FIGURE 4-7    (A) Straight-legged, good front; (B) splayfooted; (C) pigeon-toed; (D) knock-kneed, narrow front, wide base; (E) narrow base; (F) bow-kneed. [*From Bradley, 1977.*]

is subject to many injuries that are difficult to detect. Both hocks, as with all structures of the horse's legs, should appear *exactly* the same.

For power, the hock should appear wide from the side, at the top, and at the base; thick when viewed from front or rear; and clean-cut, with only the normal bony prominences. The hock should seem dense and powerful.

Ideally the hock should be set low, forming a large, open angle of about 160°. Poor angles often accompany sickle hocks (Figure 4-9). It should be possible to draw a line from both the side and the back from the point of the buttock straight down through the point of the hock parallel to the cannon bone and the fetlock. The distance from the haunches to the hock should be very long to accommodate the principal muscles providing impulsion.

FIGURE 4-8    (A) Correct, good bone; (B) pastern too straight; (C) pastern too long and flat, angle of pastern different from that of foot (coon-footed); (D) short straight pastern calf-kneed; (E) buck-kneed or over on the knee; (F) fine bone below the knee (tied in). [*From Bradley, 1977.*]

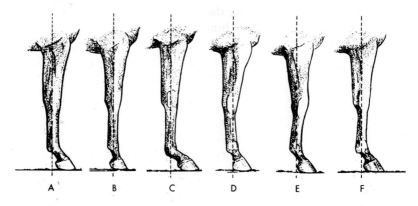

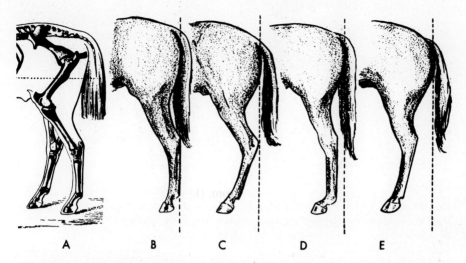

FIGURE 4-9    (A) Correct skeletal structure; (B) correct leg set; (C) excessive flexion of the hock (sickle-hocked); (D) legs that are too straight (post-legged or coon-footed); (E) camped under or stands under. [*From Bradley, 1977.*]

Almost all horses display cow hocks to a degree. Some horsemen prefer that hocks point slightly toward each other with the feet pointing slightly outward. This is insurance against wide hocks or bandy legs. However, extremely noticeable cow hocks are undesirable, from the standpoints of both action and appearance.

Bandy legs or wide-set hocks seriously deter collected action and predispose to unsoundness.

Sickle hocks are quite common and are serious because of the stress placed on the hocks in performance and the many unsoundnesses that are associated with them. View a stallion with sickle hocks with concern.

Boggy hocks are usually seen with post legs.

The *gaskin* runs from above the hock to below the stifle, and corresponds to the calf in humans. It should exhibit great muscular development. It should be long, allowing the hock to be well let down.

The *stifle* corresponds to the human knee. It is the joint lying between the femur and the tibia. It should be set close to the abdomen and slightly outward. The stifle joint connects the patella with the tibia and fibula of the gaskin. For this reason, the way the stifle joint is set determines how the hind legs are set. If the stifle is too far from the abdomen, the result will be cow hocks. If the stifle is too close, the horse will be out at the hocks or pigeon-toed (Figure 4-10).

The *croup* transmits impulsion from the hindquarters through the spinal column. It should be relatively long, approaching the horizontal, and be wide, muscular, and thick.

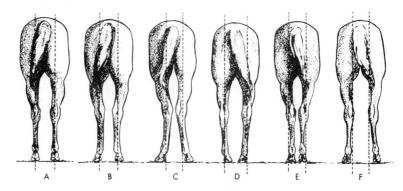

FIGURE 4-10 (A) Straight-legged; (B) slightly cow-hocked; (C) extremely cow-hocked, splayfooted; (D) bowlegged or bandy-legged or "too wide"; (E) narrow base or stands close; (F) wide base or stands wide. [*From Bradley, 1977.*]

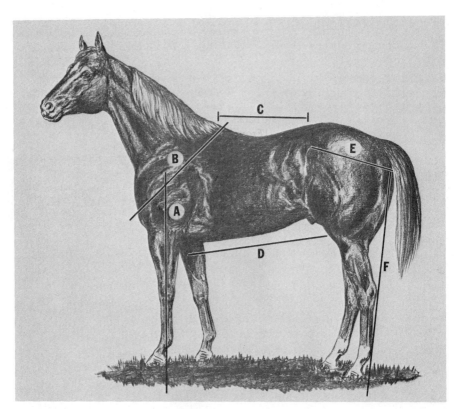

FIGURE 4-11 Observe the side view of a horse for long sloping shoulders; short, strong back; long underline; and long, rather level croup. These characteristics increase the probability that our horse is, or can become, a good "athlete." [*American Quarter Horse Association, drawing by Orlin Mixer and adapted by Doug Ross.*]

To be strong, the *back* should be short. The *ribs* should spring outward and backward from the spine. If the ribs are properly sprung and the back is sufficiently short, there should be room for about one man-sized fist between the last rib and the point of the hip.

Short backs with long underlines move the fore and rear legs farther apart, tend to raise the croup and head, contribute to style and action, and increase height and length of stride. The short back is usually more muscular (Figures 4-11, 4-12, and 4-13).

The length and shape of a horse's neck and the size of its head affect action. Fine throats facilitate breathing and allow maximum flexion of the chin without binding the jaws on the neck. Short-necked, thick-throated horses steer hard and may sling the head, as a result of jaw pressure, when pulled up short. The size of the head should be in accord with breed requirements.

*Quality* is indicated by refinement of head, bone, and joints, and hair coat. It is reflected in thin skin, and prominent veins, and in the absence of coarseness, especially in the legs. Good circulation in the legs is important to durability. Coarse, meaty legs indicate poor circulation, and tend to stock, puff, bog, and become unsound.

FIGURE 4-12 Insist on a short back for strength; the horse is less likely to tire under heavy weight or long use. Short backs usually are associated with short, strong couplings and more stylish horses. [*From Bradley and Slemp, 1976.*]

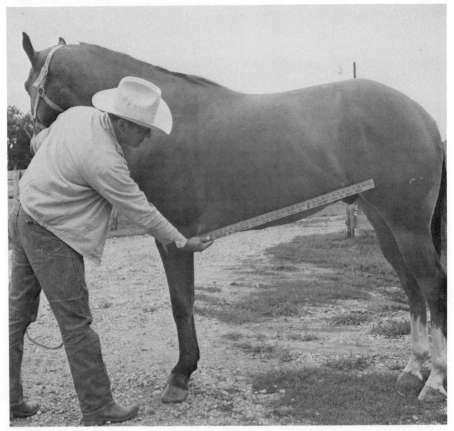

FIGURE 4-13  A long underline keeps the forelegs and rear legs farther apart, increases length of stride, and contributes to style. [*From Bradley and Slemp, 1976.*]

The *chest* area between the forelegs must be of good size—an essential indicator of adequate room for vital organs as the heart and lungs.

The *withers* should be relatively high, clean-cut, and prominent, and should run well back, disappearing nicely into the rest of the back. Such withers guarantee that the saddle will stay in the right place. Low, excessively rounded, short, or mutton-shaped withers indicate a horse is poorly balanced and possibly clumsy.

The topline should be as graceful and appealing as possible—the neck should seem to flow into the withers, the withers into the back. The back should be raised slightly at the croup. Overall, the distance from the point of shoulder to the stifle should be greater than from the point of hip to the withers. The length of the horse's head should be equal to or slightly less than the line of shoulder.

Finally, the *forehead* should be broad and flat, with prominent, well-set *eyes* (Figure 4-14). The eyes should be clear and bright. The *ears* should

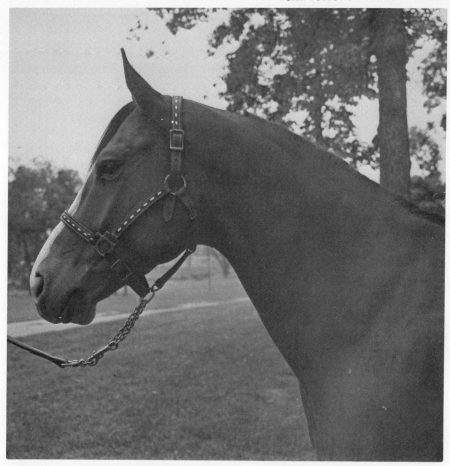

**FIGURE 4-14**  Head and neck contribute to the balance, style, and flexibility of a horse. The head should be clean-cut with refined features. The neck should be long, slightly arched, refined, and clean at the throatlatch. [*From Bradley and Slemp, 1976.*]

be relatively short, and clean-cut, and active. *Lips* and *nostrils* should be fine and soft, the *muzzle* clean and not loose-lipped. The *mouth* should be examined for bit injuries and age determination (see Appendix 4-1). The *neck* should be fairly long, well-directed, and muscular.

## JUDGING ACTION

Good action is determined largely by the set of the feet and legs, the slope of the shoulders and pasterns, and the shortness of back and coupling relative to the length of underline or belly. Good action reflects relative structural straightness, physical fitness, and confidence gained from systematic training.

## The Judging Procedure

Try to see the horse before it is warmed up, to see its natural, relaxed movement in its stall or while walking quietly around the barn area. The steps
should be even and true, never quicker on one foot than the others. *Listen
to the rhythm* of the walk and trot. *Examine the track* in a well-raked, soft
surface. *Observe the horse's action* from the front and from behind (on the
approach and going away).

The feet and legs of a horse at the walk or trot should move straight
ahead, parallel to an imaginary center line in the direction of travel (Figure
4-15). The feet should rock upward from the heel and break over squarely
at the toe, and they should rise with a snap. They should be carried forward
in a straight arc, with the highest point of the arc occurring at the center
of travel or when the supporting leg is passed. They should be set solidly
and squarely on the ground with toes pointing straight ahead. Any deviation from this procedure is a defect of action. This is not to say that all good
horses must have perfect action. Many compensate by intelligence, willingness, and practice; however, correct action would make them better horses.

THE GAITS    Knowledge of the correct characteristics of the various gaits is a
prerequisite to judging action. *Speed, beat,* and *footfall pattern* are the
variables used to describe each gait. There is a characteristic average speed
for each gait; however, the athletic, well-trained horse will be able to
demonstrate well-balanced speed versions of each—a slow trot as well as a

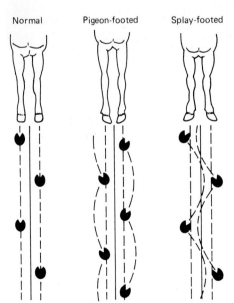

Normal        Pigeon-footed        Splay-footed

FIGURE 4-15 *Left to right:* Straight
legs usually move straight forward.
Pigeon toes swing outward at the height
of stride and "rope walk" on the
ground. Splayfeet swing inward in
stride and may interfere with or strike
the supporting ankle. [*Art courtesy of
Doug Ross, Columbia, Mo.*]

working trot; a slow, collected canter as well as a faster, more extended canter. Beat refers to the number of individual beats in each gait, be it two, three, or four. Rhythm must be maintained in all versions of the gait. Footfall pattern refers to the order in which the feet move in producing each gait.

*Two-beat gaits*

*Trot.*   Diagonal forefeet and hind feet rise and fall together (Figure 3-15). The body travels in a straight line, but rises and falls with an uncomfortable jar to the rider. It is the gait for distance riding although it is tiresome to the rider.

*Jog.*   A slow, skimming trot rather easy on rider and horse, common to western stock horses.

*Pace.*   A fast gait with lateral feet paired (Figure 3-11). All four feet leave the ground briefly at speed. Pacers move from side to side as well as up and down, rendering a most uncomfortable ride. The gait is used in harness racing with Standardbreds and ponies.

*Amble.*   Walk at the pace in short strides. It is a very rough and usually slow gait, and occurs more often going down a slope or hill. It is common to natural gaited horses. All horses should be discouraged from developing and using this gait.

*Three-beat gait*

*Canter.*   A slow- to medium-speed gait. The term *lead* refers to which forefoot strikes the ground last; e.g., a horse is said to be on the right lead when its right forefoot is the third beat. The footfall pattern of the canter of a horse on the right lead would be as follows:
    *Beat 1.*   Left hind pushes off.
    *Beat 2.*   Right hind and left fore strike the ground simultaneously.
    *Beat 3.*   Right fore strikes the ground.
Horses exhibiting good *cadence* (energetic rhythm expressed by springiness) will usually show a brief period of suspension after the third beat of the canter. Horses with the more comfortable "rocking chair" canter show little or no period of suspension. For the footfall pattern of a horse at the canter on the left lead, simply reverse the above procedure, with the right hind pushing off on beat 1.

*Four-beat gaits*

*Gallop.*   A fast, four-beat canter. The gallop is also characterized by right or left leads, but the diagonal pair which would, in the canter, hit the ground simultaneously, strike separately instead (Figure 3-12). There is invariably a period of suspension in the gallop, in which all four legs are off the ground. The gallop is a demanding gait and should be used only on horses in good physical condition. It is the racing-speed gait of almost all horses.

*Fox trot.* A broken trot at medium speed where the hind foot leaves the ground slightly later and reaches the ground later than the diagonal forefoot. The horse is "walking in front and trotting behind." A good fox trot is easy on both horse and rider. It has an intermediate nod of the head. This is a popular gait for trial riding. It is the major gait of Missouri Fox Trotters (Figure 3-16).

*Running walk.* A medium to fast speed gait that tends to pair lateral feet more nearly than diagonal feet. In the show ring, the back feet glide with great length of stride and overreach. One foot must be in contact with the ground at all times—no trotting is allowed. Front feet must have the "big lick," i.e., rise high, fold well, and reach far without pointing (Figure 3-20). Nodding of the head is exaggerated. This is the main gait of Tennessee Walking Horses. The show gait is one of the easiest on the rider, but rather demanding on the horse because of the speed demanded and the heavily weighted front feet. Less speed and trappings under pleasure riding conditions demand much less of the horse. Many Tennessee Walkers can perform the gait for hours under conditions of pleasure or competitive riding.

*Paso gait.* Broken pace in which the two lateral legs move almost together, but the hind foot reaches the ground slightly ahead of the front foot. Exaggerated "termino" (winging out) of the front feet is encouraged. The gait is very easy on horse and rider and is performed by the legs with little rise or lateral body movement. It is performed at three speeds—paso fino, a collected show gait (Figure 3-18); paso corto, more relaxed and slightly faster; and paso largo, the speed gait.

*Rack (formerly called single foot).* A fast, flashy gait in which each foot strikes the ground separately at equal intervals. Three feet are either in the air, contacting, or leaving the ground, with most of the weight borne on one foot, hence the name "single foot" or "a walk turned upside down." It is very easy on the rider, but hard on the horse. The rack is required of five-gaited Saddlebred horses (Figure 4-16).

*Stepping pace (slow gait).* A slow gait in which the lateral feet rise together (or almost together), but the front foot arches high and reaches the ground later than the lateral hind foot. When this gait is performed well, the horse 'crouches" behind and "rises" in front, indicating great style. A fairly easy gait to ride but tiring to the horse, it is most useful for showing. It is a requirement of five-gaited Saddlebreds (Figure 3-13).

*Walk.* A slow gait with alternate feet moving forward at equal intervals of time. Three feet are in partial and/or complete contact with the ground, with one in the air moving ahead. Although described as "slow," it should be prompt, animated, and true.

**FIGURE 4-16**  This student-owned Saddlebred horse displays the rack (single-foot) in a practice ring at Stephens College. The left front foot is in contact with the ground (hence, the common name single-foot) while the others are in action off the ground. The rack is a fast, flashy, four-beat gait of equal intervals that is smooth for the rider, but demanding on the horse. [*Photograph by Ligibel, courtesy of Stephens College, Columbia, Mo.*]

Some common defects of action are as follows:

1  *Winding or rope walking.*  A tendency to swing the striding leg around and place it in front of the supporting leg
2  *Dishing or winging in.*  The striding foot swings inward in motion, then outward again at completion of stride
3  *Interfering.*  Striking the supporting leg, usually near the fetlock, with the foot of the striding leg
4  *Paddling.*  An outward deviation in the forefoot and lower leg at flection
5  *Winging.*  Exaggerated paddling, most noticeable in high-going horses
6  *Forging.*  Striking the heel or undersurface of the shoe of a forefoot with the toe of a hindfoot
7  *Rolling.*  Excessive lateral shoulder motion as with wide-fronted horses

8  *Pointing.*  A low, long stride
9  *Dwelling.*  A perceptible pause in flight of the foot before it reaches
the ground
10  *Trappy gait.*  A quick, high, short, jolting stride
11  *Pounding.*  Heavy contact, sometimes resulting from a heavy stride

Straight underpinning does not guarantee good action but it increases the
probability of it.

## JUDGING SOUNDNESS

A horse must be sound of wind, sight, and limb.

Any abnormal deviation in the structure, sight, or wind of a horse can
render it partly or completely useless. Therefore, any defect that affects
serviceability is considered an *unsoundness.*

Those defects that detract from appearance but do not impair serviceability are considered *blemishes.* Blemishes are looked upon with great
disfavor in gaited, parade, and some pleasure horses. Blemishes are more
common in stock horses and tend to detract from their value less than other
types.

An important part of selecting a horse is the ability to recognize common unsoundnesses and blemishes, and the faulty conformation that tends
to predispose the animal toward unsoundness and blemishes. Some horses
become unsound at an early age because of coarse, crooked legs, whereas
others remain useful for years. As with automobiles, abusive treatment,
excessive use, and poor care will render any horse unsound.

### The Judging Procedure

It is not easy to make an accurate diagnosis of a horse's soundness. Often
professional assistance is needed. Whenever possible the horse should be
taken on a trial basis for use under the conditions to which it will be subjected under new ownership. Most horsemen can increase their competence
in identifying unsoundness and blemishes by practicing a system of
inspection.

Whenever possible, *examine the horse in its stall under natural conditions.* Note the manner of tying—the horse may be a halter puller. If
metal covers the manger or feed box, cribbing should be suspected. Look
for signs of a strap around the throat. Note the arrangement of bedding. If
the horse paws, the bedding will be piled up near the back feet. Slight lameness may be detected by movement of bedding caused by pointing. Signs of
kicking may be noted. Move the horse about in the stall, and observe signs
of slight founder, stiffness, and crampiness, and stable attitude.

*Lead the horse from the stall and observe the eyes closely* for normal dilation and color. Test eyesight further by leading it around obstacles, such as bales of hay, immediately after coming out of the stall into bright light. Back the horse and observe hock action for stringhalt and crampiness. Stiff shoulders and/or stiff limbs are indicated by a stilted, sluggish stride.

*Examine for lameness in motion.* Lameness in a front limb is indicated by a nod of the head when weight is placed on the sound limb. The croup drops when weight is shifted from a lame hind limb to a sound one. Splint lameness usually gets worse with exercise, whereas spavin lameness may improve. The horse should be examined when cool, when warmed up, and when cooled off again, at both the walk and trot.

*Check for soundness of wind under conditions of hard work.* Be alert for roaring and heaves or the appearance of a discharge from the nose. Cocked ankles may appear after sharp exercise, and weak fetlocks and knees may tremble.

*Make a general examination with the horse at rest.* He should not point or shift his weight from one forelimb to the other. Stand directly in front of the horse and observe the eyes for signs of cloudiness, position of the ears for alertness, and the face for scars or indentation indicating diseased teeth. Pay particular attention to the knees, cannons, and coronary bands for irregularities.

Move to the side at an oblique angle and note the strength of back and coupling, signs of body scars, and the shape and cleanness of hocks, cannons, fetlocks, and coronary bands. Look for capped hocks, elbows, and leg set from a side view. Stand behind the horse and observe the symmetry of hips, thighs, gaskins, and hocks, and the position of the feet. Move to the opposite side and the oblique angle previously described for a final visual inspection before handling any part of the horse.

The wall of a good hoof is composed of dense horn of uniform color without any signs of cracks in it or rings around it.

*Pick up each foot and look at the bearing surface.* The frog should be full and elastic and help bear weight. The bars should be large and straight. The sole should be arched and should not appear flat as with "dropped sole." Check for hard heels or sidebones, ringbone, corns, contracted feet, and thrush. If the horse is shod, *check for wear on the shoe* from the contraction and expansion of healthy heels.

Examine the hocks (with care, for safety) for swelling, spavins, puffs, curbs, or other irregularities, by feeling when necessary.

A thorough examination combined with a week's trial will identify almost any unsoundness or blemish.

## Limbs

The front feet and legs of a horse bear about 60 percent of its weight. Healthy horses stand at rest with weight equally distributed on both front legs. Lameness in the foot or leg will cause "pointing" (Figure 4-17). Pointing

FIGURE 4-17 Pointing indicates lameness. One foot is positioned ahead of the other in an effort to reduce weight on the affected side. Weight is habitually shifted from one hind limb to the other by healthy horses during rest and does not indicate lameness. [*From Bradley, 1975.*]

refers to a state of rest with one foot positioned about 10 to 12 inches ahead of the other in an effort to reduce weight on the affected side.

Healthy horses habitually shift weight from one hind limb to the other during rest.

As a major shock-absorbing mechanism the feet are subjected to great stress. Horses that work hard most of their lives may acquire one or more unsoundnesses of the feet to varying degrees as they get older. Wide, deep heels and dense horns, combined with proper care and shoeing, will reduce the chances of these conditions developing.

NAVICULAR DISEASE  This condition (it is not truly a disease) is one of the most common causes of lameness, especially in heavy-bodied horses with small feet. Dry, contracted hooves, poor shoeing, and hard work—especially at roping, racing, or trotting on hard surfaces—cause it. (See Chapter 14 for more details.)

A horse with navicular disease tries to relieve the pressure when standing by shifting weight from side to side and by walking on its toes. Both front feet are usually affected. Back feet seldom are (Figure 4-18).

Early stages of the condition are hard to diagnose since x-rays appear normal. Hoof testing locates the area of soreness and may yield early evidence of the developing condition. Later stages result in extreme pain. Treatment consists of rest, therapeutic shoeing (usually raising the heels), and consideration of nerving (posterial digital neurectomy). Posterior digital surgery requires serious consideration, for it is not always successful,

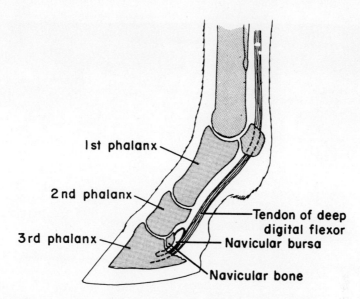

1st phalanx

2nd phalanx

3rd phalanx

Tendon of deep
digital flexor

Navicular bursa

Navicular bone

FIGURE 4-18   Navicular disease is a serious unsoundness. It starts as an inflammation of the deep digital flexor tendon. Erosion of the articulation or junction between the navicular bone and the second and third phalanges results in lameness in advanced cases. [*From McClure, Kirk, and Garrett, 1974.*]

and complications are not uncommon. It may be the only alternative to relieve the horse of pain.

Navicular disease is a serious unsoundness, and horses suspected of having it should be avoided.

SIDEBONES   This is a common unsoundness, especially in gaited horses, resulting from wear, injury, or abuse. On each side of the heel extending above the hoof are elastic cartilages just under the skin that serve as part of the shock-absorbing mechanism. They are commonly termed lateral cartilages (Figure 4-19). When they ossify (turn to bone), they are called sidebones. In the process of ossification they may be firm but movable inward and outward by the fingers. The horse is then considered "hard at the heels." Sidebones are more common to the front outside lateral cartilage than to other locations.

Treatment consists of rest in the early stages of sidebones to prevent prolonged irritation and increased calcium deposition. After 3 to 6 months lameness may cease, and the horse may become serviceably sound. However, if large sidebones develop, lameness may recur each time the horse is used on rocky or irregular terrain. Lowering the hoof wall on the affected side decreases the risk of injury on rough surfaces.

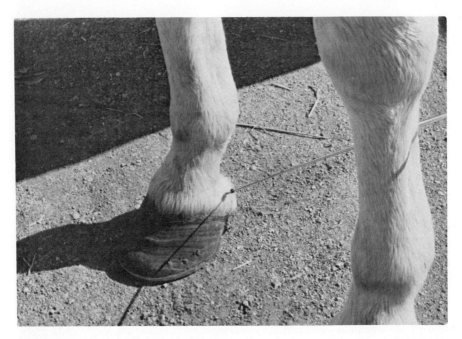

FIGURE 4-19  This prominent sidebone at the top of the hoof head is a result of ossification (turning to bone) of the lateral cartilage. This much ossification usually causes lameness. [*Photograph by the author.*]

LAMINITIS (*FOUNDER*)  Laminitis is an inflammation of the sensitive laminae which attach the hoof wall to the fleshy portion of the foot. When horses gain access to unlimited amounts of grain, founder often results. Other conditions conducive to founder are retained placenta after foaling and lush grass. All feet may be affected, but front feet usually suffer the most.

Symptoms of laminitis include lameness (usually in both front feet), stiffness, settling back on the hind feet to get weight off the forefeet, heat in the hooves, and bounding pulse in the arteries at the back of the pastern. The wall of the hoof separates from the sensitive laminae allowing the coffin bone to rotate within the hoof wall. Because the hoof can no longer grow normally at the toe, the heel outgrows the toe. In long-standing chronic cases, the hooves will turn up (Figure 4-20).

In serious cases, the third phalanx or coffin bone may tilt downward and penetrate the sole of the foot. This type of acute case must be treated immediately. A delay of 24 hours may cause irreparable damage regardless of the treatment given. However, most cases of laminitis can be corrected with proper veterinary attention.

Therapeutic trimming and shoeing can greatly improve chronic cases where founder has caused separation of the hoof wall and curling of the

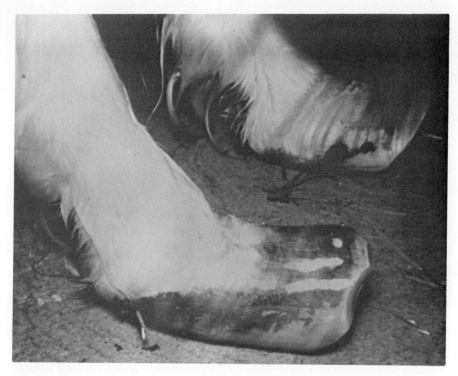

FIGURE 4-20   Laminitis (founder) renders many horses useless for riding and suspect for breeding each year. [*Photograph courtesy of James R. Coffman, D.V.M.*]

toes. In such cases the affected hoof wall can be trimmed away and a replacement made with acrylic. (See Chapter 14 for more details.)

CORNS   Corns appear as reddish spots in the horny sole, usually on the inside of the front feet, near the bars. Many corns lie under the shoe. Advanced cases may ulcerate and cause severe lameness.

There are many causes, but bruises, improper shoeing, and contracted feet are the most common. Reponse to correct treatment and shoeing is usually satisfactory.

HOOF CRACKS   When hoof cracks extend upward to or near the hairline, lameness often results. When well established, the condition is difficult to arrest and cure. Cracking can be prevented in most hooves by proper trimming and shoeing.

If serious, a competent farrier may lace the crack closed with strong wire, fill it with acrylic and use a shoe with clips to prevent opening of the crack.

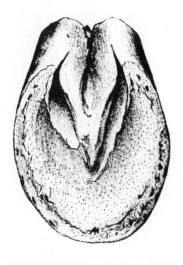

FIGURE 4-21 Contracted feet usually result in lameness if not corrected. This foot has lost its ability to expand and contract in normal shock absorbing action. [*From Salmon, 1886.*]

CONTRACTED FEET   This condition results from continued improper shoeing, prolonged lameness, or excessive dryness. The heels gradually lose their ability to contract and expand when the horse is in motion (Figure 4-21). Horses allowed to overgrow their shoes, and horses with long feet and congenitally narrow heels, are susceptible to contracted feet. Close trimming, leaving the horse unshod, adding moisture, or corrective shoeing usually effects sufficient cure to restore the horse to service. (See Chapter 14 for more details.)

THRUSH   Thrush is a filth disease caused by the anaerobic decomposition of stable manure around the bars and frog of the foot. It may cause lameness. Thrush usually responds promptly and completely to treatment, and cleanliness will prevent recurrence.

SCRATCHES OR GREASE HEEL   Scratches are characterized by inflammation and scab formation on the back surface of the fetlocks above the bulbs of the heels. Thorough cleansing with mild, plain water and careful, complete drying of the area is the best treatment. Infections of the area respond to antibiotic ointments. Grease heel is a similar affliction, mainly found in draft horses and heavily feathered breeds.

RINGBONE   Ringbones are not very common, but are serious unsoundnesses. These bony deposits usually appear just above the coronary band on a front foot, although hind feet may also be affected. High ringbone occurs nearer the ankle. In severe cases the long and short pastern bones may fuse together causing terrible pain and lameness (Figure 4-22).

Any enlargement of the pastern may be ringbone. Ringbone may appear

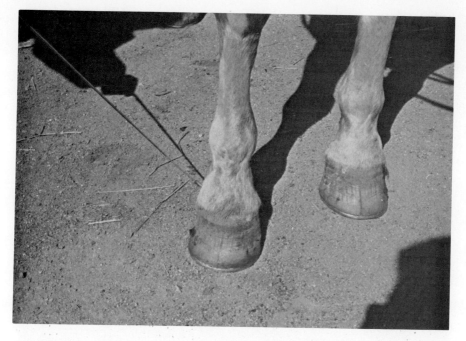

FIGURE 4-22  Ringbones are serious unsoundness. They are bony outgrowths just above the cornary band (low ringbone) or midway to the pastern joint as shown (high ringbone). [*Photograph by the author.*]

on only one or all four feet. Treatment is usually ineffective or only mildly effective. Rest is probably the best treatment, enabling the afflicted horse to return to intermittent light work.

SPLINTS  These are bony deposits that usually appear on the upper inside border of the front cannon (Figure 4-23). They seldom cause protracted lameness, but occasionally a high splint may interfere with the action of the knee and cause unsoundness. Young horses stressed by play or training may pop a splint. If lameness persists more than a few days, a veterinarian should be called.

Some horses have splints on the back legs. Splints occasionally appear on the outside of both front and rear legs.

BOWED TENDONS  Bowed tendons appear as a thickening of the back surface of the leg immediately above the fetlock (Figure 4-24). One or more tendons and ligaments may be affected, but those commonly involved are the superficial flexor tendon, deep flexor tendon, and suspensory ligament of one or both front legs. Predisposing causes are severe strain, wear and

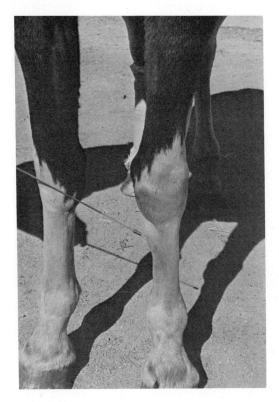

FIGURE 4-23 Splints are bony outgrowths that occur most often on the inside front cannons. They occasionally appear on the outside or inside of either the front or hind cannons. They are usually blemishes. [*Photograph by the author.*]

tear with age, and relatively small tendons attached to light, round bone. They are common to horses that race.

Bowed tendons usually cause severe initial unsoundness, but usually respond to treatment and become sound.

WINDPUFFS OR ROADPUFFS  Small swellings around the ankles and lower cannons are common to horses that are used heavily or trailered a lot, and to older animals. Those with adequate flat bone, well-defined joints, and prominent veins usually have sufficient substance and circulation to withstand wear better than horses with coarse round bones and meaty legs with poorly defined joints and veins.

LACERATIONS  These may appear all over the body, but the front legs, chest, and all four feet bear the brunt of injury, usually because of contact with barbed wire. Scars are usually considered blemishes, but severe cuts around the ankles may sever tendons, resulting in permanent deviation of gait and unsoundness. Some cuts around the coronary band result in misshapen hoof growth and lameness.

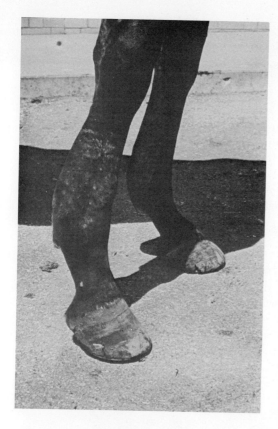

FIGURE 4-24 Bowed tendons usually cause temporary lameness. Stress, overwork, and neglect of the horse's feet induce bowed tendons in young race horses. [*Photograph by the author.*]

CAPPED ELBOW OR SHOE BOIL   This condition is a blemish at the point of the elbow—a puffiness usually caused by pressure from the shoe when the front leg is folded under the body while the horse is lying down. Shoes with calks (heels) cause more damage than flat plates.

The hock is a vulnerable joint; therefore, it is important to examine the hock carefully for unsoundness. Most of the power of a pulling horse is generated in the hindquarters and transmitted to the collar by contact with the ground via the hocks. Working stock horses, jumpers, and dressage horses must bear most of the weight on their hind legs by keeping their hocks well under them if they are to attain maximum flexibility. Degree of finesse is determined in gaited and parade horses by how well they move off their hocks.

Structurally sound hocks, then, should be reasonably deep from top to bottom; well supported by fairly large, flat, straight bone; characterized by clean-cut, well-defined ligaments, tendons, and veins; and free from induced unsoundness and blemishes.

BONE OR JACK SPAVIN   Bone spavins are common unsoundnesses in light horses, especially those with sickle hocks and/or shallow hock joints from top to bottom surmounting fine, round bone. Such conformation is a serious fault in a working stock horse.

A bony enlargement at the base and inside back border of the hock may be a bone spavin (Figure 4-25). Inspect the horse by bending or squatting in front of it and looking between the front legs at the face of the hocks, or by standing near a front leg and looking under the belly at the opposite hock. Before passing judgment, assume the same position and look at the opposite hock. If both hocks are alike, the horse is probably normal. In the early stages, lameness may be apparent only when the horse has remained standing for a while. Bone spavins, like ringbones, may fuse bones and render joints inarticulate.

CURBS   Curbs can be seen best from a side view of the hock. They appear as swellings on the back border of the base of the hock. They result from inflammation and thickening of the sheath of one of the important tendons. Shallow, sickle hocks predispose to development of curbs. They may or may not cause lameness but are not severe unsoundnesses.

FIGURE 4-25   Bone spavins are located at the base of the inside face of the hock. They usually interfere with articulation of the joint, which results in lameness. [*Photograph by the author.*]

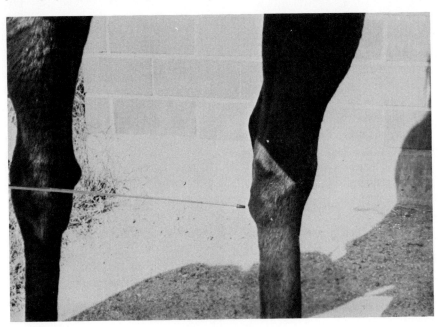

CAPPED HOCK  A thickening of the skin or large callus at the point of the hock is a common blemish. Many capped hocks result from bumping the hocks when trailering in trailers that are too short or are unpadded.

STRINGHALT  Crampiness of the hind leg(s) is a disease of the nervous system resulting in spasmodic flection of one or both hocks when the horse is first moved after standing or when the horse is backing. The hock is raised abnormally high.

Stringhalt occurs more frequently in older animals and may not render the animal unserviceable. New surgical techniques may correct it.

BOG SPAVIN AND THOROUGHPIN  Bog spavins are soft swellings on the inside front area of the hocks that may result from the presence of synovial fluid ("joint oil"). Blemishes of this type are more common to heavy horses than light ones, although individuals of low quality in any breed are susceptible to the condition.

Thoroughpins are blemishes that appear as soft swellings above and in back of the hock joint just in front of the large tendon. The synovial fluid can be pressed from side to side—hence the name.

COCKED ANKLES  Cocked ankles may appear in the front legs but are more common in the hind legs. Severe strain may result in inflammation and/or shortening of the tendons and a subsequent forward position of the ankle joints. Advanced cases of this unsoundness impair movement and decrease usefulness.

STIFLED  When the patella of the stifle joint is displaced, the animal is "stifled" (an upper fixation of the patella). Nature endowed the horse with an elaborate locking mechanism of the hind limbs, enabling it to relax the leg and sleep in a standing position (probably for quick escape from enemies). The two patellar ligaments form a loop that permits the patella to lock over the bony projection of the lower end of the femur or thigh bone (Figure 4-26). Whenever the horse is unable to unlock this loop from above the bony projection, its hind leg will be locked in a stiff, forward position on the ground. Simple surgery severs the medial ligament to correct the condition.

POLL EVIL  This acquired unsoundness results from a bruise or persistent irritation in the region of the poll. Its cause is *brucella abortus*, the same organism that causes Bang's disease in cattle. An early symptom is swelling, and the animal may become touchy about the head and ears when being bridled. Severe inflammation, eruption, and bad scars may result in neglected cases. Poll evil is not seen often.

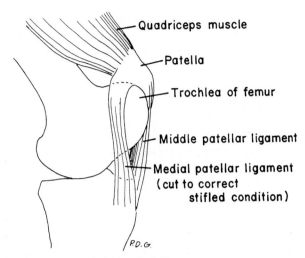

Medial View of Stifle Joint

FIGURE 4-26    Upper fixation of the patella results in stifling. When the horse cannot unlock the patella from this upward position, the horse is stifled. Surgery in which the median patellar ligament is severed corrects the condition. [*From Mc-Clure, Kirk, and Garrett, 1972.*]

FISTULA    Fistulated withers is a serious unsoundness. It is an inflammation of the withers affecting the region in much the same way that poll evil affects the poll (Figure 4-27). It may be present on one or both sides of the withers. It should be treated early; otherwise, the disease can linger on, resulting in severe infection and occasionally in a "crestfallen" condition of the neck immediately in front of the withers. Saddles with low gullets that rest on the top of the withers often trigger this serious unsoundness.

SWEENEY    Sweenied horses experience atrophy or a decrease in the size of a muscle or group of muscles. It is common in the shoulder muscles extending from the withers downward about two-thirds of the distance to the point of the shoulder. Sweeney is not very common in light horses but appears frequently in draft animals. It may be associated with lameness from another source in the same limb.

KNOCKED-DOWN HIP    A fracture of the external angle of the hip bone (ilium) results in a lowering of the point of the hip. It can be identified best by standing directly behind the horse. Hurrying through narrow doors, crowding in trailers, and falling, and injury from other causes may be responsible for this condition. Usefulness is seldom impaired, but appearance is greatly affected.

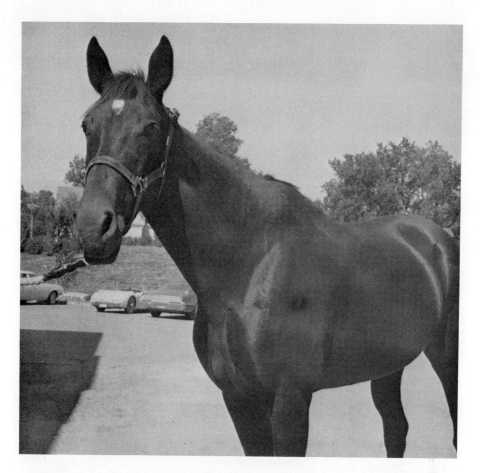

**FIGURE 4-27**    Fistula is an inflammation of the withers. Ill-fitting saddles are a major cause. [*Photograph by the author.*]

SCARS    Attention is usually directed to scars because of the presence of white hairs. Working stock horses with scars are not discriminated against very much, but gaited and parade horses are seriously faulted.

HERNIAS    These swellings may appear on any portion of the abdomen, but are more common near the umbilicus. They are seldom serious enough to cause an unsoundness. Most are operable.

## Sight

BLINDNESS    Blind horses are seriously handicapped. Blindness is usually characterized by cloudiness of the cornea or a complete change of eye color to white. Pale blue, watery eyes may indicate periodic opthalmia (moon blindness). Watery eyes may also indicate vitamin A deficiency. These conditions are not common to horses on pasture.

Even if blind in only one eye, the horse is a bad risk, for it tends to shy from objects and mistrust horses on the blind side.

## Wind

HAY ALLERGY   Some horses are allergic to hay with small amounts of mold in it. In the early stages of the allergy a mild cough may linger for months when the horse eats moldy or dusty hay or when it is exercised. It usually develops into an allergy to all types of hay and later into heaves unless hay is withdrawn from the diet. Grazing, hay pellets, and grain may arrest its development for years.

HEAVES   A loss of elasticity of the lungs, resulting from a breakdown of the walls of a portion of the air cells, causes heaves. The condition is characterized by an apparent extra contraction of the flank muscles during expiration. The expiration process can be seen, and often heard, to proceed normally to about two-thirds of completion, where it stops. The flank and lower rib muscles contract briefly, and then expiration continues to completion. Dusty hay and/or the atmosphere, severe exertion of out-of-condition horses, and respiratory infections are common causes of the disease. It is a serious unsoundness.

ROARING (WHISTLING)   A paralysis or partial paralysis of the nerves that control the muscles of the vocal cords may result in a roaring or whistling sound when air is inhaled into the lungs. The condition is seldom apparent when the horse is at rest, but it becomes obvious upon exertion. Roaring may be limited to one nostril and can be determined by plugging each nostril alternately.

Roaring may respond to surgery. Unless corrected it is an unpleasant, serious unsoundness.

## Stable Vices That Affect Usefulness

Vices are habits acquired by some horses that are subjected to long periods of idleness. Hard work and freedom from close confinement are preventatives. Windsucking, cribbing, weaving, and stall-walking horses are hard to keep in condition. The latter two types are often fatigued; the former tends to colic more readily than other horses.

WINDSUCKING   A windsucking horse finds an object on which to press its upper front teeth while pulling backward and gulping air into its stomach.

FIGURE 4-28  Wind sucking is a vice or habit that some idle horses develop. The upper teeth are pressed downward on an object while air is sucked into the stomach. Windsucking interferes with eating. [*From Bradley, 1976.*]

This behavior is usually accompanied by a prolonged grunting sound. The habit is practiced even while eating, thus causing loss of food (Figure 4-28). Confirmed offenders will suck wind even when on pasture, and will practice the habit when tied, as the opportunity is presented. Windsucking is a contagious habit in a stable of bored confined horses.

CRIBBING  Crib-biting horses grasp an object between their teeth and apply pressure, gradually gnawing the object away if it is not metal. Windsucking and crib biting are usually associated, although a horse may practice one without the other. Cribbing wears away the incisor (front) teeth severely.

Both cribbing and windsucking may be partially prevented and sometimes stopped by a cribbing strap fitted sufficiently close about the throatlatch to compress the larynx when pressure is borne on the front teeth. Normal swallowing is not impaired.

WEAVING  Weaving is a rhythmical shifting of the weight from one front foot to the other. It is not a common vice, but when carried to extremes it renders a horse almost useless, for the constant movement causes fatigue and poor condition. Its cause is obscure but its occurrence is correlated with enforced idleness in confined quarters. Some horsemen condemn vertical bars that can be seen through, and others consider chain halter shanks that rattle when moved as predisposing causes.

STALL WALKING    This uncommon vice impairs the horse's conditioning and induces fatigue. Offenders wear an obvious path in the bedding of their stall.

KICKING    Occasionally horses will learn to destroy partitions or doors in stalls by kicking. Some kick only at feeding time, thus giving vent to their impatience. Usually they do not kick outside the stall. Padding the stall has been known to stop some kickers, for some horses kick merely because they enjoy the noise.

BITING    Stallions often acquire the habit of nipping at the attendant for want of something to do. Gentle horses can be encouraged to nip when too much pressure is applied in grooming or during cinching of the saddle girth. Many show horses learn to bite in self-defense when agitated by pokes from well-wishers as they rest in their stalls on the show circuit. Removing the cause will usually correct the condition.

TAIL RUBBING    Tail rubbing often starts because of irritation from parasites and continues from habit. Parasite control and tail boards prevent it.

HALTER PULLING    When a horse becomes confident of being stronger than the rigging that secures it, it becomes a halter puller. Young horses in training will not gain such confidence when secured by strong halter equipment tied to stationary objects. (Bridles should never be used for tying horses.)

The habit may be broken in its early stages by tying a slip noose about the flank, with the rope shank passing between the forelegs, through the halter ring, and then fastened securely. Pulling backward will then cause pain. A second rather successful method is to pass the halter rope through a tie ring in the stall and fasten it to a hobble placed on a fore pastern.

## JUDGING DISPOSITION

If riding is to be a joy and safety a requirement, a horse with a good disposition is a must. Disposition may be both "born" and "made." Some breeds are more docile than others, and wide differences exist among individuals within breeds. Any horse appropriately trained will have a satisfactory disposition for normal riding. Conversely, horses of excellent dispositions can be spoiled by improper handling.

Watch the ears and eyes of the horse for nervousness and resistance. Have the owner handle its feet. Ride the horse (if it is trained) to see if it is dependable and adequate for your purposes. Take the horse on a trial basis if possible.

Courage or heart is necessary in horses used for racing and sporting events. Intelligence or ability to learn is an asset in any horse. These can be easily identified in horses trained or in training and may be predicted in part by pedigree or family relationships.

A horse with the conformation and disposition described is physically able to be an effective performer, provided it is fed appropriately and kept healthy.

## JUDGING SUITABILITY

### Age and Training

The decision is often made by beginning riders of all ages to buy an unbroken or "green broke" horse because it is gentle and economical. One or both of these assumptions usually prove erroneous.

A 10-year-old rider and 2-year-old horse "learning together" are an unsatisfactory, dangerous combination. Neither one is physically, mentally, or emotionally mature enough to make decisions or handle emergencies that may arise. The younger or less experienced the rider, the older and more experienced the horse should be. Inexperienced riders need "kid" or "foolproof" horses. Even if they are not injured, beginning riders become discouraged or fearful with mounts that take advantage of them and make them look amateurish in front of their friends. "Kid" horses are less numerous now than they were a few years ago because of the expanding use of older horses for manufactured products such as pet food and glue, but experienced, safe horses can be found and should be sought out.

Those having the time, desire, and sufficient horse experience should train some young horses because there are never enough well-trained horses. Such people can often start with yearlings and with patience produce good horses that make money.

Experienced horsepersons who have busy schedules will usually be glad they bought finished horses even at higher prices because they seldom have the time to "make" a young horse.

### Price

Most any 1,000-pound healthy-looking horse will bring $250 to $300 for slaughtering purposes; however, many horse owners will accept less money if assured that their horse is getting a good home. The cost of run-of-the-mill, unregistered horses ranges from $200 to $500. Some are good beginner's horses. Those that are very talented may bring from $750 to $1250, depending on breed and activity. The cost of registered horses of above-average conformation that show well in small shows may exceed this amount. Reasonably good hunters and jumpers may cost $2000 or more, and talented registered horses are very expensive.

In general, for youngsters light enough to ride ponies, useful ponies can be found that are cheaper than horses. But ponies will be outgrown unless younger family members can take them over, and ponies have less resale value than horses. Be sure you don't buy a spoiled pony!

Since horses are long-term investments, buy the best. The big cost of horse ownership is feed, and a good horse eats no more than a poor one.

## Grade or Purebred

Grade or unregistered horses are cheaper than comparable purebreds. However, since they can perform as well as purebreds, grades may be the best choice if showing is not planned.

Registered horses may enter both open and breed shows and may have higher resale value. A breeding program must involve registered horses.

However, there are many purebred horses for sale at rather low prices because they are culls from poor breeding programs. Such horses have no advantage over grade horses, since they should not be bred because of deficiencies of conformation likely to be transmitted to their offspring.

## Sex

Geldings (castrated male horses) are more even-tempered and more predictable than mares and stallions. Mature, well-trained geldings are in demand by many knowledgeable horsemen and may be higher priced than comparable mares.

Some mares can be temperamental at different stages in their heat cycles; at those times they do not perform as well and exhibit a general attitude of mareishness. Most mares at the peak of estrus can be nuisances in crowds of horses, especially around stallions. However, some mares are completely stable and exhibit few signs that they are in heat except to a teasing stallion. Many are extremely intelligent and responsive to commands, and consistently try hard to perform well.

Many new horse owners buy mares to breed, hoping to recover all or part of their cost. This practice may be justified by the experience gained from it, but it is usually doomed to economic failure with the new horse owner because of inadequate facilities and inexperience. It takes a long time and a lot of money to breed a mare and raise the foal and get it into production. Many young horses do not return the money invested in them. Furthermore, the new horse owner usually has a lot of riding time planned, and mares in late pregnancy should be ridden lightly, if at all. Riding a mare with a nursing foal poses all kinds of problems: if the foal tags along, automobiles are of great concern; if stabled, the foal may injure itself, and the mare may become overanxious to return to the stable during rides.

Historically, stallions have been the most prestigious horses to ride. The ability to conquer and manage a stallion impresses friends and enemies alike. Some horsemen and horsewomen prefer the nerve and resiliency of stallions. Well-trained stallions in the hands of experienced men and women are completely safe, but the management involved usually is a high price to pay for casual horse activities.

Unless there is a need for a stallion in a breeding program, they are not worth the extra bother to keep just for riding. They require more watching, more discipline, and more work when used in general horse activities. Some group events prohibit them, e.g., 4-H activities and many commercial trail rides.

If the price is favorable, stallions may be gelded and become excellent mounts.


## APPENDIX 4-1   DETERMINING AGE OF HORSES BY THEIR TEETH

The art of determining the age of horses by inspection of the teeth is an old one. It can be used to a considerable degree of accuracy in determining the age of young horses. The probability of error increases as age advances, and becomes a guess after the horse reaches 10 to 14 years of age. Stabled animals tend to appear younger than they are; whereas those such as range horses, which graze sandy areas, appear relatively old because of wear on the teeth.

Age determination is made by a study of the twelve front teeth, called *incisors*. The two central pairs above and below are called *centers*, pincers, or nippers. The four teeth adjacent to these two pairs are called *intermediates*, and the outer four teeth are designated as *corners*.

*Canine teeth or tusks* may appear midway between the incisors and molars at 4 or 5 years of age in the case of geldings or stallions, but they seldom appear in mares. *Wolf teeth* (small teeth that sometimes appear between the incisors and jaw teeth) may appear in either sex. Adult horses have twenty-four molar teeth.

There are four major ways to estimate the age of horses by appearance of their teeth: (1) occurrence of permanent teeth; (2) disappearance of cups (see section below); (3) angle of incidence; and (4) shape of the surface of the teeth.


### Occurrence of Permanent Teeth

Horses have two sets of teeth, one temporary and one permanent. Temporary teeth may also be called "baby" or "milk teeth." Temporary incisors tend to erupt in pairs at 8 days, 8 weeks, and 8 months of age (Figure A4-1).

A well-grown 2-year-old may be mistaken for an older horse unless permanent teeth can be accurately identified. Permanent teeth are larger, longer, and darker in color, and do not have the well-defined neck joining root and gum that temporary teeth have (Figures A4-2, A4-3, and A4-4).

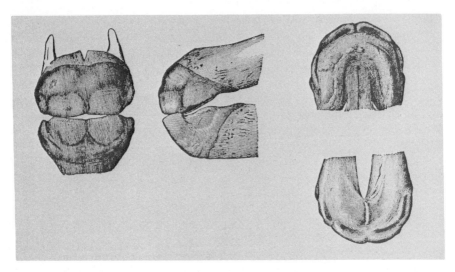

FIGURE A4-1    The teeth of a foal at birth. None of the teeth have penetrated the gums. [*From Gabaux and Barrier*, The Exterior of the Horse.]

The four center permanent teeth appear (two above and two below) as the animal approaches the age of 3 years, the intermediates at 4 years, and the corners at 5 years. These teeth constitute a "full-mouth" (Figures A4-4, A4-5, and A4-6).

FIGURE A4-2    One year of age. All temporary teeth are present. The corners are not yet in wear. [*From Gabaux and Barrier*, The Exterior of the Horse.]

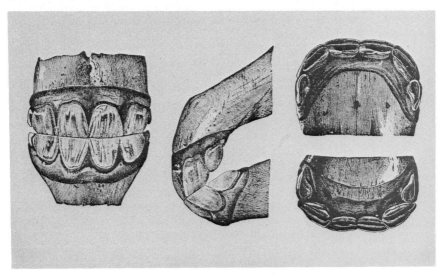

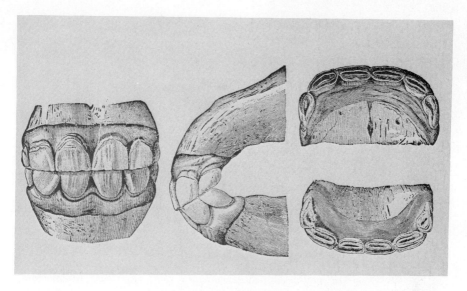

FIGURE A4-3   Two-year-old mouth showing corners in wear. Temporary teeth may be identified by the well-defined neck joining root and gum. They are smaller and lighter in color than permanent teeth. [*From Gabaux and Barrier*, The Exterior of the Horse.]

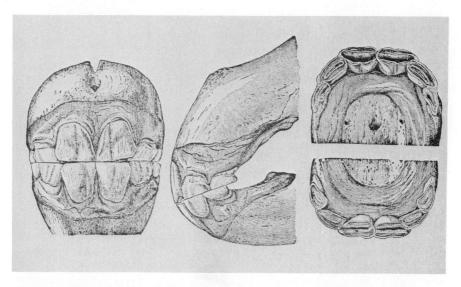

FIGURE A4-4   A typical 3-year-old mouth, showing the large permanent center teeth, both upper and lower. Contrast these with the small, light-colored temporary teeth adjacent to them. [*From Gabaux and Barrier*, The Exterior of the Horse.]

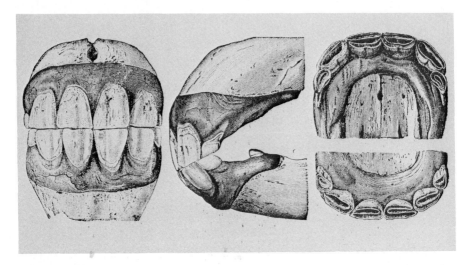

FIGURE 4-5   Note the well-developed permanent centers, immature intermediates, and milk teeth at the corners in this 4-year-old mouth. Tusks or canines have appeared. [*From Gabaux and Barrier,* The Exterior of the Horse.]

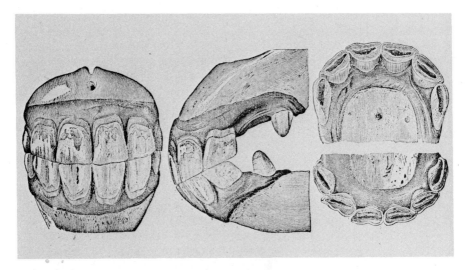

FIGURE A4-6   At 5 years all the temporary teeth have been replaced by permanent teeth. This complete complement of teeth is called a fullmouth. Although the corner teeth are well matched from a profile view, they show very little wear in the view of the upper jaw. The upper centers are beginning to appear round on the inside back surface. Cups are very plain, both above and below, with little wear appearing on them. [*From Gabaux and Barrier,* The Exterior of the Horse.]

## Disappearance of Cups

Young permanent teeth have deep indentures in the center of their surfaces, referred to as *cups*. Cups are commonly used as reference points in age determination. Cups in the upper teeth are deeper than in the ones below; hence, they do not wear evenly with the surface or become smooth in equivalent periods of time. In general, the cups become smooth in the lower centers, intermediates, corners, upper centers, intermediates, and corners at 6, 7, 8, 9, 10, and 11 years of age, respectively. A "smooth-mouth" theoretically appears at age 11 (Figures A4-7; A4-8; A4-9; A4-10; A4-11 and A4-12). A few horsemen ignore cups in the upper teeth and consider a 9-year-old horse smooth-mouthed. Although complete accuracy cannot be assured from studying cups, this method is second in accuracy only to the appearance of permanent teeth in determining age.

As cups disappear, dental stars appear—first as narrow, yellow lines in front of a central enamel ring, then as dark circles near the center of the tooth in advanced age. (Study Figure A4-17.)

## Angle of Incidence

The angle formed by the meeting of upper and lower incisor teeth (profile view) affords an indication of age. This angle of incidence or "contact"

FIGURE A4-7 This 6-year-old mouth shows some wear on the corner teeth as viewed from the side. Cups in the center teeth of the lower jaw should be worn reasonably smooth at this age. The cups in this figure show relatively less wear than is customary in the normal 6-year-old mouth. Note that the canines are immature as contrasted to those in Figure A4-6. The dovetail or notch is apparent but the angle of incidence shows little change. [*From Gabaux and Barrier*, The Exterior of the Horse.]

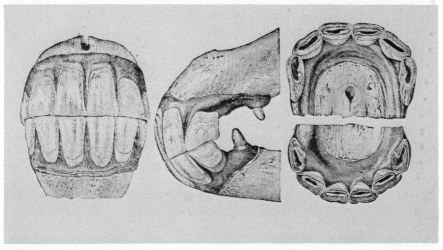

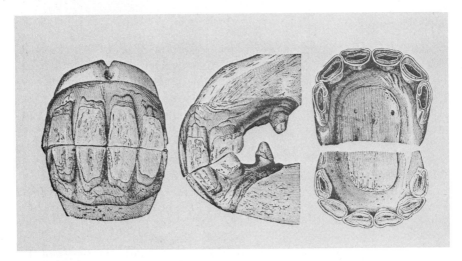

FIGURE A4-8   At 7 years the dovetail has usually developed to its maximum. The rounding corner in this picture does not give it the appearance that is ordinarily seen in a 7-year-old mouth. The angle of incidence is not very sharp, and perhaps is typical for this age. Cups are disappearing from the lower centers and intermediates, with very prominent cups still showing in the corners and in all the upper teeth. Dental stars have not appeared. [*From Gabaux and Barrier*, The Exterior of the Horse.]

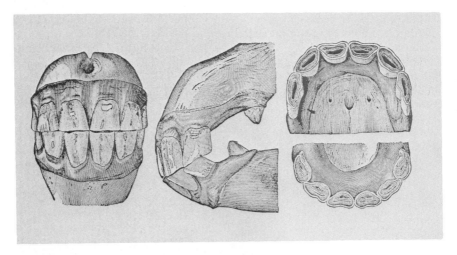

FIGURE A4-9   This 8-year-old mouth shows the notch almost gone from the upper corner tooth. Cups have all disappeared from the lower jaw, but none in the upper jaw have worn out. The teeth are becoming much more oval on the back surfaces, and the angle of incidence is becoming sharper. Dental stars have appeared in four lower and two upper incisors. [*From Gabaux and Barrier*, The Exterior of the Horse.]

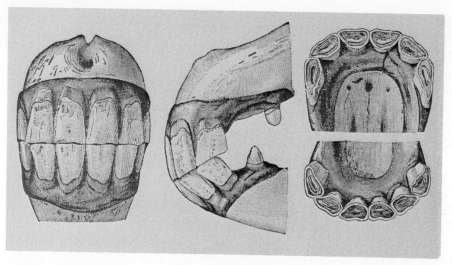

FIGURE A4-10   A front view of this 9-year-old mouth shows a tendency toward narrower and longer teeth. The profile view shows a steeper angle of incidence; however, this angle does not appear to be as steep as that of a typical 9-year-old mouth. Cups are gone from the lower jaw and the two centers above. All teeth except the upper corners are tending toward more ovalness. Dental stars are merging with central enamel rings, which are becoming small and round. [*From Gabaux and Barrier*, The Exterior of the Horse.]

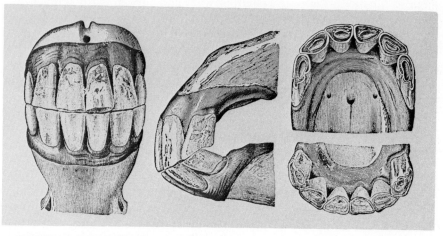

FIGURE A4-11   This 10-year-old mouth shows a typical angle of incidence with reappearance of the notch on the upper corner. Ordinarily cups are gone from all teeth but the upper corners at 10 years of age. Back surfaces of upper centers are changing from ovalness to angularity. [*From Gabaux and Barrier*, The Exterior of the Horse.]

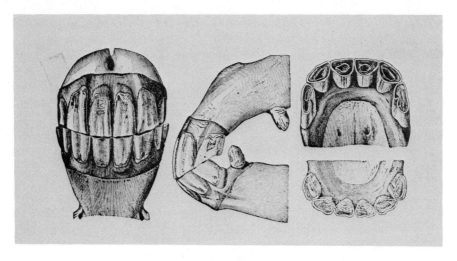

FIGURE A4-12   In this 11-year-old mouth, the length of the teeth, relative to their width, continues to increase. A profile view shows a considerable angle of incidence, with the upper corners almost missing the lowers. Cups are all gone, and centers and intermediates are assuming angularity. [*From Gabaux and Barrier*, The Exterior of the Horse.]

changes from approximately 160 to 180° in young horses to less than a right angle as the incisors appear to slant forward and outward with aging. Compare Figures A4-5; A4-9; A4-12; A4-13; A4-14; A4-15; and A4-16. As the slant increases, the surfaces of the lower corner teeth do not wear clear to the back margin of the uppers, so that a dovetail, notch, or hook is formed on the upper corners at 7 years of age. It may disappear in a year or two, reappear around 12 to 15 years, and disappear again thereafter (Figures A4-8; A4-10; A4-12; A4-14 and A4-15). The condition varies considerably between individuals, but most horses have a well-developed notch at 7 years of age.

## Shape of the Surface of the Teeth

The shape of the teeth undergoes substantial change during wear and aging (Figure A4-17). The teeth appear broad and flat in young horses. They may be twice as wide (side to side), as they are deep (front to rear). This condition reverses itself in horses that reach or pass 20 years of age. From about 8 to 12 years of age, the back (inside) surfaces become oval, then angular at about 15 years. Twenty-year-old teeth may be twice as deep from front to rear as they are wide. (Study these differences in Figures A4-3; A4-10; A4-15; and A4-16.)

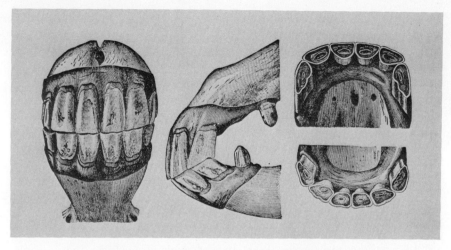

FIGURE A4-13   This 12-year-old mouth cannot be differentiated from the 11-year-old mouth in Figure A4-12, except for cups in the upper corners and a decrease in the size of the central enamel rings. When a horse is completely smooth-mouthed, factors other than age will determine its usefulness. Perhaps the best way to ascertain the physical condition of a horse that is being considered for purchase is to take it on a trial basis. [*From Gabaux and Barrier,* The Exterior of the Horse.]

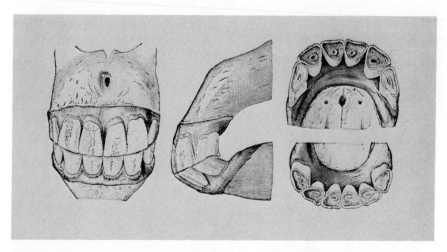

FIGURE A4-14   A 15-year-old mouth. All the cups are gone. The central enamel rings are prominent but are very small and round. All teeth have become angular. [*From Gabaux and Barrier,* The Exterior of the Horse.]

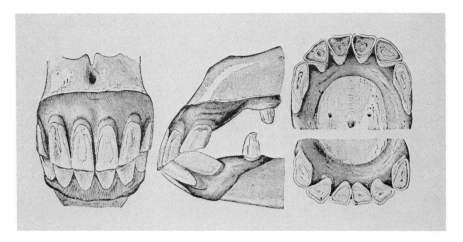

FIGURE A4-15  Extremely long teeth, an acute angle of incidence, and triangular surfaces characterize this 21-year-old mouth. Spaces have appeared between the teeth. [*From Gabaux and Barrier*, The Exterior of the Horse.]

## Abnormal Teeth Conditions

*Parrot mouth* is a result of the upper and lower incisors not meeting because the lower jaw is too short. This condition is rather common and may seriously interfere with grazing and bitting (Figure A4-18).

FIGURE A4-16  A 30-year-old mouth showing characteristics of old age, although spaces between the teeth are absent. [*From Gabaux and Barrier*, The Exterior of the Horse.]

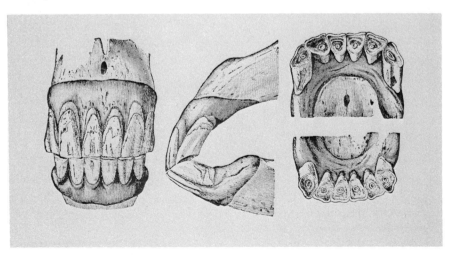

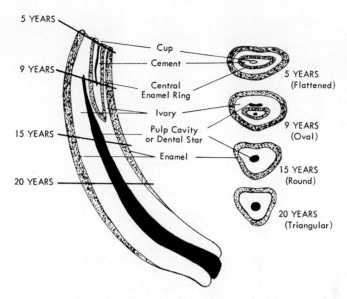

**FIGURE A4-17**  A permanent middle incisor tooth at different ages and stages of wear. The reasons that wear causes a change in the angle of incidence and the shape of the table surfaces, the disappearance of cups, and the appearance of dental stars are evident in this figure. As wear progresses, surface enamel is worn away, leaving two enamel rings, one around the margin of the table surface and the other around the cup. As wear continues, the cup almost disappears and the dental star or pulp cavity makes its appearance (at about 8 to 10 years). The tip of the dental star first appears as a wide thin yellow line in front of the internal enamel surrounding the cup. In old age the dental star appears dark and round, and is centered in the tooth. Changes in shape from oval to angular as wear progresses toward the root are shown in the cross-sectional views. [*From Gabaux and Barrier,* The Exterior of the Horse.]

*Monkey mouth* is the opposite of parrot mouth and is seldom seen in horses.

*Wolf teeth* are small, easily removed teeth that appear in some horses during the first year in front of the jaw teeth. There may be only one or up to four such teeth in either male or female. They are usually in the way of the bit and should be removed before the horse is bitted. They are the cause of much pain and head slinging or unnecessary head motion in many young horses.

*Cribbing* is a habit common to stabled horses which damages incisors by chipping or breaking them.

*Bishoping* is tampering with cups to make the horse appear younger than it is.

*Floating* is filing high spots in molars to facilitate chewing. Molars

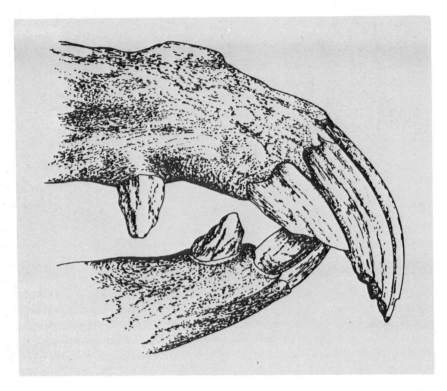

**FIGURE A4-18** A neglected case of severe parrot mouth. [*From Bradley, 1975.*]

should be checked regularly by veterinarians or professional equine dentists. Caps should be removed in the young horse, and molars should be kept floated as needed thereafter.

*Galvayne's groove* is a groove which often appears at the gum margin of the upper corner incisor at about 10 years of age. It extends halfway down the tooth at 15 years, and reaches the table margin at 20 years. It then is said to recede and disappear at 30 years.

## BIBLIOGRAPHY

Bradley, Melvin, and William H. Slemp: *Fundamentals of Conformation and Horse Judging,* Science and Technology Guide no. 2837, University of Missouri Cooperative Extension, Columbia, 1976.

Bradley, Melvin: *Leg Set: Its Effect on Action and Soundless of Horses,* Science and Technology Guide no. 2443, University of Missouri Cooperative Extension, Columbia, 1977.

Bradley, Melvin: *Determining Age of Horses by Their Teeth*, Science and Technology Guide no. 2842, University of Missouri Cooperative Extension, Columbia, 1975.

Bradley, Melvin: *Unsoundness and Blemishes of Horses: Feet and Legs*, Science and Technology Guide no. 2840, University of Missouri Cooperative Extension, Columbia, 1975.

Bradley, Melvin: *Unsoundness and Blemishes of Horses: Head, Body, Respiratory Tract and Stable Vices*, Science and Technology Guide no. 2841, University of Missouri Cooperative Extension, Columbia, 1976.

McClure, Robert C., D.V.M., Gerald R. Kirk, D.V.M., and Phillip D. Garrett, D.V.M.: *Functional Anatomy of the Horse's Foot*, Science and Technology Guide no. 2740, University of Missouri Cooperative Extension, Columbia, 1974.

# BEHAVIORAL PSYCHOLOGY OF THE HORSE IN NATURE AND IN TRAINING

an is inferior to the horse in size, strength, and speed, and yet the horse has been man's more or less willing servant for thousands of years. Modern horse psychology attempts to predict the probable behavior of horses under various conditions and to establish those conditions that encourage horses to respond as handlers wish.

## PHYSICAL PARAMETERS

The horse is a sensitive creature of tremendous physical strength, great speed, and quick reactions. It has great ability to adapt to unfamiliar situations because its ancestors evolved during periods of constant, stressful change (see Chapter 2).

The ancestors of the modern horse depended on hiding and running away for their survival. The tools the horse developed for survival in the past are in evidence in its reactions today. Those tools of survival include

FIGURE 5-1    If your horse is neurotic, it may have a "people problem." When an angry rider punishes a horse by spurring it, and then jerking it back when it moves forward, the rider leaves the horse little alternative but to rear, buck, or become neurotic. [*Courtesy of Doug Ross, Columbia, Mo.*]

sight, reflex for flight, memory, gregarious nature, ability to feel ground vibrations, hearing, smell, and skin sensitivity.

## Sight

By human standards, the horse has poor vision. Its eyes have a "ramped retina"[1]; that is, the retina does not form a true arc; therefore, parts of it are closer to the lens than other parts. The horse adjusts its range of vision by lowering and raising its head, much as a human does wearing bifocal glasses.

The size and position of the eyes and the width of the head determine the horse's field of vision (Figure 5-2). With its head up in normal position, there are blind spots at both ends of the horse. With its head down in grazing position, the horse enjoys a 340° field of vision—most convenient for spotting enemies. Frontal vision will vary slightly between horses depending on width of forehead and where the eyes are set.

Most horses probably do not see objects nearer than 3 feet directly in front of their faces without moving their head. With their heads in normal

[1]R. H. Smyth, M.R.C.V.S., *The Mind of the Horse*, The Stephen Green Press, Brattleboro, Vt., 1966, p. 46.

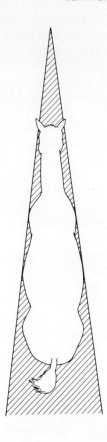

FIGURE 5-2    There are areas (shaded triangle), both in front of and behind a horse, that it does not see without moving its head or body. One should speak to a horse when approaching from any direction, but especially when approaching from directly behind. [*Courtesy of Douglas Ross, Columbia, Mo.*]

position they do not see the feed they eat or where the forefeet are landing. This visual arrangement is most convenient for grazing and watching for enemies at the same time, but it is a real handicap in judging height and distance. As a horse approaches a strange jump, it lowers its head, searching for a groundline and, then raises it to appraise the height of the jump.

"Pig-eyed" horses, or those with sunken eyes, see less in front and behind than others. Many pig-eyed horses are normal and useful, but one researcher suggests that those growing up in groups of foals may be picked on more than others and therefore develop disposition problems. (Most horsemen discriminate against them.)

The horse sees completely different images with each eye. The input from these images may be processed either separately and alternately or independently. Probably the only area in which the horse has classic depth perception begins about 10 feet beyond its nose when looking straight ahead. Although most of the visual input it receives is flat, the horse infers three dimensions as a learned response and functions accordingly.

The horse can see and function well in the dark, but its eyes grow accustomed more slowly to changes of light than do a human being's. Horses taken from a brightly lighted area for loading into a dark trailer, for example, may lower their noses to the floor of the trailer, then raise their heads rather high for loading. In addition to smelling the trailer for identification, they may be trying to find the head position that gives them the best possible vision.

Still objects convey very little information to the horse's brain. A sitting rabbit or bird may be seen readily by the rider, but may remain obscure to the horse until it moves. Horses see movement instantly, however, and react according to their temperament, experience, and confidence in the rider.

Lining the retina of the horse's eye are two different kinds of light-sensitive bodies—rods and cones. While the rods are used primarily for night vision, the cones generate neural impulses when stimulated by daylight and color. The presence of cones in the retina of the horse does not prove that the horse perceives color, but the cones may be an indication that its visual world is not the totally drab one formerly suspected.[2] Some ability to differentiate colors may have been a positive survival trait, useful when other senses, such as hearing and smell, were at a disadvantage because of wind direction.

Because it doesn't see the ground, the horse must be allowed to concentrate while traversing rough terrain. Undoubtedly some stumbling results when the horse does not watch the area over which it travels and therefore does not remember where the obstacles are.

## Flight Reflex

Quick reflexes and panic characterized the prehistoric horse. Indeed, its life depended on them. Horses are endowed with an extensive system of ligaments which permit them to sleep while standing. They will panic into flight without much consideration for the need or consequence of such an action. Young horses particularly, fleeing with or without riders, may be severely injured from running into objects or from total exhaustion. Today's runaway horse is simply carrying out the same kind of behavior that allowed its ancestors to survive. As the horse gets older it tends to outgrow this tendency; some never do, however.

The horse's speed and its willingness to serve its owner, even at great sacrifice, have made the horse most useful to man. These qualities also pose some problems.

Flighty horses should be handled with strong equipment and must not be hurried into new and strange situations. Even horses who are controllable at home may not be easy to control in strange surroundings. The object of the handler must be to impose his or her will on the horse without provoking an unmanageable confrontation.

[2]*Horse Lovers' National Magazine*, February 1977, pp. 21ff.

Ears thrust forward is a sign of interest or suspicion. Some horses in new surroundings show an interest in everything they see without being frightened. Such horses maintain a good attitude and seem to enjoy their work. Others keep their ears forward and eyes open, just looking for something to shy from.

Eyes and nostrils show emotion and reflect temperament. Dilated nostrils reflect interest, curiosity, or apprehension. When the eyes flash, the nostrils dilate, and the muscles tense, the horse is likely to react. The reaction might be only a slight start, a reverse in direction, or both. If the cause of fright intensifies, the horse may bolt, rear, or buck.

## Memory

Horses are usually considered to have memories second only to elephants.[3]

In the wild state, if an attack came at a certain place, the herd avoided that spot in the future. This caution is still practiced by wild horses in the United States. If it were not for the horse's good memory, it would be considerably less useful to man. A well-trained young horse never forgets its training; neither does a poorly trained one. For this reason bad habits should be recognized and corrected before they become fixed.

The performance of horses on limited intelligence tests has not been outstanding, although horses do very complex things routinely when trained.

You may have known an old horse that was considered highly intelligent because it could open most gates and doors on the farm. Idle horses tend to seek activity, some of which may involve gate latches. Once they succeed in opening the latch, their good memory keeps them trying to open doors. When they succeed in getting the grain bin open, however, they later remember only the joy of eating. They don't associate overeating with the bellyache from colic or the pain from founder.

## Gregarious

Horses are gregarious by nature; that is, they band together. This tendency has practical implications. Wild horses in the center of the herd were safer from attack. This behavior can be seen today in zebras in Africa. Wise old ranch horses learned they were more likely to be roped from the remuda for the day's work if they were near the edge; therefore, they sought the center of the group.

This tendency to be gregarious can be taken advantage of in training young horses. Group riding brings out a tendency toward herd obedience in horses, for they all tend to do what others do. For example, if one enters a stream the others tend to follow.

[3]Moyra Williams, *Horse Psychology*, 5th ed., Barnes, South Brunswick, N.Y. 1969, p. 1430.

## Feeling Ground Vibrations

Horses can feel the ground vibrate through their feet. This sensitivity to vibration was an essential part of the prehistoric horse's early warning system. It can be a headache to the modern horse owner, however, as horses often react to the pounding of other horses galloping far out of human sight and hearing.

One manifestation of this sensitivity may be an overcautiousness about footing—to the point where some horses will negotiate soft ground slowly and with apprehension, if at all.

## Hearing

The finely shaped, active ears perched on top of the horse's movable head on the long neck represented an excellent adaptation for survival. Horses can hear both high and low tones not perceptible to human ears. Fear of parade bands, loud machines, and gunshot noises may result from actual pain to the horse. United States Cavalry mounts used on pistol ranges often completely lost their hearing after a few years.

## Sense of Smell

Most animals in the wild state have a good sense of smell; horses also have keen noses. Domestic stallions can identify mares in heat from great distances downwind. In one research project conducted in England, horses that had been circled in closed trailers were nevertheless able to head directly homeward from a downwind distance of 5 miles.

Young horses being saddled for the first few times should be allowed to smell the saddle and the blanket before saddling. This reassures them that the trappings are not dangerous and that they have been used by other horses.

Smell probably dictates grazing habits of horses, although it does not always keep them from eating poisonous plants when forage is abundant.

To intensify and perhaps identify unfamiliar or enjoyable smells, horses of both sexes can frequently be seen lifting their upper lips and breathing in very deeply. The somewhat comical appearance they present at such times is frequently mistaken for a clownish propensity to make faces.

## Skin Sensitivity

The skin of the horse is a very highly specialized sense organ—in fact, it is the largest sense organ of all.[4] It tells the animal whether something is hot or cold or hard or soft, and whether the object causes pain. Nerve endings in

[4]Roger Molesworth, *Knowing Horses*, 4th ed., Arco, N.Y., 1973, p. 21.

human beings are more abundant in the mouth, feet, and hands. The areas of greatest sensitivity in the horse seem to be the mouth, feet, flanks, neck, and shoulders.

The mouth is sensitive to pain rather than light pressure. Bitting should be done with care and reins handled with light hands; otherwise, sensitivity in the mouth is lost and a hard mouth is the result. Some horses will learn to check an electric fence daily with the hairs on their upper lip, and then promptly tear it down when the battery fails.

Some horses are so sensitive to contact in the flank that they promptly buck when heels are applied there.

Application of the whip requires great reserve and good judgment if the learning situation is to be constructive for the horse. Using the whip on the shoulders of a running horse will tighten the shoulder muscles and shorten its stride. Application of the whip near the flank or directly along the ribs may cause a move sideways. Many horses hump up and consequently slow down under heavy use of the whip when they are running.

Probably the most pain horses have to bear is caused by ill-fitting saddles. There are about as many shapes of saddle trees as there are of shoes; and, like feet, the backs of all horses are not the same (Figures 7-5 and 7-6).

Horses vary greatly in skin sensitivity. Some love to be groomed and have their backs scratched. For some thin-skinned horses, it is necessary to select mild grooming equipment. Currycombs and shedding blades should have fine teeth.

Communication between rider and horse is accomplished through voice, hands, and legs. Voice cues for starting and stopping are easy to give and easily understood by the horse. Rein cues are more complex for both rider and horse, and signify a more complicated maneuver than simple starts and stops. Leg cues are needed for most complex responses, such as rollbacks. Because of the sensitivity of a horse's skin it can react to light pressure of the rider's leg.

## NORMAL BEHAVIOR OF DOMESTIC HORSES

### Agonistic Behavior

*Agonistic behavior* includes all aggressive, conflict-related actions—fighting, submission, and escape attempts.

The first thing a group of new horses does when turned together is to begin to establish a *dominance hierarchy*, or *pecking order* (Figures 5-3 to 5-8). Severe conflict or fighting may be required before dominance hierarchy is established, but more often it is established with no more than some lost hair and hide or a few cuts and bruises.

FIGURE 5-3    Maintenance of dominance hierarchy, or peck order, is illustrated in Figures 5-3 to 5-8. The middle gelding blusters when a gelding that has formerly dominated him is released into his domain. He is not anxious to surrender the affections of the mare or the pile of hay they have been sharing. (The straps suspended from their browbands are face fly protectors.) [*Photograph by the author.*]

FIGURE 5-4    When frontal threats fail to stop the advance of the dominant gelding, he turns heels to the intruder for further intimidation. [*Photograph by the author.*]

FIGURE 5-5   Boldness has rewarded the dominant gelding with the hay pile without contact or struggle. While the dominant gelding eats, the loser psyches himself into one final challenge. [*Photograph by the author.*]

FIGURE 5-6   The dominant gelding meets the loser's charge with resolve. The loser's final challenge is stopped short when his courage fails. [*Photograph by the author.*]

FIGURE 5-7    The dominent gelding flails the air with his heels to emphasize control of the situation, while the loser retreats. [*Photograph by the author.*]

FIGURE 5-8    The dominant gelding will retain complete, unchallenged dominance, without loss of hair or hide, by means of intimidating glares. Without dominance hierarchy, evolution of the horse would have been impossible. Without dominance today, horses would require separate housing. [*Photograph by the author.*]

Stallions do not normally submit to dominance easily and may fight to the death if in small pastures. However, a ranch in Wyoming runs mature stallions together in a large pasture. When a new stallion is purchased, it is turned into the pasture to be greeted by an agonistic reception committee. Once a dominance hierarchy is established, each stallion accepts its position in the pecking order and maneuvers its band of mares according to its rank at the water holes and on the range.

One must manage horses with such behavior in mind if the horses are to stay healthy. Obviously, a horse low in the hierarchy should not be tied where others can reach it. Square corners and barbed wire in small lots and places where timid horses can be hemmed in should be avoided.

Many horses are dominant, but not very aggressive. They rule by means of pinned ears, threatening gestures, and intimidating charges at other horses, with little intent to make contact. In some groups of horses such little dominance is displayed that the members eat together throughout their lives.

### Sexual Behavior

Fillies become sexually mature at about 20 months or 2 years of age and cycle every 21 days during spring, summer, and fall thereafter, unless pregnant. They urinate frequently and will accept the stallion for a few days at the peak of the estrous cycle. Stallions reach sexual maturity much younger and may breed mares as yearlings. The routine behavior of uncastrated horses changes more than that of the castrated male. The intact male becomes much more aggressive and may require more restraint, both in hand and under saddle. Stronger, higher fences may be needed in pasture and paddock.

The old custom with draft horses of not castrating until the animals were yearlings or 2-year-olds to enhance spirit and neck development hardly seems necessary with modern riding horses. Indeed, it is doubtful that the practice ever had any effects on drafters, either.

Some geldings, although not many, are sexually aggressive enough to tease mares and may become very possessive of these mares and agonistic to other horses about them.

### Epimeletic Behavior

*Epimeletic behavior* is the concern of one animal for another animal's needs. Mares care diligently for their foals and will fight horses that are higher in the hierarchy without hesitation if they approach the mares' new foal.

Horses that do not associate with each other very much during most of the year may stand head-to-tail during fly season and swish annoying flies

FIGURE 5-9   Epimeletic behavior—caring for another's needs. Mutual back-scratching sessions are common among horses whether or not they are good friends. Horses often stand head to tail and switch flies off each other. [*Photograph by the author.*]

from each other. When the fly season ends, so does the friendship, and the dominant horse resumes its role of aggression at least to some degree (Figure 5-9).

Breeding stallions seldom exhibit epimeletic behavior.

## Et-Epimelectic Behavior

*Et-Epimeletic behavior* involves signaling for care and attention. All horses call for care, companionship, or food. Weanling foals call frantically for their dams, as do dams for their foals, when separated.

Horses call welcomes to grooms at feeding time and to each other when one returns after a period of separation. They will recognize a pickup truck that feeds them on pasture and will meet it regularly at the appointed time of feeding.

*Pair bonding* is a nuisance with many horses, and especially with a mare and gelding combination. When separated they may call for each other to the point of embarrassment for their handlers. Some pairs are so anxious when separated on rides that they almost become unmanageable. If one horse becomes sick in old age and gets down in an area of the pasture, its friend may stand over it for hours awaiting a change.

## Ingestive Behavior

The stomach of a horse is small; therefore, the horse prefers to eat often and in small amounts. Whether or not a prehistoric need to move on while watching for predators still stimulates horses is unknown, but they like to cover ground in grazing. This is apparent when grazing a horse on a halter shank or when watching horses at pasture.

## Eliminative Behavior

All experienced horsemen have hauled horses that could hardly wait to get back to their stalls to urinate. Why do horses pollute their own stalls? Some people attribute this action to "marking out territory," but it is more likely a result of prior management. Horses confined to stalls for long periods of time, such as show horses, have no other alternative, and it becomes a habit. Conversely, those reared in large pastures are better "housekeepers" if given the option of open stable and paddock. Research with swine has shown that certain forced-air-movement systems and building designs help control where confined hogs defecate in their quarters. Perhaps research with horses will someday lead to effective sanitary management.[5]

Stallions in stables with available paddocks will often defecate outside the stall in the same spot every day. They back up to the location and make a high pile. Most turn around and smell it and some paw at the pile. They seldom do this when pasture-mating with mares.

Grazing mares and geldings on reasonably sized pastures defecate and urinate wherever and whenever the need arises. In small pastures horses often urinate and defecate in only one or two spots in the pasture. This may be a form of natural parasite management; at the very least, the horses may be unconsciously trying to control the distribution of parasites.

## Investigative Behavior

Horses are curious and they constantly investigate their surroundings and what is going on in them.[6] They frequently find an open bin, gate, auto window, or other things to meddle with. They may also use the senses of touch, hearing, and smell to identify aspects of their surroundings their inadequate eyesight has not clarified.

[5]Gary D. Potter and B. F. Yeates, *Horse Behavior and Management*, 1st National Horseman's Seminar, Program Proceedings, Fredericksburg, Virginia, 1976, p. 126.
[6]Moyra Williams, *Horse Psychology*, Wiltshire Book Company, North Hollywood, Calif., 1973, p. 45.

## ABNORMAL BEHAVIOR OF DOMESTIC HORSES

Almost any difficult maneuver that is required of a horse by a human is "abnormal" behavior from the horse's point of view (Figure 5-10). The fact that horses adapt to such activities so willingly is a tribute to their flexibility and to their trainers' skills.

Not all horses do adapt, however. Like humans, some are unable or unwilling to adjust to their environments and are classified as outlaws or as rebels against the "system." Some horses are neurotic—in a more or less con-

FIGURE 5-10    Almost any difficult maneuver a horse performs for a human is "abnormal" behavior from its point of view. No amount of conditioning will induce a domestic feline to subject itself to the kinds of indignities that a horse will allow. [*Courtesy of the American Paint Horse Association.*]

stant state of irresoluteness and mental conflict. Some are just stupid and cannot perform the routine activities expected of them. Others are erratic and are upset in certain activities with certain handlers and quite relaxed and normal under different management regimens.

Granting that there are hopeless mental cases among horses and that retraining many problem horses is uneconomical, the problem of such abnormal behavior must be approached from the preventive standpoint of reducing conflict, uncertainty, and restriction.

Research psychologists use conflict, uncertainty, and restriction to test individuals and species of animals. These conditions are routinely imposed on many horses in normal usage.

## Conflict

Mental conflict results from two opposing urges, both of which are equally strong. A classic example was demonstrated in an experiment in which cats were confined to small cages and fed at the ringing of a bell.[7] When a blast of air in the face was substituted for food, cats became frantic and exhibited various types of abnormal behavior, ranging from scratching themselves to attacking their caretakers.

Such a frustrating environment can be seen at many small shows. A partially trained young horse forced to run the poles in a game class before learning to neck-rein is an example. The horse is urged to race at top speed in a frontal direction. Just as it responds, its head is plow-reined hard in the opposite direction so that the horse will miss a pole. Before it fully collects itself, it is jerked in the other direction, etc., until the course is finished. While some horses learn to cope with such training remarkably well, most do not. They become anxious to avoid the event or get it over with to the point of losing control. Some appear to go completely crazy and many find other undesirable ways to reduce tension and relieve frustration.

## Uncertainty

Horses exhibit abnormal behavior when faced with problems beyond their power of resolution. For example, when a rider in anger punishes a horse by spurring it, and then jerking it back when it moves forward, the rider leaves the horse little alternative but to rear or buck (Figure 5-1).

The uncertain but willing horse may offer all sorts of responses to its rider-trainer's unclear or conflicting demands. The good trainer must not only know how to ask for the desired response but must also be sensitive enough to know when a poor response is the result of confusion rather than

[7]Charles W. Conrad (ed.), *Understanding Horse Psychology*. The Farnam Horse Library, Omaha, p. 35.

FIGURE 5-11 Active horses confined without exercise to box stalls try to relieve boredom by engaging in a variety of stable vices—many of which persist a lifetime. These habits include cribbing, weaving, stall-walking, kicking, pawing, eating bedding, and many more. [*Courtesy of Duane Dailey, Columbia, Mo.*]

resistance on the horse's part. Such treatment eventually results in timid, hostile horses.

## Restriction

Horses build a mental defense for restrictive conditions (both inside and outside their stalls) and relieve anxiety or boredom by abnormal behavior. The unexercised confined horse develops stable vices from sheer boredom that continues even when activities are increased or when boredom ceases. Cribbing, weaving, stall-walking, kicking, pawing, and eating bedding are only a few. Almost all of these are management-induced by lack of exercise, care, and proper feeding habits (Figure 5-11).

## THE PSYCHOLOGY OF THE HORSE HANDLER

Because of the goodwill and good memory of the horse, it is important to remember that a horse is being trained each time it is handled in any way. Therefore, the subject of horse psychology is not complete without a discussion of human psychology as well.

One might facetiously classify horse handlers into four general categories: "naggers," "passengers," "coexisters," and "progress makers."

To the nag, a horse can do no right. The nag must always "correct" the horse by means of whip, voice, heels, and/or reins from the start to finish of every ride. Their horses usually develop neuroses or become "zany," and develop habits such as head-slinging, jigging, and moving sideways to the line of travel, which cause them to stand out in a group. Strangely enough, nags are not always beginning riders, although both nags and beginners often exhibit a common countenance of unhappiness during a ride. Both rider and horse seem glad when the ride ends. However, some good riders may be mounted on zany horses, and some horses are remarkably tolerant of constant annoyances inflicted on them by their riders.

The passenger is a well-intentioned person, usually a beginner, who allows the horse to do almost exactly as it wishes. Fortunately they are usually mounted on gentle horses—survival would be difficult otherwise—but these riders do pose a dangerous problem in group riding by crowding and often causing someone to get kicked or stepped on. In this case, a horse and rider pecking order has been established, with the horse number 1. Such riders need more confidence and firmness, which are usually gained with more experience and formal training.

Coexisters include a majority of fairly new weekend riders as well as some others. They ride various types of horses for the sheer fun of riding and the companionship that goes with it, without concern for improving the horse in the process. They are experienced enough to handle their horses adequately for reasonably safe riding, without strict adherence to prescribed horsemanship practices. Their horses have usually not been extensively trained. In other words, these riders have a give-and-take relationship with their horses, and they are only interested in enjoying the occasion. The horses are not subjected to undue stress, and any strain is usually more physical than psychological.

Horses handled by progress makers are better horses as a result of their experience. These good horse handlers are of many types and achieve results by many different techniques. Some are amateur and some professional trainers, some are young people with patience and love, and others are just good, experienced horsepersons who are able to improve the performances of good horses and work out the problems of bad ones.


## PSYCHOLOGY OF TRAINING

The value of a horse is determined largely by how much training or desirable modification of its behavior has taken place. Well-trained horses undergo extensive schooling based on positive and negative reinforcement (reward and punishment) to achieve high levels of performance. The accomplished rack of a gaited horse, and the feats of the successful show jumper and western reining horse are the results of genetically and physically well-endowed individuals that reach a predetermined level of performance through a training process that takes manipulation of environmental stimuli and reinforcement to achieve desired responses.

A *response* is that part of behavior that refers to an action taken by the horse. It may be a small segment of an intended major maneuver (e.g., jumping a course), where many responses will collectively result in the major maneuver.[8] For example, the running walk of Tennessee Walking Horses is achieved by the following process: shoeing and teaching to pace; then reshoeing and gradually changing to the desired gait; then gaining finesse through constructive, correct repetition. The importance of encouraging *approximations* of desired responses is obvious, because the major maneuver (e.g., running-walk gait) is a result of numerous responses built upon each other. If the trainer does not recognize the approximate responses, the horse's major manuever is seriously jeopardized.

A *conditioned response* is established by a stimulus or *cue*. We say "whoa" to a young horse on the lounging rein and follow the verbal cue with a sharp jerk to get the horse to stop. The young horse soon learns it is easier to stop than to experience repeated sharp jerks.

New cues are learned best when paired with those the horse already knows. For example, the horse that responds to "whoa" will quickly learn to stop with bit pressure—the important procedure is to present the new cue (bit pressure) first, followed by the known cue ("whoa"). Soon the old cue can be discontinued. Leg pressure can later be added to bit pressure in signaling the horse that a cue to stop is coming. Trainers must be skilled in giving cues, whether by voice, hand (reins), leg, or weight.

*Reinforcement* must be employed to ensure learning. A *natural or primary reinforcement* is feed. The presence of feed in the trailer of the hard-to-load horse, who then learns to expect to find it there, strengthens the horse's response to this stimulus. Primary or natural reinforcements can be overdone, however, and are not used extensively in horse training.

*Learned or secondary reinforcements* are more important than primary reinforcements, but require time and skill to teach. Examples are a kind tone of voice, or dismounting and ceasing training immediately following a good performance. Such action is called *positive reinforcement* or *reward training*. There is little doubt that most good, finished horses have gained much of their polish from this technique rather than from the opposite technique—*negative reinforcement* or *aversive stimuli*. Nevertheless, aversive stimuli are a necessary part of the procedure in training and handling of all horses.

---

[8]B. F. Yeates, *Applying Principles of Psychology to Horse Training*, Proceedings of Horse Production Short Course, Texas A&M University, College Station, Texas, 1974, p. 77.

Negative reinforcement is of three types:

1   *Punishment*   The horse makes an undesirable response without a cue, e.g., might attempt to buck. If an aversive stimulus is applied, such as a few sharp cuts with a whip, the horse has a choice of ridding himself of this temptation. It may promptly stop bucking in order to terminate the punishment, and may not start bucking again at a later date if it expects to be punished.
2   *Escape*   The crop is applied to the jumper whose rider is convinced the horse is considering refusing the jump. The horse's alternative is to take the jump in stride.
3   *Avoidance*   A trained horse ignores a cue or responds poorly to it and is punished, e.g., a reining horse may respond slowly or incompletely to a spin or rollback. The aversive stimulus of a light whip on the shoulder away from the direction of the turn may correct the problem. The horse moves away from the placement of the whip.

There are many types of aversive stimuli: whips, reins, spurs, heels, voice, etc. Horses vary tremendously in their response to them. Some are crushed when shouted at. Others require even more proof of the trainer's resolve. No horse should be abused or receive extended punishment however. One or two applications are usually sufficient. All negative reinforcement must be *contingent* (immediate) on the punishable behavior, and the horse must have at least one alternative response. If the punishment is applied a few minutes too late, the horse cannot associate it with the offense; the horse becomes fearful, and cannot concentrate on learning or performing. If there is no alternative response available to the horse, or if the horse is physically incapable of or does not understand the alternative response sought, negative reinforcement may worsen a bad situation.

Negative reinforcement is a two-way street. If the trainer hits a thoroughbred with a whip for bucking and is unseated by the resultant jump, the horse's bad behavior (bucking) is reinforced, and the horse will probably attempt to buck even more vigorously the next time.

*Shaping behavior* is accomplished by reinforcing any approximation of desired responses. It is especially important to recognize these approximations. When gaiting a horse in early training, for example, an approximation may occur only once, if at all, in a half-hour session. Once the approximation is performed, it is often a good idea to pet the horse, dismount, and casually remove the saddle and put the horse away. Do not quit on a sour note.

In early training (acquisition phase) the horse is reinforced often or *continuously* either by reward or mild punishment. When cues are presented without reward or punishment, responses to cues diminish or are honored only when their execution pleases the horse. Williams (1969) trained a young horse to start, stop, and turn both ways by signaling the horse on the withers.[9] She used no reinforcement. Response to cues were instant and accurate if the cues pleased the horse. Otherwise, they were totally ignored.

As training proceeds, reinforcement diminishes; *continuous* reinforcement becomes *intermittent*. The horse will begin to perform better and for longer periods of time with no reinforcement. Such is the case with finished horses, although finesse will diminish with repetition in most of these horses, until reinforcement is initiated.

Regardless of terminology used, horse training boils down to patience, common sense, uncommon communication, repetition, and a healthy horse, mentally and physically willing and able to respond. There are no short cuts in the production of a finished horse.

## BIBLIOGRAPHY

Blake, Henry: *Talking with Horses*, Dutton, New York, 1976.

Conrad, Charles W., ed.: *Understanding Horse Psychology*, The Farnam Horse Library, Omaha, 1976.

Jackson, Laurie: "To See and Not to See—The Special World of Equine Vision," *Equus*, vol. 16, February 1979.

Molesworth, Roger: *Knowing Horses*, 4th ed., Arco, New York, 1973.

Smyth, R. H., M.R.C.V.S.: *The Mind of the Horse*, The Stephen Green Press, Brattleboro, Vt., 1966.

Williams, Moyra: *Horse Psychology*, 5th ed., Barnes, South Brunswick, N.Y., 1969.

Williams, Moyra: *Horse Psychology*, Wiltshire Book Company, North Hollywood, Calif., 1973.

[9]Williams, *Horse Psychology*, 1969, p. 100.

# SAFE BASIC
# HORSE HANDLING

orses rarely intentionally injure people. Indeed, they will avoid stepping on a fallen rider at great risk to their own balance and security. However, horses are large, heavy animals, and any horse will bite or kick under certain circumstances; therefore, caution should always be exercised when handling horses. It is the responsibility of the horse owner to give the horse the best care in the safest possible way.

## PROPER APPROACH TO HORSE HANDLING

Good horsemen and horsewomen exhibit an attitude of underlying calm and skillful watchfulness no matter how exciting or enjoyable the activity.

The handler's calmness will go far to engage the horse's cooperation in any circumstance. An excitable handler and an excitable horse are a dangerous combination.

Almost everyone gets stepped on sooner or later. Sturdy shoes reduce the likelihood of discomfort from bruising as well as more serious injury.

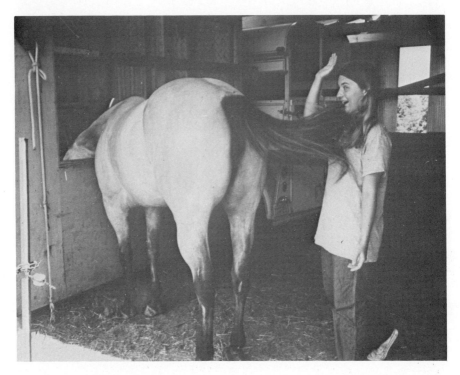

**FIGURE 6-1** Horse safety does not start this way. It could end here! Never surprise a horse from behind, particularly when its head is in a manger. Speak to the horse when approaching from the rear before you are in range of a startled horse's heels. [*Photograph by Duane Dailey.*]

Tennis shoes should not be worn around horses; platforms and open-toed sandals are an invitation to disaster. Comfortable long pants protect the legs from the scratches and itchiness of bedding and the chafing of riding.

Good, safe horsemastership simply requires an understanding of the nature of the animal—without overestimating or underestimating the horse—and habitual practice of safe procedures coupled with good judgment and common sense.

## PRACTICAL CATCHING, LEADING, GROOMING

### Approaching the Horse and Haltering

Whether the horse is loose in a field or paddock or confined in a stall, speak to the horse when approaching. Horses have restricted vision, particularly directly behind, but they hear well (Figure 6-1).

Whenever possible, approach the horse from the left shoulder rather than from behind, with the halter shank in the hand nearest the horse and the halter in the other hand (Figure 6-2).

Read the horse's intentions by the attitude of head, neck, and ears. A snaking neck and laid-back ears indicate a bite or a kick may be coming, but a firm word may prove that this is just a bluff. Rubbing the shoulder may help reassure the animal. If the horse shows signs of moving away, move toward it more slowly.

Ease the halter shank over the horse's neck and hold it there gently. Standing beside the horse between shoulder and head and facing the front, slowly open the halter so that it will slip over the nose easily without hitching. Holding the noseband with the left hand and the headpiece and the ends of the shank with the right, pass the noseband of the halter over the nose of the horse. Do not drag it on; dragging may cause the noseband to get hung up over a nostril or tickle the whiskers of the lower nose and muzzle, causing the horse to raise its head and move away. Carefully feel the way up the far side of the head with the headpiece, slip it over the head behind the ears gently and without slapping or sudden motion, and fasten it on the left side.

FIGURE 6-2   When catching a horse, approach from the shoulder. A horse that insists on turning its heels toward you in a box stall should get a few light taps around its ankles with a whip to discourage this habit. [*Photograph courtesy of Duane Dailey.*]

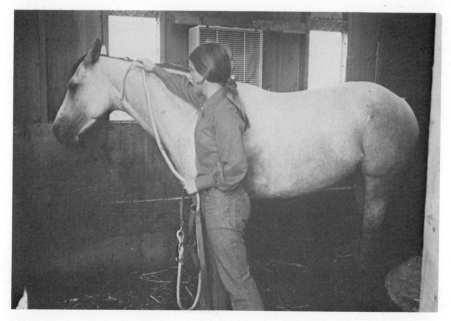

An important factor is using a halter that fits. An excessively tight halter will cause a horse to fight the haltering process. The headpiece or crownpiece should lie flat behind the ears. The throatlatch should lie flat at the swell of the cheek with no big gaps when the horse is viewed from the front. The jawpiece should show about 2 finger widths of room when viewed from the side. The noseband should lie 2 to 3 finger widths below the cheekbone and should show about 3 finger widths below the gullet so that the horse can eat and graze comfortably. (However, whenever possible horses should be turned out and stabled without halters, for many horses die or are injured each year from getting hung up in their halters.)

A box-stalled horse that insists on turning its heels to the handler when approached for haltering should be firmly but gently disciplined with a few light taps around the ankles with a long whip. This correction should not be overdone or it may escalate a mere threat or bluff into a real battle.

A corralled or pastured horse should be approached in the same way as one that is confined. Move toward the horse slowly and quietly, but positively and with confidence. If the handler is anxious and shows nervousness, the horse will be quick to pick it up and will prove hard to catch. The best cure for the hard-to-catch horse is to make the catching and the resultant work as pleasant for it as possible, so that dealing with the handler seems less like punishment and more like fun. See Chapter 8 for other hints on the hard-to-catch horse.

The horse confined in the standing or tie-stall must be taught to move over when the handler enters for haltering or feeding.

## Leading the Horse

The horse should always be led from the left side. The right hand grasps the halter shank at a point about 18 inches from the horse's head, while the left hand holds the balance of the length of the shank, with the excess looped in a figure 8 pattern, and placed across the palm of the hand. The bight (excess) of the shank should *never* be wrapped around the hand; should the horse bolt, the handler may not be able to get free in time and may be dragged some distance; should the horse rear, the handler could be pulled under the front legs. Looping the bight in figure 8s lets the handler feed the shank out should the horse act up while still keeping safe control (see Figure 6-3).

While the disciplined riding horse can usually be led on a halter, with the shank snapped to the lower ring of the halter, livelier horses, and probably all stallions, should be handled with the extra care their unpredictability warrants. A strong leather shank with about a foot of chain at the fastening end should be used. This chain can then be run over the nose from left to right through the side rings and fastened at the upper (high cheek) ring on the right side. This procedure gives the added control of nose pressure.

FIGURE 6-3    Fold the bight (end) of the halter shank into loops and hold it in the left hand when leading. Walk at the shoulder of your horse and change directions by turning toward the horse (right). These safety precautions prevent your hand from becoming entangled in the shank, reduce the risk of getting bumped from behind, and save the feet from getting stepped on. [*Photograph courtesy of Duane Dailey.*]

The horse should walk beside the handler when being led, and should not be allowed to mosey along behind or chug away in front. Handler and horse should be approximately shoulder to shoulder. The handler should walk with head up, but be mindful of his or her feet, keeping them out of the horse's path (Figure 6-3). With right arm near or against the horse's shoulder, the handler will be able to feel the horse's actions and anticipate its moves.

To change directions, turn right (toward the horse). This safety procedure is a requirement in halter show classes and should become a habit of all horse handlers.

The horse who drags behind its handler is dangerous because the handler cannot see what the horse is doing. The horse may try to run off to the left of the handler and wind the handler up in the shank. If the horse bolts, it may run into the handler from behind. A stallion may try to mount the handler if allowed to dawdle behind. The horse allowed to range way out in front may successfully cow-kick (kick forward and out with a hind leg), and connect with its handler.

## Tying the Horse

The safest way to tie a horse is to cross-tie in an alley or stable aisle. Quick-release snaps are now available for extra safety. The stable ends of the cross-ties should be fastened to a solid support at about the height of the horse's withers; the snap ends go to the side rings of the halter. A horse should not be tied by a bridle.

Another good way to tie is with a slipknot to a solid post against a solid wall or corral fence. If the wall is solid, the horse is less likely to be distracted or spooked by other horses, at least on that side (Figure 6-4). If the horse

FIGURE 6-4   Tie with strong equipment at the height of the horse's withers. Use a slip knot that can be untied easily in an emergency. [*Photograph courtesy of Duane Dailey.*]

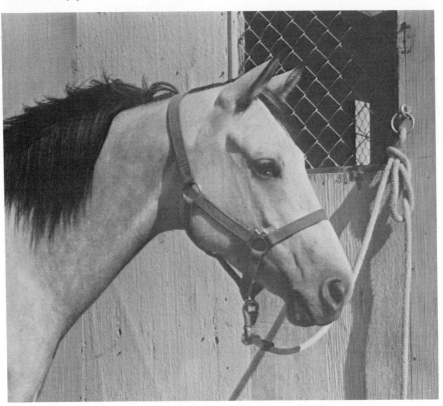

is tied to a corral post, the handler must take care not to get caught between horse and fence.

When tying by a shank to a post the handler should consider the following:

1   Tie rather short. A horse tied too long can step over the tie and get tangled.
2   Tie at approximately the level of the withers.
3   Tie with a quick-release slipknot, but not so loosely that the tie can slip down the pole.
4   Tie to a sturdy support, not to a crossrail that can splinter, break, or be jarred loose.
5   Do not tie the horse to a wire fence, for it may get cut or hurt someone trying to release itself from entanglement (Figure 6-5).

FIGURE 6-5   An alarming number of horses can be seen tied like this at many horse events. If the horse gets tangled in the halter shank and struggles, it may cut itself on the fence, and anyone trying to rescue the horse also risks injury. [*Photograph courtesy of Duane Dailey.*]

Always untie the horse before removing the halter. When turning the horse loose, lead the horse completely through the gate of the corral or the door of the stall (box), and turn the horse around to face the direction from which it came. Make the horse stand quietly before releasing it. Avoid letting a horse bolt away and kick out.

## Grooming the Horse

The tools for grooming the horse are simple to use and safe when used with care. Essential are (see Figure 6-6) the rubber currycomb, a coarse-bristled brush, a fine-bristled body brush, a rubrag, a mane and tail comb, a hoof pick, a sweat scraper, and a sponge.

Every horse should allow its feet to be handled with no fuss or struggle. An owner or groom who must battle a horse to handle its feet is not likely to give it the daily foot care it needs. If the only foot care comes every other month when the farrier shoes the horse, the chance of lameness is increased.

FIGURE 6-6   Top: Shedding blade for mud and shedding hair. Second from top: Rubber currycomb for body; coarse brush for legs; two fine (dandy) brushes for body, face, mane, and tail. Third from top: Fine comb for mane and tail; sweat scraper. Fourth from top: Coarse comb for mane and tail; sheep shearing blade for thinning tail; and fine mane comb. Bottom: Cloth for cleaning bit; hoof pick; sponge for cleaning nose and eyes. [*Photograph by the author.*]

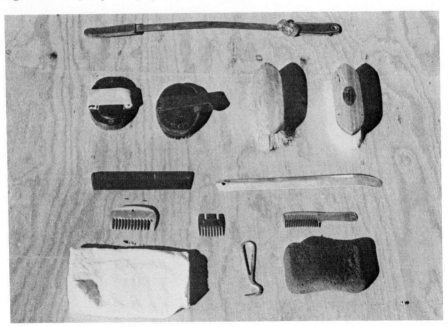

Every foal should be taught to have its feet handled and should not have a bad experience in the process. Teaching a horse to have its feet handled requires patience. Almost any mature, nervous horse can be taught to submit to daily foot care without danger or struggle if the handler has the patience to convince the horse it will not be hurt.

Be considerate when handling the back feet of an old horse. Many are stiff, crampy, or have had injuries, so that their feet cannot be jerked off the ground and folded over the handler's knee. When an old, stiff horse's foot is picked up, the horse will pull it forward. Simply wait with it in that position and gently bring it backward without hurrying. If a gentle horse allows its back foot to be held up a while and then begins to fight to get it down, it may have muscle cramps. Some heavy-muscled horses cramp when their feet are held up too long.

HOLDING THE FOOT   Start with the horse on level ground in a balanced position with all four feet reasonably well placed under it. Work with the left front foot because the horse will be accustomed to a person on that side. Place the left hand on the horse's shoulder about two-thirds up to the withers, and rub the forearm with the right hand. As the right hand goes down the leg, feel for muscle tenseness with the left. If the horse is nervous, go more slowly. If not, move the right hand down to the ankle, then grasp the pastern from the front side as you push the horse away with the left hand. This tends to relieve the weight from that foot, which can readily be raised from the ground as the leg is folded at the knee. If the horse struggles and jerks the foot away, calmly surrender it and start all over again.

After the horse allows its foot to be held in this position, change hands on the pastern in preparation for passing the foot behind you with the left hand. Place the foot between your knees with the right hand, and grasp the foot with your knees. This frees both hands to work on the foot. Contrary to popular opinion, there is more danger to the handler or farrier working on the front foot than the back. This is because the horse can rear, strike, bite, or lift you off the ground if you have the foot between your knees with a firm grip on it. For this reason, make a concentrated effort not to clamp down on the front foot of a horse when it struggles; otherwise, it may raise you parallel to the ground and drop you, face first.

Handling the back foot should begin on the left side also (Figures 6-7 to 6-9). With left hand on hip and right hand stroking the horse in the gaskin area, work toward its lower cannon with the right hand. If you expect trouble, have a handler hold the horse on the same side you are working from and point the horse's head to the left, which will tend to keep the quarters away from you. It is most important that you remain at the side of the horse and do not get behind it in a struggle. Again, you can tell how tense the horse is by feeling its muscles with the left hand. If the horse shows signs of anxiety as you go down the leg, go slowly and repeat the process

FIGURE 6-7    A procedure for safe handling of horses' feet is shown in Figures 6-7, 6-8, and 6-9. With one hand on the horse's body to determine muscle tenseness and to "push off" with if needed, stroke down its hind leg to the lower cannon. [*Photograph by Duane Dailey.*]

FIGURE 6-8    Push horse's weight onto supporting leg with free hand as cannon is pulled forward. When foot rises, step under hock with your inside leg. [*Photograph by Duane Dailey.*]

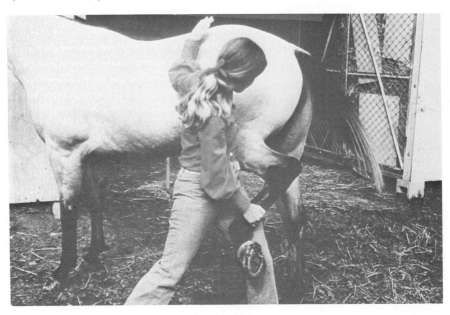

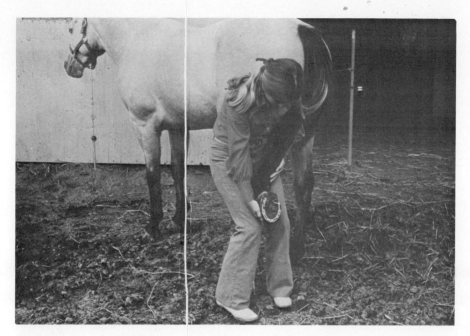

FIGURE 6-9  Lock hock under inside elbow. Keep knees together, toes turned in, and hands free to work on foot. [*Photograph by Duane Dailey.*]

starting at the gaskin. When the horse allows you to rub it below the hock down toward the fetlock, pull its leg *straight forward* by grasping behind the cannon just above the fetlock. Lift forward and upward in one easy motion.

If the horse does not struggle at this time, step forward (toward the quarters) with the left leg underneath the hock of the horse, and extend its foot backward. While moving to this position, slip the right hand over the front of the foot and fold its ankle with the sole of the foot turned upward. The horse cannot kick in this position. The final position is with the horse's leg extended comfortably behind it, hock tucked under the left elbow, cannon resting on top of the handler's left leg, and both of the handler's knees together with feet pointed inward. The right hand still holds the pastern folded in a locked position. If the horse is quiet at this point, both hands can be relaxed to do whatever is necessary with the foot.

Extremely difficult or mean horses may require professional help until they submit to handling. A horse should willingly surrender its feet to be cleaned or handled except when caustic or painful medications are used. In those cases restraint is required.

CLEANING THE FOOT  Stabled horses should have their feet cleaned daily, and those that are working should be checked for stones, cuts, or other injuries at the end of each work day. Use the hoof pick from heel to toe. Hold

FIGURE 6-10   Stabled horses should have their feet cleaned daily to reduce risk of thrush and to identify injuries. By picking from heel to toe the risk of injury is reduced from the hoof pick hanging in a crevice should the horse jerk its foot free and step on it. [*Photograph by Duane Dailey.*]

the hoof pick coming out of the back of the hand away from the thumb side (Figure 6-10). The reason is to keep the hoof pick from hanging in a crevice if the horse jerks its foot free and steps on it. Clean the entire ground surface of the hoof and get in the crevices, down the center of the frog, on each side of it, and around the bars (see Figure 15-1).

After the foot is cleaned, pay particular attention to thrush, nails, foreign objects, cracks, dry feet, contracted heels, and contamination of seedy toes if the horse has been mildly foundered. Any oozing of pus and a pungent odor suggest thrush. If you see a nail that has not pierced the quick, pull it and disinfect the nail hole. However, if it has reached the quick, a veterinarian should be contacted to treat it and administer a tetanus booster shot.

THE BODY   Start grooming with the currycomb, which is designed to lift deep dirt and loose hairs away from the skin, on the left side at the top of the neck. Work backward, against the lay of the hair, being careful to face the rear of the horse and to watch where you put your feet. Use elbow grease, but work carefully in areas where bones are near the surface. The currycomb is never used on the head or the legs, and should be used carefully on the belly.

It is best to use a coarse brush after currying to sweep the dirt and loose hairs away. If the horse is very dirty, it is wise to periodically brush the hairs of the coarse brush through the currycomb to clean the brush. A coarse brush is used in the direction of the hair on the body.

The fine bristles of the body brush are excellent to polish the haircoat from head to lower legs to tail. Most of the dirt and dust should have been removed by the currycomb and the coarse brush. Follow the lay of the hair.

The mane can be styled according to the breed with the mane comb, and the hairs of the tail untangled with the fingers or gently with the comb.

The entire job is polished off with the rubrag, rubbing hard and long with the lay of the hair. The rubrag will bring up the oils of the coat and put a shine on a horse better than any fancy conditioner.

Stay quite near the horse while working from front to rear, and be sure to always face the hindquarters.

Walk well back and away from the horse when changing sides. This is particularly important with a horse you have never groomed before. However, with an older, safer horse who enjoys grooming, you can move closely

FIGURE 6-11    Bend at the hips when grooming the feet and legs of a horse. If it moves, you can also move, with little risk of getting stepped on. [*Photograph courtesy of Duane Dailey.*]

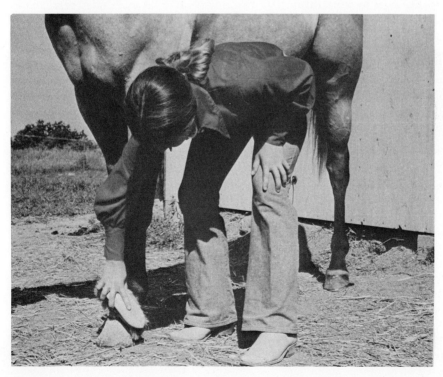

to the rear of the horse when passing behind. If the horse should kick, you will avoid the full thrust of the blow.

Never climb over the halter shank of a tied horse. You would be passing from the line of vision of one eye to the other, through the frontal blind spot. If the horse were to become startled and pull back, you would be in an uncompromising situation indeed: for when a horse is thwarted in pulling back, its next move is often to charge forward.

Untie the horse before grooming the head. Hold the halter in one hand and begin with a soft brush on the forehead by the ears. Move down over the face and around the eyes without brushing over the eye. Work around the mouth and nose as needed, but use care. Some horses are extremely sensitive in those areas, and cannot bear even the softest brush and lightest hand. A well-folded, soft rag may be needed to clean these delicate areas.

Brush both front and hind legs by bending at the hips (Figure 6-11). The lower legs are quite delicate, and a very coarse brush should not be used.

Particularly when in a hurry with a known horse, the handler may have a tendency to squat down under the horse when grooming the legs. This can be a dangerous breach of safety standards, for it is difficult to move quickly from this position.

Working directly behind a horse is not safe. Stand to the side and pull the tail over to work on it.

## Special Grooming Procedures

Blanketing, bathing, shedding out, and protecting against flying insects are a few of the more common special grooming duties. More complex jobs, such as clipping and trimming, and pulling and braiding manes and tails, are best learned by watching experienced horsemen at work preparing the breed or type of horse in question.

BLANKETING   During show season many campaigning horses are stabled in light sheets to protect the haircoat from dirt, scrapes, and the annoyance and unsightliness of fly bites. During winter, many stabled horses, especially if clipped, are sheeted when the temperature drops below 40°F at night, and blanketed when the nighttime temperature drops into the teens or low twenties. During fly season some owners like to protect their thin-skinned stabled charges with a fitted fly sheet as well as fly spray. After work and after bathing, horses are usually protected for a period of time by a woolen cooler of varying weight according to the season. All these pieces of horse clothing, employed for whatever reason, can and should be applied in such a way as to increase the horse's comfort and minimize fear and safety hazards.

BATHING   Bathing a horse can be called a necessary evil because, although it does tend to remove the natural oils from the hair coat, it is indispensable in treating certain pathological conditions of the skin, such as lice infestation (see Chapter 14) and fungus, in soothing generalized muscle soreness, and in thoroughly cleansing the thoroughly dirty horse!

Although many horse owners can be seen hosing down their horse, it is best to take the chill off the water, no matter how hot the day, if only by letting the filled wash buckets stand in the sun to warm up.

There are very good horse shampoos on the market, some of which include antibacterial and antifungal ingredients. Most commercial horse shampoos can be added directly to the wash water and the suds sponged on the horse. Do not merely pass the sponge over the horse's body; work it back and forth so that the soap can penetrate the surface grime and oils and clean the skin. Proceed in the same careful way as when grooming with brush and rag. Be thorough and reach every area. Work carefully around the face and eyes. Rinse the horse thoroughly with a clean, unsoapy sponge and warm water (the tail may have to be hosed out, but most horses will stand for this if it is done with tact and from the side with a slow, steady stream of water). Use the sweat scraper, curved end toward the horse's head, to "wring" the excess water from the horse's coat. Be especially careful with the sweat scraper on the belly. If it is windy or if there is a chill in the air, the horse wil benefit from being lightly toweled before the cooler is put on. Walk the horse out to speed the drying process. Check under the cooler frequently; if the belly is still very wet after 15 minutes, towel it off again or rub it with straw. The cooler can be folded back as soon as the hair on the neck is dry to facilitate drying the mane, which usually takes longer.

Although many racehorses are bathed daily no matter what the season, it is best for the average horse owner to avoid winter bathing. If, because of lice infestation, a bath is unavoidable, then special precautions must be taken to keep the horse from catching cold.

SHEDDING OUT   As the days grow longer in the spring, the horse's winter coat will begin to shed out. If the horse has been allowed to grow a fuzzy, protective coat, the whole process can seem disconcertingly long. Each year new products appear on the market designed to make the shedding process easier. There is no substitute for elbow grease, however, and a frequently applied currycomb.

The shedding blade (Figure 6-6, top) is a flexible piece of metal with tiny, closed-spaced teeth on one side. This can be used in short strokes along the grain of the hair to remove loose hair and dirt. It must not be used on the legs or the face.

There is a rubber mitt with a knobby surface available that is soft enough to be used on face and legs and belly. The loose hair clings to the little knobs and must be knocked out frequently, but the mitt does an excellent job on these delicate places.

Currying twice a day—say, before and after riding—helps to speed up the shedding out process and puts a lovely bloom on the emerging sleek spring coat.

PROTECTING AGAINST FLYING INSECTS    Flying insects are an annoying health hazard (see Chapter 14) which should not be allowed to distress the horse. There are many insecticides designed specifically for use on horses. Some water-based ones can be sprayed on, while the oil-based ones are meant to be applied with a rag or soft mitt.

Many horses do not like or fear the sound of spraying. If the handler proceeds patiently, some will learn to tolerate spraying, especially of the legs and belly. Never attempt to spray around the face or directly into the eyes. Water-based insecticides may tend to wash out with sweat.

Oil-based insecticides are rubbed on lightly with the grain of the hair. Work carefully around the face and eyes. Do not allow the same "fly-wipe" rag to be used on every horse—that practice encourages the spread of skin disease.

Some thin-skinned horses may suffer from flies so terribly that they may require a light fly sheet as added protection. Keep such horses indoors during the day in darkened stalls. Search out and destroy the breeding areas of flying pests; pick up stalls more frequently during fly season (see Chapter 14). Besides providing comfort for the horse, it is a courtesy on the part of the farrier to protect the horse from fly annoyance before going to work on the shoes.

## Practical Saddling and Bridling

Before tacking up, check the equipment to be sure it is equal to the occasion. Tack must be clean and must fit the horse if injury or discomfort is not to follow riding activities.

SADDLING    The horse should be haltered and secured in one of the ways discussed above. While preparing the horse, lay the saddle well back and away from the horse. Be sure there is nothing between you and the horse to stumble over when you pick up the saddle to put it on.

Place the blanket well forward over the withers and pull it slowly and gently toward the rear of the horse. Be sure there are no wrinkles in the blanket or saddle pad.

Do not approach the horse carrying a saddle with dragging girth or cinches and flapping stirrups. Not only is there danger of frightening the horse, but there is also a real danger of tripping on the dragging rigging. On an English saddle, the girth is best removed entirely and the stirrups run up to the top of the stirrup leathers; on a western saddle the cinch and fenders should be folded up, with the right stirrup hooked over the saddle horn and the cinches laid back over the seat of the saddle. With the saddle prepared in this way there is no chance that girth or cinch and stirrups will get caught up under the saddle or knock the ribs and legs of the horse when the saddle is placed on its back.

Raise the saddle as high as possible and forward of where it should lie. Ease it back onto the blanket or pad gently and settle it. Walk well behind the horse to be sure the saddle is centered.

Move to the far side to let the cinches and stirrup down on a western saddle and to attach the girth of an English saddle. Do not release cinches and stirrups of the western saddle from the near side, for they will bruise and bang the horse's ribs and leg.

Move back to the near side. Reach under the horse with the left hand to catch the front cinch of the western saddle or the girth of the English saddle. With the left hand under the buckle to prevent its pinching the horse, pull the cinch or girth up firmly but not too tightly with the right hand. Make sure that the cinch or girth is tight enough to prevent the saddle from slipping out of position but not tight enough to ride in at this point. You will finish the tightening process later.

On the western saddle with a roping or back cinch, reach under the horse again with the left hand to bring this cinch over to the near side. When tightening the back cinch, leave enough room to insert a hand freely under the cinch. The back cinch should not be so tight that it touches the horse's belly when air is inhaled or so loose that a back foot might get caught in it.

After a few minutes, tighten the front cinch or English girth another hole or two. Secure the end of the cinch strap of a western saddle through the keeper. Although most cinch straps are not long enough to step on, they should not be allowed to flap annoyingly.

The stirrups of an English saddle should be kept run up until the rider is ready to mount. If pinched-looking folds of skin can be seen around the girth, the horse's front legs should be lifted up gently just above the knee to help settle the girth and avoid chafing.

For unsaddling, reverse the above procedures.

BRIDLING    Bridling a horse safely starts with untying the horse. Drop the noseband of the halter off the nose but refasten the headpiece around the neck. This will give you something to hold on to if it is necessary to restrain the horse.

Be certain that nosebands, curb straps, and throatlatches are unfastened in the bridle about to be put on. Take the reins in the right hand and slip them over the neck of the horse. Standing beside the horse to the left and facing front as in the haltering process, spread the crown of the bridle with the right hand and grasp the bit in the left. Move the right hand with the crownpiece slowly up the right side of the horse's head. Keep the cheek-pieces and headstall out of its eyes. With the bit pushed lightly against its teeth, insert the left thumb behind the incisors at the bars of the horse's mouth. An obliging horse will often open its mouth automatically, without your having to insert your thumb into the mouth.

As the bit slips into the mouth, continue to move upward with the right hand holding the crownpiece, toward the ears. Once the bit is in the mouth, be especially sure not to jerk the bridle hard, causing the hard bit to bang the front teeth or gums.

With the thumb of the right hand move the right ear of the horse slightly forward and slip the crownpiece over it. With help from the now-free left hand, insert the left ear carefully. Fasten the throatlatch, leaving 3 to 4 finger widths of room.

The bit should be high enough in the mouth to create one or at most two small wrinkles at the corners of the horse's mouth.

Unbridling is the reverse of the above procedure.

## Safe Riding Procedures

Certain observations and generalizations can be made about riding the horse which will enhance the safety of the experience, no matter what "school" or style of riding is followed.

MOUNTING   Now that the horse is saddled and bridled, you are ready to lead it out and away from the building and other objects for mounting.

Check the area where you are mounting. Stay away from buildings, fences, and trees. Also, ground objects, rough or slippery footing, other horses, and people may cause the horse to spook. Before mounting, recheck the cinch to be sure it is not too loose or too tight. If the horse is fat and the saddle narrow at the gullet, ride with a breastcollar for safety's sake.

The following is the best way to mount safely (Figure 6-12). Slack should be pulled out of the reins. Hold the reins in the left half. Face the rear of the horse. Twist the stirrup facing you to receive the left foot. Watch your horse. If it tends to wander away or start up, pull the reins and have it stand in place.

With the right hand on the cantle, take one hop on the right foot and rise in the saddle. Restrain the horse if it tries to move forward. Be sure your left toe is not pushing into its forerib. With the right hand still on the cantle of the saddle, rise up close to the horse.

Stand straight on the left leg in the stirrup. Raise your foot and leg well over the rump of the horse. Do not drag your foot on its rump. This causes anxiety in young horses, and causes older ones to move off before you are seated in the saddle.

Bear weight in the stirrup with the right foot before you drop into the saddle. Don't drop into the saddle and then fish for the stirrup. Such actions will sometimes trigger a cold-backed horse to buck. Also, be in command of

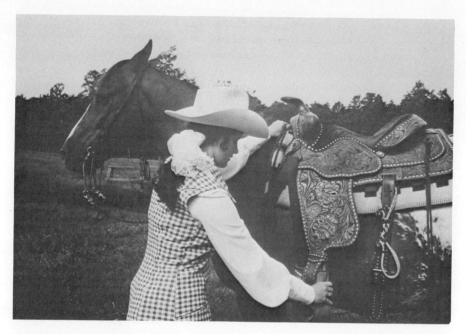

FIGURE 6-12   One safe way to mount is to face the rear of the horse, insert the left foot in the stirrup, take one hop on the right foot, and rise into the saddle while the horse is controlled with the reins in the left hand. [*Photograph courtesy of Duane Dailey.*]

the reins. If the horse tries to charge forward, don't allow it to lower its head to buck. Teach it to stand while you mount, and to wait until you ask it to move off.

RIDING    Ride the horse in the area with which it is familiar in order to work its energy down before riding off in another direction. Feel the horse out in its own surroundings. If there is any bucking tendency, it will come early after mounting with most horses. When the horse is quiet, it is ready to go out and field-ride or work.

When riding on a road, be sure you know on which side your state requires horsemen to ride. Some states require riders to face traffic, as foot traffic does, and others require them to travel with the traffic. Riding on roads where there is high-speed traffic is extremely hazardous and should be avoided whenever possible.

To be safe, dismount when crossing pavement or hard road surfaces, because of their slickness. This is particularly important when they are wet or if there are oil spots on them. If you ride across hard-surfaced roads, do so at a walk. Give yourself adequate time to cross between speeding vehicles.

Your horse does not see the surroundings in the same way that you do. Each eye has a separate field of vision, and the horse sees only varying amounts of reflected light in a drab mosaic landscape. It may show fear at strange objects.

A rider should acquaint the horse with each situation without increasing its fear. Urge the horse gently up to the object of its fear. Don't punish the horse. Give it time to see and smell. Speak to the horse quietly. If hurried or whipped, the horse's original fear will be reinforced and its reaction to the next experience worsened.

When you ride with a friend, ride side by side if the terrain allows it. This is better for visiting and is safer for the horses. Horses that crowd each other or travel close together in a line may tend to get kicked.

If you ride in a group, remember that horses don't like to be left behind. For example, if one person drops behind to close a gate, that horse will become anxious to catch up. In this case it is a good idea for all of the party to wait before starting away. Young horses are particularly impatient when left behind, because of the natural herding instinct. Some may even panic.

When riding a trail single-file, keep one horse length between horses. If you ride up on the rear of another horse, you and your horse may be kicked, or your horse may step on the other horse's heels and substantially injure them.

Don't canter by a rider at the walk unless you know the rider has a well-trained horse. The nature of a horse is to join the group when other horses start to run. This evolutionary trait saved their lives from prehistoric predators. It is not uncommon for young, green horses to panic and buck when other riders gallop by if they are not allowed to join in the chase.

Riding double is a common practice; however, it is not as safe as it looks. Be sure the back rider is an experienced horseman or horsewoman before letting the person mount behind you. If a horse shows anxiety from a rider behind the saddle, the tendency is to squeeze in with the legs. This flanks the horse and worsens a bad situation.

Don't wear shorts when riding horses. If a rider wearing shorts is thrown, skinned knees and injured legs may be the result.

Few riders need spurs or are adept in using them. Spurs should not be used for dress. Indeed, they should be used only for a specific purpose, and sparingly at that. Although it may be stylish to put spurs on youngsters whose feet come only partway down the side of a horse, the tendency is for these spurs to gouge the ribs of the animal and create an unsafe situation.

Clowning and horseplay increase the probability of accidents. Good riders seldom feel a need to exhibit their horsemanship skills by clowning; indeed it may actually indicate poor riding ability.

Allow the horse plenty of time and free rein in crossing obstacles. Free rein allows the horse to lower and raise its head to judge height and distance, and to improve balance with its head and neck.

Don't hurry a horse over rough terrain. Give it time and a loose rein. Then it can pick its footing much more safely than if held on a tight rein and urged at speeds that do not allow time to adjust if it steps on a rolling stone.

Don't allow your horse to run back to the barn with you. This creates anticipation of being turned loose and will make the horse "barn-sour." A good idea is to walk back the last one-fourth mile at the end of the ride. This also allows you to loosen the cinch, permitting blood to flow back in the area under the saddle at a slower rate than if you dismount and quickly jerk the saddle off.

English-type horses may be more spirited and stronger-willed than western horses, and are more likely to spill their riders. Be sure you are not overmounted when hacking or hunting. Get the edge off by longeing or ring-riding the horse until it settles down.

Most hunt seat riders live in more heavily populated areas and must watch for vehicles and slick paved roads.

There is some element of risk to hunting and jumping. Wear a protective helmet with sturdy chin strap and always wear boots. Don't jump objects beyond your skill and that of your horse. Have someone along when you jump and never try to jump barbed wire. If in a group, give the rider plenty of space to clear the jump in front of you, and space your horse one full length behind the horse in front when traveling.

Remember, good position, balance, and control of the horse all contribute greatly to safety (see Chapter 7).

## Hauling a Horse

GENERAL SAFETY PROCEDURES   Some horse activities may involve hauling the horse. If so, be sure your hitch is strong and that your trailer is fastened securely to it. Use a strong chain to secure the trailer to the towing vehicle. Before loading the horse, check tires, brakes, and turnlights.

If you are hauling one horse, load the horse on the left side. This is because the road is higher in the middle and you have better control of the load (Figure 6-13).

If the trailer floor is wet and slick, the horse may be fearful of being loaded.

When loading a young horse, you can give it more confidence if you enter first on the opposite side of the partition. Never go into the same stall you want the horse to go into unless there is an escape door. Eventually, the horse should be trained to go into a trailer alone. Hang the rope up on the horse's neck and let the horse walk in on its own. Horses that expect a small amount of grain when they load will do so readily. This takes the risk out of loading and prevents a nuisance when a horse is difficult to load.

Promptly fasten the bar or chain behind the horse. This prevents it from

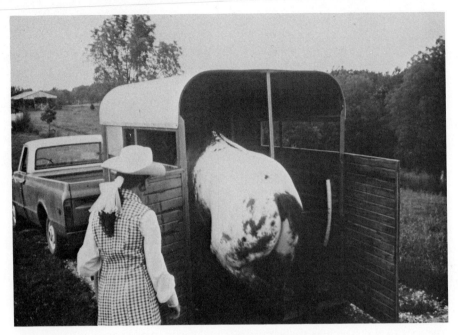

FIGURE 6-13  Your young horse's education is incomplete until it learns to load promptly and haul well. [*Photograph by Duane Dailey.*]

backing out when there is no food or from deciding that maybe it did not want to go after all.

Be sure the gate is secure, both at the top and bottom. Check latches to be sure they are tight and won't bounce up and come loose. There are many types of door latches on trailers. Be sure the type you are using can't come unfastened.

When on the road stay back from the vehicle in front of you so you have adequate room to stop. Hard stops tend to throw horses down. Even if not injured, they may become fearful and trailer-sour, which will make them difficult to haul. Always drive slowly on the curves so your horse can maintain balance.

When you arrive at your destination, be careful where you unload. Leave enough room behind for unloading. Also, carefully observe the condition of the footing on the ground as well as footing around the trailer.

With the rope up over the horse's neck, you are in position to catch the horse when it unloads. Be sure you have untied the horse before you release the tail chain. Horses that get part way unloaded and find their heads caught tend to panic and injure themselves.

Don't stop being careful going home. Be sure the trailer is secure and that your horse is loaded and fastened before you start. Inspect the hitch, lights, and tires before you start and at every rest stop you make. Be in control of the rig, by driving defensively at all times. Drive slowly until you are used to the trailer and then stay back away from vehicles so that you have adequate room to stop. (See Chapter 9 for specific tips on trailering.)

## BIBLIOGRAPHY

Harris, Susan E.: *Grooming to Win*, Scribner, New York, 1977.

*Horse Safety for the Hunt Seat Rider*, Management, MGMU-3, 4-H Horse Project, National Service Council, Chicago, Ill.

*Horse Safety Guidelines*, USDA Extension Service, in Cooperation with the National Horse and Pony Youth Activities Council, Washington, D.C., February 1970.

*Safety: Catching, Leading Grooming*, Management, MGMU-1, 4-H Horse Project, National Service Council, Chicago, Ill.

*Safety: Saddling, Bridling, and Riding Western*, Management, MGMU-2, 4-H Horse Project, National Service Council, Chicago, Ill.

# HORSEMANSHIP

## WHAT IS HORSEMANSHIP?

orsemanship means different things to different people. To some it means skill in the management, care, and handling of horses; to others it means the art and science of riding. Finally, others think of it only as "horsemanship" (equitation) classes in shows where bored horses repeat dull routines as their anxious riders await the decision of a judge. We support such show classes, but contend that horsemanship is much more.

Good horsemen are not new to our generation. Xenophon, Greek scholar and student of Socrates (circa 430–355 B.C.), was a superb horseman.[1] As a soldier, he depended for his survival upon staying well mounted on a fast, healthy horse with enough courage and confidence in its rider to outmaneuver its enemies in close combat. His detailed descriptions of the health, psychology, management, training, bitting, riding, and care of horses in *The Art of Horsemanship* emphasized the need for and appreciation of good horsemanship even at that early date.

In every horse crowd, there are good horsemen like Xenophon, and

[1]Xenophon: *The Art of Horsemanship*, M. H. Morgan (trans.), Little, Brown, Boston, 1893.

FIGURE 7-1   Two 3-year-olds exhibit championship form at Sunset Arena, Kansas City, Missouri. Stephanie Coones, barely three years old, rides with a bath towel saddle blanket to allow her feet to cue Jokers Diamond Hank. [*Photograph by Paul C. Dowling, Olathe, Ka.; Courtesy of the Appaloosa Horse Association.*]

there are those who are not so good. Good horsemen and horsewomen are patient, experienced persons skilled in the art of psychology and communication, with sufficient scientific knowledge to offer their charges a top nutrition and health management program. They have keen observation, attend to details of preparation, and are masters of equitation. They anticipate problems before they happen and act to prevent or diminish their effects. Good horsemen and horsewomen see when they look, and act when they see.

## Careful Observation

It is amazing how some riders can ride and associate with sick or injured horses day after day and never know their horses are not normal.

Horsemanship begins with a thorough knowledge of a normal horse. If you observe a horse for normality, any deviation is readily seen. For example, if one of your horse's eyes is watering, it is easier to see this than to start looking the entire horse over for something wrong. This is especially true of temperature or other early indications of disease. If you go to the stable and your horse skips some of its normal greeting routine, it may feel ill. Its ears may sag, its eyes may appear listless, and its attitude may be dull. If it appears to be its "cheerful self," has no hide missing, eats aggressively, has no cough, and has normal-looking droppings, it is probably well.

The first step in becoming a good horseman is to develop keen observation, based on a thorough knowledge of the appearance of a healthy horse.

## The Normal, Healthy Horse

Age and activities affect the health and soundness of most horses. Because of their vigorous activities at play and lack of immunity to disease and parasites, young horses, under close scrutiny, may show signs of abrasion, parasitization, or coughs from infection.

Hardworking horses may be lame, sore, fatigued, overheated, or chafed by equipment. Old horses may be obese and may have bad hearts, poor circulation, chronic lameness, poor eyesight, and bad attitudes from feet that hurt from lack of exercise.

Young, healthy horses will spend much time together at play. If a young horse does not join the group activity its behavior is not normal. Young horses and foals with fevers will breathe more heavily than others when romping. Count their respiration rates by observing their flanks or nostrils. Normal rates at rest are 9 to 12 per minute for yearlings and older horses. Foals have higher rates. If rates of 50 or more per minute are reached in play, horses usually stop for a "breather" for a few moments during which time respiration rates decline sharply toward normal. If one or more counts remain high, check temperature with a thermometer (see Chapter 14).

Normal horses blow their noses routinely in dusty conditions, but they do not cough much, if at all. Coughs indicate infection of the lungs or respiratory system, allergies, or in older horses, heaves. Infection produces temperatures, but allergies and heaves do not.

Breathing at rest should be free, soft, effortless, and inaudible.

Defecation usually occurs eight to ten times daily when the horse is eating dry feed and more often if the horse is on good pasture grasses or during work. Defecation may be triggered by anxiety or stress, or may be part of a hungry horse's greeting routine. Horses on restricted water or poor-quality hay or with bad teeth may void hard feces. Soft feces may indicate intestinal irritation (as with internal parasites), "washy" high-moisture grass, or laxative feeds. When whole grain is consumed by horses with bad teeth much of it will appear in the feces undigested. However, some whole grain passes through all normal, healthy horses.

Urination frequency varies between individuals, but most horses urinate two to four times daily. Urination too may be a part of the greeting routine. Mares in heat urinate frequently and in small amounts around other horses. Urine should flow easily and in abundance from healthy horses. If geldings dribble urine they may have a "bean" (smegma or sebaceous accumulation) obstructing the flow of urine from the urethra that can be easily removed by a veterinarian or other experienced person.

Normal horses have bright eyes, alert ears, and soft, pliable skins. Their hair coats appear glossy, depending upon season, and should be uniform without indication of abrasion from scratching or rubbing. If one horse in a group is noticeably less conditioned than the others, it has a problem. It should be separated from the competition of others and given extra feed, care, and medication, if needed.

Train yourself to be a keen observer of the normal horse. When a horse is "off" (not normal), you will be able to identify it quickly and to effect recovery without permanent damage or excessive stress to the horse.

## TACK AND EQUIPMENT

Tack is any article or piece of equipment used in riding or driving a horse. Saddles, bridles, halters, blankets, tie-downs, breast collars, and martingales are only a few of an endless list of items horsemen feel they need in handling their horses. Basic equipment consists of a saddle, bridle, bit, halter, shank (lead rope), pad or blanket, and grooming equipment. It is essential that items used on the horse fit well and be kept clean and carefully adjusted. For this reason each horse should have its own equipment. Badly adjusted, inappropriate equipment signals uncomfortable horses, unsafe riders, and poor horsemanship.

An inspection of many tack rooms would reveal a variety of bits, halters, bridles, blankets, and numerous pieces of miscellaneous tack and equipment such as gag reins, draw reins, martingales, and pieces of correctional equipment too numerous to mention.[2] One wonders what a nineteenth century Plains Indian, a superb horseman with only a thong around the lower jaw of his horse, would think if he could see and have these items explained to him. He might think they were gimmicks designed to shortcut basic training of the horse. While some are, most are beneficial if carefully selected, appropriately used, and discontinued when results are obtained.

However, there are few shortcuts to a well-trained horse, and substitution of equipment for wet saddleblankets and hard work is not one of them.

### Saddles

Your saddle is one of the most expensive pieces of tack you will buy. It largely determines your and the horse's comfort and may affect your safety. If it is a quality saddle, it will outlast several horses and perhaps its owner.

Quality saddles are the best buy in the long run. They not only wear longer, but fit the horse and rider better. Quality saddles are built on good trees, covered with good leather, and manufactured with good workmanship. They can seldom be bought new for under $400 and may range upward many times more than this. However, their resale value is good and depreciation is minimal.

Saddles can be classified into four usage categories: hunter-seat, Lane Fox (English), stock or western, and miscellaneous.

[2]Sam W. Sabin, *Miscellaneous Tack and Equipment*, Miscellaneous, MSMU-15, 4-H Horse Project, National Service Council, Chicago, Ill., p. 1.

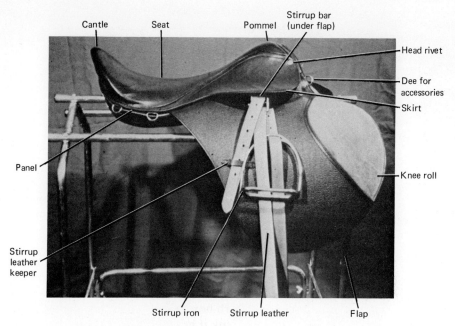

FIGURE 7-2  Forward seat saddle.

Hunter-seat saddles are for forward and balanced-seat riding, such as hunting, jumping, and polo (Figure 7-2). They are light and easy to handle, and a number of styles are available.[3] They allow the rider to sit close to the horse and therefore to communicate with it through leg cues better than do stock saddles. When used in vigorous hunting and jumping activities, hunter-seat saddles require better balance of the rider to maintain a secure seat than stock saddles. For this reason, they result in better equitation form and balance than are achieved by most stock-seat riders.

*Lane Fox* saddles are used extensively in showing gaited horses and in exhibition classes of a few nongaited breeds (Figure 7-3). They are briefer and lighter, and allow the rider to sit closer to the horse than most other saddles. They have long, flat seats and allow the rider to sit back toward the loin of the horse to give a more stylish appearance to the horse's "forehand." They are not used as much for pleasure riding as other types, although American Saddlebred horses are usually pleasure ridden with Lane Fox saddles.

*Stock or western* saddles are used with western horses for roping, cutting, equitation, and general-purpose use (Figure 7-4).

[3]Sam W. Sabin, *Selecting and Using a Saddle*, Miscellaneous, MSMU-12, 4-H Horse Project, National Service Council, Chicago, Ill., p. 2.

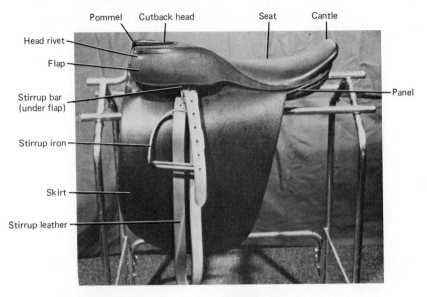

Pommel   Cutback head        Seat        Cantle

Head rivet

Flap

Stirrup bar
(under flap)

Panel

Stirrup iron

Skirt

Stirrup leather

FIGURE 7-3   Lane Fox saddle.

Good western stock saddles wear well. The old story of the cowboy gambling away everything but his saddle was mostly true, because he could afford only one or two in a lifetime. Recent trends in weight have greatly reduced the old 60-pound roping saddle to a more manageable weight of 36 to 42 pounds. Western saddles tend to isolate the rider from the horse because of their thickness. They make leg communication more difficult than do lighter English saddles. However, they offer a great deal of security for the beginning rider and are more versatile, durable, and rugged than other types.

*Miscellaneous* saddles are used for special purposes, such as dressage, racing, sidesaddle riding, trick riding, and parade use. They are of a variety of types and styles ranging from a pound-and-a-half racing saddle to heavy, complex police saddles. Saddles for running gymkhana (games on horseback) events, such as barrel racing and pole bending, can be found in a number of light weights and a variety of styles.

Since competitive and distance riding have become popular, special saddles for these events have been built. The distance saddle usually has a substantial tree with enough surface area to prevent hurting the horse's back. Brief in skirts and fenders, it has no horn but has adequate pommel and cantle to give support to the rider. Such saddles are flat in the seat so the rider can sit forward, especially going uphill.

Many so-called equitation saddles have been designed to improve the appearance of the western rider and horse in show classes. These saddles also

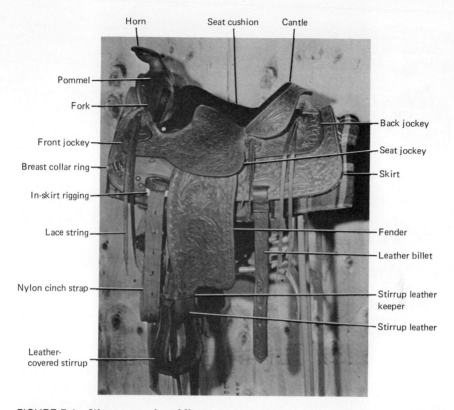

Horn    Seat cushion    Cantle

Pommel

Fork

Front jockey

Breast collar ring

In-skirt rigging

Lace string

Nylon cinch strap

Leather-covered stirrup

Back jockey

Seat jockey

Skirt

Fender

Leather billet

Stirrup leather keeper

Stirrup leather

FIGURE 7-4    Western stock saddle.

have flat seats to allow the rider to sit forward, and in some cases the stirrups are mounted forward on the bars.

Major considerations in buying a saddle are that it fits the horse and rider, is appropriate for the activities desired or to be engaged in, and is of sufficient quality to withstand extensive use.

COMPONENT PARTS OF SADDLES    The most important part of any saddle is its tree. It determines both how well the saddle fits rider and horse and how long the saddle will last, and is indicative of the quality of leather and workmanship throughout the saddle. A variety of materials are used in saddle trees, and an infinite number of shapes. Like shoes, saddle trees vary in size because, like feet, no two horse's backs are the same.

English saddles, both hunt-jump and Lane Fox, are built on steel-reinforced wooden trees.[4] Recently, spring trees have been developed to permit the tree to lie closer to the horse's back (Figure 7-5).

[4]Sam W. Sabin, *English Saddles: Structure and Construction*, Miscellaneous, MSMU-14, 4-H Horse Project, National Service Council, Chicago, Ill., p. 1.

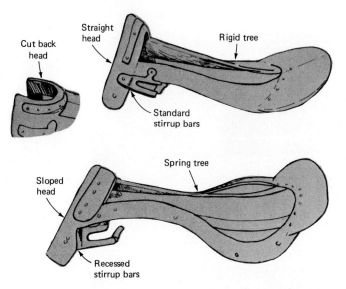

FIGURE 7-5    Straight-head, cutback-head, and sloped-head English saddle trees for Hunter seat and Lane fox saddles. [*Art by Jane S. Tutton; courtesy Animal Science Department, Cornell University.*]

High-withered horses require sloping head, semi-cutback or full cutback trees. Hunt-jump saddles often have straight-head, semi-cutback trees. Lane Fox saddles utilize straight-head, full cutback trees (about 4 inches) that result in a low silhouette, enhancing the appearance of the forehand of the horse, and accommodate high withers.

Length of seat of an English saddle is measured from the head nail (on either side of the pommel) to the center of the top of the cantle. Seat sizes of 19 to 21 inches are standard for Lane Fox saddles, and 17 to 19 inches is standard for hunt-jump or forward seat saddles.

Historically, western saddle trees were made from laminated wood and were covered with beef or bull hide. Bull-hide trees are used for heavy roping and are found in saddles weighing 45 to 60 pounds. Beef-hide-covered trees are lighter in weight and not quite as strong, but are adequate for most light roping and all general use. Recently, extruded plastic has been shaped into a number of saddle "forms" that are guaranteed for five years and have competed well with heavier trees. These forms include the tree and the ground seat that normally is built on a wooden tree and therefore require less labor to construct. They are strong and most are warp-free (Figure 7-6). Other trees are made of fiberglass-covered wood, cloth-covered wood, or simple, bare wood. Saddles with such trees may be satisfactory for light riding, but the trees will fail when pressure is applied, especially when an animal is roped or when the saddle is stepped on.

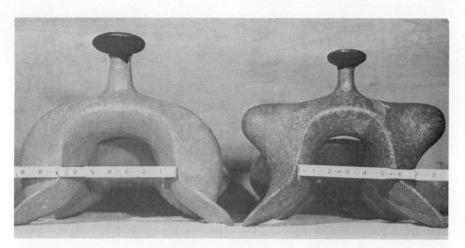

FIGURE 7-6   Extruded plastic "forms" (trees) for two types of horses. *Left to right:* wide (7-inch) low gullet with relatively flat bars for thick-withered, wide-backed horses; narrow (5½-inch) high gullet with steep bars for high-withered, narrower-backed horses. [*Photograph by Duane Dailey.*]

There are four important measurements of the tree of a western saddle: length of the seat, width and height of the gullet, and shape of the bars. Length of the seat is considered for the comfort of the rider (Figure 7-7). Most adults ride 15- to 15½-inch seats. Larger people may want a 16-inch seat, and youth seats range from 12 to 14 inches. The comfort of the horse is dependent upon the other three dimensions. A broad-backed, low-withered horse needs a 6½- to 7-inch wide gullet (Figure 7-6). This prevents pinching the horse's withers. The tree should also have flat bars, such as Quarter-Horse or semi-Quarter-Horse bars. Height of the gullet is not a problem with low-withered horses. Since Arabians have wide, round backs with wide-sprung ribs, these dimensions are critical in Arabian saddle trees. Many Arabian trees have 7-inch-wide gullets and shorter and flatter bars than trees designed for Quarter Horses. Conversely, narrow-bodied, high-withered horses can be severely injured with wide trees that allow the top of the gullet to rest on the withers, causing fistula and other injuries (Figure 7-6). When mounted, you should be able to insert two fingers beneath the gullet of your saddle and above the withers of your horse. Narrow-bodied horses can use 6-inch-wide gullets with heights of 6 to 6½ inches, and the bars must have less flatness than trees for round-ribbed horses. Remember that a saddle must accommodate a blanket, so allow more width than is needed for the horse alone.

Another consideration is the surface area of the bars. Generally speaking, the more surface area, the less weight per square inch and the less risk of a sore-backed horse.

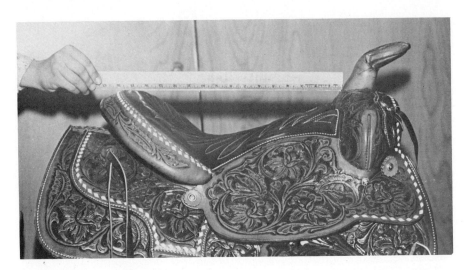

FIGURE 7-7　Seat length is measured from back of pommel to front of cantle. Most adults use 15- or 15½-inch seats. Sixteen-inch seats are available for larger adults, and youth saddles with 12 to 14 inch seats are also available. [*Courtesy Animal Science Department, Cornell University.*]

Other considerations with saddle trees are the width and bulge of the pommel and the width and height of the cantle. The so-called "roping" tree is narrow at the pommel without noticeable bulges. Some ropers have a "slick-forked" tree that tapers from horn to bars. Since the roper must dismount quickly, cantles on roping saddles are lower and smaller than those on "cutting" saddles, and may be no more than 3 inches high. Conversely, cutting saddles may have large bulges on the pommel, claimed to help keep the rider in place under strenuous activity of the horse. Many good cutting-horse riders scorn wide-bulge saddles and depend upon balance for stability in their saddles.

The main requirements of a tree are that it fits the horse, is adequate for the job without being excessively heavy, and remains straight. Many wooden trees warp and cause the saddle to ride off-center at the back. If you have a saddle that consistently rides to the left or right of the backbone of your horse, this may be the problem. Extruded plastic trees are free from warp, but the variety available is limited compared to wooden trees.

There are many styles of western saddles with varying degrees of decorations (Figure 7-8 and Table 7-1). Two major skirt styles are round and square. Round skirts are popular in the range country and are cooler and just as secure on the horse as other shapes. Square-skirted saddles are used more in other localities and outnumber all others. Most show saddles have square skirts with buck stitching, and some are adorned with varying amounts of silver.

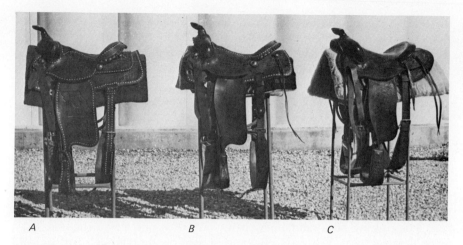

A                              B                              C

FIGURE 7-8  Three styles of western stock saddles: (A) cutter; (B) trail rider; (C) roper.

Skirt sizes in saddles vary. Older saddles usually had back jockeys (Figure 7-8). Many new saddles, especially for trail riders, omit them, but the skirts may extend farther behind the cantle to accommodate an item tied to the saddle. Such a skirt design is called a "Mother Hubbard." Seat

TABLE 7-1  DESCRIPTIONS OF THREE STYLES OF WESTERN STOCK SADDLES.

|  | *(A) Cutter* | *(B) Trail Rider* | *(C) Roper* |
|---|---|---|---|
| Tree style and uses | Cutting, show, pleasure | Trail riding, show, roping | Roping, general use |
| Rigging | Full, double, in-skirt | ⅞, double, in-skirt | ⅝, double, dee rings |
| Skirts | Square: front, seat, and back jockeys | Square: front, and seat jockeys, "Mother Hubbard" | Round: front, seat, and back jockeys |
| Seat | Padded, bicycle style | Padded, bicycle style | Plain |
| Decorations | Stamped, some engraving, buckstitched, name plate | Stamped, some engraving, buckstitched, name plate | Stamped |
| Cinch and rigging | Nylon cinch strap, 17-strand girth, 3″ back girth | Nylon cinch strap, 17-strand girth, 3″ back girth | Latigo cinch strap, 27-strand girth, 3″ back girth |
| Stirrups | 3″ standard, leather covered | 3″ standard, leather covered | 4″ roping, leather covered |
| Blankets | 1″ orthopedic pad | 1″ quilted pad | 2″ orthopedic, roping pad |

styles also vary. Most western riders prefer padded seats for more riding comfort. The extensively padded "high front cutter," popular a few years ago for casual riding, has largely been replaced with less extensively padded seats (Figure 7-8). The popular "bicycle seat" is padded on the inside of the cantle at the back of the seat, and tapers to about 4 inches in width at the front, where it widens again as it contacts the pommel.

Many saddles are stamped with elaborate decorations and the more expensive ones are extensively hand-tooled. Cheap saddles, extensively embossed by stamping, may have hidden faults in the leather that would show if not embossed. Many working saddles have rough-out (inside-out leather) for all or part of the visible portion of the saddle. They are less popular than formerly because they are hard to clean and when new cause the rider's clothes to climb upward.

The rigging on a saddle may be in-skirt or it may be on the tree. Rigging may be located directly under the bulge of the pommel (full-rigged) or it may be halfway back on the tree from pommel to cantle (commonly called "center-fire"). Saddles are also rigged ⅝, ¾, and ⅞. Location of the rigging is very important depending upon use of the saddle. Full-rigged saddles are used for roping. Roping saddles must also have a back cinch that prevents the saddle from rising behind. Many pleasure riding saddles are ⅞ rigged. This moves the girth back from the elbows of the horse and helps prevent cinch (girth) galls. Distance riding saddles are usually center-fire or ⅝ rigged. Distance horses are vulnerable to cinch sores because of prolonged extended trotting. Western saddles used on gaited horses with long shoulders that slope well backward should be ⅞ rigged or full-rigged. If they are not, the cinch tends to pull the saddle too far forward onto the withers of the horse.

There are at least three types of western stirrups to choose from. The standard 3-inch tread stirrup is used mostly for pleasure riding; the deep, wide-tread roping stirrup for quick dismounts; and the narrow oxbow stirrup for cutting or for riders whose weight is borne on the instep of the boot. There is a trend to use oxbows on show saddles instead of the standard 3-inch tread, and roping stirrups are used with alarming frequency by riders other than ropers. Roping stirrups are inappropriate on a cutting saddle and are unsafe for small feet and riders without boots, because the feet can slip through them and become caught.

Standard western girths are 30 inches long. Girths ranging in length up to 36 inches can be obtained for large horses. Many are made from a combination of mohair and nylon and have seventeen strands. Roping girths may be all mohair and range up to twenty-seven strands for added strength.

The best English girths are chafeless, folded leather. Economy girths of web are less satisfactory, but cost only a small amount compared with leather. Most range in length from 38 to 52 inches. Each horse should have its own girth because of variations in size. When fat, your horse may require a girth extension or a different girth for appropriate fit.

Saddles should be tried both on the horse and by the rider before purchase. Some old saddles have so endeared themselves that their riders never want to part with them. Conversely, if a good saddle is unsatisfactory to its owner it can find a ready market, because it may be exactly what another person wants and needs. (See Chapter 6 for a safe saddling procedure.)

## Bridles

Bridles must hold bits at the proper position in the horse's mouth and furnish reins for control and communication.

Bridles vary from a single-leather-strap headstall to complex Weymouth bridles with two bits, four reins, and caveson. Most utility bridles have a headstall, browband, throatlatch, bit, and reins (Figure 7-9). The browband and throatlatch keep the headstall positioned and help prevent the horse from getting its bridle off.

TYPES OF BRIDLES   There are appropriate bridles for each of the three styles of riding, hunter-seat, saddle-seat, and western; and there are many varieties within each style. Hunter-seat riders engaged in hunting and showing on the flat often use a medium-sturdy hunting snaffle bridle with headstall, brow-

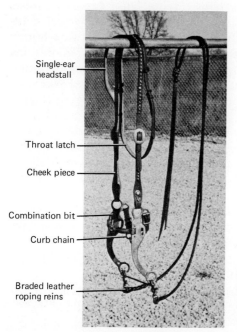

Single-ear
headstall

Throat latch

Cheek piece

Combination bit

Curb chain

Braded leather
roping reins

FIGURE 7-9   Western single-ear bridle (instead of browband) with braided leather roping reins and loose jaw combination snaffle-curb bit. The curb strap is a nylon-chain combination. [*Photograph by the author.*]

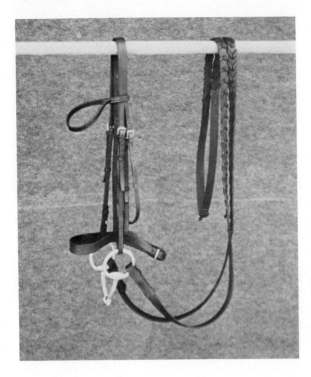

FIGURE 7-10    Hunting snaffle bridle with laced reins. Hunter seat classes on the flat (no jumping) may also be shown in Pelham or full bridles, but most judges agree that well-trained horses are most often shown in hunting snaffle bridles. [*Photograph by the author.*]

band, noseband, and laced hunting reins (Figure 7-10). Legally, hunters may "use a snaffle bridle, a Pelham bridle with single bit and double reins or full bridle[5] (Figures 7-11 and 7-12) for showing. However, if your hunter is well schooled and obedient, showing it in a snaffle bridle removes any doubt that it needs more severe equipment for good performance and control.

American Saddlers, Morgans, and Arabs shown under Lane Fox saddles show in Weymouth bridles with double bits, reins, and a caveson (Figure 7-12). Browbands and cavesons may be stitched leather or they may be decorated with a color inlay. Tennessee Walking horses wear Lane Fox saddles and Weymouth bridles, with a single rein and long-shanked walking horse bit. Fox Trotting horses show in western saddles and Tennessee Walking horse bridles, but their browbands and cavesons are often ornate and studded with sets or covered with "glitter" (Figure 7-13).

Western bridles vary much more than others, but usually have single reins and curb bits. Most western bridles are of the single-ear headstall type, with throatlatch and narrow reins. Show bridles may be ornately decorated with silver and gold inlay. Curb straps are usually leather or leather and chain combined (Figures 7-9 and 7-14).

[5]*Rule Book*, The American Horse Shows Association, Inc., 527 Madison Avenue, New York, annual.

FIGURE 7-11 Pelhem bridle with four reins and caveson; Pelham bit with mouth piece, twisted curb chain, and leather lip strap. Hunters often use this bit to gain more rider control than snaffle bits offer. Pelham bits used on American saddlebreds have longer shanks and use ports instead of bar mouth pieces. [*Photograph by the author.*]

Many western horses are trained in a hackamore. True hackamores utilize bosals. They also have a headstall, browband, fiador, and mecate. A fiador (fee-ah-door) is a light, doubled-rope throatlatch that rests behind the horse's ears, is knotted under the horse's throat, and is attached to the

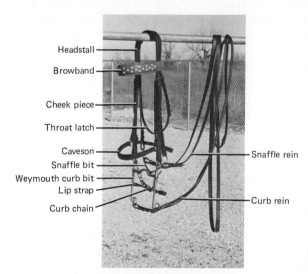

Headstall
Browband
Cheek piece
Throat latch
Caveson
Snaffle bit
Weymouth curb bit
Lip strap
Curb chain
Snaffle rein
Curb rein

FIGURE 7-12 Weymouth bridle with curb and snaffle bits and four reins. Curb bit has standard twisted chain and round leather lip strap. Snaffle reins are always wider than curbs, ⅜ to ½ inch in this case. A snaffle bit is supported by its own ½-inch strap headstall. American saddlebreds and some other breeds show and work in Weymouth bridles. [*Photograph by the author.*]

FIGURE 7-13 A Missouri Fox Trotting or Tennessee Walking horse bridle with plain caveson and ¾-inch reins. The bit is an "Elmer Hicks" Fox Trotting horse bit with leather-chain curb strap. [*Photograph by the author.*]

heel knot of the bosal to keep it level.[6] A mecate (meh-kah-teh) is horsehair or soft rope attached in front of the bosal heel knot to form both reins and lead line (Figure 7-15).

Bridles and halters used on Arabians are brief and minimal, and many are rolled; that is, parts of the cheek pieces, browband, nose piece, and reins are round.

Well-trained horses need very little headgear to do their jobs well.

ASSEMBLING AND ADJUSTING BRIDLES  Western bridles are easy to assemble and adjust because they are relatively simple. When the browband and throatlatch are in place on the headstall, add the bit and attach the reins and curb strap. Make sure you have allowed enough room for these to go on your horse's head. Before final adjustment, the next step is to bridle the horse as described in detail in Chapter 6.

[6]Warren J. Evans, Anthony Borton, Harold F. Hintz, and L. Dale Van Vleck: *The Horse*, Freeman, San Francisco, 1977, p. 648.

FIGURE 7-14       Simple, single-ear western stock horse bridle with lightweight bit, leather-chain curb strap, and ⅝-inch split reins. It is light, handy, and good for routine ranch work. [*Photograph by the author.*]

Double bridles with two bits are more complicated to assemble and fit to your horse than western bridles (Figure 7-12). The snaffle bit, called a bridoon, usually has its own separate crown with a single cheek piece. It is assembled underneath the headstall of the curb bit with the single cheek-piece buckle on the left side. Next comes the caveson crown strap, followed by the throatlatch on the bottom next to the horse's head. The curb-bit cheek pieces are in front of the bridoon cheek pieces in the assembled bridle. Most English bridles have hooks and curb chains, and many have lip straps. The hooks are attached to the headstall rings of the bit, with the hook on the outside. The curb chain is attached and twisted so that it will lie flat under the chin of the horse. The right hook is clamped closed on the chain, but the left one is left open so the curb chain may be disengaged. Loops on the shanks of the curb accommodate the small leather lip strap which is passed through the ring in the center of the curb chain. With the bridoon-bit rings hanging about an inch above the bar of the curb, bridle the horse as previously described. After the bridle is in place, be sure to hang the bits correctly in the horse's mouth. The bridoon bit will hang higher in the

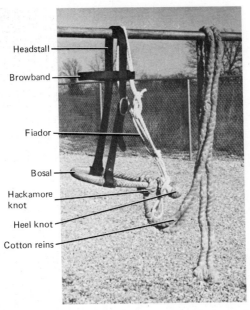

Headstall

Browband

Fiador

Bosal

Hackamore knot

Heel knot

Cotton reins

FIGURE 7-15 A simple hackamore that has been used to train some good western stock horses. It has the heavy bosal for control and response; the reins are made of soft, braided cotton. [*Photograph by the author.*]

mouth than a single bit would, but the curb bit should hang approximately at the level it would without a bridoon.

Bosal adjustment is also very important. If too high on a horse, it is ignored, if too low, it damages the soft cartilage on the nose. It should hang approximately 3 inches below the cheek bone. Also, the size of the bosal should be adjusted either by the reins or by a small leather strap, to accommodate the size of the horse's nose.

## Bits

Bits are used for control and communication. They range from very mild to very severe. The mildest bit possible that will control the horse should be used, and severe bits must be used with great reserve. There is a tendency to "overbit" and "undertrain"—to try to substitute a complex bit for training or schooling time before the horse is physically or mentally ready for the desired maneuver.

Bits should fit the horse's mouth. Most are 5 inches wide, with 4½- to 5½-inch sizes available in some types.

Mouth pieces are made from copper, stainless steel, aluminum, mild steel, many other metals, and hard and soft rubber. The first three materials will not rust—a requirement one should demand of most bits. The debate on which material horses tolerate best continues.

Copper and stainless steel are much more expensive than aluminum bits, but are preferred by most trainers and horsemen.

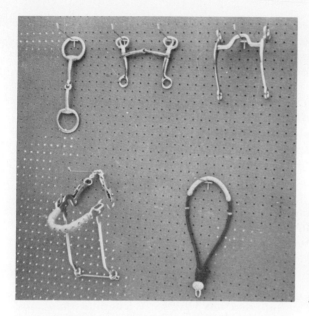

FIGURE 7-16 Four basic types of bits and bosal. *Left to right:* snaffle, combination (both curb and snaffle), curb, hackamore and lightweight bosal. [*Photograph by the author.*]

Four basic types of bits—snaffle, curb, combination, and hackamore—with many variations of each, and a variety of bosals (not really bits) are used with horses (Figure 7-16).

*Snaffle bits* are jointed in the center, with rings at each end (Figure 7-17). They are the most widely used bit in the world and one of the easiest on a horse's mouth. Their severity depends upon the size of the mouth piece, the larger being less severe. Most work stock, horses beginning training or schooling, race horses, and active hunters use snaffle bits. Rings in snaffles may be round, racing dee, egg-butt, and half- or full-cheek. Full-cheek snaffles are good for training because they seldom pull through the horse's mouth.

*Curb bits* have extensions above and below the mouth piece that utilize a curb strap or chain to give the rider leverage through the reins (Figure

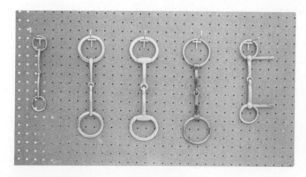

FIGURE 7-17 Snaffle bits. *Left to right:* Bridoon snaffle, from Weymouth bridle; hunting snaffle with flat rings; racing Dee snaffle; work bridle snaffle; and half-cheek driving snaffle. [*Photograph by the author.*]

7-18). Degree of severity depends upon length of shank and ratio of the two extensions. A long-shanked bit combined with a short extension above the mouth piece gives greatest leverage. It should be emphasized that no bit is severe until it gets into rough hands.

The mouth pieces of most curb bits are arched, have various heights of arches (ports), or have straight mouth pieces (bars) with or without spades (extra high port). Arched and ported mouth pieces allow room for the tongue, with most of the pressure applied to the bars of the mouth. Spade and high-port bits exert pressure on the roof of the mouth in addition to the bars and chin from the curb chain or strap. These potentially severe bits must be used with tight curbs and very light rein pressure to prevent injury to the horse.

Horses shown in Lane Fox saddles, especially American Saddlebreds, wear two bits—a bridoon (snaffle) and a moderate-length, straight-shank curb bit referred to as a Weymouth bit (Figure 7-12). Weymouths use chain curbs and lip straps. The curb bit sets the head and neck, is used for control, and may be used to signal certain gaits. The bridoon guides and directs the activities of the horse.

Walking and Fox Trotting horse bits have more length of shank and consequently more leverage than others. The extra leverage is utilized to

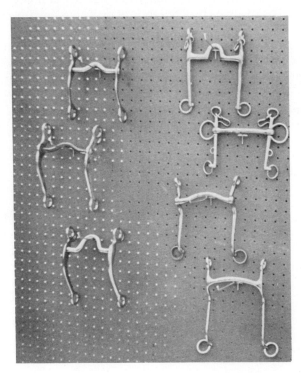

FIGURE 7-18    Western and English curb bits. *Top to bottom:* Light aluminum western curb bit with short shanks and low port; aluminum shanks, copper low-port mouth piece grazing (shanks bent backward to allow horse to graze) bit; polished stainless steel high-port grazing bit. *Second column:* "Tom Bass" American saddlebred curb bit with medium port; Pelham, straight-bar bit; "Eldonian" walking horse bit with low port; "Elmer Hicks" Fox Trotting bit with arched mouth piece. Made from polished stainless steel. [*Photograph by the author.*]

encourage the "big nod" and the "rocking chair" canter of Tennessee Walkers (Figure 7-18). Western horses use moderate-length shank curb bits but more severe ports for extremely light rein pressure compared with more bit contact with gaited horses and hunters.

*Pelham curb bits* have a single mouth piece, but four rings to accommodate two sets of reins. They are used by hunters, on polo ponies, for pleasure riding, and in training (Figure 7-18).

*Combination bits* employ both curb and snaffle action (Figure 7-16). They have jointed mouth pieces and curb shanks. Reins may be attached at the mouth piece in early training then moved to the loops in the end of the shanks in later training. They are often used in this manner by Western trainers, and many are used on reining horses.

*Hackamore bits* have no mouth pieces (Figure 7-16). Their action is based on a wide strap, with or without a metal core around the nose, a small chain under the chin, and two long shanks that permit application of enormous pressure to the nose and chin. Their major use is with western horses in gymkhana and rodeo events, and with horses that are hard to hold, hence the nickname "bear-trap." They are useful on trail horses that drink better without a bit in their mouths and in improving stops on western horses.

*Bosals* are not bits, but are included because they are a useful training tool and are a pleasant change for some well-trained horses that tend to open their mouths excessively.

Most bosals are made of braided rawhide on a rawhide or cable core (Figure 7-16). There are various sizes, from the 4-plait "pencil" show bosal to the stiff, heavy, ¾-inch, 12-plait training size (Figure 7-16). Many good bosals are homemade from old lariat ropes, stiff new rope, horsehair, and other material. All should have heel knots to add weight for quick release when reins are slackened.

A correctly adjusted bosal applies pressure on the nose and under the chin when slack is taken from the reins.

## Halters and Lead Shanks

Halters should not be taken for granted. Each horse should have a halter of its own that fits its head (Figure 7-19). If too large, a halter can catch a hind foot when the horse scratches its head; if too small, it can cause open sores to develop at friction points.[7] Most halters are adjustable, and different sizes of each kind are available. (See Chapter 6 for details of halter adjustment.)

Halters should be strong if the presence of a loose horse creates danger. Tying near busy roads or on trail rides in wilderness areas where a loose

[7]Sam W. Sabin, *Haltering and Tying Horses*, Management, MGMH-11, 4-H Horse Project, National Service Council, Chicago, Ill., p. 1.

FIGURE 7-19        Halters
should not be taken for
granted. Each horse should
have its own, and the halter should fit the horse's
head. A variety of sizes,
strengths, uses, and prices
are available. [*Photograph
courtesy of Duane Dailey.*]

horse could be lost is safest with nylon web halters and neck ropes. Nylon
halters are strong, economical, washable, and available in many sizes and
colors. Their edges are abrasive and tend to wear off spots of hair if worn
constantly by grazing horses.

Leather halters are soft and easy on a horse's head and are more attractive than other materials. They are used on show horses and can be decorated with buckstitching and silver. They are too weak for a large horse that
halter-pulls, are expensive, and require continuous maintenance and repair.

Sash-cord rope halters are inexpensive, light, and easy on the horse.
However, they are not strong and will shrink badly when wet. New rope
halters should be preshrunk in hot water before use.

Halter shanks or lead ropes come in a variety of sizes,lengths, and materials. Soft cotton ropes ⅝ or ¾ inch in diameter with bull snaps braided into
one end make excellent lead ropes. They are strong, easy to tie, and easy on
the hands. Nylon rope and web are strong, but abrasive when pulled through
your hands, and some are stiff enough not to tie well.

Leather shanks are attractive and easy to tie, but are not strong enough
for secure tying.

Most shanks are 7 to 9 feet long.

## Pads and Blankets

The purpose of a saddle pad is to protect the horse's back. If your horse is
working hard, the pad must be thick or more than one must be used to fulfill
this requirement. This fact can be appreciated by observing horses under
hard, continuous use, such as roping horses, distance horses, and those
used under saddle every day for ranch work. Some English show classes
prohibit the use of pads.

FIGURE 7-20 Pads must be thick to protect the horse and should be easy to keep clean. They are available in various colors to match horse color and rider's clothing. *Left to right:* 2-inch "therapeutic" roping pad; 1½-inch "synthetic" work and show pad; 1½-inch quilted work pad with leather reinforced wear points; 1-inch foam rubber pad for light riding. [*Photograph by the author.*]

Pads are available in a variety of types, sizes, and colors (Figure 7-20). Years ago most were folded blankets. The military used a single army blanket folded into nine thicknesses. A single blanket is seldom enough padding for a hard-used horse. Show horses are often shown in highly decorated blankets. These are attractive and can be matched to the color of the horse.

When selecting a pad or blanket, give special consideration to how easily it can be cleaned. There are a number of materials that can be washed in a standard washing machine. Many blankets and some of the materials used in saddle pads meet this requirement; however, many do not.

Genuine Navajo blankets made from wool by Southwestern Indians are in great demand by western horse exhibitors. They are expensive and must be dry-cleaned, and the desired color may be hard to find. All blankets have a tendency to wrinkle when used on high-withered horses. "Therapeutic pads" have been produced from synthetic fibers recently in various sizes and colors and have met with ready sales. A good therapeutic pad should be at least an inch thick, and some are thicker. They are washable and are available to both western and English riders. Foam rubber pads are also well received by English and western riders, although lower-priced foam pads deteriorate rapidly. Many working western pads are of quilted material with a variety of fillers. Some are stuffed with hair. Better ones are an inch or more thick, with leather wear points at the gullet and billets. These pads are economical and quite satisfactory, but they cannot be laundered and are hard to keep clean.

The best English blanket or pad is made from sheepskin with a long dense fleece, shaped to fit the saddle, and reinforced at strain points. It can be washed with cold water, but is easily kept clean by brushing or combing the fleece side after each use. Good sheepskin pads are expensive. There are imitation sheepskin pads that are adequate and much cheaper.

## Grooming Equipment

Good grooming is basic to good horse management (see Chapter 6 for grooming details).

## Miscellaneous Tack and Equipment

Most horsemen use a variety of miscellaneous tack and equipment. Among them are breast plates, breast collars, hobbles, martingales, tie-downs, longe lines, driving lines, leg wraps and bandages, and other items.

Horses with low, round withers do not hold a saddle well and should be ridden with a breast plate or breast collar in vigorous activities. Otherwise the rider risks injury if the saddle should turn or slip backward. A breast plate consists of straps extending from a central "Y" at the center of the chest to the top of the shoulders on each side (Figure 7-21). Breast plates are used in English riding, especially with eventing horses, steeplechasers, and polo ponies. Breast collars are more common to western horses (Figure 7-22). They extend around the chest and attach to cinch rings or breast-collar rings in the corner of the saddle skirts. There are many types of breast collars and breast plates.

FIGURE 7-21      Breast plates lie in the "collar bed" of the shoulders. They help secure English saddles and may be used with both English and stock saddles with "tie downs." [*Art by Jane S. Tutton; courtesy Animal Science Department, Cornell University.*]

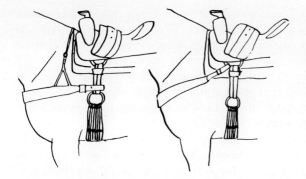

FIGURE 7-22 Breast collars are used with stock saddles for security, especially with flat-withered horses. Some have dee rings to accommodate tie downs. [*Art by Jane S. Tutton; courtesy Animal Science Department, Cornell University.*]

Almost all horses should be trained to hobbles. Horses so trained will struggle less if caught in wire, can be restrained while they graze, and can be taught more easily to stand still while being mounted. Most hobbles have straps for each ankle with a central chain connector. Many are homemade from burlap sacks.

Martingales and tie-downs are useful in training horses and in some cases in correcting bad habits. Running martingales are becoming popular with western riders after decades of use with English horses. Running martingales are attached to the cinch between the horse's legs and are split at the top with a ring on each of the straps for the reins to pass through (Figure 7-23). Most have a strap going around the horse's neck to maintain the martingale in proper position. Their use tends to lower high-headed horses and gives better head control. Results derived from using a running martingale may continue after it is removed.

Tie-downs attach to the girth, as do martingales, but their upper end attaches to a caveson or nose band, thus preventing the horse from thrusting

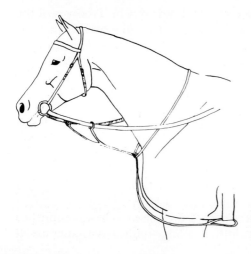

FIGURE 7-23 Running martingales are useful training tools. They are used on both English and western saddles. Standing martingales (tie-downs) have a single "lead-up" and engage a caveson or nose band instead of the reins. [*Art by Jane S. Tutton; courtesy Animal Science Department, Cornell University.*]

its head and nose forward. Tie-downs are preventive equipment and usually do nothing to eliminate a horse's bad habits. They are used extensively in western gymkhana events and with roping horses. Their counterpart in English horses is a standing martingale, used on many jumpers.

Many horses are exercised on a 30-foot line, which allows them to circle their handler. A longe line is a good training device with young horses and an excellent way to exercise trained horses when the handler does not wish to ride. Most are web with a snap at one end.

Driving lines are essential in training young horses and are useful in improving head carriage of trained horses. Two longe lines make excellent driving lines. Since they are made of flat webbing, they will burn the hands unless gloves are worn. With this arrangement, horses can be driven at least part of the time in a circle, much as they would travel on a longe line. If a bitting harness is not available, driving lines can be passed through the saddle stirrups to keep the lines from getting tangled in the horse's feet.

Horses that are hauled or are used in strenuous work may benefit from leg wraps or leg bandages. Most of these are simple 4-inch strips of cotton, 15 feet long, pinned with safety pins, taped, or fastened with Velcro fasteners. Care must be exercised not to cut off circulation by wrapping leg bandages too tightly.

Each trainer or handler has different ideas about miscellaneous tack and equipment. What works for some may not be satisfactory for others. Trial and error may indicate which is best.

## Caring for Tack

Good tack deserves good care. If properly cared for, it can last a lifetime. If not, leather items dry out and crack and saddle pads collect hair and filth that abrades the skin of your horse.

How often should cleaning be done, and how much? Troopers of the U.S. Cavalry cleaned leather items with warm water and soaped them with saddle soap or a glycerin bar after each use. Indeed, peacetime daily training schedules often included 1 hour for grooming, 2 hours of riding time, and 1 hour for equipment cleaning. Bridles and saddles were taken apart, cleaned with sponge and warm water, and extensively saddle-soaped by working lather into the leather. This method counters claims that soap should be used sparingly because excessive soap "closes pores" in leather. Some military saddle straps cleaned by this method over 60 years ago are in use to this day.

Excessive labor need not be used to keep leather equipment clean and soft. Frequent attention with minimum effort is adequate and is better for tack than extensive cleaning two or three times a year.

Daily cleaning of leather surfaces next to the horse can be accomplished by wiping them clean with a moist cloth or sponge immediately after use. If wet from sweat or rain, they should be soaped, and if they are used frequently, thorough cleaning weekly or every two weeks is indicated.

Bits should be wiped clean and dried after each use.

New or neglected leather items require extensive preparation before they can be restored or be prepared for heavy use. The task is made easier and is more likely to get done with proper equipment.

## EQUIPMENT FOR CLEANING SADDLES AND BRIDLES

1 A good saddle rack. It can be used to store the saddle as well as to clean it, and may conveniently contain a compartment for cleaning equipment storage.
2 A hook, peg, or rack mounted rather high for hanging the bridle for cleaning.
3 A gallon pail for warm water and a mild detergent for cleaning and rinsing.
4 Two sponges of different colors, one for cleaning, the other for applying saddle soap.
5 Two or three preservatives. Saddle soap and pure neat's-foot oil are essential. A glycerin bar is the cheapest preservative, but requires more labor because of the difficulty of keeping your sponge at the exact moisture content for good application.

   Many products are designed to give a sheen or "new look" to leather. If they contain wax, they reduce the absorptive response of leather to saddle soap.
6 A chamois and a woolen cloth to dry wet leather and shine finished leather when it dries.
7 A 2-gallon covered bucket for soaking leather items in neat's-foot oil is justified if you have a lot of equipment, and an electric wire buffer is handy for cleaning bits or rusted buckles and other metal.

## HOW TO CLEAN SADDLES AND BRIDLES

1 Assemble cleaning equipment on a table near work location.
2 Disassemble item(s) to be cleaned. Dirt around buckles and access to folds in leather cannot be reached otherwise. (Sponging of leather next to the horse after daily use may make disassembly unnecessary.)
3 Remove all dirt by thorough cleaning with warm water, mild detergent, and sponge.
4 Wipe item(s) partially dry or let dry while cleaning another item before applying leather preservative.
5 Most commercial saddle soaps maintain good spreading consistency

when used with a damp sponge. If too wet, soap clogs holes and lodges in crevices, and if too dry, not enough is applied. Two or three moderate applications with drying time in the sun allows good absorption by the leather.

Neat's-foot oil penetrates better than saddle soap, but will darken leather and soil clothes unless extreme care is used. Saddles are often soaped on visible surfaces and oiled on the underneath side.

6    Wipe off excess preservatives and buff by rubbing with a woolen rag.

## Storage of Tack

A major consideration in tack storage is that it should be safe from theft. Isolated buildings with good locks may not suffice. For this reason, much tack is stored over winter in basements with rather high temperatures and low humidities, both of which speed the drying of leather.

Ideally, tack should be stored in a cool, dry, clean place away from rodents, dampness, and ammonium from manure.

Ammonium rapidly deteriorates leather, and dampness fosters mildew, which is equally destructive.

### STORAGE SUGGESTIONS

1    Place the recently cleaned and soaped saddle on a rack with all parts hanging freely as they would on the horse.
2    Use a stirrup bar to train stirrup leathers of western saddles.
3    Cover saddle with plastic sheet or cloth cover to keep it clean.
4    Hang clean bridles on 4-inch rounded crown hangers with all straps straight and metal parts buffed free of rust and coated with petroleum jelly. Cover bridle.
5    Replace broken parts and have all repairs made in adequate time for next use.
6    Do not forget to reclean and soap after 3 or 4 months in storage.

### EQUITATION

Writers have penned more paragraphs about this topic than any other subject relating to horses. Instruction in equitation and horsemanship began before recorded history, but it is a large and important part of today's horse industry. Discipline, regimentation, and long apprenticeships characterized the early schools. Even today the Vienna School of Riding, now more than 200 years old, refuses to hurry training of its horses and students. In this country, the "military seat" was learned in detail before cavalrymen

were allowed "free" riding time with their horses. It was designed to maximize the energy and life of military horses without very much consideration for their riders. Nevertheless, the person who mastered this style of riding was a good rider.

Often described as "the posture one uses to sit a saddle," equitation
should be broadened to include the rider's ability to control, communicate with, and get the best possible responses from the horse.

The American Horse Shows Association describes the procedure in
detail for the three riding styles (Figure 7-24). Its description reflects riding style and posture as they relate to "horsemanship" show classes. Riding
styles vary between and within breeds and from one rider to another, but
good equitation form is similar for each style of riding. Serious riders
should take instruction in the riding style they prefer under a competent
instructor at an early age (Figure 7-1). "Horsemanship" is a large part of
any breed's program and an important division in its show classes. While
casual riders who have been formally trained may not continue the posture that wins horsemanship classes, they are better riders the rest of their
lives for having had equitation training.

The center of gravity of the horse lies just behind its front elbow.
Changing the center of gravity in the appropriate direction by the rider's
shifting his or her weight greatly aids the horse in certain activities. For example, the race horse is ridden forward while the jockey leans low to reduce wind resistance. Distance riders also ride forward, especially negoti-
ating hills, to reduce fatigue in their mounts. Conversely, horses that work
off the hindquarters, such as cutting horses and American Saddlebreds,
are ridden farther back to release the front end by removing some of the
weight from it.

An appropriate seat in the saddle is basic to all successful activities
with horses. It also indicates sophistication in horsemanship and helps
the rider to be in balance with the mount. Vigorous activity requires that
the rider's body be in rhythm with the motion of the horse and not interfere with the action by being ahead or behind the motion. Good equitation
blends the action and motion of horse and rider into a coordinated unit
that maximizes the performance of the horse.

One's horsemanship and equitation can usually be improved by re-
viewing the following passage from *Horsemanship and Horsemastership*,
by the U.S. Cavalry School.[8]

> The base of support is formed by those parts of the rider's body in contact
> with the saddle and horse, from the points of the pelvic bones, down along
> with inside of the thighs, to and including the knees, legs, and stirrups.

[8]*Horsemanship and Horsemastership*, vol. 1, part one, *Equitation of the Rider*, U.S. Cavalry
School, Fort Riley, Kan., 1935, p. 4.

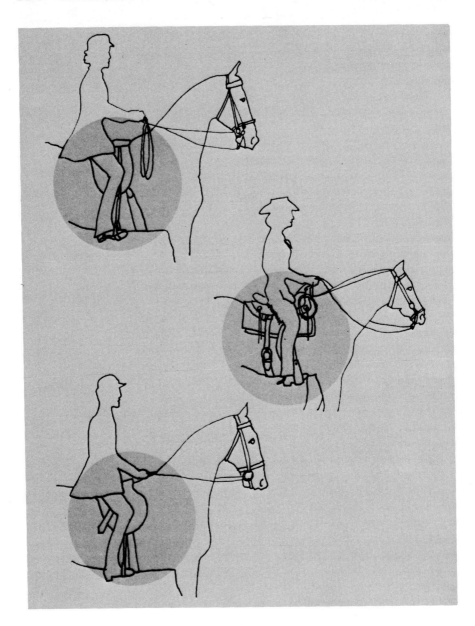

**FIGURE 7-24** The three riding styles, saddle seat, stock seat, and hunt seat, differ in details, but are basically the same. Saddle seat riders sit farther back to enhance the "forehand" of their horses. Stock seat riders sit "deep" in the middle of their saddles for athletic activities, and hunt seat riders sit forward for running and "taking fences" and jumps. [*Courtesy of Sabin, MSMU-12.*]

It is quite evident that the rider's body, receiving impulses from the horse, is constantly tending toward a state of unstable equilibrium, and can remain stable only by balance and the clinging of the knees and thighs, reinforced by a sufficiently strong leg grip.

Balance requires that the center of gravity of the rider's upper body remain as nearly as possible over the center of its base of support.

A study of Figure 7-25 reveals more backward slope in the legs from the knees down and the center (weight) of the body more nearly over the stirrup treads than in most riding styles.

Another point of much discussion with trainees was "in balance or with his horse":

> In forward movement the degree of forward inclination of the upper body varies with the speed of the horse. It should always be such that the rider remains in balance over his base of support. When the inclination of the upper body is not sufficient to maintain this balance, the rider is not "with" but "behind" his horse. When it becomes excessive, the rider is not "with" but "ahead" of his horse.

These words are well written and easier said than done, but mastery of a good "seat" and development of good "hands" are essential to all types of successful equitation form and good horsemanship.

FIGURE 7-25 The U.S. Cavalry seat was "forward," with preservation of the horse first in priority. Theoretically, the center of the rider's weight was over the stirrup treads, requiring more bend in the knee than other riding styles. [*Courtesy Field Artillery*, Elementary Mounted Instruction, *1933*.]

## Hunter-Seat Equitation

No other style of riding requires more body balance and grip of the legs than hunter-seat riding. If the body leans too far forward or does not lean forward soon enough at a jump, the horse's rhythm and timing may be lost, resulting in a bad jump or a refusal. Grip at a jump reassures the horse and prepares the rider for the unexpected as well as aids in maintaining balance over the jump. Class routines in hunter-seat equitation and shows may or may not include performance over jumps.

Good hunter-seat position begins with a saddle that fits the rider and with properly adjusted stirrups (Figure 7-26a). When the legs hang relaxed in the saddle, the irons should strike the boots at the ankles or slightly above. This allows appropriate knee position in the pockets and low heels in the irons (Figure 7-26b). The rider sits forward in the saddle with an erect body position, both shoulders back, eyes, head, and chin up. He or she should be poised, alert, attentive, and relaxed. The rider's legs should bend at the knees, with knees firmly pressed into the pockets and thighs in contact with the horse at all points. Legs from the knee down are kept approximately parallel to the girth, with calves in light contact with the horse, heels down, and balls of the feet over the center of the stirrup treads or thrust all the way "home," depending on rider preference. Reins are held in both hands, with the hands low over the withers in line with the elbows and bit and turned about 30 degrees inside the vertical (Figure 7-26c). The reins should be held in a relaxed manner and hands should always be light and supple.

One of the most difficult challenges is to maintain balance with the motion of the horse without changing pressure on the reins. Good "hands" are a must in hunter-seat riding. When the horse is standing or in motion at the walk and slow trot, the body of the rider should be vertical. As the horse enters the trot when traveling in a circle to the left, the rider's body inclines slightly forward and rises with the outside front leg of the horse (posting). When the horse is cantering, the body of the rider should be halfway between the position of a posting trot and walk. When the horse is jumping or galloping, the rider's body is inclined forward to the position of the posting trot.

The appropriate mounting procedure is to take up the reins in the left hand and position hand and reins on the withers.[9] Slack should be out of the reins for control of the horse. Position the left stirrup iron with your right hand to receive your left foot. Swing quickly into the saddle from one hop on the right foot (for tall horses) by aid of the right hand on the pommel of the saddle. Hold the reins as in Figure 7-26c according to the number of reins used and the activity undertaken.

[9]James J. Kiser, *What the Judge Looks for in Equitation Classes,* Science and Technology Guide no. 2838, University of Missouri Cooperative Extension, Columbia, 1975, p. 2.

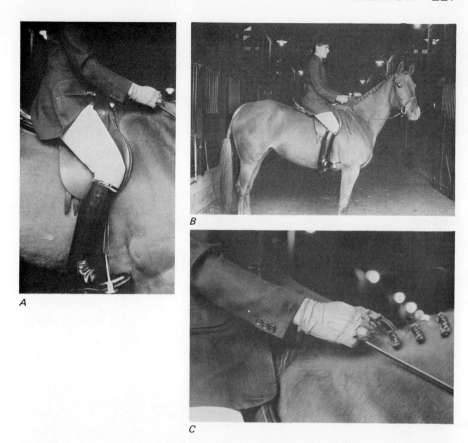

FIGURE 7-26  (*A*) Sit forward in the hunter-seat saddle with thighs and knees in firm contact with flaps and knee-rolls and heels lower than toes. (*B*) Back is arched, shoulders are back, chin is up, and eyes look well ahead over horse's ears. (*C*) Reins are held as shown; hands are turned in at 30 degrees with elbows, hands, and reins in straight line. [*Courtesy Kaiser, 1976.*]

It takes practice, discipline, and physical fitness to assume and maintain hunter-seat position. When these are achieved, it is a comfortable position to ride and one that maximizes maneuverability of the rider and horse.

## Saddle-Seat Equitation

Basic saddle-seat equitation does not vary greatly from hunter-seat equitation except that the rider sits farther back on the horse, rides with slightly longer stirrups, and has two bits and four reins to handle.

To take a basic position, sit comfortably in the center of the saddle with the inside of both knees and thighs contacting the saddle, feet and legs hanging under the body in a relaxed, natural position. Properly adjusted stirrups will rest between the ankles and insteps of your feet, depending on your build. The irons should then be placed under the balls of your feet (not toes or "home") with even pressure on the entire width of the boot soles (Figure 7-27a). Foot position should be neither extremely in nor

FIGURE 7-27    (A) Saddle-seat show riders sit farther back in their saddles to enhance the "forehand" of their horses. Their knees and calves are in close, toes pointed ahead, heels down, and stirrups adjusted for appropriate knee bend. (B) Posed horse and rider should look stylish, poised, calm, and in control. (C) Reins are held in this manner, with snaffle rein outside of curb and elbows, bottom of hand, and bit all in line. (D) "Addressing the reins" or picking up reins preparatory to taking reins in both hands. [*From Bradley and Hardwicke, 1975.*]

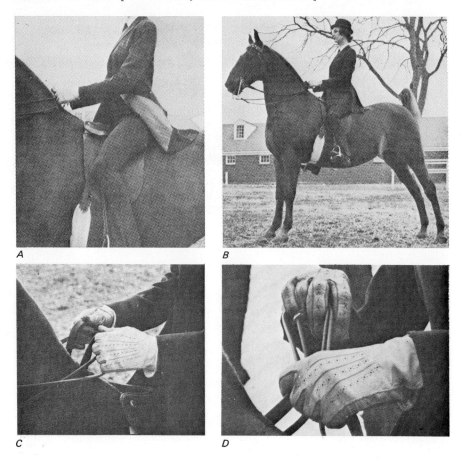

A

B

C

D

extremely out. Ankles and insteps should be flexible, with heel positions lower than toes. Much of the success of good riders can be attributed to this position.

Figure 7-27*b* shows a good posed position of both horse and rider.

The rider's hands should be held in an easy position, neither perpendicular nor horizontal to the saddle, and should show sympathy, adaptability, and control. Height above the horse's wither is determined by how and where the horse carries its head. Figure 7-27*c* shows the most common position of holding the reins, with snaffle reins on the outside of curb reins and the bight on the right side of the horse. Elbows are held at your sides in a natural position, neither in too tight nor out too far.

Judges sometimes use tests of horsemanship in deciding final placings.[10] One common test requires the rider to "address the reins" or "pick up reins." With the reins on your horse's neck, pick them up according to Figure 7-27*d* and hold them as shown in Figure 7-27*c*.

When asked to mount or in routine mounting, address the reins as in Figure 7-27*d* (except that the rider is dismounted) and hold them with the bight on the right side, left hand on withers, while right hand positions the stirrup over the left foot.

With your left hand firmly on the withers, grasp the off side of the cantle with your right hand, take one or two hops on your right foot to attain momentum, and swing your right leg clear of the horse's hips. Position the right foot in the stirrup before easing the body weight into the seat of the saddle.

Dismounting is the reverse of mounting. With snaffle reins tighter than curbs, left hand on withers holding reins, right hand on pommel, support yourself in the stirrups in preparation to dismount.

Swing your right leg over the horse's back and place your right hand on the cantle in preparation for stepping or sliding to the ground. It is correct either to step down or slide down from this position, depending on the size of the horse and/or rider.

Good saddle-seat equitation enhances style, beauty, and motion of the performing horse. Accomplished riders minimize their horse's mistakes, maximize their horse's speed without losing form and motion, and capitalize on their horse's style and beauty by their position in the saddle and the height of their hands to enhance "forehand" and head carriage. To do these things, they do everything possible to divert attention from themselves to their horses. This is why conservative clothing is worn in society shows.

---

[10]Melvin Bradley, and Shirley Drew Hardwicke, *English Equitation: Mounting Correct Seat, Dismounting*, Science and Technology Guide no. 2875, University of Missouri Cooperative Extension, Columbia, 1977, p. 1.

## Stock-Seat Equitation

A correct seat in the western saddle is basic to successful horsemanship, not only for appearance, but because of the quickness and athletic activities of western horses. Because western saddles have more height of pommel and cantle than English saddles, they offer more to cling to. However, a correct seat in the saddle should not be neglected by beginning riders, because balance is just as essential in western saddles as other types (Figure 7-28).

More variation exists throughout the country in methods of mounting, riding, holding the reins, and carrying the free hand and arm than in other styles of riding. However, some basic fundamentals are agreed upon and are acceptable for showing.

As with English riding, sit relaxed in the center of the saddle (not on the cantle) with legs hanging down for stirrup adjustment. The stirrups should fall approximately halfway between the ankle and instep to allow a slight knee bend and to permit the heels to be lower than the toes. This adjustment allows flexibility in the ankles and insteps to accommodate the motion of the horse; it is particularly important in jogging. The thighs, knees, and calves are in light contact with the horse and the feet are pointed almost straight ahead, depending upon the build of the rider. The motion of the horse tends to move the rider back on the cantle of the saddle with too much bend in the knees, resulting in high heels and toes pointed toward the ground. Some riders overcompensate, resulting in "dashboard" riding. That is, they bring their feet too far forward in the stirrups with knees nearly straight and brace against the cantle of the saddle.

The phrase "tall in the saddle" is a good one. One should sit deep in the seat of the saddle, back erect, chin up, eyes up, shoulders back, and elbows comfortable at the sides. Although training is done with two hands, showing is limited to one. The hand holding the reins is in line with the elbow and the bit held slightly above and forward of the saddle horn.

There are three permissible ways to hold the reins when showing western horses: closed, split, and romal (Figure 7-29a, b, c). Closed reins enter the top of the hand and are held between the first finger and thumb, with the bight on the same side of the horse as the hand holding the reins. Split reins are held in the same manner, except divided by the first finger. A romal enters the bottom of the hand and comes out at the top between the first finger and thumb, with the bight held in the other hand at least 16 inches from the reining hand.

When closed or split reins are used, the opposite hand (usually the right) is carried either along the thigh or at the belt, with folded elbow. Wherever the arm is carried, the rider must look relaxed. A ramrod-stiff, erect rider not in motion with the rhythm of the horse detracts from the best-performing horse and violates the intent of the activity.

There are two positions from which most riders mount. It is safer to mount a green or fractious horse by holding the left hand on the withers

FIGURE 7-28    (*A*) Stock-seat riders sit "tall in their saddles," positioned between pommel and cantle, thighs and knees in contact with the horse, and heels down as with other riding styles. Upper body is erect at the walk, chin up, shoulders square with neither shoulder in front of the other. (*B*) To jog, the body inclines slightly forward at the waist to be "with the motion of the horse." (*C*) Loping is accomplished with further forward position of the upper body without changing position of the legs and feet. [*Art by Bill Culbertson.*]

with no slack in the reins. While the rider faces the rear of the horse, his or her right hand positions the stirrup to receive the left foot. With one or two hops of the right foot, and right hand on saddle horn, the rider rises into the saddle with a continuous motion. The second way, more commonly used, is simply to face the horse at the side, reins in left hand on withers, and raise the left foot into the stirrup while the right hand on the saddle horn aids mounting.

The most important point in any type of riding is not that you fulfill the requirements of show rules (although you must if you are competitive), but that you ride in cadence and rhythm with the motion of the horse. Good horse handlers and trainers have learned to do this either formally or

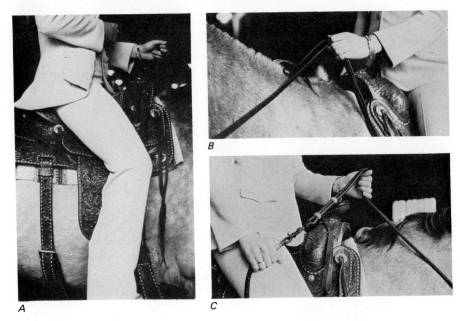

FIGURE 7-29   There are three permissible ways to hold the reins when showing western horses: (A) closed reins; (B) split reins; and (C) romal. Closed reins enter the top of the hand and are held between the first finger and thumb with the bight on the same side of the horse as the hand holding the reins. Split reins are held in the same manner, except that they are divided by the first finger. A romal enters the bottom of the hand, comes out at the top between the first finger and thumb, and the bight is held in the other hand at least 16 inches from the reining hand. [*Courtesy Stephens College, Columbia, Mo.*]

informally. The cowboy working cattle, and the trainer schooling a hunter or working the rough spots out of the gaits of a Saddlebred horse, have established good bases of support and are in motion with their horses even though they may not carry head, hands, and feet according to prescribed "horsemanship" show rules. They have modified the three basic seats into their own riding styles that work best for them.

## Modified Riding Styles

Since most horse classes are judged for performance, not equitation, riding styles are not judged in them, but the horse is judged completely on its own performance (supposedly). Riders doing the same thing with a gait tend to look alike. However, there are wide variations in equitation form with different uses of the gait. For example, endurance riders stand at the trot, cowboys sit, and American saddle horse riders post. Endurance riders lean forward and learn to balance standing up, simply to spare themselves and their horses so they can finish the event. Western stock horse riders sit erect when showing and bear weight on the stirrups as they flex their ankles to take part of the bounce out of a rough jogging horse, hoping to make it appear smoother.

There is a tendency in speed-gaited classes, such as racking, for riders to thrust their legs forward and outward, elevate their hands and elbows, and thrust their chin and head forward to give the impression of speed, power, and boldness.

Riders of soft-gaited horses in the same class may have dramatic contrasts in riding styles. Some may be riding in "good" form while others tend to ride with extremely long stirrups with toes pointed toward the ground to emphasize to the judge that they are not riding hard spots out of a rough traveling horse by bearing weight in the stirrups. These extremes may be unnecessary, as good equitation form usually gains more favor with the judge and spectators than radically modified individual riding styles. However, before condemning such riders as clods we should be aware of their intent, whether or not we agree with it.

Some mistakes that amateur riders often make are listed below:

1  Flapping elbows
2  Heels higher than toes
3  Humpback or slouching position
4  Not in rhythm with the horse
5  Daylight under the knees
6  Reins held too long or too short
7  Hands too high or too low
8  Riding the cantle of a western saddle
9  Wrong adjustment of stirrups
10  Ill-fitting saddles for rider or horse

## PREPARATION AND SHOWING

Growth in horse shows in recent years has been spectacular. They appeal to both showmen and spectators alike. Exhibitors show horses for two main reasons, fun and profit, though seldom for both. Many people haul horses to shows throughout the show season for the challenge of competition and enjoyment of winning, without any thought of regaining expenses. Trainers and those whose economic survival depends on the horse business must show to advertise, to accumulate points on a horse, or to appraise the quality of stock of their competitors.

Successful showing requires a well-trained horse, a knowledgeable horse person, expense money, and hard work. Showing can be a very

FIGURE 7-30 Horse showing should be fun. It is, with a good horse and competent rider who is not compelled to "win at all costs." The rider enjoys a good performance by her five-gaited American Saddlebred horse as she posts the trot on the right diagonal. [*Photograph by Morris; courtesy of Stephens College, Columbus, Mo.*]

pleasurable activity. For this to be so, it requires a certain competency of horse and rider (Figure 7-30). Any time a person participating in horse shows feels compelled to win every class and becomes offended when he or she does not, horse showing ceases to be fun. When it is no longer fun, it should be stopped and another horse activity engaged in that is less competitive. Experienced exhibitors know they have won classes they should not have and lost some they should have won. Therefore, they accept the judges' decision quietly if not cheerfully, because in the long run placings tend to average out about where they should be.

### Preparation for Showing

Competition is so keen that horses are usually shown only in one or two events. Needless to say, a very well trained horse is required. If such a horse is purchased by a beginner, it will be expensive and will not show as well for its new owner as it did for the professional person who showed it. Therefore, new owners should not expect to buy the top horse in a community or state and expect it to continue winning at that level, until they have acquired considerable skill and knowledge.

When training your own horse, school it in routines you intend to use it in until it makes no mistakes. Remember, both horse and rider are likely to be nervous in new surroundings at the show and may perform below the average of their performance at home. One should not take a half-trained horse to a show and be embarrassed by its ineptness compared to other horses in its class. When your horse is doing routines at home without mistakes, have it evaluated by a friend or enter a small horse show to find out what someone else thinks about its performance before entering strong shows.

Show horses must be well groomed and trimmed. Grooming starts weeks ahead of the show by proper nutrition (see Chapter 6 for grooming and Chapter 13 for feeding), adequate exercise, and endless brushing. Most show horses are kept inside a barn out of the sun through the show season, so their hair coats do not sunburn or get abraded. This also allows their owners to keep them under blanket and keep their coats blooming. Some breeds must be shod specifically for their activities, and some must be kept in tail sets during the show season.

Trimming a horse must conform to breed requirements (observe fitted horses in Chapter 3). Two kinds of electric clippers are convenient for trimming: a large type that trims fetlocks, bridle paths, and the body, if needed; and the small animal electric clipper to trim around the nose, throat, ears, and areas where noise affects the horse. Small clippers do not have enough power to adequately trim the body, mane, or fetlocks.

## Show Rules

Most shows comply with the American Horse Shows Association rules. There are some very large breeds for which there are elaborate extensions of the American Horse Show rules to be followed.

Before the aspiring exhibitor goes to a show, he or she should be thoroughly familiar with the rules applying to the particular classification and division, and should also resolve with the show management any questions on special rules the local show may be using before the class starts. Further, if the judge modifies procedure or explains the way the class is to be shown, the exhibitor should listen carefully to these instructions and abide by them. The excuse of not understanding the rules or "not knowing what I was supposed to do" usually is insufficient to satisfy a judge or ringmaster after the class is placed.

## Performance Classes

Performance classes are so numerous and varied that they include almost everything imaginable.

Hunter-seat horses formerly included mostly thoroughbred horses, but recently most western breeds and many others have hunter-seat classes. Hunter-seat horses are shown in forward-seat saddles. Nonjumping horses are required to walk, trot, canter, and hand gallop both ways of the ring.

They must execute individual figures according to the American Horse Shows Association and are judged largely on good balance, even pace, and maneuverability.

Hunters that take jumps are scored on faults (that is, striking the jump with any part of the body), uniform pace, manners, and speed, or time it takes to complete the course.

Saddle-seat showing has long been associated with the American Saddlebred horse. More recently, as in hunter-seat showing, exhibitors of other breeds, especially Arabs and Morgans, are showing their horses in Lane Fox saddles. The image prompted by saddle-seat riders is of horses with much style and motion (high action) doing the walk, trot, and canter both ways of the ring, and, if five-gaited, performing a slow gait and rack. Riders post the trot in both hunter- and saddle-seat classes and must be sure they are posting on the correct diagonal—i.e., as the circling horse's outside front foot rises, the rider rises in the saddle, and sits in the saddle as the inside front leg rises (Figure 7-30).

## Showing at Halter or in Hand

Each breed differs in equipment worn and emphasis placed on judging these classes. Western horses are shown in halters, many elaborately decorated, while gaited horses are most often shown in bridles. These classes are usually called model or in-hand classes. They are all judged on type, conformation, quality, soundness, style, and straightness of legs. They are shown posed, walking, and trotting in a straight line toward and away from the judge. Their leaders always walk at the left shoulder of the horse and turn them to the right for safety reasons. Stylish breeds may be followed by a second person with a whip to help keep them alert and exhibiting high action or motion.

Halter and model classes may be shown according to age and sex and by groups such as produce of dam (two animals from the same dam) or get of sire (three animals by the same sire).

## Showing under Saddle

After the horse has been hauled to the show, has rested, and is prepared or partially prepared, it should be warmed up. Warm-up rings are usually available. Some horses require extensive warm-ups and others no more than casual walking. If a western horse tends to be "hot" (overactive), it may need extensive riding before its class. On the other hand, an old horse that makes no mistakes but tends to be "ouchy" or prone to get lame may need little warm-up. Your goal is to have your horse make no mistakes and give an above-average performance of its capabilities. You cannot expect a top performance from your horse each time it enters the show ring, although this is what you are hoping for.

FIGURE 7-31   Western pleasure show classes outnumber all others. Riders by the thousands haul horses far and near throughout the long show season to vie for trophies, ribbons, and points with their horses. [*Courtesy Animal Science Department, Texas A&M University.*]

Listen to the instructions of the announcer and watch the signals of the ringmaster. Prompt compliance without hurrying or making your horse nervous is sufficient. If you feel nervous, the horse will sense this and will likely respond in kind. If you expect the best from your horse, you are likely to get it; and if you expect the worst, it is likely to follow also. Be alert when the horses are performing, and stay out of bunches. Although a judge usually sees the kind of horse he or she wants to use in a class, it is possible that horses with solid colors might be obscured in groups. You are trying to place your horse in a position that can be easily seen by the judge without being too bold or obvious about it. A good judge appreciates an exhibitor who shows a horse to the best of his or her ability, is courteous to the competition, does not constantly try to conceal obvious faults of the horse, and does not try to take unfair advantage of other exhibitors.

Western pleasure and stock horse show classes outnumber all others without a close second. Western pleasure horses must walk, jog, and lope both ways of the ring in good form and balance (Figure 7-31). They must back straight, stop hard, and neck rein well. All cues given to western horses are imperceivable or minimal, as these horses must be totally obedient without giving signs of nervousness, opening the mouth, anticipating maneuvers, or wringing their tails. The judge may ask finalists to do extensive ring work in trying to determine which horse to place first.

Trail classes also include the walk, jog, trot, and lope both ways of the ring. In addition, the horse must work on a loose rein around and through a series of obstacles that might be encountered on the trail. Some of these include opening and closing gates, water traps, cavalletties, bridges, backing around obstacles, and almost any other imaginable test for a horse going cross-country. The horse is scored on performance, manners, and how it performed the maneuvers asked of it. Conformation is also part of the score.

Reining stock horses must execute one of a series of reining patterns that include flying changes of leads, hard stops, rollbacks, and spins, followed by standing still on a loose rein.

The American Quarter Horse Association approves six reining patterns; most stock horses run one or more of them.

One seldom buys a finished horse, quickly learns to ride, then promptly captures most of the top awards on the show circuit. It takes experience, skill, knowledge, discipline, resolve, and an attitude and willingness to continue to improve. The person who "makes" a finished horse and keeps it competitive is not only a master of equitation, but a genuine horseman.

# MANAGING ADULT
# HORSES

n excellent horseman nearing the end of his career once said, "You can count the truly great horses you have owned on the fingers of one hand."

Most objective horsemen would agree. Such horses are priceless to their owners, and every possible management practice should be employed to extend their usefulness. It is sad to see a grieving owner who underpriced such a horse or who allowed its usefulness to terminate through neglect, accident, or bad management.

Many adult horses (5 years old and older) not used for breeding are kept for use in an athletic activity (Figure 8-1). Some have had extensive training and are very competitive performing their specialty. However, most adult horses are not extensively trained or economically essential but are held in high esteem for occasional rides or as comforting companions. The longevity, and therefore productivity, of all horses depends upon regular feed and care, adequate housing, a healthy environment, and knowledgeable management practices. Almost everything that terminates a horse's usefulness is management-induced or management-influenced.

FIGURE 8-1  Stabled and show horses live in managed environments. They must be fed a ration that supplies all needed nutrients without gain or loss in condition, be exercised to prevent bad attitudes and stable vices, and be used enough to maintain proficiency of performance. [*Courtesy of Stephens College; photograph by Duane Dailey.*]

Idle adult horses (but not growing foals, lactating mares, or hardworking horses) are among the easiest animals to manage. When mixed animal species suffer under mismanaged conditions, adult horses are usually the last to go, because they are hardy and many of the feeds they consume meet their nutrient needs. Horse owners and managers are often overconcerned with "magic" feeds and health remedies that are advertised and underconcerned about basic feeds, effective parasite control, and proven immunization practices. Internal parasites and diseases destroy more horses than improper feeding and cause misery and pain to many horses that manage to live and faithfully serve their owners. The objective of this chapter is to summarize information on feeding, management, and health that will result in long, useful service from adult horses. Extensive discussions of feeding and health will be found in Chapters 11 to 15.

## MANAGING THE FEEDING PROGRAM

The goal in feeding well-conditioned adult horses a balanced diet is to have no gain or loss in weight; to furnish all required nutrients; and to produce no colic, wood chewing, or other stable vices—all for a reasonable price. This is quite an order when considering the varying needs of horses of different sizes in the herd or stable, the effects of the hierarchy on pastured horses, and the amount of exercise each receives.

## Essential Nutrients

A strange but widespread misconception of many horse owners is that their animal is not covered by the basic principles governing the amount and kind of nutrients needed by other animal species, whose nutritional needs have been well researched. Therefore, some of the horse's basic nutrients may be slighted, or even ignored, so long as it gets a "spoon" of this or a pinch of that—provided the spoon and the pinch are extensively advertised and excessively expensive. How dangerous a practice this can be is well documented in other species. Indeed, if confined swine or poultry are denied even a small amount of a major nutrient or are offered an unbalanced ration, production ceases and their peaceful social order is violently disrupted and may even result in cannibalism.

The first requirement of horse feeding is that the nutrient needs of the animals be met by using the proper quantity of quality feeds. The horse requires *energy* (calories) for maintenance of the body cells and work; *protein* for tissue repair and disease resistance; *minerals* for bone growth, acid-base balance, and enzyme functions; *vitamins* for vital chemical reactions; and *water* for nutrient transport and temperature control (see Chapter 11 for more details).

*Nutrient Requirements of Horses*, published by the National Research Council[1] lists minimum nutrient requirements of horses of different ages and sizes at various stages of work and reproduction (Table 12-1). These tables are the basis of all nutritional research studies of the horse and of all good commercial feed formulations. They should be understood by all horse feeders, because when carefully followed, most of the guesswork and much nutritional misinformation is eliminated from horse feeding. As important as art and common sense are in horse feeding, unless a feeding program is based on an understanding of the horse's nutrient needs, results will be unsatisfactory. Retarded growth, poor condition, below-peak performance, or temporary or permanent unsoundness result from ignoring the horse's basic nutrient needs.

## General Considerations for Feed Regulation and Exercise

The importance of maintaining athletic condition in adult horses and preventing obesity is hard to overemphasize. While this is not a serious problem with certain nervous breeds and animals engaged in strenuous activity, most idle adult horses are overfed and underexercised (Figures 8-2 and 8-3).

[1]*Nutrient Requirements of Horses*, 4th rev. ed., National Research Council, Washington, D.C., 1978.

FIGURE 8-2   Coley Al as an old horse in working condition but not fitted for show. [*Courtesy of the Animal Husbandry Department, University of Missouri.*]

FIGURE 8-3   Coley Al in obese condition. Showing has stopped and forced exercise has ceased. Fat horses, like fat people, are not very athletic and are often unhealthy. [*Courtesy of the Animal Husbandry Department, University of Missouri.*]

Horse owners tend to feel compelled to feed grain to every adult horse. If in thin condition or working, the horse needs grain; if inactive and overweight, it needs no grain. Indeed, obese horses are as susceptible to health problems associated with overweight as are humans—including premature unsoundness of feet and legs resulting from carrying extra weight.

As horsemen watch the proud, parading Anheuser-Busch Clydesdales, it is easy to credit their beauty to high condition. Condition is but a small part of their beauty. They are also stylish, high-stepping, elegantly matched in flashy colors, immaculately clean, expensively harnessed, and professionally handled. Their secret to maintaining superb condition without founder, heart damage, and lameness is regular, forced exercise. Even the stallions at Grants Farm, where the breeding herd resides, routinely work among mares in pairs on feed wagons and manure spreaders to gain both exercise and good manners.

In a real sense, horses are born energy-deficient, and many remain so if raced or worked hard in early life. As adults, energy needs tend to decline with cessation of growth and with reduced activity, while available energy supplies tend to increase from overfeeding.

Feed regulation and/or forced exercise are indicated for most adult horses. The extent of feed regulation is influenced by size, activity, and individuality. Few animals show as much variation in feed efficiency and preference for different feeds as do horses. A 900-pound horse, individually fed, may require 30 percent more nutrients to maintain a condition comparable to that of a stablemate that outweighs it by 200 pounds. The feeder must discern the needs of each individual animal and feed accordingly.

Picky horses may refuse a variety of feeds readily consumed by others. Such horses usually eat most feeds well enough to maintain condition at rest or light work, but lose weight and strength at hard work unless they are separated and their tastes are catered to in the feeding program.

How much to feed? This question has no easy answer, but there are guidelines.

Easy-keeping idle adult horses may maintain body condition on 1.5 to 3.0 percent of their body weight on good quality air-dry hay; that is a 1000-pound idle horse eating 15 to 30 pounds (weighed—not guessed at) of quality hay may need no grain. Bad keepers (horses that tend to lose weight and conditioning) and old horses may require one-third more hay or 4 to 5 pounds of grain to maintain a comparable condition.

The main objective in regulating feed intake is to keep the horse in a stable condition (not too fat or thin) at whatever activity the horse engages in.

The adage, "The eye of the master fattens his cattle" is more appropriate for horses than the cattle it was created for in antiquity. One must learn to "eyeball" horses and recognize slight changes in weight or condition soon after they occur if feed intake is to be regulated in order to prevent more serious changes in condition from taking place.

The following factors must be considered when planning feeding and management programs for the adult horse:

*What is the workload?*   Is the horse idle, working 2 to 4 hours daily, in heavy racing, or at hard work? Are mares dry or in peak lactation? *If stabled, what is the exercise program?* Is it regular and adequate for the temperament of the horse, or is it intermittent or only on weekends?

*Is there supplemental feed,* such as pasture? (Pasture may supply part or all of the needed nutrients and decrease mental stress of confinement as well.)

*What are the characteristics and personality of the horse?*   Is it young or old; does it have good or bad teeth; is it an easy or poor keeper; aggressive or picky eater; dominant or dominated in the pecking order?

*Compare costs and availability as well as quality of feeds.*   Are both legume and nonlegume hays available at reasonable prices? What is the relative nutrient value of various grains available?

In summary, three factors bear heavily on results of the adult horse feeding program. They are: (1) amount and kind of forage or pasture available that yield both feed and exercise, (2) degree of confinement (box, or stall with paddock), and (3) temperament and keeping condition of the horse.

## Some Suggestions for Management of Feeding

*Quality feeds.*   The basis of an adult horse feeding program is quality hay—without mold or too much age and unspoiled by rain—or good quality pasture. When these make up half of the nutrients in the ration, few things go wrong with the feeding program. Grains should not be moldy, dusty, dirty, or finely ground.

*Balanced rations.*   All essential nutrients must be offered the horse through the feed it eats. This is done (with the exception of salt and water) when horses are given good pasture, but nutrients must be supplied in the diet of those that are confined. Quality hays usually supply all but salt. Grains and hays complement each other in mineral balance. Unless corrected for calcium deficiency, a high-grain ration has a bad mineral imbalance.

*Feed for the athletic look.*   The amount of feed a horse should get depends to a large extent, upon its work load, age, and general health. If you can count most of the horse's ribs, it is too thin. If indications of the last two or three back ribs cannot be seen, the horse is too fat (Figures 8-2 and 8-3).

*Keep teeth functional.*   Horses 5 years and older should be checked annually by a veterinarian to see if their teeth need floating (filing). Sharp edges on upper teeth cut cheek muscles. Those on the lower teeth may lacerate the tongue. After a horse is 12 to 14 years of age, it may have infected jaw teeth.

If the horse has a tooth problem, it is likely to hold its head sideways when chewing and spill feed from its mouth. The horse may refuse to eat.

*Parasite control.*   Horses with heavy parasite loads cannot be fed into appropriate condition. Follow a good parasite program based on advice of a veterinarian (see Chapter 14).

*Feed salt free-choice to all horses at all times.*   If horses are consuming legumes or trace minerals in commercial feed, white salt will suffice. If not, use trace-mineralized salt after consulting with the local county extension agent about soil conditions in the area.

*Feed calcium and phosphorus free-choice to all horses at all times.*   Calcium and phosphorus should not be force-fed in the horse's salt. If horses are consuming mostly roughage, the ratio of calcium to phosphorus should approach 1:1. If they are consuming a lot of grain, the ratio should be 2:1, unless they are consuming a fourth or more of their diet from legume hay. In that case, the ratio can remain 1:1 (Figure 8-4).

*See that the stabled horse gets exercise.*   The horse will eat better, digest its food better, and be less likely to colic. It will also have a better attitude and will be less likely to form bad stable habits.

FIGURE 8-4   An important management practice is to supply salt, calcium, and phosphorus free-choice to all horses at all times. The white salt block (*left*) contains no trace minerals and is fed with rations containing trace minerals, such as commercial grain rations or when "conditioners" are added. The brown salt block (*center*) has trace minerals and is used as the salt source for most horse feeding when grass and hay are the main source of diet. The block on the right has a ratio of 15 percent calcium to 14 percent phosphorus for feeding with a high roughage diet. If 6 or more pounds of grain are fed with no legume hay, the ratio should be 2:1 or 15 percent calcium and 7.5 percent phosphorus. [*Photograph by author.*]

*Feed according to the individuality of the horse.*   Some horses are hard-keepers and need more per-unit weight. Others are timid and must be separated from fast, aggressive eaters. Others have ravenous appetites that result in overweight.

*Feed by weight, not volume.*   A gallon of different grains may vary 100 percent in nutrient yield. Some commercial grains are very light per unit volume. The adult horse needs a minimum of 1½ pounds of feed per 100 pounds of body weight. When working very hard, it may need 4 or more pounds (split between grain and hay).

*Minimize fines in a prepared ration.*   If a ration is ground fine, horses will be reluctant to eat it, and the chances of colic will increase when they do. It should be prepared coarsely to form a loose mass in the stomach.

*Offer plenty of good water, no colder than 45°F.*   Free-choice water is best. Horses should be watered at least twice daily. Water containers should be cleaned frequently and water should contain no foreign matter, such as nitrates, worm eggs, or other contaminants.

*Watch for choking.*   If horses tend to choke or eat greedily, feed in a large box, and scatter 3-inch smooth stones or hard wood blocks in the feed to slow their intake. Whole oats choke horses worse than any other feed.

*Change feeds gradually.*   When changing from a low-density (low-grain), high-fiber ration to one of increased density, do so gradually over a period of a week or more. Do likewise when changing one grain for another.

*Start on feed slowly.*   Horses on pasture should be started on dry feed gradually. Start this on pasture if practical, and gradually increase the feed to the desired amount in a week to 10 days.

*Tired or hot horses.*   Do not feed grain until tired or hot horses have cooled and rested, preferably 1 or 2 hours. Instead, feed hay while they rest in their blankets or out of drafts.

*Feeding before work.*   Hungry horses should be finished eating at least an hour before hard work. It is best not to feed heavy grain feeds if work is anticipated.

*Frequency of feeding.*   All confined horses should be fed at least twice daily. If horses are working hard and consuming a lot of grain, three times is mandatory. Those horses working extremely hard should be fed grain four times daily, with an hour's rest after each feeding before work.

*Hay feeding.*   Half of the hay allowance should be given at night, while the horses have more time to eat and digest it. Feed above the ground when possible, except in range areas where parasites are not numerous. Stalled horses should not eat from the ground because they recycle parasites and may learn to eat bedding. If the bedding is sand, this management practice is particularly important in order to avoid sand colic.

*Feed at the same time each day.*  Stabled horses can guess the time within a few minutes. They get nervous and anxious for their feed when feeding time arrives. If late, more digestive upsets result.

*Extremely heavy feeding.*  If horses consume large amounts of feed to meet their energy requirements, the ration must be extremely palatable, high in nutrient density, fed frequently, reduced by half on idle days, and prepared often to avoid staleness. Even with all these precautions, some horses cannot be maintained on such a program because of digestive disorders and going off feed.

## Feeding Management of Idle Adult Horses

The minimum requirements in the diet of the idle adult horse are 7.7 percent crude protein (CP) 0.27 percent calcium (Ca), and 0.18 percent phosphorus (P) (see Table 12-1). The idle horse consuming good quality hay should require no additional vitamin supplementation. If enough feed is fed (1½ to 3 percent of body weight) to maintain condition, nutrient needs are met. Indeed, the nutrient content of most *good* hays will usually exceed these minimum requirements until the horse starts working. Therefore, good hay or good pasture will actually abundantly feed a healthy, idle adult horse.

However, it must be remembered that the NRC *Nutrient Requirements for Horses* are *minimum* requirements determined from research with idle horses confined to individual metabolism stalls under carefully controlled management conditions. In practice, there is often competition for feed, some wastage, different ages, dominance hierarchies, and actual activity to be considered. Therefore, 10 to 20 percent more feed per horse than NRC tables list is a suggested way to start the feeding program. Many feeders simply select a good-quality hay and offer all that their horses will clean up twice daily. If hay is scarce, three-quarters of its weight in grain can substitute for up to half of the hay diet.

RANGE HORSES  Range horses are easiest to feed because they usually have pasture to graze that supplies all or most of their protein and energy requirements and induces forced exercise as well. In addition, they eat frequently and in small amounts and, when parasites are controlled, seldom if ever experience colic. Since dominance hierarchies are quickly established, range horses know exactly how to function in the system without indecision, stress, or anxiety.

Range horses seldom become obese or experience laminitis because they travel great distances for food and water. Their condition tends to be uniform because the same amount of time is spent grazing by all members of the herd.

Blizzards and droughts plague Northwestern range horses; drought and disease-carrying parasites affect those in the Southwest. Horses in snow country should have access to supplemental hay feeding. All the good quality hay consumed in an hour when snow covers the ground or during extended drought will suffice.

Range horses, like all other horses, should be fed salt and minerals (calcium and phosphorus) free-choice, but separately, their entire lives. Horses should not be forced to eat other minerals in the same block or mixture in fulfilling their salt requirements. Trace-mineralized salt instead of plain salt is preferred on most ranges, but a check with the local county extension agent for soil conditions and mineral needs for livestock in the area is well worth the time.

The mineral block (or loose mineral) must contain the appropriate ratio of calcium to phosphorus. Most range forages produce adequate calcium and inadequate phosphorus; achieving a ratio of about 1:1 is desirable. Check mineral feed tags until finding one that indicates 15 percent calcium to 14 percent phosphorus or near that ratio.

Salt and mineral blocks should be placed in areas where the herd spends most of its time, such as near shade and water. Supply enough salt blocks for timid horses to get their turn at them. One per ten horses may suffice. Each block in dry (but not hot) climates may supply salt for 400 horse-days. One mineral block for fifty horses may suffice in areas of good forage. Indeed, a lack of interest in them may indicate the feed the horses are eating is adequate in calcium and phosphorus.

Pasture forages during drought conditions are unpalatable, low in digestibility, and low in vitamin A. If supplemental hay is unavailable or of low quality, vitamin A feeding is indicated. An average of 12,500 IU per head per day in the mixed ration would undoubtedly be adequate.

Since vitamin A is stored in the liver and fat tissues, it may be fed satisfactorily two or three times weekly in grain, in salt (when mixed every 2 weeks), or as range cubes. The effectiveness of injectible vitamin A, popular a few years ago, is now under scrutiny. It has not proven very dependable in cattle research.

Southwestern range horses may suffer more from vitamin A depletion than other horses because of the extended nature of droughts and extensive use of Bermudagrass hay supplemental feeding instead of legume hay.

Stores of vitamin A in the body may last 3 to 6 months before being depleted if horses are grazed on green grass for that length of time. However, risk of a deficiency is not worth taking because supplemental vitamin A is cheap and abundantly convenient.

Be sure to use a concentrated form of vitamin A and not a diluted coat conditioner that furnishes only a few units of the vitamin. Most vitamin A supplements will have 4 to 5 million IU *per pound of supplement*. If such a supplement also contains vitamins D and E in addition to A, so much the better.

A dependable source of clean water is a problem on many ranches. It should be reasonably close to grazing areas, should be ample for the entire herd, and should be checked frequently for adequacy, cleanliness, pump failure, or other problems. Shade at the water location helps relieve heat and insect stress.

FARM HORSES   Farm horses tend to be used hard when used, but spend much time in idleness. Many are not saddled at all during winter months. Most have pastures to graze that furnish abundant feed during early spring, are dormant in summer, and absent in winter, necessitating extensive periods of hay feeding.

Sixteen to twenty pounds of good-quality hay per head per day will fill most protein, energy, and vitamin requirements for most idle farm horses, provided all horses have access to it and it is not wasted (Figure 8-5).

FIGURE 8-5   The nutrients that idle, adult horses need (except salt and water) are contained in this good-quality brome grass and red clover hay, which chemically analyzes as 54 percent TDN (total digestible nutrients), 14 percent CP, 0.9 percent Ca, and 0.25 percent P (dry-matter basis). The feeder must manage horses so that each horse gets the amount it needs to maintain condition, usually about 2 to 2½ pounds per 100 pounds of body weight. [*Photograph by author.*]

Farm horses occupy the area of our country of abundant hay production and high rainfall. Most of the country's beef cattle are also found in part of this area. Since most hay is baled for cattle under threats of rain and the pressure from attention to grain crops, it is usually baled with too much moisture for horses, resulting in moldy hay. Moldy hay seldom bothers cattle, but may cause colic, hay allergy, or heaves in horses. It will abort pregnant mares.

If horses winter in high condition, some are likely to founder on lush spring grass. Condition should be regulated in winter, when more expensive feeds are fed, by separating fat horses and reducing their feed.

The manager of farm horses must supply unfrozen water year-round and must feed hay when forage is unavailable because of snow cover, damage by drought, or overgrazing (Figure 8-6). Salt and the minerals calcium and phosphorus should be supplied free-choice.

STABLED HORSES    The manager of confined or stabled horses faces two major challenges: (1) to furnish all the nutrients the horse needs without contributing to obesity, and (2) create an environment acceptable to the horse without producing undue stress that results in bad stable habits. Unfortunately, the nervous, animated breeds tend to receive most of the confinement. However, many are better off under management regimens than their ancestors, who had to forage for food and take care of shelter, health, and safety needs themselves, when in the wild.

Confined horses are more difficult to feed because of boredom and its resultant manifestations. Even though exercised an hour daily, many nervous horses soon become restless and bored and develop bad stable

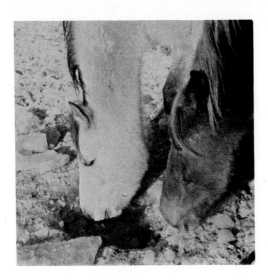

FIGURE 8-6  This is the worst possible way to water horses because the cold temperature of the water reduces consumption, and if the water freezes the horse is unable to drink. Horses should be watered at least twice daily with water no colder than 45°F. [*Photograph by author.*]

habits, such as windsucking, cribbing, weaving, pawing, stall walking, kicking, and endless other undesirable ways to relieve their frustration. Composition and type of diet and frequency of feeding directly affect all of these habits.

Since all the stabled horse's feed is selected for it, the feeder assumes substantial responsibility. Feed must not be moldy or excessively dusty and must contain all the nutrients the horse would get if making its own grazing choices (see Chapter 11). In addition, the horse should be fed often, at least twice daily, and the amount given should balance with the horse's exercise program, resulting in little weight gain or loss.

Supplying a diet of two kinds of hays and at least one grain or grain mixture, instead of a single source of hay, makes feeding a stable of idle horses easier (Figure 8-7). One hay should be a good legume and another nonlegume. Legumes are readily eaten and are higher in protein, energy, minerals, and vitamins, but may prove fattening to easy keepers. The ratio of legumes to nonlegumes may be regulated to maintain desired condition.

FIGURE 8-7    Two kinds of hays and one grain make feeding a stable of mixed horses easy. Five pounds of legume (*left*) can serve as a base to furnish most of the protein, part of the energy, and all the calcium and vitamins your horse needs. Less palatable nonleguminous hay (*middle*) can be offered free-choice to supply many nutrients and reduce wood chewing. Grain may be added as needed to "hard keepers," old horses, and horses working to maintain condition.

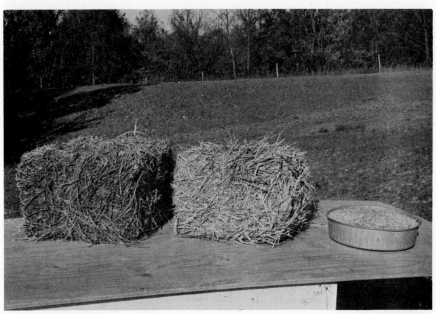

Old horses or bad keepers may be given 3 to 4 pounds of grain in addition to all the hay they will eat.

If only legume hay is fed, aggressive eaters will consume their portion in a few minutes and may use the remainder of the day to develop undesirable stable habits if no other hay is offered. For this reason, a less palatable nonlegume will last much longer, resulting in less wood chewing. When bored, the horse simply eats a small amount of the hay instead of its manger or partition.

An all-pellet diet fed to idle horses usually results in extensive wood chewing, coprophagy (eating feces), and other bad stable habits (Figure 8-8), as does an all-grain ration. Kentucky researchers fed 13.2 pounds of grain versus 17.6 pounds of long hay to confined known wood-chewing adult Quarter horses for 8 days.[2] Each group had access to an untreated 1-inch

[2]Judy G. Willard, S. A. Walfram, and J. B. Baker, "Effect of Diet on Cecal pH and Feeding Behavior of Horses," *Journal of Animal Science*, vol. 45, no. 1, July 1977, p. 87.

FIGURE 8-8    Pellets reduce dust and help control heaves and hay allergies, but an all-pellet diet fed to confined horses usually results in extensive wood chewing, coprophagy (eating feces), and other bad stable habits. [*Photograph by author.*]

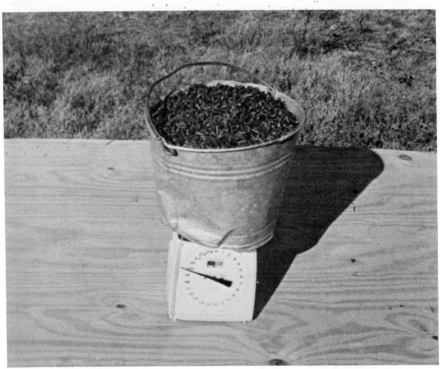

by 8-inch by 5-foot pine board. Horses eating only grain consumed an average of 18.66 pounds of wood during the 8-day test, compared with 5.28 pounds for those eating long hay. Eating time for the long hay group was 9.48 hours in 24, compared with 0.81 hours for those consuming only grain.

Results of this research appear reasonable when one considers that the horse's digestive tract (see Chapter 11) may have a capacity of 40 to 50 gallons, and when only a few gallons are fed, the horse remains hungry and vigorously pursues fiber for food. The solution lies in feeding at least half of an idle adult horse's nutrients in the form of long hay, increasing exercise when possible, and feeding frequently.

BACKYARD HORSES   For backyard horses having access to 1 or 2 acres of improved, regularly fertilized pasture per horse, the feeding program is similar to that for farm horses—the horses should be fed grain when they work and furnished hay when snow covers the pasture.

If grass is poor quality, sparse, or mixed with weeds, feed as for stabled horses; however, because the horse can exercise at will, two types of hay are unnecessary and once-a-day feeding will suffice.

Internal parasites are a big problem with backyard horses (see Chapter 14) because of population density and short grass (most worm larvae stay on the bottom 3 inches of the plant).

## Feeding Management of Working Adult Horses

Some adult horses work hard, 6 to 8 hours daily, day after day. In the youth of our country all were expected to do so. Racing and competitive and distance riding have required duplication of many of the feeding and management requirements that many early horsemen faced. Consequences to the modern horseman of failure to meet these nutritive challenges are significant although far less than those encountered by his counterpart who traveled the plains with his family in a covered wagon and whose life depended upon maintenance of a healthy team.

The mature, 1100-pound horse in *moderate work* may be the extensively used pleasure horse, that spends equal time at walk, fast trot, and canter. Other horses in this category may be used for ranch work, roping and cutting, barrel racing, jumping, etc. The same horse at *hard, stressful work*, e.g., the race horse, polo pony, or circuit show jumper, would be spending most of its time cantering, galloping, and jumping.

As energy (caloric) demands increase, the problems of colic, weight loss, and appetite change. A number of modifications are indicated in the feeding management of hardworking horses.

INCREASING NUTRIENT DENSITY   First, grain must replace part of the roughage to increase nutrient density of the ration because of the bulkiness of hay and high water content of grass. The horse cannot eat enough hay to fulfill its increased needs. Grass may be the first to go, with hay remaining as a source of nutrients and fiber (bulk). An all-grain ration is dangerous and difficult to feed without causing colic, founder, or other problems.

Some nutritionists recommend that quality hay supply half of the nutrients that hard working horses consume and that grain supply the remainder. Many racehorses and distance horses are fed this way. For example, if good hay is 50 percent and grain 75 percent digestible, an 1100-pound, moderately hardworking horse consuming 18 pounds of *total digestible nutrients* (TDN) (see Chapter 12) could do so from 17 pounds of hay and 11.32 pounds of grain. Some careful feeders use grain for three-quarters of the needed nutrients and hay for one-quarter, or 8 pounds of hay and 16 pounds of grain fed in 3 feeds.

PALATABILITY   Second, if large amounts of feed are to be consumed, *the ration must be palatable to the horse.* Palatability depends upon quality ingredients, coarsely prepared with liquid molasses added to reduce dust and fines and kept fresh by frequent preparation and disposal of refused feed. Clean feed troughs are a must.

FREQUENCY   Finally, if they are to be kept on feed, free of colic, *horses should be fed often and in small amounts.* They should be fed lightly before work and be rested before receiving grain or a large amount of a palatable feed.

AMOUNT AND KIND TO FEED   Most working horses will maintain condition on 1 to 1¼ pounds of grain plus 1 to 1½ pounds of quality hay per 100 pounds of body weight, feed in three feeds daily on work days. Reduce grain by half on idle days to prevent azoturia (see Chapter 14), and increase the hay by 1½ times the amount of grain reduction.

TWO BALANCED GRAIN MIXTURES   Following are two nutritionally balanced grain mixtures for moderately hardworking to hardworking horses fed non-legume hay free-choice.

Table 8-1 gives a customized ration fed to equitation and show horses in a large women's college. It has built-in safety in protein, mineral, and vitamin levels as only one ration is fed to horses of different ages and to new horses that may arrive in different conditions. Condition is regulated by changing the amount of grain fed. If properly formulated, this ration will weigh 1987 pounds and have 13.0 percent crude protein, 0.52 percent calcium, and 0.45 percent phosphorous on a dry-matter basis.

Table 8-2 gives a popular commercial ration that has a large percentage of sales in a heavily populated horse area. Sales were built on satisfied customers, not advertising.

TABLE 8-1   GRAIN MIXTURE FOR STABLED
COLLEGE RIDING HORSES (AS FED BASIS)

| Feedstuffs | Amount, lb |
|---|---|
| Corn, coarsely cracked* | 850 |
| Oats, crushed or rolled† | 850 |
| Soybean meal, 44% protein | 100 |
| Molasses, blackstrap‡ | 150 |
| Limestone | 25 |
| Salt, trace mineral | 10 |
| Vitamins, premix§ | 2 |
| | 1987 |

*Corn must be cracked coarsely. Fine particles are
unacceptable.
†Crush, crimp, or roll oats, or leave them whole. Do
not grind them. They must weigh at least 32 lb per
bushel.
‡Blackstrap molasses required. Molasses pellets unsatisfactory.
§The proper amount of premix will provide 4000 IU
of vitamin A and 400 IU of vitamin D per pound of
mixed feed.

## PSYCHOLOGICAL MANAGEMENT OF ADULT HORSES

One of the most difficult management challenges is to create and maintain
an environment that results in good attitudes in adult horses that are relatively idle, mostly confined, inadequately exercised, and abundantly fed.
Horses in their natural state do not live solitary lives, graze in one spot,

TABLE 8-2   COMMERCIAL GRAIN MIXTURE (AS
FED BASIS)

| Feedstuffs | Amount, lb |
|---|---|
| Corn, coarsely cracked | 600 |
| Oats, crushed | 1000 |
| Soybean meal, 50% | 100 |
| Alfalfa pellets | 100 |
| Molasses, blackstrap | 150 |
| Limestone | 20 |
| Salt, trace mineral | 10 |
| Vitamins, premix* | 2 |
| | 1982 |

*The proper amount of premix will supply 4000 IU
vitamin A and 400 IU vitamin D per pound of mixed
feed.

eat low-fiber diets once or twice daily, or accept what food is at hand, be it abundant or scarce. Instead, in the wild, horses belong to a group, graze wide areas (10 to 40 miles), eat a high-fiber diet, graze often eating small amounts (at least half of each 24 hours), and feel few pressures because they know exactly how to function in their position in the dominance hierarchy.

Because of these evolutionary conditions, horses find solitary confinement more frustrating than do humans. It is not realistic to expect horse owners to duplicate nature's offering to its horse herds, but most can make a horse more content and, ultimately, responsive by following these healthy practices: (1) give the horse as much range, pasture, paddock, arena, or lane as possible; (2) exercise the horse ½ to 1 hour daily by riding, longeing, ponying (leading), driving, or by using a hotwalker; (3) be firm, but patient and kind, when using the horse; (4) house the horse next to a friend in a stall where it can see out in three or four directions, if possible; and (5) feed and water at least twice daily.

Horses kept for companionship that are seldom used but well cared for and allowed to satisfy their own need for exercise seldom develop psychological problems. Indeed, such lucky horses fit well into this environment because nature prepared them for it. When horses are confined without companionship, overfed without exercise, overused before preparation, and abused without an alternative, they *and* their owners develop problems.

An equally bad situation results from the domination of a timid owner by the horse. A pecking order will emerge in any relationship between human and horse, hopefully with the human first in the hierarchy. When appropriately trained or schooled, horses submit to gentle but firm domination with minimum resistance and trauma. If a clear communication system is established and horses are not pushed beyond their physical capabilities, they may submit to most human dominance throughout life. It is a pleasant experience not to be able to recall the last time a favorite horse was disciplined—even by voice—providing the horse remained equal or improved in performance.

Horses vary even more in temperament than they do in nutrient requirements, and therefore require different handling techniques. Some breeds, such as Thoroughbreds and Arabs, have more red blood cells per unit volume (supposedly for maximal oxygen exchange) than others, giving rise to the old terms "hot-blooded" and "cold-blooded," the latter referring mostly to draft and work horses. Without doubt some breeds are more highly strung and more nervous than others, and some activities tend to unnerve horses more than others. Spirited horses are required in some events while quiet, sedate horses are preferred in others. Speed events, such as racing, chasing, and gaming, create "hot" horses that require patience and reserve from their riders. Society show horses must be animated and stylish, but must be well-mannered as well. The majority of horses are used for casual pleasure activities and are appreciated most when they relax, drop their heads, and respond to cues and the demands of the activity without fuss. Flawless performance of a horse and rider combination tells the observer that horse and rider are compatible; that both are comfortable and competent at this activity; that the horse is well trained, physically able, and mentally having a good day.

The horse should be ridden with minimum correction. When it performs well, it should be rewarded. When it deliberately disobeys, it must be punished promptly, but only enough to correct the condition. Even good horses have bad days, but patience and work will eventually produce a positive response.

One must realize that adult horses vary in talent and willingness; some are intelligent athletes and some are not; and some have been well trained while others have been neglected or spoiled into dangerous, belligerent horses.

MINIMIZING AND CORRECTING BAD HABITS   A bad habit to one person may be a good habit to another. The serious bucking horse may not suit a working cowboy but may be considered a real prospect by the rodeo contractor. The jigging, charging, spirited horse may be more than the casual rider wishes to cope with, but may fulfill the needs of a youngster who rides hard and often with friends.

Coping with ingrained bad habits or responses is the primary chore of the handler of adult horses. If the fault developed with the owner, retraining by a professional may not prevent its recurrence when the horse returns to the same environmental conditions that caused the problem in the first place. Nonetheless, many annoying and most dangerous habits can be corrected by a professional and prevented by experienced riders.

Emphasis in horse use and handling should always be on avoiding conditions that develop difficult problem horses. The conditions to be avoided are:

1   Trying to hurry horses into maneuvers they are neither mentally nor physically prepared for
2   Allowing excessive energy to develop from inactivity and overfeeding
3   Failing to establish clear-cut communications and appropriate reinforcement of good responses

Horses are physically and mentally immature until they are 5 or 6 years old. If *pressured* into competition, even as adults, horses may become fearful and frustrated, and attempt to avoid consequences resulting from the activity. They may suffer pain from obscure lameness, sore muscles, or overexertion, in addition to the punishment inflicted by their riders.

Most handlers will never be capable of successfully training a young horse for complex maneuvers until they have successfully handled an older horse in the same activity.

Horses must not be starved into submission. A well-balanced workload, a good feeding program, the hands of a firm, patient handler—these factors produce or reclaim good adult horses.

Horses respond well to cues they understand. Cues must be given the same way each time. Horses must understand the consequences of their responses to these cues: if they respond positively they will be rewarded; if not, they should expect punishment. Handlers should be firm but gentle. They must recognize the beginning of problems early and act to alleviate them before they become fixed. Handlers must be sensitive to the underlying cause of the problem, which is not always readily apparent.

TEN COMMON BAD HABITS    The ten most frequently mentioned annoying habits from a survey of two large horse course audiences were: (1) jigging or prancing, (2) refusal to leave the barn (barn-sour horses), (3) halter pulling, (4) rearing, (5) bucking, (6) resistance to saddling (cinchy horses), (7) shying, (8) kicking, (9) running away, and (10) being hard to catch.

The responses of six trainer-instructors were pooled and condensed into the following discussion of these bad habits.

The *prancing* horse excessively fatigues itself and its rider and is an annoyance to people and horses alike that are around it. Since the horse does not jig when turned out, one can assume it feels pressure, excitement, competition, or pain—or merely wishes to go back home where it can reasonably expect to relax, eat, and rest.

Crowds of horses and people excite some horses, probably creating a feeling of claustrophobia they cannot suppress. Some gentle horses trail ridden for several years by good riders suddenly develop anxieties under trail conditions that they cannot cope with. This is especially true in groups that spawn spontaneous horse races at every open field.

Some events, such as racing, gymkhana, and fox and bird hunting, create pressures. The horse must compete with other horses or with a stop-watch, and may be punished in the process even when it is doing its best. To ask a horse from the racetrack to settle down in a noisy mob and walk on a loose rein is asking a lot, although some will.

Few game horses escape the jigging syndrome if started young in competition, although many can become relaxed enough for pleasure riding alone or in small groups. Few western horses will compete well in both games and pleasure classes during the same season.

Ill-fitting equipment causes horses to jig. High-strung horses with ill-fitting saddles pressing on their backbones will try to escape and get back to the stable for relief, as will thick-backed horses with narrow gullet saddles cinched so tightly they can hardly breathe.

Most horses prefer the peace and comfort of their stable and may jig when turned in that direction. However, most will consent to walk toward the stable after a short distance of jigging, unless provoked by punishment from their riders.

Most jigging horses have been spoiled by getting their way—they know if they prance, crow-hop, and run sideways long enough, their riders will allow them to explode to the front of the line or dash back to the stable and be released. Other personality types expect a confrontation from their owners on every ride, and will jig until they get it.

The jigging horse's environment must be varied as much as possible, and it must be exercised 2 to 4 hours daily on a hotwalker or under saddle with a patient rider. Ring riding bores horses and tends to settle them down. Most of all, the saddle must fit, and all equipment must be properly adjusted. To avoid creating a jigging habit in an adult horse, the following rules are helpful:

1  Do not game (gymkhana) a horse meant for pleasure.
2  Do not race outside of organized racing conditions.
3  Do not ride with ill-fitting equipment.
4  Do not allow a horse to increase speed or change gaits until cued for the change.
5  Do not practice the same routines until they are anticipated.
6  Do not expect the overfed, underexercised horse to exhibit the same good manners it does when fit and routinely worked.

The *barn-sour* horse refuses to leave the barn; it rears, sulks, circles, and runs backward or sideways. It is often, but not always, an untrained or undisciplined horse that has been permitted to have its way. Some well-trained horses have developed this condition late in life under loose management because they expect the consequences of their refusal to be less than the discomfort of the trip.

The overriding cause of the barn-sour condition is allowing the horse to run back to the barn, where it is promptly unsaddled and fed. Such management practices reward and reinforce the barn-sour attitude.

On the positive side, anything that makes the ride a pleasant experience will help alleviate the barn-sour attitude. If the ride is an ordeal from ill-fitting equipment, bare feet on stones, or abusive treatment, no progress will be made.

Some trainers tie and feed the horse away from the stable at a neighbor's or at a prearranged site where they have located a trailer with one of the horse's equine friends for company. Others ride to a grazing site, dismount and give the horse 15 minutes or so to graze and relax (while the trainer holds onto the reins!).

To avoid creating the barn-sour horse, the following rules are helpful:

1  Do not allow a horse to run toward the stable.
2  Do not allow a return to the stable to be so pleasant that the horse cannot wait to get there the next time. Enter the warm-up ring and canter until the horse is thoroughly tired before quitting.

3   Do not follow the same routine, but vary it; i.e., dismount and walk the last half mile or ride past the stable, then dismount and return.
4   Do not overlook the opportunity to periodically challenge the horse to seek the stable by riding straight away 100 yards and then straight back. Repeat until there is no speeding up at the far turn. It may take as many as thirty to fifty trips.
5   Do not become impatient or angry. Be as patient and gentle as possible but demand obedience. Ring-riding routines help.

*Rearing* is one of the most dangerous habits a horse can develop. While a rearing horse is easy to sit by leaning forward in the saddle, the danger lies in inadvertently tightening the reins at the peak of the rear and pulling the horse over backward. Inexperienced riders and rearing horses are a dangerous combination.

Rearing is natural for many horses when restrained or frustrated. It is learned by others from harsh bits in rough hands. Barn-sour horses often rear when pressured to leave the barn; jigging horses tend to rear when restrained as other horses run by them. Many rearing horses have been used in pressure situations such as barrel racing and timed events.

Rearing can usually be cured and is easy to discourage in the beginning by a threatening voice or a sharp cut of the quirt or bat. If encouraged or tolerated because it is cute or showy, rearing can develop into a dangerous habit.

Prevention of rearing in the adult horse consists of the minimization of anxiety, good basic training before engaging in pressure activities, light hands, mild bits, and conservative use of the whip.

*Bucking* comes in various degrees—ranging from the playful horse that crow-hops with its head up to the serious bucker who "boggs" its head with every intention of ridding itself of its rider. Most horses have no tendency to buck and never learn to, while others need no coaching in the art, from the first mounting throughout their lifetimes. Nervous, athletic breeds tend to buck. The tendency to buck is likely an inherited characteristic, for strains are bred by rodeo stock producers for their bucking skills.

However, more buckers are made than born. Almost all can be managed and used without developing into serious bucking horses. The horse can sense fear, and will take advantage of the rider in achieving its own purposes. Almost all horses signal their intent before they buck: the muscles tense, the eyes and nostrils flare, and some even hump before lowering their heads for serious bucking.

Most older horses simply need some energy worked off before being mounted. Longeing, driving, or ponying (leading from another horse) usually suffices. Allowing horses to romp in an enclosure is also helpful. Excess energy, cold weather, and idleness are the most common predisposing causes.

Keep the horse's head up and give it a few sharp cuts with a whip or bat along its shoulders when it bucks. Intimidate the horse with your voice, and show displeasure with its behavior.

To avoid creating a bucking habit in an adult horse, some form of punishment should be administered at the first sign of bucking, even if its intent is of a playful nature. Be sure the horse is always tacked up with a well-fitting saddle and is given a lot of riding with an appropriate amount of feed.

When the horse learns that it is stronger than the equipment securing it, it is well on its way to becoming a *halter puller.*

Almost every horse has halter-pulled one or more times in its life, from fear, ignorance, or panic. However, many are encouraged to do so by being tied by the bridle reins.

Halter pullers vary sharply in resolve and determination. Some respond promptly and effectively to treatment without loss of hide or hair, while others must seemingly learn the hard way.

Different trainers use different disciplinary methods. However, most use the body rope and halter method. A strong, soft rope 18 to 20 feet long with a stout loop in one end encircles the horse's body, with the shank end extending forward between the front legs. It is then passed through the ring in the halter and tied in a slip knot at the height of the horse's withers (never above!). To test this method trainers either wait for the horse or deliberately spook it back into the rope so that they may give assistance or release the rope in an emergency. A normal response is for the horse to sit back hard on the rope, usually about half a minute, until pain prompts it to leap forward for relief.

Not all horses respond normally. Some will fight, it would seem, to the death. For this reason smooth ground is best and a solid wall prevents hanging a foot when they rear and lunge forward.

Do not be in a hurry to release a horse that is down having a fit of anger unless it is in serious danger. If released, promptly repeat the procedure until it stands with a loose shank.

To avoid creating an adult halter puller, the following rules are helpful:

1   Do not tie by the bridle.
2   Do not tie with light, weak halters and shanks; do not tie to loose rails or weak, doubtful fixtures.
3   Do not encourage pulling by tying in dangerous places, such as around loose horses or in frightening locations.

*Cinchy* horses resist being saddled because they associate the activity with discomfort. Although most simply halter-pull and try to avoid having the girth tightened, some rear and even fall over backward. When they reach this stage, they are hard to retrain.

This condition is caused by hasty saddling and promptly cinching the saddle too tight. Some 2-year-olds can be cinched so tight with western saddles that they cannot breathe normally and thus may even fall to the ground.

Round-backed horses with narrow gullet saddles are prone to excessive cinching to keep the saddle from turning. The saddle should be changed for one that fits, and a breastplate or collar may be necessary to secure it.

If the proper saddling procedure is used, horses will not become cinchy. Get a saddle that fits and position it in place gently while an assistant holds the horse. If you work alone with a tied horse, it may struggle and hurt itself. If extremely hard to saddle, hobbles or some other kind of restraint may be necessary. A light English saddle is easier to handle when a horse resists than a heavy western saddle. Attach the cinch only tight enough to hold the saddle in place and let the horse stand, maybe a half hour if resolutely resistant. Next, tighten the cinch slightly and walk the horse around for a few minutes. After walking, tighten the cinch a third time, tight enough for mounting. Ride the horse calmly 10 or 15 minutes, dismount, and tighten the cinch once more, usually only one hole, before engaging in athletic activities.

To avoid creating a cinch-tightening problem in an adult horse, the following may be helpful:

1   Never tighten the cinch or girth so tight you cannot get a hand under it.
2   Do not have a tugging, swelling duel with the horse, i.e., it expands its belly for protection against the tightening of the girth. Wait a while, catch the horse relaxed, and ease the cinch tighter.
3   Do not ride with an ill-fitting saddle that must be overcinched to stay in place.
4   Do not fail to use a breastcollar when needed, instead of overcinching.

*Shying* horses are a nuisance, especially those that find real or imagined spooks to avoid at all costs by leaping sideways every hundred or so yards of the trip. Individuals of some gaited breeds are especially prone to this habit.

While it is natural for young horses to jump, spin, and dash away when startled by sudden noises and moving objects, the normal adult horse, through years of exposure, should act more reasonably. The fearful older horse, however, may not shy often or reverse directions when startled, but may refuse to approach big machinery, bright objects, and unfamiliar surroundings that it may perceive to harbor potential danger. This and the first type of horse usually walk gingerly through soft footing and reluctantly, if at all, over bridges.

Horses shy for three major reasons:

1   It is their nature to be wary of strange objects and noises and to burst into flight when in doubt of the consequences.

2   They undoubtedly have limited vision that makes resolution of objects slower and less sharp than human eyes. (Many horses could probably use glasses.)
3   Riders may inadvertently encourage their horses to shy. If the horse is punished when concentrating on a fearful object, it thinks the object caused the pain and its fears are reinforced. If the rider tenses and increases leg and rein pressure, the horse knows it and probably thinks "since we are both scared we had better escape."

Gain confidence and control of the horse in familiar surroundings by regular exercise and routine riding. If it is normally responsive and disciplined, its reaction to fearful objects will diminish.

Repeat the horse's exposure to objects of fear. If it has a mortal fear of a parked road machine, patiently and repeatedly urge the horse up to the machine and have it stand by the machine until its fears subside. If the horse knows it must march up to an object and stand by it 5 or 10 minutes each time it makes an escape response, time and intensity of shying will greatly decrease. Indeed, as horses gain confidence that their riders will not urge them into dangerous situations, they may shy, then march up to the object and stop of their own volition as if to "get it over with" and be on their way.

If a horse must cross a bridge a number of times each time it refuses to cross it, it will soon accept an initial crossing to this alternative, albeit down the center on tiptoes.

The horse that shies every hundred yards responds least to retraining. Group riding helps some horses. Riding in line beside a nonshying horse is helpful.

Tired horses and those in pursuit shy less than others. Nervous, energetic horses ridden alone may shy sharply going away from the stable but little if any when fatigued and anxious to get back home. Fox-hunting horses seldom shy in the heat of the chase, nor do bird hunters when cantering to the point.

It is tempting to accuse shyers of "orneryness" and punish them for their behavior, but patience and perseverance are the best treatments.

To avoid creating a shying problem in an adult horse, these rules may prove helpful:

1   Do not strike or punish a fearful horse.
2   Do not ride in a fearful environment, such as a parade, until the horse is well trained and settled.
3   Do not hurry a fearful horse. Dismount and lead it if necessary.
4   Do not trigger an unwanted response by tensing and tightening hands and knees. If a move is made, let the horse start it. The horse may not move at all!

*Kicking* horses are of three kinds: (1) defensive, (2) exuberant, and (3) malicious. The victims of kicking horses are other horses and/or humans.

Startled horses may kick without malice, or they may defend their foals or food by kicking. A mare will defend the newborn foal by kicking or fighting another horse higher in the pecking order, and many horses will kick when surprised while eating. Some even kick intermittently with one foot, with head buried in the feedbox as they munch their grain. Trail horses, never otherwise known to kick, can be provoked to do so by charging horses from behind that step on their heels.

Horses may kick each other in exuberance as they romp and play. It is natural for a horse to kick, buck, and run when released to pasture. Therefore, the alert handler faces the horse back toward the gate before releasing it and is prepared to step quickly backward to avoid flying heels.

The malicious horse that kicks with deadly intent at another horse or human is quite another matter. Malicious kicking may be a learned trait used by certain horses to dominate other horses and humans, or it may be an expression of the sour, uncooperative disposition of a horse that wants to be left alone. Malicious kickers are dangerous animals. They must not be tolerated.

Most horses telegraph their intent to kick: they lay back their ears at horses passing or standing in line, or they watch the horse behind them for an opportunity. A threatening word or gesture usually prevents the horse from kicking. If it succeeds, sharp punishment at the time of infraction will usually eliminate or discourage the response. If allowed to strike out without punishment, the horse will eventually injure another horse or person and may have to be put down or removed from use.

To avoid establishment of the kicking habit in an adult horse, the following rules are helpful:

1  Do not allow a horse to kick without punishment.
2  Do not risk life and limb of other horses and people by riding a malicious kicker in groups of horses and riders.
3  Do not ride an occasional kicker with other horses without a red cloth tied around its tail.
4  Do not tolerate a dangerous kicker that may severely injure humans or animals. Have it retrained or destroyed.

The *runaway* horse may be more of a nuisance than a danger. Competitive speed horses may get out of control and run out of the ring or back to the stable. Many U.S. Cavalry mounts would take the bit in their teeth and run back to the stable despite the pulling of their strong-armed riders.

The horse learns through disobedience to gain control of the situation and ignore signals from the rider. Good riders may experience a partial runaway with a spoiled horse before they get it under control. Control depends upon manners, a responsive mouth (as opposed to a hard mouth), and bitting appropriate for the activity and the horse.

Draw reins are mild on the horse's mouth, but can double it at the first few lunges by turning it in its tracks. The horse can easily be circled in ever-smaller circles until the rider is in complete control. If surprised without draw reins, circle the horse if there is room by the cheekpiece of the bridle, if necessary.

If horses run away in bosals or snaffle bits, they may need more severe bits while being retrained and ridden.

To avoid creating the runaway response in the adult horse, the following rules may be helpful:

1  Do not game or race a horse not completely trained.
2  Do not allow the horse to begin running away—stop or circle it in the beginning before it gains control.
3  Do not tolerate an undisciplined horse. Teach it the meaning of "whoa."

To a rancher with lariat, corrals, alleys, and pens, it is difficult to imagine a *hard-to-catch* horse, but to the suburbanite with a loose horse in a 60-acre field with other running horses and no catching equipment, it may be a major problem.

Horses become hard to catch for two reasons: (1) they fear or mistrust humans, or (2) they anticipate a bad experience when caught.

Do something the horse enjoys when it allows itself to be caught, e.g., feed it, groom and pet it before riding. Repeat this procedure, without riding, until it can be caught with a pan of grain.

Any pasture should have a lot or pen in which to catch horses. Even so, some cannot be driven into such enclosures except by mounted riders if they do not wish to go. Patience is the key word in catching wary horses. If you hurry they become suspicious and dash away. They must learn trust and expect the treat they get for consenting to be caught to exceed the consequences of the trick they are expected to pay in return.

To avoid the hard-to-catch syndrome in the adult horse, the following rules may be helpful:

1  Do not punish the hard-to-catch horse for running when it is caught.
2  Do not saddle up promptly and ride hard after catching. Feed the horse, groom it, or do something pleasant for it.
3  Do not ride each time the horse is caught.
4  Do not hurry when catching a horse.

In summary, bad habits ruin good horses, but the blame lies mostly with the horse handler. While some horses cannot cope with every situation, there are situations in which every horse can perform well. If a bad habit is ignored and allowed to continue, another and yet another may develop until the horse is almost useless and the cost of professional retraining becomes prohibitive.

The problem must first be recognized in its early stages. Second, it must be corrected in a humane way, calculated to leave the horse better off for the correction, not further traumatized.

## HEALTH MANAGEMENT OF ADULT HORSES

The adult horse will have fewer diseases and accidents, unless used in a high-risk activity, than will the younger horse. This is because it has built up some resistance to communicable diseases and to roundworms, one of the major parasites. The adult horse also has learned to live in its environment with fewer accidents, partly because its activities have declined. However, as it ages, unsoundnesses tend to increase from wear and tear, and work loads borne by the 5- to 12-year-old horse should not be expected from those approaching 18 to 20 years. Regardless of age and use, all horses should receive health management practices that protect them from internal parasites, communicable diseases, and bad teeth. For a detailed health discussion, see Chapter 14.

INTERNAL PARASITES    More than 150 parasites have been identified on postmortem of horses. However, only four usually cause them much trouble. Of the four, only two are usually lethal. The four parasites are: *Strongyles vulgarus* or bloodworms, ascarids or roundworms, pinworms and bots.

By far, the major killer and cause of most colic in horses is *Strongyles*. Since a horse never builds an immunity to this parasite, it must be protected against it throughout life. Ascarids will kill young horses by plugging the intestines and causing colic, but horses build substantial immunity to these parasites by the time they are 3 years of age. Pinworms seldom cause serious health problems in horses; however, they irritate the anus and cause itching. The horse backs against an object and scratches the hair off its tail head, resulting in a very unsightly condition. Bots hatch from yellow eggs laid by the bot fly under the chin and along the chest and front legs. The horse ingests them through the mouth from scratching these locations. Bot larvae migrate through the tongue and lips and are swallowed to the stomach. Heavy infestation can result in death.

All horses need routine worming. Few conditions exist that allow them to escape the bot fly, exposure to their own manure, or worm eggs in contaminated feed and water. Prevention from worm contamination is more important than treatment, because of the extensive migratory phase of the worm's life cycle in body tissues where they are immune to most worm treatments. However, treatment is very essential and is a part of total internal parasite management.

ALLERGIES AND HEAVES   Hay allergies and heaves affect a few horses in most stables. Symptoms usually result from months of eating moldy feeds and standing in dusty bedding. Some horses are very susceptible, while others are very resistant to these conditions.

Early symptoms are coughing when slightly musty hay is offered, when first exercised, or when the bedding gets dry and dusty. The condition improves or disappears when turned out on pasture. Feeding pellets, good hay, or sprinkling the hay with water usually helps. Unless their environment or management is changed, such horses usually develop heaves, a serious unsoundness.

IMMUNIZATION   Immunize against at least two diseases annually. These are tetanus and encephalomyelitis, or sleeping sickness. A horse that has not been immunized against tetanus will require 2 shots about 2 weeks apart for immunity and a booster shot each year thereafter. Two shots are required annually for immunity against encephalomyelitis. The vaccine immunizes against both eastern and western strains of the disease.

Show horses and horses that are moved frequently or live in contaminated areas may require other immunizations. Discuss these possibilities with a veterinarian.

TEETH CARE   Just as human teeth need regular maintenance, so do those of horses. Adult horses need their teeth checked annually. Since the upper jaw is wider than the lower, upper jaw teeth are worn faster on the inside and lower jaw teeth on the outside. This results in upper teeth occasionally having long, sharp edges on the outside that cut the cheek muscles, and lower teeth on the inside that may pierce the tongue (Figure 8-9). Floating or filing these by a veterinarian or equine dentist will remove the problem. A horse that holds its head sideways when eating has a tooth problem. However, some horses may have substantial tooth problems without these symptoms. Jaw teeth decay in older horses and some become infected and erupt on the cheek or under the lower jaw. They need a veterinarian's attention before they reach this stage.

Constant loss of condition may signal molar teeth problems. A change to grain, succulent feed, or finely chopped hay may temporarily correct the condition. If no changes are made in the ration, the horse will literally starve to death.

FOOT CARE   Three-fourths of the causes of lameness are located in the feet. Many of them can be prevented. Navicular disease, sidebones, and other

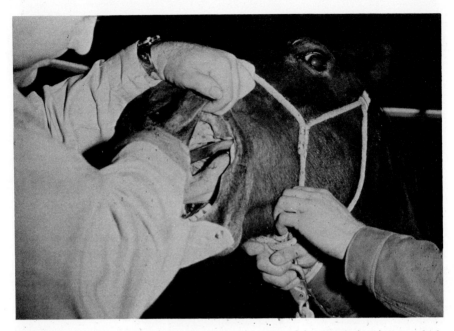

FIGURE 8-9   Have your adult horse's teeth inspected by a veterinarian regularly and floated (filed) as needed to ensure good mastication (chewing) and digestion, and to reduce colic. [*Courtesy of the Animal Husbandry Department, University of Missouri.*]

lamenesses resulting from old age or wear and tear are not totally preventable. But most are delayed with a good foot care program. For a detailed discussion of foot care, see Chapter 15.

Daily foot inspection while the horse's feet are being cleaned with a hoof pick is a major part of adult horse management, for almost all foot problems result from neglect.

If a horse is not working and is not exposed to sharp rocks, it should not be shod. The only reason to shoe a horse is to protect its feet from abrasive footing and excessive use, which wears then down faster than they can grow back. Going barefoot improves frog pressure and circulation and restores the hoofs to near-natural condition.

Two of the biggest mistakes owners make is to leave shoes on a horse until they fall off and to allow the hooves to become too dry. If the horse is not used for 6 or more weeks, shoes should be removed and the walls of the feet trimmed for going barefoot. When barefooted, trimming should be repeated every 6 to 8 weeks, or more frequently depending on growth and condition. Frequent foot checks of pastured horses is vital to health and good management.

Dry feet crack, contract, and encourage lameness. Horses on pasture tend to lose moisture in dry seasons, but regain it from the ground in wet weather. Sawdust bedding removes moisture quickly from stabled horses' hooves. Those with long hooves tend to stay dry. Front feet are drier than back feet in stabled horses because moisture from urine is more available to back feet. Mud packs, mud baths around outside water troughs or ponds, and hoof dressings are all used by horsemen as treatments for dry feet.

Humane management consists of practiced methods of handling, housing, and using your horse that result in the least amount of distress (stress) commensurate with the horse's contribution (work, companionship, etc.) toward paying for its keep. Simply stated, it means use but do not mentally or physically abuse your horse and it will serve you well year after year.

# MANAGING YOUNG HORSES

he growing and training phases of horse management are the two most important aspects of the horse industry. The grower must produce bones, feet, and muscle to last a lifetime, and the trainer must condition and educate the young horse to be a useful performer. For purposes of discussion, this chapter will consider the weaned foal through the trained young horse, usually 2 or 3 years of age, ready for sale or use.

Since training is often a low-return, high-risk, highly speculative business, why do so many aspire to enter the business? There are at least five reasons:

1  They expect to save money.
2  They expect to make money.
3  They expect to train the kind of horse they like.
4  They need the experience in training to become a better horseman or professional trainer.
5  They may produce a champion.

FIGURE 9-1   Millions of Americans are "rediscovering" horses as an escape from their pressurized environment and as a means of enjoying nature's beautiful scenes. Many good riders prefer to train a young horse in the activities they engage in rather than search for one already trained to their liking. [*Photograph by the author.*]

The person who looks to the young horse with an eye to saving money in producing a satisfactory finished animal is frequently doomed to failure. There are no shortcuts in horse handling. The value of the finished horse is in direct proportion to the quality of management invested in it.

However, for the good horseman who has the time, training may become a successful business venture. It is necessary to be a good judge of weanlings and yearlings as well as a good feeder. Buying well-bred yearling fillies and managing them well is a good way to get into the breeding stock business. A shrewd buyer with an eye for the potential of thin animals can grow out young horses and sell them as unbroken or broken 2-year-olds at substantial profits.

Many good riders prefer to train a young horse in their specialty rather than search for those already trained to their liking. Many young horsemen hope to make horse training their life's occupation, and they wish a trial run with two or three young horses. Of course, it is assumed they have had substantial experience with older horses and various horse activities before undertaking the training of young horses.

## MANAGEMENT CONSIDERATIONS

### Definitions

For convenience, most horsemen (no matter what breed is involved) adopt the terminology of The Jockey Club in describing horses, as follows:

*Foal.*   A horse or pony from its birth to January 1 of the following year.

*Filly.*   A female foal up to 3 years of age.

*Colt.*   A male foal up to 3 years of age.

*Yearling.*   A horse or pony during the first year after the January 1st following its birth.

*Long yearling.*   A yearling after 18 months of age and up to 24 months of age.

*Stallion.*   Also called *horse;* a whole or uncastrated male horse or pony after 3 years of age.

*Mare.*   Female horse or pony of any age after 3 years.

*Gelding.*   Castrated male horse or pony of any age.

### General Considerations

More facilities and equipment are required for growing and training young horses than are needed for adults. Rather large, well-fenced paddocks and pastures with abundant shade, clean water, and good forage are essential. When these are combined with a good winter feeding program, adequate shelter, and minimum accident exposure, young horses thrive. Their feet will require regular trimming; they must be protected against internal and external parasites; they must be immunized against contagious diseases. Yearlings and weanlings must be separated, and horses that are doing poorly removed from competition, to be fed individually or in small groups.

Where young horses are bought may be an indicator of the type of feeding, parasite, and immunization practices they have been subject to. If purchased at *public sales*, good management practices may have been minimal. Certain health standards may have been required for horses sold at *consignment sales*, and *breeder's sales* usually offer animals that have been under good care and management. When buying registered animals, be sure to get their registration papers. Transfer of these papers to buyer from breeder or seller is the buyer's responsibility.

Before hauling, make the conveyance vehicle as comfortable for the young horses as possible. A veterinarian may give them some antibiotics for protection in transit. Upon arrival at the farm, house them in well-bedded stalls. Let them rest a few days on a good-quality hay with little or no grain, unless they were already consuming grain. Find out from the previous owner the amount and kind of feed they were eating and try to duplicate it during the first weeks of adjustment to the new environment. When young horses are settled down and comfortable in their new quarters, consider the type of immunization and worm treatment they need before trying to improve their condition with heavy feeding. Talk this over with the veterinarian. It is likely that they will need worming, and they should be vaccinated for sleeping sickness, tetanus, influenza, and any other diseases that may be prevalent locally. Most young horses need worming before they are ever started on a conditioning program. If there is any question about their health, keep them isolated from the other horses, both young and adult, for 30 to 60 days.

## Shade, Water, Pasture, and Minerals

No environment is as good for young horses as a large pasture with abundant forage, good shade, clear water, and an appropriate mineral-feeding program. Traveling among the racing farms of Kentucky, one is impressed with young horses romping in this environment—it not only improves strength of muscles, soundness of bones, agility, and endurance in action, but it creates a psychological environment that results in a happier, better-adjusted horse. In the early days, Kentucky's success in horse production was attributed to a limestone base in its soils that produced abundant bluegrass pastures. With modern technology and fertility, these conditions can be duplicated in almost any state. Recent inroads on track records made by racehorses from other states is perhaps proof of this statement. Chapter 11 describes varieties of pastures and how to utilize them.

Even when pastures are utilized, feeding *supplemental grain* to yearlings and weanlings is a good practice. The grain can be hand-fed by stabling the horses individually each evening and feeding according to size and need. If in groups on pasture, yearlings need abundant trough space, and if fed in individual feeders, there should be one extra feeder to accommodate timid animals.

The *water* supply should be clean and free of chemicals, and should not be a site of disease or worm-egg contamination. Low spots of stagnant water or ponds that animals can get into should be drained or fenced. Only clear-running freshwater or water supplied in a controlled waterer or tank should be offered. If possible, location of water near shade will result in more frequent use than if in a hot, sunny place.

The same location should be supplied with a weatherproof *mineral* feeder containing both calcium and phosphorus, in one compartment, and *salt* in another. As pastures tend to be inadequate in phosphorus, the mineral offered should have a calcium to phosphorus ratio of 1:1. The other compartment should supply trace-mineralized loose salt. If no such weatherproof feeder is used, these minerals can be offered in block form, although there will be substantial wastage in areas of high rainfall.

## Insect Control

Insects annoy all horses. Biting insects may cause the young horses to expend as much energy stomping and fighting them as they would in 4 hours' daily walking time. Therefore, biting insects should be controlled through spraying, fogging, or offering a horse a dark stall during the high point of insect activity. Stable flies and face flies are active throughout the day and late evening. Face flies can be especially annoying and can produce swollen eyes and impaired vision (see Chapter 14 for details). Horseflies are early-morning and late-evening feeders. Contact the county extension agent for latest insect control recommendations for the area.

## Housing the Horses

Loose housing for growing horses of the same age is desirable. If they have an option of coming or going to an outside pasture, paddock, or lot, so much the better. About 60 square feet is required for 1 loose horse, and 100 square feet or a 10-foot by 10-foot box stall is sufficient for 2 young horses. Heated stables are not desirable because they tend to increase respiratory diseases. The stalls should be free from drafts and sharp objects young horses can injure themselves on, and must be kept clean to prevent manure buildup and heating from its fermentation. Housing should be fireproof. It should be designed so that the caretaker does not have to enter stalls to feed groups of loose horses and incur the risk of being kicked. Good housing will supply adequate feeding space and will have available clean water at temperatures above 45°F.

## Identification

There must be a method of positive identification for all horses. A color photograph showing the detailed markings of each horse is excellent. Pictures of maturing horses should be kept current. If there is a scar or unusual color marking, take a close-up picture of it for the file.

The registration certificate should adequately describe the color and markings of the horse. However, it is not sufficient for identification in cases of disputed ownership, and many horses have about the same color patterns. Therefore, one of the other methods of identification is recommended.

Over the years a number of methods for identifying animals have emerged. These range from ear notching, hotbranding, freeze branding, and lip tattooing to "fingerprinting," or taking an imprint of the horse's chestnuts (the horny growths on the inside of each of the forelegs).

Before any permanent brand is applied, it should be registered with the owner's name, usually with the State Department of Agriculture, through a county official at the county courthouse. It is unlawful, in most states, to use a nonregistered brand.

Ear notching and ear cropping were extensively used in England as means of identifying horses. Cropping was also used in this country in the early days to identify work stock, especially mules belonging to some of the larger companies. While permanent in nature, it is easily duplicated and disfigures the animal.

Hot branding with breeds that do not discriminate against blemishes is a very positive and permanent method of identification. Ranches have long used this method, and in many states it is the only officially recognized legal method of identification of animals. It does disfigure the animal, however, and cannot be changed when ownership is changed. Branding irons that are heated in an open fire are still available, but electric branding irons are handier for horses. Comply with state law on size (such as a letter or numeral that is $^3/_{16}$ by 3 inches high).

Freeze branding is a relatively new method of identity developed by Dr. R. Keith Farrell, of Washington State University. A branding iron is submerged in a bath of dry ice and alcohol at –80°C (Figures 9-2 and 9-3). After 2 or 3 minutes the iron is removed, blotted on a cloth, and applied to the clipped area of the horse where the brand is desired. Contact time on the skin depends upon the color of the horse and the temperature of the iron. Usually the time ranges from 30 to 60 seconds. The brand is usually placed under the mane near the top of the neck, midway between the poll and withers. Compared to hot-iron branding, freeze branding is relatively less painful. Therefore it requires less restraint and is more convenient to apply. However, permanency or readability of the brand has been questioned, and light-colored horses are hard to brand well enough for permanency. Freeze branding has been accepted by the Arabian Horse Registry as the official method of identification of Arabs.

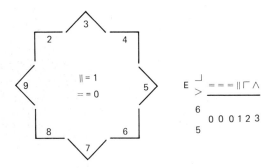

FIGURE 9-2 Right angles and straight lines represent Arabic numerals in the freeze-branding system developed by R. Keith Farrell, D. V. M., of Washington State University. The octagon shows the numerical values of the angles and lines.

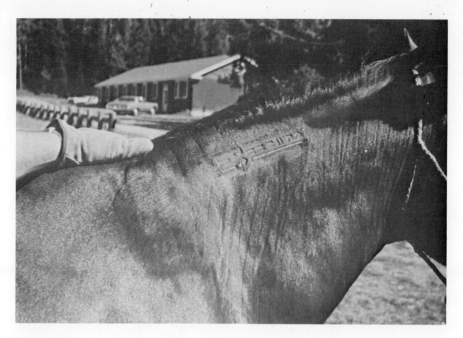

FIGURE 9-3  A freshly applied freeze brand. The brand is interpreted as follows: E = equine; stacked symbols = year of birth; remainder = horse's number. Thus the brand reads "equine, born in 1965, number 000123." [*Photograph by the author.*]

Dr. Farrell has formulated an elaborate numbering system based on angles that show year of birth, registration number, and most any other needed statistic.

The American Jockey Club requires a lip tattoo for Thoroughbred horses that race. The tattoo is placed inside the upper lip with a letter denoting the year of birth and numbers denoting registration numbers. This is a positive identification system, designed to prevent substitution in a race of one horse for another. Lip tattoos may be hard to read. However, they serve their purpose well for owners and stewards of racetracks.

In addition, the Jockey Club relies heavily on accurate description of cowlicks and chestnut patterns for foolproof horse identification. Cowlicks or whorls are the patterns of hair growth going against the grain of the hair coat. No two horses, no matter how similarly colored and marked, will have the same cowlick pattern.

The chestnuts of horses are like fingerprints in humans—no two are alike and they tend to remain the same from an early age throughout life. These are photographed and classified according to size and distinctive patterns.

## Castration

Weanling colts can be castrated any time that both testicles have dropped enough for the veterinarian to reach them. The younger a horse is castrated, the less shock it will suffer. The old custom of waiting until the horse was 2 years old for castration seems hardly justified in this day of few drafters and mostly riding horses. It was thought that leaving the colt whole until 2 years of age would increase neck development and aggressiveness—neither of which contribute much to the modern-day riding horse. Most 2-year-olds and a few yearlings will show sufficient secondary sex characteristics to be obnoxious around fillies, and, indeed, many will breed them. Therefore, the sooner castrated the better, provided a future champion is not being hastily neutered.

## FEEDING MANAGEMENT OF WEANLINGS, YEARLINGS, AND 2-YEAR-OLDS

One of the grower's biggest challenges is to feed growing horses an adequately balanced ration for optimum growth. There is a trend toward breeding for large size in most breeds. The larger the horses are, the better chance they have of winning a halter class. The more developed young racehorses are, the more training and racing they can often endure as yearlings and 2-year-olds.

Feeders aware of this demand tend to get yearlings as large and heavy as they can for shows and sales. However, some old-fashioned, thick-type horses are not genetically programmed to be 16 or 17 hands tall and weigh 1400 pounds at maturity. Offspring from these tend to become fat and thick instead of tall and trim under heavy grain feeding as yearlings. Many such horses become lame, and obesity has been blamed as the reason. In some cases this contention is correct, but in most cases lameness is a result of an improperly balanced ration, too low in calcium and protein and too high in phosphorus and carbohydrates. This condition is not new in horse raising. It has also been experienced by those raising poultry, swine, and, to some extent, large-frame beef cattle. As the type and growth rate of these species changed, so did their nutritional needs.

Horses, like other animals, should be fed so that they will achieve their genetic growth potential, but they must be fed a ration that will develop bone and muscle in addition to increasing weight. If horses become obese as yearlings, something is wrong with the feeding and/or breeding program.

### Feeding Management of Weanlings

It is imperative that all the essential nutrients needed for fast-growing animals be offered in a balanced ration of sufficient palatability for *each weanling* to satisfy its nutritional needs. Fast-growing, large breeds that work hard as 2-year-olds, such as racing Thoroughbreds, are seriously and permanently damaged from a badly balanced mineral ration or one deficient in one of the basic nutrients. The well-fed, well-grown yearling has 80 to 100 pounds of dense, hard bone that must stay sound for a lifetime. The horse must get it from a mother well fed in late pregnancy and from eating a weanling ration with 0.7 to 0.8 percent calcium and 0.5 to 0.6 percent phosphorus in addition to 14 to 16 percent protein (see Table 12-1).

If the horse is not fed enough calcium and phosphorus for strong bone formation, its bones will be porous and weak, resulting in unnecessary lameness and susceptibility to fractures throughout its lifetime.

If protein is deficient, growth and muscle development are retarded and the horse will be more susceptible to disease. If energy, or total feed intake, is inadequate, the horse will be underweight or permanently stunted.

A well-balanced ration, especially in minerals, does not occur by accident under practical feeding conditions. It must be planned! Excellent timothy hay and the best of oats fall far short of adequate mineral and protein levels for feeding confined weanlings. If fed equal parts of timothy and oats by weight, the nutrients supplied will only be 0.24 percent calcium, 0.32 percent phosphorus, and 11.3 percent protein. A spoon of a conditioner or tonic may improve vitamin levels, but does little to correct the basic deficiency. If excellent legume hay, such as alfalfa or red clover, replaces timothy hay, the percentages of calcium, phosphorus, and protein are 0.7, 0.32, and 16, respectively (Figure 9-4).

Because of the importance of feeding adequate quantities of a balanced ration, ration evaluation and ration balancing must be mastered (see Chap-

FIGURE 9-4  Excellent timothy (*left*) or nonleguminous hay fed with oats falls far short of the nutrient requirements of weanlings. Excellent alfalfa (*right*) or leguminous hay fed with oats almost meets weanlings' requirements.

TABLE 9-1   NUTRIENT REQUIREMENTS AND NUTRIENTS SUPPLIED WITH
(A) TIMOTHY AND OATS AND (B) ALFALFA AND OATS DIETS

|  | Crude protein, % | Calcium, % | Phosphorus, % |
|---|---|---|---|
| Nutrient requirements, weanling | 14.5 | 0.60 | 0.45 |
| (A)   In timothy-oats, equal parts of each | 11.3 | 0.24 | 0.32 |
| (B)   In alfalfa-oats, equal parts of each | 16.0 | 0.70 | 0.32 |

ters 12 and 13) when feeding growing horses. Do not be influenced by sales pitches encouraging you to feed a particular product to a young horse, especially if its expected nutritional contribution cannot be calculated. At best, a supplement may be worthless; at worst it may be toxic. Chapter 12 provides actual field cases of induced nutritional toxicities and mineral imbalances resulting from such additive feeding.

GROWTH RATE   How fast should weanlings grow and at what age should growth cease? There are a number of measures of growth, but weight and height are the two most used in research and professional discussion.

Trowbridge and Chittenden noted that, in draft horses, about 55 percent of the increase in weight and 72 percent in height at the withers occurred by 12 months of age.[1] They compared full grain-fed weanlings to those fed half the amount of grain eaten by the full-fed group. Both groups received all the excellent "pea green" alfalfa hay they would eat. Abundant, quality pasture was available for both groups in summer. Daily gains approached 3 pounds for each group until weaning and approximated 1.75 pounds for the heavy grain-fed group and 1.5 pounds for the other group during their first winter. Their observations were that at 1 year of age there was little difference in height and weight, but by 2 years of age heavy grain feeding had increased height 1 inch and weight (mostly fat) by 100 pounds, and enhanced salability or buyer appeal by producing fatter horses. They also noted increased cost, increased lameness, more fatigue, and less production when these heavy grain-fed horses began working. This hard lesson remains to be learned today by most buyers because they want young horses fatter than is healthy for soundness and work, and are willing to pay accordingly.

Some very comprehensive research on growth in Arab horses has been reported by Norman K. Dunn and associates at California State Polytechnic University.[2] They observed that males and females grow at about the same

[1]E. A. Trowbridge and D. W. Chittenden, "Horses Growth on Limited Grain Rations," *Missouri Agricultural Experiment Station Bulletin 316*, 1932.
[2]Kandee R. Reed and Norman K. Dunn, "Growth and Development of the Arabian Horse," *Proceedings of the 5th Equine Nutrition and Physiology Symposium*, University of Missouri, Columbia, 1977, p. 76.

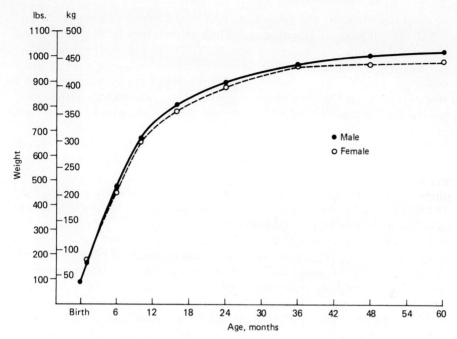

FIGURE 9-5    Growth curves for Arabian horses: age-weight relationship for males and females. [*From Reed and Dunn, 1977.*]

rate until 18 months of age, but males are 40 pounds heavier at maturity (Figure 9-5).

Growth curves in Figure 9-5 show rapid increase in weight up to 1 year of age, then a sharp slowdown ending at 5 years. Females weighed 83 pounds at birth, gained 2.1 pounds per day until weaning at 6 months, and 1.13 pounds per day the next 6 months, resulting in average weight of 657 pounds at 1 year. These horses were 37.1 inches tall at birth and 53.7 inches at 1 year, a growth of 16.6 inches. Height at 5 years was 58.4 inches. By 1 year of age, 65 percent of mature weight and 84 percent of mature height had been reached. Arabs are reputed to be late-maturing and therefore slow-growing animals. These data demonstrate unusual early growth and slow but sustained growth from 1 to 5 years, emphasizing the need for a good diet the first year of life.

KIND AND AMOUNT OF FEED    Daily amount of feed will depend on the size of weanling being fed, its ultimate mature size, rate of maturity, and its own individuality. A few individuals from large breeds,[3] such as Thorough-

---

[3] Jim C. Hierd, "Characteristics of Growth and Development in Horses," *1975 Production Short Course Proceedings*, Texas Agricultural Extension Service.

breds, Standardbreds, and some Quarter Horses, may be 15 hands tall and weigh 1000 pounds at 1 year of age. Their growth may be 99 percent complete at 24 months.

However, most growers are satisfied with winter gains after weaning of 2 to 2½ pounds daily, resulting in a 60 to 70 percent mature weight at 1 year. Amounts of 1 to 1¼ pounds of grain per 100 pounds body weight, and free-choice feeding of quality hay (legume), are sufficient to achieve this growth rate.

To get good gains, a palatable ration must be fed. Palatability depends on quality grains, variety, physical preparation, freshness, and probably the development of a taste for sweetness.

Oats vary in quality more than any other grain and must be carefully monitored in weanling rations. Commercial rations usually utilize corn and oats as base grains with small amounts of barley added in the northern part of the United States where it is grown. There are a variety of ways to process grain (see Chapter 12), but it must not be finely ground for horses. Indeed, the fewer fines, the more readily horses eat it. Freshly prepared grain is preferred, although daily or even weekly preparation may be impractical. Feed troughs should be kept clean of leftover grain. Horses, like humans, develop a sweet tooth for molasses in grain mixtures. Molasses also reduces dust and masks odors.

Quality hay depends on variety, degree of maturity, leaf-to-stem ratio, fragrance, and purity. Legumes, such as alfalfa or red clover, are much preferred by weanlings to nonlegumes like timothy, bromegrass, or orchardgrass hays. Mature hays are high in fiber, low in digestibility, and not well eaten. Leaves are higher in nutrients and lower in fiber than stems and are more readily consumed. Fragrance of newly mown hay stimulates horses' appetites. Good fragrance also indicates freedom from mold and is associated with greener color and higher vitamin potency. Finally, purity from weeds and other plants results in better consumption and less waste.

The grain ration fed should match the hay. For this reason, it is best to seek and purchase enough quality legume hay, usually alfalfa, to supply 10 pounds per head per day for each weanling through the first winter. Such hay will broaden the choice of grain and correct other nutritional deficiencies so often associated with weanlings because it will be high in protein, calcium, vitamins, and palatability.

Use a commercial grain sold for weanlings or one customized for them, since grain for weanlings must be higher in protein, minerals, and vitamins than adult horse rations. Homegrown grain can be fed with good legume hay to achieve a satisfactory growing ration. Satisfactory growth, however, cannot be expected of confined weanlings fed on homegrown grains or even most commercial grains with nonlegume hays such as timothy. They are too low in protein, calcium, and vitamin levels, unless a protein and mineral supplement is added to the ration, as described in Chapter 12.

TABLE 9-2   WEANLING RATION*

| Feedstuffs | Amount, % |
|---|---|
| Corn, cracked | 30 |
| Oats, rolled | 40 |
| Wheat bran | 10 |
| Soybean meal (50% crude protein) | 15 |
| Brewers' grain | 2 |
| Limestone | 1.5 |
| Dicalcium phosphate | 1 |
| Salt, trace mineralized | 0.5 |
| | 100 |
| Vitamin A, D, E (to supply 5000 IU vitamin A per lb of feed) | |

*The ration is 18.6% crude protein, 0.88% calcium, and 0.59% phosphorus. This ration is too high in protein for yearlings.

TWO CUSTOM CREEP AND WEANLING RATIONS   Table 9-2 gives a grain ration *with legume hay* that was used with success by a university for their Quarter Horse foals from 2 weeks to 8 months of age. Foals are creep-fed (see Chapter 10) on pasture and confined from weaning to approximately 1 year of age in exercise lots and open sheds. If some do not compete or eat well, they are separated and fed in small groups.

Table 9-3 gives another ration, one that is used from 8 to 16 months. It has less protein, calcium, and phosphorus because diets of 14 to 16 percent protein are eaten more readily than higher levels, and much of the muscular and bone development of foals is complete by their yearling year.

TABLE 9-3   EARLY YEARLING RATION*

| Feedstuffs | Amount, % |
|---|---|
| Corn, cracked | 40 |
| Oats, rolled | 40 |
| Soybean meal (50% crude protein) | 10 |
| Molasses, blackstrap | 7.5 |
| Limestone† | 1 |
| Dicalcium phosphate | 1 |
| Salt, trace-mineralized | 0.5 |
| | 100 |
| Vitamin A, D, E (to supply 4000 IU vitamin A per lb of feed) | |

*This ration contains 15.21% crude protein, 0.68% calcium, and 0.65% phosphorus on a dry-matter basis.
†Leave out if fed with all-legume hay.

Excessively high protein feeding may also reduce calcium utilization. This ration may be fed with mixed hay, legume hay, or good quality nonlegume hay. It is readily eaten, well balanced, reasonably inexpensive, and convenient to feed. It may also be fed to adult horses successfully if price is not a serious consideration, but there are more economical adult horse rations that are satisfactory (see Chapter 8).

## Feeding Management of Yearlings

Yearlings that romp with their friends on lush pasture with some supplemental grain their second year of life develop strong bones and muscles and good attitudes, and learn how to get along well with each other. This experience is especially beneficial to young horses scheduled for racing and other mentally and physically demanding activities.

Yearlings do not compete well with older horses for food and shelter. They have not developed much immunity for ascarids (roundworms) and are easily infested with these damaging parasites. For these reasons, this stage of their lives has been referred to as "the neglected age."

Yearlings and long yearlings require 12 percent protein, 0.5 percent calcium, and 0.35 percent phosphorus in their diets, respectively (see Table 12-1). These requirements are most nearly filled by quality, improved pasture, and supplemental grain feeding. The digestible protein in grazed early season Kentucky bluegrass, for example, is 12.4 percent, with 0.56 percent calcium and 0.40 percent phosphorus. For the nutrient composition of other forages, see Appendix Table 12-1.

## Some Additional Suggestions for Yearling Management

1  Separate yearlings from older horses and run them together on excellent pasture if possible. If not, full-feed a quality hay to the pastured yearling.
2  Feed 1 pound of a grain ration daily per 100 pounds body weight.
3  If on crowded pastures, worm every 8 weeks through the summer; worm 3 to 4 times with sparse yearling populations, or if confined.
4  Prevent lacerations by avoiding barbed wire, except on ranges and very large pastures. Remove all machinery and other sharp objects where yearlings romp.
5  Keep immunized against contagious diseases, and reduce exposure by isolating new horses before adding them to the herd.
6  Keep feet and legs growing straight by routine trimmings 4 to 6 weeks apart.
7  Remember, starvation never pays. Growth gains with young horses are more economical than they ever are again in the horse's life.

## Two-Year-Olds

Two-year-old horses are difficult to manage because they are still growing, and yet most are in training. Unfortunately, many are pushed too hard for shows and racing purposes as 2-year-olds.

Two-year-olds, even those in light training, are under stress and must be fed high-energy rations to maintain the condition and strength needed to avoid interruption of training or performance.

A 2-year-old in light training requires a diet with a minimum of 9 percent protein, containing 0.40 percent calcium and 0.30 percent phosphorus (see Table 12-1). Some suggestions are as follows:

1   Use only quality feeds.
2   Supply half of the nutrients in a coarsely prepared, dust-free mixed grain source, usually 12 to 15 pounds daily.
3   Feed a balanced diet for better consumption. Offer all the excellent legume hay the horse will eat, except 2 hours prior to work.
4   Feed grain three or more times daily.
5   Reduce grain by half and increase hay on days of rest.
6   Keep feed troughs clean and offer clean water free-choice.
7   Work quietly but efficiently with hardworking young horses and be sure they are given every opportunity to rest and relax.
8   Continue an immunization and worming program as in the yearling year.
9   If the 2-year-olds are valuable, ensure them against accident, death, and theft.

## TRAINING OR SCHOOLING THE YOUNG HORSE

For purposes of discussion, the assumption is that training starts with a weaned foal already gentle from having been taught to lead and tie (these phases are explained in Chapter 10).

The words "training" and "breaking" are used mostly in a discussion of western horses, and "schooling" with English types. The term "breaking" is an old one that sophisticated horsemen may associate with the rough handling procedures of some years ago when horses were wild, cheap, and handled abusively by some cowboys and owners. This term is still used by draft horseman and mulemen, although the process is patiently carried out over a long period of time with minimum trauma, the same as the training and schooling of other horses.

## How Much Training?

Ideally if the best were bred to the best, all horses would have the athletic potential to justify a careful, expensive, and extended training period. Unfortunately, this is not the case. Many low-grade horses are bred together, resulting in offspring of such poor conformation and predisposition to unsoundness that the cost of an extensive training program is simply not justified. To expect modestly priced horses with substantial conformation faults to perform at a level that will repay a year or more of constructive training is unrealistic. However, most any horse should be given a fair opportunity to find a useful place in some person's horse activities. Even though most horses learn very quickly and try hard to fully cooperate with their riders, some do not. Therefore, a basic training program involving a minimum of 100 constructive hours over a period of 6 months to a year will give the average horse an opportunity to be a useful worker and earn good care, though it will not yield a finished horse. Many horses do not have even this opportunity and yet develop surprisingly well, while others with substantially more training never become very useful.

Some professional trail riders who are also excellent horsemen will saddle a 3-year-old and start on a week's trail ride to train their horse as they go. This procedure demands a lot, both mentally and physically, from the animal, and requires patience and skill on the part of the rider-trainer. Most owners prefer less traumatic training methods.

Many professional trainers use three or four major steps in their training programs. They may train the horse in longeing, then teach it to line-drive, to ride, and finally to perform a specific function (e.g., jump). Although some trainers leave out one or more of these steps, there is a healthy trend back toward spending more time in training and schooling horses before pressing them into service.

It is important to realize that there are many ways to produce well-trained horses. However, there is no technique that produces fully trained horses in a very short period of time.

## Longeing

In longeing the horse travels around the trainer in a large circle on a long strap or line. The intent is to shape the behavior of the young horse by reinforcing successive approximations and punishing undesirable actions. This is accomplished through teaching the horse to start, stop, stand, walk, trot, canter, back, and stay on the perimeter of the circle or come in, all by voice commands. The idea is to do as much training from the ground as possible before mounting, for longeing gives the young horse an opportunity to find its balance, develop stride, and learn to be obedient to voice commands before it carries the weight of a rider. (Longeing also allows the owner of an older horse to give it some exercise quickly and conveniently.)

Longeing can start after weaning, but care must be taken not to let young horses hurt themselves by being jerked off balance on a longe line. Horses occasionally are injured this way, so some good trainers and veterinarians object to longeing for these and other reasons.

EQUIPMENT NEEDED AND TRAINING AREA    Although a horse can be longed with a halter and long rope, minimum equipment should be a well-fitting halter, a 30- or 35-foot nylon longeing line, longeing whip, and halter shank. If enough horses are involved, it may be worthwhile to go to the expense of buying a longeing caveson, as seen in Figure 9-6.

A training ring is also very convenient for longeing and other training activities. These are usually round, 35 to 40 feet in diameter, and have solid walls 7 feet high. Most have 6 inches of sand in the bottom or are worked frequently with machinery to keep the dirt loose. This reduces the possibilities of injury to the horse and rider and provides good footing for training maneuvers.

FIGURE 9-6    Lead the young horse around the longeing area until it is thoroughly relaxed before teaching it to adapt to the longe. Use fly spray if needed and remove distractions for a better learning experience. [*Animal Science Department, Cornell University, photograph by Duane Dailey.*]

Horses can be longed almost anywhere if the footing is not slippery. Any earthern area that receives a lot of trampling, such as horse lots and paddocks, becomes almost impervious to water absorption; therefore, a light shower or rain can cause the surface to be extremely slick, resulting in a fall or sprain to playful young horses on the longe line. Wet grass is also slick, and mature grass on extremely hard, dry soil has enough juices in it to be slick underfoot. The best longeing surface is one that is dry and soft from a sandy texture or cultivated earth.

TECHNIQUES    The young horse is led to the longeing area with a well-fitting halter or longeing caveson and a halter shank snapped in the lower ring. If the horse has not seen the enclosure before, turn the horse loose in it and do not try longeing it until the animal is thoroughly comfortable at this location. Remove distractions that might take its mind away from the lesson. Control flies with a repellent and try to limit objects it would be interested in, such as friends grazing in a nearby pasture. Some people start a young horse with an assistant; some prefer to start it alone. A round training pen facilitates working alone.

The longeing line is snapped in the cheek ring of the left side of the caveson or halter. With the folded longeing line in the trainer's left hand and the whip in the right, the trainer starts walking in a circle to the left with the young horse (Figure 9-7). Gradually the trainer will drop back from the horse's shoulder, urging it gently forward and saying "walk," with the whip in the right hand as its head is pulled slightly to the left (Figure 9-8).

Some trainers "push" with the whip in the area of the haunches, while others tap lightly, when needed, around the hind cannons. In either case, the trainer must be patient and urge only enough to start the horse. If the horse dashes away and turns to face the trainer, the process must be repeated over and over until the horse gets the idea. If the horse seems particularly afraid of the whip, an assistant may be needed while the horse learns that use of the whip merely means "go forward." The ultimate goal is to make the horse responsive to voice command alone, with the whip relegated to brief reinforcement, as a "pointer." As the horse learns to walk forward, restrained by the longeing line from dashing away and urged forward by the whip from behind when it stops, the distance between trainer and horse is gradually increased by feeding out the longe line. In 10 or 15 minutes in a training pen, the horse should be circling rather well at a sustained walk, while the trainer describes a smaller circle near the center of the horse's circle. This is a good time to quit for the day—the attention span of a young horse seldom exceeds 10 or 15 minutes.

The assistant can lead the young horse from the right side while the trainer is positioned on the left with whip in hand as if alone. The assistant will gradually drop back toward the hindquarters. When completely re-

FIGURE 9-7 Start the young horse to the left by using the whip in the right hand and the longeing rein in the left as you walk with it in a circle. [*Animal Science Department, Cornell University, photograph by Duane Dailey.*]

leased, the young horse will continue to walk without the assistant. If it stops and faces the trainer, the procedure should be started over again.

The second lesson begins much like the first, with the horse being brought to the location, groomed until it settles down, and sprayed for flies if necessary. The horse should be started to the left as before. After it settles down and quits trying to run, the young horse will probably remember its previous lesson and perform well. Some trainers like to start and stop the horse quite a lot, going to the left before they change directions, while others will change directions frequently.

To teach the horse to stop, the trainer will say "whoa," loud and clear, and give a little jerk on the longeing line. At first the horse may respond in a number of different ways: It may stop as asked; it may stop and face the trainer; it may speed up; or it may try to change directions. Whatever the result, the trainer is in complete control and will be careful to remain calm, to repeat the command in the same tone of voice each time, and to

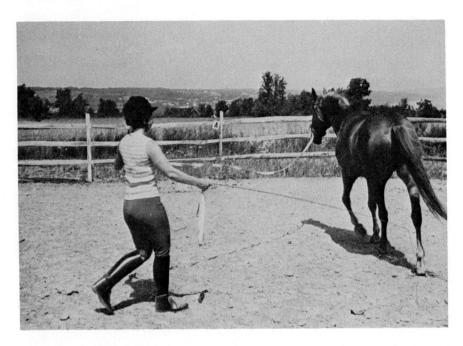

**FIGURE 9-8**   Reduce the size of the circle you travel as the line feeds out. Keep the horse moving with the whip and control speed with the longeing rein. [*Animal Science Department, Cornell University, photograph by Duane Dailey.*]

reward even the slightest approximation of the stopping response. After 2 or 3 days of patient work the horse should start and stop well on command and walk without breaking into a trot.

Changing direction to the right may well cause total confusion at first. Some horses will try to turn and go left. After one or two lessons going right, however, the horse will be going well both ways, moving out when asked and stopping on command while standing in the direction of travel at the perimeter of the circle.

Every horse will show a preference for working to one side or the other. This is because horses, like people, are right-sided and left-sided. This side preference is termed *asymmetry*. The *right*-sided horse will find it easier to *canter* to the *left* because it pushes off with its stronger right hind leg and "falls" on its left shoulder.

Although it is never possible to completely erase the effects of asymmetry, some trainers suggest working the horse a little more to the more difficult side.

In about a week, the horse is ready to trot. The trainer will use a rather small circle, and urge the horse forward more vigorously with the whip, saying "trot." The horse's first response is likely to be to burst into an explosive gallop. This should be controlled by small jerks with the command "whoa." One must be careful not to jerk a young horse off balance or have it fall. Repeat starting and stopping until the horse will trot in a large circle without coming in or pulling outward on the longe line. It has had enough experience by this time to go in both directions at the trot the first day, but do not expect perfection and do not work the horse more than 15 or 20 minutes. The best trainer will stop on a positive note.

When the young horse is starting and stopping well, and trotting in both directions in a balanced and calm manner, it is ready to canter (Figure 9-9). The trainer will establish the daily routine of walking and trotting in both directions before asking the horse to canter. The trainer will also know by now which lead is most natural for the horse and will start it in the most comfortable direction. The trainer will ask for a trot, then urge the horse faster by talking to it, or by the whip, until it breaks out of a fast trot into the canter. At first the horse may wander in and out and may try to run off. It may take a great deal of patience to get the right lead from the young horse going to its weak side. However, many well-balanced athletic horses will pick up the correct lead the first time when entering it from a fast trot. The

FIGURE 9-9   When cantering with good form and balance, a horse should not pull on the longe or decrease the size of the circle. It should lead with the inside front foot and not try to bolt or run away. [*Animal Science Department, Cornell University, photograph by Duane Dailey.*]

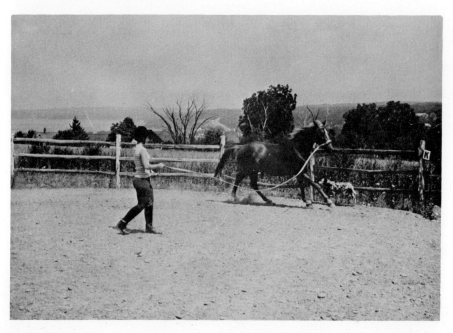

horse should be drilled in the canter in successive lessons until it has both leads going in good form at a reasonably slow, calm pace, in response to voice command alone.

The next lesson might be to back, although some trainers prefer to teach this from the very beginning, using light jerks on the longe line while the horse is standing at the perimeter of the circle.

One way to teach a horse to back is to stand straight in front of it and say "back." Jerk very lightly on the halter and if the horse does not respond, tap it gently around the ankles with a small whip. Be satisfied with only one or two steps, as backing is a difficult maneuver for a young horse to learn. Guide the horse so it backs straight. For the first lesson, be satisfied with any response it shows to the voice command. After a few lessons, it will back on voice command a few steps without any artificial stimulation.

## Line-Driving

More and more trainers are *line-driving* (*long-reining* or *ground-driving*) young horses (Figure 9-10). Gone are the days, even in the West, where the

FIGURE 9-10   More and more trainers are line-driving young horses. It teaches many basic maneuvers without undue stress to horse or rider. This horse is being driven with a bosal and a western saddle. [*Texas A&M University.*]

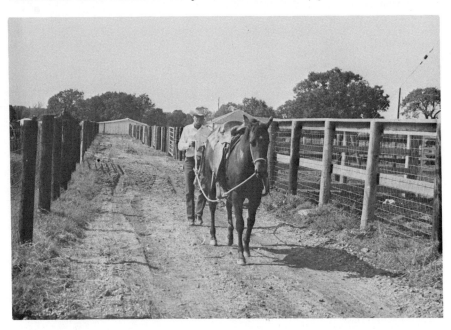

cowboy snubbed the wild horse to a post, blindfolded it, cinched on his saddle, mounted, and whipped furiously hoping the horse would run instead of bogging its head and bucking seriously. Such training produced horses that maintained their fear and distrust of humans throughout their lives, although some of them were very good horses in the hands of skilled riders. Training by degrees without any trauma produces a much more satisfactory mount. If the young horse has been appropriately longed, line-driving is merely a continuation of its education. If not, more time will be required in its basic education.

WHEN TO LINE-DRIVE   Most horses are driven when they are 16 to 18 months old, although slow-maturing or small breeds may be started at about 2½ years. A well-grown yearling should be 75 to 90 percent of its mature height and should be ready to drive about any time during the yearling year, even though it is not mature enough to ride. For best results, the horse should already be responsive to voice commands on the longe.

THE CART   Not many people drive with a training cart; however, those who do like it very much. The cart should be light, strong, and relatively free from noises and should have as few wooden parts as possible to reduce the chance of splintering in case of a struggle. Use of a cart will require a strong training harness that can also be used as a surcingle when starting the young horse in line-driving.

If a cart is used, the young horse should be thoroughly trained in line-driving before being hitched to the cart. When the horse is hitched, a strong-armed helper should stand at its head. The assistant can move the horse forward, then stop it. Some young horses become frantic when they see something the size of a cart pursuing them; however, with a little care they will respond calmly to the cart. A horse so trained is worth more the rest of its life because of the resurgence of the horse-drawn vehicle and the increasing number of vehicle classes in horse shows. Some breeds are trained routinely to carts for show purposes.

TO BIT OR NOT TO BIT   A decision must be made whether to line-drive in a soft bit or a hackamore (see Figure 7-15). Hackamore training has certain advantages:

1   There is less risk of injury to the horse's mouth.
2   A horse so trained can be rested from a bit later in life when it tends to get sour if excessively worked or shown.
3   Distance horses will usually drink better on the trail without a bit.
4   Some of the world's best-handling western horses have been trained with hackamores.

There are, however, some disadvantages:

1  Most show classes require the horse to be shown with a bit.
2  A training pen is more essential with a hackamore because the horse can resist and buck more seriously, or it can run away more easily when out in the open.
3  Some trainers feel it takes more time to prepare a horse for show that has been trained with a hackamore and that must then be switched to a bit before being shown. (Others might claim this to be an advantage.)

In any case, if a hackamore is used, the bosal should be the large size to start with. It should be carefully adjusted and should be used with the same gentle touch as if a bit were being used. In general, as training proceeds, the heavy training bosal will be removed for one of the lighter weights. When the horse is well advanced, an attractive pencil bosal may be substituted for appearance and for lightness to the horse and ease of handling for the rider.

Many bits are used for training. In general, they should have large rings, large bars, and should be jointed in the middle—such a bit is called a *snaffle* (Figure 7-17).

If the horse has an unusually soft mouth, a large rubber mouthpiece is recommended. The main thing is not to get into a tugging contest with the horse. Rough handling can damage the bars of the mouth and make hard-mouthed, headstrong, unresponsive horses. Trained western horses and English horses should respond instantly to light bit pressure. Gaited horses, whose heads are set and who wear double bits, are ridden with more bit pressure and are seldom required to respond quickly to rein and bit signals.

There are a number of bitting devices designed to prevent damage to the horse's mouth. Many go around the nose and attach to the bit rings to eliminate jerks or hard pulls on the mouth in case the horse jumps, but light hands on the reins beats them all.

The horse must be accustomed to the bit or the bosal before it is driven. Many trainers put a bridle on a horse with a throatlatch and bit in its mouth or bosal around its nose 4 or 5 days prior to driving. Some leave the bit in (under watchful supervision) for an hour or until such time as the horse stops chewing and working with it. Watch the horse to prevent its getting tangled or getting the bridle off. The same procedure may be done with a hackamore and bosal.

OTHER EQUIPMENT NEEDED   In addition to the equipment used in longeing, a bridle or hackamore, a second longeing line, and a surcingle, saddle, or training harness are necessary. A surcingle is a strap padded at the top that fastens around the body of the horse. It has side rings to accommodate the lines, and a ring at the top to attach a rein to.

A number of trainers start line-driving western horses by using a western saddle as the surcingle. They tie the stirrups under the belly to keep them from flopping and run the lines through the stirrups for driving. This is a good procedure; however, it is easier to teach the horse to line-drive with a training harness or regular surcingle because the tendency to buck is less with a regular surcingle and there are usually rings to receive the lines in two locations. That is, a pair of side rings low on the surcingle for low-headed breeds and a pair near the top of the back for breeds who normally carry their heads high.

HOW TO LINE-DRIVE   Repeat the procedure of taking the young horse where it has been worked, grooming it, protecting it against flies, and getting it settled down before driving. An assistant will help prevent an unmanageable situation. The assistant will stand at the horse's head until the right line is passed through the ring in the surcingle, over the back, and to the left side of the young horse. The left line should be attached to the bit but should not at first be passed through the ring. In this way the right line can be secured while the left line serves as a shank.

The horse trained with a longeing line will probably move off readily to voice command. As it travels around the perimeter of the pen, the trainer

FIGURE 9-11   If the horse's head "overtucks" (if its chin is in too far), there is too much pressure on the lines, because of either heavy lines or "heavy" hands. [*Animal Science Department, Cornell University, photograph courtesy by Duane Dailey.*]

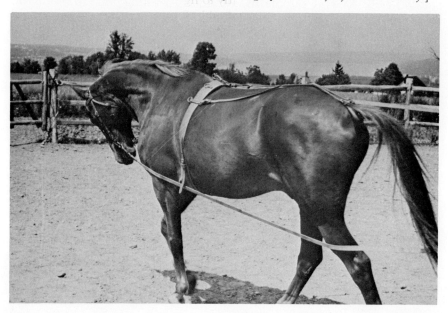

will move with it, beginning to guide with the lines, starting and stopping the horse a few times. When the outside, or right, line drops down around the horse's buttocks and hind leg (the trainer will be positioned almost behind the young horse at this time), it may get frightened and try to kick. However, a horse that has been longed should drive well in both directions the first day it is driven. Drive the young horse a few days in each direction at the walk; have it stop, stand, and back. When you back, pull one line and then the other as you clearly and loudly say "back." If the horse responds with a few steps the first few times, be satisfied. This would be a good note on which to stop the lesson. If the horse will not back, have an assistant stand in front of it with a small whip used around its ankles when it refuses. After a week in a training pen with the young horse going good in both directions at the walk, starting, stopping, and backing promptly, you are ready to trot. This can be done inside the ring with the trainer standing near the center just as you would with a longe line. Teach the horse to trot, stop, stand, and eventually to canter from this position.

Watch the position of the horse's head. If it is overflexed (chin in), either the lines are too heavy, or the hands are keeping too much pressure on mouth or nose (Figure 9-11). If the horse pokes its nose out, side reins may be indicated. A surcingle with elastic side reins is excellent, but bridle reins tied evenly to the surcingle or western saddle stirrups may suffice.

## Riding the Young Horse

SACKING OUT    *Sacking out* means introducing a young horse to various objects, which may or may not have an odor or make noises, by rubbing these objects over the horse's body. The objective is to get the horse to feel at ease when touched on any part of its body, to reduce its tendency to jump or cringe. Sacking out is particularly useful for nervous, jumpy animals and for those that are wild or have not been handled much.

In the old days sacking out was a routine part of breaking range horses. They were caught and snubbed, and in some cases the hind leg was tied up while the cowboy rubbed the saddle blanket over the body of the horse. Some modern trainers use saddle blankets, canvas, tarpaulins, plastic sheets, raincoats, tincans, etc.

An assistant *must* hold the horse while sacking. Most horses will profit from this experience, especially if they are to be used in parades, on trail rides, or as pack animals.

SADDLING THE YOUNG HORSE    When the horse is thoroughly gentle, has been sacked out, and has been either longed or driven or both, it is ready to be saddled. Go through the daily routine of catching, grooming, and putting the horse at ease, and take it to a familiar location for saddling. An assistant should hold the horse during the saddling process. If it has been driven with a surcingle, the task will be easier and less frightening to the young horse. The horse should be thoroughly comfortable with a blanket on its back. A saddle pad with cinch and stirrups is even better. These weigh only a few pounds and cannot be distinguished from a blanket by the young horse. If none is available, an English saddle with stirrups run up, without a blanket, is to be preferred to a heavy western saddle.

The saddle is placed gently on the horse's back. The horse should not resist, but in case it does, the trainer will hold on to the saddle firmly to prevent its falling. When the horse is thoroughly at ease with the saddle resting on its back, move to the other side and let the girth down gently. (It should not be pushed over from the near side and allowed to fall heavily on the off side.) The girth should be tightened only enough to keep the saddle from turning should the horse move.

Let the horse stand with the saddle on for a few minutes. If it shows no anxiety, the girth can be cinched a little tighter. When relaxed, the horse can be moved forward a few steps. When the horse is thoroughly relaxed, lead it around for a while, then tighten the cinch enough for mounting. After leading some more, discontinue the lesson for that day. The procedure is repeated until the saddle becomes a routine part of the longeing and driving routines. After the horse goes through its routine normally with the saddle in place, if it is old enough and large enough, it is ready to be mounted.

MOUNTING THE YOUNG HORSE  There are a number of ways to mount a young horse for the first time. There is no one best procedure for all horses and riders. The main objective is to avoid frightening or provoking the young horse to buck. Most horses allow mounting without trouble, but some have bucking tendencies and the trainer must be prepared for this eventuality. If you have done your groundwork well, there is only a remote possibility that the young horse will become frightened or annoyed when mounted. You may wish to mount without an assistant by having the reins in position, left hand on withers, right hand on pommel of saddle, rise slowing in the stirrup to a standing position. If this frightens the young horse, promptly step down. If not, stand a few seconds in this position without any attempt to mount; then slowly lower your weight to the ground. You may want your horse's head in the corner of a board fence for this procedure or some riders prefer an assistant standing at the head of the horse, depending much upon how the training has gone to that point.

After standing in the stirrup three or four times without any concern on the part of the young horse, put your right leg over gently and find the stirrup with the right foot, then let your weight down gently on the back of the horse, according to the safe mounting procedure discussed in Chap-

FIGURE 9-12    The method used to mount by this trainer is to rise and stand in the stirrup while holding the bridle cheek-piece. When resistance ceases, the mounting process is completed. [*Animal Science Department, University of Missouri.*]

ter 6. Reassure the horse with pats and talk reassuringly to it. Sit quietly a minute or two, then dismount. This procedure can be repeated three or four times and the lesson should be terminated on a good note (Figure 9-12).

RIDING PROCEDURES    The same mounting routine is practiced until the horse is calm. The objective in early riding is to start and stop the horse a number of times at a walk without any excitement or undue anxiety. The lessons are always stopped on a good note. The good trainer will be quite sure the horse is going well at the walk before asking it to trot. The horse is still urged forward by voice, and now leg pressure is added to get the trot. Speed, balance, and coordination control are achieved slowly in successive lessons. Trotting is a natural gait and usually comes easily. After 2 or 3 weeks of walking and trotting, the horse is ready to canter.

Most horses can be urged into the correct lead from a fast trot on a rather small circle. The horse will probably take the correct lead. If it does not, but is an athletic horse, it will probably change and get into the correct lead rather soon. The trainer will allow the horse to calmly canter around the circle two or three times, and then will slow to a trot and stop. He will speak reassuringly to the horse and reward it for its good performance.

Be prepared for a horse to buck the first time it is urged into a canter. You should have the slack out of your reins and not allow the horse to get its head down. More than likely one or two hops will conclude the bucking experiment. If this activity is done in an enclosure, it is much safer for both rider and horse. If not, an assistant is necessary as a safety precaution.

If the horse has trouble taking a lead and canters one time around the ring in the right lead, perhaps this is enough training for that day. Before many lessons the horse should go the other way and take leads in both directions just as it did on the longe line. From then on it is a matter of balance and getting it slowed down to a reasonable speed at the canter or lope. Do not expect a young horse to canter a slow, balanced canter without weeks of training and hours of patient handling.

Western horses, Thoroughbreds, and some other breeds canter naturally. Gaited breeds have more problems, especially those that are naturally gaited. Fox Trotters, for example, show only at the walk and fox trot as 2-year-olds. Most are not taught to canter until the end of the show season of that year or the beginning of their third year. Many 3-year-olds are not very well trained to hold and maintain a good square canter without some hint of pace, rack, or other gaits showing in it; and some never eliminate these tendencies from their canters. The more natural gaited the horse is, the more trouble it has with the canter.

The high, rocking canter of the American Saddlebred is performed at a rather fast pace and is relatively less rewarded in the show ring compared with the other gaits. The Tennessee Walking Horse has the most extreme action in the rocking motion of its canter. This is a learned gait that if done well at slow speed requires extensive training to perfect.

## The Finished Horse

Top performing horses seen at horse shows, race tracks, field events, and other competitive activities are largely professionally trained or "finished" and shown. When you have completed basic training of your horse, you must decide "Where to from here?" If you need the horse and its performance pleases you, fine. If the horse shows good aptitude for an event or activity beyond your time schedule or ability, it may justify the cost of professional training. A 3-month training period with a good trainer is sufficient to appraise the potential of most horses. Those with talent may repay training costs many times over in owner satisfaction and added value if sold.

The trainer you select is very important. He or she must have a good reputation of success in the event(s) your horse needs training for and must manage, handle, and feed his or her charges in a manner that ensures good public relations and owner satisfaction. Go to the trainer's stable and see if the facilities are adequate and if the horses in them look well-fed and groomed. Find out if the trainer or an assistant works the horses and how often. Watch the workouts and note trainer-horse relationships and whether the environment is conducive for learning. Finally, talk with other customers about their experience and evaluation of results with their horses.

Good trainers are seldom cheap and may have waiting lists, but are usually worth the extra cost and inconvenience of scheduling.

## SPECIFIC TIPS ON TRAILERING OR TRANSPORTING HORSES

The young horse's education is incomplete until it learns to load promptly and haul well. Foals are often hauled beside their dams for rebreeding, showing, and other reasons soon after birth. However, they are not able to compete for space in crowded quarters and may become injured if not protected in a separate compartment. If not transported by their yearling year, plans to engage them in such training should begin.

There are many ways to move a horse from one location to another. They may be flown, trucked, vanned, hauled in various types of trailers, or be driven or ridden. The major point of concern is that they arrive safely and are stressed or distressed as little as possible during the trip. This is especially important for horses that travel thousands of miles annually and whose usefulness depends upon such travel. If their experience in transit is bad, they will eventually become trailer-sour and almost impossible to haul without temporary or permanent injury.

TOWING VEHICLES   By far, the greatest number of horses in this country are transported behind automobiles or pickup trucks in standard two-horse, four-wheel trailers or in larger fifth-wheel trailers pulled by pickup trucks. This is a good way to move your horses because it is convenient, reasonably inexpensive, and quite safe when pulled by a sturdy vehicle with adequate motor and braking power and good hitch. Motors on most automobiles and trucks that pull as many as two horses should be equipped with towing packages, heavy frames, and springs and be especially dependable in their brakes and hitches.

NEW TRAILERS   Standard two-horse trailers come with many options. They should all have four wheels, brakes, and appropriate lights, and be large enough to give your horses substantial room. Most are 6½ feet tall, but 7-foot-tall trailers with 6 inches additional length are more appropriate for horses 16 hands and taller. They should have spare tires and wheels, mats in the floor for good footing, and adequate ventilation systems. A carrying rack on top is convenient, and extra length in the tongue will make them easier to back and handle.

There are two schools of thought on the advisability of a partition to divide the horses and whether or not the trailer should have a letdown ramp in back or be constructed so that the horse steps up in the trailer to load. Solid partitions are essential for hauling small horses and foals. However, they make it harder for a horse to balance on turns and create more trailer-sour horses in the hands of speedy drivers on curves than does the 2 inch by 12 to 14 inch divider located stifle-high to adult horses. This divider discourages the kind of climbing that occurs on a center partition, although it has the drawback of allowing horses to step on each other's feet.

Some people prefer a ramp that lets down at the top for the horse to walk up as it enters the trailer. Thoroughbreds and gaited horses are often hauled this way. On the other hand, those who prefer the horse to step up the 10-inch height of the other type of trailer point out that horses often step off the edge of the ramp in loading and injure their feet or legs.

USED TRAILERS When buying a used trailer, be sure and check some critical points of wear. These are the floor, brakes, axles, tires, and paint. Many older model horse trailers did not have creosoted floors, and rotting floor boards at the back of the horse near its hind feet may be serious. Unless you inspect the trailer from underneath, it is difficult to detect rotten floor boards. If a horses' back legs go through the floor in transit, they can be severely abraded or even lost before the horse can get them back into the trailer. Brakes always seem to be a headache on trailers. The worst condition is where one engages and the other does not. They require constant maintenance and there are not many good technicians to correct them. Test your used trailer by standing behind it when you signal a driver to apply the brakes. Both wheels should skid the same amount. Axles on many trailers are bent. This may come from curbing or from whipping. The safest way is to have these checked by a shop that straightens axles on trailer rigs. The cost will be small and well worth the expenditure and satisfaction. Trailer bearings also are a source of weakness. These can be checked by a mechanic when they are packed; if not, they can cause substantial whipping, and in some cases serious accidents. Tires on trailers should be checked frequently and should be replaced when worn. Finally, the condition of the paint job may tell not only how much care the trailer has had but the general quality of the entire trailer. Cheap trailers tend to be poorly painted and soon show blisters and rust spots.

The easiest trailer to drive, and perhaps the safest from the standpoint of control, is the fifth-wheeler or gooseneck trailer pulled by a pickup truck. Usually, four or more horses are hauled this way. It is more expensive, but is roomy, convenient, safe, and probably more comfortable for the horse than almost any other trailer.

Some horses are hauled in pickup or larger trucks. This is not a very comfortable way for a horse to ride. Even if protected from the wind and weather with a good ventilation system, the horse is high enough in the air to receive a lot of swings and jerks and general discomforts. This has been shown by shrinkage in cattle hauled in pickups or straight trucks compared to low-slung tractor trailer vans with a smoother ride and less sway. Therefore, vans prepared for horses that ride low to the ground are indeed very acceptable modes of transport, although very expensive.

Horses that move long distances may find flying less traumatic than hauling. However, the risk of turbulence is always present, and, in spite of the best preparation, takeoff and landing are rough.

Rail transportation was the order of the day in years gone by. Circus horses were transported in this manner for their entire lives. In those days, it was handled safely and comfortably by trained engineers; the tracks were smooth and the stock cars well prepared. Today, horse owners are unlikely to choose to transport a large number of valuable horses by rail.

TEACHING TO LOAD   There are a number of ways to teach horses to load, but there are no quick ways, employed by impatient people, that result in willing loaders and quiet haulers.

Some people let young horses teach themselves to load. One breeder has elevated single horse size stalls for weanlings to be fed in. Foals enter an alley loose, one at a time when learning, and are driven into whichever stall they choose. They are promptly fastened in and fed while being petted and rewarded for their compliance. After one or two lessons they promptly go in a stall of their own free will to get the food they know is awaiting them. After a few weeks each foal learns its own location and need not be fastened in the stall while being fed. Another horseman parks a stock trailer with a wide door that is low to the ground against the wall to teach his yearlings to load. In the front is tied an old horse calmly munching on feed. Soon the inquisitive yearlings get in the trailer to see what is going on. After a few days, they will promptly load in the trailer to be fed.

Not all horsemen have this kind of equipment and must load in a regular two-horse trailer or something similar. The young horse should be gentle and thoroughly trained to lead by its yearling year. Park the two-horse trailer near a wall, and use a gate on the other side in loading the young horse. If the trailer has a ramp, loading may be easier; if not, have someone at the head of the horse to control the halter shank just enough to keep the horse headed in the right direction. You cannot tug the horse in. A person at the back urging the horse forward may result in its promptly stepping into the trailer.

If the horse does step in and promptly backs out, let it. Do not try to force it to stay in and bang it in a hurried attempt to slam the door. After loading two or three times it is likely to stay in and munch on feed you have prepared at the front in the feed trough of the trailer. If it does not go in readily but stands looking in near the trailer, move its front feet forward one at a time. Occasionally when loading in a step-up trailer, one can place a front foot up on the back of the floor and the horse will promptly go in. In no case do we hurry the horse, become excited, start whipping it, or use extensive force. If it is reluctant to enter, consider loading an old gentle horse on one side to give it some reassurance. If the horse has not loaded in a half hour, it may be necessary to cross ropes behind it to prevent its running backward and getting too far from the trailer. A soft rope tied to each side of the trailer crossed at its breeching area and held by two assistants will prevent the horse from running backward. With its head pulled into the stall you wish it to load into, wait several minutes. It is likely when the horse sees it can not escape by backing, it will promptly climb into the trailer. If not, tighten the ropes, place the front feet in the trailer one at a time, and propel it forward into the trailer. Do this two or three times the first time it loads until it stands in the trailer reasonably comfortably. After two or three days of such education, after which the horse is fed in the trailer, it is likely to go in with no trouble.

Loading a spoiled horse is another matter. There are many prescribed ways. Some of them involve line-driving the horse up to the trailer parked as described before and driving it in. Others involve securing the horse's head where it can not get loose and using the whip around the ankles. Still others involve using brooms to scare the horse into jumping in, cross-ties to force it in, blindfolds, and various other devices. The point is not to create conditions that make your horse fearful of loading and hauling. Almost any horse that expects to be fed when it gets in the trailer and that has not experienced severe bruising on the ride will load into a trailer when the doors open and when the halter shank is draped across its crest (see Figure 6-13). All horses should be taught to load in this fashion.

DRIVING THE LOADED HORSE    Horses fight trailers from fear or from an accurate knowledge that they are going to be bruised in the hauling process. After your young horse learns to promptly load and stand in and get out of the trailer, it should be initiated to the vehicle in motion. Load the horse as before in its pasture or where it feels comfortable. Move the rig forward only a few feet and gently stop it. Do this a number of times before you make turns. Let your first turns be large, slow turns. Indeed, every turn with a loaded horse should be a slow turn. After 3 or 4 days of various types of turns and stops at home, take the horse on a short trip. Always drive slowly on sharp curves. Give yourself a lot of room to stop. Watch traffic far ahead. Remember your horse can balance rather well forward or backward, but its balance from side to side is poor. When taking a trip check the rig over carefully for safety. Check the brakes, tires, lights, and especially turn signals, and drive slowly the first few miles until you are in complete control of the rig. Be alert for larger vehicles that will speed past you. They will push your rig to the right. Usually this is of no consequence if you maintain a firm grip on the wheel and accelerate slightly. Before stopping warn the horses with slight pressure on the brake. This will let them brace. Travel with as much room between you and the vehicle in front as is practical. Never tailgate. Avoid getting into situations that require sharp stops and jammed brakes. This makes horses scramble and fight and creates wall climbers. Load your heavy horse on the left side because the center of the road is higher and heavy weight can be controlled better on the upper side.

The main points in driving a trailer are to drive defensively, to not hurry, and to have good equipment. Anticipate problems as much as possible before they happen.

If you are making long hauls, particularly out of state, have appropriate health certificates prescribed by your veterinarian. Keep the horses comfortable in terms of temperature. In winter, this requires blanketing, and in summer, good ventilation. Modern trailers with all closed-in back gates and doors are hotter than most that have no upper doors. If this is the case, take these doors off in hot weather to increase ventilation. Remember, few trailers have good ventilation systems at speed. Leg-bandage your horses if they have far to go, and protect their feet with shipping boots if they are riding in a trailer without a solid wall between horses. Water at every stop you make while you have them loaded. If you have an extremely difficult horse to haul, tranquilizers may be justified. Relieve boredom by offering small amounts of hay in transit. If you are going very far, tie with panic snaps or quick-release buckles. The amount of time a horse can haul without undue stress is quite debatable. Some people haul 10 or 12 hours without stopping; others unload every fourth or fifth hour. If you unload that frequently, you should consider breaks of 2 hours' duration; otherwise the horses may be reluctant to load after having been in the trailer for a while. Some horses will not urinate in transit and may require more frequent stops than others.

During insect season use an appropriate insecticide to repel flies before loading and during transit. If flies are loaded with the horse, it has little protection against them.

Make transporting the horse as comfortable and painless as possible, and it will reward you with a lifetime of prompt loading and pleasant hauling in any rig.

## BIBLIOGRAPHY

Amaral, Anthony: *How to Train Your Horse*, Winchester Press, New York, 1977.

Fillis, James: *Breaking and Riding*, J A Allen, London, 1969; reprinted from original edition of 1902.

Podhajsky, Alois: *The Complete Training of Horse and Rider*, Doubleday, New York, 1967.

Ricci, A. James: *Understanding and Training Horses*, Lippincott, Philadelphia, 1964.

Self, Margaret Cabell: *Horsemastership*, Arco, New York, 1973.

Stanier, Sylvia: *The Art of Long Reining*, J A Allen, London, 1974.

# Ten

# MANAGING THE HORSE-BREEDING HERD

egardless of whether a single mare is bred for the experience of the wonder of nature in creating a new life, or whether a herd of mares is bred for a given market, the venture must be treated as a business. The successful breeder will (1) have a plan, (2) keep good records, and (3) carry out the plan by adjusting it to encourage the phases that show profit and eliminate those that do not. The breeding business requires elimination or control of sentiment and a realistic evaluation of progress toward a predetermined goal.

Before that favorite backyard mare is casually bred to the neighbor's stallion, the owner should ponder these questions: What will be done with the foal? Can it be kept, or must it be sold? If it must be sold, what kind of home can it be expected to find? If the parents are ordinary horses, the foal is likely to be the average of these parents. If the parents are good-quality individuals, they may produce a foal that will have good buyer appeal and therefore justify good training and management. What will it cost to raise this foal? It is a rare 2-year-old of even undistinguished parentage that has not encumbered its owner with costs of $1500 in feed, stud fee, medicine,

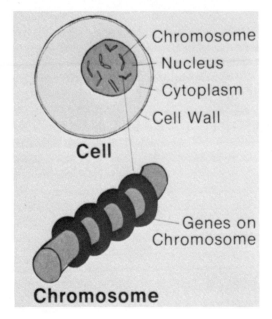

**Cell**

Chromosome
Nucleus
Cytoplasm
Cell Wall

Genes on
Chromosome

**Chromosome**

FIGURE 10-1   The nucleus of horse cells contains 32 pairs of chromosomes, one in each pair coming from each parent. Many different genes, the determiners of inheritance, are carried on each chromosome. The mathematical probability of producing unalike offspring from the same parents is great, making breeding an exciting challenge. [*From John F. Lasley*, Genetics of Livestock Improvement, *Prentice-Hall, Englewood Cliffs, N.J., 1972.*]

and labor. The realistic answer to the question, to breed or not to breed, therefore, is usually negative. On the other hand, good-quality backyard horses may produce useful and rewarding offspring when bred to outstanding stallions, when these offspring are trained to their genetic potential.

The person who starts a horse-breeding enterprise must first be a successful horseperson, or else be willing to hire someone who is and let them exercise much judgment in selection and management of the horses. While many horse enterprises are accused by the Internal Revenue Service of being tax write-offs, most affluent people that enter the business genuinely feel they can contribute to it, produce a winner, or make money from it. To do so, the horse breeder must treat it with the same dedication and energy as any other business and often must develop skills and judgment beyond those required to succeed in many other fields.

## Costs, Returns, and Business Considerations

INVESTMENT   Minimum investment for a reasonable horse enterprise in land, buildings, machinery to work the land, and equipment to use the horses ranges from $2000 to $3000 per mare. This does not include purchase cost of the animals or labor to work the enterprise, or the cost of having horses shown, raced, or professionally handled off the premises. In the final analysis, it is not unrealistic for a quality breeding business operating on fixed and variable costs to estimate a cost of $10,000 or more per mare. Of course, if much of this expense is clear or secured with collateral, cash flow is a minor consideration. If not, cash flow can be a major problem during years of low income or unbudgeted expenses.

CASH FLOW   There is a continuous flow of dollars through the horse business. Income is mostly from sales; outgo occurs in the form of payment for operating expenses, new investments, taxes, veterinarian payments, interest, living expenses, and many other commitments. The operator with high payments on indebtedness obviously is in greater danger of foreclosure during the early phases of the horse business, when waiting for sales to begin, and during bad years of low sales than the operator with a long-term, low-payment loan. Therefore, this jeopardized type of operation requires some provision to borrow money during hard times. Opportunity for supplemental employment, such as training boarding horses, may be a consideration in a fiscal emergency.

EXPECTED RETURNS   Obviously returns must pay outstanding debts and payments on commitments, and furnish a living for the family and some opportunity for growth. If these expenses are $150,000 a year, and the size of the enterprise is 50 mares, a 60 percent foal crop must sell for approximately $5000 per head average as yearlings to recover expenses. One-fourth of a breeder's horses usually return half of the income from sales. When breeding replacements are needed, they must come from this best group, resulting in reduced income from an expanding herd unless some horses also yield income from competition.

RECORDS   Some records must be kept because the Internal Revenue Service demands it. The successful horse manager will keep far more detailed records than are demanded for tax purposes, however. These will include all expenses and income, plus detailed breeding and performance records of each horse. There are a number of private and public farm record-keeping systems available to horse breeders. These may range from expensive computer records available through accounting firms, lawyers, or farm management consultants, or they may be less expensive records computerized in an extension service program available through the county extension agent.

Breeding, medical, and performance records are usually adapted to specific farm needs, and vary substantially from one breeding operation to another.

INSURANCE AND LIABILITY   A horse-breeding establishment should carry adequate insurance on the buildings and breeding herd. If outside mares are bred at the breeding establishment, sufficient liability insurance must be carried. The amount of liability depends upon the number of persons on the premises and the value of mares brought there for service. Many establishments use $1 million coverage. Horses that are hauled to shows or raced, or that otherwise engage in activities that require stress and strain either in performance or transit, should be insured. There are now a number of good companies that are happy to supply information on their programs.

ADVERTISING   The purebred breeder, who depends upon the enterprise for a living, must advertise. There are many ways to make the public aware of your stock: breed journals, consignment sales, shows, production sales, good public relations, and an attractive show place are only a few. In the long run, however, the best advertisement is good horses. There are some old establishments that simply use reputation as the basis for merchandising their animals.

The breeder of purebred horses must have unique patience in dealing with the public. These breeders must smile in the face of criticism, replace animals under conditions they feel may not be their responsibility, and above all, must be honest and consistent in judgments, even under circumstances in which there are few rules and guidelines to follow.

BREED SELECTION   Before selecting a breed of horses, there are a number of factors to consider. First, the breed must be one the breeder likes, and second, it must be one with growth potential. Many breeders have chosen a rare breed in the hope of seeing it greatly expanded. In some cases they have seen such a result, but in many more they have not. Some breeds have yearling sales averaging in the five-figure bracket. While it takes more money to get into the breeding business at this level, the potential for return is substantially greater than starting with a herd of cheap thousand-dollar mares.

When the breed has been chosen, and the mares carefully assembled, a breeder can select a stallion to purchase and mate to them, or arrange to have the mares bred to "outside" stallions owned by another person or firm. Even if the breeder owns a stallion, it may be desirable to breed some of the mares to another stallion because of its quality, the mares' relationship to the home stallion, or other potential advantages of outside mating. The mate chosen for the mares should be acceptable in terms of conformation and bloodlines, and current popularity within the breed. Although more expensive, offspring from such a mating should pay for the additional cost.

## GENETICS

The science of *genetics* is the study of how characteristics are passed along from parents to offspring. *Inheritance* determines the upper limits of performance (speed) a horse can ultimately achieve. *Environment* (training, feed, health) determines how closely this upper limit is approached. The study of genetics has great practical significance to the horse breeder. However, it does not ensure a champion, because there are an infinite number of possible gene combinations from matings between two horses.

## Units of Inheritance

The genetic material which determines characteristics and which is passed from parents to offspring is contained in the chromosomes.

*Chromosomes* are microscopically visible, threadlike bodies present in the nucleus of each body cell. Chromosomes occur in pairs in body cells except reproductive cells. Horses and ponies have thirty-two pairs (sixty-four individual chromosomes) of chromosomes. The members of these pairs are not exact duplicates. When a body cell divides to form two new cells, the chromosomes self-replicate as well, ensuring genetic continuity within the organism.

Located along the chromosomes in discreet positions are the *genes*, the biochemical *determiners* of the expression of characteristics. Because the chromosomes are paired, the genes are also paired. The members of each gene pair are not necessarily identical, giving rise to important modifications and a nearly infinite variety in the expression of traits. Nonidentical genes paired at the same locus on a chromosome are called *alleles*.

Genes are complex protein molecules of deoxyribonucleic acid (DNA). Genes send "coded" messages through another complex protein, ribonucleic acid (RNA), which determines the assembling of amino acids into a protein structure, ultimately resulting in muscles and other structures in the individual. Any deviation in or interruption of this code results in a mutation, and may result in genetically deformed offspring.

THE REPRODUCTIVE CELLS  The only link of inheritance an offspring has with its parents is through two tiny cells that unite at fertilization—the egg cell from the female and the sperm cell from the male.

These germ cells are produced in the body by the process of reduction division or *meiosis:* two cell divisions result in reproductive cells having only *half* the normal number of unpaired chromosomes, and thus only half the number of genes. When egg and sperm unite in fertilization—each containing thirty-two chromosomes—genes and chromosomes are again paired, one member of each pair donated by the father, one by the mother.

SEX DETERMINATION  The chromosomes determining the sex of the offspring are known as X and Y types. Mares possess two X chromosomes, while stallions possess an X and a Y. Presence of the Y chromosome causes the foal to be a male. The egg cell can only transmit an X chromosome; the sperm cell transmits either Y or X, with equal probability, and therefore is the

TABLE 10-1  MATHEMATICAL PROBABILITY OF
HOMOZYGOUS CROSS

|  | Parents | Offspring | |
|---|---|---|---|
| Stallion | BB | BB | BB |
| Mare | BB | BB | BB |

determiner of the foal's sex. The Y chromosome, however, is microscopically
smaller than the X chromosome, and is thought to possess less hereditary
material (fewer genes). Therefore, male foals may obtain more hereditary
material from their mothers than their fathers, whereas females obtain an
equal amount from each parent.

The area of sex-linked traits has been much studied in many species.
Hemophilia, for example, is a trait determined by a gene appearing only
on the X chromosome.

TABLE 10-2  MATHEMATICAL PROBABILITY OF
HETEROZYGOUS CROSS

|  | Parents | Offspring | |
|---|---|---|---|
| Stallion | Bb | BB | Bb |
| Mare | Bb | Bb | bb |

$$Bb \times Bb = BB + 2Bb + bb$$

GENOTYPE   The genetic makeup of an individual is termed *genotype*. An animal having identical genes for a specific trait, say *BB*, paired at a specific locus on the chromosome, is said to be *homozygous* for that trait. An animal having nonidentical genes, *Bb*, paired at an equivalent locus, is said to be *heterozygous* for that trait. (Genes affecting the same trait and occurring at the same locus on a chromosome pair are called *alleles*.)

The reproductive cells of the homozygous individual described would contain only *B* genes for that trait. The reproductive cells of the heterozygous individual, however, would be split 50-50, half containing *B* and half *b*. Tables 10-1 and 10-2 show the statistical genotypic outcome of matings of homozygous and heterozygous individuals.

## Types of Gene Action

The visible expression of genotype is called *phenotype*. Phenotype may be expressed (1) *nonadditively*, and (2) *additively*.

Nonadditive gene expression includes *dominant, recessive, partially dominant, overdominant,* and *epistatic* gene action. Additive gene action results in one or more pairs enhancing the action of one or more other pairs.

NONADDITIVE EXPRESSION   Results of nonadditive gene action may appear early in a breeding program. Certain matings of colors are predictable, while others are very complex and little understood. For example, the inheritance of greys, blacks, and browns is nonadditive and their matings predictable, while Appaloosa-pattern inheritance is complex and uncertain.

*Dominant and Recessive Action.*   If one gene of a pair *masks* the expression, or phenotype, of another, it is said to be *dominant*, while the one masked is *recessive*. Black coat color is a good example. If capital letters represent dominance, a *homozygous* (both genes for color are alike) black horse would be represented as *BB*. If the homozygous black horse were bred to a sorrel mare (*bb*), the offspring would all be *heterozygous* black because the sire would transmit only dominant *B* genes. All offspring would be heterozygous (one *B* and one *b*) for coat color. Such a homozygous dominant individual is said to *breed true* (Figure 10-2).

When two black heterozygous horses are mated, the mathematical probabilities for coloring are 25 percent homozygous black, 50 percent heterozygous black, and 25 percent homozygous sorrel (Table 10-1). There are two phenotypes, black and sorrel, and three genotypes, homozygous black, heterozygous black, and homozygous sorrel.

*Partial Dominance.*   When one gene of a pair *modifies* the expression of another, the effect is *partial dominance*. The dilution gene $c^{cr}$ (cremello),

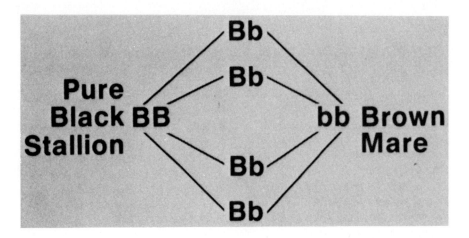

FIGURE 10-2   A homozygous (*BB*) black stallion bred to a brown or chestnut mare (*bb*) can produce only black-colored offspring, but all are heterozygous (*Bb*) for black coloring. [*From John F. Lasley*, Genetics of Livestock Improvement, *Prentice-Hall, Englewood Cliffs, N.J., 1972.*]

when paired with *bb* (chestnut) produces palomino color. The heterozygous palomino does not breed true for color.

The expected mathematical percentages from mating palominos together are: 25 percent $c^{cr}c^{cr}bb$ (cream or cremello colored), 50 percent $Cc^{cr}bb$ (palomino) and 25 percent $CCbb$ (chestnut).

*Overdominance.*   Overdominance may be expressed by labeling genes $A^1$ and $A^2$. Phenotypes expressed as $A^1A^2$ are more desirable in color or performance than either those of $A^1A^1$ or $A^2A^2$. Many pairs of overdominant genes with unlimited combinations may affect performance of horses.

*Epistasis.*   In *epistasis*, one pair of genes masks the phenotypic expression of another pair in another place on the chromosome. For example, genes for the inheritance of white coat are found at a different locus from the genes for any other coat color and are therefore inherited separately, but they nevertheless mask the expression of any other coat color.

ADDITIVE GENE ACTION   Additive genes not only contribute their influence but enhance the action of genes in other pairs. Additive gene action affects many traits of economic importance in horses and other animal species. An example is racing speed. It is not known how many pairs of additive genes are involved in speed, but assume two pairs, genes $A$ and $B$, could represent good speed, and $a$ and $b$ slow speed. Two pairs of genes give sixteen possible genotype combinations with a ratio of 1 : 4 : 6 : 4 : 1.

1 {*AABB* great speed

4 {*AABb* good speed (2)
   {*AaBB* good speed (2)

6 {*AAbb* average speed (2)
   {*aaBB* average speed (2)
   {*AaBb* average speed (2)

4 {*Aabb* below average speed (2)
   {*aaBb* below average speed (2)

1 {*aabb* slow speed

Each addition of an *A* or *B* gene increases speed over *a* and *b* genes. Unfortunately, science cannot positively identify the number of desirable genes in any given horse, but breeders must resort to performance records, family relationships, and breeding systems to increase the probability of breeding a good performer.

## Lethal Genes

Individuals from all populations carry lethal genes. These genes are recessive and therefore depend for expression upon chance combination with a similar gene at mating. Since individuals may carry different lethals, the chance of a combination of similar lethals is remote in large populations unless inbreeding is practiced. The way to prevent lethal expression is to outbreed, or avoid breeding an animal that has parented a recessive lethal. If a stallion sires but a single lethal, it is a carrier and capable of transmitting that gene at the next mating. If the mare is not a carrier, there is no problem. If, however, the mare *and* the sire are carriers, the chance is 1 in 4 of producing the homozygous recessive lethal expression. A few common genetic defects are discussed below. There are many more lethals and dozens of defects inherited by horses.

LETHAL WHITE   The homozygous genotype for white, *WW*, is lethal and causes death of the homozygous individual in the uterus in the early embryo stage. When white heterozygous adults are mated, expected results are 25 percent lethal deaths in utero, 50 percent white foals, and 25 percent colored foals. Note that the gene pair *Ww* will alter the expected black color of a cross with *BB*, resulting *WwBB*, which phenotypically is white.

COMBINED IMMUNODEFICIENCY   This is an apparent genetic condition found only in as much as 25 percent of all Arab and part-bred Arab foals, with 2.3 percent lethally affected. These affected foals are unable to develop antibodies for normal disease resistance and perish soon after weaning as a result of adenoviral infection of the respiratory system. They may appear normal at birth and during lactation because of antibodies in milk. No cure is known. The genetic action is unclear, but is thought to be autosomal (non-sex-linked) recessive. It may have begun as a genetic mutation in a single stallion.

WOBBLES   An arsenal of conditions (some may be genetic and some environmental) may affect the central nervous system by restricting or compressing the spinal cord. Incoordination or holding the head to one side is an early symptom. If caused from an injury or infection the condition may respond to time or antibiotics. Many afflicted young horses simply degenerate into a condition that requires euthanasia.

ANAL ATRESIA AND ATRESIA COLI   Foals born without anal openings are seldom saved by surgery. Fortunately this condition is rarely seen. Atresia coli, incomplete development of the intestine, is also rare but results in death from colic a few hours after birth. It has been reported in Thoroughbreds, Percherons, and white foals.

## Qualitative and Quantitative Inheritance

*Qualitative* inheritance is a result of only one or a few pairs of genes, resulting in a distinct and predictable phenotype. The black coat color explained earlier is a good example.

*Quantitative* inheritance involves many pairs of genes, most of which remain obscure. Phenotypes are difficult to distinguish from each other, and have a tendency to blend together. Environment further complicates this type of inheritance by its interaction with it. Racing ability is an example that is affected by complex inheritance and environmental differences in training, health, nutrition, and psychology.

## Heritability Estimates

The effects of heritability and environment combine to account for all of the horse's traits. A heritability of 5 percent for breeding efficiency is low, assigning 95 percent to environment or management. This would mean that 95 percent of the improvement in a large foal crop must come from better management practices rather than selection of replacement fillies from regular producing mares.

If speed were 60 percent heritable, one could expect progress by breeding to a stallion whose speed is faster than the average speed in your herd.

Here is how it works. If a Standardbred mare that averages 2-minute 10-second (2:10) miles is bred to a 2-minute stallion (2:00), how much improvement in racing speed from this mating can be expected? To find out, divide the difference in speed by one-half times the heritability. Difference

(10 seconds) ÷ ½ × 60 percent = 3 seconds. Average speed from this mating should be 2:07 for the mile.

Of course some offspring will be faster and some slower than "average."

## Superior Foundation Animals

It is imperative, if progress is to be made, to use superior breeding animals. Robert Bakewell, famous English foundation breeder of cattle and sheep, said two centuries ago, "Don't buy breeding animals from someone with better grass than yours." He was aware of the environmental effect (fat, sleek hair coat, etc.) from good feed and care in masking genetic worth.

Knowledge of the performance of the individual and/or its close relatives is very beneficial. A progeny test of an older stallion or mare is excellent, but these horses are rare and expensive when located. Leading sires of performance horses are genetically superior, but they are often only bred to good mares, which also helps performance of their offspring.

Close relatives, such as parents or half-siblings, that perform well are very positive indicators, while a distant ancestor who performed well contributes little genetic value. A fourth generation (great-grandson) may receive only 12.5 percent of its inheritance from its famous great-grandsire. Inheritance from relatives farther back is usually unworthy of consideration.

Do not select the only good individual from a family of sorry horses Because of its heterozygosity, it seldom breeds true.

## Breeding for Improvement

If animals carrying the greatest number of desirable genes could be identified, and if the genes could be programmed to unite for the maximum possible benefit at breeding, superior offspring would be assured. Unfortunately, this is impossible. The main objective of a breeder, then, is to combine maximum numbers of desirable genes and eliminate undesirable animals and those that produce undesirable gene combinations. (Since undesirable gene combinations are often masked, this is a difficult task.) The main tools breeders have to accomplish their objectives are *selection, culling*, and a variety of *mating systems*. The fewer traits a breeder selects for (speed versus head, style, color, etc.), the faster progress will be.

Breeding is a very challenging undertaking. The upper limits of performance appear not to have been reached, and rewards await those persons who can make genetic improvement in their animals.

## MATING SYSTEMS

Choose a mating system to combine desirable genes of parents in their offspring. Genetic variation permits the concentration of both good and bad genes, which enables horse breeders to cull poorly performing horses and select the best ones for the breeding program. The long generation interval and low reproductive rate of the horse makes progress slow at best. It is not an enterprise that tolerates many serious mistakes (e.g., wrong studs), nor does it allow a constant change of goals. It is a lifetime challenge and may take years to achieve measurable progress.

## Inbreeding

*Inbreeding* results from mating animals together that are more closely related than the average population. Breeds differ in the degree of their relationship, with Arab being more closely related than most others. Related individuals carry more homozygous gene pairs than others—hence the relative ease of getting recessive genes paired. If recessives should prove to be inferior individuals, they can be identified and culled. Dominant individuals may be superior and selected.

The closer the relationship, the faster the progress, but there is also more danger of uncovering lethals and "genetic trash" that may render the animal worthless. Also, close inbreeding, e.g., between full brother and sister or between parent and offspring, results in loss of vigor in early life that may substantially reduce viability. For this reason, most breeders avoid close matings.

## Linebreeding

Linebreeding is a form of inbreeding, but it maintains a high degree of relationship to one outstanding ancestor without the often drastic consequences of inbreeding. One can actually concentrate 50 percent of a great-grandsire's inheritance in a foal with only 12.5 percent inbreeding. Most linebreeders mate no closer than half brother–half sister matings from the outstanding parent.

There is little danger of excessive "genetic trash" surfacing by using this method, but one must be absolutely sure the ancestor's blood being concentrated is excellent.

## Outbreeding

Most breeders outbreed: they simply select a stallion within their breed that is unrelated or generations removed from mares in the herd. Outbreeding improves vigor and those traits related to physical fitness. It masks recessive genes by producing heterozygous individuals. These offspring usually look better than they breed because of the number of masked recessive genes they carry and transmit to their offspring, although there are notable exceptions.

## PHYSIOLOGY OF REPRODUCTION

### Mare

The role of the female in reproduction is to supply an internal and external environment for the new life in addition to supplying half of its genetic material. Because of this double role, complex hormonal actions and interactions require near perfect cooperation from other body systems. When adverse conditions affect other systems, the reproductive mechanism may also be affected and may not function properly until the related condition is corrected. Even under conditions of apparent good health and care, wide variations in reproductive behavior in mares are the rule rather than the exception.

REPRODUCTIVE ORGANS OF THE MARE   The *ovaries* produce eggs that unite with the sperm to begin the new individual. They also secrete the hormone estrogen, which induces heat (estrus) and produces other hormones that condition the reproductive tract for implantation and maintenance of the fetus (Figure 10-3).

The *Fallopian tubes* are the customary site of fertilization of the ovum (egg) by the sperm, and serve as a connecting link between the ovary and uterus.

The *uterus* consists of a *body, cervix,* and two *horns,* one of which receives the fertilized ovum for development.

The *vagina* receives the sperm during mating and functions as a passageway during parturition.

THE REPRODUCTIVE CYCLE   The mare is a seasonally polyestrous breeder. *Polyestrous* means that the mare has four reproductive heat periods during

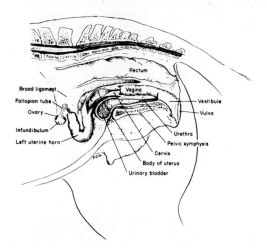

FIGURE 10-3   Reproductive organs of the mare. [*Drawn by P. G. Garrett, from M. Bradley, 1978.*]

the season. The peak of breeding efficiency coincides with the longest day of the year, or June 21, and the anestrus or quiescent season of the cycle coincides with December 21, the shortest day of the year. Most mares do not come into heat at this time.

Hormones, activated by increased daylight, improved nutrition (from more abundant forages), and warmer temperatures control the estrus cycle. All the hormone activators are associated with spring. Upon stimulation, the pituitary gland, located at the base of the brain, secretes the follicle-stimulating hormone (FSH), which travels to the ovaries via the blood system to stimulate development of an egg follicle (proestrus phase). The follicle itself in turn secretes estrogen, which prepares the reproductive tract for mating and affects behavior and receptivity of the mare for breeding. Estrogen also acts on the pituitary to inhibit further FSH release (which would stimulate another egg to ripen) during the estrus phase.

The egg is released during the very last part of the estrus phase, which usually lasts 5 days and is the period during which the mare will accept a stallion.

Continuing estrogen secretion after ovulation causes the production of the luteinizing hormone (LH). LH in turn stimulates the formation of the corpus luteum (yellow body) at that place on the ovary where the egg was released. This corpus luteum functions during the metestrus phase, secreting progesterone to prevent the maturing of new follicles.

If the egg is fertilized by a sperm, pregnancy follows. The corpus luteum is maintained and continues to secrete progesterone, which maintains the pregnancy.

After about 2 weeks, if no embryo is present in the uterus, the uterine endometrium (lining) then secretes the hormone prostaglandin which destroys the corpus luteum. This causes a reduction of progesterone and allows FSH levels to rise again and repeat the cycle.

This very complex process is absent or erratic in most open mares in winter, tending to stabilize near mid-June. Even at the peak of the breeding season the only consistency about cycles is their inconsistency.

The results of research by Andrews and McKenzie in 2 seasons with 35 light mares (grade Thoroughbreds) are given in Table 10-3.

In addition, about 15 percent of the mares showed *split estrus*, characterized by an initial heat period of 1 day or more followed by 1 or 2 days of a nonreceptive period, then a subsequent return to heat for 1 or more days, at which time ovulation occurred.

*Silent heat* was identified in about 5 percent of the mares that were nonreceptive to the regular teasing stallion.

CONTROLLING THE ESTRUS CYCLE    Man has constantly tried to rearrange the heat cycle of the mare. Show and racing classes are based on the calendar year—therefore, the nearer January 1 the foal is born the larger it will be

TABLE 10-3   VARIETIES IN REPRODUCTIVE CYCLE

|  | Range, days | Average, days |
|---|---|---|
| Duration of estrus (heat) | 1–37 | 5.3 |
| Appearance of foal heat* | 2–30 | 11.4 |
| Length of cycle | 13–37 | 22.0 |
| Length of interestrous period | 5–33 | 16.0 |

*Thirty-three mares observed. (Foal heat is the estrus cycle occurring 2–18 days after foaling.)
SOURCE: Frederick N. Andrews and Fred F. McKenzie, "Estrus, Ovulation, and Related Phenomena in the Mare," *Missouri Agricultural Experiment Station Research Bulletin* 329, May 1941.

and the more successful it is expected to be in shows and racing. To foal near January 1, the mare must be bred about February 1, a condition contrary to its natural heat cycle.

Natural and chemical persuasion has been used extensively in attempts to reverse normal heat cycles. Mares have been moved from one continent to another to take advantage of light, nutrition, and sunshine in an attempt to have them produce foals near January 1 on their original continent. Artificial light, heat, and improved nutrition are furnished to stimulate summer conditions. All of these have some beneficial effects, but are not always dependable or very profitable.

More recently chemical control with hormones has shown promise. These control techniques require synchronizing ovulation with estrus or heat to successfully inseminate or naturally breed the mare. If ovulation and heat can be synchronized, one mating of the mare, near ovulation, should result in a high settling percentage. Such a procedure would save endless labor in teasing, palpation, record keeping, and other chores commonly required by normal breeding. Colorado researchers have used two hormones to achieve this goal—human chorionic gonadotropin (HCG) an ovulation-inducing hormone, and prostaglandin, an estrus-inducing hormone.[1] In general, their results showed a shorter breeding season, fewer services, and more mares foaled with the hormone treatment. However, no attempt was made to advance the breeding season toward January 1. Each year progress is made in hormone treatment, and it is likely to continue. However, mares must be cycling normally before hormone treatment can be effective. At this time the major goal of advancing the peak of the breeding season to near February 1 remains elusive.

[1] J. L. Voss and R. W. Pickett, "Reproductive Management of the Broodmare," *Colorado State University Experiment Station and Animal Reproduction Lab General Series* 961, November 1976.

PRACTICAL BREEDING PRACTICES    Mares should be 3 years old and in good condition at the time of breeding. Ideally, they are bred the day the egg is released from the ovary. Knowing the day of release is a problem. We have already seen that heat may extend to 37 days, may come as a split cycle, or may be silent.

Ovulation usually occurs about 24 hours before cessation of visible signs of heat. Since neither the egg nor spermatozoa live long at body temperature, time of breeding relative to egg release is critical. It is little wonder that low settling percentages result from the practice of "noticing signs of heat," taking the mare to the stallion, and returning her to pasture for the rest of the season. Experienced veterinarians can predict date of ovulation quite accurately by daily palpation of the ovaries, and breeding can be synchronized with release of the egg.

Serious horse breeding involves breeding the mare daily or at least every other day until heat ceases, followed by regular and frequent teasing for at least two heat periods (45 days). Boarding the mare at the farm of the stallion owner, or pasture mating is preferred.

Mares with silent estrus must be identified by physical examination and bred by artificial insemination when possible. In such cases, settling percentages may be quite satisfactory.

Older mares and those that are diseased require special diagnosis and treatment. Sometimes they can be restored to normal or partial fertility. Obviously, the expenses incurred dictate restoration only of those of greatest value.

PROBLEMS WITH BROODMARES    Maintaining the health of the mare's reproductive system is one goal of the breeder. Mares in poor condition seldom breed regularly. Adequate feed intake, phosphorus, and vitamin A are necessary. All of these are supplied in abundance in good pasture or in good feed.

Exercise may not be essential for the broodmare, but it does improve the muscle tone of confined mares, and tends to prevent obesity, which can be dangerous in pregnancy.

A number of diseases affect the reproductive tract. Large breeding establishments usually require a health certificate from a veterinarian before breeding an outside mare.

Infection is quite common, especially with older mares. It may be detected by a qualified veterinarian on physical examination or by use of cultures. Some infections can be eliminated by appropriate antibiotic treatment before breeding starts.

Mares that have difficulty at parturition, retain the placenta, or show abnormal discharges should not be bred until the condition is corrected.

Breeding at foal heat is risky. The reproductive tract has not had time to return to normal, opportunity for infection is increased, and settling percentage is lowered. Andrews and McKenzie noted more than a 50 percent decrease in conception rate with mares bred at foal heat as compared with those bred at the second or later heat periods after foaling.

## Stallions

The stallion must deliver healthy spermatozoa into the vagina of the mare at time of service. He should have enough libido or sex drive to service frequently, and should be able to sustain production of healthy spermatozoa throughout a concentrated breeding season.

THE REPRODUCTIVE SYSTEM OF THE STALLION   The male reproductive system consists of two *testes*, three accessory *sex glands*, and a series of *tubules* through which spermatozoa are transported to the female reproductive tract (Figure 10-4).

Spermatozoa are produced in small, coiled seminiferous tubules in the testes that can be extended 400 to 500 feet in length. Since these developing cells cannot live at body temperature, heat regulation of the testes is critical. Scrotal muscles contract and expand as temperatures change, thereby regulating the temperature of the testes. Ridgeling, or cryptorchid, horses are sterile in the testis maintained in the too-warm body cavity, but are fertile in the suspended testis. Since this condition is hereditary, such a horse should not be bred. Castration of a cryptorchid horse is usually a serious operation.

The accessory sex glands are the *seminal vesicles, prostate gland,* and *Cowper's gland.* These furnish alkaline fluid secretions to transport and neutralize the urethra. Spermatozoa are transported from the epididymis

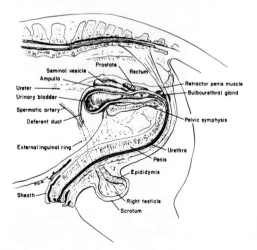

FIGURE 10-4   Reproductive organs of the stallion. [*Drawn by P. G. Garrett, from M. Bradley, 1978.*]

through the urethra, which terminates at the end of the male genitalia, the *glans penis.*

The volume of semen per ejaculate in stallions is 60 to 300 milliliters. The total number of spermatozoa in the ejaculate is about 6 billion, and the average number of spermatozoa per milliliter is 60,000.

The lifetime of the sperm in the mare's tract is from 24 to 48 hours. Only in highly irregular or exceptional cases can the sperm live longer. Sperm have been found in the Fallopian tubes 15 to 18 minutes after coitus, but the normal time to travel from site of deposit to the Fallopian tubes is 5 to 8 hours. The average lifetime of the egg is also only 5 to 8 hours.

Because of the mare's long but uncertain estrous cycle and the short life span of the spermatozoa and egg, it is not uncommon to have a lower than 50 percent conception rate among horses.

## CARE AND USE OF A HEALTHY STALLION

*Breeding rates.* Yearlings should not be depended upon for breeding. Two-year-olds may settle 10 mares, three-year-olds may settle 30 mares, and mature stallions 50 mares when hand-mated. About half this number can be pasture-mated. A short breeding season will reduce the number, and sexual individuality of the stallion will greatly affect its siring ability. Some stallions routinely breed 100 mares per year in a long breeding season.

*Feeding and management.* The breeding stallion should be fed like a horse at hard work. An estimate is 1½ pounds of grain and 1 pound of hay per 100 pounds of body weight. If the stallion is worked hard under saddle, more feed will be required. Because a stallion is easily distracted, a ration high in palatability may be necessary for some stallions to get adequate nutrition.

Regular exercise usually results in increased vigor (libido) and fertility; inactivity and obesity often reduce it.

Regular grazing, even for short periods of time, is recommended.

For safety's sake, fences should be strong and tall when stallions are grazed loose, and mares should not be in adjoining pastures unless extremely tall, safe fences are used.

## MANAGING BROODMARES

Mares can be classified into three types—maiden mares, producing mares, and barren mares. Mares having regular heat cycles are considerably easier to settle. If not, a number of breedings are necessary, involving much time and labor. Generally speaking, stud farms that breed a number of outside mares find that settling percentages increase with the advance of the breeding season. There is a tendency to breed too early in order to approach January 1 with the birth of the offspring, also resulting in low fertility. Late seasons (extension of winter into spring) will affect heat cycles in general, retarding normal cycling and resulting in later birth of the majority of foals.

*Maiden mares* in healthy condition usually settle easily. They require considerably more time and patience in the breeding process because of fear, anxiety, and difficulty in adjusting to new surroundings when sent out to a stallion. However, most stud handlers prefer to breed them because of their high settling percentages.

*Producing mares* are those nursing foals. Since they are proven breeders, the owner's main objective is to provide a nutritional plane adequate to supply energy for the production of milk and to bring the mare back into heat. When the plane of nutrition is low, nursing mares do not recycle. This is especially true of first-foal mares.

For this reason there is a trend to "flush" (increase the level of nutrition) such mares before rebreeding. If the foal comes in the middle of the grazing season, the mare is automatically flushed on good pasture. If not, soon after foaling the grain ration can be increased from 5 to 6 pounds to 10 to 12 pounds daily. If foal heat is skipped, the feeder has time to slowly increase grain feeding 28 to 30 days after the foal is born. Of course if the mare is obese, she is likely to have trouble foaling and should not be flushed for rebreeding.

The *barren mare* is the biggest challenge. If such a mare is cycling normally and was not bred the previous year, she may settle readily. If there was a problem the prior year, it will probably remain unless steps were taken months ahead of the breeding season to correct it. Barren mares should be watched in the fall prior to the breeding season and a record kept of their heat cycles. A veterinarian should be called upon to check the reproductive track for infections. The veterinarian may identify organisms that respond to antibiotic treatment and get the mare healthy without prolonged infection.

Older mares tend to have an abnormal angle of the vulva, or a recessed anus. This results from a relaxing of the muscles. It is common to breeds that have level croups, such as Thoroughbreds. Such conditions cause *pneumovagina*, or air in the vagina, which in turn gives rise to *chronic vaginitis*, an infection greatly decreasing conception rate. In most cases the infection can be cleared prior to breeding. Suturing the vagina (known as Caslick's operation)—closing the upper half of the vulva—after breeding will greatly reduce the chance of abortion from new infections.

*Cervical atresia*, or closure, is a result of healing of tears of the cervix during foaling, and is a common cause of infertility. The condition may be hard to correct with surgery and requires a lot of time for healing when it is corrected. The surgery is usually performed only on valuable mares.

*Rectovaginal fistula* results from difficult births. The foal's hoof rup-

tures or penetrates through the roof of the vagina into the rectum. These
tears can be treated rather easily surgically to prevent fecal material from
passing into the vagina and causing infection.

It is important with a *barren mare* to start examination and treatment
early. The mare should be on a good plane of nutrition because infections
heal slowly under stress conditions. The mare's progress should be monitored throughout the breeding season by constant teasing and adequate
breeding, either artificially or, when possible, naturally.

## Heat Detection

In the wild state or in pasture-mating the stallion detects heat very efficiently
and breeds the mare at the appropriate time of ovulation. However, heat
detection is quite another challenge to the person who owns one mare and
wishes to breed it or to the stud man who must detect heat in the stable of
mares that come to his breeding service. Indications of heat include *relaxation of the external genitals, frequent urination, mucus discharge*, and an
obvious *desire for male company*. Single mares may walk the fence and look
down the road as if they expect another horse to appear. If there is another
horse near, ready mares may assume the breeding stance—the characteristic
raised tail, hind legs spread apart, and relaxed pelvis. In the presence of
another horse they urinate frequently, and eversion of the clitoris, commonly referred to as *winking*, is frequently observed. However, the best way
to detect heat is with a teaser stallion.

TEASING   Large breeding establishments have a teaser stallion in addition to the stallions they breed with. Most teasers are of modest economic
value, but must be aggressive without being difficult to handle and manage. Some establishments use Shetland pony stallions as teasers.

When mares are teased, safe equipment for both horses and handlers
should be used. There are many teasing stalls and breeding stocks used in
the teasing and breeding process. Figure 10-5 shows a teasing stall. The main
purpose of a teasing stall is to keep the stallion and mare separated without
injury to them or their handlers. There is usually a 3-foot-wide aisle, approximately 3½ feet tall, allowing the stallion to nuzzle the head and upper
body of the mare to detect her response. Hard hats worn by the handlers decrease the probability of a serious accident. With the mare in place, the
handler approaches slowly with a well-mannered teaser. Mares not in heat
will kick and show great desire to keep the stallion away or to escape. If in
heat, the mare will respond as described previously.

With most mares, detection of heat by a teaser stallion is very simple,
but some exhibit negative behavior most of the time, with very few signs
of receptivity. Reading the response of the mare and the attitude of a teaser
stallion is an art developed to a very high degree by some stud handlers.

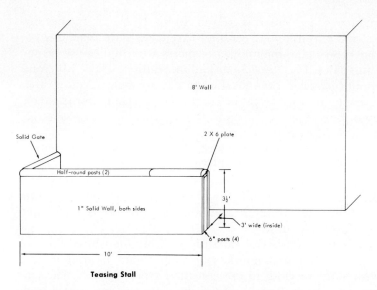

8' Wall

Solid Gate

2 X 6 plate

Half-round posts (2)

1" Solid Wall, both sides

3½'

3' wide (inside)

6" posts (4)

10'

**Teasing Stall**

FIGURE 10-5  Teasing stalls vary on most stud farms. They should be strong, safe for both horses and handlers, and conveniently located. [*From M. Bradley, 1978.*]

Such persons keep a detailed record of the behavior of the mare either in their mind or on paper, and can detect even the smallest changes in attitude.

Large numbers of loose mares can be teased together. They may be driven into a 3-foot-wide chute having solid doors between each mare. The teaser stallion is brought to them and checks each one by going down the line. Group teasing is a very great time-saver where an owner or rancher is breeding a large number of mares by hand mating.

In another teasing procedure the teaser is led out in the pasture to check loose mares, but this procedure is very dangerous to both handler and teaser. There is always the possibility of the teaser escaping and breeding a mare unless the stallion wears a blanket secured around its body to prevent such an occurrence. Vasectomy prevents this possibility, and vasectomized stallions are becoming more popular as teasers.

Finally, a cage for the teaser stallion may be made, giving interested mares safe access to it. Many breeders keep their stallions separated from the herd of mares by a tall corral fence. Mares in heat often will seek out the stallion.

To maintain aggressiveness in teasers, they should be mated occasionally to grade or inexpensive mares.

## Breeding Procedure

There are two general ways of mating horses: (1) naturally, by pasture mating, and (2) by hand mating.

Pasture mating reduces labor, is convenient for the owner, catches shy-breeding mares, and affords a high settling percentage. Pasture mating has the disadvantage of reducing the number of mares a stallion can serve, and obscures breeding dates. There is some risk to the stallion. Those who must be shown without blemishes cannot safely be pasture-mated. Young studs to be used in pasture mating should be taught the procedure by an old experienced mare in heat. They will then learn that when they are too rough, their progress is slowed by mare resistance.

Most expensive horses are hand-mated; that is, the mare is restrained to prevent injury to the stallion while the stallion is allowed to pursue the breeding process under control of handlers. The mare is restrained in a breeding stock or in breeding hobbles (Figure 10-6). This prevents the mare from seriously kicking the stallion. In addition one front foot is often raised and a twitch applied to the nose.

Breeding sanitation consists of carefully washing the genital areas of both the mare and stallion with a mild soap solution and binding the tail of the mare with gauze or cloth to prevent interference of hairs. The stallion should approach from directly behind the mare and receive aid from the handler who guides the stallion's penis into the vulva. It is especially important from a safety standpoint not to have a rearing, striking stallion during this process.

After ejaculation the stallion will usually flag his tail (switch it up

FIGURE 10-6   Safety for the stallion is essential for his survival when hand-mating. Hobbles on the mare reduce the risk of his getting seriously kicked. [*From M. Bradley, 1978.*]

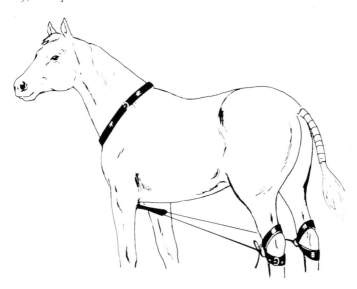

and down) before dismounting. Some stallions will dismount before they ejaculate. If in doubt, pressure on the urethra can surface semen at its end before the postbreeding, washing, and disinfecting process.

Finally, a good way to get a high settling percentage is to hand-mate the mares until near the end of the breeding season, and then turn the stallion out with them to identify and pasture-mate shy breeders and those that may have returned to heat.

## Care of Pregnant Mares

After the breeding season mares should be checked to determine which ones are safely in foal. This is usually done 45 days after breeding by a competent veterinarian. Those not in foal can either be rebred or separated from the pregnant mares who will require a different management regime.

NUTRITION   The pregnant mare should be fed as an idle horse during *the first two-thirds of pregnancy* (Chapter 8). Now is the time to regulate condition—not to create obesity or to deplete body stores of essential nutrients by malnutrition. Ideally, mares should be permitted to graze good pasture, be fed minerals free-choice, offered shade, and kept free of parasites during this early phase of pregnancy.

Obviously, conditions do not always afford these opportunities. Confined mares need regular exercise and must be supplied essential nutrients. Their nutrient needs are not different in *early pregnancy* than they would be if not pregnant. A foal at birth weighs 60 to 100 pounds, most of which is water. Since most of the foal's development comes during late pregnancy, the mare has few additional nutritional needs until then.

However, the breeder is anxious to have the mare enter late pregnancy with no lost body stores of nutrients. Feeding in *late pregnancy* requires sufficient nutrients to maintain the physical condition of the mare and supply those used by the developing fetus and accompanying membranes.

The nutrient requirements for the mare in late pregnancy are a minimum 10 percent crude protein, with 0.45 percent calcium and 0.30 percent phosphorus (see Table 12-1).

As the fetus develops in size, space for additional feed decreases within the mare. The mare should have access to feed most of the time and should be fed a more concentrated diet of grain rather than all coarse roughages. As foaling time approaches, the feeding program should include a laxative feed such as bran, high-protein feed, or lush pasture.

MANAGEMENT   During early pregnancy extra space is not needed by mares. As they advance in term they tend to become more hostile to each other and need more privacy. Since they are more awkward in their movements, they should not be subjected to stress caused by being chased, crowded, kicked, or pursued by other mares. It may become necessary to separate timid mares from a large herd. If the mares are kept crowded, abortion from being kicked is a very real possibility. Mares in heavy pregnancy should not be ridden hard, nor should they be required to negotiate deep mud, soft sand, and other areas of insecure or slick footing. They need adequate room, protective shelter, and individual areas they can retire to for relaxation. Confinement should be in individual or large lots, and foaling should occur alone in a clean pasture or in a foaling stall.

## Foaling

Mares should be given privacy when foaling. The mare is expected to foal approximately 344 days after the last service. However, terms vary as much as 30 days, depending upon the individual mare. If a mare has a long gestation, e.g., 1 year, she is liable to have long gestations in future pregnancies. Although a level pasture without obstacles that the foal might wander into may be a good place to foal, competition from other animals and horses should be limited or eliminated. Some barren mares, and even some geldings, will annoy the new mother by trying to claim the offspring, causing her or another horse to hurt the foal in the scuffle. For this reason, a private pasture or other area is desirable. However, this should not be so far removed from the herd that it causes the expectant mother nervousness or anxiety. It is best to get the mare accustomed to her foaling area 2 weeks to a month prior to the end of pregnancy.

Expensive horses confined on purebred establishments foal in box-stalls that have been sanitized and prepared for them. They are often observed through closed circuit television or one-way windows by veterinarians who must be present during foaling. If a mare knows she is being watched, she will put off giving birth as long as possible.

SIGNS OF FOALING   There is about as much variation in signs of foaling in mares as in signs of heat cycles. Two to four weeks prior to term, the udder of most mares will begin to enlarge; this condition may not appear until a few days prior to foaling in some mares and may be developed extensively in others. Good milk-producing mares under good nutritional conditions usually show a lot of udder development a week or more prior to foaling. The teats may be engorged with a watery liquid just prior to foaling, or they may be filled with colostrum that drips or streams. Some excellent milking mares may actually lose enough colostrum prior to foaling to greatly reduce the antibodies badly needed by the foal.

Mares usually show relaxation of the muscles around the anus, vulva, and over the rump and croup. As foaling time approaches, there may be visible uterine contractions (Figures 10-7 to 10-21). The mare may look at her sides as if she has colic and lie down and rise often. The mare may sweat, walk the stall, paw, and show visible signs of annoyance and a desire to be alone. Such signs may be very brief, or they may extend over a period of a few hours.

Then the water bag breaks, and 2 to 5 gallons of water are expelled. The mare may lie down and give birth to the foal immediately by exerting tremendous contraction pressure, or she may begin to foal first with a contraction or two and then rise and lie down again before completing the process. Usually, foaling comes very quickly and almost always successfully.

The tendency on the part of the owner lucky enough to see the event is to try to hurry to give help when indeed things are progressing normally. First to appear are the front feet of the foal, with the nose following closely between the cannons.

On rare occasions foals have been born safely with breech presentations. A breech birth is easy to detect because of the direction the feet are pointing when the hind feet appear. The breech foal should be promptly helped through the birth canal; otherwise it will suffocate if the umbilical cord is broken or closed off from pressure.

If a mare is having a difficult birth, a veterinarian should be called although the veterinarian may not arrive in time to save the life of the foal. Because of the tremendous pressure of contractions an abnormal birth or

FIGURE 10-7   A restless mare just prior to foaling. She lies down, rises, sweats, appears uncomfortable, and turns her head to the side (also a symptom of colic). Muscles on the croup are relaxed, the tail is elevated, and milk may be dripping from the udder. [*All photographs in foaling sequence 10-7 to 10-21 courtesy of the American Morgan Horse Association, Inc.*]

FIGURE 10-8   Strong uterine contractions have initiated the foaling process by expelling a portion of the placenta. Many mares will complete foaling approximately 10 minutes from this point. If over 30 minutes are required, the mare may need professional help.

FIGURE 10-9   Front feet and nose of foal have appeared in normal position. Some ·mares will rise at this point, but most will complete foaling lying in position.

FIGURE 10-10   The emerging foal has broken the placenta with a front foot but has not freed its head and initiated respiration.

FIGURE 10-11   The birth process is almost complete, but the head is still covered with the placenta. Weak foals die at this point unless they are helped or they can muster enough strength to free themselves.

FIGURE 10-12 The foal has freed its head from the placenta and has initiated breathing.

FIGURE 10-13 The mare nuzzles the foal in an attempt to free him and dry him off. She should expel the placenta ½ to 2 hours postpartum. If not, infection is a real hazard without a veterinarian's attention.

FIGURE 10-14     The alert foal will soon attempt to rise while the mother rests in the background.


FIGURE 10-15     Strong foals struggle to rise 10 to 30 minutes after birth. Small foals appear to accomplish standing sooner than large ones; however, most stand within 30 minutes.

FIGURE 10-16 Unable to succeed in the normal way, the foal rises behind first like a member of the ass family instead of in front like a horse . . . but it worked!

FIGURE 10-17 After rising the foal may remain in this position for several minutes before attempting to move.

FIGURE 10-18   The foal seeks to find the teat, a natural instinct, while the mother continues to dry him off.

FIGURE 10-19   Not all mares are this affectionate. Some will disclaim their foals and harm them unless prevented from doing so by an attendant.

**FIGURE 10-20** Nursing colostrum (first milk) is essential to the foal's life because colostrum contains antibodies that fight or ward off infection.

**FIGURE 10-21** Foals a few hours old will run beside their dams if necessary and will nibble grass with them when only a few days old.

malpresentation must be corrected very soon or the fetal legs may be pushed through the uterine, vaginal, or rectal walls.

After foaling the mare will often lie in a recumbent position with the umbilical cord still attached to the placenta. This phase is important because the foal may receive up to a liter of oxygen-rich blood from the mare during this period. The umbilical cord should not be cut by the attendant, but should be allowed to rupture when the mare stands. It usually severs naturally a few inches from the abdominal wall of the foal.

As soon as the foal is born, make sure that it is breathing and has none of the fetal membrane obstructing its nostrils. If not breathing, artificial respiration may well start the process and save the foal's life. Rubbing the body with a cloth and drying it off often aids sluggish respiration. The stump of the naval cord should be dipped in a 10 percent iodine solution as soon as feasible to reduce the possibility of infection through this opening.

*Navel ill* is a serious foal disease that may result from lack of sanitation at birth. Whether to administer 5 milliliters of combiotic to the newborn foal is an option of the owner. This process is controversial but is practiced by most veterinarians as a preventive measure against digestive upsets. Most agree that administration of tetanus antitoxin to mare and foal is good routine practice. However, if the mare has been given a tetanus booster shot a month prior to foaling, it will have sufficient antibodies to protect both itself and foal during early postpartum.

After the foal has been dried off, treated with tincture of iodine and administered the necessary shots, it will try to stand—within about thirty minutes. If the mare does not mind, the foal can be helped to get to its feet.

Many handlers tend to hurry the foal to its feet to nurse. If the foal has shown no indication of nursing after 2 or 3 hours, it should be pointed in the direction of the udder. Young mares are sometimes sore and worn out and will not allow a newborn foal to nurse immediately without being restrained. It is important that the foal get colostrum reasonably soon; its digestive tract is conditioned to receive the large dose of colostrum antibodies, but this condition changes after the first 36 hours. Most foals will learn to nurse quickly. If the attendant hurries the process, trying to place the foal's head on the teat, time may actually be lost.

The placenta is expelled by the mare from 20 minutes to 2 hours after foaling. If it has not been released by this time, the mare may need medical attention, for infection is a very likely possibility. When the placenta is passed, it must be spread out on the ground to see that all of it is present. If even the smallest portion is retained, the mare will surely become infected and suffer an extended period of infertility. For this reason, the placenta should be carefully saved for the veterinarian's inspection.

The foal's yellow fecal excrement should pass within 4 to 8 hours. This *meconium* or first droppings may be hard, creating constipation. It is important to be sure the foal does not retain the meconium. If constipated, the foal will persist in straining with elevated tail. An enema of 1 or 2 quarts of warm soapy water given at frequent intervals will help the yellow feces pass.

MILK PRODUCTION   Some mares foal with little or no milk. This can be anticipated by milking the mare the day before foaling and soon after foaling. However, take precautions not to waste colostrum in checking the milking ability of the mare. If the mare has little milk, the foal will nurse often or almost constantly and will dehydrate and lose condition rapidly, resulting in onset of disease or death within a few days. In the central part of the country where mares have been grazed on fescue pasture, *dry milk syndrome* is a very common condition. Treatment consists of sharply increasing the grain in the mare's ration, even at the risk of laminitis or founder. Three feeds of 3 to 5 pounds of grain daily may be indicated.

Occasionally foals are orphaned. If at all possible, transfer them to another mare with colostrum, or feed them colostrum that has been refrigerated for that purpose. Veterinary clinics may have colostrum available for such an eventuality. Raising an orphan foal is a high-labor, low-return enterprise, although some foals are well worth the effort. Orphan foals have been raised in many ways. Some have been fed cow's milk after receiving mare's colostrum and some have nursed goats, but perhaps the best way is to go to a reliable commercial feed company that has an equine milk substitute available with directions for its use.

## Nutrition and Care of Mare and Young Foal

After the mare has passed the placenta and the foal is feeding and appears healthy and normal, the mare may be turned out to pasture with other horses or may be individually cared for for a week to 10 days. Be sure the mare is milking well. About the third day begin to increase the mare's grain ration.

A milking mare must consume an enormous amount of calories, protein, calcium, and phosphorus to meet the needs of her own body for rebreeding and to supply milk for the fast-growing foal.

During the first 3 months of lactation the mare requires 12.5 percent crude protein, with 0.45 percent calcium and 0.30 percent phosphorus. From the fourth month through weaning, when the foal is beginning to consume more and more creep feed, these requirements drop only slightly to 11 percent crude protein, 0.40 percent calcium, and 0.25 percent phosphorus.

If the mare is eating good grass pasture, these requirements will be supplied. However, few mares can get enough grazing to maximize milk production. If the mare is in dry lot, she should be fed free-choice quality legume hay and 10 to 12 pounds of grain. If fed nonlegume hay, use 12 to

TABLE 10-4    GRAIN MIXTURE FOR
LACTATING MARES*
(Dry-matter basis)

| Feedstuffs | Amount, lb |
|---|---|
| Oats | 485 |
| Corn | 485 |
| Soybean meal | 30 |
| Limestone | 12 |

*Plus vitamins A, D, and E to furnish
5000 IU of A per pound of feed.

14 percent crude protein grain ration. The grain mixture listed in Table 10-4 is a good example.

When the foal is about a week old, a creep should be made that the foal can enter without competition from its mother to eat grain and hay as it wishes. It is important that this creep be located where the mare spends a lot of time. The very best alfalfa or legume hay will attract the foal. A creep grain ration, as discussed in Chapter 9, should be provided. Grain for foals should always be fresh (Figure 10-22). Mare and foal should be halterless when running loose because the foal can rear and get its leg caught in the mare's halter or get its foot caught in its own halter.

FIGURE 10-22    Grain should be offered to foals from a creep from 1 week of age through weaning. Creeps should be located near where mares congregate, such as areas of shade and water. [Photograph by Duane Dailey.]

The foal should be taught to be handled and to tie and lead at an early age. Some owners catch foals when they are 3 or 4 days old. A foal soon learns that it will not be hurt and readily submits to handling. Indeed, scratching the neck and back often wins its confidence quickly and causes it to look forward to association with humans. If gentle to catch, the foal will probably be easy to lead. Two handlers can work together, one leading the foal and the other the mare. After getting used to this procedure the foal can be walked away from the mare with a second person trailing behind, or with a rump rope held in the hand of the leading handler. A rump rope is a small rope with a loop in the end large enough to drape over the foal's rump and fall in the stifle area. The other end of the rope is passed through the halter. When the foal stops, a light jerk will be sufficient to start it again.

When foals are tied, the attendant should stay nearby to be sure they are not hurt. Foals are best tied beside the mother with enough space between them to prevent interaction should they try to escape. Some handlers use an inner tube tied against a solid wall about 6 feet high. The bottom of the tube hangs just above the foal's withers, and a 3-foot-long tie is made to reduce the chances that the foal will rear and get its feet over the shank. Should the foal panic and get in trouble, the attendant is always there to promptly untie it. The foal is tied only a little while the first few days. Tying time is gradually extended under observation. These simple lessons are never forgotten, and almost always result in a well-mannered foal that will not try to escape or halter-pull.

Antibodies from the mare are very beneficial to the foal while it nurses, but they do nothing to prevent infestation of internal parasites. Foals are very susceptible to *Strongyles*, ascarids, and other devastating internal parasites. Since manure is the medium whereby such parasites are propagated, the cleaner the facilities, the less parasite infestation. Most foals should be treated every 2 months for these parasites unless they are in very large areas of sparse horse populations. Tests in Pennsylvania showed much improvement in gain of foals treated every 2 months through the first year of their life compared with others that received no treatment (see Chapter 15).

WEANING   Somewhere around the fourth to the sixth week mare's milk production begins to decline. While most people prefer to wean at 4 to 6 months, Tisnick of Ohio has successfully weaned them at 2 months and found no adverse effects. In any case, the foals should be eating 8 to 10 pounds of grain from the creep when weaned. If the foal must first learn to eat during the few days it is trying to adjust to weaning, the likelihood of disease, injury, or other trauma increases.

There are a number of ways foals are weaned. In one system used on many Thoroughbred farms in Kentucky, a number of foals are separated across a safe fence from their dams for part of the day. After a few hours they are returned. This practice may continue 3 to 4 weeks, with the time spent away from the dam increasing. The theory is that this method causes minimum stress. However, there is always the danger that either mother or foal will try to get back together and be injured in the process.

A second method is to remove the mares far enough from the area of the foals for them to be completely out of sight and hearing. With this method mares must often be shipped to a different farm entirely.

A third method is simply to remove the foals from the mares and house them together in a safe stable or paddock. This too requires keeping the mares out of communication distance, but it affords a good way to wean. In any case, the foal should be left with its friends. It should not be separated and confined alone unless absolutely necessary.

FOAL NUTRITION   The nutritional demands of the weaned foal are the most stringent in the life of the horse. It must have quality feeds it will eat and a balanced ration, and must not have high loads of internal parasites.

The new National Research Council nutrient requirements recommend sharp increases in protein, calcium, and phosphorus. To maintain an average daily weight gain of 1.75 pounds, the foal requires a diet of 14.5 percent protein, with 0.60 protein calcium and 0.45 percent phosphorus, in an average daily feed of 11 pounds. Vitamin A content should stay at about 9200 IU (see Table 12-1).

The protein must be of high quality, for the foal's digestive apparatus is not yet functioning at peak performance. The two rations given in Tables 9-2 and 9-3 or a commercial weanling ration from a reliable company should prove satisfactory. Foals must be watched while they eat to see that all are eating and that some are not eating all grain and others all hay. Sometimes foals require separation so that individual tastes can be catered to.

## MANAGING BREEDING STALLIONS

The more natural the environment of the stallion, the more satisfactory a breeder the stallion will be. It may not be practical to graze an expensive stallion on pasture, but it is practical to give it all the exercise it needs. Ideally the stallion will earn his keep by working at any activity other horses are used for on the ranch or farm. Indeed, most stallions should be well-mannered around mares and should not be obtrusive or obnoxious when ridden in groups of horses. Even expensive stallions can use hotwalkers safely with other horses when supervised by a competent attendant.

### Winter Care

After the breeding season, if a stallion will run with mares, it can do so with a compatible pregnant mare. If this is not practical, the stallion can be housed near other horses. The stallion should have doors or windows he can see out of readily, and as much space as possible. Ideally, he should have a large, safe corral with an open shed in it, and be able to come and go of his own free will. Such housing would ensure adequate exercise if there were other horses nearby. The breeding stallion should be fed as an idle horse.

The stallion's feet require care and trimming every 6 to 8 weeks, the same as any other horse. He should not normally be shod unless living in a very rocky area.

The stallion must be watched for colds, coughs, hay allergies, or over-exposure to inclement weather. If other horses run near his paddock he may not be inclined to use the shelter enough and may require forced housing at night.

## Spring Care

As spring approaches, provided that the stallion is not too fat, its feed is increased slightly in time for a heavy breeding season. Beginning in January monitor the semen through collection with an artificial vagina. While semen at this stage of the season may not be as high in sperm count and motility as it will be later, it should meet safe standards of fertility based on a knowledge of the stallion's sperm count, motility, and prior history. The veterinarian can perform this important task.

If at all possible let the horse be exposed to sun, fresh air, grass, and exercise. If the horse is not ridden, an hour daily on a hotwalker will do wonders to get it into condition to adequately breed mares during the breeding season. It will also improve the horse's breeding manners and probably increase settling percentages.

## Care during Breeding Season

The goal for the stallion during the breeding season is high fertility and a controlled but vigorous libido. Horsemen refer to a stallion as a sure breeder if it settles a high percentage of mares at the first opportunity or soon thereafter. Perhaps there is as much variation in fertility in stallions as there is in heat cycles in mares; they often are influenced by the same environmental conditions.

Although there is disagreement as to what values are normal in measuring fertility, four indexes are presently relied on in conjunction with one another: concentration, volume, morphology (examination of sperm for abnormalities), and motility.

The normal *volume* of one ejaculation varies from 60 to 300 ml. Lighter breeds such as Arabs may have a somewhat smaller total volume.

*Concentration* of sperm varies even more greatly—from about 50,000 per ml to 500 million per ml.

*Motility* involves two measures: first, type of movement of sperm, and second, number of motile sperm. A motility of 70 percent is considered normal; that is, 70 percent of the sperm are alive and *moving vigorously.* Very good motility is 90 to 95 percent.

The normal sperm exhibits an oval head, midpiece, and tail. A satisfactory morphological exam should reveal between 70 and 80 percent normal sperm.

A number of conditions seem to affect fertility in stallions. Some of these are: (1) abnormal sperm production (a high number of dead sperm or abnormal heads, midpieces, or tails); (2) periods of sickness of the stallion resulting in high temperature and low fertility; and (3) nutritional factors, either starvation or obesity. Most of these conditions can be corrected with adequate exercise and sound nutrition. Good psychological environment is important, too; recent Colorado studies have shown that studs have psychological hangups, just as mares and humans do.

One of the most exasperating conditions is reduced or complete lack of sexual desire. There seems to be a hereditary connection with this condition; however, most stud handlers feel it is environmental. A horse that works too hard when young may show this tendency. Indeed, if the horse is overworked as a 3-year-old, which can occur if he is bred to a large number of mares in a short breeding season, his libido is likely to decrease.

Rough handlers can often reduce the teasing and breeding effectiveness of a young stallion. The stallion may fear the person who is handling him. If he associates the sex act with pain or punishment, the stallion is likely to give up. This may also result from being kicked by mares. But probably the biggest cause of reduced libido is underexercise and excessive weight—conditions that are easy to correct.

Stallion discipline is an important part of the success of a breeding operation, but it must be achieved with forbearance. Breeding stallions are unusually alert and vigorous. A fearful handler may mistake the natural exuberance and playfulness of the stud for insubordination and become abusive. Such treatment can ruin a good stallion.

## ARTIFICIAL INSEMINATION (AI)

Artificial insemination is the deposition of semen in the mare's reproductive tract by artificial rather than natural means.

Artificial insemination has been used extensively in the improvement of dairy cattle and substantially with some breeds of beef cattle. Theoretically it is an excellent tool for genetic progress because:

1 It concentrates genes of superior individuals by insemination of many mares from a single ejaculate.

2   It reduces the risk of disease.
3   It extends the breeding life of crippled or physically handicapped horses.

Artificial insemination began with horses and has been used extensively in Russia, Japan, and China, but its use in the United States has been limited to large breeding farms as a supplement to natural service.

A survey of breed associations reflects the lukewarm attitude to its use. Some associations require one natural service on the same premises followed by artificial insemination supplementation. Many want no part of it. Some associations fear reduced demand for young stallions and the ease of abuse in record-keeping.

Breeder reluctance to embrace artificial insemination was clearly voiced by The Jockey Club when artificial insemination was disallowed in the breeding season of Thoroughbreds in 1978 to control the venereal disease, Contagious Equine Metritis (CEM).

Despite some commercial claims to the contrary, successful freezing and storage of semen has not been achieved to a satisfactory degree. Currently fresh semen extended with various buffers has given higher settling percentages than frozen semen.

## Collection Equipment and Procedure

The Fujihira model artificial vagina is used by many researchers and breeders to collect semen. It consists of an outer frame with inner rubber liner and collection bulb. Warm water (42 to 44°C) fills the space between inner liner and outer frame to stimulate vaginal temperature and pressure. A sterile lubricating jelly is applied to the liner, and a rubber collection bag is placed over the end. The same safety precautions and most of the other procedures used in natural service are employed in semen collection.

A mare in natural or hormonally induced estrus excites the stallion. He is allowed to mount while an attendant directs his penis into the artificial vagina; there pressure is applied to the glans penis when he begins to thrust. If the water pressure or temperature is incorrect the stallion will dismount without ejaculation. Adjustment of the apparatus usually corrects the problem.

Workers at Colorado State University use an estrus mare to prepare the stallion, then stand the mare beside a wooden dummy that trained stallions mount for collection—reducing risk to both stallion and mare.

Kept at a constant temperature of 102 to 105°F, semen is either extended with a diluent or used raw for insemination.

## Insemination Procedure

Ten to twenty-five milliliters of (extended) semen are inserted into the cervix through the vagina with a Chambers catheter. A speculum or hollow tube is first carefully inserted into the vagina which is illuminated by a small battery light so that the cervix can be clearly seen. The semen-containing catheter is inserted as far into the cervix as possible and its contents ejected.

Satisfactory collection and insemination require a technician trained in the art and psychology of collecting from the stallion, preparing and extending the semen, and sanitary handling and inseminating of the mare.

It is an expensive process. Therefore, its use is largely limited to large breeding studs. After one natural service, mares are inseminated daily or every other day until cessation of estrus. Artificial insemination undoubtedly extends the use of a valuable sire and results in above-average settling percentages in mares.

## BIBLIOGRAPHY

Evans, J. Warren, Anthony Borton, Harold E. Hintz, and L. Dale Van Vleck: *The Horse*, Freeman, San Francisco, 1977.

Hamilton, Samantha: "When One and One Make Three," *Equus*, no. 3, January 1978, pp. 21–27.

Lasley, John F., *Genetics of Livestock Improvement*, Prentice-Hall, Englewood Cliffs, N.J., 1972.

Willis, Larryann C.: *The Horse-Breeding Farm*, Barnes, Cranberry, N.J., 1973.

# THE BASICS OF HORSE NUTRITION

T he relatively simple-looking feeds we offer horses are composed of complex chemical substances that must undergo dramatic changes before the horse can use them. *Digestion* is the process of mechanical and chemical breakdown of food into simple chemical structures that are mostly soluble in water and readily absorbed through the mucus membranes that line the intestinal tract. Proteins are broken down into amino acids and carbohydrates into simple sugars and volatile fatty acids.

## THE DIGESTIVE SYSTEM

The digestive system of the horse is quite unique. It is neither ruminant (four stomachs like cattle) nor nonruminant (one stomach like pigs and humans), but it performs a special combination of the functions of each. It has a relatively small but efficient stomach for grain utilization like the pigs, and a large cecum and colon for roughage utilization, aided by microor-

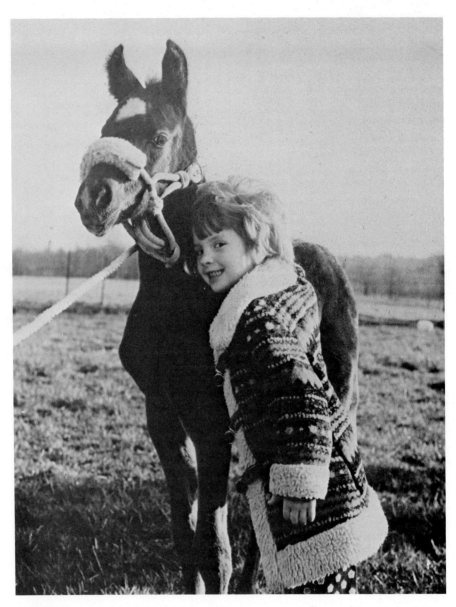

FIGURE 11-1   Good health and long life are greatly influenced by the food these youngsters will eat before they reach maturity. They must consume appropriate amounts of protein and minerals to develop bone and muscle to last a lifetime. [*Courtesy of Jim Ritchie, Tipton, Mo.*]

ganisms for energy and B vitamin production, thus functioning somewhat like the rumen of cattle (Figures 11-2 and 11-3).

The purpose of the digestive system of the horse, like that of cattle and pigs, is to process edibles as efficiently as possible into their component nutrients for absorption and utilization by the body. Horses meet their daily nutrient requirements by eating an unbelievable variety of feeds. Indeed, the mitochondria present in all cells, which produce energy from the simple sugars that are the end products of digestion, could care less what the original source of these sugars was. The sugars could have resulted form the digestion of oats, grass, an apple, or even bark from a tree.

The *alimentary canal* (digestive system) is a hollow tube more than 100 feet long starting at the mouth and ending at the anus. This muscular tube is looped on itself many times and varies in size from approximately 1 inch in diameter at the small intestine to 8 inches in diameter at the cecum and large colon. Its component parts are the mouth, pharynx, esophagus, stomach, small intestine, large intestine (divided into cecum, ventral and dorsal colons, transverse colon, small colon, and rectum), and anus. The alimentary tract, with the help of its accessory organs—the teeth, tongue, salivary glands, liver, and pancreas—prepares food for absorption and rejects and eliminates the residue.

Few foods horses eat come in simple, soluble form, such as glucose, for easy consumption and digestion. Most require substantial change by mechanical, secretory, chemical, and microbiological action.

Mechanical actions are mastication or chewing, deglutition or swallowing, intestinal movements, and defecation or elimination of residue.

FIGURE 11-2   Schematic sketch of the digestive system of the horse showing the relative size and capacity of each component part. [*Frederik Harper*, Horse Science, *National 4-H Service Council, Chicago, 1965, p. 23.*]

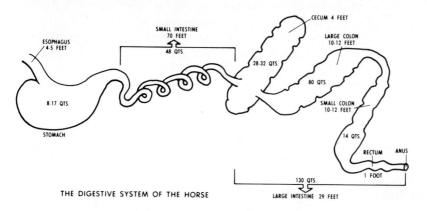

ESOPHAGUS
4-5 FEET

SMALL INTESTINE
70 FEET
48 QTS.

CECUM 4 FEET

LARGE COLON
10-12 FEET

28-32 QTS.

80 QTS.

8-17 QTS.

STOMACH

SMALL COLON
10-12 FEET

14 QTS.

RECTUM   ANUS

1 FOOT

THE DIGESTIVE SYSTEM OF THE HORSE

130 QTS.

LARGE INTESTINE 29 FEET

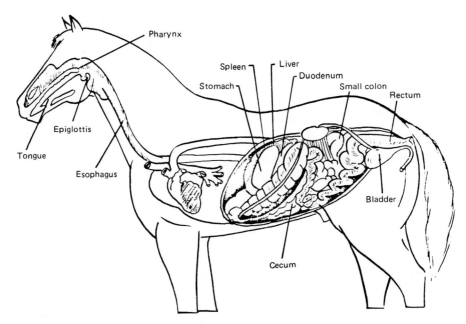

FIGURE 11-3 How the digestive system is arranged in the body of the horse. (*From* Horsemen's Veterinary Guide, *Western Horseman Books, Inc., Colorado Springs, Colo., 1965.*]

## The Mouth

*Prehension* is the grasping and conveying of food into the mouth by a sensitive, mobile upper lip. This action in the horse is so precise that horses can graze grass almost into the ground and can sort and select hay deftly from a manger.

Few systems this good are without problems when nature's plan is substantially altered. In the wild state horses wandered over vast areas biting off grass. Domestic horses still wander around the field when grazing.

Today, however, confined horses must graze in small areas and eat from a manger or off the ground in their stalls. Pursuit of the last morsel of feed and persistent action by the mobile lips during ingestion constantly agitate the feed and bedding. If the hay is moldy or dusty, such agitation creates ideal conditions for exposure of the lungs to mold spores and other foreign material. Continuous exposure can result in hay allergy, heaves, and colic in some horses.

Some horsemen eliminate this problem by letting the horses feed on the floor of the stall. This creates a worse problem because it simply recycles the worms in the horse at a dangerous pace.

MASTICATION   Chewing (mastication) reduces particle size and increases surface area for maximum exposure to digestive juices.

Males have forty teeth and mares thirty-six, which equip them well for chewing grain and coarse roughages. Indeed, mechanical preparation of grains may not increase digestibility more than 5 percent for horses with good teeth, but is essential for old horses with bad teeth.

Teeth are not trouble-free. Incisors (front teeth) start replacement at 2½ to 3 years of age and end at 4½ to 5 years of age. Biting off grass may pose a problem, especially for fall foals, whose teeth may shed at the peak of the grazing season. Jaw teeth start replacement at 1 year and end at 3½ to 4 years by growing outward and absorbing the cap (baby tooth). Often the cap falls off. Sometimes caps do not fall off, and the resulting length (height) of the tooth causes severe mastication problems.

Infection at the roots of teeth of older horses is not uncommon. Swelling on the lower side of the jawbone may be visible and soreness evident. Swelling on the face and sometimes drainage at the base of an upper tooth verify this condition. Mastication at this stage is difficult or impossible, and the horse's condition deteriorates rapidly.

Since the upper jaw is wider than the lower, upper teeth surfaces wear faster on the inside; lower, on the outside. Such wear results in sharp edges that can irritate the tongue or cheeks and interfere with chewing. Annual checks of older horses and floating (filing) by a veterinarian or equine dentist usually solve the problem.

Chewing or teeth problems are indicated when a horse chews with its head held sideways, when large amounts of grain are dribbled from the mouth, or when the horse's condition declines sharply without apparent reason.

SALIVATION   Saliva is secreted by three sets of paired glands in the mouth: the parotid, submaxillary, and sublingual glands. Saliva is mostly water, with only 1 percent inorganic salts and a very small amount of amylase, a digestive enzyme. Saliva moistens and lubricates the food mass for swallowing. During mastication hay absorbs about four times its weight in saliva and oats an equal amount by weight. Horses produce large amounts of saliva while eating (upwards of 10 liters), but do not salivate at the mere sight of food.

Greedy or fast-eating horses take too little time for chewing, thus reducing accompanying salivary production and increasing the probability of choking and impaired digestion.

## Pharynx

The pharynx is located in the upper back part of the horse's mouth where the digestive and respiratory tracts cross. It is muscular and funnel-shaped, and serves to guide food into the esophagus. Once in the pharynx, food or water cannot return to the mouth because of the blocking action of the soft palate. The epiglottis closes at the same time to prevent passage of food into the lungs. Horses cannot breathe through the mouth, and only extremely rarely can they vomit.

## Esophagus

The esophagus is a 4- to 5-foot muscular tube extending from the mouth, down the *left* side of the neck, through the diaphragm, to the stomach. It conveys food and water to the stomach by progressive waves of muscular restrictions called peristalsis. These waves are normally irreversible, another reason why a horse cannot easily vomit. Neither can the horse relieve gas pressure by belching, a mechanism that would be most useful in some colic cases. Greedy horses may wolf down dry oats in such quantity that choking occurs in the esophagus.

## Stomach

The stomach is a U-shaped sac near the diaphragm at the front of the abdominal cavity. A powerful muscle (the sphincter) regulates the opening of the esophagus into the stomach and further renders vomiting almost impossible.

The stomach of the horse is small compared to that of other animals. A stomach capacity of 2 to 4 gallons, coupled with the fact that the stomach remains partially filled with food, underscores the horse's need to be fed two or three times daily instead of just once. Since food moves rapidly through the stomach, frequent feeding in small amounts is more efficient and better satisfies the horse's appetite.

The stomach serves briefly as a reservoir for swallowed food while subjecting it to gastric digestion. Gastric juices, secreted from numerous glands in the mucous membrane of the stomach, contain hydrochloric acid and two enzymes, pepsin and gastric lipase.

Hydrochloric acid functions as an activator of pepsin by establishing a favorable hydrogen ion (pH) concentration which allows the pepsin to convert protein to proteoses and peptones. Complete breakdown of these two compounds into amino acids by digestion occurs later in the small intestine.

Pepsin is a protease—an enzyme that helps digest protein into amino acids. Lipase helps digest fat into fatty acids and glycerol, which are absorbed and used for energy just as simple sugars are.

The digestive process is continuous, but greatly increased upon the receipt of food. When two-thirds full, the stomach begins to pass food into the small intestine, and continues to do so as long as eating continues. If excessive food is consumed at one time, some of it leaves the stomach without sufficient digestive action, resulting in somewhat decreased digestive efficiency.

The age-old contention that watering a horse after feeding will wash undigested nutrients out of its stomach is not scientifically supported. Most water bypasses a full stomach by direct passage from the esophageal opening to the opening of the intestine, a detour facilitated by the U shape of the stomach.

It is interesting to watch confined animals eat dry feed when water is near. They make numerous leisurely trips between feed and water, and will more readily consume feed when water is available. When taken often and in small amounts, water probably aids salivation and the digestive process. This is a well-established research fact with swine.

The stomach is the site of a number of digestive disorders. It should be spared moldy feeds, finely ground masses, sudden changes in feed, and feast-and-famine situations. The stomach should also be kept relatively free of parasites.

## Small Intestine

The small intestine is a 2-inch by 70-foot tube that holds about 12 gallons and connects the stomach to the large intestine. It is folded into many folds and coils. The small and the large intestines are suspended from the loin region of the back by a fan-shaped membrane called the mesentery. Its blood supply enters at the stem of this fan membrane near the loin through the large mesentery artery. Unfortunately this location is where bloodworms choose to lodge and feed, producing aneurysms (blood clots), which reduce blood supply to the intestines and which result in colic and often death. A good parasite-control program eliminates this hazard.

The small intestine and its accessory organs, the pancreas and liver, supply most of the enzymes for digestion. Peristalsis of the intestinal wall ensures a good mixture of its mostly fluid contents.

Pancreatic juice contains the enzymes trypsin, pancreatic lipase, and amylase. Trypsin converts protein and peptides into amino acids that are absorbed by the small intestine and taken by the bloodstream to the site of need, e.g., muscles in growing horses and mammary glands in lactating mares. Pancreatic lipase hydrolizes fats to glycerol and fatty acids, and pancreatic amylase breaks starch down to maltose, a simple sugar that is easy to digest.

The liver secrets bile, which helps break down fat, aids in fatty acid absorption, and activates pancreatic lipase.

Villi, small projections in the small intestine, greatly increase the surface area of the small intestine for absorption into the bloodstream of a host of nutrients, such as simple sugars, fatty acids, amino acids, minerals, and vitamins. Villi severely damaged by heavy parasitization in early life probably contain enough connective tissue to adversely affect digestion for the rest of the horse's life. This may be a reason why some horses are hard-keeping.

## Large Intestine

The large intestine, composed of the cecum, large colon, small colon, rectum, and anus, conveys undigested material from the small intestine to the anus for elimination and carries out other important functions as well. With a combined capacity of 30 to 35 gallons, this 26- to 30-foot-long tube is a beehive of bacterial action; cellulose, starch, and sugars are digested into volatile fatty acids, which may supply up to one-fourth of the energy used by the horse. As a fringe benefit, bacterial action in healthy adult horses produces their daily B vitamin requirements, except in extreme stress conditions.

Production of some amino acids occurs in the large intestine, but its contribution to the horse's protein needs are less than its production of fatty acids for energy. The cecum is the primary site of water absorption.

For better utilization of roughages (hays), the passage of roughage through the cecum and large colon is delayed, depending to some degree on fiber content and amount of available water. Nature's plan for better utilization of hay backfires with poor-quality, late-cut (high-fiber) hay fed without adequate water. The result may be hay belly or sometimes impaction in the large or small colons and sometimes in the rectum, resulting in colic or other problems.

Twisted intestine may be a result of overstuffing followed too soon by hard work, or of rolling as a result of parasite-induced colic (see Chapter 14). Prevention consists of an even flow of quality feed, abundance of good water, and an adequate parasite program, and not making unreasonable demands when working the horse.

Nutrient-laden blood from the intestines is conveyed through the portal vein directly to the liver, where nutrients are chemically processed as needed for use in other areas of the body.

The rectum connects the small colon to the anus and receives feces, formed into characteristic balls by the small colon to be voided through the anus. There may be 40 to 50 pounds of feces voided 8 to 12 times daily by horses consuming standard diets of grain and hay. The shape, size, and consistency of feces give an indication of the general health of the horse. If the feces are dry and hard, the horse may be deficient in water or protein. If soft, it may be sick or consuming a diet that is too laxative. It takes about 70 hours for food to be processed from mouth to anus.

## Management Implications

A number of practical management concepts emerge from a study of the digestive apparatus of the horse.

1 Since the stomach is small and feed and water pass through it rapidly, feed and water often and in small amounts.
2 Parasites in the small intestine reduce absorption of nutrients, possibly permanently.
3 Poor hay and skimpy water result in impaction and colic.
4 A horse can not "burp" or vomit. Avoid moldy feeds to reduce risk of colic.
5 The horse should not be worked for at least an hour after heavy feeding for two reasons: (a) Muscle activity will divert blood from the digestive system, which interferes with the digestive process, and (b) twisted intestine may result.
6 The alimentary tract is 100 feet long, has a capacity of as much as 50 gallons, and is never totally empty. Slowly digested fibrous foods such as hay or grass are therefore necessary to the psychological and physiological health of the horse.
7 Bad teeth reduce digestion, resulting in poor condition.
8 Intestinal microorganisms contribute greatly to energy and B vitamin production. Sudden changes in feeds are detrimental to them.
9 Foals and young horses need easily digested quality protein because their digestive tracts are not yet developed to peak efficiency.

## ESSENTIAL NUTRIENTS

The nutrients horses need for maintenance, work, and reproduction are identical in kind to those necessary for humans, pets, and other farm animals. An understanding of nutrition for horses will, to some extent, result in understanding nutritional needs for humans and household pets.

However, the amounts horses need vary greatly according to conditions. Energy needs for a racehorse exceed maintenance needs by 50 to 100 times. A hard-working horse can perspire 2 to 3 ounces of salt on a hot day. Foals need three times more calcium because their bones are growing rapidly.

### The Five Classes of Nutrients

The essential nutrients are *water*, *energy* (carbohydrates and fats), *protein*, *minerals*, and *vitamins*.

Theoretically, it would be most convenient if a single food existed with just the right proportions of these nutrients to meet the needs of each particular horse. Its near-100-percent digestibility would be efficient; little stall cleaning would be necessary. Actually, the Morris Animal Foundation, supported by funds from the American Quarter Horse Association, developed such a synthetic diet and sustained research horses on it for 2 years (Figure 11-4).

This artificial diet met the horses' nutritional needs. It is excellent for

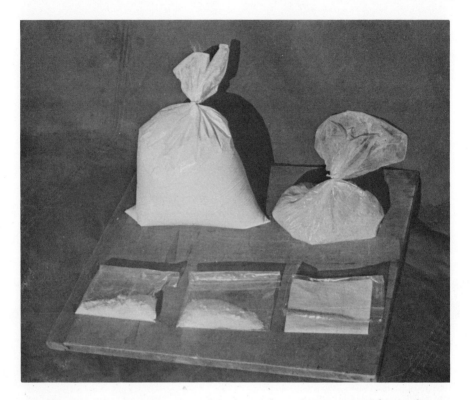

FIGURE 11-4   The correct ration of basic nutrients (except water) in nearly pure form required by a 1100-pound idle horse. Back row: left, carbohydrate (which supplys energy); right, protein. Front row: left to right, calcium, phosphorus, and vitamins. [*Photograph by author.*]

basic nutrition research and certain feeding conditions after surgery, but it is neither economical nor sufficient in bulk for routine horse feeding. The 50-gallon alimentary tract is not satisfied with 6 to 8 pounds of total feed in a day. The horse still feels hungry and will try to alleviate its craving by wood chewing or other bad habits.

WATER   Water is the most essential and often the most neglected of all the nutrients. Lack of water when a horse is suffering heat stress is dramatic and sometimes fatal. Water functions in regulating temperature; maintaining cell integrity or cell shape; transporting nutrients; assisting normal body chemical reactions; and assisting as a carrier in the processes of digestion, absorption, and elimination.

Adult horses will drink from 2 to 12 gallons daily depending on heat, work, and type of feed eaten.

Low humidity and high temperature decrease the moisture content of dry feeds stabled horses eat and increase water consumption. Sweating may result in water requirements that are double or triple normal requirements. Conversely, horses on succulent pasture, which may be as much as 80 percent water, may appear to ignore the water trough almost completely.

Water varies greatly in hardness or mineral content, but contributes little to the mineral nutrition of the horse. Calcium is usually the major mineral in water, but excess salt may also be present. If the horse is forced to drink salty water, electrolyte balance and intracellular pressure are affected, and dehydration may result. If water tastes salty to a human, it is probably too salty for a horse.

Because of different tastes and odors, different sources of water are easily identified by the horse. Some horses hauled frequently to different places may refuse to drink unfamiliar water, necessitating taking water from home.

Good water, free from contamination, should always be available, and should be warmed in winter to at least 45°F. Once-a-day ice chopping of surface water in winter is an inadequate management practice.

In rare cases overhydration (excessive drinking) may occur in sick horses. High temperature or fever increases water consumption dramatically. When the disease is corrected, consumption usually returns to normal.

There are cases on record where bored horses have developed drinking habits that resulted in bloated bodies and swollen limbs that rendered them useless. Water in such abnormal cases must be limited to regular intervals until the horses are exercised more and their environment changed.

ENERGY (CARBOHYDRATES AND FATS)   The complex organic molecules of the *carbohydrates* are formed in plant leaves by photosynthesis from carbon dioxide, water, and inorganic salts, using energy from the sun, in a process catalyzed by chlorophyll.

Carbohydrates are the main source of energy for horses and all life. They vary greatly in chemical complexity and therefore digestibility, depending upon the part of the plant, the variety of plant, and the stage of maturity when harvested. Plant leaves contain soluble carbohydrates that digest easily; stems are more chemically complex and less digestible. Plant seeds are high in starch and are highly digestible. Shelled corn, the seed portion of maize, for example, may be 80 percent digestible.

*Variety* makes a difference: legume plants and hays are digested easier than grass or nonlegume hays.

The greatest deterrent to digestibility is *maturity*. As plants approach maturity, they quickly form chemically complex carbohydrates in their cell walls called cellulose and lignin—together called *crude fiber*—that are difficult for the horse to digest. Some cellulose is digested, but little if any lignin.

Other factors that affect digestibility of carbohydrates are frequency of feeding, individuality, work load, and processing methods. The horse's condition is a good measure of carbohydrate intake. If fat, the horse is getting too much; if thin, too little.

*Fats* are solids and *oils* are liquid carbohydrates. Both are very concentrated sources of energy. The chemical formula for one common fat is $C_{57}H_{104}O_6$, illustrating the high ratio of carbon (the energy source) and hydrogen to oxygen. Fats and oils are usually composed of three molecules of fatty acids and one of glycerol to one oxygen. Fats are considered to furnish 2¼ times more energy by weight than other carbohydrates. The law of some states requires minimum fat percentage to be stated on commercial feed tags.

Fats are present in varying amounts and kinds in plants, but are highest in the seed portion. For example, alfalfa leaves are about 3 percent fat and stems 2 percent, but alfalfa seed is 10 percent fat. Oats and linseed meal are about 5 percent fat, and soybean meal 7 percent fat, depending on processing method.

Linoleic acid, one of the derivatives of fats, is necessary for a healthy hair coat on horses. Normal horse diets are marginal in this fatty acid; addition of linoleic acid to a show ration probably improves the hair coat.

MEASURES OF ENERGY CONTENT    There are a number of measures of energy content, but horse owners most frequently use total digestible nutrients (TDN) and digestible energy (DE).

MEASURES OF ENERGY    TDN is the sum of all the digestible organic nutrients (protein, nitrogen-free extract, fat, and fiber), with fat multiplied by 2.25. The digestion coefficients of these nutrients are determined by actual digestion trials with horses. Digestible energy is gross energy in the feed minus energy lost in the feces. It and TDN are very similar and can be compared by assuming that 2000 kilocalories of DE is equal to 1 pound of TDN.

PROTEIN    Protein supplies the materials from which body tissue (muscle) is made. It is especially necessary for growing foals, young horses, and lactating mares. It is also necessary for maintenance of adult horses and lactation in mares. Practical rations range from approximately 18 percent protein for early weanlings to under 10 percent for adults (see Appendix 12-1).

Work does not increase protein requirements much, if any, but rations containing 12 percent may be eaten more readily by hard-working horses than those with 10 percent or less.

Proteins are complex molecules of carbon, hydrogen, oxygen, and nitrogen made from a combination of twenty-two *amino acids*, or "building blocks." The amino acids are chemically complex nitrogenous compounds, and feeds vary in percentage content of them.

*Essential amino acids* are those the animal cannot produce in the digestive and metabolic process. Some may be insufficient in standard feeds. A *quality protein* is one containing a high percentage of essential amino acids in the proportions needed. Milk is a good example. Oats and other grains fed to young horses are deficient in the essential amino acid, lysine. Quality protein is that which is most nearly complete in essential amino acids.

Good grass and legume hay are adequate sources of protein, but the oil meals are the main sources of protein in commercial feeds. Soybean oil meal, cottonseed oil meal, and linseed oil meal are the major protein supplements.

Microbial synthesis of protein is known to occur in the cecum and colon, but the extent of its digestion and absorption remains obscure. Weanlings have been shown to gain significantly faster when standard grain and linseed oil meal diets were supplemented with either milk protein or synthetic lysine. About 0.7 percent lysine in the diet appears to be adequate for optimum growth.

Protein is often expressed in percentage of the total or crude protein (CP) or digestible protein (DP). It is expressed in pounds in the feed industry and grams in scientific circles.

A deficiency of protein is slow to appear and difficult to diagnose until too late. Growth slows or stops in growing horses. Their appetite is depressed, hair coat is rough, and shedding is delayed. Permanent stunting results from long periods of severe shortages. The milk production of lactating mares declines, and adult horses' appetites are depressed, resulting in poor condition, reduced performance, and late spring shedding.

MINERALS    Minerals are very important in skeletal development, teeth, acid-base (pH) balance, enzyme reactions, oxygen transport, regular breeding, and nerve and muscle responses. Their balance in the body is important, and some of the trace minerals are toxic at reasonably low levels.

Major minerals that are used by the horse in large amounts, but are not plentiful in standard horse feeds, are salt, calcium, and phosphorus. These are inorganic compounds (containing no hydrocarbons) that are mined, processed, and added to animal feeds or used as plant nutrients in soil fertilizers.

*Salt.* Salt should be offered free-choice to all animals at all times in a container separate from the free-choice calcium-phosphorus source. This practice prevents force-feeding calcium and phosphorus to meet the salt needs of the horse.

No other animal uses salt at the rate of a perspiring horse at hard work in high temperatures. Two or three ounces may be lost daily. Salt stimulates saliva secretion, is necessary in some enzyme reactions, and improves appetite. While the amount of salt varies depending upon the climate and the activity of the horse, a ration containing ½ to 1 percent will usually suffice for most salt needs.

Salt deficiency may trigger muscle–tie-up syndrome. Long-term deficiencies result in depraved appetite, rough hair coat, reduced growth, and reduced milk production. If excess salt is offered to a horse with a depraved appetite, it may consume toxic amounts, especially in the absence of adequate water. A salt-deprived horse should receive an ounce daily for 3 days and then double that amount until its appetite is satisfied.

High amounts of salt should not be used to regulate grain intake of self-fed horses as is customary in cattle feeding. Variation among individuals in tolerance of salt makes self-feeding of grain and salt impractical.

Salt may be fed loose or in block form. Loose salt is more readily available and may be more readily consumed by horses, especially those on range not exposed to it daily. However, loose salt erodes badly when exposed to rain. Unless fed in an all-weather mineral feeder, salt in standard 50-pound blocks is more satisfactory.


*Calcium and phosphorus.* Calcium and phosphorus are essential for sound bone development and many other body functions. Recently, they have received considerable attention in research and practical horse feeding. Although bone growth in adult horses has ceased, endogenous (metabolic) losses of these minerals continue throughout life. For this reason a 1100-pound mature horse requires approximately 23 grams of calcium and 15 grams of phosphorus daily. Standard horse diets usually yield this amount of digestible calcium and phosphorus, but diets for foals and weanlings seldom meet their needs unless these minerals have been added. Digestibility of calcium in standard horse diets ranges from 55 to 75 percent and 35 to 55 percent for phosphorus. Claims are often made of calcium and phosphorus with superior digestibility, but unless supported by research one must assume they fall within the above ranges.

The ideal *calcium-to-phosphorus ratio* is not fully agreed upon but is usually considered satisfactory if 1.1:1 minimum and 3:1 or 5:1 maximum. A 1.1:1 ratio is probably too low for pregnant or lactating mares, and 5:1 may be too high if the source is inorganic calcium. Lieb found that a 4.1:1 and 7.25:1 ratio of inorganic calcium to phosphorus were detrimental to phosphorus digestion in ponies.[1] We can successfully feed alfalfa hay indefinitely when its ratio of (organic) calcium to phosphorus is 5:1 or 6:1. A ratio of 1.5:1 or 2:1 is recommended.

In addition to adequate amounts of calcium and phosphorus in the correct ratio, *vitamin D* must be present for proper bone formation. This is not usually a problem in practical horse management, unless horses are kept

---

[1]Sandi Lieb and J. P. Baker, "Effect of High Calcium Intake on Phosphorus Metabolism," *Proceedings of the Fourth Equine Nutrition and Physiology Symposium*, 1975, p. 60.

out of sunlight for long periods of time. (See the discussion of vitamins below.)

If young growing horses receive inadequate calcium or phosphorus, they will develop crooked bones and large joints, and will have inadequate mineralization of the osteoid tissues, resulting in weak bones throughout life. Mineral-deficient adult horses have weak bones and insidious lamenesses shifting from one foot to another. Advanced cases produce osteomalacia (softening of the bones).

If an excess of either calcium or phosphorus is fed, the detrimental effects are much less pronounced if an adequate amount of the other mineral is present in the diet. A disastrous condition exists when a high amount of one of these minerals is fed in the presence of half or less adequate amount of the other.

When excess phosphorus is fed to adult horses, such as twice as much phosphorus as calcium, for long periods of time, an irreversible condition called nutritional secondary *hyperparathyroidism* or "big head" may appear. Low blood-calcium levels trigger the parathyroid gland to cause withdrawal of calcium from bones to meet the emergency. Connective tissue replaces the calcium in the bones, and facial bones are enlarged. High-grain feeding or all-grain rations cause most big-head conditions.

Excess calcium and phosphorus leave the body via the feces, urine, and sweat.

*Minor or trace minerals.*    When the calcium, phosphorus, and salt requirements of the horse have been met, other mineral feeding problems are easy to solve. Indeed, unless the horse is living in an area of unusual mineral excess or deficiency, simple trace-mineralized salt fed free-choice will solve most of its other mineral needs. Exceptions are those horses on very high grain rations or those for some reason getting little or no forage. Hays and grasses usually contain most of the trace minerals in adequate amounts to satisfy the needs of the animal. Silages, corncobs, and other rough feeds are inadequate in these minerals.

There are probably more horses adversely affected by mineral toxicities from overfeeding trace minerals than there are horses suffering from an inadequacy of these minerals. High levels of trace minerals can occur in forages, and most commercial supplements also contain them.

*Potassium* is necessary to maintain proper acid-base balance in cells. Since most diets are adequate in potassium and it is readily absorbed, there is seldom a deficiency. The National Research Council has suggested levels of 1 percent potassium for early weaned foals, or 0.4 to 0.5 percent for adult horses. Healthy horses are unlikely to display signs of low potassium. However, those afflicted with serious illnesses may exhibit hypokalemia (decreased serum potassium) and may go off feed. If so, their diets should be supplemented with potassium. Potassium toxicity has not been reported. Potassium is excreted in the urine.

*Iodine,* an important part of the hormone thyroxine, is present in the thyroid gland and controls metabolic rate. The National Research Council estimates that 1 milligram per kilogram of feed or 1 part iodine per million is required. It is considered toxic to pregnant mares at a level of 48 milligrams or more per day, resulting in goitrous foals. Excess amounts of certain kinds of seaweed have also created this condition. Both the excess and the insufficiency of iodine result in enlarged thyroid, often called goiter. In many cases this condition is fatal, especially in the young. Excessive use of iodine is not uncommon in routine horse feeding, because it may be present in three or four sources of feed, especially in conditioners and some premixes. Iodine is secreted in the urine.

The *selenium* requirement of horses is estimated to be 0.1 milligram per kilogram of diet, or 0.1 part per million. There is an interaction between selenium and vitamin E. The amount needed of each depends upon the level of the other in the ration. A selenium deficiency results in white muscle disease, a degeneration of the muscles in young foals. They are born too weak to nurse, and die of starvation soon thereafter. Although rare, the condition has been noted in New York and Kentucky.

Selenium is best known for its toxicity in dry, alkaline areas of the Northwest. Horses consuming forages from excessive selenium soils develop "blind staggers" or alkaline disease, which is characterized by loss of appetite, loss of hair from the mane and tail, and rings on the hooves. If enough selenium is present to produce advanced symptoms, paralysis, blindness, and loss of hoof occur. Toxicity has occurred in horses consuming forages containing as little as 5 milligrams of selenium per kilogram of dry matter.

Except in very limited areas, normal horse feeds are not toxic in selenium. If selenium injections are used for various muscle disorders, they should be carefully monitored by a veterinarian who understands the significance of an improper injection.

*Fluorine* is a toxic mineral that has not been demonstrated to be a necessary nutrient for the horse. Toxic levels in the ration are about 1 milligram per kilogram of body weight, or 50 parts per million. Symptoms of high fluorine are lesions on the gums, mottled, soft teeth, a Roman-appearing nose, and trouble in chewing and eating. Fluorine levels in water seldom cause toxicity, however.

*Zinc* deficiencies have occurred in foals on zinc-free diets. Their requirements are probably less than 50 parts per million. Symptoms of zinc deficiency are reduced growth, lesions on the lower extremities around the belly and legs, and reduced levels in tissue and serum. The upper tolerance for zinc is high. However, foals fed 90 grams per day or 2 percent of their diet developed lameness, stiffness, incoordination, difficulty with stepping over obstacles with their hind feet, and high zinc blood levels.[2]

*Magnesium* is an essential nutrient. An 1100-pound horse requires 4.65

[2]Harold Hintz et al., *Journal of Animal Science,* vol. 3, 1971, p. 1274.

grams daily or 0.09 percent of their ration. Growing foals require something more than this amount. Magnesium is essential for bones and teeth and, like other trace minerals, is also an enzyme activator in other chemical reactions in the body. In the presence of excess doses of calcium and phosphorus it would seem that magnesium becomes less digestible. It is excreted in the urine. Deficiency signs are common in cattle: the disease grass tetany usually results from grazing forages low in magnesium. However, horses grazing the same pasture are seldom affected with any symptoms. Research has shown that young foals on a diet of 8 milligrams of magnesium per kilogram of feed become magnesium deficient. Symptoms include nervousness, muscular tremors, collapse, and sweating. Occasionally death can result. Under practical conditions, magnesium would seem to be adequate in most horse rations.

The daily *copper* requirement is estimated at 5 to 8 parts per million. High levels of copper have been shown to accumulate in the livers of ponies, but have shown no other detrimental effects. Copper deficiency is associated with anemia in the animal and excessive bleeding or hemorrhaging in foaling mares, as well as with weakening of bones.

*Iron* deficiency will result in anemia. Iron is an important part of the hemoglobin of red blood cells, and assists in the carrying of oxygen. For this reason, many racehorses have received prerace iron injections in order to boost the oxygen-carrying capacity of the blood. Research does not substantiate the claims of this particular iron therapy, however.

Iron is absorbed from the small intestine, and most feeds are adequate in iron to meet the horse's need. In addition, the horse is a very good conserver of iron in the body because the iron is recycled. Conditions that might create iron-deficiency anemia would be heavy blood loss, as from infestation of internal parasites. The National Research Council suggests a daily dose of 50 parts per million for growing foals and 40 parts per million for adults. Iron toxicity has not been reported specifically in horses, but has been reported in most other species. Because *iron dextran* injections have killed horses, however, this compound should be avoided.

Blood serum levels of iron are actually hard to establish. The horse stores a great amount of iron-rich blood in the spleen. When the horse is working hard, the spleen actually contracts to pump vital oxygen-carrying red blood cells into the circulatory system. Racehorse veterinarians wishing to establish iron levels in an individual's system take blood samples from a horse fresh from the track after a morning's gallop or breeze.

*Manganese, sulfur,* and *cobalt* are other trace minerals appearing on feed tag labels. A requirement for manganese in the horse has not been established. Sulfur is a component of two amino acids, methionine and cystine. Adequate intake of a good-quality protein such as soybean meal eliminates any concern about sulfur. Cobalt is an important constituent of vitamin $B_{12}$, but it is naturally abundant in feed.

It is important to exercise caution in feeding trace minerals. Enough may be provided from sources such as legume hays, conditioners, vitamin premixes, and protein supplements, to create a toxic level of one or more of the trace minerals if additional sources are offered.

VITAMINS    Vitamins are organic compounds required in minute amounts in the body. Their role is so complex and varied in body functions that deficiencies manifest themselves soon in malfunctions. Like other nutrients, vitamin requirements are affected by the horse's stage of production, age, stress, and the amount of food eaten. Whether or not vitamins are added to the ration depends upon the type and quality of forage the horse consumes and the degree of synthesis in the digestive tract (and also, in the case of vitamin D, the horse's exposure to sunlight).

Good-quality forages are excellent sources of vitamins. However, most of the forages horses eat, except grass, are not good quality. The vitamin content of hays baled with too much moisture and those rained on, bleached in sunlight, and aged by more than a year of storage is questionable if not totally inadequate. Many other factors also affect the vitamin content of feedstuffs. For this reason some horse-feeders prefer to feed vitamins to confined horses most of the time. As with minerals, however, some are toxic and should not be fed in excess.

Vitamins are normally measured in international units (IU) and U.S. pharmacoepia units (USP), which are equivalent.

There are two types of vitamins: (1) fat-soluble—A, E, D, and K; and (2) water-soluble—vitamin C and the B complex vitamins. Fat-soluble vitamins dissolve in fat or fat solvents, and therefore are stored in the body either in the liver or in fat cells. Animals on good feeds with high fat-soluble vitamin levels may not need supplementation for long periods of depletion ranging from 3 to 6 months. Water-soluble vitamins are easily depleted and therefore must be ingested daily or manufactured daily in the body.

*Fat-soluble vitamins*

> And the wild asses did stand in high places, they snuffed up the wind like dragons; their eyes did fail, because there was no grass. *Jeremiah* 14:6

This Old Testament prophet might qualify as an early agricultural researcher because of his observation that grass was necessary for normal vision in wild asses and that its absence in droughty seasons caused blindness. The cause was probably vitamin A deficiency.

*Vitamin A* has been called the "anti-infection vitamin." It is necessary for maintenance and health of epithelial cells in skin, hair, hooves, and eyes. Lacrimation, or tearing, is one of the first symptoms of a vitamin A deficiency. Others are infertility, night blindness, digestive disturbances, respiratory illnesses, polyuria, and keratinization of cornea and skin.

Carotene, the yellow pigment found in green growing plants, is a precursor to vitamin A in the animal body. Although green pigment in plants masks the yellow color of carotene, grasses and hays that are green are high in carotene. However, the conversion of carotene by horses to vitamin A is not efficient, especially of the carotene found in grass foliage.

The National Research Council assumes that 1 milligram of carotene is equivalent to 400 IU of vitamin A, which may or may not be accurate in some cases. The National Research Council may also be conservative in its estimate that the daily needs for vitamin A is 12,500 IU per adult horse. It is known to be higher for cattle of the same weight. Practical horse feeders often administer 20,000 IU daily.

Research on toxicity is not specifically recorded in horses, but has been established in many other species. Steers at Iowa State University showed no detrimental symptoms at 100,000 IU per head per day but did at 10 million IU. Since the synthetic form of vitamin A is so cheap, abundant, and safe, many horse owners feed more than their horses need, giving a teaspoonful of A, D, and E from a concentrated source that supplies 40,000 IU of vitamin A per day. Adult horses maintained during most of the year on forages and hays rich in vitamin A may store up as much as a 3 to 6 months' supply of the vitamin.

*Vitamin D* is known to be a vitamin essential to proper bone growth. It is necessary for proper absorption, transportation, and metabolism of calcium and phosphorus. Vitamin D also assists in the uptake of other minerals by the bones, and functions in the synthesis of collagen, a fibrous protein holding cells together.

Maximum and minimum levels of vitamin D have not been thoroughly established. However, a diet providing 3300 IU per 1100-pound horse is safe under most conditions.

It is difficult to create a practical condition of vitamin D deficiency. Sun-cured hays are good sources; ultraviolet rays of sunlight convert the dehydrocholesterol produced by the body into vitamin D. Blanketed horses eating poor hay may show deficiency symptoms such as stiff, swollen joints, stiffness of gait, and reduction in serum calcium and serum phosphorus. These symptoms are accompanied by a reduction in bone calcification. Advanced symptoms are rickets (bowed legs) in young horses and osteomalacia (soft bones) in adults. Compared with other vitamins, vitamin D is toxic at low levels. The National Research Council states that 50 times the normal requirement may be harmful. Ponies fed 3300 units per kilogram (2.2 pounds) of body weight per day died within 4 months. Soft tissue calcification, general bone abnormality, and kidney damage were extensive. Calcification of heart valves in both horses and humans is also caused by eating too much vitamin D.

Nutritionists disagree on the need for *vitamin E* in the horse. Some feel that it is insignificant in practical horse feeding. Research foals, however, experimentally depleted, have responded significantly to vitamin E in recovery. There is no established minimum daily requirement.

Because E also plays a part in the removal of waste products from the muscles after work, studies are being conducted to see whether combinations of vitamin E and selenium will relieve tying-up syndrome. Vitamin E may have something to do with fertility in both sexes, but there is no clear research evidence to support this contention. There would seem to be no toxicity to vitamin E.

Alpha tocopherol, an alcohol substance found in plants, is the precursor of vitamin E. Most rations adequately supply vitamin E. However, substances may be present in the ration that destroy or serve as antagonists to it.

*Vitamin K* is synthesized in adequate amounts by the intestinal microflora to meet the needs of the horse. No deficiencies have been reported. Its main function in the body is to promote normal blood coagulation and prevent hemorrhages. Moldy hays, especially sweet clover and legumes, contain dicumarol, which interferes with vitamin K's function in blood clotting. Feeding such hays to horses can cause hay allergy and heaves, and can result in serious hemorrhagic disease. There is no recommended daily allowance of vitamin K.

Vitamin K supplementation is currently popular in the treatment of racehorses exhibiting bleeder syndrome (hemorrhaging from nose) after racing. Vitamin K definitely does *not* effect a cure of this condition, although it probably does not hurt, either. The only known cure for bleeder syndrome is not to run the horse.

A good commercial A, D, and E horse supplement will contain 4 to 10 million IU of vitamin A per pound of supplement. The content of vitamin D will be 4 to 10 times less than A, and the content of E 80 to 100 times less than D.

These amounts will be clearly stated on the feed tag. There are vitamin premixes with an equal amount of A and D per pound, but if these are fed to supply 20,000 IU of A per day to each horse, a toxic excess of vitamin D will result.

*Water-soluble vitamins.* The *B complex vitamins* are abundant in quality forages. In addition, synthesis in the intestines supplies sufficient amounts for most horses. Indeed a comparison of B vitamins ingested in the food and voided in the feces shows that the horse excretes more vitamins than it eats, resulting in adequate amounts unless it is under stress. Severely stressed horses such as race horses, game horses, distance horses, and others, however, may need some B vitamin supplementation. Be sure the supplement you use does not contain antibiotics; antibiotics would further decrease B vitamins produced in the cecum and colon under normal conditions. Most horse feeders and most commercial rations use little or no B vitamin supplementation.

A *thiamine* ($B_1$) requirement has not been established, but 3 milligrams per kilogram of feed is a good daily allowance. This level will maintain appetite, feed intake, body weight gains, and normal levels of thiamine in the skeletal muscles of growing horses. Some researchers have estimated that 25 percent of the free thiamine in the cecum is absorbed by the horse. Since grains and forages both contain more than 3 milligrams of thiamine per kilogram, the dietary intake coupled with that synthesized in the intestinal tract undoubtedly furnishes all of the thiamine a normal horse needs. When a thiamine deficiency is experimentally produced, symptoms are anorexia (poor appetite), loss of weight, incoordination, and low blood thiamine. Certain plants, such as brackenfern, may destroy thiamine when eaten by horses. Some drugs prescribed by veterinarians inhibit thiamine utilization. Also, poor hay fed to the horse for long periods may result in a thiamine deficiency. Supplemental feeding of thiamine or an improved ration promptly corrects the condition.

The maintenance requirements for *riboflavin* ($B_2$) are satisfied by 2.2 milligrams per kilogram of body weight. Riboflavin is an important factor in the synthesis of carbohydrates and amino acids. Moon blindness in military horses was thought to be the result of a riboflavin deficiency; however, recent research tends to refute this contention.

No *niacin* (nicotinic acid) requirements have been officially established for the horse, but about 30 milligrams per day should be a safe allowance. It can be synthesized from tryptophan (the amino acid), suggesting that a dietary source is unnecessary. Legumes and yeast are good sources of niacin. It has been observed by some researchers that horses consuming 0.01 milligram of nicotinic acid per kilogram of body weight actually excreted more niacin than they consumed. Such is the case with most of the B vitamins.

*Pantothenic acid.* This B vitamin is richly supplied by most feeds. Only under research conditions is it likely to be deficient. 0.015 percent in the diet seems to be adequate.

The requirement for *vitamin $B_{12}$* has not been determined in horse nutrition; supplemental vitamin $B_{12}$ is therefore not considered necessary. Vitamin $B_{12}$ is known to be produced by microorganisms in the digestive tract and is adsorbed from the large intestine.

*Other water-soluble vitamins. Pyridoxine* ($B_6$), *folic acid*, and *biotin* are also synthesized in the lower digestive tract of the horse. There are no known dietary requirements for these substances. When horses have been starved, they show a response to folic acid, and some stabled horses have been found low in blood levels of this B vitamin.

*Vitamin C* (ascorbic acid) is not necessary for horses (although it is for humans, monkeys, and guinea pigs), for it is readily synthesized in the intestine. Excess vitamin C will be excreted in the urine. Vitamin C is important in collagen synthesis and in maintaining capillary strength.

## FEEDS AND THEIR NUTRIENTS

Since nutrients do not come nicely packaged in just the right amounts for the job at hand, feeds must be carefully selected to supply nutrients and must be fed in the appropriate amount. Although almost every conceivable thing has been successfully fed to horses, conventional horse feeds are pastures and hays, which are roughages, and grains, which are concentrates. The optimal combination of these and the substitution of one for another—depending on the need of the horse, the availability and cost of the feed, and the convenience of purchase and storage—is the horseman's challenge.

### Forages

Forages include pastures, hays, and succulent feeds stored with high moisture contents, such as silages. Pasture grasses, when lush and growing, supply an abundance of nutrients for most horses in about the right proportions. However, dormant grass during winter or drought may be substantially deficient in protein, energy, vitamins, and palatability. In such cases, supplementation with hay, grains, or protein supplements is indicated.

Not all horsemen have pasture available for their animals, and they must turn to hay as part of the diet to replace it. High-quality hay is a good substitute for pasture. Total digestible nutrient values range from 30 to 56 percent, protein contents may vary from 3 to 20 percent, and mineral contents from 0.2 to 2 percent calcium and 0.15 to 0.4 percent phosphorus. Nutrient contents varies substantially, and palatability declines with nutrient decline in the condition under which the hay was cured and handled. Haying conditions are adversely affected by bad weather in many of the areas in which they are grown. A buyer of hays for horses must be very discriminating.

High-moisture processed feeds such as silages and hydroponically produced forages have never played a very great role in horse feeding. It is impractical for horsemen to build silos to store feed for their horses. However, if they already have a silo for cattle, some silage can be safely fed to horses provided it does not contain mold. Mold and silage are almost synonymous, however, and good management is necessary if silage is being used as feed. Troughs must be kept clean, and, to avoid molding in the trough, only enough silage should be offered in warm weather as can be eaten in a few hours. Despite the hazard of mold, much of the feed for a herd of horses can be supplied by silage through careful management. Corn silage is low in protein and calcium. Grass silage is low in protein and palatability.

Hydroponics is a very old method of sprouting grain for animals. Grain is soaked a few days to a week, and the resulting sprout and remainder of the grain is fed to the horses. This is a labor-intensive, very expensive way to feed. Cost usually dictates another method.

## Pastures

Grass is nature's way of feeding horses. No one feedstuff is more complete in nutrients than green pasture grown on fertile soil, and few feeds are fed in a more healthful environment (Figure 11-5). Grass is inexpensive, provides succulence, and furnishes minerals and vitamins that are sometimes lacking. Hardworking horses, however, need supplemental energy feeds because of the low energy content of grass. Dry grass is usually low in protein and vitamins, and crowded pastures pose a parasite problem. Lush spring grass will cause certain obese horses to founder if they are allowed to consume large amounts.

Horse pastures differ in several respects from cattle pastures, although most principles for establishing and fertilizing forages developed for cattle pastures also apply to horse pastures.

In general, horses are much more destructive to pastures than are cattle: they tear the sod, denude paths along fences and gates, and in times of excessive soil moisture, punch holes into the sod.

Many people when talking about pasture may really be referring to an exercise lot. If only 1 acre or less can be provided per horse, then that area

FIGURE 11-5  Grass is nature's way of feeding horses. This improved pasture on good soil ankle deep in growth will supply all the nutrients, except salt and water, that most horses need. [*Howell N. Wheaton and Melvin Bradley,* Horse Pastures, *University of Missouri Science and Technology Guide no. 4695, 1978.*]

can furnish exercise space but little feed. In such cases tall fescue is the choice to use. Fescue will withstand trampling, keep down dust, reduce erosion and pollution, and provide a clean and pleasant place for the horse to exercise. But the horse should be fed as if in confinement.

A minimum of 2 acres per mature horse is needed to develop a pasture system that will furnish adequate feed, exercise space, and conditions that control internal parasites. To control parasites, drug treatments should be used and horses should be rotated among pastures.

GRAZING CATTLE WITH HORSES  If at all possible combine cattle and horses for grazing purposes. Horses tend to graze in spots, undergrazing and overgrazing. Cattle will graze the otherwise wasted feed. Cattle droppings are randomly distributed, but horse droppings will be concentrated in specific areas, which become hothouses for parasites.

If cattle and horses are grazed together, pasture clipping is usually eliminated, and it is easier to control parasites and to maintain a balance between grasses and legumes.

Cattle and horses may be grazed together simultaneously or rotated, with one following the other. Generally speaking, cattle do not have the same intestinal parasites as horses, and horses are not bothered by cattle parasites. They can graze near each others' droppings without becoming infested.

MANAGING HORSE PASTURES  When pastures are continuously grazed by horses, many areas become severely overgrazed. In other parts of the pasture the forage growth becomes tall and coarse and is refused by horses.

Closely grazed areas first tend to increase in clover, but when they are grazed out or when the short stubble is killed by drought, many bare areas result. In the ungrazed areas tall grass becomes too competitive, and clover is smothered out. The best solution to this problem (other than grazing cattle) is frequent mowing and pasture rotation.

Another horse pasture problem is inadequate fertilizer. Horse pastures should be top-dressed annually. Grass-legume pastures should have a minimum of 30 pounds of phosphorus and 60 pounds of potash per acre. Straight grass pastures should be top-dressed with 90 pounds of nitrogen, 30 pounds of phosphorus, and 60 pounds of potash per acre. Usually the fertilizer is most effective if applied during winter or very early spring.

TYPES OF HORSE PASTURES  Horse farms or ranches should have four or five smaller pastures rather than one or two large ones, especially if cattle are not available to help with pasture management.

Several small lots near the barn seeded to tall fescue are good to have in addition to regular pastures. When pasture soils are wet, horses tend to damage the sod more than any other class of livestock. In these times, horses are best confined to small areas to prevent damaging regular pastures. Heavy fescue turf in small lots is ideal for this type of area.

TYPE OF FORAGE SPECIES    Ideal pasture plants should be productive over a long growing season, highly palatable, aggressive and persistent, adaptable to climatic extremes, and resistant to insects and disease. No single forage plant meets all these criteria, and more than one species must be used in a system of uniform feed supply. There are two types of pasture plants, grasses and legumes.

GRASSES    *Kentucky bluegrass.*    No other grass is held in as high esteem by horsemen as Kentucky bluegrass. In areas where it is adapted, it can become the backbone of the forage system. It is palatable and nutritious, will withstand close grazing, and will maintain its legume component if properly managed. In addition, bluegrass produces a high-quality turf that heals rapidly from damage caused by the horses.

*Orchardgrass.*    Orchardgrass is very desirable for horse pastures. It can be used in combination with bluegrass or as the only grass in a mixture with a legume. It is equal to bluegrass in quality, and outside the bluegrass area it should be first choice for horse pastures. Orchardgrass withstands closer grazing than timothy, and is less aggressive to a companion legume than fescue, bromegrass, or reed canary grass.

*Tall fescue.*    Fescue is widely grown in the United States, and thousands of horses are pastured on this hardy grass. However, it is not the best forage for horses because it is unpalatable much of the year. Horses sometimes do poorly on it unless their ration is fortified with grain. This is especially true of mares with nursing foals.

Mares grazing fescue pasture during the last 3 months of pregnancy may abort despite the fact that the mares are fed an adequate balanced grain ration. If mares are carrying extremely valuable foals, it may be safest to remove them from fescue pasture during the last 2 or 3 months of pregnancy.

A fescue-legume mixture is more desirable for horse pastures than fescue alone. Some fescue can be used in pastures for late fall and winter grazing. Late summer and early fall growth can be stockpiled and used to supplement hay and grain rations during winter.

Tall fescue should be used in small exercise lots where horses are confined in times of wet weather. It is ideally suited to barn lots, lanes, around gates and watering troughs, and other heavy traffic areas.

*Sorghum–Sudan crosses, Sudan grass, and pearl millet.*    These are not recommended for horse pastures because cystitis has been recognized in horses grazing them. Most of the cases reported have been in Texas. Nothing is known about the relationship of cystitis and pearl millet.

*Timothy.*   Timothy is well liked by horses but it does not survive close grazing. If it is used, rational grazing must be practiced.

*Bromegrass.*   Bromegrass may also be used successfully as a horse pasture in areas where it is adapted. It is somewhat sensitive to close grazing and may require more management in the form of rotation grazing, clipping, and fertilizing than other grasses to maintain a productive stand.

*Reed canary grass.*   Reed canary grass has been used to some advantage as a horse pasture in New Jersey and is well adapted to the Midwest.

*Bermuda grass.*   In many areas of the South and Southeast, Bermuda grass is used with good results in horse pastures. Oklahoma reports that it is inferior to the cool-season grasses for horses, but could be used in a system to produce some summer grazing. If it is used as part of the forage program it is important that a legume be maintained in combination with it.

LEGUMES   Any legume that is adapted to the soil and moisture conditions of an area can be successfully used as a legume in horse pastures. Horses seldom bloat, so there is little fear of using alfalfa, ladino, or white clover.

Sometimes an excessive amount of legumes in a mixture will cause excess salivation or slobbering. If the amount of legumes can be maintained at about 35 to 40 percent of the mixture, slobbering will be minimized.

The best legumes are bird's-foot trefoil, white and ladino clover, alfalfa, and red clover. Alsike clover and lespedeza may also be used.

SELECTING A MIXTURE   Keep seeding mixtures simple. For best results use only one grass and one or two legumes in a mixture. Differences in palatability and maturity dates among grasses make it highly undesirable to use more than one grass species per forage mixture. For example, tall fescue and orchardgrass seeded in the same mixture result in spotty grazing and wasted forage because of differences in palatability.

The following seeding rates should serve as guides for the proper amount of seed to plant per acre to obtain forage stands with a proper balance between grasses and legumes. Soil and climate conditions may dictate some adjustments in seeding rates from one area to another. The local county extension agent will make recommendations suitable for the area.

*Seeding mixtures (pounds per acre)*[3]

1   Alfalfa (10 lb) combined with bromegrass (10 lb), orchardgrass (6 lb), or tall fescue (10 lb)

[3]Howell N. Wheaton and Melvin Bradley, "Horse Pastures," *University of Missouri Science and Technology Guide* 4695, 1978.

2   Medium red clover (8 lb) combined with orchardgrass (6 lb), timothy (2 lb, fall), or tall fescue (4 lb, spring)
3   Red clover (8 lb) plus ladino clover (¾ lb) combined with tall fescue (15 lb)
4   Bird's foot trefoil (3 lb) combined with timothy (2 lb) or with orchardgrass (3 lb) plus Kentucky bluegrass (1 lb) (unless bluegrass was present in the old sod)
5   Lespedeza (15 lb) plus ladino clover (½ lb) combined with tall fescue (15 lb) or orchardgrass (6 lb)
6   Ladino clover (1 lb) plus alsike clover (2 lb) combined with reed canary grass (6 lb)
7   Alfalfa (10 lb) or red clover (10 lb) combined with reed canary grass (6 lb)

### Hays

By definition, hay is a feed produced by dehydrating green forages to a moisture content of 15 to 20 percent. High-quality hay is a necessary part of most horses' diets. When half or more of the nutrients horses need come from high-quality hay, few nutritional and psychological problems develop. Indeed, most horses can be maintained indefinitely on quality hay without any other feed. Only young horses, those working hard, and mares milking heavily need additional nutrients.

Since pastures are unavailable to many horsemen, they must rely on hay for its replacement. Unfortunately, much hay is harvested in a manner that renders it unsatisfactory for horses—cut when too mature and baled with too much moisture to cure properly.

Hay grown in cool areas or those of moderately high rainfall is usually baled or processed with too much moisture in it to cure well. There are a number of reasons for this. If it sells by the ton out of the field, extra water means more profit. Threat of rain may hasten the harvesting process before the windrowed hay is dry enough to cure well. Wet soil and high humidity makes curing very difficult. Much hay is not a high-value cash crop and may be neglected for one that is.

When baled, stacked, or bunched with too much moisture, hay ferments (heats), loses nutrients, and produces excessive mold. If white areas of mold or a musty odor is apparent in the inside of a bale, it should not be fed to horses. The short-run risk of colic is great, and the long-run condition of heaves in some horses is a certainty.

Late-cut hay, especially nonlegume, is high in fiber, which means it is low in digestibility (approximately 40 percent), palatability, and carotene or vitamin A activity. If forced to eat such hays, the horse will tend to develop haybelly. High fiber hay passes through the digestive tract slowly, and the horse must gorge to obtain its daily nutrient requirements.

Note in Table 11-1 the sharp decline in nutritional value of matured

TABLE 11-1   EFFECT OF MATURITY AND BALING WITH TOO MUCH MOISTURE ON
HAY QUALITY (Dry-matter basis)

| Sample | Species | EDDM,* % | CP,† % | Crude fat, % | Crude fiber, % | Date cut |
|--------|---------|----------|--------|--------------|----------------|----------|
| 1 | Fescue | 48.7 | 9.1 | 2.3 | 32.5 | May 29 |
| 2 | Fescue | 42.6 | 5.8 | 1.9 | 38.0 | July 2 |
| 3 | Orchardgrass | 40.2 | 7.3 | 2.0 | 38.2 | June 19 |
| 4 | Alfalfa–orchardgrass | 41.5 | 8.9 | 1.6 | 40.0 | May 30 (baled wet) |
| 5 | Alfalfa–orchardgrass | 58.2 | 18.0 | 2.1 | 28.7 | July 10 |
| 6 | Timothy | 46.1 | 6.4 | 2.0 | 32.1 | June 8 |
| 7 | Fescue–clover | 47.0 | 10.2 | 1.2 | 34.5 | June 5 |

*Chemically estimated digestible dry matter.
†Crude protein.
SOURCE: University of Missouri, Columbia, 1976.

fescue (sample 2). By delaying harvest approximately 1 month, digestibility (EDDM), crude protein, and fat percentages all decline, while crude fiber rises substantially compared to sample 1. Hay with this analysis is too low in protein and palatability for horses and too high in crude fiber. Such hay is often brown in color and is consumed only by very hungry horses. Conversely the May 29 cutting (sample 1) is adequate in nutrients for adult horses and will be consumed readily by most of them. Note the dramatic loss in nutritive value of sample 4, alfalfa–orchardgrass, from heating when baled wet. Mold would prohibit its use with horses, although many would gladly eat it because of the legume (alfalfa) in it.

Unfortunately "horse hay" to some horsemen more nearly resembles the poor-quality, late-cut hay shown in Figure 11-6. How often one hears a distinction made between "hay" and "horse hay" by hay sellers and horse hay buyers, with junky hay going to the horses!

THREE TYPES OF HAYS   There are three types of hays: (1) legume, (2) nonlegume and (3) mixed hays.

Legumes and nonlegumes are striking in their physical and nutritional differences. Legume plants have small nodules on their roots which, when naturally "innoculated" with bacteria, produce a high nitrogen or protein content in their leaves. Legumes are also higher in calcium, vitamins, trace minerals, leaf-to-stem ratio, and palatability. Horses love them.

Physically, legumes grow more densely on the ground, have a deep and extensive root system, yield more tonnage per cutting, and may be cut two

FIGURE 11-6   A conglomerate of late-cut grass, hays, and weeds, browned from being rained on and moldy around the pockets of the weeds (*bottom*). Unfortunately, this is considered "horse hay" by some horse owners. [*Photograph by the author.*]

to four times per season. Because of yield they are usually more profitable, and may receive better fertility management and processing care than nonlegumes.

Legumes make excellent horse feed and should be included in the rations of young growing horses, breeding horses, and adults being conditioned.

Note the great advantage in TDN, crude protein, and calcium percentages of legumes compared to nonlegumes in Table 11-2. (Please remember nutrient composition given in Tables 11-2 and 11-3 are listed on a "dry-matter basis" and the discussion of hays and grains are on an "as-fed" basis or approximately 9 to 10 percent less.) This is why legumes should complement grains when feeding animals that require high calcium and protein diets, i.e., growing foals and milking mares. Both legumes and nonlegumes are about the same in percentage of phosphorus, and both decline in nutritive value with maturity.

Are legumes hard on the horse's kidneys? Some horsemen swear by them and some swear at them. In certain areas of the country alfalfa is fed extensively because of its availability. Winners of the Tevis Cup 100-mile endurance ride are about equally divided on feeding legume and nonlegume hay.

There is considerably more protein in quality legumes than an adult

TABLE 11-2  COMPARISON OF NUTRIENT VALUES OF LEGUME AND NONLEGUME HAYS (dry-matter basis)

| Species | DE, Mcal/kg | TDN, % | CP, % | Ca, % | P, % |
|---|---|---|---|---|---|
| *Legumes* | | | | | |
| Alfalfa, second cut | | | | | |
| Early bloom | 2.42 | 55 | 17.2 | 1.75 | 0.26 |
| Midbloom | 2.29 | 52 | 16.0 | 1.50 | 0.25 |
| Full bloom | 2.16 | 49 | 15.0 | 1.29 | 0.24 |
| Clover, red | 2.16 | 49 | 14.9 | 1.49 | 0.25 |
| Lespedeza, full bloom | 2.07 | 47 | 13.9 | 1.15 | 0.25 |
| *Nonlegumes* | | | | | |
| Bermuda | 1.98 | 45 | 7.0 | 0.40 | 0.19 |
| Brome, smooth, late bloom | 2.38 | 54 | 7.4 | 0.32 | 0.22 |
| Fescue, midbloom | 2.02 | 46 | 10.5 | 0.57 | 0.37 |
| Oats, hay | 2.07 | 47 | 8.9 | 0.25 | 0.07 |
| Orchardgrass | 2.07 | 47 | 10.1 | 0.35 | 0.31 |
| Timothy | | | | | |
| Prehead | 2.20 | 50 | 11.5 | 0.50 | 0.25 |
| Headed | 1.98 | 45 | 0.9 | 0.41 | 0.19 |

SOURCE: National Research Council, *Nutrient Requirements of Horses*, National Academy of Sciences, Washington, D.C., 1978.

horse's body needs for muscle building. Therefore, extra protein is broken down for energy or fat, and the excess nitrogen (from the excess protein) is excreted in the urine. Since nitrogen is in salt form and urine stays constant in salt content, the horse must drink more water in order to increase urine volume to eliminate excess salt. It is quite obvious to the handler of a closely observed horse eating large amounts (12 to 20 pounds) of legume, especially if the handler is also cleaning the stall, that the horse is drinking a lot of water and voiding a lot of urine. Anxiety may arise about the possibility of a kidney problem when in reality such irrigation of the kidneys, at least in older horses, may be beneficial. Of course there is no need to habitually *full-feed* good legume hay to adult horses as it is expensive, causes obesity, and increases stall cleaning.

Nonlegumes are easier to cure than legumes without danger of mold because of lower leaf density, a harvest later in the season, and drier ground for growing due to less shading and warmer weather. However, almost all nonlegumes, because of the harvestor's desire to increase tonnage, are harvested too late to yield a high-quality product.

Good nonlegumes are good adult-horse hays and will sustain adult horses with no other feed if fed in adequate quantities. However, they are too low in protein, calcium, and palatability for many weanling and growing horses.

*Mixed hays* combine many of the advantages of both legumes and non-legumes. They may be midway between the two (depending on percent of each type) in protein, calcium, vitamins, and palatabilty. They are less expensive than legumes and do not produce obesity as quickly in stabled horses.

TYPES OF LEGUMES    *Alfalfa (50 to 56 percent TDN).* Alfalfa is king of the legumes. Its high nutrient content, high yield, multiple cuttings, and excellent palatability make it so. The University of Missouri–Columbia Equine Center tries to keep top-quality third- or fourth-cutting alfalfa on hand for sick horses and picky eaters. (Figures 11-7 and 11-8). If such horses will not eat good alfalfa, they are not likely to eat much of anything else.

Because of its fragrance and palatability, alfalfa is ideal for enticing foals into creeps, where they learn to eat grain. Good alfalfa is especially useful in weanling feeding because of its abundance of nutrients which are deficient in grains. It is also excellent for feeding old horses with bad teeth.

FIGURE 11-7    Good first-cutting alfalfa containing approximately 50 percent TDN and 15 percent CP. The stems are coarse. This alfalfa has a high stem to leaf ratio. Foals will often refuse the stems, and this will result in some waste. [*Photograph by the author.*]

FIGURE 11-8    Excellent fourth-cutting alfalfa containing approximately 56 percent TDN and 18 percent CP. This alfalfa has a high leaf to stem ratio, and is cured without mold. Feed it to foals and weanlings and sick or picky eaters, and use it for conditioning old or thin horses. [*Photograph by the author.*]

In some climates alfalfa will produce 5 cuttings per year, averaging ½ to 2 tons per acre per cutting. This makes it a good cash crop and therefore justifies top management attention and high priority in the work schedule.

First-cutting alfalfa is usually higher in stem-to-leaf ratio than later cuttings, may be harder to cure in certain areas because of the rainy season, and may be cut in a late stage of maturity because of competition for labor from other crops and from wet weather. Horsemen generally prefer second- or third-cuttings because of these factors and the fact that weeds, especially giant foxtail, tend to appear in fourth and fifth cuttings. However, the nutrient content, especially protein, tends to be greater in late-cut hays. If all crops of alfalfa are cut at the same stage of maturity, the early bloom stage, nutrient contents are rather uniform, provided the curing process is satisfactory. Stage of maturity greatly affects protein content of alfalfa, which may vary from 20 to 12 percent, while calcium and phosphorus remain about the same at about 1.5 percent and 0.30 percent, respectively.

The contention by some horsemen that alfalfa causes sweating and excessive overheating in summer is hard to verify. A good argument can be made that because of its high nutrient content, high digestibility, and sparing effect on grain, horses eating alfalfa under practical management conditions tend to be fatter than those eating grain and a nonlegume hay.

Another complaint that is hard to verify is that alfalfa tends to cause loose bowels. Some authorities years ago recommended that only first- cutting alfalfa be fed work horses. However, modern research shows no more likelihood of loose bowels from late cuttings than from first cuttings. It is possible that horses, when *first switched* to alfalfa, tend to have loose bowels, but this condition soon clears.

Alfalfa is not without problems. It is hard to cure and is susceptible to mold. Dense foliage and early-season maturity make the first crop come in seasons of high rainfall in most areas when it is grown.

Weevils have destroyed many fields, and recent export demand has driven prices beyond the budgets of many horse owners. When overfed to adult horses it will create obesity. If carelessly fed to extremely fatigued horses its palabatility and disgestibility may induce digestive disorders more easily than would a lesser quality hay.

Despite these problems, alfalfa is a super horse feed when used in a reasonably good horse management system.

*Clover hays (50 to 54 percent TDN).*   A variety of clovers are grown in almost every region of the nation—red, white, crimson, alsike, and ladino.

By far the most widely distributed variety is *red clover*. It is a biannual that makes two hay crops per year and yields much more tonnage than other clovers. For this reason, all but red clover has been relegated to a minor role in horse hay production.

When properly cured, red clover may be the most palatable hay fed to horses (Figure 11-9). They will eat every leaf and stem. Indeed, one can chew the stem and get a sweet taste from it. Nutritionally it is slightly inferior to alfalfa in calcium and phosphorus (1.5 percent calcium, 0.25 percent phosphorus) and is usually 1 or 2 percentage points below average alfalfa in protein. It probably is not nearly as good a vitamin source, either. Protein content can approach 18 percent, but generally ranges from 12 to 15 percent.

Red clover is very difficult to cure because of its large stems, and it is more susceptible to mold than any other hay. Draft horse owners years ago often refused to feed red clover because they said it made horses cough. Indeed, if there is mold in it, horses will cough.

First-cutting red clover comes in the middle of the rainy season in much of the country where it is grown (Figure 11-10). This makes curing especially difficult, because the ground as well as the plant may be high in moisture. It furnishes such dense shade to the ground that sun curing is difficult even after the clover is cut into a swath. It may require raking and turning more than one time before it is ready to bale.

FIGURE 11-9 This excellent second-cutting red clover hay contains approximately 54 percent TDN and 17 percent CP. Small, immature heads show the desired maturity; brightness of color indicates that the red clover is well preserved. [*Photograph by Duane Dailey.*]

Red clover is well eaten by horses of all ages in all stages of growth. However, smaller-stemmed, second-cutting red clover is preferable for foals.

Red clover normally should be cut between the half-bloom and full-bloom stages. However, the protein content is greatest when it is cut when the first blooms appear.

*Crimson clover* makes good hay and yields two crops per year. It tends to be higher in fiber than red clover, and therefore must be cut at a reasonable stage or it becomes tough and unpalatable to horses. It is adapted to the southeastern part of the United States and will grow on many different kinds of soils. It contains about 12 to 13 percent protein, 1.4 percent calcium, and 0.2 percent phosphorus.

*Alsike clover* is a fine-stemmed, low-yielding clover that is adapted to wet soil. It tends to lodge while growing and may be hard to cure. However, when well-cured it is a good hay for horses. Alsike is about 12 percent protein, with 1.3 percent calcium and 0.29 percent phosphorus.

*Ladino* is a cool-season variety of clover that is used more for pasturing than for hay because it does not grow very tall or yield very much per acre. When cured properly, it is very high in protein, about 15.6 percent, and very

FIGURE 11-10  This coarse, dark (rained on), mature, weedy, first-cutting red clover contains approximately 46 percent TDN and 12 percent CP. If white mold and musty odor are present in mature red clover, it should not be fed to horses. [*Photograph by Duane Dailey.*]

low in fiber. Ladino hay contains 1.32 percent calcium and 0.24 percent phosphorus.

*Lespedeza (48 to 52 percent TDN).*    When cut early, lespedeza makes an excellent horse hay (Figure 11-11). It is about as high in protein as red clover, having about 12 percent protein, and contains about 1 percent calcium and 0.25 percent phosphorus. It will grow on the poorest of soils and reseeds itself annually. It is often grown with a cover crop such as wheat or oats.

Lespedeza occupied a very large area in the Midwest and Southeast some years ago. It grew well on soils that had formerly produced little grazing or hay prior to its appearance in this country. However, disease has troubled lespedeza of late, and it is not a sufficiently high-yielding crop to compete with other legumes in modern intensive farming operations. When over-mature and overdried, it has tough wiry stems and is subject to severe leaf shatter (Figure 11-12).

Lespedeza can be cut early in the morning and will be dry enough to bale late in the afternoon in much of the area where it is grown. However, it is a late-season crop and does not compete very well with weeds.

FIGURE 11-11  Excellent lespedeza containing approximately 52 percent TDN and 15 percent CP. High leaf to stem ratio indicates that the plant is of the required maturity and was properly cured. [*Photograph by Duane Dailey.*]

*Bird's-foot trefoil (52 percent TDN).*  This northeastern crop resembled some of the clovers in fineness of stem and density of leaf. It is very difficult to establish as a new crop. There are two kinds of trefoil, one adapted for pasture and the other for hay production. The variety best adapted to an area should be determined by the county extension agent. Once bird's-foot trefoil is established, and a good stand achieved, it is a rather high-yielding crop. Its nutrient content is much like the clovers, about 14 percent digestible protein with 1.75 percent calcium and 0.2 percent phosphorus.

In summary, the legume hays are very beneficial for feeding foals, young growing horses, milking mares and breeding stallions, and sick or old horses that are doing poorly. The high protein and calcium content of alfalfa are particularly needed by such animals.

Conversely, alfalfa may add fat if self-fed to idle horses and may aggravate digestive upsets if carelessly fed to tired horses, especially after a large grain feed has been consumed. The buyer or harvester of legumes must constantly guard against molds as all varieties are much more susceptible to them than are nonlegume hays.

TYPES OF GRASS HAYS  There is a very large variety of grasses and small grains cut early and baled for hays. They vary immensely in palatability,

FIGURE 11-12    Late-cut lespedeza containing approximately 46 percent TDN and 11 percent CP. Bare stems show substantial leaf shatter and large weed stems indicate late cutting. [*Photograph by Duane Dailey.*]

quality, percentage fiber, and amount of weeds, because some are cut only once each year. Protein contents may range from 3 to 20 percent, but calcium and phosphorus contents remain almost constant at 0.3 to 0.4 percent calcium and 0.2 to 0.3 percent phosphorus. Stage of maturity is critical for harvesting grass hays because fiber increases sharply as the hays approach maturity and may render some of them—fescue and orchardgrass in particular—almost totally unpalatable if cut 10 days to 2 weeks too late.

Good grass hays can be fed free-choice without concern about digestive upsets from an excess of nutrients and in most cases without producing obesity. For this reason they are particularly useful in feeding stabled horses to reduce wood chewing and other bad habits resulting from idleness. Free-choice feeding of fescue will actually reduce most obese horses without producing wood chewing and other starvation-induced habits.

*Timothy (44 to 50 percent TDN).*    No other nonlegume hay is as popular as timothy. Its wide range of climatic adaptability, ease of curing, bright color, and freedom from dust and mold make it the horseman's favorite.

When timothy is cut in the early-bloom stage, its crude protein content may approach 12 percent (Figure 11-13). Although timothy deteriorates less

FIGURE 11-13    Excellent timothy containing approximately 50 percent TDN and 12 percent CP. It was harvested in mid-Missouri on June 14 before the heads (upper right) were fully grown. [*Photograph by Duane Dailey.*]

from late cutting than almost any other nonlegume, its crude protein quickly drops to 8 or 9 percent 2 or 3 weeks after the optimum harvest season. Mature, late-cut timothy is a poor feed for any class of livestock (Figure 11-14). Timothy is often grown with a mixture of other crops for hay and pasture.

Timothy hay is excellent for adult horses. It may be the only hay fed to all classes and ages of horses, however, it must be strongly supplemented with protein, calcium, and phosphorus and vitamins for weanlings, milking mares, and growing horses.

The timothy hay buyer can determine stage of maturity easily by development of the heads. If none has seed in them but show some stalks with heads in the boot stage, it can be certain it was harvested at the appropriate stage. If cut late, most of the seeds in the heads will be lost. Timothy cut at this stage should be avoided by most horse feeders.

*Bromegrass hay (44 to 50 percent TDN).*    Bromegrass is a fine-stemmed nonlegume with a wide area of adaptation. It grows densely on the field and has a high yield. Brome is easy to cure and is palatable to horses when cut in the midbloom stage. It may be slightly lower in crude protein than timothy and may not grow well in warmer southern climes. Like timothy, brome

FIGURE 11-14  Unacceptable timothy. Horses refused to eat it. Chemical analysis showed its estimated digestible dry matter to be 32 percent; CP, 3 percent; and phosphorus, 0.18 percent. Seeds are gone from the heads. This timothy was grown on poor soil, cut late, rained on, and stored for 5 years before it was sold as "horse hay" to an inexperienced owner. [*Photograph by Duane Dailey.*]

can be used in a mixture of a variety of pastures and hays. It is very good when mixed with alfalfa. For these reasons, pure brome hay is not readily available to most horsemen. The stage of maturity is not easy to detect, but in the best brome the heads are fine and the seeds are small.

*Orchardgrass.*  Orchardgrass is much like brome, but coarser and less well-liked by horses if cut late. Orchardgrass will grow on poorer soils than brome and produce a taller plant that has a higher stem-to-leaf ratio. All other things being equal, brome is a better horse hay. However, early-cut orchardgrass in the early bloom stage makes a very acceptable hay. Although crude protein percentage of orchardgrass is listed at 10.1 by the NRC, it takes an excellent hay producer to reach this level. Chemical analysis of a number of samples may show that in practice haymakers average closer to 6 percent. Since orchardgrass mixes well with legumes, it is often available in mixed hays.

*Fescue (32 to 46 percent TDN).*  Fescue is grown extensively in the Midwest and Southeast portion of the United States. It will grow in any type of soil and is almost impervious to drought and overgrazing. Indeed, there is no known way to eradicate it if you wish to eliminate it except in areas that can be cultivated. Although attacked by some insects, fescue is almost completely resistant to destruction by insects and disease.

Fescue is probably the poorest common horse hay. Part of the reason is that it is almost always cut too late. But fescue is also unpalatable to horses in hay form in almost any stage of cutting. A common management practice for fescue in Missouri, a very large fescue-producing state, includes heavy grazing through the spring, followed by removal of animals for a seed crop in mid-June, then cutting and baling the stubble for cattle immediately after the seed crop is removed. Such hay is exceedingly low in protein, perhaps only 3 percent, and totally unpalatable to all but starving horses.

On the other hand, fescue cut in prebloom stage (usually by mid-May to late May) produces an attractive, green hay which is very fine-stemmed and which has 10.5 percent protein. Even so, it is eaten reluctantly by horses, but as the saying goes, "none have been known to starve to death on it." For this reason many horsemen feed 4 to 6 pounds of good legume in winter to their adult horses and feed fescue free-choice as the only other ingredient in their diets. Fescue works well in this type of management regimen, and also with fat, stabled horses.

The buyer must be cautious to avoid late-cut fescue—its fiber content will be extremely high, its protein low, and horses are likely to waste more of it than they eat because of unpalatability.

Improved varieties of fescue are being tested at the University of Missouri. Some have shown great promise in palatability and higher protein content than varieties now available.

*Bermudagrass (42 to 46 percent TDN).*  Bermudagrass is grown mostly in southern regions of the country. Coastal Bermuda is the variety used mostly for horses. Since it may be harvested three or four times annually, the last cuttings are higher in nutrients than the earlier, having 7 percent crude protein. Bermuda hay and timothy are often compared in nutrient value, but timothy is likely to be more palatable and to be damaged less by late cutting. Like timothy, Bermuda is best for adult horses because of its low nutrient content and low palatability. Researchers are developing varieties like fescue that are both higher in nutrients and palatability.

*Prairie hay (42 to 45 percent TDN).*  Prairie hay, as the name implies, grows in the dry areas of the country in the Midwest. In years past, it was popular with draft horse owners in cities, because it could be depended upon to be cured appropriately without mold. Train loads of prairie hay from Kansas and Nebraska were shipped to most large cities in the country during the draft horse era. Recently prairie hays have lost popularity with horse people because they are not very high in any nutrients and because transportation costs render them uneconomical. However, they can be substituted for timothy hay in areas where cost is competitive. Crude protein is 6.7 percent.

*Cereal hays (45 to 50 percent TDN).*   Cereal hays come from the small grain crops, such as oats, barley, wheat, and rye, and they are preferred by horses in that order. To make good hays, they must be cut in the soft- to stiff-dough stage. Many acres are made into hay in the Northwest region of the United States. Cereal hays vary greatly in nutrient value, depending upon the development of the head or grain portion. Their average protein content may be between 8 and 9 percent, and their calcium and phosphorus contents can vary sharply depending upon the grain-stalk ratio (see Appendix 12-1). They are often low in or without vitamins. If there is little grain left on the heads, phosphorus content may be almost nil. Cereal hays vary greatly in palatability. Oat hay is relished while rye, especially if late-cut, may contain close to 40 percent fiber and be very unpalatable.

Cereal hays may be grown as a hay crop in the Northwest region of the country, but in most other areas, they are a cover crop and are made into hay to remove competition and shade from the crop they were intended to shelter. For this reason, they vary a great deal in stage of maturity, attention to harvest, and nutrient content.

*Sudangrass and other sorghum–Sudan species for hay.*   Sudan, Johnson grass, millet, and other forages of this nature are grown in hot, dry areas or as summer supplemental grazing crops. Johnson grass is seldom intentionally sown or grown and has been ruled an obnoxious weed by state law in Missouri and many other states. It is prohibited in some states from being hauled on public roads to prevent spreading of seeds. Recently a number of hybrid *Sudans* have emerged with much higher yields than the old-fashioned millet, and are being used extensively in the southern half of the United States for supplemental summer grazing and for hay. Most of these state on the feed tag "not to be grazed by horses," for some have caused a condition in horses called cystitis, which results in inflammation of the urinary bladder and eventual death.

Plants of this variety grow tall, have big stems and a small amount of leaves, and are low in protein and calcium. They may range from 9 to 3 percent crude protein, depending upon stage of maturity. If used for hay, they must be cut early, at least in early bloom if not before. If allowed to get tall they are almost impossible to cure, and nutrient content decreases sharply. Although satisfactorily used with cattle, they are more risky as horse hays, because of unpalatability, low nutrient content, and the ever-present danger of mold. However, good management can overcome these problems, and they can be satisfactorily used.

FIGURE 11-15 Excellent mixed hay, composed of brome and alfalfa. This hay contains approximately 52 percent TDN and 12 to 14 percent CP. Mixed hays are the choice of many horsemen. Mixed hay combines the high protein, calcium, and vitamin conent of legumes with the easy curing, safe feeding, and economy of non-legumes. [*Photograph by Duane Dailey.*]

MIXED HAYS Mixed hays are a combination of one or more varieties of grass hay and one or more of legume hay. They combine the good qualities of each without including much of the bad of either. Mixed hays, if about equal in varieties, are approximately 0.8 percent calcium, 0.3 percent phosphorus, and 12 to 14 percent protein. Most horsemen, especially those with a few animals of different ages, like mixed hays (Figure 11-15).

There are many varieties grown together, among them brome–alfalfa, timothy–red clover, orchardgrass–lespedeza, or combinations of any of these and many others. The fertility program can be regulated to encourage one species and discourage another if the ratio becomes unsatisfactory. One problem that buyers have is evaluating the proportion of legume to non-legume hay. When the crop is standing, it may appear to be mostly legume, but when it is baled and cured, it may appear to be mostly nonlegume.

## Hay Quality

Even though higher-quality hay is a necessary ingredient in most horses' diets, its production is difficult at best, even when proper management steps are followed to the letter throughout most of the production phase. The producer still faces a high level of risk from unpredictable wet weather, unless the hay is produced in the irrigated districts of the Southwest. Rains leach nutrients from plants, retard proper drying and curing conditions, and encourage mold growth if the producer is forced to bale hay with much more than 20 percent moisture. Hay that has been rained on will lose some leaves and much of its vitamin content. A number of factors affect hay quality. Some are stage of maturity, condition of curing, method of curing, plant species, and freedom from foreign matter.

FACTORS AFFECTING HAY QUALITY    Of all the things that affect hay quality, *stage of maturity when cut* is most important. Nutrient content in the stem portion of the plant declines sharply when lignin and cellulose content increase at maturity. The amount of nutrients in early cut hay is actually greater, even with less tonnage, than in heavier late-cut hay—and prices should but do not reflect this difference. Progressive stages of maturity are inversely proportional to the digestibility of hay. For this reason, the best hay should be at the prebloom or early bloom stage of maturity.

*Curing conditions* can greatly affect nutritive value and palatability. Even though cut in prebloom stage, if hay is improperly cured by overdrying, leaves are lost, or if baled with too much moisture, molds are encouraged. Two things are certain to happen when hay is baled wet: first, it will heat, thus losing a large percentage of nutrients, and second, the heat and moisture will inevitably support mold growth. Hay that has heated will be brown and will have lost its vitamin A content. If force-fed to horses, it will cause heaves, respiratory problems, and severe colic. Hay that has been affected in this manner cannot be recovered by additive or mechanical treatment. It should be removed from the stable and be fed to cattle that have a very much higher tolerance for moldy hay than horses. It should not be used for bedding, because hungry horses may eat it, and if a legume, it must not be hauled to the ditch on the "back forty" because horses will eat rotten legume and develop colic.

The curing process is a trade-off between leaf loss and reduction of moisture in the hay. The moisture content must be reduced from approximately 80 percent to approximately 15 to 20 percent without excessive leaf loss from overdrying or from constant agitation in the windrow by mechanical means to hasten drying of the stems. Mechanical hay conditioners cut hay-drying time in half by cracking the stems at uniform intervals (approximately 4 inches apart) to expedite moisture evaporation. Without proper management, leaves overdry and stems underdry before hay can be safely baled. Heavy, tight bales may indicate too much moisture and possible mold. If hay is baled wet, a loosely tied bale will cure much more completely than one tightly baled.

*Plant species* greatly affects hay quality, as was discussed in the comparison of legume and nonlegume hay. Even though legumes are usually higher in nutrient content and more palatable, the best of the nonlegumes processed in the prebloom stage will have more palatability and protein than the worst of the legumes cut too late and improperly processed. Therefore, the horseman who cannot grow or buy legumes because of climate and soil conditions may well be able to produce or buy quality hays made from nonlegumes by early cuttings and proper hay-making procedures.

Finally, hay quality depends to some extent on the *amount of foreign matter* in the hay. Weedy hay indicates sparsely populated plants or late maturity. While toxic weeds are seldom present in hay fields, the presence of weeds indicates less than optimum hay production practices. Since weeds contain more moisture than most hay plants, there are usually mold pockets around them in hay bales. If horses are fed enough hay, the weeds will be sorted out and cause little trouble. However, if hay is limited to the point where horses must eat mold pockets, the horse will be in trouble. Some hay appears dusty or dirty (not as a result of mold). Usually dustiness indicates that the hay was rained on in the swath before raking and may subsequently show low levels of carotene, leaf loss, and loss of palatability. There is not much danger in feeding such hay when appropriately supplemented, although it will not be consumed as readily as bright, clean hay. Foreign objects are not uncommonly found in bales of hay, especially in hay cut from hay fields near road right-of-ways. Such foreign objects can pose quite a threat, especially for cattle and to a lesser degree for horses. Horses tend to sort out foreign materials in their hay better than cattle, but can be injured on the lips and tongue when sorting glass.

## THINGS TO LOOK FOR WHEN BUYING HAY

1 *Species.*   Is the hay a legume, nonlegume, or a mixture? Determine the relative amounts of each of these if buying a mixed hay.

2 *Maturity.*   At what stage of maturity was the crop harvested? This can be estimated by development of the heads and stem-to-leaf ratio. If the hay is a nonlegume, seeds will be mature or shattered out and gone if cut too late.

3 *Color and aroma.*   The color should be bright green, and the hay should smell like it is new-mown. Bright color means that there was no heating in the bale; the hay will be free of mold and have a high vitamin A content. If it is light brown, it may have been sun-bleached or baled too dry. If totally brown, it was probably rained on or baled when too wet, and has been heat-damaged, resulting in a nutrient loss of 10 percent or more. In order to check hay for color and aroma, break some bales and check the center of the bales because the outsides cure more easily.

4  *Age.*  Is it hay from the current year? If not, it will be drier, more brittle, and considerably less palatable to the horse, unless it is legume hay. It will also be much lower in vitamin content.

5  *Foreign materials.*  Weeds show easily on the edges of bales. Pull out weeds and see how much mold accompanies them. If approximately 20 percent of the bale is weeds, one will be lucky to feed 70 percent of the bale because of moisture damage around the weeds. If bull nettles or other thorny-type plants are in the bale, avoid it because the thorns can cause a serious problem in the mouth and lips of the horse. Although uncommon, some weeds are poisonous in bales of hay. They are clotallila, dogbane, bitterweed, and jimsonweed.

HOW TO HARVEST GOOD HAY   More and more horse owners are raising and processing their own hay. Good hay making starts with an understanding of the stage of maturity of plants and with adequate harvesting machinery and equipment. Standing hay is approximately 80 percent moisture, which must be reduced to 20 percent. This means that for each ton of dry matter baled, approximately 4 tons of water must be evaporated. Uniform drying of the standing hay crop is an essential technique of good hay making.

All mown hay should be raked without stacking a windrow on a portion of unraked hay. Windrows should be medium-sized and fluffy with the butts of the hay to the outside of the windrow and the heads on the inside. Loose, fluffy, uniform-sized windrows encourage rapid, uniform drying. Early spring cuttings of hay will probably be raked on damp ground, requiring a second turning of the windrows after the exposed side has dried to the appropriate moisture content.

Hay conditioners are an essential part of the machinery for the haymaking enterprise. The stems of the hay should be cracked, but not crushed. Rollers or crimpers of the machine should be damp as it operates, but should not squeeze excess moisture out of the plant.

Before baling, check the hay for uniformity of moisture content and appropriate dryness. While there are a number of commercial moisture testers, most producers quickly learn to determine when the plants have reached an appropriate moisture content by feeling and twisting the plant. One should avoid mowing heavy stands in the early morning, when the plants are covered with dew.

Hay will dry some in bales, especially if left in the field. However, the hazard of rain in most areas is so great that all bales produced in a day should be hauled to shelter that same day. If not, rain on unprotected bales will virtually ruin them. If baled hay can be stacked loosely in a barn to allow air to pass through it, or if it can be scattered over a wide area under shelter, it will continue to dry. If the hay is stacked tightly together (tall, deep, and wide) and if it contains too much moisture, the problems of heating, loss of nutrients, and mold will be worsened. Excessively wet hay stacked in the barn can actually cause spontaneous combustion resulting in destruction by fire of the hay and barn. Such hay would have been worthless for a horse even if it had not burned the barn. The old contention that hay must "go through the sweat" before it is ready for a horse to eat was based on a knowledge of the problem of wet hay. The fermentation process is so great that horses fed such hay actually suffer from the fermentation in progress at the time of eating the hay, and experience colic.

## Grains

Grains supplement forages in the horse's diet basically to increase energy. Hardworking horses cannot graze enough grass or eat enough hay to meet their energy needs; therefore, grain is necessary to furnish enough energy for work performed and to maintain condition. Medium-sized, hardworking horses may need as much as 12 to 15 pounds of grain and an equal amount of hay daily to maintain body weight, whereas adult idle horses may get fat on grass or hay alone.

Horses like grain. Some even bolt it down to the point of choking. Most grains are improved by grinding or rolling, but none should be ground fine. Frequent feeds in small amounts are best, with at least an hour's rest for tired horses before feeding. Continued heavy grain feeding on a day off can cause a serious illness called azoturia. In general, grain rations should be cut in half and hay increased on days that horses are idle. When substitution of one or more grains is made for others it should be done gradually.

In general, grains are average in protein content, ranging from 8 to 13 percent, very low in calcium and average in phosphorus. The seed portions of plants are high in fats and oils but poor in vitamins and trace minerals. Fortunately, the hays are strong in grains' weak points. Hays and grains complement each other well in the horse's diet.

CORN (80 PERCENT TDN)   Corn is the nation's most abundant grain. It grows in every state and is available to most horsemen. While it has some disadvantages (listed below), many backyard horse owners could supplement their horse roughage rations with small quantities of shelled, ear, or chopped corn in total safety and with great economy.

Corn's 9 percent crude protein and 0.26 percent phosphorus is adequate for adult horses, but its 0.02 percent calcium is dramatically low and must be supplemented by combining with hay, pasture, or a calcium supplement. Four pounds of corn and 12 pounds of most any kind of quality hay will suffice.

Corn has some advantages compared with oats: it is higher in energy (because it contains a large amount of carbohydrates), higher in vitamin A, more uniform in quality, and usually considerably cheaper (Table 11-3).

TABLE 11-3  NUTRIENT COMPOSITION OF SOME COMMON GRAINS AND ENERGY
SOURCES (dry-matter basis, except molasses)

| Grain | DE, Mcal/kg | TDN, % | CP, % | Ca, % | P, % | Crude fiber, % |
|---|---|---|---|---|---|---|
| Barley | 3.61 | 82 | 13.9 | 0.05 | 0.37 | 6.0 |
| Corn no. 2 | 3.87 | 88 | 10.9 | 0.02 | 0.31 | 2.0 |
| Grain sorghum | 3.52 | 80 | 13.8 | 0.07 | 0.36 | 2.8 |
| Oats | 3.34 | 76 | 13.6 | 0.07 | 0.37 | 12.0 |
| Wheat | 3.83 | 87 | 13.0 | 0.05 | 0.46 | 3.0 |
| Molasses, liquid | 3.26 | 74 | 4.3 | 1.05 | 0.15 | — |
| Wheat bran | 2.94 | 67 | 17.0 | 0.12 | 1.43 | 11.0 |
| Distillers' grain | 3.08 | 70 | 29.8 | 0.11 | 0.44 | 12.0 |

SOURCE: National Research Council, *Nutrient Requirements of Horses*, National Academy of
Sciences, Washington, D.C., 1978.

Corn is especially useful for improving condition in thin horses and maintaining condition in hardworking horses. Because of its uniform quality,
no. 2 yellow corn grown in one part of the country is almost identical to that
grown in any other part. The economy of TDN in corn is seldom matched
by any other grain, and in some areas it exceeds the economy of nutrients
purchased in hay.

Corn is only average in palatability and because of its high nutrient
density and low fiber content, can cause digestive upsets in horses more
easily than oats. Corn and oats combined in equal parts make an excellent
grain ration; most commercial horse grain rations are based on or near this
percentage. Corn can supply all the grain in a horse ration when fed according to the work the horse is performing, when large amounts are not given
at one time, and when it is introduced slowly, over 3 to 4 weeks. Indeed, in
draft horse days it was the only grain many horses ever received throughout
long useful lives. However, if large amounts of corn are fed to tired, hungry
horses, they are likely to develop colic, or else may burn out and refuse to
eat enough to maintain condition.

Some horsemen consider corn a "heating" feed in warm weather. However, "heat" or "specific dynamic action" of digestion is greater for high-
fiber feeds, such as hay and oats, than for corn. Probably a major reason for
the old misconception that corn is a heating food is that horses eating corn
tend to stay fatter than others, especially if they are not regularly exercised
and are fed by volume instead of weight (Figure 11-16). A given *weight* of
corn provides 15 percent more energy than oats, and a given volume of corn
can exceed the energy yield of oats by 100 percent, depending upon the quality of the oats.

Trowbridge did extensive research trials years ago with mules, feeding

FIGURE 11-16   Cracked corn. A coffee can that will hold 3 pounds of coffee holds 4¾ pounds of no. 2 yellow corn. Cracked corn has 80 percent or more TDN and 15 percent more energy than an equal weight of oats and may have double the energy of an equal volume of "light" oats. Feed by weight, not volume. [*Photograph by Duane Dailey.*]

one mule corn and the other oats, then switching grains.[4] After a 2-year study, it was determined that the difference in heat tolerance was indeed all accounted for by the difference in condition, and that over a season corn-fed mules maintained higher condition better and did so considerably more cheaply. However, it is much more convenient to feed oats, and an all-corn diet would not be recommended for most young horses in heavy training activities because of the risk of colic and burn out.

OATS (65 TO 75 PERCENT TDN)   Oats are the most commonly fed grain. The bulky (fibrous) nature of oats permits maximum liberty in feeding with minimum danger of digestive disorders. Oats are highly palatable. Oats are higher in protein content than corn, averaging approximately 12 percent, which makes them very useful when fed with low-protein grass hays. Oats are readily digestible and may not need any mechanical preparation,

[4]E. A. Trowbridge, "Corn versus Oats for Work Mules," *Missouri Agricultural Experiment Station Circular* 125, Columbia, Mo., July 1924.

such as crushing, crimping, or steam rolling, except for old horses with bad teeth.

Good oats are clean, heavy, bright in color and ripe, and have a low husk to kernel ratio. Oat color is usually white, but some oats are gray and even black, depending on variety. Dark kernels that are moldy, burnt, or bitter tasting, however, are poor-quality oats, and should not be fed to horses. Oats are not a good source of vitamins.

However, this excellent horse feed has some disadvantages. It varies more in quality than any other grain (Figures 11-17, 11-18, 11-19, and 11-20). While the standard weight of oats is 32 pounds per bushel, so-called race-horse oats may weigh 46 pounds and poor-grade oats may weigh 25 pounds and approach the TDN value of good hay. Oats often contain dirt or dust that tends to make the horse cough. To avoid this problem, oats must be cleaned and often recleaned to be satisfactory. Greedy horses will sometimes choke on oats. This can be avoided by placing smooth round stones in the trough that the horse must move around to get at the grain. Oats are expensive relative to feeding value and are difficult to mix with micronutrients such as limestone or vitamin supplements without concentration of the supplements due to settling. For these reasons oats are often pre-

FIGURE 11-17 "Racehorse" oats weigh about 46 pounds per bushel. Oats like these probably contain 80 percent TDN. A can that holds 3 pounds of coffee holds $4\frac{1}{3}$ pounds of super oats. [*Photograph by Duane Dailey.*]

**FIGURE 11-18**   A close-up of the above oats shows plump grains, light, clipped husks, and few immature kernels. [*Photograph by Duane Dailey.*]

**FIGURE 11-19**   There are about 25 pounds of sorry oats per bushel and oats like these probably contain 57 to 60 percent TDN. A coffee can full of sorry oats holds $2^2/_3$ pounds. Oats vary more in quality than any other horse grain. [*Photograph by Duane Dailey.*]

FIGURE 11-20  A close-up of the above oats shows an extensive husk-kernel ratio; many oats have no kernels in them. [*Photograph by Duane Dailey.*]

pared in combination with corn or another grain—plus molasses for more uniform mixing.

When buying oats check for weight or fullness of kernel and degree of foreign matter. If bought from the farm, assume that the oats must be cleaned. Many horsemen prefer "northern oats" because of their heavy weight, plumpness, and quality. Some oats will weigh up to 50 pounds per bushel; none should be considered that weigh under 35 pounds.

While oats are the favored grain of most horsemen and most horses, when cost or convenience dictates otherwise, rations can be formulated without them.

BARLEY (76 PERCENT TDN)  Barley is the fourth-ranking grain crop in North America, grown extensively in Canada and the northern United States. Good barley is clean, heavy, and has a low husk-to-kernel ratio. The kernels should be plump. The husk of processed barley, such as the steam-rolled variety, will be very light compared to the kernel portion in the best quality barley.

Barley is similar to oats in protein content and quality, but is lower in fiber.

Most barley is fed as a portion of the horse grain diet to improve its palatability. It has always been a popular feed for young racehorses, used to provide variety when encouraging them to consume greater quantities of grain.

GRAIN SORGHUM (78 PERCENT TDN)   Grain sorghums (milo) grow in areas of low rainfall, particularly in the Southwest part of the United States. While grain sorghum can be a satisfactory horse grain, there are more problems in feeding it than almost any other grain.

Although dense and high in TDN, grain sorghums vary in protein content from 5 to 12 percent and also vary greatly in palatability. The so-called "bird varieties" are unpalatable to all animals, especially horses. If much grain sorghum is to be fed, it should be tried on the horse before buying. Grain sorghum should be processed before feeding to increase digestibility, since it has a hard outer shell. It should not be finely ground, but may be rolled, crushed, or otherwise processed. Grain sorghums are very low in fiber and therefore are difficult to feed in large amounts without digestive upsets, but few problems result from feeding 4 to 6 pounds of grain sorghum per head per day. It is usually very inexpensive.

Grain sorghum may be similar to corn in many nutrient respects, but because of its low palatability and low fiber content, corn is preferable to it.

WHEAT (87 PERCENT TDN)   Whole wheat is seldom fed to horses except in the Pacific Northwest because it is expensive. It can be safely fed as part of the grain ration only when not exceeding half of the ration and when fed with a bulkier feed. It should be rolled or coarsely ground. Fines should be avoided because they produce a doughy ball in the stomach of the horse and can result in digestive upsets. Whole wheat is about 11 to 14 percent protein, 0.05 percent calcium, and 0.48 percent phosphorus.

Wheat middlings, by-products of the flour milling process, are currently popular as an ingredient in complete "textured" grains, a mixture of grains prepared with molasses. Wheat middlings are about 8 to 10 percent fiber and about 15 percent protein. Wheat middlings are by definition finely ground; despite their fiber content, when fed alone they tend to pack in the stomach and therefore must be mixed with bulkier grain.

WHEAT BRAN (66 PERCENT TDN)   Wheat bran is usually palatable to horses, quite laxative, and very bulky. Horsemen have long given bran mashes to animals that were under stress conditions or during extreme fatigue. However, the need for a bran mash in modern horse husbandry is infrequent, and its cost seldom justifies its *routine* use.

Bran is approximately 17 percent protein and 1.4 percent phosphorus and is very low in calcium. It is usually fed for bulk in a heavily concentrated diet and its cost renders it a poor buy on a TDN basis. Old-time horse people fed horses high levels of bran in combination with legume hay because of its high phosphorus content. Although the phosphorus in bran is not highly digestible, horses on a grain ration, one-fourth of which routinely is bran, are very likely to develop a severe calcium-phosphorus imbalance, unless fed legume hay or the appropriate amount of calcium supplement.

## Protein Supplements

Protein is a high-nitrogen nutrient built from amino acids. These range chemically from very simple to very complex molecules that are used to build muscles in growing horses, produce milk in lactating mares, and in many chemical reactions and bodily functions. The quality of protein is determined by the percentage or amount of essential amino acids that the young horse's body cannot synthesize or that are usually deficient in the feed (Table 11-4). The effectiveness of protein, therefore, depends upon its most limiting essential amino acid. Ideally, a protein would supply all the amino acids in exactly the amount they are needed in the body. Milk protein most closely approaches this description, with other protein sources varying substantially from it. Next to calcium, protein is the nutrient most often found deficient in the diet of growing horses and in pregnant and lactating mares. It may also be deficient in diets of horses being groomed for show and horses under stress, since stress affects appetite.

There are three sources of protein: plant, animal, and nonprotein nitrogen. The seeds of some plants are high in protein, fats and oils, soybeans, flaxseeds, and cottonseeds among them. These plants furnish almost all of the commercial protein supplements for animal feeding in this country.

TABLE 11-4  ESSENTIAL AND SOME
NONESSENTIAL AMINO ACIDS FOR
MOST NONRUMINANTS

| *Essential amino acids* | *Nonessential amino acids* |
|---|---|
| Arginine | Alanine |
| Histidine | Aspartic acid |
| Isoleucine | Citrulline |
| Leucine | Cystine |
| Lysine* | Glutamic acid |
| Methionine | Glycine |
| Phenylalanine | Hydroxyproline |
| Threonine | Proline |
| Tryptophan | Serine |
| Valine | Tyrosine |

*Lysine is the major essential amino acid that foals and young horses respond to in standard horse diets.

Different processing methods result in different protein levels in these meals. In years past, the hydraulic process was used to crush the seeds, which were then cooked and pressed by hydraulic presses as long as oil could be extracted. The residue was ground into meal that contained a relatively high percentage of fat. A second process was the expeller process: the beans were cracked and dried, then cooked by steam processing. Screw presses removed the oil and the residue was then ground into meal. This process also rendered a high fat content. A third process, and the one used currently in most oil meal production, is the solvent process. In this method, the beans are rolled into flakes, then exposed to chemical solvents that extract all of the oil and most of the fat. Generally the higher the fat the lower the percentage of protein in an oil meal, but the higher the percentage digestibility because fat is a concentrated source of energy. Fat is also a good source of the fatty acid linoleic acid, which causes the hair coat to bloom.

SOYBEAN OIL MEAL    Extensive expansion of soybean production in the corn-belt for export purposes has resulted in enormous quantities of soybean meal for the livestock industry. Most soybean meal produced by the solvent process is sold on the basis of 44 percent crude protein; in areas where poultry is produced it may be 50 percent. The fat content ranges from 1½ to 5 percent. It is a good source of phosphorus (0.7 percent), fair source of calcium (0.3 percent), and the best of the plant sources in the essential limiting amino acid, lysine (3.28 percent). It is highly digestible, low in fiber, economical in price and available almost anywhere feed is sold. Soybean meal is eaten more readily than most of the other protein sources and has less laxative effect than linseed meal. For these reasons it should be the choice protein supplement for horse feeders. Most commercial horse rations use soybean meal as a protein source.

Whole soybeans should not be fed to horses. They contain a trypsin inhibitor that prevents the proper breakdown and assimilation of the amino acid trypsin. When heated, however, the inhibitor is destroyed, and the remaining meal is easily digested. Horses do not readily eat raw soybeans; however, if exceedingly hungry they will and may die as a result of such overeating.

COTTONSEED MEAL    Cottonseed meal is used extensively for horses in the Southwest. It ranges in protein from 30 to 40 percent, contains 2 to 6 percent fat, and is a good source of phosphorus. It has about 4 percent fiber. The amino acid balance of cottonseed is not as good as soybean, but better than linseed (Table 11-5).

Some varieties of cottonseed and some methods of producing the oil meal result in a high gossypol content, which is a chemical toxic to horses. However, recent processing methods and developing a variety of cotton that does not produce gossypol have greatly reduced this risk. The buyer should

TABLE 11-5 NUTRIENT COMPOSITION OF SOME COMMON PROTEIN
SUPPLEMENTS (dry-matter basis)

| Concentrate | TDN, % | CP, % | DP, % | Lysine, % | Ca, % | P, % |
|---|---|---|---|---|---|---|
| Cottonseed meal (beef) | 75 | 44.8 | 36.3 | 1.70 | 0.17 | 1.31 |
| Linseed meal | 69 | 38.9 | 27.6 | 1.34 | 0.43 | 0.90 |
| Milk, skimmed, dried | 92 | 36.0 | 30.3 | 2.69 | 1.30 | 1.09 |
| Soybean meal | 82 | 50.9 | 35.7 | 3.28 | 0.31 | 0.70 |

SOURCE: National Research Council, *Nutrient Requirements of Horses*, National Academy of
Sciences, Washington, D.C., 1978.

determine the level of gossypol before using cottonseed meal in high
amounts in rations.

LINSEED MEAL  Flax, a plant grown in the North Central part of the United
States, produces linseed meal. Linseed meal contains from 30 to 32 percent
protein and is the most poorly balanced protein in amino acids of the oil
meals. However, linseed meal does contain 1.34 percent lysine. Linseed meal
contains 10 percent fiber, 0.43 percent calcium, and 0.9 percent phosphorus.
It has a slight laxative effect on horses and is useful where a laxative is needed.

Linseed meal had the reputation of blooming the hair coat when it was
produced by the expeller process. This is probably because of its fat content;
however, since most oil meals are now produced by the solvent method,
their effect in blooming hair coat tends to be about the same. Linseed meal
is less palatable than the other two oil meals.

COMMERCIAL PROTEIN SUPPLEMENTS  Commercial protein supplements for
horses are largely based on soybean meal proteins. In addition to protein,
these are usually fortified with minerals and vitamins. Commercial supplements may be convenient in pellet form or cubes, but they will be more expensive. For this reason price as well as convenience should be compared
when purchasing them.

ANIMAL PROTEINS  Horses can be fed animal protein, such as bloodmeal,
meatmeal, and others, but the cost of these supplements usually limit their
use in horse feeding. If animal proteins are fed, they should be purchased
from a reliable company that has the appropriate processing machinery to
destroy disease spores and other contaminants that might jeopardize the
health of the horse.

NONPROTEIN NITROGEN (NPN)  The nonprotein nitrogen most used in animal
food is urea, best known in cattle-feeding circles. Vast amounts of fertilizer
and cattle feed are produced by a process resulting in a high NPN content

that can be synthesized and utilized by microbes in the rumen of cattle fed good energy diets. Research would indicate that horses on maintenance or submaintenance diets can utilize small amounts of nonprotein nitrogen, but that horses on standard diets utilize little NPN. In light of present research NPN is not a good choice for horses. However, if they eat feeds formulated for cattle with a portion of the protein coming from NPN, no ill effects should be expected because horses can tolerate more toxicity from urea than can cattle.

## Mineral Supplements

Although common horse feeds, such as pastures, hays, and grains, may furnish all the minerals adult horses need (except salt), some horses have higher mineral needs than others. All horses should be offered a mineral mixture free-choice throughout life. The amounts of these and conditions under which various ratios of calcium to phosphorus are needed were explained above. The average horse owner would do well to buy a commercial mineral mixture because it is used in such small amounts that price is not a big factor.

The commercial sources of minerals used by most feed companies are given in Table 12-10. All-grain rations are short of calcium if not combined with legume hay, and the common source is ground limestone for almost all animal feeding. Steamed bone meal is an animal source of calcium and phosphorus, which has a very high calcium to phosphorus ratio, 27 percent calcium to 13 percent phosphorus.

In general, phosphorus is the expensive mineral in these mixtures and the one that is most commonly sought when offering a mineral mixture free-choice to horses. The largest and perhaps best source of phosphorus is dicalcium phosphate. This is a widely distributed mineral that is easily digested and usually competitively priced. The calcium-phosphorus ratio is relatively low, but may vary according to different locations. Therefore, the feed tag should be checked before levels are assumed.

Monosodium phosphate is not very widely available and may be expensive; however, it is most convenient in balancing the calcium-phosphorus ratio because it contains no calcium. The same is true of disodium tripolyphosphate.

Defluorinated rock phosphate has about 32 percent calcium and 14 percent phosphorus. This source of phosphorus has been thoroughly researched in swine and found to be slightly less digestible than dicalcium phosphate. The two minerals chosen by most feed companies in formulation of their horse rations are dicalcium phosphate and ground limestone. These have been shown to be highly digestible and are widely available and economical.

## Vitamin Premixes

There are an endless number of commercial vitamin premixes. Those containing A, D, and E are the best choice. Healthy horses, unless under stress, are producing or consuming all the B vitamins they need. Therefore it is enough to find a supplement of A, D, and E in a satisfactory ratio in concentrated form. A good ratio is 4,000,000 IU A to 1,000,000 IU D to 6000 IU E *per pound of premix*. It is very important to keep the correct A to D ratio: five to ten times less D than A. Two pounds of this premix in a ton of grain yields 4,000 IU A, 1,000 IU D, and 6 IU E *per pound of feed*. At current prices the cost is approximately 1 percent of that of the total grain ration.

## Conditioners and Supplements

Companies and salespersons sell tons of these products, some good, some worthless, but all expensive.

A known feed company that will customize the horse ration to supply the amounts of vitamins A, D, and E as described above will do so for less than $2.50 per ton. But it also sells a "miracle" product that, to supply the same amount of these vitamins, would cost $154 per ton. The unhappy truth is that horse owners are buying such products while failing to supply basic nutrients.

The nutrients in the following lists are major and trace minerals and water-soluble and fat-soluble vitamins:

| | *Minerals* | | *Vitamins* |
|---|---|---|---|
| 1 | Calcium | 1 | Vitamin A |
| 2 | Phosphorus | 2 | Vitamin D |
| 3 | Salt | 3 | Vitamin E |
| 4 | Magnesium | 4 | Vitamin $B_{12}$ |
| 5 | Manganese | 5 | Choline chloride |
| 6 | Iron | 6 | Thiamine |
| 7 | Copper | 7 | Riboflavin |
| 8 | Zinc | 8 | Pyridoxine |
| 9 | Iodine | 9 | Pantothenic acid |
| 10 | Cobalt | 10 | Niacin |
| 11 | Sulfur | | |

Although this list is a hypothetical one, it does approximate some formulas that cost 10 to 15 cents a head daily to feed.

The first three ingredients in the first column are major minerals. Calcium, phosphorus, and salt. A "spoonful" of these in low concentration falls far short of the horse's needs and will do little good.

The next eight ingredients listed (4 to 11) are trace minerals. These are rarely deficient in horse rations. Pasture and hays, especially legumes, are good sources. Indeed, toxic levels of iodine and probably others are easy to produce by force-feeding trace minerals. Decreased milk production in dairy herds is common when excess trace minerals are given by feeding from three or four sources; e.g., from salt, protein supplement, legume hay, and those conditioners spooned onto the feed.

One should not be impressed by the number of ingredients listed on the label. Trace minerals that are not needed may rate a minus.

A good way to ensure an adequate supply of trace minerals is to feed them in trace-mineralized salt. If the diet includes legume hay and another source of trace minerals, use plain white salt.

The items in the second column are all vitamins. Vitamins A, D, and E are fat-soluble—that is, they are stored in fat and in the liver for long periods. Well-grazed horses may have 3 to 6 months' storage when going into winter. Bright green hay is also a good source. If fed brown grass in winter or late-cut nonlegume hay, horses may need vitamin A supplementation. Because of oxidation most commercial horse grains have 3000 to 5000 IU per pound of feed. The daily requirement of adult horses is about 10,000 to 20,000 IU *total*. If horses are depleted of vitamin A, more should be offered. Depleted cattle are often fed 50,000 to 100,000 IU daily until recovery.

The vitamins listed 4 through 10 in the second column are B vitamins, which are water-soluble and which do not keep long in the body. Nature, therefore, prepared the horse's intestinal tract with a B vitamin production factory that runs round the clock. Normally horses need no B supplementation.

In summary, if the horse is eating (1) growing pastures, (2) green-colored hays, or (3) commercial grain mixes supplying 3000 to 5000 IUs of vitamin A per pound, the horse needs no vitamin supplement. If the horse is confined on brown, nonlegume hay, or is grazing dried-out pastures following a dry season, consider supplementing with 10,000 to 20,000 units of vitamin A daily.

## SUMMARY

- Complex "concoctions" are expensive and unnecessary.
- B vitamins are synthesized in abundance by healthy horses and are abundant in good hays.
- Trace minerals are abundant in most horse roughages and are supplied cheaply in trace-mineralized salt. To feed three or four sources may cause toxic reactions.

- Major minerals (calcium, phosphorus, salt) are essential nutrients, but are required in higher amounts and cost less from other sources than from spoon-feeding practices.
- Vitamin A (and D to some extent) is short in many practical horse-feeding programs. Safe and effective levels of A to add daily are 10,000 to 20,000 IUs. These are very inexpensive in cattle and horse premixes.
- Ninety percent or more of the weight and an equal amount of the cost of horse feeding should go for energy foods and protein. Add to this good water, a good worming program, and reasonable health management, and the feeding results will be good. Without these management practices, magic formulas cannot overcome; with them, magic is not needed.

# RATION EVALUATION
# AND FORMULATION

here are few topics today as controversial as horse feeding, even though for thousands of years uneducated handlers have successfully fed horses under conditions of hard work and great stress with few ill effects. Yet others, then and now, have ruined a horse's health in a year by improper feeding and handling because of nutritional ignorance and carelessness in management. While nutritional research on horses is less complete than for other farm animals, there is enough solid information available to horse nutritionists and feeders to effect a good feeding program for all horse activities. The problem that horse owners face is sorting accurate information from the abundance of opinions and inaccurate information that abounds.

The horse deserves a balanced feeding program, and only a knowledgeable person can supply one, by evaluating the ration and correcting any deficiencies in it.

Three mathematical methods of checking and balancing rations are offered:

1   Mathematical evaluation of percentages of nutrients based on an air-dry, or as-fed, basis.

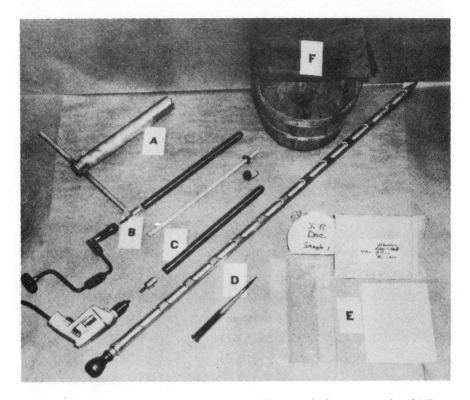

FIGURE 12-1   Equipment for sampling. (*a*) Homemade forage sample; (*b*) Penn State forage sampler with square-headed chuck to fit a breast drill; (*c*) Penn State forage sampler with chuck to fit a ½-inch electric drill; (*d*) grain samplers (grain probe, sack thief); (*e*) plastic bags (12 × 15 inches) and mailable containers; (*f*) basket and plastic sheet for mixing silage or grain.

2  Mathematical evaluation of minimum amounts of nutrients based on a 100 percent dry-matter basis.
3  The *X-Y* method, using a dry-matter basis and the metric system.

The first method, percentages, is frequently used when a large batch of feed is mixed in order to yield desired percentages of total digestible nutrients (TDN), crude protein (CP), calcium (Ca), phosphorus (P), and International Units (IUs) of vitamins. Feed companies use percentages extensively. Lay horsemen find them easy to work with in checking and balancing their own horse rations. When asked, your feed dealer may declare the composition of your favorite horse feed to be 72 percent TDN, 10 percent, CP, 0.4 percent calcium, and 0.3 percent phosphorus, with 4000 IU of vitamin A per pound of feed. Such a feed would be identified as an adult horse ration according to Table 12-1.

TABLE 12-1  NUTRIENT CONCENTRATION IN DIETS FOR HORSES
(As-fed Basis), 1100-lb MATURE WEIGHT

|  | TDN lb daily | CP, % | Calcium, % | Phosphorus, % | Digestible energy, kcal |
|---|---|---|---|---|---|
| Mature horse at maintenance | 8.20 | 7.7 | 0.27 | 0.18 | 16,000 |
| Mares, last 90 days of gestation | 9.20 | 10.0 | 0.45 | 0.30 | 18,000 |
| Lactating mare, first 3 months | 14.25 | 12.5 | 0.45 | 0.30 | 28,000 |
| Lactating mare, 4 months to weanling | 12.25 | 11.0 | 0.40 | 0.25 | 24,000 |
| Creep feed (supplemental) | . . . | 16.0 | 0.80 | 0.55 | 6,000 |
| Foal (3 months) | 7.50 | 16.0 | 0.80 | 0.55 | 13,000 |
| Weanling (6 months) | 8.00 | 14.5 | 0.60 | 0.45 | 15,000 |
| Yearling (12 months) | 8.50 | 12.0 | 0.50 | 0.35 | 17,000 |
| Long yearling (18 months) | 8.75 | 10.0 | 0.40 | 0.30 | 17,000 |
| 2-year-old (light training) | 8.25 | 9.0 | 0.40 | 0.30 | 16,500 |
| Mature working horses |  |  |  |  |  |
| Light work* | 12.00 | 7.7 | 0.27 | 0.18 | 16,000 |
| Moderate work† | 18.00 | 7.7 | 0.27 | 0.18 | 22,000 |
| Intense work‡ | 22.00 | 7.7 | 0.27 | 0.18 | 29,000 |

*Examples are horses used in western pleasure, bridle path hack, equitation, etc.
†Examples are ranch work, roping, cutting, barrel racing, jumping, etc.
‡Examples are race training, polo, etc.
SOURCE: Adapted from National Research Council, *Nutrient Requirements for Horses*, National Academy of Sciences, Washington, D.C., 1973, 1978.

The second method, minimum amounts, allows the feeder to check easily for one or more nutrients suspected of being deficient in the total feed the horse eats in a 24-hour period. This second method is useful in checking for energy in racehorse diets as well as for all nutrients that are fed in sparse amounts. It is usually calculated on a dry-matter basis, with calcium and phosphorus expressed in grams.

The *X-Y* method uses algebra to solve simultaneous equations to determine two unknowns (the amounts of each of two feeds) in ration balancing. This rather sophisticated method is used by researchers in formulating research rations as well as in nutrition courses. It often uses the metric system with energy expressed in calories, protein as digestible protein (DP), minerals in grams, and vitamins in IUs.

TABLE 12-2   NUTRIENT PERCENTAGES OF SOME TYPICAL HORSE FEEDS
(As-fed Basis)

| Feedstuffs | TDN, % | CP, % | Calcium, % | Phosphorus, % | Crude fiber, % |
|---|---|---|---|---|---|
| *Concentrates* | | | | | |
| Barley | 74 | 12.0 | 0.06 | 0.35 | 5.0 |
| Corn, No. 2, dent | 80 | 9.0 | 0.02 | 0.30 | 2.0 |
| Molasses, cane | 56 | 3.2 | 0.80 | 0.11 | . . . |
| Oats | 67 | 12.0 | 0.06 | 0.33 | 11.0 |
| Sorghum, grain (milo) | 76 | 11.0 | 0.03 | 0.30 | 2.7 |
| Wheat bran | 60 | 16.0 | 0.11 | 1.27 | 10.0 |
| Wheat grain | 77 | 12.8 | 0.04 | 0.43 | 2.7 |
| *Protein supplements* | | | | | |
| Brewers grains | 60 | 25.0 | 0.25 | 0.53 | 15.0 |
| Cottonseed meal, solvent | 41 | 68.0 | 0.15 | 1.20 | 14.0 |
| Linseed meal, solvent | 63 | 36.0 | 0.39 | 0.82 | 9.0 |
| Soybean meal, solvent | 74 | 45.0 | 0.23 | 0.63 | 7.0 |
| *Dry roughages* | | | | | |
| *Legumes* | | | | | |
| Alfalfa: | | | | | |
|   Early bloom | 53 | 16.6 | 1.13 | 0.21 | 27.9 |
|   Midbloom | 51 | 15.3 | 1.20 | 0.20 | 28.5 |
|   Full bloom | 46 | 13.9 | 1.12 | 0.18 | 30.3 |
| Meal, dehydrated | 56 | 17.8 | 1.23 | 0.22 | 24.8 |
| Lespedeza: | | | | | |
|   Early bloom | 52 | 16.4 | 1.04 | 0.24 | 22.0 |
|   Late bloom | 48 | 12.5 | 0.97 | 0.21 | 29.0 |
| Red clover: | | | | | |
|   Early bloom | 51 | 14.1 | 1.30 | 0.21 | 27.0 |
|   Late bloom | 46 | 13.0 | 1.25 | 0.21 | 28.0 |
| *Nonlegumes* | | | | | |
| Bermudagrass, coastal | 41 | 7.0 | 0.40 | 0.16 | 31.0 |
| Brome, smooth: | | | | | |
|   Early bloom | 45 | 10.6 | 0.36 | 0.20 | 29.0 |
|   Mature | 43 | 5.4 | 0.40 | 0.20 | 36.0 |
| Fescue, tall: | | | | | |
|   Early bloom | 44 | 9.3 | 0.30 | 0.20 | 29.0 |
|   Mature | 40 | 9.2 | 0.30 | 0.20 | 36.0 |
| Oat hay | 43 | 8.1 | 0.29 | 0.23 | 27.0 |
| Orchardgrass: | | | | | |
|   Mature | 42 | 9.0 | 0.27 | 0.23 | 29.0 |
|   Prairie hay | 41 | 6.0 | 0.37 | 0.14 | 30.0 |
| Sudangrass | 48 | 9.0 | 0.60 | 0.20 | 30.0 |

TABLE 12-2  NUTRIENT PERCENTAGES OF SOME TYPICAL HORSE FEEDS
(As-fed Basis) (Continued)

| Feedstuffs | TDN, % | CP, % | Calcium, % | Phosphorus, % | Crude fiber, % |
|---|---|---|---|---|---|
| | | Dry roughages | | | |
| Nonlegumes (Cont.) | | | | | |
| Timothy: | | | | | |
| Prebloom | 47 | 10.8 | 0.50 | 0.30 | 29.0 |
| Midbloom | 43 | 7.3 | 0.36 | 0.17 | 30.0 |
| Late | 39 | 7.2 | 0.33 | 0.16 | 31.0 |

SOURCE: Adapted from National Research Council, *Nutrient Requirements for Horses*, National Academy of Sciences, Washington, D.C., 1973, 1978.

## EVALUATION OF FEEDS

There are at least two objective ways to check the adequacy of horse rations. They are (1) mathematical calculations based on average feed composition tables, and (2) chemical analysis of the feed itself. They are best used together, i.e., the horse's feed is mathematically checked, and then chemically analyzed for comparison.

### Mathematical Evaluation: Percentages (As-fed Basis)

Analysis of hundreds of samples of horse feeds have been compiled by the National Research Council. Some are recorded in Table 12-2 and many others in Appendix 12-1. The horseman must assume his feed ingredients or those he buys are average when comparing them with those in Table 12-2, but that may or may not be true. Table 12-1 gives the nutrient requirements of different kinds of horses as-fed or on a 90 percent dry-matter basis. These data are compiled and updated approximately every 5 years by a committee of prominent horse researchers from land grant colleges. The requirements are *minimum* requirements chiefly designed for individually fed horses doing little or no work (unless otherwise stated). These values do not account for eating habits, peck-order effects, or extremely fast-growing foals and young horses. Therefore, the practical feeder must exceed these minimum nutritional requirements in certain cases by increasing them 10 to 20 percent or by offering more feed.

Consider the standard management practice of weaning most foals at 4 to 7 months (there are usually some of each age in large herds). To ensure separation from the dams and safety from injury in fences, weanlings are usually confined in a stable, shed, or corral. Since separation is necessary for long periods, they may remain in these facilities—without pasture—all winter or for several weeks. This is a good management practice provided foals are fed an adequate ration. Unfortunately, few are. A very large percentage of such foals are fed equal parts of good-quality oats and average-quality timothy hay or some other nonlegume hay. Some are fed two-thirds hay and one-third oats. Let's analyze a diet of half oats and half timothy hay to see if it meets the nutritional needs of weanlings.

NUTRITIONAL PICTURE   A quick but adequate way to answer this question is to average the nutrients supplied in oats and timothy hay and compare them with the requirements of weanlings. Here is how:

1   List the nutrients in oats and timothy hay from Table 12-2.
2   Add the nutrients of these two feeds together, then divide by 2 to get the percentage of nutrients in an equal-parts mixture.
3   List the requirements of weanlings from Table 12-1 and compare with those supplied by oats and timothy hay.

EXAMPLE

| Feedstuffs | TDN, % | CP, % | Ca, % | P, % |
|---|---|---|---|---|
| 50% oats | 67 | 12.0 | 0.06 | 0.33 |
| 50% timothy, midbloom | 43 | 7.3 | 0.36 | 0.16 |
| Total | 110 | 19.3 | 0.42 | 0.49 |
| Average, % | 55 | 9.7 | 0.21 | 0.25 |

| | TDN lb | TDN % | CP, % | Ca, % | P, % |
|---|---|---|---|---|---|
| Nutrients required, weanlings, 6 months | 8.00 | . . . | 14.5 | 0.60 | 0.45 |
| Nutrients supplied ½ oats, ½ timothy | . . . | 55 | 9.7 | 0.21 | 0.25 |
| Deficit | | | 4.8 | 0.39 | 0.20 |

Let's consider energy first in evaluating our findings. The requirement is 8.00 pounds of TDN daily to support good growth. By dividing 8.00 by 55 percent and multiplying by 100 (TDN in half oats, half timothy), we see that 14.54 pounds of oats and timothy must be consumed to meet energy needs. But will foals eat enough of this diet to meet their energy needs? If they are well grown (450 to 500 pounds) from creep-feeding, some will eat this much, as this is approximately 3 percent of body weight, but not all will. A better hay, higher grain-to-hay ratio, or the substitution of corn for half the oats would increase energy concentration and decrease the amount of feed needed to meet the energy requirement, but addition of corn would decrease total protein and minerals. The supply of other nutrients in this fifty-fifty oats and timothy mixture is dangerously low and would result in stunted growth and inadequate bone development. Protein is only two-thirds adequate, calcium one-third, and phosphorus only half adequate. One could offer a free-choice mineral (a good practice with all horses) in addition to what is supplied by the oats and nonlegume hay, but not enough of it would be eaten to meet weanling needs. It is often recommended to pour 2 tablespoons of limestone onto a ration of oats. Theoretically this should meet the foal's calcium needs, but many foals will not eat this much limestone, and much is lost when it sifts through the oats to the bottom of the trough.

Some feeders argue that they have fed oats and timothy with no ill effects. But the effects of soft, porous bones may appear in many forms, including immediate lameness or lameness years later. If weanlings are fed in confinement for a short time, then turned out to pasture, levels of nutrients may have been raised enough by the pasture forage to prevent visible symptoms of deficiency. However, the best solution is to drastically alter the diet by the method shown in the discussion on percentage balancing below.

What is the nutritional picture with one-third oats and two-thirds timothy hay? We can no longer add the nutrient percentages for the two feeds together and divide by 2 because twice as much hay is fed, by weight, as oats. Since there are now 3 equal parts (2 hay, 1 oats), multiply the percentage of nutrients in hay by 2, those in oats by 1, add these together, and divide by 3.

EXAMPLE

| Feedstuffs | TDN, % | CP, % | Ca, % | P, % |
|---|---|---|---|---|
| Oats (1 part) = | 67 | 12.0 | 0.06 | 0.33 |
| Timothy (2 parts) = | 86 | 14.6 | 0.72 | 0.32 |
| Total | 153 | 26.6 | 0.78 | 0.65 |
| Average (total ÷ 3) | 51.0 | 8.87 | 0.26 | 0.22 |

To get 8.00 pounds of TDN, foals must eat 15.69 pounds (8.00 ÷ 51% × 100) of hay and oats, because hay replaced part of the oats. The oat reduction also reduced the protein percentage from 9.70 to 8.87. Both are too low for satisfactory growth and maintenance of appetite. A change in the entire diet is indicated.

Compare these diets with the nutrient requirements of other types of horses shown in Table 12-1. Either diet would suffice for idle mature horses when supplemented with free-choice calcium and phosphorus, but both are deficient in protein and minerals for mares in late pregnancy and lactation and for all ages and stages of growing horses.

## Mathematical Evaluation: Minimum Amounts (Dry-matter Basis)

The horse's diet is only as good as its most limiting nutrient. If one nutrient is below the requirement, the animal cannot function at peak performance regardless of how well the diet supplies the other nutrients. One is anxious to know if each nutrient is supplied in sufficient quantity for maximum health and performance. Such information can be obtained when horses are individually fed. If the amount of feed a horse is eating is weighed, the minimum amounts of the basic nutrients supplied may be determined with accuracy.

Let us make this calculation on a dry-matter basis instead of the as-fed basis, because this method is more accurate when using high-moisture feeds. Consider the first ration (equal parts of oats and timothy hay) for the weanling. One could convert as-fed figures in the first ration to a dry-matter basis by multiplying by 0.9, but for practice let's use dry-matter figures for oats and timothy hay from Appendix Table 12-1 and compare the results with the foal's dry-matter requirements in Table 12-3.

| Feedstuffs (Appendix 12-1) | TDN, % | CP, % | Ca, % | P, % |
|---|---|---|---|---|
| 50% oats | 76.0 | 13.6 | 0.07 | 0.37 |
| 50% timothy, head | 45.0 | 9.0 | 0.41 | 0.19 |
| Total | 121.0 | 22.6 | 0.48 | 0.56 |
| Average | 60.5 | 11.3 | 0.24 | 0.28 |

If we use 7.80 pounds of TDN (12-3) as the requirement, 12.89 pounds of oats and timothy [(7.80 ÷ 60.5%) × 100] is required (dry-matter basis) to supply adequate energy for the foal. When 12.89 pounds is multiplied by percentages of protein, calcium, and phosphorus and divided by 100, the number of pounds of these nutrients consumed daily is obtained. These figures for calcium and phosphorus are then multiplied by 454 (grams per pound) for comparison with minimum requirements as listed in Table 12-3.

For example:

$$CP = \frac{12.89 \times 11.3}{100} = 1.46 \text{ lb}$$

$$Ca = \frac{12.89 \times 0.24}{100} = 0.031 \text{ lb} \ (0.031 \times 454 = 14.1 \text{ g})$$

$$P = \frac{12.89 \times 0.28}{100} = 0.036 \text{ lb} \ (0.036 \times 454 = 16.3 \text{ g})$$

TABLE 12-3 NUTRIENT REQUIREMENTS OF HORSES (Daily Nutrients per Horse),* 500-kg MATURE WEIGHT

| | Weight | | Daily gain | | Digestible energy Meal† | TDN | | Crude protein | | Digestible protein | | Cal-cium, g | Phos-phorus, g | Vitamin A activity, 1000 IU | Daily feed* | |
|---|---|---|---|---|---|---|---|---|---|---|---|---|---|---|---|---|
| | kg | lb | kg | lb | | kg | lb | kg | lb | kg | lb | | | | kg | lb |
| Mature horses, maintenance | 500 | 1.100 | 0.0 | … | 16.39 | 3.73 | 8.20 | 0.63 | 1.39 | 0.29 | 0.64 | 23 | 14 | 12.5 | 7.45 | 16.4 |
| Mares, last 90 days gestation | … | … | 0.55 | 1.21 | 18.36 | 4.17 | 9.18 | 0.75 | 1.65 | 0.39 | 0.86 | 34 | 23 | 25.0 | 7.35 | 16.2 |
| Lactating mare, first 3 months (15 kg milk per day) | … | … | 0.0 | … | 28.27 | 6.43 | 14.14 | 1.36 | 2.99 | 0.84 | 1.85 | 50 | 34 | 27.5 | 10.10 | 22.2 |
| Lactating mare, 4 months to weanling (10 kg milk per day) | … | … | 0.0 | … | 24.31 | 5.53 | 12.16 | 1.10 | 2.42 | 0.62 | 1.36 | 41 | 27 | 22.5 | 9.35 | 20.6 |
| Nursing foal (3 months of age) | 155 | 341 | 1.20 | 2.64 | 13.66 | 3.10 | 6.83 | 0.75 | 1.65 | 0.54 | 1.19 | 33 | 20 | 6.2 | 4.20 | 9.2 |
| Requirements above milk | … | … | … | … | 6.89 | 1.57 | 3.45 | 0.41 | 0.90 | 0.31 | 0.68 | 18 | 13 | 0.0 | 2.25 | 4.9 |
| Weanling (6 months of age) | 230 | 506 | 0.80 | 1.76 | 15.60 | 3.55 | 7.80 | 0.79 | 1.74 | 0.52 | 1.14 | 34 | 25 | 9.2 | 5.00 | 11.0 |
| Yearling (12 months of age) | 325 | 715 | 0.55 | 1.21 | 16.81 | 3.82 | 8.41 | 0.76 | 1.67 | 0.45 | 0.99 | 31 | 22 | 12.0 | 6.00 | 13.2 |
| Long yearling (18 months of age) | 400 | 880 | 0.35 | 0.77 | 17.00 | 3.90 | 8.58 | 0.71 | 1.56 | 0.39 | 0.86 | 28 | 19 | 14.0 | 6.50 | 14.3 |
| 2-year-old (24 months of age) | 450 | 990 | 0.15 | 0.33 | 16.45 | 3.74 | 8.23 | 0.63 | 1.39 | 0.33 | 0.72 | 25 | 17 | 13.0 | 6.60 | 14.5 |

*Dry-matter basis.
†For total caloric requirements expressed in kilocalories, multiply by 1000.
SOURCE: Adapted from National Research Council, *Nutrient Requirements for Horses*, National Academy of Sciences, Washington, D.C., 1973, 1978.

The minimum nutrient requirements from Table 12-3 are:

|  | Feed, lb | TDN, lb | CP, lb | Ca, g | P, g |
|---|---|---|---|---|---|
| Nutrients required, daily | | | | | |
| 6-months weanling | 11.0 | 7.80 | 1.74 | 34.0 | 25.0 |
| Supplied, 12.89 lb | | | | | |
| ½ oats, ½ timothy | 12.89 | 7.80 | 1.46 | 14.1 | 16.3 |
| Difference | +1.89 | 0 | −0.28 | −19.9 | −8.7 |

Most foals will manage to eat enough of this diet to meet their energy needs because this timothy hay is higher in quality, as indicated by the nutrients it furnishes, than the timothy used in the first problem. However, protein and phosphorus are low, and calcium is drastically low. If nutrients are only slightly deficient and enough feed is offered, most foals will consume enough to satisfy minimum needs. However, horses cannot be depended upon to know what nutrients they need and to eat more feed to get them—or to make wise choices in selecting from the variety of feeds that supply these nutrients.

How much must they consume of this ration to meet their protein, calcium, and phosphorus needs? If requirements are divided by the nutrients supplied and multiplied by 12.89 pounds, the number of pounds that foals must eat to fulfill their needs for normal growth are calculated. For example,

$$CP = \frac{1.74}{1.46} = 1.19 \qquad 1.19 \times 12.89 = 15.34 \text{ lb of diet}$$

$$Ca = \frac{34}{14.1} = 2.41 \qquad 2.41 \times 12.89 = 31.06 \text{ lb of diet}$$

$$P = \frac{25}{16.3} = 1.60 \qquad 1.60 \times 12.89 = 20.62 \text{ lb of diet}$$

Few foals would eat 15.34 pounds of this diet to meet their protein needs. If they did, the excess energy would produce extra weight (fat) to be carried on undermineralized bones—because no foal would consume 31.06 pounds, the amount required for minimum calcium intake. Calcium is very difficult to feed to weanlings unless it is mixed in a grain ration with molasses or unless legume hay replaces nonlegume hay in foal diets.

ANALYSIS OF U.S. CAVALRY RATION    Rations with a variety of ingredients cannot be analyzed quite so easily. Weights or percentages of ingredients must be known before calculations can be made. Let's check the TDN, protein, calcium and phosphorus of the U.S. Horse Cavalry ration fed to horses at Fort Riley, Kansas (1935).[1] The ration consisted of oats, 8 pounds; wheat bran, 2 pounds; and prairie hay, 14 pounds. As a matter of interest, the feeding and watering schedules were as follows: 5:30 A.M., 3 pounds of oats and bran; 7:30, water; 10:50, water; 11:00, 3 pounds of hay; 11:30, 3 pounds of oats and bran; 1:30 P.M., water; 4:30, water; 4:35, 11 pounds of hay; 5:00, 4 pounds of oats and bran. Such a schedule sacrifices labor in order to get maximum digestibility from the feed.

The objective is to determine TDN and protein in pounds and calcium and phosphorus in grams to see if minimum requirements were met. Multiply the percentage of the nutrient by the number of pounds of the feed and then divided by 100 to get the number of pounds of actual nutrients.

EVALUATION OF U.S. HORSE CAVALRY RATION FOR ADEQUATE
TDN, CP, CALCIUM, AND PHOSPHORUS (Dry-matter Basis)

| Feedstuffs | TDN | | CP | | Ca | | P | |
|---|---|---|---|---|---|---|---|---|
| | % | lb | % | lb | % | lb | % | lb |
| Oats, 8 lb | 67 = | 6.80 | 13.6 = | 1.09 | 0.07 = | 0.0056 | 0.37 = | 0.0296 |
| Wheat bran, 2 lb | 67 = | 1.34 | 17.0 = | 0.34 | 0.12 = | 0.0024 | 1.43 = | 0.0286 |
| Prairie hay, 14 lb | 46 = | 6.44 | 6.7 = | 0.94 | 0.41 = | 0.0574 | 0.15 = | 0.0210 |
| Lb, 24 | | 14.58 | | 2.37 | | 0.0654 | | 0.0792 |

*Note:* The number of pounds of calcium and phosphorus are changed to grams by multiplying by 454:

$$\text{Grams of Ca} = 0.0654 \times 454 = 29.70$$
$$\text{Grams of P} = 0.079 \times 454 = 35.96$$

Our calculations show 24 pounds of these three feeds yielded the following nutrients that can be conveniently compared with the requirements from Table 12-3.

| Requirements | TDN, lb | CP, lb | Ca, g | P, g |
|---|---|---|---|---|
| 1100-lb horse, maintenance | 11.00* | 1.39 | 23 | 14 |
| In U.S. Cavalry ration | 14.58 | 2.37 | 29.70 | 35.96 |

*Figure derived from *National Research Council, Nutrient Requirements for Horses,* 1973.

One cannot seriously criticize the U.S. Cavalry ration because it exceeds all of the nutrient requirements that modern researchers have established for 1100-pound adult horses at maintenance. Although the workload

[1]*Horsemanship and Horsemastership, Part Three. Animal Management,* The U.S. Cavalry School, Fort Riley, Kan., 1935, p. 122.

is not indicated, these garrison horses were probably doing medium amounts of work. The extra protein was probably beneficial as supplemental energy. However, bran was an expensive source of energy; the excess protein may have been a result of biases of the era toward bran feeding. Of more concern is the calcium to phosphorus ratio of 29.70 g of calcium to 35.96 g of phosphorus. Adult horses can probably perform indefinitely on a 1:1 ratio, but pregnant mares and growing horses cannot. It would be better if the ratio of calcium to phosphorus were reversed or if it were 1½ or 2:1.

## Chemical Analysis of the Horse Ration

Although chemical analysis of feeds is not sanctioned by all nutritionists, it is recommended by most of them. Its opponents point to a high rate of sample error; its proponents attempt to minimize error and list a number of advantages of chemically monitoring the feeding program. Among them are these:

1   Chemical analysis increases the accuracy of feed formulation.
2   It helps to identify good-quality feed ingredients.
3   It monitors the accuracy of the feed mixing service.
4   It identifies inadequate rations before damage occurs.

Routine monitoring of ration ingredients by chemical analysis should be a part of every nutrition consultant's services and of most competitive horsemen's feeding programs. Table 12-4 is a typical chemical analysis of the grain ration from Grant's Farm, home of the Anheuser-Busch Clydesdale breeding herd. Grant's farm sought a single grain ration to be fed with excellent alfalfa hay that would suffice for weanlings as well as for horses of all ages, in order to eliminate the risk of stable hands getting different rations confused and thereby of weanlings getting grain rations formulated for adult horses. An adult horse ration with less protein, calcium, and phosphorus and less complex ingredients would also be cheaper. This ration was formulated to be 14 percent CP, 0.60 calcium, and 0.60 phosphorus (as-fed basis). When two-thirds grain is fed with one-third alfalfa hay, foals consume 14.7 percent CP, 0.90 calcium, and 0.53 phosphorus. Table 12-4 verifies two things: (1) accurate ration formulation, and (2) accurate feed mixing procedures.

A study of Table 12-4 shows a lower-than-average moisture content of 7.39 percent. This is because the ration was stored in a heated room. The 13.73 percent protein, 0.60 calcium, and 0.56 phosphorus are near calculated levels. The 10.80 percent fiber is higher than most horse grain rations, reflecting the high percentage of wheat bran used.

Reputable feed companies have quality control programs whereby all large shipments of feed ingredients are chemically analyzed. Adjustments

TABLE 12-4   EXAMPLE OF CHEMICAL ANALYSIS OF THE GRAIN RATION FROM GRANTS FARM

| SAMPLE NO<br>SAMPLE I.D. | | 78-7-I-13<br>FEED #2 | |
|---|---|---|---|
| | | *As-fed*<br>*basis* | *Dry-matter*<br>*basis* |
| MOISTURE ........ | o/o | 7.39 | 0.00 |
| DRY MATTER ..... | o/o | 92.61 | 100.00 |
| PROTEIN ......... | o/o | 13.73 | 14.82 |
| ADJ C PROTEIN ... | o/o | | |
| ADF-NITROGEN .. | o/o | | |
| PEPSIN D PROT ... | o/o | 11.92 | 12.87 |
| A. D. FIBER ........ | o/o | 10.00 | 10.80 |
| N. D. FIBER ....... | o/o | | |
| T.D.N. ............. | o/o | 74.39 | 80.33 |
| N E MILK .... THMS/LB | | .84 | .90 |
| CRUDE FAT ....... | o/o | | |
| PH ................ | o/o | | |
| ASH .............. | o/o | .82 | .89 |
| NITROGEN ....... | o/o | 2.20 | 2.37 |
| CALCIUM ......... | o/o | .60 | .65 |
| PHOSPHORUS .... | o/o | .56 | .61 |
| MAGNESIUM ...... | o/o | | |
| POTASSIUM ....... | o/o | | |
| SODIUM ......... | o/o | | |
| SULFUR .......... | o/o | | |
| IRON ............ | PPM | | |
| COBALT .......... | PPM | | |
| COPPER ......... | PPM | | |
| MANGANESE ..... | PPM | | |
| ZINC ............. | PPM | | |
| ALUMINUM ....... | PPM | | |
| NITRATES ........ | o/o | NEGATIVE | |
| NAME ................. | GRANT'S FARM | | |
| ADDRESS ............. | | | |
| SUBMITTED BY ........ | DR. MELVIN BRADLEY | | |
| ADDRESS ............. | MUMFORD HALL,<br>COLUMBIA MO. | | |

SOURCE: K-C AGRICULTURAL LABORATORY SERVICE, NEVADA, MO., Sept. 18, 1978.

can be made in feed formulation to ensure adequate nutrients in the finished feed. It is amazing how much accuracy can be achieved when the supplier mixing the feed knows that the product will be routinely chemically analyzed. "Nutritional accidents" beset the University of Missouri swine evaluation station ration before chemical tests of each batch began. None have happened since. Knowledge of the CP, calcium, and phosphorus of hay, in particular, greatly aids accurate ration balancing and may result in substantial savings in supplemental feed costs. Unless the diets fed to young horses have been formulated by a person competent in nutrition, most of them will fail a chemical test, because they will not supply nutrients in the correct amounts and ratios.

SAMPLING FEEDSTUFFS FOR ACCURATE CHEMICAL ANALYSIS   A chemical analysis cannot correct sampling errors. The sample must be representative of the feed sampled. Appropriate sampling equipment improves accuracy and reduces sampling time. Figure 12-1 shows various types of items useful in sampling. The Penn State forage sampler is very handy for baled hay. It is listed in farm supply catalogs. However, a good sample can be taken without it by cutting hay to 3-inch lengths. Sampling technique involves taking six to twelve samples from random, scattered locations (bales, sacks, etc.), mixing them thoroughly in a container, and then taking small amounts from random locations in the container until there are 1 to 2 pounds to submit to the chemical lab.

Dr. George Garner, Agricultural Chemist at the University of Missouri, lists these further steps to be followed for maximum accuracy and minimum confusion.[2]

1   Sample size should be a minimum of 1 quart (be sure the sample is representative). All forages should be chopped to a length of 3 inches or less.
2   Pack tightly to exclude air. Seal airtight. Use plastic bags in all cases, except very dry samples.
3   Send samples to the laboratory as quickly as possible. Indicate nature of analysis desired by letter or with appropriate form, if part of an organized program.
4   All letters, instructions, checks, or money orders should be put in a first-class mail envelope and attached to the mailing container. The sample container can go as fourth-class mail.
5   Address both letter and sample container with correct laboratory address and return address.

Horsemen usually sample for CP, calcium, and phosphorus, but a knowledge of the moisture level is essential when buying and storing grain,

[2]George B. Garner, "Sampling Feedstuff for Chemical Analysis," UMC Science and Technology Guide 9650, 1978.

as well as of the nitrate level in hays. Grains may heat and be ruined in areas of high humidity if stored under conditions of much over 12 percent moisture; furthermore, buying excess water in feed is uneconomical. Hay grown on fertilized land with heavy application of poultry or dairy manure may be high in nitrate. If hay has over 0.5 percent nitrate on a dry-matter basis, it is too dangerous to feed except in very small amounts. Most laboratories automatically report moisture content and many screen forages for nitrate. Carotene (the vitamin A precursor) is seldom tested in grain because it is assumed to be present in small or nonexistent amounts, unless added in commercial mixtures; cost of the analysis would purchase enough vitamin A, D, and E to feed the horse for a year.

Table 12-5 shows typical services offered and the atypically low prices

TABLE 12-5   K-C AGRICULTURAL LABORATORY PRICE LIST FOR
ANALYSIS SUGGESTED ON FEED TESTING DATA SHEET
(Other prices can be obtained from the laboratories)

| K-C Agricultural Lab.[1] | Effective Nov. 1, 1977 (Prices subject to change without notice) |
|---|---|
| 5.50 | DRY MATTER, CRUDE PROTEIN, and ACID DETERGENT FIBER (ADF) or neutral detergent fiber (NDF). (Recommended for all hays and silages). For Heat Damaged Forages see last item. |
| 4.00 | DRY MATTER, CRUDE PROTEIN (recommended for grain and grain rations). |
| 2.00 | CALCIUM (recommended to check formulation on rations and on forages containing legumes to be fed to dairy animals). |
| 2.50 | PHOSPHORUS (recommended to check formulation on rations and mature forages fed to beef animals). |
| 2.00 | POTASSIUM (recommended for "stocked piles" grasses in winter for beef cows). |
| 3.00 | NITRATE (all forages will be screened for nitrate. If test is positive a quantitative analysis will be conducted). |
| 8.00 | IVDMD (recommended for low-quality forages in addition to dry-matter, crude protein and acid detergent fiber or neutral detergent fiber). |
| 3.00 | ADF PROTEIN (heat damaged forages should have ADF protein in addition to DM, Crude Protein and ADF). |

[1]Will bill at the time results are returned.
SOURCE: K-C Agricultural Laboratory Service, Nevada, Mo.

charged for them by a lab that services most of Missouri's livestock industry. In Table 12-5, the analysis requested and paid for was dry matter, CP, calcium, and phosphorus. Other calculations listed were furnished without charge.

Most chemical laboratories avoid analysis for toxicity in feeds for two reasons. First, the suspected feed more often than not is not guilty; second, laboratories are not anxious to take time for litigation. However, some laboratories do specialize in toxicity sampling and charge accordingly for identification of the toxin and time spent, if any, in litigation.

SAMPLING BALED HAY    Core-sample fifteen to twenty randomly selected bales with a Penn State core sampler. Sample from the end of square bales by using the full length of the sampler. Repeat this procedure for each different kind and cutting of the hay used.

SACKED FEED    Take samples from five or six sacks according to sampling procedure above. Most sacked feeds have been well mixed; however, use of a small probe gives a representative sample. Reputable companies with quality control programs seldom deviate from specifications; however, the conscientious horseman will carefully observe each sack of feed as used.

BULK FEED    Unless molasses is included, bulk feed is difficult to sample because of separation by particle size. Get samples from ten to fifteen areas and from as many depths as possible. A grain probe may be helpful. If the grain ration is customized, "grab-samples" can be taken as it is poured into the grain bin.

Many state extension services have feed analysis programs. If not, the county extension agent will know of private chemistry labs or land grant college agricultural chemistry departments which can analyze feeds.

## Other Tests for Nutritional Adequacy

BLOOD LEVELS    Blood analysis is used extensively by veterinarians in diagnosis. Blood levels of nutrients are useful but must be interpreted with some caution because of the homeostatic mechanism of the body, which attempts to maintain normal serum levels. Calcium blood level is not a very good indicator of calcium intake, but phosphorus, potassium, and magnesium blood levels more accurately reflect the animal's nutritional state with regard to these nutrients.

Most researchers doubt racehorses' need for iron to the extent that injections are now given. They conclude that the normal range of serum iron is so broad that tests are not very dependable and that the amount of iron contained in the spleen at the time of testing may affect results. (See Chapter 11, "Iron.")

HAIR ANALYSIS  Chemical analysis of hair probably more nearly reflects the diet at the time of hair growth than at the time the sample was taken. If the kinds and amounts of nutrients consumed are carefully monitored through calculation and chemistry, the less accurate measurements of blood and hair may well be unnecessary.

## COMMERCIAL HORSE FEEDS AND RATIONS

The owner of one or a few horses should probably buy a commercial horse grain from a reliable company to be used with whatever roughage can be found. Pasture is not available to many owners, and good hay is very expensive and difficult to obtain in many areas. Companies have "complete feed" pellets and hay wafers or cubes that meet nutritional needs, but these may create wood chewing in the absence of roughage. If only 5 pounds of long hay are fed daily, such stable vices may be avoided. With some effort, inexpensive satisfactory hay can almost always be obtained.

There are many brands of commercial horse feeds, all containing roughly the same basic ingredients, and almost all claiming to be substantially superior to the rest. Even if a researcher's job depended upon showing significant differences among horses using recommended feeds from various reputable companies, such data would be difficult to supply. But this is not to say that all commercial rations are good.

There are many ways to identify a reputable feed company. Does the company have a horse nutritionist? Ask the dealer who the nutritionist is. He may be located in another city. Companies seriously formulating horse feeds have at least one nutritionist who specializes in horses. If the nutritionist must divide his or her time between horses, beef cattle, dairy cattle, swine, and poultry, he or she may not have time to keep abreast of current developments. How many horse feeds does the company offer? Do they have an orphan foal ration? A 14 to 16 percent protein weanling ration? A 12 to 14 percent growing or breeding ration? A 10 percent adult horse ration? Do they have a "complete feed" (grain and roughage)? A large horse-breeding operation may require most of these. Feed companies committed to this extent almost always have sound ration formulas and appropriate milling machinery to prepare them.

Beware of a sideline horse feed formulated by a company that listens to what "horse people" want and mixes it without checking the nutrients for adequacy and balance and the trace minerals and vitamin levels for sufficiency without toxicity. The following mix is an example:

| Ingredient | Amount, lb |
|---|---|
| Oats, whole | 500 |
| Corn, chopped | 1150 |
| Soybean meal, 44% | 33 |
| Wheat bran | 120 |
| Molasses, blackstrap | 180 |
| Trace minerals | 5 |
| Salt | 12 |
| Cattle premix | 0.5 |
| Total | 2000.5 |

A glance at this list of ingredients arouses two suspicions: this ration must be toxic in trace minerals and deficient in calcium. Calculation confirms both suspicions. The reason for suspicion is that pure trace-mineral mixtures are more concentrated than trace-mineralized salt. Five pounds of trace-mineralized salt, for example, would have aroused no suspicion. A grain ration with this much corn (low in calcium) and wheat bran (high in phosphorus) must be supplied with a source of calcium, such as 15 to 20 pounds of limestone.

### Sample Checks

The annual report of the state feed law enforcement agency, the state department of agriculture, reports what percentage of each company's feed samples have met their registered formula specifications. Be suspicious if a high percentage of samples failed.

Another way to check the adequacy of commercial horse feeds is to take a close look at them. What is the physical character of the grain mixture? Are the oats rolled, not ground, and the corn cracked or rolled, not hammered to dust? Are there fines? Fines are no problem with hungry horses fed small amounts, but they pose serious palatability and digestive problems with young horses and with those consuming large amounts of grain.

Serious horse ration preparation requires specific milling machinery. Where is the feed prepared? Is it made in one or a few locations and distributed to dealers? Or is the trade name furnished, with each local dealership doing its own preparation? If the latter, samples will vary in quality among locations.

### Feed-Tag Analysis

State laws vary slightly, but tags offer some useful information. A grain mixture "guaranteed analysis" will include minimum crude protein and fat and maximum crude fiber. For example:

*Brand X Horse Feed—50 lb net*
"Guaranteed Analysis"

| | |
|---|---|
| Crude protein, not less than | 12.00 percent |
| Crude fat, not less than | 3.00 percent |
| Crude fiber, not more than | 5.00 percent |
| Vitamin A, not less than | 4000 IU/lb |

"Ingredients—oats, corn, wheat bran, soybean meal, linseed meal, vitamins A, D, and E, salt, dicalcium phosphate, calcium carbonate, cane molasses."

Twelve percent crude protein in this formulation suggests a general-purpose horse ration for mixed ages of horses. As with all grain rations for mixed groups, it provides more protein than adult horses need (although it will not hurt them) and too little for weanlings. The crude fat content of 3 percent is good enough for reasonable bloom on the hair coat. The low crude fiber percentage reveals an absence of hay additives and suggests good digestibility. A rule of thumb used by some nutritionists in analyzing commercial grains is to subtract the percentage of crude fiber on the feed tag from 75 percent to get an estimate of digestibility—70 percent in this case. The 4000 units of vitamin A per pound are about standard for horse feeds and are good insurance against vitamin A deficiency. If an adult horse needs 20,000 IU of vitamin A daily, and half or more comes from its other feed (even with poor-quality hay), a mere 2½ pounds of this grain would meet the requirement.

Ingredient lists usually list the most abundant ingredient first—in this case there are more oats than corn and wheat bran. Dicalcium phosphate (dical) and calcium carbonate (limestone) are choice sources of calcium and phosphorus. Although the levels of these two minerals are absent from the feed tag, one could assume at least 0.5 percent calcium and 0.4 percent phosphorus in this grain mixture, which is standard for commercial horse grains of this protein level. The molasses keeps down dust, stabilizes fines in the ration, and makes it tasty.

If the price were right, one would not hesitate to purchase a few sacks of this feed to try with one's horses. If inspection of its physical properties shows grains to be coarsely prepared with enough molasses to hold it together, it can be fed with confidence to all types of horses except weanlings. If the same company has a weanling ration that is higher in protein, calcium, and phosphorus, it might be a good choice. If not, the regular grain can be supplemented with soybean meal, dicalcium phosphate, and limestone to meet weanling needs.

## BALANCING HORSE RATIONS

The experience that is acquired in building a custom ration is hard to duplicate in any other way. It is sometimes possible to build a better ration than
is available commercially, and it is almost always less expensive. The feed
company must be furnished with a list of ingredients and the number of
pounds of each desired in order to give an accurate mixture. However, unless there are enough horses to consume a ton of feed in 2 or 3 months, it
may not remain fresh enough to be practical.

### Trial-and-Error Balancing

The feeds and the nutrients they supply can be taken from Table 12-2. When
a rough estimate of actual nutrient totals is compared to nutrient requirements as listed in Table 12-1, excesses and deficits may become apparent.

There are certain rules of thumb that are helpful in trial-and-error
balancing:

1  Heavy feeding of grain supplies excess phosphorus but deficient calcium, trace minerals, and fiber.
2  If wheat bran composes one-quarter or more of the grain ration, excess
   phosphorus is likely to be present.
3  Good legume hays supplement the excess phosphorus in grains with
   abundant calcium, and also supply trace minerals and vitamins.
4  Legumes are excellent for growing horses but may create obesity in confined adults and must be given to them in only limited amounts unless
   they are working.
5  Two-year-old hay has lost most of its vitamins and requires vitamin A
   and D supplementation.
6  Use high-quality feeds. Feed no moldy hay or "dusty" oats.

The trial-and-error method is adequate for adult rations but is not
accurate enough to use with foals and growing horses.

### Percentage Balancing

The feed industry formulates rations in bulk based on minimum percentages of each nutrient. To do so they must calculate in pounds the exact
amount of each ingredient to add to the mixture. Following are the steps
necessary to formulate a ration based on percentages.

1  List the nutrient requirements of horses to be fed (see Table 12-1).
2  Select the feeds to be used.

3 Calculate the grain to protein ratio.
4 Calculate mineral quantities: present in the feed; required in the total; and needed as mineral supplements to supply requirements.
5 Calculate vitamin needs and add them.

Let's formulate a ration for a 6-month-old weanling. Standard requirements and feed sources for weanlings are listed below:

| | TDN, lb | CP, % | Ca, % | P, % |
|---|---|---|---|---|
| Requirement for weanling | 8.00 | 14.5 | 0.60 | 0.45 |
| *Feedstuffs* | | | | |
| Oats | | 12 | 0.06 | 0.33 |
| Corn | | 9 | 0.02 | 0.30 |
| Soybean meal | | 45 | 0.23 | 0.63 |
| Molasses, blackstrap | | 3.2 | 0.80 | 0.11 |
| Dicalcium phosphate | | — | 24.0 | 19.0 |
| Limestone | | — | 36.0 | — |
| Salt | | | | |
| Vitamins, IU/lb of premix | | | | |
| A = 5,000,000 | | | | |
| D = 1,000,000 | | | | |

## Grain-Protein Ratio

How should oats, corn, and soybean meal be combined to yield a 14.5 percent CP mixture? Start by deciding the ratio of the two grains. It could be two-thirds oats, one-third corn, or half of each. Let us use half of each and average their protein percentages:

| Feedstuffs | Crude protein, % |
|---|---|
| Oats | 12 |
| Corn | 9 |
| Total | 21 |
| Average | 10.5 |

Use of the *square* method with protein in grain (10.5 percent) at the upper left, protein in soybean meal (45 percent) at the lower left, and the desired percentage of protein (14.5 percent) in the center of the square allows cross subtraction (in the direction of the arrows) that gives the correct ratio of soybean meal to use with oats and corn for a 14.5 percent final mixture. For example:

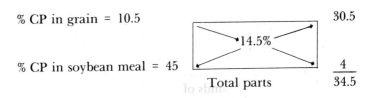

% CP in grain = 10.5                                           30.5

% CP in soybean meal = 45                                       4
                                                               ——
                                        Total parts            34.5

By subtracting protein in the grain (upper left) from desired amount (center), we determine that 4 parts of the total will be soybean meal.

If we subtract 14.5 (center) from 45 (soybean meal, lower left), the figure in the upper right corner, 30.5 parts, represents grain. If 30.5 parts of grain are mixed with 4 parts of soybean meal, the final mixture will be 14.5 percent CP. This ratio can be expressed in percentages, i.e., 11.6 percent soybean meal, 88.4 percent grain, but in the feed trade the size of the batch to be mixed is known and the number of pounds of each ingredient it contains must be given to the mill operator.

Let us use the square a bit further to get the number of pounds of oats, corn, and soybean meal to be mixed in a 2070 pound batch mixer. The batch could be any size; 2070 is an arbitrary number.

1   Divide 2070 by 34.5 to get the total number of pounds per part of ration—in this case, 60.
2   Multiply the number of pounds per part by 4 to get the number of pounds of soybean meal required.
3   Multiply the number of pounds per part by 30.5 to get the number of pounds of grain, then divide by 2 to get the number of pounds each of oats and corn.

% CP in grain = 10.5

$$30.5 \times 60 = \frac{1{,}830}{2}$$
$$= 915 \text{ oats}$$
$$= 915 \text{ corn}$$

% CP in soybean meal = 45

$$\frac{4}{34.5} \times \frac{60}{2070} = 240 \text{ lb soybean meal}$$

Result:

| | |
|---|---|
| Oats | 915 lb |
| Corn | 915 lb |
| Soybean meal | 240 lb |
| Total | 2070 |

This grain and supplement mixture meets the 14.5 percent CP need of weanlings. Unfortunately, many similar home-mixed preparations are fed to all sizes and ages of horses—with disastrous results.

## Mineral Calculation

Before supplementing a grain mixture with minerals, three determinations must be made: (1) the amount of minerals contained in the grain and protein supplement, (2) the total pounds of minerals needed in the final mixture, and (3) the number of pounds of mineral supplements to be added to the ration to supply the needed minerals. Use Table 12-10 for mineral quantities per source.

1 List ingredients in kind and amount.
2 Find percentages of calcium and phosphorus in Table 12-2.
3 Multiply amounts of ingredients by percentages of each and add them together.
4 Divide by 100 to get number of pounds.

|  |  |  | *Ca* |  |  | *P* |  |
|---|---|---|---|---|---|---|---|
|  |  | % | *lb* |  | % |  | *lb* |
| Oats | 915 lb × 0.06 | = | 54.9 |  | 0.33 | = | 301.95 |
| Corn | 915 lb × 0.02 | = | 18.3 |  | 0.30 | = | 274.50 |
| Soybean meal | 240 lb × 0.23 | = | 55.2 |  | 0.63 | = | 151.20 |
|  | 2070 |  | 128.4 |  |  |  | 727.65 |

$$\text{Pounds of calcium} = \frac{128.4}{100} = 1.28$$

$$\text{Pounds of phosphorus} = \frac{727.65}{100} = 7.28$$

Thus 2070 pounds of this mixture yields only 1.28 pounds of actual calcium, or 0.06 percent, which is exceedingly low. The mixture has 7.28 pounds of P, or 0.35 percent, which is a sizable contribution. The ratio of calcium to phosphorus is drastically wide—in the wrong direction! Foals consuming high levels of grain rations such as this without calcium supplementation develop sore legs and swelling at the ankles and knees, and their tendons contract, standing them on their toes. Thumb through any western horse magazine and note the erect pasterns of breed-winning halter show horses. Shoeing may account for some steep pasterns, but it would be interesting to know if these horses had eaten large amounts of grain without adequate calcium supplementation.

The solution is to add the appropriate amount of calcium to the grain mixture to meet the requirements of the horse and to match the type of hay with which it will be fed. How many pounds of calcium and phosphorus should there be in 2070 pounds of mixture? Multiply the percent requirements by 2070 and divide by 100 to get the number of pounds needed.

$$Ca = 2070 \times 0.60 = \frac{1242}{100} = 12.42 \text{ lb}$$

$$P = 2070 \times 0.45 = \frac{931.5}{100} = 9.32 \text{ lb}$$

The amounts needed in the mixture are therefore 12.42 pounds of calcium and 9.32 pounds of phosphorus.

As ingredients are added, the total weight of the mix increases, and we are in effect diluting the percentages slightly. This must be corrected in swine and poultry rations because of the demands of high production and limited feed intake. However, this dilution is usually ignored in horse grain rations.

It is well to note that the number of pounds of calcium in a ton of horse feed must range between 5.5 minimum and 16 maximum; phosphorus must range from 4 to 11 pounds, depending upon the age of the horses for which it was prepared.

How much dicalcium phosphate and limestone must be added? If one had pure sources of minerals, the solution would be easy, but limestone is only one-third calcium and dicalcium phosphate about one-fifth phosphorus and one-fourth calcium. Because of the "bonus" calcium supplied in dicalcium phosphate, we calculate phosphorus need first by subtracting the phosphorus supplied by the feed from the need and dividing by the percentage of phosphorus in dicalcium phosphate. Then we calculate the contribution of calcium in the dicalcium used and add it to the calcium in the feed before calculating the number of pounds of limestone in the same way.

$$P = \frac{\text{need} - \text{in feed}}{\% \text{ in dical}} = \frac{9.32 - 7.28}{0.19} = \frac{2.04}{0.19} = 10.74 \text{ lb dical}$$

$$\text{Ca supplied by 10.74 lb dical} = 10.74 \times 0.24 = 2.58 \text{ lb}$$

$$\text{Total Ca} = 2.58 + 1.28 = 3.86 \text{ lb already present in feed}$$

$$Ca = \frac{\text{need} - \text{in feed}}{\% \text{ in limestone}} = \frac{12.42 - 3.86}{0.36} = \frac{8.56}{0.36} = 15.29 \text{ lb limestone}$$

Thus 10.74 pounds of dicalcium phosphate and 15.29 pounds of limestone should bring the grain mixture to 0.6 percent calcium and 0.45 percent phosphorus. For practical purposes, the figures can be rounded off to 11 pounds of dicalcium phosphate and 16 of limestone.

Grain rations usually contain 0.5 percent salt. (For example, 2070 × 0.5% = 103.5 ÷ 100 = 10.35 pounds of salt.) Thus 10 or 11 pounds of salt should be added—probably trace-mineralized salt unless trace minerals are coming from more than one other source.

## Adding Vitamins

FAT-SOLUBLE VITAMINS    Grain rations should be formulated to contain approximately 5000 IU of A, 500 to 1000 IU of D, an optional 10 units of E, and no K per pound of mixed feed. Ask the feed dealer for a concentrated source of vitamin A with appropriate D and E. Read the label carefully, it may reveal the exact amount to use in a ton of feed. Do not be fooled with a long list of unneeded ingredients. Verify how much to use in a ton of feed with the following calculations:

1  Read label for amount of A per pound of premix.
2  Check ratio of D to A (5 to 10 times less).
3  Check ratio for E (if any) to D (80 to 100 times less).
4  Divide amount of A by 2000 pounds to determine IU of A per pound of mixed feed.

Consider a premix that has the following concentration of A, D, and E per pound:

$$IU \ A = 5,000,000$$
$$IU \ D = 1,000,000$$
$$IU \ E = 1000$$

Note quickly that the ratios are correct. Now divide 5,000,000 IU of A by 2000 pounds (ton) = 2500 IU of A per pound of mixed feed. Since 5000 IU per pound is standard, use 2 pounds of the premix to furnish the correct amount in a ton of mixed feed.

Table 12-6 was prepared for convenience in quickly checking a vitamin premix or conditioner for the amounts of vitamins A and D required in a ton of feed to yield desired levels per pound of feed.

One-pound vitamin premixes containing 10,000,000 IU of A and 2,000,000 IU of D yield 5000 units of A per pound and 1000 units of D when mixed in a ton. Thus 3 to 5 pounds of this feed supply the horse's daily requirements. If the horse is eating 10 pounds of grain, half this amount per ton will suffice. When a commercial grain with good levels and balances of vitamins and minerals is "cut" or reduced by half and replaced with oats or another grain, vitamin levels are also reduced by half and calcium is greatly reduced while phosphorus is reduced little, if at all.

If the last premix (Table 12-6) of 100,000 IU of A and 20,000 of D were used, how many pounds of it would be required to give 5000 units of A and

TABLE 12-6 VITAMIN A AND D LEVELS PER POUND OF MIXED FEED WHEN DIFFERENT CONCENTRATIONS IN A POUND OF PREMIX ARE ADDED TO A TON OF FEED

| Concentration of A per lb premix | IU of A per lb mixed feed | Concentration of D per lb premix | IU of D per lb mixed feed |
|---|---|---|---|
| 10,000,000 | 5000 | 2,000,000 | 1000 |
| 9,000,000 | 4500 | 1,800,000 | 900 |
| 8,000,000 | 4000 | 1,600,000 | 800 |
| 7,000,000 | 3500 | 1,400,000 | 700 |
| 6,000,000 | 3000 | 1,200,000 | 600 |
| 5,000,000 | 2500 | 1,000,000 | 500 |
| 4,000,000 | 2000 | 800,000 | 400 |
| 3,000,000 | 1500 | 600,000 | 300 |
| 2,000,000 | 1000 | 400,000 | 200 |
| 1,000,000 | 500 | 200,000 | 100 |
| 900,000 | 450 | 180,000 | 90 |
| 800,000 | 400 | 160,000 | 80 |
| 700,000 | 350 | 140,000 | 70 |
| 600,000 | 300 | 120,000 | 60 |
| 500,000 | 250 | 100,000 | 50 |
| 400,000 | 200 | 80,000 | 40 |
| 300,000 | 150 | 60,000 | 30 |
| 200,000 | 100 | 40,000 | 20 |
| 100,000 | 50 | 20,000 | 10 |

1000 units of D per pound of mixed feed? If 1 pound of the premix yields 50 units of A per pound (column 2, Table 12-6), then 100 pounds would yield 5000 units per pound of feed. No one will pay the price to supply ample vitamins if 100 pounds of premix are required, yet a majority of horse conditioners and many premixes yield this amount or less—some as little as 10,000 IU of A per pound!

If you are spooning a premix directly onto feed, calculate from the label how much is being fed. In a premix with 5,000,000 units of A per pound, how much A is in a heaping teaspoon? Ideally this amount should be weighed on a gram scale. Sometimes the dealer offers this service. If not, soybean meal vitamin carriers weigh approximately 4 grams per heaping teaspoonful. 5,000,000 ÷ 454 = 11,013 IU of A per gram or 44,052 IU per teaspoonful. This amount supplied every other day would be adequate, since it is stored in the body. It could be placed on top of the grain ration, fed alone in a trough, or mixed in loose salt for range horses (if it were mixed every 2 weeks to reduce the effects of oxidation).

TABLE 12-7   STABILITY OF VITAMIN A IN COMMERCIAL FEEDS

| Month and year | Stock block A | Stock block B | Beef concen-tration A | Beef concen-tration B |
|---|---|---|---|---|
| February 74 | 32,700 | 34,000 | 58,200 | 75,300 |
| March 74 | 31,000 | 28,800 | 56,500 | 74,700 |
| April 74 | 30,100 | 28,800 | 55,000 | 70,900 |
| May 74 | 26,300 | 22,800 | 47,900 | 58,700 |
| June 74 | 25,100 | 25,100 | 45,200 | 55,700 |
| July 74 | 20,400 | 23,900 | 42,500 | 50,600 |
| August 74 | 20,400 | 21,600 | 41,200 | 48,800 |
| September 74 | 17,000 | 18,000 | 28,400 | 35,900 |
| October 74 | 15,000 | 17,000 | 23,000 | 28,400 |
| November 74 | 15,000 | 15,000 | 22,300 | 24,200 |
| December 74 | 16,000 | 16,000 | 24,100 | 24,400 |
| January 75 | 15,000 | 15,000 | 22,900 | 25,000 |
| Percent Lost | 51.1 | 55.9 | 60.7 | 66.8 |

*Note:* The vitamin A contents are expressed as USP (IU) units per pound.

It is important to note that vitamin premixes lose potency with age and should be used or replaced after about 6 months. Table 12-7 shows the results of research in South Dakota on storage loss of vitamin A.[3] The loss would be much greater in warmer, more humid climates.

CONDITIONERS AS SOURCES OF VITAMIN A AND D   An interview with horse feed dealers in one medium-sized town showed that "conditioners" (those supplements advertised to ensure greatness for the horse) *outsold* vitamin premixes ten to one, were approximately ten times *more expensive* than premixes, and contained ten or more times *less* vitamin A and D! The ranges in these vitamins were 9500 to 800,000 units of A and 1370 to 80,000 units of D per pound of conditioner. All contained long lists of major minerals, trace minerals, and B vitamins. There are situations such as recovery from disease or emaciation where conditioners may profitably be used, but they should be used to supplement vitamins, protein, and minerals—not to replace them.

If one were wealthy enough to meet a horse's vitamin A and D needs from conditioners, more than half of the conditioners surveyed would supply toxic levels of trace minerals and/or vitamin D. One described above

[3]S. K. Dash and J. D. Michell, "Storage, Processing Reduce Vitamin A," *Animal Nutrition and Health*, October 1976, p. 17.

would produce iodine toxicity at 2 pounds of mixed feed and vitamin D toxicity at 6 pounds. Toxic materials sold to the public must be diluted because of the notion entertained by some people that "if a little is good, much more must be better." Conditioners are no exception.

WATER-SOLUBLE VITAMINS   Researchers are divided in opinion on the need of stressed horses for B vitamins. If, indeed, there is a need, it can be projected on the basis of research with other monogastric animals, as has been done in human nutrition. However, the amount of supplement needed is uncertain because B vitamin production undoubtedly continues in the intestines of stressed horses.

Swine are very exact in their requirements for riboflavin, niacin (nicotinic acid), panothenic acid, and vitamin $B_{12}$. Thiamine, pyrodixine, and choline are assumed to be abundant in swine (and horse) feeds.

Table 12-8 is not an endorsement of B vitamin feeding. It is merely the amount of these vitamins that swinemen would use for a 1000 pound weight of bred females. If these amounts are compared to those in most horse conditioners, they may equal or exceed the entire amount contained in a pound of many conditioners designed to feed a horse for weeks.

One large reputable feed company advertises the following amounts of B vitamins supplied daily in its conditioner when fed as directed:

Thiamine, 100 mg

Riboflavin, 40 mg

Niacin, 100 mg

Pantothenic acid, 120 mg

TABLE 12-8   DAILY VITAMIN B REQUIREMENT OF SWINE AND PROJECTED AMOUNTS (IF ANY) FOR HORSES

|  | Daily amounts | |
|---|---|---|
|  | 200-lb swine | 1000-lb horse* |
| Thiamine, g | 3.0 | 15.0 |
| Riboflavin, g | 8.0 | 40.0 |
| Niacin, g | 44.0 | 220.0 |
| Pantothenic acid, g | 33.0 | 165.0 |
| $B_{12}$, $\mu$g | 28.0 | 140.0 |

*Projected from first column by multiplying by 5.
SOURCE: Adapted from National Research Council, *Nutrient Requirements for Swine*, National Academy of Sciences, Washington, D.C., 1973.

Folic aid, 2.5 mg

Vitamin $B_{12}$, 0.4 mg

Note that these units are in milligrams (mg), 1000th of a gram, compared to the grams listed in Table 12-8.

B vitamins are often injected into horses by veterinarians. Old, thin, weak, wormy, and recuperating horses may need them. The label on an injectable form of vitamin B might look as follows:

B vitamin complex solution (for use by veterinarians only) Each cc contains:

| | |
|---|---|
| Thiamine | 100 mg |
| Niacin | 100 mg |
| Panthenol | 10 mg |
| Riboflavin | 2 mg |
| Pyrodixine | 2 mg |
| Vitamin $B_{12}$ | 2 $\mu$g |

This mixture is designed for a variety of animal species and contains vitamins that some species may not need. Directions for horses are "10 to 20 cc; repeat as indicated." A single injection of 15 cc would far exceed most of the needs as projected from swine requirements in Table 12-8. However, these vitamins are absorbed slowly.

A number of research questions must be answered before it makes sense to supplement rations with B vitamins. Do horses need any? Most researchers think not. Do they require supplementation when stressed such as when racing? Most racehorse owners and some researchers think so. If so, how much? It would seem likely that intestinal fermentation under stress does not cease and that absorption from food continues; therefore, the small amounts offered in the best conditioners may make up the difference. Research with hardworking draft horses failed to show a need for B vitamin supplementation, but these horses were not excited, were traveling slowly, and were consuming large quantities of roughage. Whether the high-strung young racer, possibly eating little roughage, needs them remains a mystery. If so, the owner is confronted by many decisions, because feeds and conditioners vary in the amounts they furnish as widely as has been shown for those supplying vitamins A, D, and E.

## X-Y Balancing

Researchers and graduate students must balance rations according to the amount of each nutrient consumed daily, weigh and measure quantities carefully, and report research findings in the metric system (Table 12-9).

TABLE 12-9 WEIGHT UNIT CONVERSION FACTORS

| Units given | Units wanted | For conversion multiply by | Units given | Units wanted | For conversion multiply by |
|---|---|---|---|---|---|
| lb | g | 453.6 | μg/kg | μg/lb | 0.4536 |
| lb | kg | 0.4536 | Mcal | kcal | 1,000. |
| oz | g | 28.36 | kcal/kg | kcal/lb | 0.4536 |
| kg | lb | 2.2046 | kcal/lb | kcal/kg | 2.2046 |
| kg | mg | 1,000,000. | ppm | μg/g | 1. |
| kg | g | 1,000. | ppm | mg/kg | 1. |
| g | mg | 1,000. | ppm | mg/lb | 0.4536 |
| g | μg | 1,000,000. | mg/kg | % | 0.0001 |
| mg | μg | 1,000. | ppm | % | 0.0001 |
| mg/g | mg/lb | 453.6 | mg/g | % | 0.1 |
| mg/kg | mg/lb | 0.4536 | g/kg | % | 0.1 |

*Note:* Weight equivalents are as follows:

1 lb = 453.6 g = 0.4536 kg = 16 oz
1 oz = 28.35 g
1 kg = 1,000 g = 2.2046 lb
1 g = 1,000 mg
1 mg = 1,000 μg = 0.001 g
1 μg = 0.001 mg = 0.000001 g
1 μg per g or 1 mg per kg is the same as 1 ppm.

SOURCE: Adapted from National Research Council, *Nutrient Requirements for Horses,* National Academy of Sciences, Washington, D.C., 1973.

The *X-Y* method is often used. It involves solving for two unknowns with simultaneous equations. The method is very accurate, but it is only useful for two feeds, for one feed in a mixture, or for two mixtures. For this reason a given amount of a feed to be used may be subtracted from the animal's requirement, and two other feeds can be used to supply the remainder of the required nutrients.

Let us consider the 6-month-old weanling again, to be fed timothy hay, oats, and soybean meal. List its requirements from Table 12-3 and subtract a fixed amount of a selected feed from them, that is, 3 kg of timothy hay (Appendix 12-1). Oats and soybean meal are the two unknowns to be solved for.

| Knowns (Requirement) | DP, kg | | DE, Mcal |
|---|---|---|---|
| 6-month foal | 0.52 | | 15.60 |
| 3 kg timothy, bloom @ 4.8% DP = | 0.14 | @ 1.98 = | 5.94 |
| Deficit | 0.38 | | 9.66 |

The deficit of 0.38 kg of digestible protein and 9.66 Mcal of digestible energy supplied by oats and soybean meal are determined as follows. We have the following quantities:

|  | DP, % | DE, Mcal/lb |
|---|---|---|
| Oats | 10.5 | 3.34 |
| Soybean meal | 35.7 | 3.60 |

Let $X$ = kg of oats to use and let $Y$ = kg of soybean meal to use.

*Equation (A): Protein.*   $X$ lb of oats times DP in oats + $Y$ lb of soybean meal times DP of soybean meal = DP to be supplied from oats and soybean meal = $0.105X + 0.357Y = 0.38$.

*Equation (B): Digestible energy.*   $Y$ = lb of oats times DE in oats + lb of soybean meal times DE in soybean meal = $3.34X + 3.60Y = 9.66$.

Calculating a factor to remove one unknown:

$$0.105X + 0.357Y = 0.38 \qquad \text{(A)}$$
$$3.34X + 3.60Y = 9.66 \qquad \text{(B)}$$
$$\text{Factor} = \frac{3.60}{0.357} = 10.08$$

Multiplying the factor times Equation (A):

$$(0.105X \times 10.08) + (0.357Y \times 10.08) = 0.38 \times 10.08$$
$$= 1.06X + 3.60Y = 3.83$$

Subtracting (A) from (B):

$$3.34X + 3.60Y = 9.66 \qquad \text{(A)}$$
$$- \underline{\quad 1.06X + 3.60Y = 3.83} \qquad \text{(B)}$$
$$2.28X + \quad 0 \quad = 5.83$$

Solving for $X$:

$$2.28X = 5.83 \quad \text{or} \quad X = \frac{5.83}{2.28} = 2.56$$

$$X = 2.56 \text{ kg of oats}$$

Substituting the value of $X$ (2.56) in Equation (B) for $X$:

$$3.34X + 3.60Y = 9.66$$
$$(3.34 \times 2.56) + 3.60Y = 9.66$$
$$8.55 + 3.60Y = 9.66$$
$$3.60Y = 9.66 - 8.44 = 1.11$$
$$3.60Y = 1.11$$
$$Y = \frac{3.60}{1.11} = 0.32$$

$$Y = 0.32 \text{ kg of soybean meal}$$

Substituting values of $X$ and $Y$ for unknown in Equations (A) and (B) to check accuracy.

$$(0.105 \times 2.56) + (0.357Y \times 0.32) = 0.38 \qquad \text{(A)}$$
$$0.269 + 0.114 = 0.38$$

$$(3.34 \times 2.56) + (3.60 \times 0.32) = 9.66 \qquad \text{(B)}$$
$$8.55 + 1.15 = 9.70$$

We have determined that 3 kg of timothy, 2.55 kg of oats, and 0.32 kg of soybean meal meet the protein and energy requirements of weanlings. We must check for calcium and phosphorus and add vitamins. The percentages of calcium and phosphorus (Appendix 12-1) are:

Oats, grain:
2.55 kg $\times$ 0.07% = 0.179 kg Ca        2.55 kg $\times$ 35% = 0.944 kg P

Soybean meal:
0.32 kg $\times$ 0.31% = 0.099 kg Ca        0.32 kg $\times$ 0.70% = 0.224 kg P

Timothy, bloom:
3 kg $\times$ 0.41% = $\dfrac{1.230 \text{ kg Ca}}{1.508 \text{ kg Ca}}$        3 kg $\times$ 0.18% = $\dfrac{0.570 \text{ kg P}}{1.738 \text{ kg P}}$

Dividing by 100 and multiplying by 1000, we have 15.08 g calcium and 17.38 g phorphorus. But the calcium and phosphorus requirements for a 6-month-old foal are 34 and 25 g, respectively (Table 12-3). To determine how to supplement the ration with dicalcium phosphate and limestone, first list their percentages (Table 12-10).

|  | Ca, % | P, % |
| --- | --- | --- |
| Dicalcium, phosphate | 24 | 19 |
| Limestone | 36 | — |

TABLE 12-10  MINERAL SUPPLEMENTS

| Supplements | Ca, % | P, % | Mg, % |
|---|---|---|---|
| Bone meal, steamed | 32.3 | 13.3 | 0.6 |
| Calcium carbonate | 36.7 | 0.5 | 0.3 |
| Dicalcium phosphate | 24.0 | 19.0 | — |
| Limestone, ground | 36.0 | — | 2.1 |
| Monosodium phosphate | — | 25.8 | — |
| Monodicalcium phosphate | 16.8 | 22.1 | 0.5 |
| Phosphate, difluorinated | 31.7 | 13.7 | 0.3 |
| Sodium tripolyphosphate | — | 25.1 | — |

SOURCE: Adapted from National Research Council, *Nutrient Requirements for Horses*, National Academy of Sciences, Washington, D.C., 1978.

Calculate as before by determining the need less what is in the ration divided by percentages in the mineral supplements.

$$P = \frac{need - in\ ration}{\%\ in\ dical} = \frac{25 - 17}{0.19} = \frac{8}{0.19} = 42.11\ g\ dicalcium\ phosphate$$

$$Ca\ supplied\ by\ 42.11\ g\ dical = 42.11 \times 0.24 = 10.11\ g\ Ca$$

$$Total\ Ca = 15.08 + 10.11 = 25.19\ g\ Ca$$

$$Ca = \frac{need - in\ ration}{\%\ in\ limestone} = \frac{34 - 25.19}{0.36} = \frac{8.81}{0.36} = 24.47\ g\ limestone$$

Thus, this daily ration requires 42.11 g of dicalcium phosphate and 24.47 g of limestone to meet minimum mineral requirements. The difficulty of feeding these minerals is readily apparent. If this amount of minerals is mixed with whole or processed oats, it will promptly settle to the bottom and some will be refused. An easy solution is to feed legume hay with oats or to feed processed grain with liquid molasses, which contains minerals and vitamins.

Feed 0.5 percent salt in the ration or feed it free-choice. Add fat-soluble vitamins as discussed earlier to supply 5000 IU of A per pound of ration.

## Computer Ration Formulation

Feed companies and researchers use computers to formulate rations. They are especially useful where ingredients may be substituted for each other as prices change. However, cost and access to computers have restricted their use to relatively few people until recently.

Regardless of what process is used in deciding on what to feed the horse, it should be based on fact—not opinion or hearsay. It should stand the test of routine chemical analysis. The horse must like the ration and eat it in sufficient quantity to sustain condition for the task at hand. It should create no negative nutrient balance that will reduce long-term efficiency, and it should be competitively priced—because of improved analytical equipment and technique, no feed company has a secret formula or magic ingredient that can remain unknown to its competitors for very long. The "magic" of horse feeding is the result of the knowledge that every nutrient needed is supplied in the feed and that none is offered in imbalance or excess.

## FEED PREPARATION

Most processing of feed is done for the convenience of horse owners, not necessarily for the horse, because there is little improvement in digestibility or palatability to be gained for horses with sound teeth.

### Forages

Good grass is the choice feed for idle horses and quality long hay for most that are confined, both idle and working. Some horse owners have neither of these feeds available to them, and their plight is not likely to improve, because the cost of processing, curing, transporting, storing, and distributing long hay in bales is prohibitive in many areas. Indeed, finding a dependable, economical source of roughage for pellets and other "complete" horse feed is one of a feed company's greatest challenges. To meet it, both forages and grains are pelleted and hays are cubed and wafered.

PELLETING FORAGES    Pelleting is used far more with grain and complete feeds than with hay alone. However, alfalfa and, to a lesser degree, red clover are pelleted where they are grown. Guaranteed protein content is usually 17 and 14 percent, respectively, and dry matter exceeds 90 percent. Processing costs usually increase the price $20 to $30 per ton.

A few years ago great hope was held for pellets by horsemen and feed companies. Its advantages were listed as these:

1  Reduced dust (good for horses with heaves).
2  Complete ration formulation with all nutrients present in correct amounts.
3  Less waste.
4  Ease of handling, transportation, and storage.
5  Less "haybelly" for show horses.

These are indeed attractive features, but cribbing and restlessness soon revealed themselves to be major shortcomings of pellets. For this reason, companies that sell pellets often recommend that a minimum of 4 to 6 pounds of long hay be fed with them.

Most pellets are ½ inch by approximately 1 inch. They can be composed of almost anything, but those made from alfalfa and clover by reliable companies with consistent processing methods are high-quality forages and are of uniform nutritional value. If pellets are overheated in processing, some nutrient loss is likely, especially of vitamin A.

Use of pellets for one-quarter to one-half of the diet of a stable of horses will postpone hay allergies and heaves in some horses. Unfortunately, it will likely hasten wood-chewing and cribbing in others.

CUBES AND WAFERS   Machinery has been developed to compress coarsely cut hay in the field into cubes or wafers about 1½ by 2 to 3 inches in size. Some are larger. High energy costs in processing dictate that this method be used with good-quality forage (alfalfa) and in dry areas. California is the leading state in cube processing.

Cubes and wafers have many of the advantages of pellets. Research by Johnson and Hughes at Washington State University (1974) showed no wood-chewing or cribbing, good weight gain, fewer feces, and a saving of grain when comparing cubes to long hay.[4] However, cost is excessive in most areas of the country. It is not uncommon for prices of alfalfa wafers in some areas to exceed prices of horse grain mixtures. Foreign demand has stimulated cube and wafer production, and this has helped to establish a price above some horsemen's budgets.

## Grains and Complete Feeds

Grains have been processed for humans and horses for centuries. They have been soaked, ground, cooked, rolled, steamed, flaked, popped, micronized, exploded, extended, and pelleted. These methods involve mechanical reduction or reshaping of particles, addition or reduction of moisture, and application of pressure and heat in an attempt to gain some slight advantage in digestibility and palatability, mostly for feedlot cattle. All processes are useful in some phase of the industry. However, breakthroughs that substantially increase digestibility remain to be achieved.

Less information is available on feed preparation for horses than cattle, but the figure used most often is a 5 percent increase in digestibility. This would vary by type of feed and age and type of horse. There are other good reasons for processing, such as the convenience of using additives without fear of separation, decreased palatability, or increased dustiness.

[4]R. J. Johnson and I. M. Hughes, "Alfalfa Cubes for Horses," *Feedstuffs*, Oct. 21, 1974, p. 31.

PELLETING GRAIN AND COMPLETE FEEDS   It is difficult to argue for the merits of pelleting grains when other methods of preparation are less expensive and more acceptable to the horse. However, it is a great advantage to many horse owners to be able to buy an expertly formulated ration in the form of a complete horse feed, as is available from some feed companies in the form of pellets. Nevertheless, grain pellets may be expensive, may pose a wood-chewing problem unless supplemented by small amounts of long hay or pasture, and may create anxiety over what the pellet contains.

A good complete feed is usually made from a grain to roughage (hay) ratio of approximately 40:60 and all ranges between. It will be properly supplemented with minerals, vitamins, and protein to allow some additional grain feeding if the horse needs more energy.

Although the importance of nutrient balance for growing and finishing swine is widely recognized, Rea[5] found thirteen of twenty-six samples of commercial swine feeds from "good" producers unsatisfactory on the basis of a chemical analysis check and recheck. Some had not been fed according to directions, but most had.

FLAKING   Flaking is a rather new method developed for cattle that is also well received by horses. The grain is steam-rolled and subjected to enough heat to increase its temperature. This increases digestibility and produces light, fluffy particles that are relished by horses. The bulky mass reduces digestive disorders and results in stable feed intake with hardworking horses. Flaked horse grains are available in cattle feedlot areas, but may be hard to find elsewhere.

GRINDING   Grinding is an old method that breaks grain into particles as flailing knives rotate over a metal screen whose holes allow particles to pass through when they are reduced to an appropriate size. Grinding equipment is cheap compared with most other processing equipment, and the process is simple, which results in less cost to horse owners. It can be done satisfactorily for horse feeds, but it is one of the least desirable feed preparation methods because it creates dust and fines. A careful operator will use a large screen to increase particle size and a slow machine speed, if possible, to reduce fines.

WETTING, SOAKING, COOKING   Bran mashes, when fed to tired, stressed horses, undoubtedly increase feed intake under some conditions where feed would have been refused. Bran is soaked in hot water for about 10 minutes before feeding. Soaking grain overnight was a common practice of hog feeders

[5]John C. Rea, "A Report of Swine Feed Analysis," Unpublished data, Aug. 18, 1975.

years ago. It probably increased feed intake during the years of "flint" corn production. Soaking is dangerous for horses because of the risk of mold. Show cattlemen often cooked grain. Some still do, thinking it results in firmer finish and more glossy hair coats.

Recent research does not support any of these methods as high-priority management practices among horsemen. The choice of a processing method should be based on cost, convenience, and acceptability to the horse rather than increased digestibility, except when feeding old horses with bad teeth. Hungry horses will eat small amounts of grain in any form, while those working hard may be enticed to eat more by reducing fines with more refined processing methods.

## BIBLIOGRAPHY

Ensminger, M. E.: *Horses and Horsemanship*, Interstate, Ill., 1969.
Equine Research Publications: *Feeding to Win*. Grapevine, Tex., 1973.
National Research Council: *Nutrient Requirements of Horses*, National Academy of Sciences, Washington, D.C., 1973, 1978.

## APPENDIX 12-1 COMPOSITION OF FEEDS COMMONLY USED IN HORSE DIETS—DRY BASIS (Moisture-free)

| Line no. | Feed | International feed number | Dry matter, % | DE, Mcal/kg | TDN, % | Crude protein, % | Digestible protein, % | Lysine, % | Crude fiber, % | Cell walls, % |
|---|---|---|---|---|---|---|---|---|---|---|
| | **ALFALFA** | | | | | | | | | |
| | *Medicago sativa* | | | | | | | | | |
| 1 | grazed, prebloom | 2-00-181 | 21 | 2.51 | 57 | 21.2 | 15.6 | 1.06 | 22 | — |
| 2 | grazed, full bloom | 2-00-188 | 25 | 2.29 | 52 | 16.3 | 11.4 | 0.65 | 33 | — |
| 3 | hay, s-c, early bloom | 1-00-059 | 90 | 2.42 | 55 | 17.2 | 13.4 | 0.94 | 31 | 48 |
| 4 | hay, s-c, midbloom | 1-00-063 | 89 | 2.29 | 52 | 16.0 | 11.6 | 0.90 | 32 | 50 |
| 5 | hay, s-c, full bloom | 1-00-068 | 89 | 2.16 | 49 | 15.0 | 10.1 | 0.64 | 34 | 52 |
| 6 | meal, dehy, 15% protein | 1-00-022 | 91 | 2.42 | 55 | 16.3 | 11.8 | 0.66 | 33 | 51 |
| 7 | meal, dehy, 17% protein | 1-00-023 | 92 | 2.46 | 56 | 19.7 | 13.9 | 0.96 | 27 | 45 |
| | **BAHIAGRASS** | | | | | | | | | |
| | *Paspalum notatum* | | | | | | | | | |
| 8 | grazed | 2-00-464 | 30 | 2.11 | 48 | 7.9 | 4.2 | — | 32 | — |
| 9 | hay, s-c | 1-00-462 | 91 | 1.89 | 43 | 5.8 | 2.5 | — | 30 | — |
| | **BARLEY** | | | | | | | | | |
| | *Hardeum vulgare* | | | | | | | | | |
| 10 | grain | 4-00-549 | 89 | 3.61 | 82 | 13.9 | 11.4 | 0.48 | 6 | 19 |
| 11 | grain, Pacific Coast | 4-00-939 | 90 | 3.48 | 79 | 10.7 | 7.0 | 0.35 | 7 | 21 |
| 12 | hay, s-c | 1-00-495 | 89 | 1.89 | 44 | 8.5 | 4.7 | — | 27 | — |
| 13 | straw | 1-00-498 | 90 | 1.63 | 37 | 4.0 | 0.9 | — | 42 | 80 |
| | **BEET, SUGAR** | | | | | | | | | |
| | *Beta vulgaris, B. saccharifera* | | | | | | | | | |
| 14 | pulp, dehy | 4-00-669 | 91 | 2.86 | 65 | 8.0 | 5.0 | 0.66 | 22 | 59 |
| | **BERMUDAGRASS** | | | | | | | | | |
| | *Cynodon dactylon* | | | | | | | | | |
| 15 | grazed | 2-00-712 | 39 | 2.20 | 50 | 9.1 | 5.2 | — | 28 | — |
| 16 | hay, s-c | 1-00-716 | 91 | 1.98 | 45 | 7.0 | 4.2 | — | 34 | 80 |
| | **BLUEGRASS, KEN-TUCKY** | | | | | | | | | |
| | *Pao pratensis* | | | | | | | | | |
| 17 | grazed, early | 2-00-777 | 31 | 2.46 | 56 | 17.0 | 12.4 | — | 26 | — |
| 18 | grazed, posthead | 2-00-782 | 35 | 2.20 | 50 | 11.6 | 7.4 | — | 27 | — |
| 19 | hay, s-c | 1-00-776 | 90 | 2.20 | 50 | 11.0 | 5.1 | — | 30 | — |
| | **BREWERS** | | | | | | | | | |
| 20 | grains, dehy | 5-02-141 | 92 | 2.99 | 68 | 27.0 | 20.9 | 0.95 | 16 | 42 |
| | **BROME** | | | | | | | | | |
| | *Bromus* spp | | | | | | | | | |
| 21 | grazed, vegetable | 2-00-892 | 32 | 3.00 | 68 | 18.3 | 12.6 | — | 24 | 60 |
| 22 | hay, s-c, late bloom | 1-00-888 | 90 | 2.38 | 54 | 7.4 | 5.0 | — | 40 | 72 |
| | **CANARYGRASS, REED** | | | | | | | | | |
| | *Phalaris arundinacea* | | | | | | | | | |
| 23 | grazed | 2-01-113 | 27 | 2.38 | 54 | 12.0 | 7.5 | — | 29 | — |
| 24 | hay | 1-01-104 | 91 | 2.16 | 49 | 12.3 | 7.6 | — | 33 | — |
| | **CITRUS** | | | | | | | | | |
| 25 | pulp wo fines, dehy | 4-01-237 | 90 | 2.99 | 68 | 6.9 | 3.6 | — | 14 | 23 |
| | **CLOVER, ALSIKE** | | | | | | | | | |
| | *Trifolium hybridum* | | | | | | | | | |
| 26 | hay, s-c | 1-01-313 | 89 | 2.11 | 48 | 14.8 | 10.1 | — | 29 | — |
| | **CLOVER, CRIMSON** | | | | | | | | | |
| | *Trifolium incarnatum* | | | | | | | | | |
| 27 | grazed | 2-01-336 | 17 | 2.42 | 55 | 17.2 | 12.1 | — | 27 | — |

| Line no. | ADF, % | Cellu-lose, % | Lignin, % | Cal-cium, % | Cop-per, mg/kg | Iron, mg/kg | Mag-nesium, % | Manga-nese, mg/kg | Phos-phorus, % | Potas-sium, % | So-dium, % | Sul-fur, % | Zinc, mg/kg |
|---|---|---|---|---|---|---|---|---|---|---|---|---|---|
| 1 | — | — | — | 2.26 | 10 | 200 | 0.25 | 28 | 0.35 | 2.35 | 0.20 | 0.50 | 18 |
| 2 | — | — | — | 1.53 | 9 | 330 | 0.27 | 25 | 0.27 | 2.15 | 0.15 | 0.31 | 15 |
| 3 | 38 | 28 | 10 | 1.75 | 15 | 200 | 0.30 | 32 | 0.26 | 2.55 | 0.15 | 0.29 | 17 |
| 4 | 40 | 29 | 11 | 1.50 | 13 | 180 | 0.29 | 29 | 0.25 | 1.90 | 0.14 | 0.28 | 17 |
| 5 | 42 | 30 | 12 | 1.29 | 12 | 170 | 0.31 | 27 | 0.24 | 1.80 | 0.14 | 0.26 | 17 |
| 6 | 41 | 29 | 12 | 1.40 | 11 | 330 | 0.30 | 31 | 0.24 | 2.50 | 0.10 | 0.20 | 22 |
| 7 | 35 | 24 | 11 | 1.50 | 10 | 400 | 0.39 | 31 | 0.26 | 2.70 | 0.10 | 0.26 | 22 |
| 8 | — | — | — | 0.45 | — | 60 | 0.25 | — | 0.19 | 1.45 | — | — | — |
| 9 | — | — | — | 0.45 | — | 60 | 0.19 | — | 0.22 | 1.45 | — | — | — |
| 10 | 7 | — | — | 0.05 | 9 | 90 | 0.15 | 19 | 0.37 | 0.45 | 0.03 | 0.18 | 17 |
| 11 | 9 | — | — | 0.05 | 9 | 80 | 0.13 | 18 | 0.37 | 0.58 | 0.02 | 0.17 | 17 |
| 12 | — | — | — | 0.21 | 4 | 300 | 0.19 | 39 | 0.31 | 1.49 | 0.14 | 0.17 | — |
| 13 | 59 | 37 | 12 | 0.24 | 10 | 300 | 0.15 | 17 | 0.05 | 2.01 | 0.14 | 0.17 | — |
| 14 | 34 | — | — | 0.75 | 14 | 330 | 0.30 | 38 | 0.10 | 0.20 | 0.23 | 0.22 | 10 |
| 15 | — | — | — | 0.49 | — | — | 0.19 | — | 0.27 | — | — | — | — |
| 16 | 35 | 23 | 12 | 0.40 | — | — | 0.17 | — | 0.19 | 1.57 | 0.44 | — | 20 |
| 17 | — | — | — | 0.56 | 10 | — | 0.20 | 79 | 0.40 | 2.20 | — | — | — |
| 18 | — | — | — | 0.46 | 9 | — | 0.18 | 68 | 0.39 | 2.01 | — | — | — |
| 19 | — | — | — | 0.30 | 9 | 260 | 0.16 | 93 | 0.29 | 1.70 | 0.14 | 0.13 | — |
| 20 | 23 | 18 | 5 | 0.30 | 24 | 270 | 0.17 | 42 | 0.58 | 0.09 | 0.28 | 0.34 | 30 |
| 21 | 31 | 27 | 4 | 0.55 | 5 | 100 | 0.18 | — | 0.35 | 2.32 | 0.02 | 0.20 | — |
| 22 | 44 | 36 | 8 | 0.32 | 7 | 100 | 0.13 | 106 | 0.22 | 2.00 | 0.02 | 0.20 | — |
| 23 | — | — | — | 0.42 | 9 | 150 | — | — | 0.35 | 3.64 | — | — | — |
| 24 | — | — | — | 0.37 | 9 | 150 | 0.31 | 106 | 0.25 | 1.86 | 0.39 | 0.41 | — |
| 25 | 23 | — | — | 2.07 | 6 | 170 | 0.16 | 7 | 0.13 | 0.77 | 0.10 | 0.07 | 16 |
| 26 | — | — | — | 1.32 | 6 | 260 | 0.41 | 69 | 0.29 | 2.46 | 0.46 | 0.17 | — |
| 27 | — | — | — | 1.33 | — | 250 | 0.29 | 317 | 0.32 | 2.51 | 0.40 | 0.28 | — |

## APPENDIX 12-1, *continued*

| Line no. | Feed | International feed number | Dry matter, % | DE, Mcal/kg | TDN, % | Crude protein, % | Digestible protein, % | Lysine, % | Crude fiber, % | Cell walls % |
|---|---|---|---|---|---|---|---|---|---|---|
| 28 | hay, s-c | 1-01-328 | 89 | 2.16 | 49 | 18.0 | 13.1 | — | 32 | — |
|  | CLOVER, LADINO |  |  |  |  |  |  |  |  |  |
|  | *Trifolium repens* |  |  |  |  |  |  |  |  |  |
| 29 | hay, s-c | 1-01-378 | 90 | 2.24 | 51 | 21.0 | 15.6 | — | 20 | 36 |
|  | CLOVER, RED |  |  |  |  |  |  |  |  |  |
|  | *Trifolium pratense* |  |  |  |  |  |  |  |  |  |
| 30 | grazed, early bloom | 2-01-428 | 20 | 2.51 | 57 | 21.1 | 12.0 | — | 19 | — |
| 31 | grazed, late bloom | 2-01-429 | 26 | 2.42 | 55 | 14.5 | 9.8 | — | 30 | — |
| 32 | hay, s-c | 1-01-415 | 89 | 2.16 | 49 | 14.9 | 10.0 | — | 30 | 56 |
|  | CORN |  |  |  |  |  |  |  |  |  |
|  | *Zea mays* |  |  |  |  |  |  |  |  |  |
| 33 | cobs, ground | 1-02-782 | 90 | 1.36 | 31 | 2.8 | 0.5 | — | 36 | 89 |
| 34 | distillers grains, dehy | 5-02-842 | 92 | 3.08 | 70 | 29.8 | 21.0 | 0.87 | 12 | 43 |
| 35 | ears, grnd | 4-02-849 | 87 | 3.26 | 74 | 9.1 | 5.6 | 0.20 | 10 | — |
| 36 | grain | 4-02-985 | 88 | 3.87 | 88 | 10.9 | 8.5 | 0.30 | 2 | — |
|  | COTTON |  |  |  |  |  |  |  |  |  |
|  | *Gossypium* spp |  |  |  |  |  |  |  |  |  |
| 37 | hulls | 1-01-599 | 91 | 1.45 | 33 | 4.2 | 1.1 | — | 50 | 90 |
|  | FESCUE, MEADOW |  |  |  |  |  |  |  |  |  |
|  | *Festuca elatior* |  |  |  |  |  |  |  |  |  |
| 38 | grazed | 2-01-920 | 27 | 2.29 | 52 | 11.5 | 7.3 | — | 29 | — |
| 39 | hay, s-c | 1-01-912 | 88 | 2.02 | 46 | 10.5 | 5.8 | — | 33 | 65 |
|  | FLAX |  |  |  |  |  |  |  |  |  |
|  | *Linum usitatissimum* |  |  |  |  |  |  |  |  |  |
| 40 | seeds, meal, solv extd (Linseed meal) | 5-02-048 | 91 | 3.04 | 69 | 38.9 | 27.6 | 1.34 | 10 | — |
|  | LESPEDEZA |  |  |  |  |  |  |  |  |  |
|  | *L. striata, L. stipulacea* |  |  |  |  |  |  |  |  |  |
| 41 | grazed | 2-02-568 | 31 | 2.20 | 50 | 14.9 | 10.2 | — | 38 | — |
| 42 | hay, s-c | 1-08-591 | 91 | 2.07 | 47 | 13.9 | 9.3 | — | 32 | — |
|  | LINSEED—see FLAX |  |  |  |  |  |  |  |  |  |
|  | MILK |  |  |  |  |  |  |  |  |  |
|  | *Bos taurus* |  |  |  |  |  |  |  |  |  |
| 43 | skimmed, dehy | 5-01-175 | 94 | 4.05 | 92 | 36.0 | 30.3 | 2.69 | 0.3 | — |
|  | MOLASSES |  |  |  |  |  |  |  |  |  |
| 44 | beet, sugar, mn 48% invert | 4-00-668 | 78 | 3.17 | 72 | 8.7 | 5.3 | — | — | — |
| 45 | sugarcane, molasses, dehy | 4-04-695 | 94 | 3.17 | 72 | 9.3 | 5.8 | — | 5.0 | — |
| 46 | sugarcane, molasses, mn 48% invert | 4-04-696 | 75 | 3.26 | 74 | 4.3 | 2.0 | — | — | — |
|  | OATS |  |  |  |  |  |  |  |  |  |
|  | *Avena sativa* |  |  |  |  |  |  |  |  |  |
| 47 | grain | 4-03-309 | 89 | 3.34 | 76 | 13.6 | 10.5 | — | 12 | 31 |
| 48 | grain, Pacific Coast | 4-07-999 | 91 | 3.34 | 77 | 10.1 | 6.5 | — | 12 | — |
| 49 | hay, s-c | 1-03-280 | 90 | 2.07 | 47 | 8.9 | 5.1 | — | 32 | — |
| 50 | straw | 1-03-283 | 92 | 2.11 | 40 | 4.3 | 2.5 | — | 40 | 70 |
|  | ORCHARDGRASS |  |  |  |  |  |  |  |  |  |
|  | *Dactylis glomerata* |  |  |  |  |  |  |  |  |  |
| 51 | grazed | 2-03-439 | 19 | 2.42 | 55 | 18.4 | 13.2 | — | 27 | 55 |
| 52 | hay, s-c | 1-03-438 | 89 | 2.07 | 47 | 10.1 | 6.1 | — | 36 | — |
|  | PANGOLAGRASS |  |  |  |  |  |  |  |  |  |
|  | *Digitara decumbens* |  |  |  |  |  |  |  |  |  |
| 53 | grazed | 2-03-493 | 19 | 2.24 | 51 | 12.5 | 8.1 | — | 29 | — |

| Line no. | ADF, % | Cellu-lose, % | Lignin, % | Cal-cium, % | Cop-per, mg/kg | Iron, mg/kg | Mag-nesium, % | Manga-nese, mg/kg | Phos-phorus, % | Potas-sium, % | So-dium, % | Sul-fur, % | Zinc, mg/kg |
|---|---|---|---|---|---|---|---|---|---|---|---|---|---|
| 28 | — | — | — | 1.39 | — | 300 | 0.29 | 200 | 0.20 | 2.00 | 0.39 | 0.28 | — |
| 29 | 32 | 25 | 7 | 1.32 | 9 | 600 | 0.29 | 200 | 0.24 | 2.80 | 0.39 | 0.18 | 17 |
| 30 | — | — | — | 2.26 | — | 300 | 0.51 | — | 0.38 | 2.49 | 0.22 | 0.17 | — |
| 31 | — | — | — | 1.01 | — | 306 | 0.43 | — | 0.27 | 1.96 | 0.20 | 0.17 | — |
| 32 | 41 | 30 | 10 | 1.49 | 11 | 310 | 0.45 | 73 | 0.25 | 1.66 | 0.18 | 0.17 | 17 |
| 33 | 35 | 28 | 7 | 0.12 | 7 | 230 | 0.07 | 6 | 0.04 | 0.91 | — | 0.47 | — |
| 34 | — | — | — | 0.11 | 48 | 200 | 0.08 | 20 | 0.44 | 0.20 | 0.10 | 0.46 | 35 |
| 35 | — | — | — | 0.05 | 8 | 80 | 0.16 | 6 | 0.26 | 0.56 | 0.05 | 0.22 | 18 |
| 36 | — | — | — | 0.03 | 4 | 30 | 0.03 | 6 | 0.60 | 0.35 | 0.01 | 0.14 | 21 |
| 37 | 71 | 48 | 23 | 0.15 | 13 | 150 | 0.14 | 10 | 0.08 | 0.87 | 0.02 | — | 16 |
| 38 | — | — | — | 0.60 | 4 | — | 0.37 | 27 | 0.43 | 2.34 | — | — | — |
| 39 | 43 | 37 | 6 | 0.57 | 4 | — | 0.59 | 24 | 0.37 | 1.74 | — | — | — |
| 40 | — | — | — | 0.43 | 28 | 360 | 0.67 | 42 | 0.90 | 1.53 | 0.15 | 0.44 | — |
| 41 | — | — | — | 1.10 | — | 310 | 0.29 | 154 | 0.28 | 1.26 | 0.31 | — | — |
| 42 | — | — | — | 1.15 | — | 330 | 0.25 | 184 | 0.25 | 1.03 | 0.30 | — | — |
| 43 | — | — | — | 1.30 | 1 | 10 | 0.13 | 2 | 1.09 | 1.66 | 0.50 | 0.34 | 68 |
| 44 | — | — | — | 0.21 | 22 | 100 | 0.30 | 6 | 0.03 | 6.20 | 1.52 | 0.61 | 18 |
| 45 | — | — | — | 0.87 | 73 | 240 | 0.43 | 52 | 0.20 | 3.68 | 0.19 | 0.46 | 33 |
| 46 | — | — | — | 1.05 | 80 | 250 | 0.47 | 57 | 0.15 | 3.80 | 0.22 | 0.46 | 30 |
| 47 | 17 | 14 | 3 | 0.07 | 7 | 80 | 0.19 | 43 | 0.37 | 0.44 | 0.18 | 0.38 | 33 |
| 48 | — | — | — | 0.11 | 6 | 90 | 0.19 | 42 | 0.34 | 0.44 | 0.16 | 0.23 | — |
| 49 | 36 | 30 | 6 | 0.30 | 4 | 400 | 0.75 | 120 | 0.26 | 1.23 | 0.17 | 0.30 | — |
| 50 | 47 | 34 | 13 | 0.25 | 10 | 200 | 0.19 | 37 | 0.07 | 2.37 | 0.40 | 0.23 | — |
| 51 | 31 | 28 | 3 | 0.57 | 7 | 170 | 0.19 | 40 | 0.54 | 3.27 | 0.04 | 0.21 | 17 |
| 52 | — | — | — | 0.35 | 14 | 110 | 0.20 | 40 | 0.31 | 3.01 | — | 0.26 | 18 |
| 53 | — | — | — | 0.45 | — | — | 0.14 | — | 0.35 | — | — | — | — |

## APPENDIX 12-1, *continued*

| Line no. | Feed | International feed number | Dry matter, % | DE, Mcal/kg | TDN, % | Crude protein, % | Digestible protein, % | Lysine, % | Crude fiber, % | Cell walls, % |
|---|---|---|---|---|---|---|---|---|---|---|
| 54 | hay, s-c | 1-09-459 | 88 | 1.98 | 45 | 9.6 | 5.7 | — | 27 | — |
| | PRAIRIE | | | | | | | | | |
| 55 | midwest, hay, s-c | 1-03-191 | 90 | 2.02 | 46 | 6.7 | 3.2 | — | 33 | — |
| | RYE | | | | | | | | | |
| | *Secale cereale* | | | | | | | | | |
| 56 | grain | 4-04-047 | 88 | 3.52 | 80 | 13.8 | 9.9 | 0.48 | 3 | — |
| | SORGHUM | | | | | | | | | |
| | *Sorghum vulgare* | | | | | | | | | |
| 57 | grain | 4-04-383 | 90 | 3.52 | 80 | 12.6 | 8.8 | 0.28 | 3 | — |
| | SOYBEAN | | | | | | | | | |
| | *Glycine max* | | | | | | | | | |
| 58 | hay, s-c | 1-04-558 | 89 | 2.11 | 48 | 15.9 | 11.0 | — | 34 | — |
| 59 | hulls | 1-04-560 | 92 | 2.64 | 60 | 12.0 | 7.7 | 1.61 | 40 | 67 |
| 60 | seeds | 5-04-610 | 91 | 4.05 | 92 | 43.2 | 31.7 | 2.93 | 6 | — |
| 61 | seeds, meal, solv extd | 5-04-604 | 90 | 3.60 | 82 | 50.9 | 35.7 | 3.28 | 7 | 14 |
| | SUNFLOWER | | | | | | | | | |
| | *Helianthus* spp | | | | | | | | | |
| 62 | seeds wo hulls, meal, solv extd | 5-04-739 | 92 | 3.12 | 71 | 50.3 | — | 1.85 | 12 | — |
| | TIMOTHY | | | | | | | | | |
| | *Phleum pratense* | | | | | | | | | |
| 63 | grazed, midbloom | 2-04-905 | 30 | 2.15 | 49 | 9.6 | 5.2 | — | 31 | — |
| 64 | hay, s-c, pre-head | 1-04-881 | 89 | 2.20 | 50 | 11.5 | 7.2 | — | 31 | 64 |
| 65 | hay, s-c, head | 1-04-883 | 88 | 1.98 | 45 | 9.0 | 4.8 | — | 32 | 70 |
| | TREFOIL, BIRDSFOOT | | | | | | | | | |
| | *Lotus corniculatus* | | | | | | | | | |
| 66 | hay, s-c | 1-05-044 | 91 | 2.20 | 50 | 16.0 | 12.5 | — | 30 | 45 |
| | WHEAT | | | | | | | | | |
| | *Triticum* spp | | | | | | | | | |
| 67 | bran | 4-05-190 | 89 | 2.94 | 67 | 17.0 | 14.4 | 0.68 | 11 | 45 |
| 68 | grain, hard red winter | 4-05-268 | 89 | 3.83 | 87 | 14.4 | 10.7 | 0.42 | 3 | 40 |
| 69 | grain, soft red winter | 4-05-294 | 89 | 3.83 | 87 | 13.0 | 9.2 | 0.57 | 3 | 30 |
| 70 | grain, soft white winter | 4-05-337 | 89 | 3.83 | 87 | 11.5 | 7.5 | 0.35 | 3 | 14 |
| 71 | hay, s-c | 1-05-172 | 89 | 1.89 | 43 | 8.7 | 4.9 | — | 29 | 68 |
| 72 | straw | 1-05-175 | 89 | 1.50 | 34 | 4.2 | 1.0 | — | 41 | 85 |
| | YEAST | | | | | | | | | |
| | *Saccharomyces cerevisiae* | | | | | | | | | |
| 73 | brewer's, dehy | 7-05-527 | 93 | 3.30 | 75 | 48.3 | 32.8 | 3.33 | 3 | — |

SOURCE: Adapted from National Research Council, *Nutrient Requirements for Horses*, 1978.

| Line no. | ADF, % | Cellu-lose, % | Lignin, % | Cal-cium, % | Cop-per, mg/kg | Iron, mg/kg | Mag-nesium, % | Manga-nese, mg/kg | Phos-phorus, % | Potas-sium, % | So-dium, % | Sul-fur, % | Zinc, mg/kg |
|---|---|---|---|---|---|---|---|---|---|---|---|---|---|
| 54 | — | — | — | 0.37 | — | — | 0.13 | — | 0.23 | — | — | — | — |
| 55 | — | — | — | 0.41 | 23 | 100 | 0.28 | 48 | 0.15 | 1.01 | 0.04 | — | — |
| 56 | — | — | — | 0.07 | 8 | 70 | 0.14 | 62 | 0.36 | 0.52 | 0.03 | 0.17 | 36 |
| 57 | — | — | — | 0.03 | 11 | 50 | 0.20 | 17 | 0.33 | 0.39 | 0.03 | 0.16 | 16 |
| 58 | — | — | — | 1.22 | 9 | 290 | 0.79 | 101 | 0.28 | 1.02 | 0.09 | 0.24 | 24 |
| 59 | 46 | 44 | 2 | 0.45 | 18 | 320 | — | 14 | 0.15 | 1.03 | 0.05 | — | 24 |
| 60 | — | — | — | 0.28 | 17 | 90 | 0.31 | 32 | 0.66 | 1.77 | 0.13 | 0.24 | 18 |
| 61 | 10 | 8 | 2 | 0.31 | 30 | 130 | 0.30 | 32 | 0.70 | 2.19 | 0.31 | 0.48 | 48 |
| 62 | — | — | — | 0.41 | 4 | 40 | 0.81 | 25 | 1.10 | 1.10 | 0.44 | — | — |
| 63 | — | — | — | 0.28 | 11 | 200 | 0.15 | 190 | 0.25 | 2.40 | 0.19 | 0.13 | — |
| 64 | 37 | 33 | 4 | 0.50 | 6 | 200 | 0.15 | — | 0.25 | 1.92 | 0.18 | 0.13 | — |
| 65 | 45 | 34 | 11 | 0.41 | 5 | 140 | 0.16 | 46 | 0.19 | 1.60 | 0.18 | 0.13 | — |
| 66 | 34 | 25 | 9 | 1.75 | 9 | 230 | 0.51 | 15 | 0.22 | 1.80 | 0.18 | — | 77 |
| 67 | 12 | 8 | 4 | 0.12 | 14 | 190 | 0.59 | 130 | 1.43 | 1.60 | 0.04 | 0.25 | 120 |
| 68 | — | — | — | 0.05 | 5 | 40 | 0.17 | 44 | 0.48 | 0.45 | 0.03 | 0.18 | 43 |
| 69 | — | — | — | 0.05 | 7 | 30 | 0.11 | 36 | 0.46 | 0.46 | 0.02 | 0.12 | 48 |
| 70 | 4 | — | — | 0.05 | 8 | 40 | 0.11 | 40 | 0.45 | 0.41 | 0.02 | 0.13 | 30 |
| 71 | 41 | — | — | 0.15 | — | 200 | 0.12 | 40 | 0.19 | 1.00 | 0.28 | 0.24 | — |
| 72 | 54 | 39 | 15 | 0.21 | 3 | 200 | 0.12 | 40 | 0.08 | 1.10 | 0.14 | 0.19 | — |
| 73 | — | — | — | 0.5 | 36 | 100 | 0.25 | 6 | 1.52 | 1.86 | 0.08 | 0.41 | 42 |

# SPECIAL FEEDING CONSIDERATIONS

ome nutritional situations are so specialized that they justify individual attention. Among them are racing, distance riding, blooming show horses, and the care of convalescent, old, starved, or hard-to-condition horses.

## FEEDING RACEHORSES

There is little room for nutritional error in racehorse feeding. Racehorses start training in prepuberty, exert extreme physical and mental effort as adolescents, and may break down before they reach maturity. Not all lamenesses and track accidents can be avoided, but proper mineral feeding of young racehorses could substantially reduce them. Cornell researchers feel that unbalanced nutrition may be at the root of many racing problems.[1]

---

[1]"Horse Nutrition Is Catching Up," *Animal Nutrition and Health*, November–December 1978, p. 7.

FIGURE 13-1   A starved 2-month-old colt weighing 100 pounds. This colt could barely stand without assistance, and could move and balance himself only by wedging his hocks together. His head was unusually large. He had a severe potbelly, and was down at the pasterns. [*Photograph by Nancy Rucker.*]

John E. Longden, famous jockey and trainer, deplores the way many racehorses are fed when compared to college athletes, who are required to eat at a special training table food that was prepared under expert nutritional supervision. He expresses concern about the feeding to racehorses of "concoctions of questionable value, if not downright harm."[2]

A survey of race rations and management practices brings to light many good feeding and management programs and some that are not so good. There is a keen awareness of the need for good-quality grain and hay among racehorse feeders; some establishments routinely chemically analyze their grain rations and hays. Oats is the base grain, with many farms using small amounts of corn and barley. Alfalfa hay is the choice of the legumes, and it may be the only hay that is fed in many areas where it is grown.

Many racehorses are fed high levels of bran. When bran is fed with alfalfa, a mineral imbalance is unlikely; however, a high P to low Ca ratio is a dangerous and likely consequence of bran feeding unless supplemental calcium is added when no alfalfa is fed.

[2]John E. Longden, "Training Horses," *Stud Managers Handbook*, vol. 13, Agriservices Foundation, Clovis, Calif., January 1977, p. 191.

Some feeders of racehorses are notoriously independent, with strong opinions and biases about feeding. Many are unimpressed with sound basic nutritional feeds offered by reputable feed companies and knowledgeable nutritionists, but are quick to try anything claiming to give a horse an advantage in a race. In this way, well over $100 per horse per year can be spent for concoctions to feed, inject, or rub on the horse with no regard to cost, nutritional content, or consequences.

## Mineral Levels and Balances for Racehorses

Since bones are where most permanent mechanical failures occur, they should be given every opportunity to develop fully. NRC requirements may not be sufficient for large, fast-growing yearlings or for 2-year-olds in heavy training. Undoubtedly 0.75 percent Ca and 0.55 percent P in a grain ration would provide a safe margin in cases of high grain intake. The ideal ratio would be 1.5:1 or 2:1. Racehorse feed should be chemically analyzed to verify nutrient content. Finally, the veterinarian should x-ray the cannon bones for epiphyseal closure and advise on how much training and racing is safe for each horse.

There is great risk of mixing home grain rations without knowledgeable mineral supplementation. Most grain mixtures yield approximately 1¼ to 2 pounds of Ca and 6 or 7 pounds of P per ton. If the young horse in racing training needs 0.75 percent Ca and 0.55 percent P, there must be 15 pounds of Ca and 12 pounds of P in a ton of mixed grain. Although hay feeding with grain improves mineral deficiencies, there is no way that a high percentage of young racehorses could remain sound on a mineral diet unbalanced to this extent. Considering the investment one has in a racehorse, it is indeed risky to take chances with the mineral feeding program.

## Protein for Racehorses

Protein builds muscles that propel growing horses around the track in racing. Sixteen percent protein diets for weanlings and 14 percent for yearlings provide suitable margins of safety. These amounts should not be doubled nor should excess protein be consistently fed—it can reduce growth rate and interfere with Ca absorption. Nursing foals should have a good-quality protein creep feed, i.e., one containing essential amino acids, especially lysine. Their diets should contain 0.7 percent lysine because their digestive tracts are not yet developed sufficiently to utilize poor-quality protein. Mares' milk declines in quality as well as quantity a few weeks after foaling. Creep rations containing 2 to 5 percent dried skim milk supply good-quality protein. Many commercial feed companies prepare them. One company has devised a milk and soy supplement suitable for racehorses throughout their lives.

## Energy for Racehorses

Compared to assuring the energy requirements of the racehorse, mineral and protein feeding is easy. Racehorses must consume 25,000 to 30,000 kilocalories (kcal) per day. Many high-strung young horses cannot be kept in constant training and racing because they will not eat enough high nutrient density feed to maintain strength and condition. There is much more art than science in feeding energy, and many racehorse feeders are artful in keeping their charges on feed. They must administer to both the physical and psychological needs of their animals.

PHYSICAL RACE RATION QUALITIES

1 Use feed with a high nutrient density: if most of the feed is oats, the oats should be at least 38 pounds test weight or heavier. Corn is a good conditioner if the horse will eat it. Twelve to 16 pounds of grain may be required to sustain condition on horses in training.
2 Feed only the best quality hay. Ship hay with the horse when racing out of state. If hay is purchased at the track, check every block for quality and mold. Alfalfa hay is the best choice to ensure both palatability and good nutrients, and all that the horse can eat should be offered. In addition, timothy or other light hays should be available at all times for the psychological benefit they provide. Hay bellies are virtually unknown in young racehorses in training.
3 Feed grain often (three to four times daily) and at the same time on each occasion.
4 Keep feed troughs immaculately clean with daily washing. Allow the horse ½ to 1 hour to eat grain, then remove it.
5 Use the best processing methods available to prepare grains.
6 Feed each horse as an individual. Discover the grain it prefers, and adjust mineral requirements to it.
7 Avoid sudden changes in grain or hay. Take a week or more to make changes.
8 Feed a balanced ration—it is more readily eaten than an unbalanced one.
9 Clean water buckets once a day and fill them at each feed or at least three times a day. The trainer must know how much water each horse is consuming. High nutrient density diets require immense amounts of water for proper digestion.

PSYCHOLOGY OF KEEPING RACEHORSES ON FEED

1 Use patience, kindness, and care. Many are extremely high strung and respond only to kind, patient treatment.
2 Have compatible grooms, exercise persons, and handlers. Some horses

and some people never like each other, and neither is at fault.

3   Keep horses happy and as comfortable as possible in transit, training, and when stabled.
4   A companion animal may be helpful. Dogs, goats, burros, chickens, cats, and others have been used.
5   Grooming by a person that the horse likes is relaxing for it.
6   No exercise on days off with reduced grain keeps a horse's appetite active.
7   Grazing grass a few minutes daily may be helpful. Sunshine stimulates vitamin D synthesis.
8   Feed only feeds with known or describable components. Two or three different unknowns may produce toxicity, upset mineral balance, or depress appetite.

## Vitamins for Racehorses

FAT-SOLUBLE VITAMINS (A, D, AND E)   Since racehorses consume high levels of grain, commercial mixtures with 5000 IU of A, 1000 IU of D, and 10 IU of E should suffice. If plain oats or other grains are fed with nonlegume hay, consider feeding a tablespoonful of A, D, and E daily. Good legume hay is a good source of vitamins.

WATER-SOLUBLE VITAMINS   B vitamins are essential in energy metabolism, but are manufactured in the horse's intestines. Whether or not they should be added to race rations is debatable. If they are added, a known amount should be fed—enough to do some good. Brewer's yeast is a good source of riboflavin and thiamine (Table 13-1). Five pounds are often included in a ton of race rations.

Table 13-1 also shows the carotene (provitamin A), riboflavin, thiamine, and vitamin E content of some common horse feeds. In general, this table emphasizes the low levels of vitamins present in grains and nonlegume hays (except E) compared with that in legumes.

The racehorse fed small amounts of nonlegume hay, especially of average quality, and any kind of unsupplemented grain is in great danger of being deficient in Ca and in vitamins A, D, and E and possibly in some of the B vitamins. Racehorses exhibiting epistaxis (bleeding from the nose after exertion) or hemoptysis (bleeding from the lungs) are often treated with vitamin K and C supplements, to little proven avail. Also, the notion held by some racehorse handlers that their horses need something "unknown" rather than the known basic nutrients is indeed dangerous. Stressed horses in athletic activities are in great need of nutritionally sound feeding programs.

For additional problems involving salt intake and electrolyte imbalance in the racehorse, see *Electrolytes and Dehydration* below.

TABLE 13-1   VITAMIN CONTENT OF SOME COMMON HORSE FEEDS

| Feed | Carotene (Provitamin A), mg/kg | Riboflavin, mg/kg | Thiamin, mg/kg | Vitamin E, mg/kg |
|---|---|---|---|---|
| Alfalfa hay, midbloom | 26.1 | 10.6 | 3.0 | 90.0 |
| Alfalfa meal, 17% protein | 131.1 | 14.4 | 3.7 | 134.8 |
| Barley, grain | 1.0 | 1.8 | 5.0 | 18.0 |
| Brewer's grains | . . . | 1.4 | 0.6 | 28.1 |
| Clover hay, ladino | 20.0 | 15.0 | 4.2 | 70.0 |
| Clover hay, red, sun-cured | 19.8 | 17.8 | 2.2 | 60.0 |
| Corn, grain | 2.5 | 1.5 | 2.3 | 25.7 |
| Linseed meal | . . . | 3.1 | 8.6 | 18.0 |
| Oats, grain | 0.1 | 1.7 | 7.2 | 18.5 |
| Oat hay, sun-cured | 15.0 | 5.3 | 3.3 | 12.5 |
| Rye, grain | 1.0 | 1.8 | 3.4 | 17.2 |
| Skimmed milk, dehydrated | . . . | 20.4 | 4.0 | 10.0 |
| Soybean meal | 0.2 | 3.3 | 6.2 | 2.3 |
| Timothy hay, sun-cured | 9.0 | 12.4 | 1.7 | 63.1 |
| Wheat bran | 2.9 | 5.4 | 7.3 | 13.4 |
| Brewer's yeast | . . . | 39.2 | 100.0 | 2.4 |

SOURCE:  Adapted from National Research Council, *Nutrition Requirements of Horses*, National Academy of Sciences, Washington, D.C., 1978.

## FEEDING DISTANCE HORSES

Distance horses compete in endurance and competitive rides.

Endurance ride courses cover a minimum of 50 miles and most approximate 100 miles in a 24-hour period, usually over rough terrain. Horses are judged on the basis of both speed and condition. Winners must finish in the required time, remain sound, and be in good condition as judged by veterinarians at checkpoints along the way and at the finish. There are awards for horses who finish first and also for those who finish in the best physical condition. The best-condition award is as popular as the award to the first horse to finish.

Competitive rides may be 1 to 3 days in length, covering distances of 25 to 40 miles daily. Horses are judged on soundness and condition, and some are judged for manners and way-of-going. The importance of a good feeding and conditioning program is apparent for these superb athletes.

Since distance riding is a relatively new horse activity, it has attracted many new horse enthusiasts, both with and without much horse experience. The success such amateurs have had in selecting, preparing, and riding their horses 100 miles over rough terrain in a single day or in a 3-day competitive ride has left the "traditional" horse fraternity dumbfounded.

How do they feed these horses? Colorado researchers[3] surveyed a number of distance riders to answer this question. They found a variety of satisfactory methods and feeds used with winning horses. Thirty-eight percent were fed alfalfa hay and 21 percent were fed grass hay (nonlegume) with others feeding mixed hay. Only 23 percent of those horses fed "special supplements" were top finishers. Five-time winner of the Tevis Cup, the Arabian Witezarif,[4] was fed alfalfa. The point is that good rations can be formulated with any basic feed if the horse will eat it in sufficient quantity to sustain condition over a long training period.

Although feeding race and distance horses is similar in that both must consume an enormous amount of energy, some feeding and management practices are dramatically different between them. This is because distance horses (senior division) are mature—5 years or older—and many compete successfully into their teens. Bones are therefore set, and the problems of growth are not seen.

## Feeding Suggestions for Distance Horses

Like racehorses, distance horses may require, depending on size, 12 to 16 pounds of grain daily in three to four feeds, in addition to high-quality free-choice hay. When idle, they should have their grain ration cut by one-half to two-thirds to reduce the risk of azoturia. Mineral levels are far less critical with these adult horses than with young racehorses, and will be adequate if half of the hay is legume. Standard A and D vitamin levels discussed in Chapters 11 and 12 will feed the distance horse adequately.

Recent research by the Colorado group casts doubt on high-protein diets, but encourages 9 percent added fat in the ration. This theory is biologically sound and should be further studied. However, continued feeding of fat has increased cholesterol serum levels in horses, which may not be desirable. The distance rider would do well to seek a 10 to 12 percent protein level and no higher, because many experienced riders and veterinarians feel that higher levels increase sweating and induce dehydration, fatigue, and muscle tie-up. A good alfalfa and high-quality oat diet may average 15 percent or more in protein. There are few good, high nutrient density feeds under 10 percent protein that are readily eaten by horses.

Salt is absolutely essential for distance horses. It should be fed free-choice in loose form at a convenient location at all times.

[3]Larry M. Slade and Peter L. Hambleton, "Feeding the Horse for Endurance," *Stud Managers Handbook*, vol. 12, Agriservices Foundation, Clovis, Calif., January 1976, p. 140.
[4]Virginia Weisel Johnson and Thula Johnson, *Distance Riding: Start to Finish*, Houghton Mifflin, Boston, 1976, p. 61.

Many horses in California are fed oat hay and oats for grain. Oat hay must be supplemented with vitamins A, D, and E and with trace minerals.

## Electrolytes and Dehydration

Electrolytes are the mineral salts dissolved in the body fluids. They are Na, K, Ca, Mg, Cl, $PO_4$, and others that are trace elements. Electrolytes are essential for cell integrity, body functions, and life. They are supplied in good-quality hays and grains and are lost by horses through sweating under extended periods of work, such as distance riding. Few pleasure horses need supplemental electrolyte feeding, but distance horses should constantly be checked for dehydration when working hard in hot climates.

Pinch the skin on the horse's neck. If it stands up when released, the horse is becoming dehydrated. Pinch further back on the shoulder and sides —these areas should show less tendency to stand than the neck.

Veterinarians dispense electrolytes in powder or tablet form to be fed on grain or mixed with water. Use electrolytes only as needed and under veterinary supervision, but do not hesitate to use them when needed. They are natural food constituents required by some horses in greater quantity than a normal diet supplies.

## BLOOMING SHOW HORSES

A glossy hair coat and healthy look add dollars to sale horses and ribbons to a show string. Feeding alone will not achieve a glossy hair coat, but it will help. Nature increases the length of daylight and the temperature and saturates the horse with an abundance of nutrients in blooming its hair coat during the spring. Grooms can simulate nature and do much more.

## Feeding

Horses' hair coats cannot bloom if any essential nutrients are deficient. The feeder must be sure that all nutrients are present in adequate quantities. A 12 to 15 percent protein diet with double the requirements of vitamins A, D, and E and enough energy to produce gain helps to shed a horse. When preparing for an early spring show or sale, start 10 to 12 weeks in advance with horses that are thin enough to stand added weight gain.

Recent research shows a response in hair coat from most horses to the feeding of linoleic acid. This is a fatty acid that is marginal or low in standard horse diets. Its best source is corn oil, sold by most grocery stores. One or two tablespoonsful once or twice daily placed on the grain will suffice.

## Exercise

All horses need exercise, but it is especially beneficial to show horses. It helps their attitude, improves their digestive processes, and gives them the athletic look that cannot simply be "fed on" a horse. Many show horses in training get abundant exercise, but halter and "in-hand" horses may require planned exercise programs because of intensive feeding practices.

## FEEDING CONVALESCENT, OLD, STARVED, AND HARD-TO-CONDITION HORSES

Certain management practices apply to all horses in this group.

1 Reduce competition. House them alone if necessary.
2 Keep them comfortable and protected from the elements. Keep them warm in winter, out of drafts, and indoors during poor weather.
3 Except for the convalescent horse, worm them promptly, frequently, and adequately. Don't wait to begin until they are better. If a horse is emaciated, internal parasites are probably part of the problem.
4 Know the condition of the teeth. Have a veterinarian check and float them as needed.
5 Feed only top-quality feeds in small amounts and often.

### Feeding Convalescent Horses

Convalescent horses differ in their needs, depending on the conditions from which they are recovering. However, almost all require continued medication upon return from the clinic or from treatment by the veterinarian, and many require special restraint or housing. Watch for their steady recovery. Monitor temperature, count coughs, if any, and watch for reactions to medication. Feed excellent feed in "recovery quantities" and keep the stall comfortably bedded and free of flies.

### Feeding Old Horses

It is a sad day when old age overtakes one's favorite horse and it begins to decline in condition. The five general management practices outlined above are essential to the battle for its survival. Since all of its body functions are less efficient, its feed should be prepared in a form that is easily swallowed and digested. Consider feeding at weanling levels excellent-quality alfalfa hay with processed grain that is well fortified with minerals and vitamins. Graze an old horse on lush pasture, if possible, but not in competition with

FIGURE 13-2   (*Top*) The starved 2-month-old colt shown in Figure 13-1. (*Bottom*) The same colt 4 months later, at about 300 pounds. After drastic deworming, a bout with pneumonia, and good nutrition management, this colt began to respond well and put on weight. [*Photographs by Nancy Rucker.*]

bully horses. Bran mashes may be more useful to this type of horse than any other. Remember bran's high P content, and offset it with added limestone or legume hay.

When the gallant old warrior is beyond help, it should be spared the indignity of long suffering by a courageous owner who, with the concurrence of the veterinarian, decides to end the struggle peacefully.

## Feeding Starved Horses

Badly starved horses should be examined by a veterinarian before being moved, lest they fall in transit and be unable to rise. Some humane societies have conveyances with suspensions for transporting such horses. The veterinarian will undertake a specific deworming program of rather unusual intensity and, if necessary, antibiotic treatment. She or he may also administer B complex injections.

The starved horse is especially prone to pneumonia. Its body temperature is generally subnormal, and it will probably spend much time lying down. For this reason it must be kept out of drafts and very warm, no matter what the weather (within reason). The chill must be taken off its water. Keeping the horse warm with blankets and/or a heat lamp is the first step to recovery from starvation.

Many emaciated horses will refuse to eat the best of feeds. Different kinds of high-quality feed must be offered in small amounts until it is possible to slowly switch to a balanced diet as appetite improves. Extra feed must be consumed to restore nutrient reserves. Total restoration to good health may require 4 to 6 months or even longer, if recuperation is interrupted by pneumonia or other infection (Figures 13-1 and 13-2).

## BIBLIOGRAPHY

Equine Research Publications: *Feeding to Win*, Grapevine, Tex., 1973.
Knickerbocker, Jan, with Laurie Jackson: "Case Report: The Long Road Back," *Equus*, no. 17, March 1979, pp. 18-23.
Lieberman, Bobbie: "The Thin Horse Blues," *Equus*, no. 7, May 1978, pp. 44-51, 66.

# BASIC HEALTH CARE OF THE HORSE

o be useful, the horse must be healthy. To be healthy, the horse must rely on his human caretaker. Good food and shelter, regular exercise, foot care, worming, and vaccination, and protection from accidents and from exposure to contagious diseases are the interdependent elements of a comprehensive equine health program.

The good horseman will know instantly when his horse is off and will know when he can let the problem take care of itself, when he can treat the animal by himself, and when he must call a veterinarian (see Chapter 7).

## THE VITAL FUNCTIONS

### Temperature

Table 14-1 gives the rectally determined body temperature ranges of the horse in health and in sickness. Because of the wide range of normal temperature, the horseman should take pains to ascertain what is normal for

464    CHAPTER FOURTEEN

FIGURE 14-1   To be useful, horses must remain healthy. They must depend upon
their owners for immunization, parasite control, food, shelter, and exercise. Neglect
of any phase of horse management may result in loss of service when the horse is
needed most. [*Photograph by the author.*]

each horse in his care. Especially in the case of young horses in intensive
training, temperature is best taken daily before schooling begins, to avoid
subsequently straining a weakening system.

TAKING THE TEMPERATURE   All horse owners should own an animal thermometer. This is a large thermometer with a loop in one end through which
a leather thong or string is threaded, which in turn is attached to a clip.

Shake the mercury down below 98°F, lubricate the bulb in petroleum
jelly, and insert it gently full-length into the horse's rectum (Figure 14-2).
Attach the clip to some hair on the rump so that the horse does not expel the
thermometer, losing it in the bedding. The first few times the horse's temperature is taken, an assistant may be needed. Stand to the side of the hind

TABLE 14-1   BODY TEMPERATURE OF
THE HORSE (Rectal)

| Condition | Temperature range, °F |
|---|---|
| Normal | 99.5–101.5 |
| Mild fever | 101.5–102.5 |
| Moderate fever | 102.5–104.0 |
| High fever | 104.0–106.5 |
| Extreme fever | Over 106.5 |

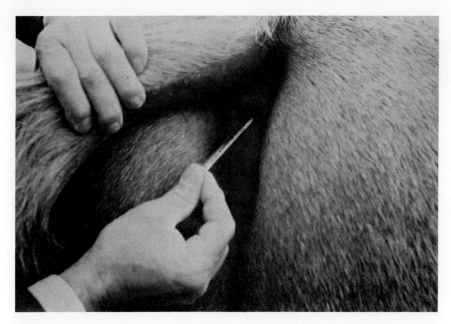

FIGURE 14-2    Every horse owner should own and use an animal thermometer. Stand at the side of your horse's hip. Insert the thermometer full length. Keep it in position 2 to 3 minutes before reading. Readings over 102°F in a resting horse may indicate the beginning of a sickness that will improve with rest or treatment and worsen with work. [*Photograph by Duane Dailey.*]

leg (preferably the left) facing the rear while the assistant holds up the front leg on the same side. Insert the thermometer slowly until the horse ceases to resist and relaxes. After two or three times most horses will allow their temperatures to be taken without resistance.

After at least 2 minutes, remove the thermometer and check the reading as indicated by the height of the mercury bar. If it is above 101 degrees, there may be something wrong. If it is 102 degrees or more, the horse probably should not be ridden; its temperature should be carefully monitored. If it rises to the vicinity of 103 degrees, a veterinarian should be called.

The veterinarian will need to know the normal temperature pattern of the horse and any other changes in behavior, feeding, or management to help him decide whether the trip is necessary and perhaps what to bring along if it is. Temperature may indicate infectious disease, toxic problems, or a respiratory condition. If temperature remains at 105 degrees or above for 2 or 3 days, dire consequences may result. Some horses will seriously dehydrate even sooner at an even lower temperature.

TABLE 14-2 RESTING PULSE
RATES OF THE HORSE

| Ages | Pulse/min |
|---|---|
| Foals to 2 weeks | 100 |
| Foals, 4 weeks | 70 |
| Colts and fillies, | |
| 6 months–1 year | 45–60 |
| 2-year-olds | 40–50 |
| Adults | 30–40 |

## Pulse

As the heart contracts to push blood through the arteries, wave upon wave of rhythmic throbbing can be felt—*pulse*. Table 14-2 gives normal pulse rates of the horse at various ages. Pulse is the most accessible indicator of heart activity. Pulse rate is easily felt in the arteries running along the inside of the jaw (maxillary), by the horse's elbow, and at the back of the fetlock.

Each horse's pulse should be taken under normal conditions several times to establish the normal rate. This should be recorded for each horse, along with the normal temperature range, on a permanent stable card available for comparison with counts taken under hard work or when checked for illness. Pulse rate will vary with excitement, pain, nervousness, increased body temperature, shock, and infectious disease.

TAKING THE PULSE   To take the maxillary pulse (if you are right-handed), stand on the left side of the horse and place the right hand just above the chin piece of the halter with the fingers wrapped around and under the jawbone. The artery will feel like a pulsing cord about ⅛ inch in size. Pulse counts are timed by the second hand on a standard wristwatch. If the horse has both elevated temperature and pulse and has not been working recently, it should remain under surveillance for a few hours, and both checks should be repeated.

Pulse rate is one of the best indications of condition or fitness. A fit working horse may have a very high pulse rate under strenuous exercise, but it will return to normal within 15 minutes to an hour. Well-conditioned distance and cross-country horses may arrive at a checkpoint with 125 pulses per minute and recover to below 70 in 10 to 15 minutes.

## Respiration

Respiration, or rate of breathing, is easily checked by watching the horse's flank rise and fall. Normal respiration depends to some extent on temperature, but most horses will breathe 9 to 12 times per minute at rest in cool weather. Respirations are tripled when the horse is walking; and if extensively exercised in high temperatures, respiration may rise to 120 per minute. However, the rate should decline to 40 or 50 within 10 or 15 minutes in well-conditioned horses.

The ratio of heart beat to respiration in horses is usually about 4:1; that is, the heart beats four times faster than the horse breathes. Under conditions of extreme stress, respiration rate may exceed the heart rate; such a situation is called an "inversion." This signals a lack of oxygen and the horse should be stopped and rested until the condition corrects itself.

Respiration will increase as a result of pain, fever, toxicity, or illnesses, in addition to work.

Coughing can signal a number of conditions; a few of which are normal, but most of which are not. Some respiratory diseases that raise temperature are accompanied by a cough. On the other hand, horses with heaves may have normal temperatures but a cough in direct proportion to exposure to moldy feed, dusty grain, dusty bedding, or other objects in the environment to which they are allergic. While an occasional cough may be quite normal, as with a human, persistent coughing never is.

## WORKING WITH THE VETERINARIAN

Selecting a veterinarian and maintaining a positive relationship with him or her are very important. The crucial criteria are competence with horses, availability, and willingness to treat the horse in emergencies. In return, he or she should be promptly paid in full after each call and should be cultivated as a friend and consultant in the horse health program. Most veterinarians are happy to advise on preventive management rather than only be invoved in crises.

The veterinarian is most effectively used only for important cases, and should not be bothered with trivia. Sometimes the difference is hard to distinguish. If a horse has colic, is injured and bleeding, gets choked, or is having a difficult birth—obviously, these are real emergencies. And yet, many times the horse owner fails to ask for professional help in time to save the horse. Any condition that affects the eye, for example, needs prompt professional attention. If care is not received in time, the iris and lens may grow together and cause blindness. In general, then, use the same good judgment in determining the need for a veterinarian as you would in calling a personal physician.

## THE HORSE'S DEFENSE MECHANISMS

The horse has a number of defense mechanisms to ward off infections, fight infections that do invade the body, and help it to combat or to adjust to various physical, physiological, and psychological intrusions.

## Physical Defenses

The physical condition of the horse determines to a great extent how much disease resistance it has when exposed to stress or infective disease organisms. The horse's first line of defense is a good feeding program, as outlined in Chapters 11 through 13. When large numbers of horses are brought together from different areas for strenuous exercise or competition, such as trail riding, distance riding, and shows, those under the poorest nutritional programs are the first to get sick and be withdrawn from competition. Well-fed horses withstand inclement weather without shelter much better than thin horses because they can draw upon enough energy stored in fat tissues to keep them warm and healthy. They also have better hair coats that shed water more effectively (Figure 14-1).

Horses that are given a reasonable work load ward off diseases better than underused or overused horses. Exercise helps all the body systems to function maximally. The underused, obese horse is not nearly in as good condition to ward off stress as is the physically fit horse.

## Physiological Defenses

Although a foal is born without immunity, the foal that gets colostrum from its mother receives antibodies that ward off many diseases until its own immunological system is developed. The immunity imparted by colostrum is called "passive" immunity as compared to the "active" immunity developed by the individual in its own body. After about 2 weeks the foal begins to develop active immunity against some diseases; however, no horse is immune to all diseases.

The body, when stimulated by certain organisms or toxins, begins to produce antibodies and antitoxins that may overcome particular disease-producing organisms. The body has numbers (some 8,500 to 10,000 per cubic millimeter) of large white blood cells called *leukocytes* to fight invading organisms. The leukocytes fight the infection by phagocytosis, actually ingesting the invading microorganisms. The involvement of protein in disease resistance is substantial; for this reason animals on a low-protein diet may be less resistant to disease than those that are fed adequate amounts of protein.

IMMUNIZATION   Vaccines simulate as closely as possible the immunity developed following natural infection—without creating the disease itself.[1] An effective vaccine will stimulate the body to immunize itself, and this should protect the horse if exposed to the disease. While any immunization program should be based on the advice of the veterinarian, there are some

---

[1]Dr. C. J. Issel, "Your Horse Is at War," *Equus*, no. 3, January 1978, p. 32.

diseases so common and so devastating that all horses should be immunized against them each year.

## Psychological

Undoubtedly the horse has psychological mechanisms that help it cope with the environment and remain healthy. Happy, content, quiet horses seem to be more healthy than very nervous, high-strung, hyperactive types. This is probably because they eat more regularly and do not wear themselves out fretting; they are therefore in better physical condition to meet the rigors of their activities and environment. Quiet handling, companionship, and reasonable work will reduce sickness in all types of horses.

## INTERNAL PARASITES

More than 150 internal parasites are known to invade horses. Of these, large and small strongyles, ascarids, pinworms, and bots are the most numerous and devastating.

While terminal diseases are obviously dramatic, insidious internal parasites are actually the biggest killers of horses, directly and indirectly. Strongyle infestations kill many horses each year directly and cause many more to die from terminal colic. Ascarids destroy many young horses before they have built up immunity to them. It therefore behooves the horse owner never to relax in the fight agains these parasites; the horse invariably becomes infected with them soon after birth and harbors some parasites throughout life. A general knowledge and understanding of the nature of these parasites and their development is essential for the necessary prevention and control measures to be effectively applied.

The injury inflicted on the horse by worms is related to (1) the kind of parasite involved (2) the number involved and (3) the amount of time that the parasites are harbored.[2] *Strongyles* are the most injurious parasites; ascarids, bots, and pinworms are generally less harmful. A few parasites may be tolerated by the horse without apparent ill effect, but larger numbers are apt to be harmful. Acquiring a large number within a few days may overwhelm and kill a horse; the invasion of a constant number over a period of weeks or months is generally much less harmful.

The horses most seriously affected by internal parasites are sucklings, weanlings, and yearlings. Generally speaking, ascarid and threadworm infections are problems restricted to young horses. This is because resistance or immunity is built up by the time a horse is 2 or 3 years old, in most cases.

[2]J. H. Drudge, Bonnard L. Moseley, and Melvin Bradley, "Controlling Internal Parasites of Horses," *University of Missouri Science and Technology Guide 2854*, 1978.

TABLE 14-3 LOCATION, AGES AFFECTED, AND SYMPTOMS
OF INTERNAL PARASITES OF THE HORSE

| Parasite | Location | Ages most affected | Injury and symptoms |
|---|---|---|---|
| Strongyles | Larvae—arteries, liver, and gut wall<br>Adults—large intestine | All ages, but young horses are especially susceptible | Retarded growth; loss of weight, poor appetite; rough hair coats; general weakness; anemia; constipation; diarrhea; recurrent colic; death |
| Ascarids | Larvae—liver and lungs<br>Adults—small intestine | Horses younger than 2 years of age | Retarded growth; pot belly; rough hair coat; digestive upsets (colic); pneumonia; death (caused by ruptured intestine) |
| Bots | Eggs—hair<br>Larvae—tongue<br>Bots—stomach | All ages | Excitement (caused by flies); digestive upsets; retarded growth; poor condition; death (caused by stomach rupture) |
| Pinworms | Larvae—large intestine<br>Adults—large intestine and rectum | Larvae—all ages | Digestive disturbances; retarded growth; tail rubbing |

SOURCE: J. H. Drudge, B. L. Mosley, and M. Bradley, "Controlling Internal Parasites of Horses," *University of Missouri Science and Technology Guide 2854,* 1978.

On the other hand, strongyles and bots affect horses of all ages. Even so, the young are much more severely affected than older horses. Table 14-3 is a brief outline of the location, ages most affected, organs injured, and symptoms of internal parasite infestation. The symptoms should always be discussed with a veterinarian, as they can also indicate other problems.

## Life Cycles

Each species of parasite has a specific life cycle. Fortunately, from a control and treatment standpoint, the four major species are rather similar, having five stages, two of which occur inside the horse and three on the ground (Figure 14-3). Since all of the parasites pass out in the droppings, manure disposal goes a long way toward keeping parasites under control.

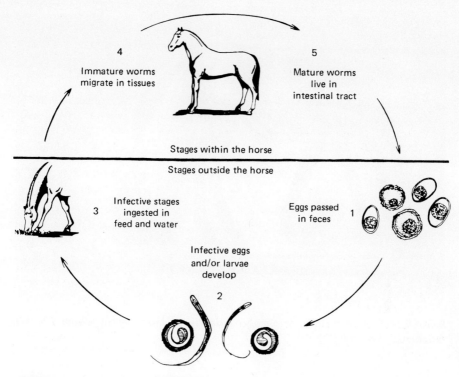

**FIGURE 14-3**  The general life cycle of the internal parasites; including strongyles, ascarids, and pinworms. [*From Drudge, Mosley, and Bradley.*]

In stage 1 of the general life cycle, the eggs are passed out in droppings on the pasture; in stage 2, the eggs hatch and become infective larvae; in stage 3 the larvae crawl up grass stems and are ingested by the horse, completing development outside the animal. Stage 4 is the migration of immature worms through the tissues. Stage 5 is the reproductive stage, in which mature worms occupy the intestinal tract and lay eggs.

## Strongyles

Strongylid (Figure 14-4) eggs (*stage 1*) leave the horse via the feces and contaminate the ground, paddock, or pasture. Under optimal conditions (warm, humid weather), strongyle eggs hatch and develop into infective larvae in 1 week (*stage 2*).

These larvae are encased in a thin sheath which protects them to some extent from the environment, and they may live for several months. They are quite active, and crawl up on grass or other pasture forage, to be consumed by the horse (*stage 3*) in grazing. Some larvae may gain access to water and thereby be ingested during drinking.

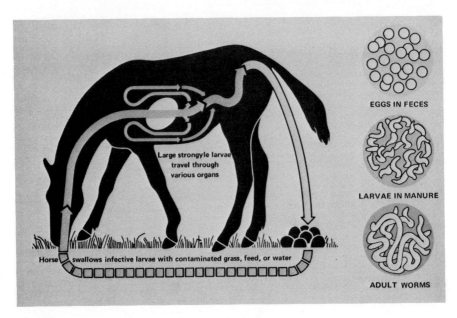

EGGS IN FECES

Large strongyle larvae travel through various organs

LARVAE IN MANURE

Horse swallows infective larvae with contaminated grass, feed, or water

ADULT WORMS

**FIGURE 14-4**   Life cycle of *Strongylus vulgaris*, or blood worm. [*From Loomis, Hughes, and Bramhall.*]

After strongyle larvae are swallowed, further development occurs, but there are marked differences between large and small strongyles during this stage (*stage 4*). Larvae of the large strongyle, *Strongylus vulgaris*, commonly called bloodworms, migrate extensively within the walls of the arteries that supply blood to the gastrointestinal tract, traveling against the flow of blood toward the heart. Within 2 weeks some larvae may have reached the aorta and heart. Damage to the arterial walls by this parasite causes inflammation of the blood vessels; severe, prolonged infestation causes thrombosis and sometimes aneurysm, particularly in the mesenteric artery. Blood clots or thromboses restrict or shut off the blood supply to the intestine and result in colic. The blockage of the arteries may be complete and sudden, in which case the animal dies. Aneurysm, the balloonlike weakening of arterial walls, is another cause of sudden, unpredictable parasite-induced death. Other types of large strongyles are less damaging because they spend less time in the arteries, concentrating mainly in the liver, pancreas, and intestines.

The large strongyle larvae require a prolonged period of time—between 6 and 11 months—to reach sexual maturation. The adult worms (*stage 5*) attach themselves to the inner surface of the large intestine and are quite active bloodsuckers. The females lay eggs which leave the body in the feces to complete the life cycle.

Small strongyle larvae (*stage 4*) penetrate the wall of the intestine and spend their entire lives there. Their development causes nodule formations in the walls. When the nodules rupture, ulcerations occur in the intestinal walls. This injury is relatively less serious than that caused by large strongyle larvae, but it is important in interfering with digestion nonetheless. The development of small strongyle larvae is also relatively rapid in comparison with the large strongyles, requiring about 6 to 12 weeks. Mature small strongyles (*stage 5*) also live in the large intestine, but for the most part they are not attached to the lining and do not suck blood. The mature females lay eggs which are also discharged in the feces like those of the large strongyles.

## Ascarids

The ascarid (Figure 14-5) cycle is also initiated by the passage of eggs in the feces (*stage 1*). Under favorable conditions, ascarid eggs develop to the infective larval stage (*stage 2*) in 2 weeks. Ascarid larvae remain in their thick, tough eggshells, which are quite resistant to environmental conditions, so pastures, paddocks, and stables may remain infested for years.

The horse becomes infected (*stage 3*) by grazing or by drinking water that was contaminated with infective ascarid eggs. Inside the stomach the

FIGURE 14-5    Life cycle of *Parascaris equorum*, or large roundworm. [*From Loomis, Hughes, and Bramhall.*]

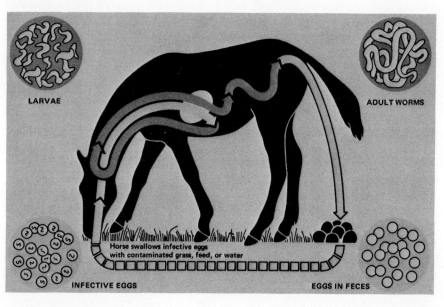

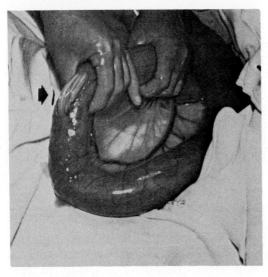

FIGURE 14-6    Intestinal obstruction in foal by large roundworms. [*From Loomis, Hughes, and Bramhall.*]

eggs hatch and the larvae penetrate the walls. They migrate (*stage 4*) through the bloodstream to the liver and the lungs. After a short period of development, during which those organs are damaged, the larvae are coughed up and swallowed. This brings them back to the small intestine, where they develop into mature worms (*stage 5*) and start egg production in about 10 weeks to complete the cycle.

Ascarids do not suck blood, but they are the largest of the parasites of the horse, attaining lengths of 10 to 12 inches in a very short time. Masses of ascarids may rupture the small intestine (Figure 14-6) and result in peritonitis, usually a fatal consequence.

## Pinworms

Pinworm (Figure 14-7) eggs (*stage 1*) are deposited under the tail by rupture of the gravid female, or are voided in the feces. The eggs are sticky and adhere to stable walls, fixtures, fences, bedding, etc. Development of the infective stage (*stage 2*) is quite rapid, requiring 3 to 5 days. The infective eggs are swallowed (*stage 3*) in contaminated feed or water or by licking and chewing on walls, fences, and so forth.

Larval development (*stage 4*) takes place in the large intestine, but without penetration or migration through tissues. Development of mature worms (*stage 5*) takes about 5 months. The principal damage from pinworm infection is the irritation to the anal region caused by the egg deposits from ruptured females. Thus the affected horse rubs its hindquarters on any

**FIGURE 14-7**  The life cycle of *Oxyuris equi*, or pinworm. [*From Loomis, Hughes, and Bramhall.*]

available object, and this results in a loss of hair from the base of the tail and frequently in secondary infections.

### Bots

The bot is not a worm, but rather a fly. However, its life cycle is similar in many respects to that of worm parasites. The adult bot fly attacks the horse and deposits eggs (*stage 1*) on the hairs, principally on the legs, chest, neck, throat, and around the mouth, causing much agitation to the horse. Development of infective larvae in the eggs (*stage 2*) takes one week, stimulated by warmth and moisture. These eggs hatch and the larvae gain access to the horse's mouth (*stage 3*) either by active migration or when the horse bites or chews at its legs. Inside the mouth, the larvae invade the tongue, gums, or cheeks (Figure 14-8).

After a developmental period of 3 weeks, the larvae migrate to the stomach and attach themselves to the lining. These larvae in the stomach are commonly referred to as bots. They remain attached to the stomach for 10 to 12 months, feeding on blood and tissue. In essence, this period spent in the stomach is a mechanism for overwintering. Ulcers form on the stomach lining at the site of attachment.

In the spring and summer, the bots detach themselves from the stomach wall and are passed to the outside in the feces. The discharged bots burrow

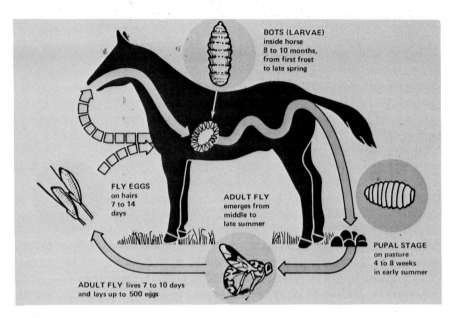

**FIGURE 14-8** Life cycle of *Gasterophilus intestinalis*, the common horse botfly. [*From Loomis, Hughes, and Bramhall.*]

into the ground and pupate. After about 5 or 6 weeks, the adult flies emerge from the pupae to complete the cycle. In temperate regions, one bot cycle is completed each year.

### Prevention and Control of Internal Parasites

Sanitation and management practices are invaluable in controlling internal parasite infections. Foals are born free of internal parasites, and the extent to which they develop parasitic infections is related to their degree of contact, either direct or indirect, with older animals carrying the infections. All the worm parasites discussed here utilize feces or manure to spread themselves, thereby contaminating feed and water supplies or the environment.

Transfer stages of these worm parasites do not actively seek the host to complete the infection process. Instead, they rely on chance to be picked up and swallowed. Thus only a very small percentage actually complete this hazardous step in the life cycle. To compensate for this, female worms produce large numbers of eggs to start the transfer process.

Sanitation and management practices aid in controlling or minimizing the spread of the infections. These practices assist natural destructive forces such as sunlight and drying during the transfer stages. Also, susceptible animals should have limited contact with contaminated pastures, paddocks, or stables. A checklist of sanitation and management practices that has been found effective in reducing numbers of parasites includes the following:

1  Proper manure disposal:
   a.  Stable manure—compost before spreading on pasture, or spread on cropland and other ungrazed areas.
   b.  Small corrals or paddocks—pick up all manure every few days and compost or dispose of as above.
2  Pasture management:
   a.  Mow and chain-harrow frequently.
   b.  Avoid overstocking for grazing purposes.
   c.  Rotate pastures at 1-month intervals as much as is practicable.
   d.  Graze young animals separately from older horses.
   e.  Graze cattle or sheep before returning horses to the same pasture.
3  Feed:
   a.  Provide mangers, racks, or bunks for hay and grain.
   b.  Do not feed on the ground.
4  Water:
   a.  Provide a clean water supply.
   b.  Avoid sources contaminated with feces.
5  Remove bot eggs: clip egg-bearing hairs, sponge affected areas with warm water, or scrape eggs off with bot scraper.

### Treatment of Internal Parasites

In addition to the foregoing practices, it is necessary to treat the animals with specific drugs, commonly referred to as *anthelmintics,* to gain effective control. These drugs remove the worms from the intestinal tract. Thus the treated animal is relieved of the immediate damage caused by parasites. But probably more important, the removal of the parasites breaks the cycle, which reduces contamination of the environment with transfer stages and thereby limits the spread of the infections and protects animals from reinfection.

### Understanding Anthelmintics

Horse wormers are quite different from each other. Some have broad-spectrum activity (effective against many worm species) and some have a very narrow spectrum. Diagnostic laboratories post numbers of horses killed each year by large strongyles that were routinely treated with a highly advertised anthelmintic—that had no efficacy against strongyles. Some drugs are very slightly toxic and others are quite highly toxic. Some are safe when used concurrently with other drugs, such as fly sprays or tranquilizers, but others are toxic under similar conditions. Finally, modes of action differ widely among classes of compounds; some only interrupt egg production of adult worms; some kill adults in the intestinal tract; and some kill adults and also have some larvicidal effect (killing immature worms in tissues). The combinations of these various drugs form an endless number of products sold by different companies under various trade names. Undoubtedly this list will grow, because of the need to rotate wormers to avoid developing resistant parasites.

Although having a veterinarian administer a liquid wormer by stomach tube remains a good treatment technique, recent production has shifted toward feed and paste wormers (Figure 14-9). Companies have developed paste wormers, deposited on the back of the horse's tongue by the "caulking gun" technique, and have developed a variety of powder, pellet, granule, and liquid carriers of anthelmintics to be top-dressed on the grain feed. Some products are consumed more readily than others, and variation in acceptability of the same compound with the same horses from one time period to another is not uncommon.

Broad-spectrum wormers, formerly available only for administration by stomach tube, are now available in paste and other carriers for top-dressing feeds. This allows the horse owner to use a broad-spectrum wormer in fall and spring, or as bot treatments are needed, and narrow-spectrum worm-

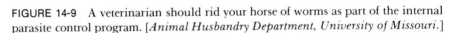

FIGURE 14-9    A veterinarian should rid your horse of worms as part of the internal parasite control program. [*Animal Husbandry Department, University of Missouri.*]

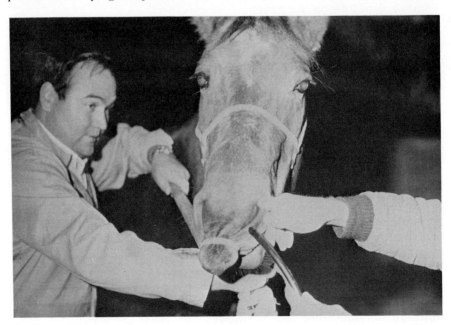

ers during the grazing season when strongyles and ascarids require frequent treatment.

CLASSES OF COMPOUNDS    For convenience, the chemical classes of anthelmintics can be grouped into: (1) benzimidazole carbamates; (2) organophosphates; (3) tetrahydropyrimidines–pyrantel salts; and (4) piperazine-carbon disulfide-phenothiazine complex.

*Benzimidazole carbamates.*    Included in this class are Cambendazole, Carbamate, Fenbendazole, Mebendazole, and Thiabendazole. These drugs are excellent wormers for several species of adult intestinal worms including large and small strongyles, ascarids, pinworms, and threadworms, but are ineffective against bots unless used with another drug. Because these compounds are safe, veterinarians may recommend dosage levels four to ten times higher than normal to produce strongyle and pinworm larvacidal benefits. Compounds of this class are usually readily eaten by horses and since they are not organophosphates, they can be safely used with other selected drugs, such as carbon disulfide, piperazine, or trichlorfon to broaden the spectrum to include bots.

After benzimidazole carbamates have been continuously used, some strongyle species build resistances to them and cross-resistances between them, requiring a switch to another class of drugs for effective control. There are some restrictions on use with pregnant mares for some of these products. Read directions before use.

*Organophosphates.*    Dichlorvos and trichlorfon are organophosphates. Dichlorvos is effective against strongyles, ascarids, pinworms, and bots. Trichlorfon is the drug of choice for bots. These two drugs appear in many commercial horse wormers, singly, together, and in combination with other appropriate drugs. However, they are dangerous when used indiscriminately. Read their directions carefully and treat according to body weight of the horse; spare pregnant mares 30 days from foaling and do not treat at too close intervals. Avoid use within 7 to 10 days of exposure to an organophosphate insecticide, muscle relaxant, phenothiazine-derived tranquilizer, or central nervous system depressant, or within 30 days of scheduled surgery (emergency surgery is excepted). Improper use of organophosphates results in cholinesterase inhibition, symptoms of which are depression, diarrhea, increased respiration, and lack of coordination. Veterinarians use Atrophine as an effective antidote.

Equigard® and Shell are sold in resin pellets. Palatability has been a problem with some horses, but not with others. Trichlorfon is quite palatable. Organophosphates are totally safe when used as directed. They are excellent wormers and should be used in many horse herds.

TABLE 14-4   SELECTED EQUINE ANTHELMINTICS, SPECTRUM AND EFFICACY
(not listed in order of preference)

| | | | | Efficacy* | | | | |
| | | | | Strongyles | | | Pin | |
| Trade name | Company | Chemical(s) | Method used | Large | Small | Ascarids | worms | Bots |
| --- | --- | --- | --- | --- | --- | --- | --- | --- |
| Equivet-14 | Farnam | Thiabendazole, trichlorfon | In feed | +++ | +++ | +++ | +++ | +++ |
| Tridex, pellets | Ft. Dodge | Dichlorvos | In feed (pellets) | +++ | +++ | +++ | +++ | +++ |
| Equizole B | Merk | Thiabendazole, trichlorfon | In feed | +++ | +++ | +++ | +++ | +++ |
| Equigard or Shell | Shell | Dichlorvos | In feed | +++ | +++ | +++ | +++ | +++ |
| Dyrex TF | Ft. Dodge | Trichlorfon, phenothiazine, piperazine | Tube | +++ | +++ | +++ | +++ | +++ |
| Parvex Plus | Upjohn | Piperazine, carbon disulfide, phenothiazine | Tube | +++ | +++ | +++ | ++ | +++ |
| Parvex | Upjohn | Carbon disulfide | Tube | ++ | ++ | +++ | ++ | ++ |
| Rintal | Haver-Lockhart | Febantel | Paste | +++ | +++ | +++ | +++ | |
| Cutter Paste Wormer | Cutter | Febantel | Paste | +++ | +++ | +++ | +++ | |
| Strongid T | Pfizer | Pyrantel Pamoate | In feed (liquid) | +++ | +++ | +++ | +++ | |

| Brand | Manufacturer | Drug | Administration | | | | | | |
|---|---|---|---|---|---|---|---|---|---|
| Banminth | Pfizer | Pyrantel Tartate | In feed (pellets) | +++ | +++ | +++ | +++ | +++ | |
| Equivet-TZ | Farnam | Thiabendazole | Paste | +++ | +++ | +++ | +++ | +++ | +++ |
| Equizole A | Ft. Dodge | Thiabendazole, piperazine | In feed | +++ | +++ | +++ | +++ | +++ | +++ |
| Camvet | Merk | Cambendazole | In feed, paste, tube | +++ | +++ | +++ | +++ | +++ | |
| Panacur | National Laboratories | Fenbendazole | Syringe, tube | +++ | +++ | +++ | ++ | +++ | |
| Telmin | Pitman-Moore | Mebendazole | Paste, in feed, tube | +++ | +++ | +++ | +++ | +++ | |
| Equizole | Merk | Thiabendazole | Paste | +++ | +++ | +++ | + | +++ | |
| Wonder Wormer | Farnam | Piperazine | In feed (pellets) | + | ++ | ++ | +++ | ++ | |
| Equiverm | Texas Pheno. Co. | Phenothiazine | In feed (bolus) | +++ | +++ | ... | ... | ... | |
| Negabot Paste | Cutter | Trichlorfon | Paste | ... | ... | ... | +++ | +++ | +++ |
| Anthon | Chemagro | Trichlorfon | In feed | ... | ... | + | + | ++ | +++ |
| Combot | Haver-Lockhart | Trichlorfon | Paste | ... | ... | ... | ... | +++ | +++ |
| Carbon Disulfide | Upjohn | Carbon disulfide | Tube | ... | ... | ... | ++ | ... | +++ |

*Efficacy: +++ = 90–100% adult worms
++ = 75–80% of adult worms
+ = 50–60% of adult worms

Notes: Some of these efficacies were obtained on small numbers of research horses. They may or may not be accurate. Read and follow direction on labels carefully. Indiscriminate use may kill your horse.

*Tetrahydropyrimidines–pyrantel salts.* These are pamoate and tartate salts, derivatives of imidazothiazole. They are effective against strongyles, ascarids, and pinworms, but not against bots unless used with another drug. Relatively new on the market, few parasites have developed strains immune to them. They are available in paste, feed, and tube form. Potency is lost rapidly in aqueous solutions if exposed to sunlight; therefore, unused mixtures should be destroyed and only fresh mixtures used for tubing.

These drugs act upon the digestive system of the worm as neurotransmitters, and, in the horse, cause intestinal spasm and prompt expulsion from the digestive tract. Only a small amount of the drug is metabolized by the horse, which permits use with pregnant mares, breeding stallions, and all ages of horses, but not with those in debilitated condition.

*Piperazine-carbon disulfide-phenothiazine complex.* Piperazine has been used for years with different species for ascarid treatment and control. It is low in toxicity. Phenothiazine salts were formerly used extensively with salt mixtures to prevent egg production in large and small strongyles, but individual variations in intake among horses and resistance developed by worms after prolonged use limited their effectiveness. Carbon disulfide is an ancient but effective bot treatment that, because of its malodorous and irritating characteristics, is combined with other products and administered by tube by a veterinarian.

Table 14-4 lists trade names, drugs and drug combinations, efficacies, and the companies that produce them. Select from it those that best fulfill the horse's need. Remember:

1 Read labels.
2 Rotate drugs.
3 Practice prevention. Considerable tissue damage results from migration during maturity of some parasite species. Drugs are ineffective during most of the migratory phase of the helminth life cycle.
4 Do not wait. The drug that damages the horse most is the one it failed to get when it needed it. There is a safe drug for every stage of production and reproduction of horses.

DEWORMING SCHEDULE   There are no simple deworming recommendations appropriate for all horse herds. For this reason, discuss control with a veterinarian who is familiar with your herd. Keep these facts in mind when formulating your deworming program:

1 Young horses are most susceptible to internal parasites. Old, weak, or thin horses are also very susceptible.
2 Large horse populations encourage parasite buildups.

TABLE 14-5 DEWORMING SCHEDULE (Heavy Infestation)

|  | Schedule |
| --- | --- |
| Foals | Every 60 days to weaning |
|  | At weaning |
| Yearlings | Every 8 to 12 weeks in summer |
| Adults | Spring and fall and twice in summer |
| Pregnant and lactating mares | One month before foaling and at 2- to 3-month intervals while lactating |

3  Parasites thrive in warm, humid weather and are consumed mostly on short grass (under 3 inches tall).

4  A horse herd of mixed ages requires regular treatment to protect the young.

5  Fecal egg counts are useful when taken monthly, but a single count may be useless. Stress or large populations of intestinal parasites may depress or stop egg production entirely.

6  Combine treatment with good prevention management, as discussed earlier in this chapter.

7  Alternate drugs and match them to need; i.e., use bot-effective drugs two or three times in fall and winter and strongyle-effective drugs in warm seasons.

8  In general, all adult horses should be dewormed twice yearly and four to six times yearly in circumstances favoring heavy infestations. Weanlings and yearlings will thrive on four to six annual treatments unless crowded or mixed with older horses; then intervals of every 6 to 8 weeks are indicated (see Table 14-5).

Parasitic infections are inherently insidious and tenacious. Success in controlling them requires a determined and sustained effort.

## EXTERNAL PARASITES

External parasites annoy horses, and they may infect them with deadly diseases or cause them to panic and injure themselves in flight (Figure 14-10). Blood-sucking parasites may weaken the horse, affect feed efficiency, and produce raw sores that become infected and result in death if not cared for properly. Some general preventive measures are removal of feces, filth, and soiled bedding to reduce breeding opportunity for these pests. Darkened

FIGURE 14-10    Louse damage of this severity may weaken a young horse to such an extent that invasion of another disease may kill it. [*From* "Horse Science," 1965, *4-H Service Committee.*]

stalls should be available for horses to escape certain flies. Chemicals applied to fly-breeding areas should be used judiciously, according to directions on the label.

### Mites

Mites (Figure 14-11) are microscopic parasites that burrow into the skin and cause a condition called "mange." There are several types of mite. One type (sarcoptic and demodectic) burrows in tunnels under the skin, and the other lives in colonies on the surface (psoroptic and chorioptic).

Sarcoptic mites usually attack the head, neck, and shoulders. As they burrow, crusts form on the surface of the skin, which eventually thickens. On the neck characteristic thick crusty folds may form. Demodectic mites live in hair follicles and accompanying sebaceous glands. They concentrate on the head, particularly around the eyes. Psoroptic mites produce moist scabs under the forelock, mane, and tail. Psoroptic mange is extremely contagious. Chorioptic mites concentrate on the lower legs of the horse, particularly on heavily feathered fetlocks. The skin thickens and secondary infections frequently set in.

Mites mate on the skin. The female lays one to two eggs daily during a

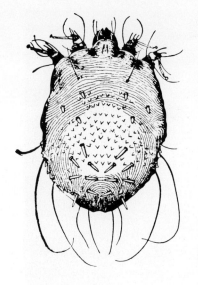

FIGURE 14-11   *Sacroptes scabiei*, or mange mite. [*From Bradley and Craig*, University of Missouri Science and Technology Guide 2853.]

lifespan of up to 2 weeks. These hatch in about 4 days and the immature mite reaches maturity in another 2 weeks. All mites are highly contagious.

Mange caused by any species of mite is very difficult to eradicate. The state extension entomologist, county agent, or veterinarian should be consulted about what treatment to use. It is most important to isolate infected horses and keep the equipment they use separate from others. Most mange treatment involves dipping or washing the affected animals. Good grooming and maintaining good condition are preventive measures, as mites thrive on run-down, poorly cared for animals.

## Lice

There are three species of lice that live permanently on horses. One is a blood-sucking louse called *Haematopinus asini* (Figure 14-12). The two biting lice are *Karichodeces tilosus* and *Damalinia equi*. Lice mature rapidly on horses and will cause itching and loss of hair from rubbing if left unchallenged. Symptoms of louse infestation are extreme aggravation, biting, and loss of appetite. A severe infestation of blood-sucking lice can cause anemia.

Eggs are deposited on the hair where they hatch after about 2 weeks. After feeding for 2 weeks, the growing nymph becomes an adult and mates in another week. The female may lay from 50 to 100 eggs each day for the rest of her life, i.e., another 4 to 5 weeks.

Dense louse infestation is more common in winter when hair is long. Some horses seem more susceptible to louse infestation than others and may be carriers. Louse transfer from an infected horse to another usually

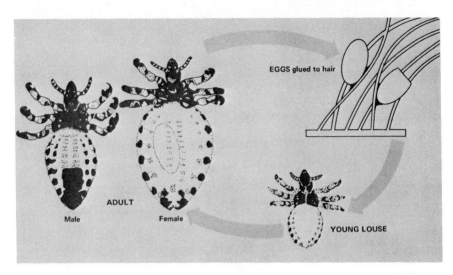

FIGURE 14-12   Life cycle of the bloodsucking louse. [*From Loomis, Hughes, and Bramhall.*]

occurs during physical contact in close quarters, since lice do not live long off their host. Lice may be seen by raising the mane and rubbing the hand up the neck opposite to the lay of the hair. In heavy infestations they are all over the body and are readily observed.

Do not wait until spring to treat for lice. Get the appropriate treatment (often malathion) as recommended by the veterinarian or entomologist and apply it by hand—dusting, spraying, or dipping—until the horse is thoroughly covered. Inclement weather, of course, will affect the time and place of this operation. Since treatment does not affect eggs, a second application 2 weeks later is necessary to kill those lice that have just hatched. It will also be necessary to treat saddle blankets and other objects that the horse has worn to rid them of nymphs and eggs.

## Ticks

Ticks are parasites which attack mammals. They lie in wait on plants and trees for a host to pass. It has been found that a component of mammalian sweat, butyric acid, attracts ticks and enables them to zero in on their hosts.

Ticks are dangerous bloodsucking carriers of several serious diseases such as encephalomyelitis and babesiosis (piroplasmosis).

Ticks are protected by a very hard outer shell, and in addition, they are fairly insecticide-resistant. The best treatment is to check horses daily in tick season (May to September), particularly if they are turned out in deep pasture or are trail-ridden. Favorite hiding places are fetlocks, ears, manes, and tails. The tick will usually detach quickly to avoid suffocation when covered in oil. The veterinarian can suggest a bath or spray for additional protection against ticks. Immunization against tickborne disease is required in heavily infested areas.

## Housefly

*Musca domestica* is the common housefly. It closely associates itself with both horses and man. Houseflies swarm around stables and are the major species seen on ceilings and walls in horse barns.

They depend upon decomposed plant material, soiled bedding, stacked horse manure, and other damp materials for food and life-cycle completion. Females may hatch from eggs and be in full production themselves within 1 week under ideal conditions. Unless checked, they become exceedingly numerous and annoy horses, by swarming and landing on their bodies. This causes constant switching, stomping, and shaking as well as subsequent loss of condition. In addition, houseflies figure as an intermediate host in the transmission of stomach worms to horses: after feeding on infested manure, they land on open sores, contaminating the wound with eggs or larvae.

Residual sprays on ceilings and walls give good control. Electrical traps and fly bait are helpful. Since houseflies do not wander far from their food supply, sanitation is the best way to reduce their population.

## Stable Fly

The stable fly is a vicious blood-sucking attacker of horses. This fast breeder (30- to 60-day cycle) feeds in the early evening hours when the weather is warm and humid. Stable flies annoy horses more than houseflies. Like houseflies, they crawl over manure and spread stomach worms to open wounds, causing slowed healing and secondary infection. Stable flies prefer manure and urine-soaked filth to reproduce in; therefore removal of soiled bedding and pasture droppings helps to control them. They are controllable through application of appropriate chemicals as well.

## Face Flies

*Musca autumnalis* is an annoyance to horses. Face flies swarm tenaciously around horses' eyes in such numbers that eye irritation and infection result. Although face flies enter dark stalls reluctantly, they may pursue horses inside if populations are heavy enough. Most states have face fly populations, but they are more abundant in the north and northeast. They are especially abundant around cattle, and horses that run with cattle may be heavily attacked.

FIGURE 14-13   A face-fly mask made from scrap leather gives good protection. The appropriate browband length is 15 to 17 inches, and straps should be ½ by 12 inches. [*Photograph by Duane Dailey.*]

Control of face flies, unlike house flies and stable flies, is very difficult. They travel great distances and multiply in fresh cattle droppings. Although these flies transmit few if any diseases, they annoy horses to the point of loss of weight and may attack the eyes, nose, nostrils, and even fresh wounds to the point of driving the horse to panic.

There are numerous chemicals to apply to the horse to reduce face fly annoyance. About the only effective control is an inexpensive face fly mask (Figure 14-13). Some owners mount these on the horse's halter in early spring and remove them in the fall only after the last face flies have disappeared.

## Blowflies

*Pthormia regina* are the most numerous blowflies. These flies lay eggs in wounds of horses, where the larvae hatch. Since these larvae do not feed on live tissues, they are less dangerous than screwworm larvae. They are easily killed with chemicals in aerosol sprays. Wound protection is essential to avoid secondary infections.

## Screwworms

Screwworm flies, the larva of *Cochliomyia,* lay eggs in fresh wounds on all types of domestic and wild mammals. These flies are more numerous in the southwest, although the U.S. Department of Agriculture screwworm eradication program has greatly reduced their numbers. Their larvae attack living tissue by burrowing through wounds and will kill animals unless caught in time. Infected animals on large ranches in the gulf coast region often die before their need for treatment is discovered.

## Horseflies and Deerflies

*Horseflies* attack horses in the evening and early morning. They are large bloodsuckers that cause great distress and pain to horses. Large numbers can devastate the skin of a horse, causing substantial loss of blood and making open wounds that other flies feed on. *Deerflies* are considerably smaller but attack horses with vigor.

Both types reproduce in swamps or other watery areas where they lay eggs on plants, stones, and twigs near water. After hatching the larvae burrow into muddy areas where they feed and grow for about 9 months before they transform into a pupal or resting stage (nonfeeding). Two to 4 weeks later they emerge as adult flies. They ravenously attack horses with their scissorlike mouthparts, which literally slice the skin open and permit blood to flow. Control is very difficult, since their habitat and breeding area is usually not known and since there is no satisfactory fly repellent that lasts longer than a few minutes. Loose horses can do a fair job of fighting off these annoying flies, but tied horses cannot compete well. If horses are kept in swampy areas with heavy horse fly infestation, they may be lightly sheeted in the evening and spared part of the agony of feeding the horse and deer flies.

## Mosquitoes

Some species of mosquitoes are carriers of viruses and bacterial infections (e.g., encephalomyelitis). They breed and lay eggs in huge numbers on water, in mud, and on the ground. When the rains come, or when the eggs are moistened, they hatch.

Control of these bloodsucking insects, if they pose a large problem, requires the help of local agencies. Drainage of stagnant water is important. Commercial flysprays and wipes are effective, but to work best they must be carefully applied according to directions.

## WOUNDS AND ACCIDENTS

A wound is any injury disrupting the tissues. A wound may or may not break the skin. There are six types of wounds.

1   Incision. The edges of the incision are clean-cut, and the bleeding which results can be quite severe. Incised wounds are usually caused by sharp-edged objects.
2   Laceration. The edges of the laceration are jagged, torn, and rough. Tissue may actually have been torn away, as by barbed wire. Bleeding is usually not severe, though these wounds tend to drain for some time as the disturbed layers of tissue are regenerated.
3   Punctures. By their very nature, puncture wounds are not always visible—the edges of the puncture often fold back over the opening, creating an anaerobic atmosphere ideal for the growth of tetanus and other bacteria. Puncture wounds are frequently caused by nails, pitchforks, stakes, or thorns.
4   Abrasion. An abrasion is usually a minor wound in which the very surface of the skin is rubbed or broken. Infection is rarely a problem.
5   Burns. Chemicals, cold, and electricity can cause burns, in addition to fire. Burns are extremely susceptible to infection and dehydration. A veterinarian should be called immediately.
6   Contusion. A contusion is a bruise. There may or may not be extensive bleeding beneath the skin and swelling. In horses contusions are most often caused by kicks and falls.

### General Treatment Procedures

When an injury occurs, the horseman must judge its seriousness and decide whether or not a veterinarian should be called. In most cases deep, incised wounds should be evaluated and treated by a veterinarian because they may involve injuries to tendons, bones, joints, or other vital parts. On the other hand, superficial wounds, such as skin abrasions, may be treated by the horseman. Lacerations on the lower legs are hard for the layman to treat because they may involve tendons or ligaments and they are much more susceptible to development of granulation tissue (see *Miscellaneous Diseases and Problems*).

If there is any possibility that suturing may be required, it is very important not to apply greasy medication, powders, strong antiseptics or other treatments that might cause necrosis (death) of tissues as a result of granulation development. Whenever in doubt, call the veterinarian.

Excessive blood loss may produce shock and cause death to a horse; however, if the horse is not experiencing shock, it can lose 2 gallons of blood before its life is endangered. A horse in shock has a rapid pulse and shallow, rapid breathing, and shows signs of anxiety. It should be covered with a blanket and kept calm while awaiting the veterinarian. To prevent blood loss, pressure bandages may be applied to reduce bleeding until the veterinarian arrives. Pressure applied directly to a bleeding wound on the body with bandages or sterile cloth will reduce arterial blood loss and probably stop venous bleeding entirely. (Arterial bleeding comes in bright red spurts; venous bleeding comes in a dark red steady flow.) Tourniquets can be used on wounds on the legs if necessary to reduce blood pressure from the body side of the wound, but they should be left on only 5 to 10 minutes and then released slowly to allow blood circulation to the leg. While loss of a horse from excessive bleeding is very rare, horses have been lost by gangrene infection after a too-tight tourniquet.

Superficial wounds must be cleaned before being treated. One of the best ways is with a hose and clear water at body temperature. Sponges and very mild soap or a mild saline solution can also be used. One must be sure that no foreign matter or dirt is left in any wound. Veterinarians usually give a tetanus booster shot simply to ward off the possibility of tetanus. They may also give the horse an antibiotic to prevent infection.

Depending on the position of the wound, bandaging can speed the healing process and protect the wound from flies and secondary infection. If the wound is on the leg and needs a wrap, apply an antibacterial ointment and a nonstick surgical wound covering, followed by sterile gauze pads, a cotton combination bandage, and a wrap to complete the job. The amount of pressure applied is very important: it should be just enough to hold the bandage in place and not enough to impair circulation. It is best to be instructed by a veterinarian before attempting to bandage a leg. Change the bandage when it gets visibly wet; or change it every second or every third day.

The healing process can be monitored by the amount of improvement in the horse's activity, reduction of swelling, lack of seepage around the wound, and whether or not the horse tries to bite or scratch the wound. Horses tend to gnaw at slow-healing wounds, especially if the wound develops granulation tissue. In such cases it may be necessary for the horse to wear a neck brace. Often a small wound can simply be cleaned and medicated with an ointment or powder. The important thing is to keep proud flesh from invading the wound and growing to such proportions that surgery is necessary.

Many kicks result in deep, open, bruised flesh. Kick wounds pose drainage problems in healing and problems of cleaning because they often have foreign matter deep within them. While many large wounds can be treated by the horseman, most should be checked by a veterinarian and sutured. If wounds are not treated properly, large scars often follow slow healing, and many days are lost.

## Accident Prevention and Preparedness

Many accidents involving horses are man-made or result from neglectful management. Many pastures, barnyards, and areas where horses are kept are potential battlegrounds. They may be strewn with old farm machinery, parked vehicles, scattered baling wire, broken glass, cans, pitchforks, protruding boards, broken-off tree limbs and other dangerous objects lying in wait for the excitable, thin-skinned horse. Regularly inspect the areas where horses spend time as well as all pasture fences, routinely removing hazards. Barbed wire is the horse's constant enemy. It should be used only with caution in large, open areas—if at all—and should never be used around small lot fences where horses are penned. Some horses do not seem to see it until they are wound up in it. Dominant horses will chase others into it, and many horses will paw into barbed wire while impatiently awaiting feed. Some horses will play across any type of fence and constantly keep themselves injured. Like certain people, some horses seem prone to injury and will devise ingenious ways to get themselves into trouble. Of course, a very few accidents are totally unavoidable. It is important to maintain insurance policies on valuable horses.

FIRST-AID KIT   The horse owner should have a first aid kit containing a variety of items in the stable for handy use. Kits may be purchased in handy carrying cases or items may be assembled according to the horseman's anticipated needs. The well-stocked bandage kit will contain a gauze roll, antibacterial medication, cotton padding, adhesive elastic-type outer bandage, nonstick surgical gauze pad, self-adhesive velcro wrap, sterile surgical gloves, field cotton, primary wrap, and other aids, depending upon the horseman's skill. A twitch should be kept in the tack room and can be used as needed in treating wounds.

## COMMUNICABLE DISEASES

There are a number of diseases of the horse produced by organisms that may be ingested, inhaled, or injected by flying insects. These can be classified into two categories, viral and bacterial, although both may be present at the same time.

Viruses are extremely small; most can be seen only with the aid of a sophisticated electron microscope. Each virus is made up of a core of nucleic acid and has a tough outer coat of protein. Viruses must attach themselves to other living cells (hosts), find a way to enter, and take over the life system of the cell to reproduce themselves. New particles of virus leave the damaged cell, seeking new host cells to invade in order to repeat the cycle.

Viruses therefore depend upon a living host for survival. Some spend their entire life cycle in a horse, and others depend on intermediate hosts. For example, encephalomyelitis virus is harbored by wild animals and birds, who show no ill effects from the virus. Through the bite of a mosquito, this virus is transmitted to horses and humans, for whom it is harmful.

Bacteria, unlike viruses, are large microorganisms. Some can live indefinitely outside the host. For example, tetanus bacteria may spend years dormant in barnyard soil and yet remain quite capable of infecting horses or humans upon entry into the bloodstream. Bacteria, like viruses, are parasitic in nature, living on a horse's body fluids and destroying cells directly or producing toxins that destroy them. When toxins reach the bloodstream, serious infection results.

Certain types of viruses and bacteria respond to immunization while others do not. Antibiotic treatment may be ineffective or have little effect against viruses, whereas specific antibiotics are quite effective against bacteria. Since viruses do not survive outside the host very long, direct contact or close proximity is required for their transmission. Bacteria are much more abundant outside the body than viruses, and may be more easily acquired through contaminated water, soil, air, or other sources.

## Bacterial Diseases

STRANGLES (DISTEMPER)  One of the most common diseases in horses is strangles. It is caused by a pus-forming organism called *Streptococcus equi*. Strangles is highly contagious and spreads rapidly through a stable or through horses on pasture. Strangles usually affects horses from 1 to 3 years of age; however, any age can be affected, especially after direct exposure and stress. Horses taken to shows, hauled during inclement weather, or subjected to the disease in the form of the nasal discharge of sick horses (as might be found in contaminated feed or water troughs) may easily contract the disease. The strangles organism may be viable for a month after onset of the disease, contaminating water troughs and pastures.

Symptoms are increased temperature and respiration, loss of appetite, lassitude, and rapid appearance of a purulent nasal discharge. The discharge is very thick and may run profusely from each nostril. Painful coughing may accompany the condition and last for 3 to 4 weeks. After a few days, lymph nodes in the upper respiratory tract may begin to swell. If not effectively treated, after 10 days to 2 weeks these lymph nodes discharge a thick, cream-colored pus and may rupture. During this time, swallowing is hard for the horse; the lymph nodes under the jaw in the throat and behind the ears are sore and sensitive to the touch.

*Treatment.*  Control consists of early identification and strict isolation of the sick from the healthy. All contaminated quarters and utensils must be disinfected, especially common water troughs.

Good nursing care is absolutely essential for prompt recovery. If left untreated the condition may linger for many weeks. It is essential not to work the sick horse, but rather to give it plenty of rest, clean, fresh water, good feed, and shelter from drafts. Veterinarians usually prescribe antibiotics to lessen the effects of the condition, especially if it is caught before abscesses begin to form. Warm compresses may be applied to abscessed nodes to coax drainage. The horse should continue to be medicated and rested for at least 2 to 3 weeks after fever and discharge cease, to be sure no pockets of infection linger.

*Prevention.*   The only sure way to prevent strangles is to avoid contact with infected animals or contaminated quarters. The condition is prevalent worldwide. Perhaps vaccination should be a routine practice for those horses hauled to shows and mingled with other horses—usually this vaccination requires three injections at weekly intervals. Horses that have had strangles enjoy some immunity for about 6 months. Such horses can be immunized with a booster shot to finish the rest of the show year.

TETANUS (LOCKJAW)   Tetanus is one of the deadliest known diseases of horses, mules, and donkeys. It is caused by *Clostridium tetani*, an anaerobic sporulating bacterium. The tetanus spore can lie dormant in the soil for many years provided it has a minimal amount of moisture. For this reason tetanus is known throughout the world and is especially prevalent around stables in manure and moist surrounding soils. A puncture wound, especially in the feet, is an ideal way for tetanus spores to enter the body. In foals, the spores gain admittance through untreated umbilical cords. Inside the body the proliferating organisms produce a neurotoxin which affects the central nervous system by way of the peripheral nerve trunk as well as through the common route of the lymph system and bloodstream.

Early symptoms are stiffness and a stilted gait, followed by fixed, erect ears, elevated tail, stiff, braced legs, and great difficulty moving the head in any direction. Since eventually the horse cannot open its mouth, eating is impossible. In advanced stages, muscles are rigid, breathing is difficult, and prolapse of the third eyelid may occur.

*Treatment.*   When horses reach the advanced condition, euthanasia is indicated. However, in early phases with good nursing the prognosis is fair. The affected horse should be placed in a safe, dark stall and be protected from the consequences of spasms and convulsions. Massive doses of antitoxin are given; sedation is essential and tranquilizers may be helpful in reducing muscle spasm. Affected horses must be fed via stomach tube. Some must be treated for urine retention and constipation as well when these functions are interrupted in the course of the disease. Bran mashes and soft feeds are indicated when the horse begins to recover.

*Prevention.*    Since this is one of the easiest diseases to prevent, immunization should be a part of every horseman's program with every horse that is owned. Many veterinarians will give a tetanus booster shot anytime they treat a puncture wound. This gives immediate protection and greatly reduces the chance that tetanus will affect the horse. Some veterinarians inject tetanus toxoid boosters annually, and in a high-risk tetanus area they may do so every other month.

THRUSH    Thrush is a condition known to almost every horseman. It is a contagious anaerobic bacterial infection usually caused by the organism *Spherophorus necrophorus*, although other bacteria and a fungus have been identified in thrush infections. These bacteria live in damp areas, especially in horse feces in damp or unsanitary stables. For this reason, stables should be kept clean and a horse's feet should be cleaned daily with a hoof pick to prevent the build-up of filth which might encourage the proliferation of thrush.

A dark, foul-smelling discharge is noticed in the cleft or groove of the frog when cleaning the thrush-infected foot. This is the beginning of a degenerative condition that may destroy the horn of the frog and in severe cases can affect the navicular bone and joint. Lameness is seldom seen in the early stages of thrush, but it characterizes later stages.

*Treatment.*    Clean out the foot well and remove loose tags on the frog and heel that harbor manure and filth. Trim out the sole so that medicine can reach the infection more easily. Thrush responds to a number of drying agents: 7 percent iodine; half-strength chlorine bleach; 4 percent formaldehyde; copper sulphate; and several more. After 3 or 4 days, recovery should be apparent. After a week of steady treatment the area should appear dry and hardened. Healing can be hastened by removing the horse from wet footing or by thoroughly cleaning the stall and bedding it deeply with sawdust or straw. In severe cases, the spot may require packing with a cotton wad saturated with medicine, followed by the application of a horseshoe with a pad. The new EasyBoot is especially helpful for treatment of thrush because it slips on and off easily and permits frequent changing of a medicated pack. Severe cases may require systematic antibiotic injections or even surgery to remove dead or dying horn.

*Prevention.*    Thrush is easy to keep under control with daily stall- and hoof-cleaning, occasional liming of the stall and application of good, dry bedding.

JOINT ILL (NAVEL ILL)    This disease is usually limited to foals because of their great susceptibility to infection. It gets its name from the localized swelling of joints responding to the invasion of a number of different bacteria. A common invader is *Shigella equirulis* (*Actinobacillus equili*). Navel ill often appears in new-born foals as a result of infection through the umbilical cord. For this reason, the umbilical cord should not be cut short soon after birth. It usually severs naturally 6 inches to a foot from the body; when disinfected promptly, this stump will dry up and fall off, reducing the opportunity for bacteria to enter.

Symptoms are fever, diarrhea, rapid respiration, sleepiness and enlarged joints that are warm to the touch and painful to the animal. Enlargement may be limited to one or both hind legs. Since its joints are extremely sore, the foal will be very lame. Often the first symptom is a slight lameness in one or both hind legs. When this occurs the veterinarian should check it immediately because navel ill is a very likely suspect at this stage of life. Temperature may rise to 105 or 106°F. The foal will stop nursing, remain lying down, and will get up only with great difficulty.

*Treatment.* Veterinarians occasionally give a blood transfusion from the dam to the foal, and administer antibiotics, corticosteroids, or a bacterin. Successful treatment depends on an early start. If symptoms are present within a few hours of birth, death usually occurs within 7 days.

*Prevention.* Cleanliness and good husbandry, especially at birth, are prerequisites to a low incidence of navel ill. For this reason, Thoroughbred establishments often have a veterinarian and team of workers stand by to catch the newborn foal in a sterilized cloth before it hits the ground. Other horsemen prefer to let the mares foal in clean pastures to reduce the occurrence of the disease. In any case, the umbilical cord should be disinfected as soon as possible after birth, because approximately half of the infected foals do not survive. Mares who produce contaminated foals are suspect and should be treated.

CONTAGIOUS EQUINE METRITIS (CEM) A venereal disease in Thoroughbreds rocked the horse world in 1977 when it was discovered in about twenty of the stallions at the English National Stud at Newmarket.[3] Intensive efforts were made to isolate the infective organisms. During this time the American Horse Council and the U.S. Department of Agriculture were observing the spread of the disease in Europe and decided to place an embargo on European horses. Before the embargo went into effect, however, two French stallions were imported to Kentucky. Despite extensive tests, these stallions were silent carriers of the highly contagious bacterial disease. It appears now that the disease is caused by coccobacillus. The possibility exists that other bacteria and even viruses may be involved.

Stallions show no symptoms but are carriers. Mares return to season

[3] *American Horse Council Newsletter*, vol. 4, no. 10, October 1977.

after having been bred and show a profuse vaginal discharge. Culture of the cervix may be negative while a urethral culture is positive. Stallions may show positive from urethral fossa, prepuce, and preejaculate secretion cultures. Mares may settle and abort at 40 to 60 days and not come back in heat again that breeding season; therefore, they are lost to production that year. Some mares, however, may carry full-term and produce normal foals, be rebred, and therefore become silent carriers.

*Treatment.* The condition appears to clear up after a few months' breeding rest. It is also sensitive to a number of antibiotics, including penicillin, ampicillin, chloramphenicol, chlortetracyclines, oxytetracyclines, furazolidone, and neomycin. It is resistant, however, to streptomycin.

Control requires isolation of infected animals. CEM in mares will often clear up spontaneously if they are given rest from breeding. It appears that the disease has been contained now, however; there is little likelihood that it will be as devastating to the American Thoroughbred industry as it was to the European.

SCRATCHES (GREASE HEEL)   Scratches is an inflammation of the skin on the back part of the pasterns, fetlocks, or hooves just above the bulb of the heels. Horses with white legs or with long feathers are more susceptible to it. Deep mud, damp conditions, or filth tend to abrade the skin and permit invasion of microorganisms, such as various bacteria and fungi. Thickening of the skin, granulation, and lameness can result if the condition is neglected.

*Treatment.* Thoroughly clean the affected area with warm water and clip off the hairs over the scabby area. It may be necessary to soften scabs with petroleum jelly or another bland ointment for a few days before they can be removed so that the real medication can penetrate to the deepest layer of infection. If the infection is serious, an antibiotic is indicated. A treatment for scratches can be obtained from the veterinarian that may contain zinc oxide, nitrofurazone, or steroids. If a steroid is applied, follow directions carefully; prolonged use of steroids can delay healing.

*Prevention.* Keep the ankles and fetlocks clipped so they do not collect filth. Keep the horse on dry, clean bedding as much as possible. Grease heel is considerably less troublesome in the hot, dry summer than in the rainy seasons of spring and fall.

## Viral Diseases

ENCEPHALOMYELITIS (SLEEPING SICKNESS)   A number of different viruses can cause encephalomyelitis. In the United States and Mexico there are three regional types: eastern (EEE), western (WEE), and Venezuelan (VEE). Eastern and western encephalomyelitis are common to the United States; Venezuelan encephalomyelitis is found more in Mexico and Latin American countries. Sleeping sickness has drawn much attention because humans can be affected by it. EEE and WEE are transmitted to both horse and man by the bite of a mosquito, but they are not transmitted directly between horse and man. Wild animals and birds are the intermediaries. In 1971 Venezuelan encephalomyelitis first occurred in the United States in epidemic proportions near the Mexican border. VEE is directly transferrable between horse and man.

The disease has been called brain disease, resulting in marked depression, high temperature (104 to 106°F), and poor coordination. Although the animal is reluctant to move, when it does it tends to stagger—hence the name "blind staggers." Affected horses may walk aimlessly about, crashing into objects, and may appear to sleep for short intervals with their eyes partially closed. They become periodically hypersensitive to sounds and touch. In advanced cases they often circle with lowered heads and eventually they get down and are unable to rise. At this stage they may grind their teeth and be unable to swallow from paralysis of the lips and throat. Urination and defecation are interrupted or cease altogether. Death usually occurs in 3 to 6 days following extreme symptoms and should not be postponed; humane considerations dictate that the animal should be destroyed.

Not all animals die from sleeping sickness. The western strain usually has a low mortality rate, something like 20 to 30 percent, while the Venezuelan and eastern strains may destroy 90 percent of the animals affected.

*Treatment.* About the only treatment after symptoms appear is to make the animal as comfortable as possible. One can keep the animal from running into things by padding its stall and protecting it from falling upon objects. Veterinarians often inject electrolytes and fluids to counteract the fever. Because of the rapid onslaught of the disease, specific therapeutic treatment is unknown.

*Control.* Every horse should be immunized against EEE and WEE, and VEE in southern border states (Figure 14-14). Immunization is very effective. There may be epidemics of the disease when mosquitoes are present in large numbers; therefore, mosquito control is mandatory. Those horsemen who do not immunize their horses each year should be especially attentive to the news media and to their veterinarians for signs of the disease approaching their area. They may have sufficient time to vaccinate; however, the best plan is to make immunization a routine practice.

EQUINE INFLUENZA  Equine influenza is caused by a group of viruses related to the human influenza virus, type A. Influenza may affect all ages of horses, but foals and the young are particularly susceptible. Influenza is highly in-

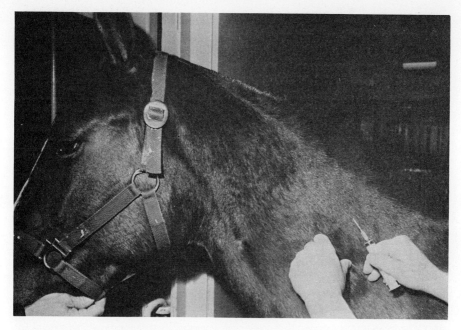

FIGURE 14-14   Every horse should be immunized annually for Encephalomyelitis (sleeping sickness), tetanus, and any local diseases reported by your veterinarian. [*Animal Husbandry Department, University of Missouri.*]

fectious, and may pass through a stable affecting 90 to 100 percent of the horses. However, it is seldom fatal, though it may linger and render horses useless over extended periods.

The disease starts with a rapidly rising temperature that may reach or exceed 106°F for about 3 to 10 days. Most horses evidence a cough characteristic of influenza—dry and frequently repeated. Most horses also show depression, loss of appetite, rapid breathing, and watery discharges from their eyes and nostrils. The discharge is usually yellow.

*Treatment.*   Stop working the horse immediately and continue rest and good care until the cough disappears. In some cases the influenza may linger for several weeks or even a few months. Veterinarians, after first culturing the discharge to determine the exact components of the infection, may use antibiotics or sulfa drugs to reduce or prevent secondary infections that delay recovery.

*Control.*   Isolate the sick animal and hope the disease does not spread to the entire barn. Avoid transmitting the virus through contaminated feed buckets, feeds, clothing, bridles, water buckets, or other utensils.

When a new horse is brought home from an auction or dispersal sale, isolate it for at least 2 weeks, for the incubation of equine influenza does not usually exceed 10 days.

RHINOPNEUMONITIS    Rhinopneumonitis is caused by a herpes virus, the same group that causes fever blisters, cold sores, and mononucleosis in man. Although it is seldom fatal to mature horses, it does cause substantial sickness in very young and old horses, and abortion in mares at almost any stage of pregnancy.

There may be few signs of the condition other than abortion in pregnant mares, or it may manifest itself with a high temperature (102 to 105°F) that lasts up to 6 days. Occasionally there is a clear nasal discharge, coughing (which may persist up to 3 weeks), swelling of eyelids, and loss of appetite. Abortions usually occur in the last third of pregnancy and they may occur with every pregnant mare on the farm. Recurrence and secondary infection are real possibilities, especially in young horses.

*Treatment.*    There is no effective treatment, however, antibiotics are often used to control secondary bacterial infections.

*Control.*    There is as yet no safe, dependable vaccine against rhinopneumonitis; researchers are still trying to develop one. There is a vaccine available now, but it is controversial and should be discussed with the state veterinarian before use, because it may produce the disease in some horses. Some breeding farms use a program of planned infection that consists of injecting the live virus into horses during June and October. Recovered animals are immune for several months. Farms employing such a method are quarantined for 3 weeks. An occasional abortion may occur despite this controlled immunization procedure.

PNEUMONIA    Pneumonia is an inflammation of the lungs, the result of an infection usually caused by a virus or a bacteria. It may be triggered by a predisposing factor, such as lowered resistance following another disease, or a mechanical injury, as when fluid enters the lungs during improper use of a balling gun or stomach tube. Infection starts in one or both lungs and spreads from the bottom upward.

Symptoms include elevated temperature (102 to 105°F) and difficult breathing. The breath often comes in rapid, short gasps. There may be some nasal discharge, a cough, audible lung congestion, loss of appetite, breath odor, and quickened pulse. Pneumonia is difficult to diagnose, as a number of preexisting or concurrent conditions can mask it. The veterinarian will often rely heavily on the case history of onset.

*Treatment.*    Horses with pneumonia should receive the best of care. They should be made comfortable in a clean stall without drafts and be given total rest with good feed. Since their appetites are depressed, their favorite feed should be offered. If the condition is caused by bacteria, and many are, it will respond promptly to antibiotics.

*Prevention.*   Since pneumonia often accompanies a depleted physical condition, as might be the result of another disease or overexertion, difficult conditions should be minimized or eliminated. Older horses, young horses, or those in thin condition should be spared exposure to the elements caused by inadequate shelter, drafty conditions, or being hauled in cold weather.

EQUINE INFECTIOUS ANEMIA (EIA, OR SWAMP FEVER)   Few diseases have received the publicity and aroused the emotions of people like EIA. Recognized as a definable disease in France in 1843 and in Canada in 1881, it was first diagnosed in the United States in 1888.[4] EIA is a virus disease caused by one of the group of viruses called "retraviruses." These viruses seek the centers of living cells and are capable of changing their own structures when attacked by the horse's natural defense, which makes development of a vaccine very difficult. The virus can coexist quite peacefully with a horse for years without causing any apparent effects, and then spread rapidly in the animal bringing on symptoms which often terminate in death. Stress tends to trigger this condition; therefore, EIA is found more often in horses that undergo routine stress, such as racing.

Although EIA attacks a very small percentage of animals in our horse population, a near-epidemic did occur in 1947 at Rockingham Park in New Hampshire. About 10 percent of the horses at this track either died or were destroyed. This tragedy prompted race horsemen to seek a control program from the U.S. Department of Agriculture that would lessen their losses from such an eventuality. It was not until Dr. Leroy Coggins, veterinarian at Cornell University, discovered an accurate test for infected animals and carriers that such a program was possible. The Coggins test, perfected in 1970, is an agar gel–immunodiffusion (AGID) test. It does not detect the EIA virus itself, but detects the presence of antibodies or virus-fighting units in the blood of the animal being tested. It has a very high degree of accuracy. Dr. Knowells, of the U.S. Department of Agriculture, classified the disease a "reportable disease" in 1973. He designated the Coggins test as the official test to determine the presence of EIA, identified laboratories at which to test the blood of horses, and prohibited interstate transportation of EIA-positive reactors except to an approved slaughterhouse or quarantine facility. At the urging of the American Association of Equine Practitioners, 41 of 50 states passed laws to control EIA. Some required a Coggins test if a horse was to be hauled on a public road, while others had no laws at all. Many had laws that required a horse entering the state to be Coggins-tested.

[4]"Equine Infectious Anemia (Swamp Fever)," *Equus Special Report* no. 1. Equine Health Publications Co., Gaithersburg, Pa., p. 9.

The net result in some states was to confine positive horses to a fly-proof stall or destroy them. A number of horses were tested and slaughtered until public emotions reached fever pitch, particularly in Florida. When a child tested his apparently healthy horse and found it to be a carrier that had to be caged or destroyed, emotions soared. As a result, five state laws were repealed or liberalized to accommodate the "inapparent" EIA carrier. A reappraisal of many state laws is underway.

There are three classifications for symptoms of EIA: inapparent carriers and acute and chronic cases. Inapparent carriers, about 85 percent of infected horses, test positive to the disease yet show no symptoms. They may remain totally healthy throughout life. Such horses have been accumulated as test horses, have mixed with and been bred with negative animals, and have produced foals without any apparent signs of the disease. They remain positive to the test throughout life. Why should such inapparent carriers be destroyed, when testing programs result in destroying more horses than the disease would in decades? On the other hand, it is known that an occasional inapparent carrier under stress will develop acute symptoms and thereby become a transmitter of the disease at that point.

Horses with acute and chronic forms of the disease show visible illness and transmit it. Acute symptoms are an extremely high temperature, often approaching 108°F, depression, depressed appetite, and prompt and extreme loss of weight. Edema may appear on the lower body surfaces, particularly in the scrotum, abdomen, and limbs. Red blood cells are destroyed and the horse may soon die.

The chronic form results in a lingering unthrifty horse that lacks stamina and gradually weakens. It may have attacks of anemia and a high temperature that may subside and seem to disappear only to reappear in 3 weeks to a month. The disease is transmitted by any transfer of blood from one horse to another, such as bloodsucking vectors, especially horse flies, unsterilized vaccination needles, or other instruments used from one horse to another.

*Treatment.*    There is no successful treatment for EIA.

*Control.* Most states require isolation for Coggins-positive horses. Some require isolation distances of only 200 yards while others demand either a vectorproof screened stall or slaughter. The horse owner must closely watch horses for signs of high temperature and weight loss. Such horses should be promptly isolated and tested. Reduction of flies around the stable should be helpful and every horse brought into the herd should be Coggins-tested before purchase. Most expensive horses are now purchased on the condition that they test negative for EIA. Since there can be some error in the testing procedure, two tests are usually taken if the first one shows positive. If the second one shows negative, a third should be taken to verify one of the tests.

Although this is a highly emotional subject, undoubtedly reasonable laws will be passed and others modified to help keep the disease under control. Meanwhile, intensive research for a cure is needed.

WARTS   The cause of warts is now considered to be a virus or viruses. Warts can range in size from tiny single warts on one location of the body to large clusters at any location. They are nuisances if they are in the way of a piece of equipment, such as the crown of the bridle. During the summer flies tend to give them special attention. They may become infected and require veterinary attention. When they reach sufficient length to break over and hang down they are called *papillomas*.

*Treatment.*   Treatment consists of immediate attention—do not let them reach the large cluster stage. Veterinarians have medications that can be purchased and applied to the warts. They may be tied off with a rubber band or fine string, which will stop their blood supply and cause the warts to fall off. This method may offer an entry for tetanus organisms, however, and a tetanus injection may be indicated.

*Prevention.*   Isolation of the horse with warts will reduce the chance of spreading the infection to other horses. While some warts simply go away, it is usually safer to isolate and correct the condition before it gets out of hand.

RABIES   Rabies is a rare but deadly disease of horses and most warm-blooded animals. It is usually transmitted from a dog, cat, or skunk that bites the horse and deposits the virus into its bloodstream. Symptoms vary from mild forms of excitement and antagonism to hostility. Horses with rabies run high temperatures and must be destroyed when diagnosed because there is no treatment for rabies, and humans are susceptible to the disease.

*Prevention.*   Since it is such a rare condition, little prevention is practiced. However, if wild animals, especially skunks, reside in or near the stable, chances of rabies are greatly increased. Rabies vaccine is available in such contaminated areas.

VIRAL ARTERITIS   Viral arteritis is caused by a herpes virus that attacks the upper respiratory tract. It causes abortion in pregnant mares. Symptoms include high temperature, ranging up to 105°F, watery nasal discharge, watery and inflamed eyes, depression, loss of appetite, coughing, colic, diarrhea, and leg edema. It affects mature horses and is difficult to diagnose because its symptoms are similar to influenza and rhinopneumonitis. The mortality rate of horses is low; however, abortions may approach 50 percent. Although the disease is less common now then it was in the past, it may spread through a group of horses and require blood tests to determine its presence. Left untreated, viral arteritis causes severe arterial wall damage and death.

*Treatment.*   Complete rest in a warm, draft-free stall is necessary. A course of antibiotics is usually administered, as well as electrolyte therapy in cases of lingering fever. Secondary infection is common and must be guarded against.

*Prevention.*   In areas of the country plagued by viral arteritis, an effective vaccine is now available.


## MISCELLANEOUS DISEASES AND PROBLEMS

### Colic

Colic is a word used to describe abdominal pain in a horse. Although there are different kinds of colic resulting in different consequences, almost all are management-induced. Equine practitioners tend to find colic cases coming in bunches, precipitated by weather conditions affecting feed intake, seasons associated with more vigorous horse activities such as shows, and seasons that encourage heavy internal parasite infestations.

Some authorities group colics into three broad categories: (1) parasitic colic, (2) flatulent (gas), or digestive, colic, and (3) obstructive colic. Recent studies and observations have led some veterinarians and researchers to attribute 80 to 90 percent of colic cases to high parasitic infestations, especially by strongyles. While it has been known for a long time that foals and young horses would accumulate enough ascarids or roundworms to thoroughly block the intestinal tract and thereby die of colic, only recently have the devastating effects of strongyles and the resultant attacks of colic been appreciated.

Colic causes either intermittent or constant excruciating pain. In an attempt to relieve it, the horse may paw, look at his sides, rise, lie down and roll, stomp with his back feet, break out in a cold sweat, have increased temperature, or injure itself thrashing about in a stall trying to find relief.

PARASITIC COLIC   Migrating larvae damage the blood vessels, and cause hemorrhages, thereby impairing the supply of blood to the intestines. The resulting swelling may also pinch the nerves. When nerves are under pressure a horse may be in only partial control of its back legs. As blood supply to the intestines is blocked, all the digestive processes are slowed, and impaction and obstruction can result. The production of gas starts the pain and initiates the symptoms of colic. At the first sign of any kind of colic, it is usually wise to call a veterinarian and to keep the horse on its feet. If it rolls and thrashes about, it may hurt itself, and some feel that this activity is a major cause of twisted intestine, which often results in death.

DIGESTIVE COLIC   Flatulent, or digestive, colic results from a number of conditions, especially overfeeding, sudden changes in feed, moldy feeds, or erratic ingestion of feed during periods of stress, such as hauling to a show or changes in the weather. This type of colic usually produces gas and causes excruciating pain. While it is the least dangerous of the three types of colics, it still warrants the attention of a veterinarian.

OBSTRUCTIVE COLIC   A number of things obstruct or delay the passage of material through the digestive tract of the horse. Most common among them is impaction resulting from high-fiber feed and inadequate water, and most deadly is a twisted intestine, probably resulting from rolling for relief from a lesser type of colic.

Veterinarians in cool climates where horses are fed rough, high-fiber hay and watered from iced-over ponds find the highest incidence of impaction (Figure 14-15). Coarse, dry, high-fiber hay passes through the digestive

FIGURE 14-15   A horse will die faster from a lack of water than from the absence of any other essential nutrient. Water deficiency decreases digestion and increases impaction. These horses eating dry feed cannot get adequate water through a hole in the ice. [*Photograph by the author.*]

tract slowly; the horse eats more and packs it on top of an already packed digestive tract. Add to this a shortage of water and conditions are ideal to produce impaction. Minor cases may be relieved by laxative feeds or application of oils into the stomach or through the rectum; however, if left without attention very long, surgery may be indicated.

Horses occasionally ingest foreign objects (allotriophagy). When a rubber "stretch" fence appeared on the market a few years ago, a number of horses died from colic and were found to have large amounts of this product in their intestines. Young horses, especially, exhibit allotriophagy and consume large volumes of strands of cord unraveled from these rubberized fences.

Wood-chewers are in constant danger of colic and obstruction from enteroliths. They may ingest a small particle, smaller in size than a toothpick, which lodges in the intestines. Natural body processes attempt to protect the horse from the sharp edges of foreign objects by depositing minerals around them, and so the particle may reach the size of a baseball or even a football.

Sand colic is common in Texas and other states where horses are bedded in sand or fed on ground which has sand as a major constituent of the soil. Sand is ingested into the intestines to the point of actually distending the abdomen. It remains at the bottom of the abdomen and obstructs the passage of the normal products of digestion.

TWISTED INTESTINE   The most devastating and dangerous colic is a twisted intestine. Twisted intestines are hard to diagnose and require very serious surgery. Speed is of the utmost importance. Twisted intestines are suspected when the pulse rate reaches 80 to 100 beats per minute. There are many ways intestines twist or deviate from normal (Figure 14-16), and there are many locations where this may occur. The two most common ways are volvulus and torsion (Figures 14-17 and 14-18). *Volvulus* means the bowel simply rotates, resulting in a twist in the mesentery. *Torsion* is a twist in the longitudinal axis of a bowel, as when a rope is grasped in both hands and each end is twisted in opposite directions. The result of either twist is a blockage or partial blockage of feed passage and blood supply. After about 90 minutes of blockage the animal begins to develop endotoxic shock from toxins produced by bacteria in the intestine lumen (inside the intestine). Successful surgery must locate the twist and correct it. If tissues have necrosed, the twisted portion is removed and the ends joined together. Only about a third of the cases at the University of Missouri veterinary clinic survive, because many arrive too late for survival and some would be irreparable even with early treatment.

There are other conditions with the same symptoms that are not actually twisted intestines. They are intestinal hernias, tumors in the bowels, nodes or growths in the mesentery that reduce or restrict blood supply, and lipoma, which is a fat tumor that suspends from a portion of the intestines (or ab-

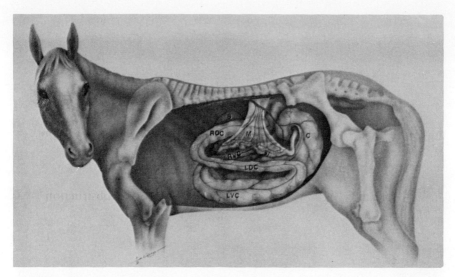

**FIGURE 14-16**  Anatomy of a normal horse's stomach and intestines. S = stomach; C = cecum; M = mesentery. (The mesentery consists of membranes that extend from the dorsal wall of the abdominal cavity to the intestinal area. Blood reaches the intestinal and stomach areas by passing through the mesentery.) SI = small intestine; RDC = right dorsal colon; RVC = right ventral colon; LDC = left dorsal colon; LVC = left ventral colon. (The RDC, RVC, LDC, and LVC compose the large intestine.) [Western Horseman. *Caption by Ted S. Stashak, D.V.M., Chairman, Department of Surgical Sciences, Miller Health Center, University of Florida, Gainesville. Art by Dennis Giddings, medical illustrator, Ft. Collins, Col.*]

dominal wall (Figures 14-19, 14-20). When this is wrapped around the intestine it may obstruct it and produce the same results as twisted intestines.

*Prevention.*  (1) Keep strongyles under control; (2) keep teeth in good condition; (3) avoid sudden changes in feeding practices; (4) feed and water regularly and reasonably often; (5) study the stool of the horse. If it is hard, the horse may not be getting enough water, may be consuming too much dry, high-fiber hay, or may need a laxative feed, such as bran or a high-protein feed; (6) do not work hard a horse that has been heavily fed; feed grain 1 hour prior to work and not much hay before strenuous exercise; (7) keep the horse comfortable and quiet in transit and at work or at horse shows. The horse that regularly eats the correct amount is less likely to develop colic; and (8) feed no moldy feeds; only good-quality feeds can safely be consumed by horses.

*Treatment.*  Do not try home remedies for colic; call a veterinarian. He or she has a number of tools with which to diagnose and treat the horse to encourage normal peristalsis to resume.

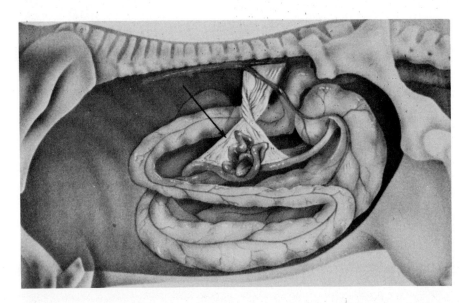

FIGURE 14-17  Here is a volvulus twist (*see arrow*) in the small intestine. Volvulus means that the bowel twists at right angles upon itself. As a result, the mensentery becomes twisted, which blocks the blood supply to the small intestine. [Western Horseman. *Caption by Ted S. Stashak, D.V.M., Chairman, Department of Surgical Sciences, Miller Health Center, University of Florida, Gainesville. Art by Dennis Giddings, medical illustrator, Ft. Collins, Col.*]

LAMINITIS (FOUNDER)  Laminitis has been known in horses as long as they have been domesticated; however, the condition has accelerated during recent years because of intermittent use, overfeeding, and underexercising. The term "laminitis" simply means inflammation of the foot. The insensitive lamini of the hoof wall dovetail, or interlock, with the sensitive lamini of the inner portion of the foot that supports both the coffin bone and much of the weight borne by the wall of the foot when in contact with the ground. When the outer wall of the hoof is removed from the inner portion, these lamini can be seen as tiny ridges and valleys running vertical to the ground. They carry blood and nutrients to the foot and are stimulated by a pumping action when the horse walks. Even mild laminitis causes swelling of the lamini and congestion of blood with reduced circulation resulting in great pain. Obviously the horse is reluctant to rise, stand, or walk. Front feet are affected most, and back feet are brought forward under the body to reduce the weight on them.

*Kinds of laminitis.*  Some authors distinguish between laminitis and founder, considering laminitis to be the first, or acute, phase and founder to be the chronic, or late, phase that results if the condition is neglected,

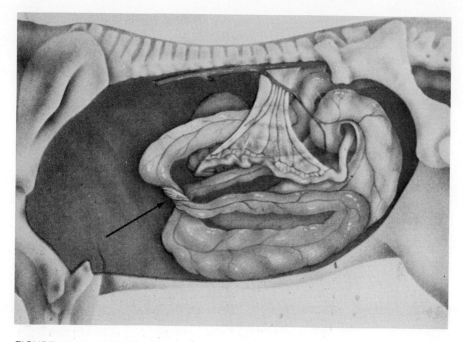

FIGURE 14-18   This illustration shows a torsion (*see arrow*) in the large intestine. In a torsion twist, the bowel twists on its long axis. [*Western Horseman. Caption by Ted S. Stashak, D.V.M., Chairman, Department of Surgical Sciences, Miller Health Center, University of Florida, Gainesville. Art by Dennis Giddings, medical illustrator, Ft. Collins, Col.*]

whereupon the insensitive lamini of the outer hoof wall separate from the sensitive lamini of the inner part of the foot at the front, allowing the sole to sink. The unsupported coffin bone then rotates or points downward, even punching a hole through the sole of the foot in bad cases. There are varying degrees of rotation of the coffin bone. In severe cases, the outer hoof wall actually grows upward at the toe resembling a sled runner, if neglected. A small amount of separation at the white line is called "seedy toe." It is important to prevent rotation of the coffin bone. Some rotation can be tolerated without permanent damage; however, prompt and proper veterinary attention can reduce the degree of rotation in most cases.

*Symptoms.*   Symptoms of founder are easy to identify. First you should be aware of the horse's probability of foundering. If it is fat, underexercised, and overfed with a heavy crest on its neck, it is a prime candidate. There appears to be a low metabolic rate in heavy-crested horses because of a low level of thyroxin. If such a horse is suddenly exposed to a large amount of

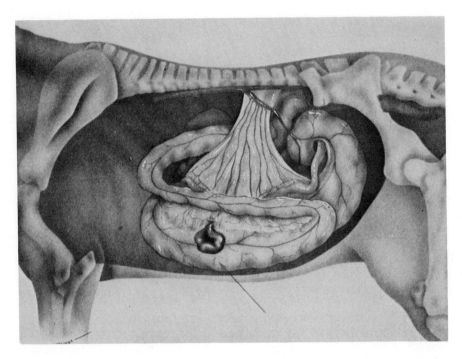

FIGURE 14-19 This illustration shows an internal hernia, which is sometimes incorrectly diagnosed as a twisted intestine. [Western Horseman. *Caption by Ted S. Stashak, D.V.M., Chairman, Department of Surgical Sciences, Miller Health Center, University of Florida, Gainesville. Art by Dennis Giddings, medical illustrator, Ft. Collins, Col.*]

food (carbohydrates) such as lush spring pasture, or gets into the feed bin, it is likely to founder. First signs are refusal of food, listlessness, sweating, and reluctance to move. The horse often takes the founder stance, with weight on the hind feet. One can feel a tremendous thumping or pulsing and distention of the digital artery on the inside of the front pastern. This is because the lamini are partially closed, preventing blood from flowing freely through the foot. The hoof will also be several degrees warmer than normal. Heart rate, blood pressure, and respiration rate are likely to be elevated, and the horse's temperature may be 2 or 3 degrees above normal. It is most important to have a veterinarian attend the horse within a period of 12 hours or less; its future soundness depends upon it. If the condition is suspected on Saturday morning, don't wait until Monday to have the horse checked.

*Cause.* There are a number of different conditions that cause founder in horses, but they all seem to have the common denominator of excessive lac-

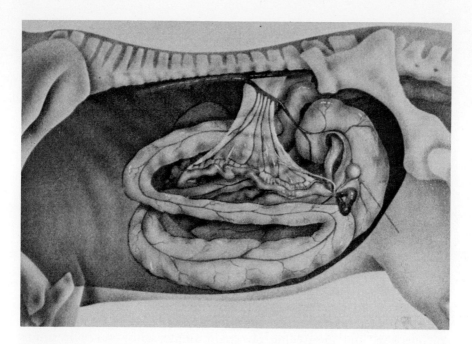

FIGURE 14-20   A lipoma is a fat tumor that forms from the mesentery. It can flip around the bowel just like a bolo, lock in position, shut off the blood supply, and block the passage of food material. [Western Horseman. *Caption by Ted S. Stashak, D.V.M., Chairman, Department of Surgical Sciences, Miller Health Center, University of Florida, Gainesville. Art by Dennis Giddings, medical illustrator, Ft. Collins, Col.*]

tic acid production in the bloodstream. Missouri researchers are able to produce founder with a measured mixture of corn starch and wood flour gruel administered directly to fistulated horses. Their research suggests that the optimal conditions for founder occur when horses consume large amounts of grain or lush spring grass that contains high levels of carbohydrate (glucose). Most horses that arrive at the University of Missouri clinic have been foundered on grass, with a large number having been grain foundered; however, there are many other causes. Any stressful condition may trigger founder in some horses that appear unusually susceptible to it. Examples are cold-water shock with an overheated horse, road founder, and foaling founder. When overheated horses are allowed to drink extremely cold water, they may fall to the ground. Founder may follow. The exact cause of water founder is unknown, but some researchers feel the microflora of the digestive system is radically changed, altering its normal role in digestion. Mares that retain part or all of the placenta occasionally founder. This is a result of infection in the uterus that affects bacterial flora in the gut. Road founder is different, as it rarely occurs quickly and intensively but rather more slowly, resulting in the same symptoms unless appropriately treated. In all of these types, there is a rise in lactic acid that plays a part in their severity or signals their seriousness. Luckily, some horses appear almost immune to founder.

*Treatment.*   The horse owner can identify the cause and remove it, but should call a veterinarian immediately for treatment. Upon arrival he or she will diagnose the condition and take steps to reduce its severity. These may start with administration of a gallon of mineral oil by stomach tube to reduce absorption of toxins in the gut and remove undigested food. Other measures may involve blocking the feet both to reduce constriction of blood vessels and ease the pain in the lower extremeties as well as increased exercise to clear the oxygenated blood in the feet and increase circulation. A tranquilizer is often used to further dilate blood vessels and allow the horse to move with less pain. Phenylbutazone (bute) is often left with the caretaker to feed to the horse to relieve pain so that exercise can be undertaken during the next several days. Many other treatments may be considered, for example, administration of electrolytes, injection of antibiotics to reduce secondary infection, and the feeding of certain amino acids, especially sulfur-containing amino acids, that may be useful in protein bonding in the laminae. Some veterinarians use antihistamines, but this practice is losing popularity as new research unfolds, and use of cortisone is now controversial.

*Prevention.*   Since laminitis is management-induced, it is easy to prevent in almost all cases. The main objective is to avoid stuffing with carbohydrates horses that receive little forced exercise. If you like a fat horse, you can greatly reduce the risk of laminitis by changing the grain-to-hay ratios in its diet. If you are feeding 15 pounds of grain and all the grass hay the horse can eat, it is in danger of foundering if it is fat and inactive. On the other hand, you can reduce the grain to 5 pounds or even eliminate it and feed a good legume hay, and the horse may consume the same amount of energy but in a substantially less soluble carbohydrate form. It is not possible to prevent obese, heavy-crested horses from foundering on lush spring pasture if they are inclined to do so. If they have foundered before, they are very likely to do it again; therefore, they must be kept off lush pasture or only be exposed to it for a short portion of each day. Of course any hardworking horse is virtually removed from the risk of feed founder unless it gets into the feed bin. The foaling mare cannot always be spared from foal founder; however, observation of her condition at foaling and ridding her promptly of the placenta will usually prevent it. Road founder may be corrected by working the horse less on hard surfaces or adapting a shoe for that type of work. Finally, shock to the microflora from cold water or other poor feeding practices should be avoided.

NAVICULAR DISEASE (NAVICULAR BURSITIS, PODOTROCHLEITIS)  Navicular disease is an inflammation of the navicular bursa inside the hoof, between the deep flexor tendon and the navicular bone. At an early stage the condition is hard to diagnose because both feet may be similarly affected and the horse may not show much lameness. X-rays may show no abnormalities. As the disease progresses, the fibrocartilage develops erosive lesions on the tendonous surface of the bone.[5] In some advanced cases the navicular bone may be eroded on its articular surface, causing extreme lameness. By this stage the surface of the tendon is usually frayed and may eventually be destroyed or ruptured.

*Symptoms.*    Horses with navicular disease may show increased lameness the day after work. They may point or rest alternate front feet in front of them to relieve weight. The horse has a short, stilted stride with toes landing first to relieve concussion at the heels, which results in excessive wear on the toe of the shoe. A hoof tester applied to the center of the frog and side of the hoof wall may locate soreness. If no other cause of lameness in the front feet can be found, the problem is probably navicular.

The disease is quite common to western stock horses with small feet. It is also associated with horses whose front feet constantly experience substantial percussion, for example, jumping horses, those traveling on hard surfaces, and horses carrying heavy weights. Since only the front feet are affected, the idea that percussion is a predisposing factor seems reasonable.

Some people feel that there is an inherited conformation that predisposes the horse to navicular disease. Upright conformation with straight shoulders and pasterns undoubtedly increases concussion and predisposes a horse to this condition. Small feet have less surface area over which to disperse concussion and shock, resulting in more pressure per square inch. Within a susceptible breed, it is uncommon to see navicular disease in a horse whose foot is one size larger than the average of the breed. A few farriers place much of the blame for navicular disease on poor horseshoeing. They claim that navicular can be avoided by maintaining the same angle of pastern and foot or by shoeing with a higher heel. The assertion that this technique will cure many horses already in some phase of the disease is indeed very interesting—but unlikely to be true. To add to the confusion, an Englishman now insists that none of these factors may be relevant, but rather that a lack of circulation in the distal sesamoid may be the cause.

[5]O. R. Adams, *Lameness in Horses*, 3d ed., Lea & Febiger, Philadelphia, 1977, p. 260.

Collin Colles presented a paper at a recent meeting of the British Equine Veterinary Association in York, England, in which he postulated that small arteries that feed the distal sesamoid bone of the foot can become clogged with thrombi (blood clots), starving the bone of nutrients.[6] The result is necrosis (dying tissue) and deterioration of the bone, resulting in rough surfaces with sharp edges. Upon feeding to twenty-six horses the anticoagulant (blood-thinning drug) warfarin, used also with humans and as rat poison, all but one recovered or showed marked improvement. His research will be tested here and elsewhere, and answers should soon be forthcoming. Obviously, careful control of dosage level would be essential.

*Treatment.* Rest will improve the condition in early stages, and horses may be effectively worked intermittently. If they can work on soft ground, serious lameness is avoided. A competent farrier should be employed, who, in most cases, will raise the heel of the horse approximately 3 degrees, either by using a tapered pad under the shoe or by shortening the toe and allowing the heels to grow longer. This takes pressure off the navicular bone and bursa and will often allow the horse to go sound under light work for a considerable length of time. Nerving, or surgically severing the requisite nerves to eliminate feeling in this portion of the foot, was widely practiced a few years ago. It has some substantial disadvantages, but on occasion it may be necessary. There is a tendency for the nerves to find a way to reconstitute themselves, and a return of lameness follows. Also, not all operations are successful. Furthermore, since that portion of the foot loses all feeling, it cannot respond to sharp objects, and the horse may thereby experience an equally undesirable injury. Regardless of the course taken, it should be under the direction of a veterinarian.

*Prevention.* Selecting a horse with a reasonably large foot that has enough slope to the walls to disperse concussion can prevent or postpone navicular disease. However, if horses are used hard on hard surfaces, wear and tear will eventually catch up with them in one way or another. One should not breed horses that develop navicular disease early in life. They may be producing conformation or predisposing effects that cause their offspring to develop the problem. Indeed, one should be very reluctant to breed to a stallion that has navicular disease. Finally, if horses can be spared extremely hard work on hard surfaces for long periods of time, they are less likely to contract the condition.

GRANULATION TISSUE (PROUD FLESH)    Proud flesh is nature's healing process gone haywire. No one knows exactly why this happens. The severed edges

[6]"British Studies in Navicular Research," *Equus*, no. 15, January 1979, p. 51.

of an open wound are cleared of dead cells by the horse's system, and then normal granulation begins. Capillaries sprout new cells that cluster and begin to fill in the wound. When a wound heals normally, the process occurs both at the bottom and the surface, and no proud flesh results. When healing occurs improperly, granulation tissue, or proud flesh, rapidly begins to grow and soon extends beyond the level of the wound. Proud flesh is covered with a scab and a matted secretion that can be soaked away in warm water and brushed with clean gauze. The rapid rate of growth and its extension beyond the wound are the hallmarks of proud flesh. If red granules appear larger in size each day, proud flesh is probably present.

*Treatment.*  Inspect wounds frequently. Bandage leg wounds. If proud flesh is suspected, treat it early. Talk to the veterinarian and obtain an agent to apply directly to the wound. If proud flesh is allowed to become sizable, surgery is almost certain, which inevitably entails an anxious wait to see if proud flesh will invade again.

AZOTURIA (MONDAY MORNING DISEASE, TYING-UP)  Monday morning disease, or azoturia, was a familiar condition in the days of hardworking draft horses. Tying-up, which is thought to be a milder form of this condition, is more common recently. The condition is called "Monday morning sickness" because hardworking horses in athletic condition that were full-fed grain on Sunday (their day off) exhibited signs of the condition soon after starting work on Monday. Recently, athletic event horses, racehorses, and other hardworking horses have exhibited a less severe but similar symptom called tying-up syndrome. After an idle period, the athletic horse is worked hard from 10 to 30 minutes before signs of azoturia or tying-up appear. The first sign may be stiffness with profuse sweating and a stiffness of gait. The muscles of the loins are tense and hard. Horses may attempt to urinate; if they succeed, the urine is coffee-colored or reddish brown, indicating muscle destruction and the loss of myoglobin.

*Treatment.*  On no account should the horse be moved or walked back to the stable. The condition is acutely painful because of the accumulation of lactic acid in muscles, and severe muscle damage and inflammation would result if the horse were forced to exercise further. In fact, if they are forced to move, horses often go down and die. A veterinarian should treat the condition. He or she will administer a relaxant, possibly cortisone, and other drugs to induce rest. Horses that experience azoturia once may do so again. They will recover from it if appropriately treated; if not, they will be permanently disabled. Tying-up is considered by some to be a mild form of azoturia. It is treated in the same way, with rest and freedom from work.

*Cause.*    Heavy grain feeding on days off is a major cause. Grain should be cut in half and hay increased for hardworking horses. Long nonstop trips in trucks and vans seem to encourage tying-up. Females are more susceptible to tying-up than males. The season may affect the condition: the cool days of early spring when horses are eager to travel may produce more problems. Also, nervous, high-strung horses are more likely to have trouble. Some veterinarians recommend blanketing a draft horse early in the morning on cold days if it must stand while a wagon is being loaded, to reduce the chance of the condition. Undoubtedly there are many important interactions among feeding, management, and environment in the etiology of these two conditions. Careful management usually prevents their occurrence. Many good horsemen have used horses throughout their own lifetimes without ever having seen either condition.

# CARE OF THE HORSE'S FEET

O f all the elements of good horse care, care of the hoof is the job most often neglected. And yet nothing could be truer than the old-timer's adage, "No foot, no horse." To indicate the importance of the hoof, it has been said that the horse has not one but five hearts—one in the normal place and one in each foot, contracting and expanding in rhythm with movement and assisting the heart in circulating blood in the extremities.

Basic foot care is discussed in Chapter 6. Here, the anatomy and physiology of the foot, stride and stance evaluation, and key elements in trimming and shoeing are discussed.

## ANATOMY AND PHYSIOLOGY OF THE FOOT

Before you trim or shoe a horse, it is essential that the structure and function of the feet be understood. For discussion, let us consider three different functional groups: (1) the hoof, or horn, that houses and protects the inner,

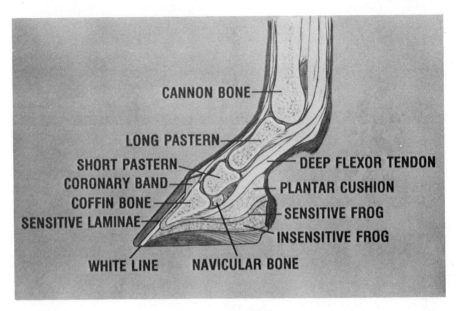

FIGURE 15-1   Anatomy of the foot and pastern. [*Photograph by Doug Ross,* Columbia, *Mo.*]

sensitive parts; (2) the bones and tendons, or structural and motor parts; and (3) the elastic, shock-absorbing structures, or wear parts.

### The Hoof Wall and Outer Structures

Familiar to all is the horny hoof wall that protects the inner sensitive structures of the foot and permits the horse to walk on rocks without pain or to stand in snow without cold feet (Figures 15-1 and 15-2). This hard, tubular, but flexible structure is composed of epithelial cells cemented together with keratin, a fibrous sulfur-containing protein. Even dense walls are approximately 25 percent water, which aids elasticity.

The hoof wall, of course, is insensitive, as are the periople, bars, sole, and frog. All these insensitive structures are produced and nourished by correspondingly named sensitive coriums lying just underneath.

Therefore, looking at the hoof wall from outside to inside we find three layers of insensitive tissue: (1) the outer, the periople or perioplic band and stratum tectorium; (2) the middle, tubular and dense; and (3) the inner, laminar layer that forms the epidermal laminae and connects the hoof to the sensitive laminae.

The periople or perioplic band functions like the human cuticle. The

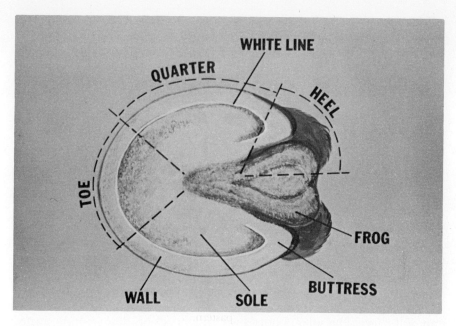

FIGURE 15-2   Ground surface of the foot. [*Photograph by Doug Ross, Columbia, Mo.*]

perioplic band lies above the hoof wall and the coronary band and is about ¼ inch wide. The periople is in turn produced and maintained by the inner sensitive structure, the perioplic corium. The perioplic band secretes a waxy substance formed of keratinized cells, called the "stratum tectorium." The tectorium, when well maintained, seals moisture in the hoof. Under conditions of dryness or when rasped by a farrier, the tectorium can become brittle and lose its protective quality.

The coronary band lies at the top of the hoof. It is produced and maintained by the underlying coronary corium. The tubular, dense, middle layer of the hoof wall is produced by the coronary band. An injury to the coronary band will result in a blemish in the hoof wall that can be traced as it grows its way down to the toe. An injury to the underlying coronary corium can result in permanently damaged hoof walls, because all growth originates there. The keratinized tubules formed by the coronary band run lengthwise down the hoof. They are hollow but, when well maintained, they contain much moisture.

The inner or laminar layer of the hoof wall ultimately connects the outer hoof to the coffin bone by a dovetailing of the outer, insensitive laminae (which in turn are covered by very fine, also insensitive secondary laminae) with the inner, sensitive structures of the laminar corium. The interlocking resembles the mingling of fine, delicate fern fronds in shape and complexity, yet it is tremendously strong.

Seen from the bottom of the foot are the wall, the white line, the sole, the frog, and the bulbs of the heel (Figure 15-2). The sole horn is produced by the sole corium, a sensitive structure located at the bottom of the coffin bone while the frog horn is produced by the frog corium. Despite its position at the bottom of the foot, the sole is not meant to bear the weight of the horse, and for this reason, it is naturally slightly concave. The important function of the sole is to protect from damage the sensitive internal structures of the foot. When the sole comes in direct contact with the ground through improper shoeing or concussion from a wedged rock, sole bruises result. The frog is an elastic shock absorber, and, because it comes in contact with the ground when the horse puts weight on the foot, it gives the foot its grip.

Like the wall, the sole consists of approximately one-third water. Its nutrients and blood supply come from the corium of the sole, which supports growth through tubules that terminate by curling near the ground surface. Dead sole is shed by constant mild abrasion from irregular ground surfaces, especially small gravel or rocks, and by expansion and contraction of the feet. The soles of horses with hoof pads or those with contracted heels (which results in little expansion) are protected, and they may require paring with a sole knife when shod.

The frog is a V-shaped structure. The sensitive or inner frog covers the digital cushion and it, in turn, is covered on the outside by the insensitive frog, which it secretes through papillae. Unlike the sole, the insensitive frog does not flake away but is shed twice yearly.

For the purposes of discussion, the wall can be divided into three parts: the toe, the quarters, and the heels. The wall at the toe is thicker than at the quarters, partly because of its greater angle, while at the heels it is thinnest—except with crooked feet. When one wall is straight and the other sloping, such as the inside wall of a splay-footed horse, the straight wall will be thinnest at the quarter. The hoof wall bends sharply back at the heels to form the "angle of wall" and resulting bars of the heels. These bars serve as braces to strengthen the walls and should not be pared away or "opened" when trimming.

The white line is an extension of the laminar corium, and it attaches the sole to the wall. It separates sensitive from insensitive tissues and serves as a guide for the farrier. Nails may be driven into or outside the white line but never inside it, lest they quick the horse. Healthy feet may show white lines (actually they are gray) of approximately ⅛ to ¼ inch wide from heel to toe. Seedy toe is separation resulting from old age or founder and may widen the white line at the toe from ½ to 1 inch or even cause enough separation to form a cavity that fills with dirt and filth. Infection in such feet is difficult to prevent and control.

## Bones and Tendons

There are four bones and two tendons in the foot. Bones and tendons are dense tissues with limited blood supplies, and they repair slowly when injured. The four bones are the first phalanx, or long pastern bone, extending from the ankle above to the second phalanx below; the second phalanx, or short pastern bone, that articulates at the bottom with the coffin bone; the coffin bone, or third phalanx; and the navicular bone.

The coffin bone sits deep in the horny wall and follows its shape to some extent. Its front and sides are rough, providing a good surface for attachment of the laminar corium that holds it firmly to and parallel with the front and sides of the hoof wall. These vertical laminae and the perforation of the coffin bone with blood vessels permit a good blood supply to nourish the foot. The secure attachment of the interlocking laminae of the coffin bone to the horny foot wall prevents the weight of the horse from literally pushing the coffin bone through the sole of the foot, a condition not uncommon when the attachment is destroyed by severe founder. The back of the coffin bone is flared into wings on each side to accommodate the attachment of the two lateral cartilages.

The navicular bone (distal sesamoid bone) is an integral part of the coffin joint that articulates with the second and third phalanges, providing a larger articulating surface area for this important joint. The front face of the navicular bone articulates in the coffin joint, and the back surface is covered with cartilage to accommodate the movement over its surface of the deep digital flexor tendon. One might say the navicular bone is "between a rock and a hard place" in the concussion chain. There is little wonder that navicular disease plagues small-footed (and small-navicular-jointed) horses that are used hard on hard surfaces. When heels are trimmed too short or toes left too long, the weight of the horse is shifted too far backward, exerting excessive pressure on the bursa of the deep digital flexor tendon and navicular bone and joint.

Tendons attach muscles to bones. They work opposite each other in the feet and legs, one extending and one flexing. The tendon of the common extensor enters the foot from above at the front of the hoof and attaches to the coffin bone near its uppermost surface. Its function is to move the foot and leg forward. The deep flexor tendon enters the foot at the back and attaches to the coffin bone on the lower back side. It flexes the foot and leg and is important in dissipating concussion.

## Shock-absorbing Structures

One must not forget the contribution of a sloping shoulder when discussing shock absorption from pastern and foot. Short straight pasterns and shoulders do not absorb concussion well and wear out both horse and rider.

Conversely, long, weak pasterns place excessive leverage on the deep flexor tendon, bursa, and navicular bone, and they encourage navicular disease. The most desirable front toe angle for western horses may be 48° to 52°, with slightly less for some gaited breeds. Any angle must be discussed in relation to the slope of pastern and shoulder as well, however.

The lateral cartilages are two large, rather thin plates of very elastic tissue extending above, and attaching to, the coronary band at the heels and to the wings of the coffin bone in the foot. Palpation of the lateral cartilages at the heels reveals their flexibility in young horses and their ossification (process of turning to bone) in old, worn-out horses with sidebones.

The digital cushion is a wedge-shaped mass of fibrous tissue extending from the heels forward on top of the sole and under the coffin bone and joint. It absorbs shock and pumps blood.

CONCUSSION   When weight is brought to bear on a front foot, part of the shock is absorbed by the shoulder and pastern, but much of it must be absorbed by the foot. Downward pressure lowers the ankle and tightens the deep flexor tendon which supports the coffin joint by supporting the coffin bone. Pressure from the coffin bone compresses the digital cushion, which flattens and widens, causing a sinking of the concave sole directly under it, which also helps the digital cushion to expand the horny hoof wall at the heels and quarters. The lateral cartilages attached to the wings of the coffin bone compress downward and spread, also aiding expansion of the hoof wall. To some extent the laminae help absorb shock. The action of fluids in the foot (blood and water) has been compared to that of a "water bed" in helping to absorb shock by dissipating it in different directions. Pressure on the foot forces blood out of veins in the digital cushion and other tissues and upward toward the ankle, to be replaced by arterial blood with moisture and sustenance for the foot. Dry, hard, or contracted feet are as much a result of poor circulation as of anything else.

Thus, we find a number of structures performing different actions, the sum of which creates a remarkable shock-absorbing mechanism.

## SHOEING

Horseshoeing is an ancient art. Physically it has always been difficult. Mentally, it is no more demanding than many other tasks, but it does require skill, which, in turn, comes from practice and a conscientious effort to improve with each experience.

The anxiety that beginners feel about injuring the horse is not necessary, provided that they follow acceptable procedures and remain alert. They fear drawing blood by nipper or knife and quicking from driven nails. It is very difficult to nip the hoof wall into the quick, and paring on the sole that

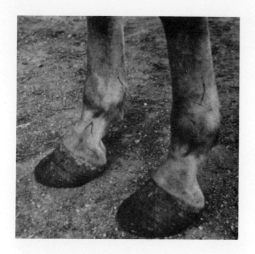

FIGURE 15-3   There is no excuse to justify leaving shoes on your horse this long. Overgrown heels invite corns; and the lowered hoof angle increases risk of sprained tendons, navicular disease, and stumbling. Most horse owners, for the sake of their horses, should learn to remove shoes and trim feet. [*Photograph by the author.*]

stops when live tissue appears is safe. Quicking with a nail occurs only when it is driven inside the white line or if it is turned backward to drift inward instead of outward. High nails do not quick horses. Beginners do get heels trimmed too low, feet trimmed crookedly, and shoes on crookedly, but none of these results in permanent lameness unless the mistake is repeated frequently.

A horse's feet grow ¼ to ⅜ inch per month. They should be trimmed every 6 to 8 weeks. To prevent irregular breaks in the wall which would result in unbalanced distribution of weight and difficult feet to shoe, do not allow this growth to exceed ½ inch before it is either trimmed or the foot is shod.

Most horse owners should be able to remove a shoe and trim feet in emergencies or while awaiting the appearance of the farrier (Figure 15-3). Many can learn to adequately cold shoe normal feet with professional supervision. No one should attempt to shoe without either some professional supervision in a reputable farriers' school or an apprenticeship with a competent farrier. The longest—or shortest—schools may not be the best—or worst; a school should be judged by the material presented and the experience gained. It is important for beginners, and indeed all farriers, to know what they can handle adequately and what they need help with. Obviously, a beginner graduating from a brief farriers' school will not wish to practice on an expensive, show-winning horse. However, he can evaluate the quality of work that his farrier does and appreciate those efforts much more after having had shoeing experience himself.

## Removing Shoes

Good tools, especially cutting tools, are essential for working on a horse's feet (Figure 15-4). Dull, inadequate tools double the time required for the

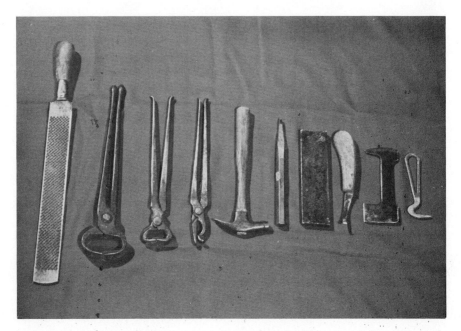

FIGURE 15-4   Good tools are essential for proper hoof care. *Left* to *right:* thin, light "race track" rasp; pinchers or "pull-offs"; professional hoof nippers; clincher; 10-ounce farrier's hammer; pritchel; clinch block; farrier's knife; clinch cutter; hoof pick. Not shown are farrier's apron or chaps for safety when nailing. [*Photograph by Duane Dailey*.]

job, and both horse and farrier get impatient, creating an environment that may precipitate an unpleasant confrontation. A hoof pick, clinch cutter, hammer, and pincher are useful in removing shoes. If the foot needs trimming, add to these three, good-quality cutting tools: nipper, hoof knife, and thin-tanged racetrack rasp and handle. A hoof level or angle to measure slope of the trimmed feet is also very useful and results in higher-quality work. (See Chapter 6 for safe foot-handling procedures.)

Clinches of old nails must be straightened to remove the shoe. If the shoe is pulled without this operation, not only will it be more difficult to remove, but the walls of the hoof and sole may also be injured. Clinches may be straightened with the clinch cutter or rasped off. This extra, "pull off" rasp is usually an old rasp no longer used to level the foot.

Place the blade edge of the clinch cutter under the clinch and straighten it for pulling with light hammer blows. If you have difficulty getting it started, lean the top out and use the back corner nearest your hand. Most commercial farriers rasp the clinches off with the fine side of the rasp, because it is faster than using a clinch cutter; however, this method results in more damage to the hoof wall. Avoid damaging the coronary band at the top of the hoof when handling the rasp. If the hoof wall is rasped above the clinches, a change in technique is indicated.

Place the shoe pullers (pinchers) under the shoe at the heel and push down toward the toe to remove the shoe. This manipulation is repeated on the opposite heel, always working toward the toe, until the shoe is completely free. Don't pry sidewise, because of danger of sprains to the horse's tendons and bruise damage to the sole of its foot. If you find this method difficult, complete the first step and then drive the shoe back down on the hoof exposing the nail heads. Nails can then be pulled one at a time.

## Trimming Feet

When shoes are pulled or lost, the wall should be trimmed; otherwise pieces are likely to break out, making reshoeing more difficult. It is important when learning to trim and shoe to work with normal, straight feet. Leave crooked feet for later. However, one should understand the effect that crookedness has on a horse's movement and how much or how little corrective trimming should be done.

PRELIMINARY EXAMINATION OF STANCE AND STRIDE  A preliminary examination of how the horse stands and moves should be made before trimming. Ideally you see straight legs under each corner of the body with toes pointed forward, but few horses are actually this straight. Stand in front of the horse to see if it is splayfooted or pigeon-toed (Figure 15-5 and Figure 4-7). If so, is the cause simply crooked ankles, or are the feet and knees also involved? If bones are seriously crooked, the horse can't be "straightened up" but may be made serviceable. If the horse is narrow-chested, base-narrow, and splayfooted interfering is likely. Look at the ankles for scars. Ask the owner if the horse interferes. If the horse is pigeon-toed, it may wing, and if shod with weight or if the hooves are left long, winging will worsen as speed increases.

Move to the side to appraise the length and slope of the shoulder, pastern, and hoof angle (Figure 15-6 and Figure 4-8). The angle of hoof and pastern should be the same; otherwise the hoof is broken forward if the heels are too high or backward if too low. If the horse has straightened pasterns, breaking it back by reducing the length of the heels to make it look more sloping (and thus presumably more acceptable to judges and buyers) may encourage navicular disease. If the side view reveals low heels and long toes in front, the horse may overreach in action. Shortening the toe and using heeled shoes may be indicated. Keep in mind the fact that a change in hoof angle changes the stride. High heels shorten but increase the height of the stride, with the highest point coming after the halfway point in foot

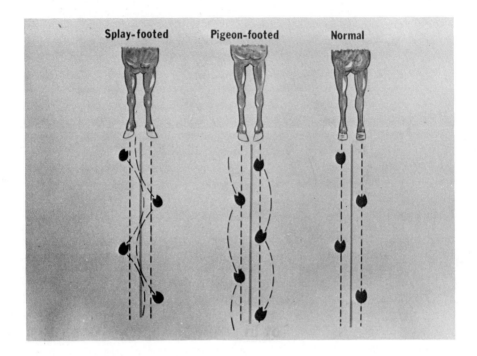

**FIGURE 15-5** "Normal" or straight-fronted horses are expected to break directly over their toes and move their feet forward in a straight line without inward or outward deviation in foot flight. They are shod "normal" with equal amounts of wall trimmed from each side of their hoofs. Splay-footed horses bring their feet inward in motion, often interfering (striking the ankle of the supporting leg). Because of disproportionate weight distribution, the inside wall wears fastest, requiring more trimming on the outside wall when shod. Pigeon-toed horses travel opposite to splay-footed horses and are trimmed opposite. [*By Doug Ross.*]

flight. They also increase break-over, i.e., a difference in the speed at which the front and back feet leave the ground. Continue the side view as you evaluate the back leg and foot. Sickle hocks and shallow heels tend to be correlated, as do post legs and high heels.

Stand behind the horse to check for cow hocks, wide hocks, and splayed feet; observe how squarely the feet meet the ground (Figure 4-10). Cow hocks may cause extra weight to be borne on the inside hoof walls, resulting in more wear there than on the outside walls. Wide hocks may cause long inside walls for the same reason. The response of the back feet to correction is less predictable and often less rewarding than that of the front feet.

Move to a distance of approximately 100 feet, and have the horse walked and trotted directly toward you and away from you. The effects of the de-

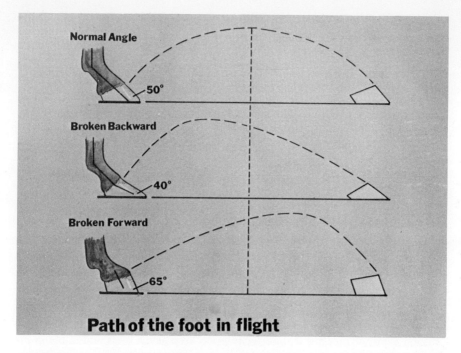

Normal Angle

50°

Broken Backward

40°

Broken Forward

65°

**Path of the foot in flight**

FIGURE 15-6   "Normal" feet reach their high point in stride when passing the supporting leg. The angle of pastern and hoof "breaks backward" in low-heeled feet causing the high point of stride to come early. Trimming the toe and leaving the heels high may improve stride, reduce stumbling, and relieve pressure on the navicular joint. Heels are high in "broken forward" feet. The stride is stilted and choppy, and feet tend to land hard. Lowering the heels is indicated. [*By Doug Ross.*]

fects that you saw standing will be magnified in action. If the horse stood splayfooted, it should swing its feet inward at both the walk and trot. If it is pigeon-toed, they should wing. Observe for closeness or possible interfering behind as it moves away from you. Move to the side to see how promptly it moves, whether its feet drag, or whether it tends to forge or overreach.

Stop the horse and review what you saw. If it is straight, it needs no correction and should be easy to shoe with a light, plain shoe. If it has broken back heels, heeled shoes may be indicated. If its feet are splayed or pigeon-toed, the long side should receive most of the trimming.

TRIMMING TECHNIQUE   Begin trimming the foot by removing the loose, shelly, or flaky, part of the bars, taking extreme care not to trim the solid part of these structures, since they are essential to the support of the hoof. Next, trim each side of the frog just enough to open the seams. This will help keep filth from collecting, which predisposes a horse to thrush. Don't lower the frog. This structure should touch the ground when the horse stands on the trimmed foot.

After the frog and bars have been trimmed, use your hoof knife to trim out the soft, flaky part of the sole in order to determine how much of the hoof wall to trim away. Observe the juncture of the sole and wall at the toe. Decide how much will need to come off the toe and how much less from the heels. Now start your nipper at the heel of the hoof at a depth halfway to the level of the sole (Figure 15-7). There is a tendency for beginners to get too deep at the heel and not deep enough at the toe. Since the wall at the heel is thin, it can be easily reduced later with the rasp if too high. Proceed around the hoof until you finish at the opposite heel. The hoof wall should not be trimmed below the level of the sole. The hoof should now appear relatively level and both heels should be the same height. A relatively level hoof that requires a minimum of rasping is not easy for beginners to achieve. The sole serves as a guide for the nippers, and there is a tendency not to lower it adequately. This results in unevenness or failure to remove enough of the wall. Such a condition is not serious, but it requires unnecessary rasping.

FIGURE 15-7   Good professional nippers facilitate hoof trimming and foot care. Uniform depth of nipping without getting too deep at the heels and dubbing the toe are important in your trimming technique. [*Photograph courtesy of Animal Science Department, Cornell University.*]

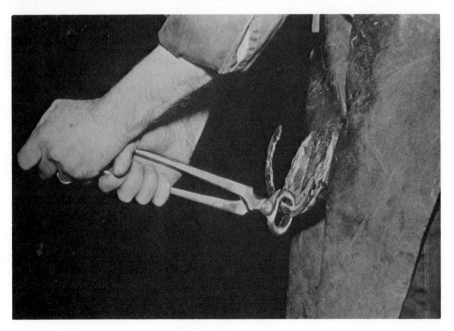

Use the rasp to finish trimming. Push the rasp from the heel toward the toe, taking care to keep the pressure equal over the entire foot without removing too much from the heels. Move the rasp around over the sides and toe, being careful not to get too deep in one spot. Use a sharp rasp for ease and speed in trimming (Figure 15-8). The rasp may be reversed and drawn from the toe toward the heel. Take special care not to apply too much pressure on the rasp at the heel. If the heels are lowered too much, the hoof will not have the correct angle.

When you think the foot is level, check levelness by sighting down the hoof from heel to toe. Drop the hoof down so it rests in a normal position with the hoof hanging free. Holding the hoof itself may result in its being slightly twisted, and it may therefore appear level when it is not. Be sure that neither heel is high and that there are no low spots around the wall.

When trimming is completed, the hoof should usually have an angle of 48° to 52°, depending on the conformation of the particular horse (slope of shoulder and length and slope of pastern). Use your hoof level to maintain the same angle of the pastern with the front of the hoof. It is very important that both front and both hind feet have the same angle. Check frequently with your hoof level as you rasp.

FIGURE 15-8    Level the foot with a sharp rasp by uniform pressure and frequent movement around the foot. Both right- and left-handed rasping technique are required. [*Photograph courtesy of Animal Science Department, Cornell University.*]

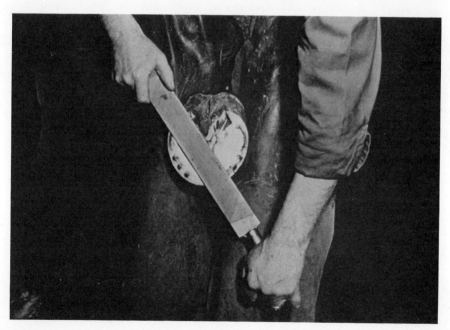

If the hoof is to be trimmed and not shod, all that remains is to round the edges of the hoof wall and lower the sole. Round the edges of the wall with the fine side of the rasp. Remove the sharp edges to about one-fourth the thickness of the wall. This reduces the chance of having pieces of the wall broken out. If the hoof is to be shod, however, this step is omitted.

Lowering the sole is important because it allows the horse's weight to be distributed on the insensitive hoof wall rather than on the sole. Since the sensitive part of the foot lies directly underneath the sole, lameness may result from failure to perform this operation. Take the curved edge of a sharp hoof-trimming knife, and lower the sole below the wall.

## Shoeing

If you aspire to shoe commercially, you may wish to take instruction in cold shoeing to confirm your intent and then enter a good school that teaches forging and shoeing. Remember, it takes months and possibly years to become competent at both. If you shoe all comers, including gaited show horses, one or more years' apprenticeship with a master farrier is indicated. Considerably less time is required to learn satisfactory cold shoeing. Although cold shoeing is denigrated by some horse owners, a very large percentage of horses can use this method quite satisfactorily, and the farrier who chooses it may be as skilled in preparing the foot and applying the shoe as his blacksmithing counterpart who forges a shoe from a steel rod. However, special corrective and therapeutic shoes must be forged, and they should not be attempted by cold horseshoers.

SELECTING SHOES, PADS, AND NAILS    Shoes are available in endless kinds, sizes, and weights. Hot shoes have long heels that are cut to fit the foot, turned out for trailers, or otherwise shaped. Cold shoes are available in plain, toe weight, heeled, aluminum plain, aluminum heeled and/or toed, rim shoes, and many more. Weights may be saddle-light, light, medium, or heavy. The numbering of shoe sizes differs among companies. Comparable horseshoe sizes are:

| Old method | A newer method |
|:---:|:---:|
| 00 | 4 |
| 0 | 5 |
| 1 | 6 |
| 2 | 7 |
| 3 | 9 |

Since the two kinds of sizes are not exactly equivalent, they complement each other, which makes "in-between" sizes easy to fit if both types are available.

Easyboots® by Les-Kare, Inc., came on the market in 1972. These are fiber and rubber boots shaped like the foot that slip over it, are clipped on with a small cable and fastener, and fastened around the ankle with a strap. The advantages claimed are ease of application and a more natural state for the horse's feet than that given by shoes. They have been used with satisfaction in 100-mile distance rides and are excellent for medicating or protecting an injured foot. Although a number of accessories are available for fitting various types of feet, they fit normal feet best. Their price may appear high, and regular foot trimming is necessary with their use.

In general, the lightest and least complex shoe that will fit the foot and support the horse without bending should be used. Cowboy or plain light or saddle-light may be indicated for foot sizes 00 to 1. However, larger-footed horses may require light to medium shoes. Flat-footed or low-heeled horses may use heeled shoes to advantage, but their use on the hind feet of hard-stopping western horses should be discouraged. Fox Trotters and some other gaited horses are often started in toe-weighted shoes.

Shoe pads, formerly all leather, are now available in a variety of plastics, rubber, and other materials. They are used mainly to protect the sole from rocks or injury and to hold wound dressings in place during recovery from an injury. Tapered pads are used with navicular disease.

Nails range in size from 3 to 9 but 5s and 6s are most commonly used. In general, size 5 fits 00 to 1 shoes and size 6 is suitable for 1s through 3s. There are two head shapes, "regular" and "city." City heads are smaller than regular heads, and they are often used with new shoes. If reset, regular heads may fit worn nail holes best. Nails are flat on one side and beveled at the point on the other to facilitate drifting out of the hoof wall when driven. The head of the nail is also beveled on the same side as the point and roughened to indicate the correct way to turn the nail when it is driven. The beveled side of the nail head is always on the inside of the foot, smooth side out, to cause the point to drift out of the hoof wall (Figure 15-9). Nail points are not all uniformly tapered. Modern manufacturing processes produce nails with varying degrees of slope at their points, ranging from none to extensively tapered. They should be checked and culled when top workmanship is required.

If you shoe, more tools are required: a caliper to measure hoof length, a pritchel to open nail holes, a clinch block upon which to clinch nails, a clincher with which to clinch them, and, above all, a farrier's apron. Never drive a nail without one, because even the gentlest horse can become excited under some circumstances and jerk a nail into you.

Anvils are expensive. Old ones can sometimes be bought at reasonable prices or satisfactory ones made from large railroad track irons. The best anvils are those made for horseshoeing with large horns and long, thin heels that accommodate the heels of shoes through the hardy hole for bending.

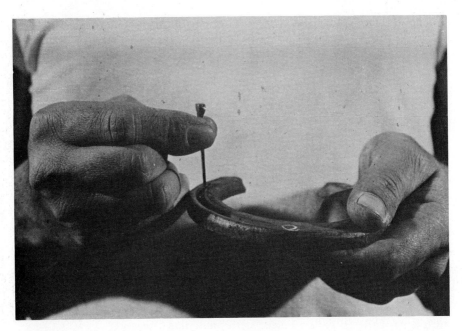

FIGURE 15-9   There are only two ways to injure or "quick" a horse with a nail: (1) if driven inside the white line; and (2) if turned backward to drift into the foot. Properly fitted shoes and technique described in the text eliminate driving inside the white line. Driving the nail, straight side out, causes the point to drift out. [*Photograph by Duane Dailey.*]

SHAPING THE SHOE   For the beginner, one of the most difficult parts of shoeing is shaping the shoe. The first rule is to shape the shoe to fit the foot. Shaping the shoe is made easier by marking the heels of the foot and making a paper tracing from heel to heel. Use a white grease pencil if the hoof is dark and mark the back of the heel where the heel of the shoe stops on each side of the foot. Trace the outline of the foot on a stiff cardboard or tablet. It is a good idea to keep tracings of your horse's trimmed hooves on hand for purchasing shoes, as some shoes are not numbered conventionally for size. A well-shaped front foot is uniformly round and wide at both heel and toe. Since horseshoes seldom come in this shape, substantial shaping will be necessary. Shaping is made easier by using the pattern. Remember to have the ground surface of the shoe down when using the pattern.

Most new shoes are too narrow for the front feet and must be spread. Place the shoe over the horn of your anvil and strike the toe. Try it on the pattern and get the correct width of toe and branches before bending the heels in. Turn the heels in by raising one heel at a time up through the hardy hole in your anvil to the point where the bend is needed. Drive it down with your hammer, then test it with the pattern.

When the shoe has been fitted to the foot, it must be leveled. Use the face of the anvil to get it level. This is an easy task for an experienced farrier, but it can be demanding on the patience of the beginner. Don't hurry; get it right. Check the levelness on the flat surface of a plywood block ¾ by 6 by 6 inches (Figure 15-10). If the shoe rocks, it has a high spot in it. With a little practice a shoe can be made perfectly level by using a board to check accuracy. Perfect levelness is desirable for both shoe and foot for equal weight distribution. High spots cause a shoe to rock and work loose, and they place undue strain on part of the hoof wall.

Although there are exceptions, most horse's hind feet are somewhat narrow and pointed at the toe. In order to shape a shoe, which is initially round at the toe, flatten each branch of the shoe near the toe on the heel of the anvil and try for size on the pattern. Upon flattening the branches, the shoe will be widened considerably at the heel and must therefore be drawn together on the face of the anvil to get the desired narrowness at the toe. The heels can then be turned in as previously described and shaping is complete.

Nail holes are too small in many manufactured shoes to accommodate the nail. Try a no. 5 city-head nail for shoe size 1 and under. Punch holes with the pritchel until the nail head protrudes about $1/16$ inch. If the nail

FIGURE 15-10  Sounder horses, convenience, and economy are results of formal training in foot care and horseshoeing. This instructor checks levelness of a shoe before the student nails it on. [*Photograph by Duane Dailey.*]

head goes flush into the shoe, it cannot be tightened. If it does not go deep enough, it will wear off and the shoe will loosen.

Turn the shoe over and file the burrs off with the fine side of the rasp. You may have sprung the shoe out of level if you hammered hard on it. Try it back on the board for levelness. Now the shoe should fit the foot nicely with no gaps between hoof and shoe. Check for high spots under the shoe by trying to rock it from front to rear and side to side. If it will rock, rasp off the high spot and lower the sole at that point. The heel of the shoe should extend ¼ inch behind the heel of the front hoof. It should be ⅛ inch wider than the heel at each branch.

NAILING THE SHOE ON    Now you are ready to nail the shoe on. Remember the white line. It marks the sensitive part from the insensitive horny hoof. Thus, any nail driven inside this line will cause pain to the horse and will result in lameness. It is therefore important to drive all nails along or just outside this line. If nails are driven very far outside the white line, they will split the hoof out and the shoe will come off prematurely. Remember, the beveled side of horseshoe nails goes on the inside or nearest the center of the foot.

When preparing to nail the shoe onto the hoof, it is important to position it so that the toe is fitted flush with the toe of the hoof. Position the shoe carefully and recheck for levelness. Don't set the shoe back and dub off the toe of the foot. Now you are ready to drive the first nail.

If the horse is gentle—and it should be—consider alternately driving two heel nails. Shoes "crawl" less with heel nails than toe nails and quicking is less likely with this procedure. Start a heel nail, flat side out in the outside, front of the back nail hole with shoe placed correctly on the foot. Drive the nail part way in with no concern about movement of the shoe. With another nail handy, reposition the shoe and start the second heel nail. If you have correctly shaped the shoe, these nails will have entered the outside of the white line and all other nail holes toward the toe will be outside it; thus the only way to quick the horse would be to drive a nail in backwards. Raise both heels of the shoe to verify this before continuing. A shoe moves both inward to the center of the foot and backward when nailed. If one heel of the shoe is out farther than the other, drive that nail first. Otherwise, alternate between the two. Twist the two nails off, and lower the foot for inspection before continuing. If the shoe is not on straight, remove it and start over again.

Next, move to the front nail. If the shoe is fuller on one side (even with or slightly beyond the wall), drive that nail first. Since the wall is steeper at the front, nails come out lower there if they are driven with the same slant as heel nails. Leaning the nail out at the top at more than a right angle to the plant of the foot should bring the nail out on the hoof wall at the appropriate height of 1 inch. Light hammer blows will drive nails deeper or higher in the wall. Hard blows bring them out sooner or lower. Three nails on a side will hold almost any well-fitting shoe and spare the wall excessive nail holes. Once through the hoof wall, safety dictates that each nail immediately be bent over with the claws of the hammer and twisted off flush with the hoof wall (Figure 15-11). Get the hammer against the foot for a short clinch on the nail. Push the nail to the bottom between the claws of the hammer for twisting off. If the previous nail end did not dislodge, you will not get a satisfactory job.

After all nails are driven, they must be set by placing a clinching block or nipper under the nail stub and striking the head of the nail. This tightens the shoe on the hoof and locks the nail head in the shoe. Excessive hammering will pull the clinches too far down to be rasped under. Rasp off the burrs of splintered hoof wall under each nail with the fine edge of the rasp next to the nail and the fine side next to the hoof. Smooth the twisted ends of the nails on top with the flat, fine side of the rasp before clinching. Although clinching can be completed with hammer and clinching bar, it is much easier done with clinchers. This tool is placed over the nail head and stub end and squeezed together, thus clinching the nail on the hoof wall. Take care to place the lower jaw of the clinchers over the nail head to prevent pushing the nail out of the hoof.

FIGURE 15-11    Safety dictates twisting the nail point off promptly after driving. [*Photograph Courtesy of Animal Science Department, Cornell University.*]

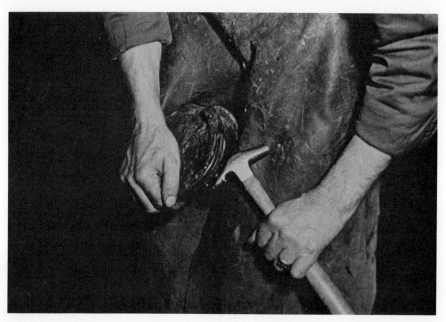

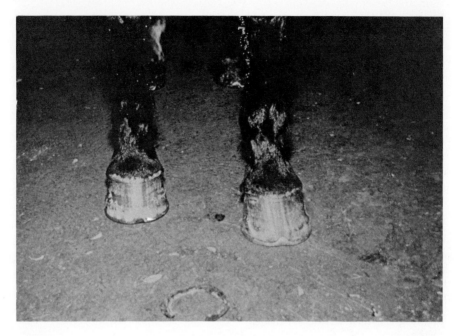

FIGURE 15-12   Right shoe has been removed, foot trimmed, and shoe reset. Left foot shows approximate maximum allowable length before resetting shoe. [*Courtesy of Animal Science Department, Cornell University.*]

FINISHING   The goal is evenly spaced nails of adequate height and a shoe fitted "full," that is, out to the edge of the hoof, with no gaps of "daylight" between hoof and shoe (Figure 15-12). If you find a space under the shoe that a knife blade could enter, you have a poor job.

After all nails have been clinched, you are ready to dress off any excess hoof which may protrude over the shoe. There should be very little, if any, of this except with foundered or flared feet. Don't rasp above the clinched nail. To do so is injurious to the hoof wall and may result in drying out or cracking of the hoof.

## Corrective Trimming and Shoeing

Corrective trimming is defined as "any reduction in hoof wall that results in a closer approach to the normal hoof." This means a long wall on one side may be shortened so as to make it equal to—but never shorter than—the opposite wall. Shortening should be done slowly, approximately $3/16$ inch at each trimming or shoeing. Excessive "corrective trimming" of badly crooked-legged horses can result in lameness from stretching ligaments on the short side and "realigning" joints when the long side of the foot is reduced too much or too quickly. However, if a splayfooted horse is totally "left to nature" and the condition not corrected, it may interfere and leave the horse useful only to a slaughterer.

Judgment must be used in corrective trimming and shoeing. Owners of halter show horses with less than perfect stances often pressure farriers to "straighten him up." A badly crooked horse with an excellent head and body is not a "useful horse with crooked feet and legs." It is a "useless horse with an excellent head and body" because crookedness is genetically determined and will be transmitted to the offspring. Most experienced farriers do some "correction," if needed, each time they trim, but they know from experience that with some horses, the results of a "tried and true" method may be different from those expected.

Corrective shoes, made by the blacksmith, adorned panel boards in most village blacksmith shops in bygone days. Although seldom used or reproduced for use, they were works of art. Included were side weight, toe weight, heel weight, side extensions, toe extensions, bar, trailer, rocker toe, rolled toe, and many others. Many such shoes have become largely historical because much of the skill in their preparation has been lost, and, in general, less correction is practiced than formerly (except with Tennessee Walking Horses). Nevertheless, some correction is given to a few horses in most stables.

SPLAYFOOTED, PIGEON-TOED   Splayed feet will break over the inside portion of the toe and quarter, resulting in greatest wear on the inside wall. As a result the outside wall will be longer, more oval at the side branch, and more sloping and thicker than the inside walls. This is because the weight-bearing wall is nearer the center of the foot, and the opposite wall is farther from a perpendicular line to the center of the leg. Being farther away (longer), it meets the ground at a sharper angle and has a thicker, more rounded wall. The combination of thick wall, high side, and less weight creates a bad situation. To correct it, simply trim more of the long wall in an attempt to move more weight toward the center of the foot (Figures 15-13 and 15-14). Trim pigeon-toed feet in an exactly opposite manner.

FORGING, OVERREACHING   In forging, a back foot may strike the ground surface of the front foot, causing a clicking sound if the horse is shod. Little damage is done, but the sound is annoying. Forging worsens when shoes are left on too long and the heels wear faster than the toe because of expansion and contraction and because they are thinner at the heels than elsewhere.

Overreaching is an extension of forging. The back foot strikes the heel of the front shoe or the bulbs of the heel, injuring or forcibly pulling the shoe. Correct overreaching by the least drastic treatment. Try lowering the front toes and leaving the heels longer by 2° or 3°. If the foot is short, use a

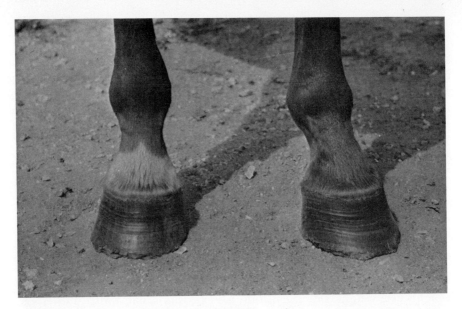

FIGURE 15-13   The farrier sees splayed feet in this horse. He or she will trim more from the long wall (outside) in an attempt to move more weight toward the center of the foot to improve stance and action. [*Photograph by Duane Dailey.*]

FIGURE 15-14   After trimming, splayed condition is improved, and action will show less tendency to interfere. Drastic correction should be avoided if possible and most correction should be done slowly by a small amount with each successive shoeing. [*Photograph by Duane Dailey.*]

heeled shoe. If more correction is needed, leave back toes long, heels lowered 2° or 3°, and the shoe fitted full at the end of the toes.

These are the two most common corrective problems that horsemen face. More serious problems, such as navicular, founder, cracks, corns, and other unsoundnesses require a professional farrier or veterinarian's help or even both. If you aren't comfortable with a problem, do seek competent help, because you are dealing with a very vulnerable part of the horse's anatomy.

## DRY FEET AND OTHER PARTICULARS

In areas of great seasonal change, horse's feet shrink and expand a small amount as moisture conditions change. It is normal in the Midwest for shoes to be removed in winter, the high moisture season, and for horse's feet to expand as a result of going barefoot. They are often shod in the spring when moisture conditions are still abundant and, as spring changes to the hot, dry conditions of summer, feet with a month's hoof growth may contract to the size they were when the shoes were applied. This condition is normal and no cause for concern. However, as summer progresses, dryness may produce quarter or toe cracks. The feet of some horses that are kept shod and not exercised much may shrink slowly and continuously. Horses that have experienced mild laminitis often develop contracted feet. Shod show horses standing in sawdust are especially susceptible to contracted heels and narrow feet.

The standard treatment used by most horsemen for dry feet is a commercial hoof dressing (Figure 15-15). Hoof dressing is painted on the outside of the hoof wall and on the sole, and is worked into the coronary band by vigorous massage with the fingers. Great claims are made in advertisements for its effect on hooves, but many horsemen nevertheless consider it to be ineffective in restoring hoof moisture. Finding the cause of dryness and eliminating it is the solution. If your farrier is rasping away the outer protective cover (periople) of the hoof, then dryness is sure to follow. If the weather is dry and the humidity low, external moisture should be added. While it is recognized that most of a hoof's moisture must come from the bloodstream, moisture can be added externally through mud packs, mud—supplied by an overflowing stock tank—for horses to walk through outside their stalls (mud must stay outside to prevent disease), or through use of Easyboots®. Easyboots® fit over the horse's feet, and water, hoof dressing, or clay packs are easily placed within them and left on the feet for a portion of each day. Such treatment may correct mild cases of dryness, but will not eliminate contracted heels. Since different horses respond differently to the various treatments for contracted heels, this condition needs the attention of a farrier or veterinarian.

FIGURE 15-15   The value of hoof dressing for dry feet is debatable, but it should be applied to the sole of the foot as well as the wall and coronary band when used. Outside mud baths, Easyboots® and mud packs are also used. Increased circulation from exercise, adequate nutrition, preservation of the periople (covering of the outer wall), and protection from careless rasping are other methods of preventing dry feet. [*Photograph by Duane Dailey.*]

The feet of racehorses are routinely packed, sometimes daily but more often after breezing (hard work) to "take the sting out" of them. Mud is placed in the foot by means of a paddle and then covered with a piece of paper. In addition to regular packing with moist clay packs, the feet of racehorses are usually washed every day after the gallop, a practice which tends to add moisture to the foot. Any hoof dressing is applied over the moist foot, sealing extra moisture in. Care is always taken to dry behind the fetlock above the bulbs of the heel to avoid the development of scratches, or of cracked or grease heel from excessive dampness.

Nutrition affects hoof growth. In general, when a horse is gaining well, growing rapidly, or receiving adequate-to-good nutrition, it has average-to-above-average hoof growth. However, excessive feeding—especially feeding of protein, such as has been shown to accelerate the growth of sheep's wool—has little, if any, effect on hoof growth. Numerous experiments have been reported on the value of feeding gelatin to stimulate hoof strength and growth; few, if any, have shown benefits from gelatin feeding. Typical is one study recently reported by K. D. Butler and H. F. Hintz of Cornell.[1] They compared gelatin-fed weanlings on both a high plane and low plane of nutrition, over a 56-day feeding trial. The consumption of gelatin made no significant difference at either level of feeding. One might conclude that, nutritionally speaking, when the nutrient requirements recommended by the National Research Council are met for each age group, additional feed is not a factor in hoof strength and growth.

Hoof growth probably does increase with exercise. Blood is pumped with each step of the foot, bringing nutrients and removing cell wastes. The hooves of foundered horses grow very slowly at first because of constricted blood supply and inactivity; indeed, many promptly display contracted feet for lack of internal moisture. Normal growth resumes upon recovery.

The strength and hardness of horses' hooves vary from extremely strong hooves that need no shoeing to extremely soft hooves that cannot function without frequent shoeing. It is not unusual for Thoroughbreds to require shoeing every 4 to 5 weeks, because their sensitive tendons and ligaments cannot take the angle change resultant from growth, and because their feet often tend to crack if the toe is left too long. Horses with white hooves have softer, weaker hooves than dark-footed horses. Some breeds have harder hooves with thicker walls—the Arab is a notable example. All horses that have been foundered tend to have soft hooves, especially soon after foundering. They tend to improve and get harder and stronger 1½ to 2 years after the founder, provided it does not recur.

[1]K. D. Butler, Jr., and H. F. Hintz, "Effect of Level of Feed Intake and Gelatin Supplementation on Growth and Quality of Hooves," *Journal of Animal Science*, vol. 44, no. 2, February 1977, p. 257.

# BUILDINGS, FACILITIES, AND BUDGETS

ood buildings and equipment provide safety and protection for the horses (Figure 16-1). Even in warm climates, stables protect horses from flies, storms, and hot sun, and they are useful in nursing sick or injured horses back to health. They are also convenient places in which to catch, groom, saddle, and unsaddle horses, as well as to store feed, tack, and the endless paraphernalia used with horses.

## LEGAL IMPLICATIONS OF HORSE HOUSING

Before starting to build, local codes, ordinances, and zoning regulations must be checked. Within certain city limits, deed restrictions, covenants between property owners, city ordinances, or township, county, state, and even national regulations may affect the stabling of horses. Regulations are seldom administered, even within a single city, by only one agency or department; sanitation, fire, water, and other authorities may all have applicable requirements.

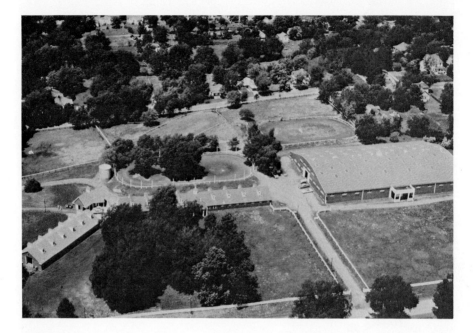

FIGURE 16-1  Good buildings and equipment provide safety and protection for horses. Shown are two stables, blacksmith shop, an indoor and two outdoor arenas, round grain bin, and lots for loose horses. [*Courtesy of Stephens College, Columbia, Mo.*]

Many ordinances deal with the nuisance potential of horses and attempt to protect property owners from horse slums, noise, or trespassing by those working with horses or the horses themselves. It behooves the ambitious horse owner to check with the neighbors about their feelings toward horses and horse activities before building or expanding.

## THE LONG-RANGE BUILDING PLAN

### Identify Objectives

Clear-cut objectives are vital to any horse operation. Knowledge of the goal will prevent drifting along in a random and ultimately costly manner. Bankers and lending agencies will lend money more readily with a well-considered and flexible plan of growth. Above all, any blueprint for a horse operation will have a logical relationship to, and be limited by, the land on which it will be established.

## Minimize Disappointments and Avoid Catastrophes

Clear-cut objectives are of no avail without adequate research on the problems of construction. Consider the 16-horse barn with varnished interior woodwork and attractive low ceiling—but no insulation in the roof or ventilation in the attic. Condensation during an extended cold winter built, on the underside of the roof, a layer of ice a foot deep, that crashed to the floor, taking the ceiling with it. Ventilation is one of the biggest problems in expensive, warm barns. Fire safety is another.

The *Horse Handbook—Housing and Equipment*, compiled by Midwest Plan Service,[1] is a comprehensive publication on horse buildings and equipment. It can be obtained from the agricultural engineering department of your state university or college of agriculture or from county extension agents. Do consider obtaining professional help. Some states have state and area extension engineering specialists that offer their services free. There are professional consultants in every area. It is also useful to visit horse farms on trips and field days and to attend equipment trade shows. When buying horses or visiting horse establishments, particular attention should be paid to buildings and equipment.

## Maximize Cost-Benefit Ratio

Any building investment must be analyzed for its possible return in dollars, pleasure, convenience, safety, and pride of ownership. If one is losing money by not having a particular building, the money should be borrowed to build it. Before building on impulse, compare the structure's contribution to the long-range plan. If it is to be used infrequently or will not be used for long, it probably should not be built.

## Maximize Safety

Time and money spent in making buildings safe for horses and the humans who work with them is always a good investment. Buildings that are not strong enough to hold a horse, or fences that allow a horse to escape are exceedingly dangerous and should not be tolerated. Horse equipment, particularly in densely populated areas, should be completely adequate to contain the strongest horse without risk of escape or injury. Equipment adequate for the mature horse might prove inadequate for foals, weanlings, or stallions.

[1]Published by the Iowa State University Press, Ames, 1971.

## Flexibility

Buildings that are flexible in construction and adapted to more than one use are the best investment. The best such buildings are well-adapted to additions and are easy to rearrange inside. A "first" building should be situated so as to facilitate eventual expansion in a long-range plan that may include a main barn, broodmare barn, barren mare barn, weanling and yearling barns, stallion barn, breeding shed, sales barn, training barn, equipment storage area, exercise area, feed storage area, office lounge, living quarters, and so on. Horse establishments, no matter how small, also need outside lots, corrals, exercise areas, and parking spaces for trailers and large vehicles. All require a distance between the buildings for fire protection and ease of access.

## Convenience

Convenience and the saving of labor should be high-priority items when arranging the new horse establishment or adding buildings to an old one. In general, layout requires more space than one suspects. One should have room to get long trailers to all buildings without great problems. Plan the facilities so that food or water must never be carried through loose horses. Buildings should be conveniently arranged so that feeds should not have to be transported far; however, it is safer from the fire hazard standpoint to have a hay shed separate from the stabled horses. Stables should be adequately and safely lighted so that horse activities can continue conveniently into the night. Foals are often born at night, and horses pick bad times to get sick and need veterinary attention.

## TYPES OF STABLES

There are two basic types of stables: (1) open shed, usually with single-pitch roof and (2) closed stable, either cold or warm type. Cold stables have no provisions to modify temperature. Warm stables may have no supplemental heat but rather depend upon insulation, tight construction, and the body heat of animals to modify the temperature or keep it above freezing in the winter. Warm stables must have forced-air ventilation systems to eliminate odors and prevent condensation. Both types may be seen on some farms, with the central warm barn housing show horses, tackroom, and work areas, the cold barn housing broodmares and other less-used horses, and open sheds housing young stock.

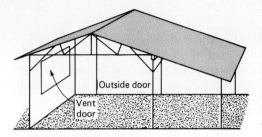

FIGURE 16-2 Open front shed, truss-post, and beam construction. Since they are free-roaming creatures of the outdoors, horses thrive with open-shed stables. [*From* The Horse Handbook, *Iowa State University Press, Ames, Iowa.*]

## Open Housing

Since the horse is a free-roaming creature of the outdoors, it probably prefers an open shed (Figure 16-2). It may be seen standing out in a snowstorm, 2 inches of snow on its back, icicles hanging from its sides, ignoring a dry, open shelter. Open housing is the least expensive type of shelter, the easiest to build, and the one most widely available in prefabricated commercial units. It may be moved or rearranged for another use if needed.

## Closed Housing

Closed housing gives horses and handlers more protection from the elements, and it allows feed, tools, and tack to be stored behind locked doors. Show horses must have the protection from sun and skin abrasions that box stalls give.

## Small Stables

The one- or two-horse open stable is satisfactory for many suburban owners with a few horses. Compatible horses running loose together in pasture may share an open shed; however, dominant horses will use most or all of the available space, and individual stalls are therefore required. Space requirements for compatible horses in open sheds are 50 to 60 square feet. For box stalls, 100 to 120 square feet are required, with a 12 by 12 foot square stall the most desirable shape. Sheds should have a 9-foot clearance on the low side and an 11- or 12-foot clearance at the entrance side. A 4- to 6-foot overhang affords extra shade and shelter, and reduces blowing elements. If blowing snow or rain is a problem, small closed sheds can eliminate it. Three 12-foot units should be considered for two horses, with one used for feed and bedding. Grain can be protected from rodents, birds, and horses in locked wooden boxes.

## Medium-sized Stables

For four or more horses, gable-roofed cold stables make useful, attractive buildings, with a 10- to 12-foot aisle in the center and 12 by 12 foot box stalls on each side. They should have a tackroom and feed and bedding storage overhead or in a stall, and some provision for sanitary manure disposal that does not create a nuisance or fly problem.

FIGURE 16-3   Large, expandable stable layout with four rows of stalls, two alleys, and inside service. With truss construction, a small riding arena can occupy one end of the building. [*From* The Horse Handbook, *Iowa State University Press, Ames, Iowa.*]

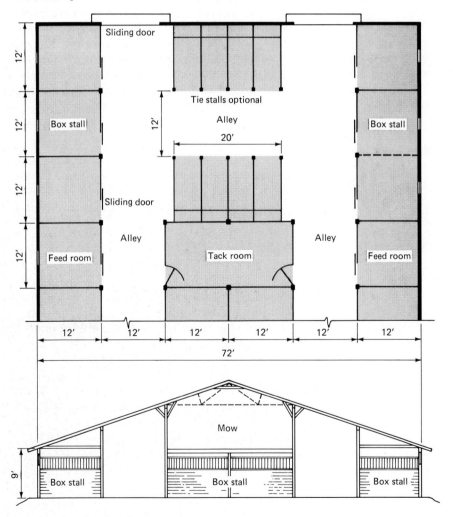

## Large Horse Stables

Large horse stables often employ the central aisle arrangement, with stalls back-to-back down the center facing 12-foot aisles. Across each aisle is a row of stalls backed against the outside wall (Figure 16-3). Feeding, bedding, and stall cleaning can be effected with the aid of machinery from these aisles. Alternatively, stalls may occupy only half of the length of such a building, leaving room for a small riding ring at the opposite end.

## SPECIAL-PURPOSE BUILDINGS, EQUIPMENT, AND NEEDS

Large breeding operations and other horse establishments must have many additonal buildings and items of equipment.

STUD BARNS   Stud barns take many forms, from expensive to inexpensive, from the octagon-shaped buildings on some Thoroughbred farms to ordinary box stalls in standard facilities. Stud facilities should be strong, safe, and well-ventilated, with 12-foot ceilings and all possible comforts, because of the amount of time the stallion is kept in them.

The stallion's stall should be at least 14 feet square, but twice this amount is useful if he does not have a paddock or is not ridden or exercised on a hotwalker. If the stallion has access to paddocks for exercise, so much the better. If not, a hotwalker should be used. Solid, double partitions from floor to ceiling should be used between stallions in stables; they should not run in adjacent paddocks outside. Paddock fences should be strong, slatted at close intervals, and 6 feet high. Chain link, pipe, and 2 by 6 inch oak boards on deep-set posts every 5 feet make good stallion paddock fences.

The stallion should be able to see other horses from his quarters. Use a solid front on the stall to a height of 5 feet, then iron pipes or bars above at 4-inch intervals to the ceiling or above his reach when rearing. Mares can be teased or checked for heat from the alley.

BREEDING SHED   The breeding shed should be close to the stud barn. The best are approximately 30 feet square with a 12- to 14-foot ceiling, with teasing equipment and a place to contain the foal in sight of the mare. It must have a storage room for equipment, hot and cold water for sanitary procedures, and a lab for the veterinarian if examination of mares is made and semen collected, evaluated, and used for artificial insemination.

FOALING BARN   In areas that experience cold winters, the foaling barn should be a closed, warm building with good insulation and forced-air ventilation. If mares are closely watched, there should be a warm room for the comfort and convenience of the attendants. The mare's modesty, ability to regulate the time of parturition, and speed in the process make birth-watching a very challenging activity. Closed-circuit television is the most reliable, but most expensive method; next may be the one-way peek-through magnifying lenses that are used in the doors of homes. Even so, the observer must be quiet and careful, lest he or she be seen and heard, only to have the predawn inspection promptly followed by foaling.

Foaling stalls should be 14 feet square if possible, although 12-foot-square stalls will do. Their floors should be level, clean, disinfected, and bedded deeply in clean straw. There should be no permanent fixtures, such as mangers, feed troughs, or waterers—only bare walls. Mares are happiest with company in the foaling barn, and more than one should occupy it at a time.

WEANLING QUARTERS   Weanling housing should be out of calling distance of the dams. Since weanlings will search frantically for their mothers, their quarters should be safe and escapeproof. Closed housing in box stalls may be safest. Many racing farms graze groups of broodmares together by day and house each mare and foal at night together in a box stall. When time to wean arrives, the mare is quietly transported out of calling distance, leaving her foal among friends in its familiar stall.

GROWING QUARTERS   Open, loose housing affords an excellent environment in which young horses can learn coexistence. They live and eat together as well as romp and play in groups. One end of a growing barn may be used for stalls or pens to feed timid or smaller horses that are not competing well in the group.

## Feed Storage and Material Handling

Most horsemen do not store and mix large quantities of grain, but depend upon bulk or sacked feeds. In a grain-growing area, properly dried grain can often be purchased and stored at harvesttime with substantial savings. Circular metal binds with auger elevators minimize handling and storage problems.

The space allocations for some common horse feeds are as follows:

| Item | Cubic feet per ton |
|---|---|
| Whole ears | 80 |
| Ear corn | 70 |
| Bulk grain | 50 |
| Baled hay and straw bedding | 200 |

Rodent control with sacked feed is very difficult without mouse- and ratproof containers or feed rooms. Cats and the systematic use of rodent poisons will control most rodent populations.

Hay is best stored in hay sheds or barns away from traffic and horses because of the fire hazard. It can be delivered daily for feeding in large stables, or a few days' supply may be stacked in an empty stall. Ground-level hay storage is more economical than loft storage. However, loft storage is more convenient and may provide insulation.

## Tackroom, Office

The tackroom should be well-organized, attractive, free of dust and dampness, and as burglarproof as possible. Many tackrooms and offices are combined into places where awards, records, and pictures of favorite horses are kept and displayed.

Tackrooms must remain dry to preserve leather items. Ammonia, dampness, and dust cause rapid deterioration and damage to leather. Each saddle and bridle should have its own rack and hanger, and every major item should be kept in its place. Wall cabinets for medicine, grooming equipment, blankets, and items not in use add to neatness.

Traffic in stolen tack and equipment has reached epidemic proportions recently. Isolated tackrooms are the main targets, although few tackrooms are thoroughly safe. Marked equipment and posted premises are helpful, but one's favorite saddle is safest in the house, when not in use. An effort is underway to issue registration numbers to be stamped on saddles and stored in a computer for easy tracing by law officers.

## Arenas

Indoor riding arenas are usually limited in size because of cost and available space. Sixty by 120 foot arenas are sufficient for most training activities, but are too small for horse shows. Arenas of 110 by 220 feet will accommodate official horse shows and most other horse activities.

Arena floors should be sloped from the center outward; surfaces may be tanbark, sand, shavings, sawdust, or mixtures of sand, dirt, and sawdust. Tanbark is the best, but it is expensive. Riding rings may be harrowed, disked, or cultivated for softer footing. Water is used to control dust; in no case should used motor oil be applied, because harmful chemicals would then be breathed into the lungs from the dust. Indoor arenas are prone to excessive moisture retention (see *Ventilation and Insulation*). Outdoor arenas are economical and should be used in suitable weather. They should be safely fenced, well-drained, and frequently harrowed. In dry weather, dusty rings should be sprinkled.

## Stalls

There are two types of stalls: (1) box, and (2) tie. New construction should concentrate on 12 by 12 foot box stalls because of their versatility: they are large enough for foaling and, with one partition removed, will house a stallion nicely.

Tie-stalls should be used only as a last resort. Docile, hardworking draft horses and hardworking academy horses may tolerate them, but spirited, underexercised, light horses will find ways to get injured in them—or may injure the groom. One might well ask: "How would you like to stand in one spot facing a blank wall for most of your life?"

Horses in tie-stalls often must be taken out to be watered if no easier system is available, but are fed in mangers at the front of the stall. Feeding is easy if there is an alley in front of the horses, but the horses must be trained to move over on command if the feed must be carried in from behind. If there is an alley in front for feeding, the space-saving advantage of tie-stalls is lost because there must also be one behind the horses. Tie-stalls are easier to clean and bed than box stalls, and they also require less bedding. Since most tie-stalls are 5 by 9 feet, they occupy less barn space than box stalls.

Regardless of the type of stall used, there should be no sharp objects, protrusions, or nail heads to injure the horse's skin or rough objects at floor level to be stepped on. Wood-chewing can be discouraged by using treated wood and by covering exposed edges with sheet metal. Rubber, plastic, and metal feeding equipment may also be used, but will not curtail wind-sucking. Wooden tailboards, used by owners of horses that wear tail sets in stalls, represent an invitation to crib. Even though the edges are covered with metal, an imperfection on their surface, such as a knot, gives the cribbing horse an opportunity to practice the vice. Metal pipes are usually more attractive. Injuries to the plywood linings of stalls also invite wood-chewing. Two-inch pressure-treated lumber, especially oak, is the material of choice for stall partitions and walls.

## Managers and Feeding Equipment

There is disagreement on what types of hay feeder, if any, to use and where to position it if it is used. Those who feed hay in a corner on the floor say that horses eat spilled feed from the floor anyway, breathe less dust in ground feeding, and incur less risk of injury from built-in mangers, but they admit that the recycling of parasites and extensive waste of hay are problems.

Corner or wall hay racks are a good compromise. Corner racks are safest and least obtrusive. Rod and strap metal feeders can be bought, or corner feeders can be made from wood. They should hold 25 to 30 pounds of hay. Wall hay feeders should be mounted at the maximum convenient height for the feeder and horse to reach. Plastic net feeders with drawstring tops are economical, but must be placed high enough so that when empty and hanging low, horses cannot paw into them. They should have breakaway strings or be mounted high on light hooks that release them when they are pawed into.

Built-in mangers should be strong enough to support the weight of a rearing horse and should have no boards with nails that horses can work loose. They should be 38 to 42 inches tall, 36 to 40 inches long, and 26 to 30 inches wide. For easy feeding, mount them next to the alley, one end against the partition wall and the other toward the stall door. It is important not to leave a rigid, square-cornered manger 26 to 30 inches wide sticking out in the stall. A rounded or angled extension on the end of the manger that attaches to the wall near the door-facing reduces the risk of injury to the horse. A 12-inch-wide by 8-inch-deep grain box mounted against the partition wall with its length matching the width of the manger almost eliminates grain spillage onto the floor. A similar box with a center partition at the other end of the manger affords separate salt and mineral feeding boxes.

Solid mangers do expose horses with hay allergies to extra dust and may result in an occasional injury to a fractious horse. They should probably not be used along the alley with some stallions. However, they save feed and labor and may result in a better mineral feeding program.

Grain can also be fed in rubber or plastic tubs on the floor or in corner-mounted grain boxes made from a variety of materials. The capacity should be 2 to 3 gallons, with large bottomed surface areas, which reduce the risk of choking compared to small, deep grain troughs, such as buckets. Some grain spillage is, of course, inevitable.

## Water and Watering Equipment

An abundant supply of good water is a requirement in choosing a location for the stable—not only for the 8 to 12 gallons of drinking water per horse per day, but also for fire fighting. Availability of water may also affect insurance rates. Rural stable planners should consider the minimum volume of water delivered before determining the main line pipe size, or they can plan to store nearby surface water.

Some stabled horses are hand-watered from buckets in their stalls, some are led to a central tank, and others drink from automatic waterers. Ideally, horses should have free-choice access to water. They seldom do when hand-watered because of spillage, freezing, or running out between waterings. Automatic waterers have been available for years but have not been used extensively in stables, partly because they are expensive, get clogged easily, are hard to keep clean, and certain types may flood the stall when a mischievous horse learns to hold their control mechanisms open. Improved varieties have overcome most of these disadvantages—except costliness. One model has a smooth-bottomed bowl with fill float and valve beyond the reach of the horse to ensure safety from overflow and make cleaning easier. It also has an electrical unit to prevent freezing. Automatic waterers should be inspected daily to be sure that water is available.

One electric waterer in a fence line will suffice for ten to twelve horses;

however, water tanks supply much more water at less cost if freezing can be avoided with electric or gas heating units. Insulation around the outsides of tanks is essential, and it should be installed on a permanent basis.

Freezeproof hydrants should be conveniently located in or near stables; they are most useful when used in combination with a water tank. They must be protected from loose horses. Connecting hoses are added fire safety measures, but they may freeze up in winter.

## Lights and Electricity

Structures should be planned to maximize natural light through windows, doors, and roof arrangement. Skylights of clear plastic are economical, but they may bend and leak under snow loads. Clear plastic may be used for siding or windows, but it may suffer wind damage more easily than metal siding. The stable must be wired according to electrical codes. It must be rodentproof, adequately wired for maximum anticipated electrical current loads, and as safe as possible. Two-way switches and well-spaced, protected outlets are convenient.

At least every other stall should have a centered fixture for a 100-watt bulb unless stalls are solid; then each should have its own light. Bulbs must have protective covers if they are in reach of horses. If the use of heat lamps in winter is contemplated, voltage and safe floor-to-fixture height must be calculated.

Aisles, tack- and feedrooms, and work areas should be adequately lighted. Night or emergency lights may be installed near fire extinguishers and exits.

## Ventilation and Insulation

The removal of moisture in closed buildings, especially old remodeled barns and houses, is a challenge not often adequately met. Professional help may well be needed in this area: it is much easier to plan and build ventilation into a new structure than to correct problems in an old one.

A 1000-pound horse releases appriximately 1500 Btu (British thermal units) of heat into the air per hour and exhales 2 gallons of water per day. When warm air drops 20°F, its water-carrying capacity is reduced by half. There is little wonder that warm, moist air rising from horses' bodies condenses on the underside of an uninsulated roof, causing constant drip, perpetual dampness, and sometimes ice formation under the roof. Some indoor riding arenas, kept wet to settle dust, almost require riders to wear raingear on cold days; the dampness also causes such areas to smell of ammonia, and it encourages bacterial growth and respiratory diseases in horses.

In moderately warm areas, open buildings are seldom insulated for moisture control, but may have 2-inch roof and wall insulation for heat modification. Most have air inlets at the top of the back wall; larger buildings may also have ridge ventilation openings. The roof and northern sides of three-sided open buildings are often insulated in northern areas, and such buildings may have drop-down doors that cover most of the open south side for wind and snow protection. Cold closed buildings should be reasonably tight, with 2- to 4-inch ceiling and wall insulation and ceiling and ridge or other ventilation. Warm buildings, when tight and well insulated, may need no other source of heat when at full capacity. There must be forced-air ventilation to rid the air of moisture exhaled by the horses, however.

One fan that moves 100 cubic feet per minute ($ft^3$/min) of air per 1000-pound horse is usually sufficient if properly located in tight walls or ceilings away from large windows or doors. Space 15- to 20-square-inch air inlets about 20 feet apart at the eaves, beginning at the end of the building away from the fan. One is needed per horse. Baffles at the eaves or down the center of a ceiling are also used as inlets. Proper forced-air ventilation is difficult to achieve. It should be supervised by a competent person.

## Location and Site Preparation

Each building should be located according to a long-range plan. Each should be accessible to all-weather roads and fire lanes, located on well-drained soil, and convenient for its intended use. Leave room to add onto the building without cramping roads and lanes. Most locations must be graded to a 5 percent slope away from the building in all directions. The amount of fill needed or the extent of grading necessary for preparation of the site greatly affect cost. Steep, rocky terrain is very expensive to prepare. Preparation should be complete and fill dirt settled before construction starts.

## MATERIALS AND CONSTRUCTION

The small horse owner can remodel, build, contract to have built, or purchase a prefabricated stable that will meet his or her needs, price, and taste. The better it looks, the more pleasing it will be to the owner and his or her neighbors. Larger units, especially in severe winter climates, may require more strength, durability, flexiblity, and economy than can be found in pre-assembled units.

There is merit in starting from the beginning because personal needs can be included. Before starting to build, a discussion of materials will save time and money and may result in better construction. It is important to be familiar with the kind of stable construction that is typical of the area and to locate contractors whose buildings reflect both high quality and horse savvy. Some materials may be abundant locally and may substitute well for others; however, none should be purchased for economy alone. Keep in mind the objective of the structure: to contain the animal in a safe, comfortable environment.

## Framing Materials

The choice of pole construction or a concrete foundation will affect the choice of framing materials. Pole construction is much more economical in terms of labor and materials. Pressure-treated poles or posts with 6- or 8-inch tops are firmly set in 4- to 6-foot holes on concrete pads to serve as well, partition, and roof supports. They can be conveniently positioned on 5- or 6-foot centers to fit 10- or 12-foot stall sizes. Correctly positioned posts along an alley can serve as partition, wall, and door supports. Poles make possible higher hay storage in gable-roofed hay mows than do trusses. Either shed or gable roofs can be built onto poles, or they can be cut to the appropriate height to accommodate roof trusses. Trusses allow clear span or open space inside to allow for riding rings or other such uses. Two-inch boards are nailed horizontally to the poles or posts to accommodate the outer siding, which is usually made of metal. It is important to begin with a pressure-treated 2- by 12-inch board placed on the ground to prevent a horse that is lying down from getting its foot under it. Pole buldings are reasonably attractive, useful, and very economical, but they are not as sturdy or attractive as frame or masonry structures.

Footings and foundation walls extending out of the ground are required for frame and masonry construction and are used in most houses and many stables. Carpenters familiar with frame construction may be reluctant to attempt a pole building. Framing or masonry structures are usually straighter, especially if round poles with slight curves are used in pole construction.

Brick veneer is attractive but less flexible, and it is exorbitant in cost. Stacked concrete blocks are equally sturdy, fireproof, and far less expensive than bricks. The concrete blocks are simply laid on top of each other and coated on each side with a fiber-containing material with strength equal to or greater than mortar. Brick veneer requires 2 by 4 framing and boarding up inside to prevent its being damaged by bumping and kicking. Blocks need the same protection against holes being made by kicks from shod hooves.

Assembled trusses can be purchased. They must be strong enough to withstand expected snow loads in the area. The design and construction of trusses will determine how closely they must be spaced and what type of sheeting must be used with them. Most are spaced on 4-foot centers.

## Roof and Siding

One of the most durable and economical roofs is zinc-coated steel or sheet iron, but it may also be the least attractive, loudest in a hail storm, and hottest if not properly insulated or ventilated. Aluminum roofing in various baked-on colors is more attractive, but not as strong as steel roofing. Asbestos shingles are attractive and have 15- to 20-year life spans, but must be nailed to solid sheeting and are subject to hail and wind damage. Both zinc-coated steel and aluminum are used extensively for siding with pole construction. Inside walls should always be boarded up 6 feet high; failure to do so with metal siding may result in a horse kicking through between two overlapping joints and suffering severe lacerations. Framed buildings usually use wood or fiberboard drop siding. For a rustic appearance, wide, rough-sawn vertical boards with 4-inch strips are attractive in plain, stained, or painted finish.

## Windows

Windows are expensive, but every stall in a closed building without an outside door into a paddock should have one. They increase light, reduce odor, aid dryness, and afford ventilation in summer. They should be placed high in the wall, be protected with welded metal screens, and open outward or slide sideways to open.

## Interior Walls and Partitions

Walls and partitions are subjected to great pressures from kicking and rubbing; add to these wood-chewing, windsucking, and the rotting effect of manure, and 2-inch pressure-treated lumber becomes a good choice. Many fir, pine, and other types of wood are strong enough for walls and stalls, but they rot and are chewed more by horses than oak if not pressure-treated. Where available, 2 by 10 or 12 inch pressure-treated oak is excellent for walls and partitions. Metal walls should be protected to a height of 6 feet. Partitions should extend 8 feet high or to a 9-foot ceiling. A 2-inch solid partition on 10- or 12-foot stalls with a bevel-edged, 2- by 6-inch vertical brace strip in the center will suffice between horses other than stallions. Stallions should have double walls from floor to ceiling. A 5-foot-high solid partition between horses and along the alley is cooler, allows more visibility, and is more pleasing to horses than solid walls. It can be extended 3 or more feet by strong and economical welded-rod swine panels, chain link fence, or strong wire mesh. The worst type of stall is totally enclosed without provision for ventilation or visibility for the horse.

Open sheds with pens or stalls may utilize board fencing, pipe, or solid partitions. If the shed is long, a solid wall every third pen will serve as a windbreak and reduce drafts from strong winds passing through the length of the shed.

## Doors

Stall doors must be strong, functional, and horseproof. They are likely to be assaulted by pawing hooves, leaning bodies, and chewing teeth. They should be 2 inches thick and treated (if wood), and should be 4 feet wide and 8 feet tall. Overhead sliding tracks mounted in the alley are preferred to hinges, and strong latches are essential. If the horse can see out but cannot get its head out to work with the latch, it is easy to contain. Most sliding doors have two brackets near the bottom to secure the door. Some are cleverly designed for safety, but many are no more than traps resulting in injury when bumped into or stepped on.

Dutch doors are very popular but not very safe, and they may be in the way when they are open. They are divided at partition height into two hinged doors with the top door often left open so the horse can extend its head and neck out over the bottom door. Horses love them. In some barns they allow visibility that would otherwise be difficult to provide. Hardware for a Dutch door must be strong and latches secure. Both top and bottom doors require three heavy butt hinges. The convenient foolproof latch short of a padlock has yet to be invented. Locks are too dangerous because of fire. Usually only one or two horses in a stable are adept at manipulating latches and their Dutch doors require an endless variety of hardware.

Sooner or later a horse may attempt to jump the lower section of a Dutch door. If the door is strongly mounted and latched, it may succeed without injury. If the door breaks or splinters it may be hurt. Stall guards, three heavy canvas strips with snaps or catches, usually used to contain horses in open door stalls, can also be used above Dutch doors to contain the chronic jumpers. Horses may rear and get caught in these; however, they do reduce the temptation of jumping out.

Most aisle, end-of-barn doors are on sliding tracks. These work well if kept the correct distance from the ground and if not situated in drifting snow areas. Since they must slide on the ground outside the building the full width of the door, drifting snow and ice and even straw debris can easily seal them closed. The solution is the more expensive overhead garage-type sliding door.

## Floors

The type of floor to be used in stalls and aisles must be decided before construction is begun. Many flooring surfaces are possible, ranging from plain dirt to indoor-outdoor carpet. Others are asphalt, clay, sand, cement, and wood.

Plain dirt, sand, and cement are undesirable and should seldom be used. Dirt easily forms mud, and sand is cold, damp, and may cause sand colic when ingested. Concrete, like sand, is damp and considered hard on hooves and legs, even when covered by deep bedding. A test of this hypothesis would make an interesting research project, because humans, with a fraction of the horse's strength and agility in the feet and legs, can spend a lifetime working in a factory on concrete with no apparent ill effects. However, the surface of concrete is slick, and it absorbs no moisture.

Asphalt and tamped clay are choice flooring materials. Both are absorbent and resilient, but hard enough to withstand pawing and hard wear. Both look good when swept down, and asphalt can be hosed clean with water. Neither is excessively expensive, but both require attention and maintenance. The edges of asphalt will crumble and in areas of heavy use, such as around water tanks, may erode and need repair in 2 or 3 years. Unless kept clean, asphalt will become impervious to water. For this reason, straw is a more suitable bedding than sawdust to cover asphalt. Clay wears out more quickly than asphalt, resulting in an irregular floor surface. It needs patching annually, and only rock-free clays are satisfactory.

Wide, 2-inch-thick boards have been used extensively for stall flooring. They should be pressure-treated, spaced an inch apart for drainage, and checked frequently for soundness because rotting is a problem. All pervious floors (except concrete) should be underlain with 12 to 18 inches of crushed rock for drainage. This should be a part of site preparation after leveling to grade.


## BUDGETING THE HORSE EXPERIENCE

Few worthwhile things in life come cheaply, and horse ownership is no exception. You will have a better horse experience if you budget this activity.


### Farm or Ranch Horses

The farm or ranch horse may be fitted into available feed and housing with little additional out-of-pocket cost. Expenses for health, miscellaneous items, and shoeing will be incurred. Such a "least-cost" budget might be like that shown in Table 16-1.

This budget is for one adult horse, involved mostly with summer activities and not being shown, using ranch or farm feeds and housing. As horse density increases, health costs will increase because of more miscellaneous

TABLE 16-1   FARM OR RANCH HORSE (LEAST-COST) BUDGET

| Item | Expense | Explanation |
|---|---|---|
| Health | | |
|   Immunization | $ 30.00 | Tetanus, encephalomyelitis |
|   Internal parasites | 25.00 | Tubing twice a year |
|   Miscellaneous | 20.00 | |
| Shoeing | 80.00 | Four shoeings in summer, barefoot in winter |
| | $155.00 | |
| Taxes and interest | | Use your own costs |
| Equipment | | Use your own estimates |

accidents and heavier concentrations of parasites. Young horses incur more expense than older ones, and so do broodmares and foals.

It is risky to cut costs on the immunization and parasite programs unless you use the new do-it-yourself kits.

BACKYARD HORSE BUDGET   The budget shown in Table 16-2 is a reasonable one for many suburban horse owners. The assumption is that this horse will be used in group riding most of the year and that all feed and grain will be purchased. Because of more activities with other horses, higher health charges were assumed than in the budget in Table 16-1.

If you have good pasture, much less hay, grain, and bedding will suffice, and you will have a much happier, better-adjusted horse. Of course, it

TABLE 16-2   BACKYARD HORSE BUDGET

| Item | Expense |
|---|---|
| Health | |
|   Immunization | $ 30.00 |
|   Internal parasites | 35.00 |
|   Miscellaneous | 50.00 |
| Shoeing | 80.00 |
| Feed | |
|   Grain, 4 lb/day @ $0.10/lb | 146.00 |
|   Hay, 12 lb/day @ $0.08/lb | 350.40 |
|   Minerals, salt, vitamins | 10.00 |
|   Pasture | |
| Bedding | 150.00 |
| Hauling (transportation) | 50.00 |
| Taxes, interest, depreciation | 50.00 |
| Total annual | $951.40+ |

may not be practical to graze show horses, but they must be exercised regularly.

A hauling or transportation charge is listed and one for depreciation of items, such as a trailer. With rising costs, horse items depreciate very little, and many used saddles sell for as much as they cost new.

There are many ways to reduce this budget. Maintenance cost per horse decreases with addition of more horses. Bulk and seasonal buying may also effect substantial savings. On the other hand, careless accidents and neglect result in sick horses, and extensive showing will also increase costs.

BOARDED HORSE BUDGET    Although boarding a horse in a stable may save time (Table 16-3), it is more expensive and less convenient for frequent use. However, stables do have the advantage of having rings, jumps, and other horse equipment, and many offer riding instructions. Some have trainers who help work out problems with an individual horse, and many offer their clients opportunities to gain experience with in-house horse shows.

TABLE 16-3   BOARDED HORSE BUDGET

| Item | Expense |
| --- | --- |
| Annual board, 12 months @ $160/month | $1920.00 |
| Health | |
| Immunization | 30.00 |
| Internal parasites | 20.00 |
| Miscellaneous | 50.00 |
| Shoeing | 120.00 |
| Other miscellaneous | 250.00 |
| Total | $2390.00 |

Centralization of horses encourages group activities such as hunt clubs, pony clubs, rodeo activities, trail-riding groups, drill teams, and others. The interaction among members provides a good educational opportunity: you get to see and discuss all types and levels of performance of horse and rider and learn how to get desired responses from your mount quicker than you could by working alone or in small groups. There is always something to be learned from watching and visiting with a good horse handler.

SHOW HORSE BUDGET    If you choose to keep a show horse in training and on the show circuit, Jordan suggests this budget (Table 16-4). Many show horses will be more expensive than this if campaigned by well-known trainers.

TABLE 16-4  SHOW HORSE EXPENSES PER HORSE

| | |
|---|---|
| 1  Stabling costs (typical charges in Minnesota, which must cover feed, labor, insurance, and stable upkeep). | $1440.00 |
| 2  Training of horse and/or rider. (The charges per month are about $100. Horses normally are not in training continuously, but on average about 25 percent of the time.) | 500.00 |
| 3  Shoeing at $25 per set would entail a minimum of 6 sets/year. (Some are reset 10 to 12 times yearly with special hand-forged corrective shoes that cost $50 to $60 per set.) | 150.00 |
| 4  Veterinary service (routine immunization, four parasite treatments, and one emergency trip). | 96.00 |
| 5  Trucking to show at $30 per trip. (In this case it's assumed the horse was entered in ten of the eighteen tri-state shows.) | 300.00 |
| 6  Entry fees of $20 per show, ten shows per year (four classes at $5 per class). | 200.00 |
| 7  Tack, equipment, and riding apparel. | 300.00 |
| 8  Insurance on horse (2 percent of horse's value). | 40.00 |
| 9  Travel, lodging, food at shows. | 600.00 |
| Total per show horse | $3626.00 |

SOURCE: Robert Jordan, "Horses' Effect on Minnesota's Economy," *The Horseman's Gazette*, vol. 3, no. 1, January 1977, p. 1.

## COMMITMENT TO HORSE OWNERSHIP

A declaration of independence for horses (or other animals) would undoubtedly include certain "inalienable rights." If a horse is to have "life, a degree of liberty, and a reasonable expectation of happiness," these must come from you, the owner. The horse cannot manage them alone—not even in the wild state (Figure 16-4).

## OBSERVATIONS

The late Will Rogers is credited with having said "the outside of a horse is good for the inside of a man."

Today, the use of horses allows many adults to escape from their pressurized environment to less-crowded conditions in scenic surroundings where they "unwind," relax, enjoy, and rejuvenate themselves.

Some psychologists and correctional institutions are using horses for therapeutic and rehabilitation purposes. Perhaps horses are best used before therapy or rehabilitation is needed.

FIGURE 16-4  The committed horse owner will see to it that the horse is well fed and cared for, not physically or mentally abused, immunized against known killing diseases, and protected from devastating parasites. The owner should also be able to spot changes in the horse which may signify the onset of illness. In return, the horse should be a consistent, willing performer in the activities for which it was trained, without reluctance, resistance, temper, or bad habits. [*Courtesy of Stephens College; photograph by Duane Dailey.*]

Young people who seek the horse "dimension" should be encouraged to do so because it may give them pleasure and enjoyment throughout life (Figure 16-5). They may find a friend in their horse; and as they develop confidence, skills, discipline, and horsemanship, they may gain some admiration from their peers. Responsibility for an animal develops love, understanding, and tolerance for all biological creations.

Horse ownership is a status symbol. It offers membership in an exclusive club of less than 10 percent of our nation's population. Horse persons justifiably take great pride in owning, exhibiting, or riding a good horse. Some families are drawn together by horse interest and totally committed to horse activities.

One father has confided "my daughter and I have been able to communicate from the backs of two horses since she was eleven years old . . . without saying a word."

FIGURE 16-5 The horse "dimension" is never lost. This 87-year-old man and his 85-year-old wife spent 17 days traveling in their covered wagon on the Bicentennial wagon train. [*Courtesy of Mr. and Mrs. L. E. Mayberry, Wentworth, Mo.*]

Almost any inexperienced person can become a good enough horse handler to "fit into a horse group"—it happens every day. If you have always wanted the "horse experience," find a good equitation instructor and start riding lessons. Who knows, it may open new doors in your life!

# Index

Heart rate (*Cont.*)
  respiration rate compared with, 465
Heat cycle of mare, 317–318, 320,
    322–323
  controlling, 318–319
  detection of, 324–325
  foal heat, 320–321
Heaves, 132, 267, 465
Heritability estimates, 314–315
Hernias, 131
Hidalgo (horse), 64
Hierd, Jim C., 281
Hintz, Harold F., 210*n.*, 362*n.*, 541
Hip, knocked-down, 130
History, U.S., horses in, 13–19, 25, 32,
    43–44, 47, 51
Hobbles, 219
Hocks, 107–109, 127
  blemishes, 129
  unsoundnesses, 128
Hoof dressing, 539
Hoof pick, use of, 181–182
Hooves:
  cracks, 123
  growth factors, 540–541
  hardness, 541
  in laminitis, 122–123, 509
  structures, 518–520
  trimming, 527–530
    corrective, 536–539
Hopkins, Frank J., 64
Hopper, Jack, 3*n.*
Hormones:
  control techniques, 319
  of mare, 317, 318
Horse racing, 4
  (*See also* Racehorses)
Horse Registry Association, 21
Horseflies, 489
Horsemanship, 195–238
  definition, 195
  equipment (*see* Tack)
  equitation, 222–233
  observation of horses, 196–198
  showing, 233–238
Horseshoes:
  corrective, 537
  leveling, 533
  removal, 524–525
  selection, 530–531
  shaping, 532, 533
  shoeing procedure, 522–525, 534–536
Hot branding, 276
Houseflies, 487
Housing for horses, 543–555
  construction, 555–557

Housing for horses (*Cont.*)
  young horses, 275
Hughes, I. M., 441
Hunter-seat equitation, 226–227
  bridles, 207–208
  saddles, 199
    trees, 201–202
  in shows, 235–236
Hunting mules, 89–90
Hydroponics, 368
Hyperparathyroidism, 361

Identification of horses, 275–277
Immunity to disease, 468
Immunization, 267, 468–469, 494, 495,
    498, 500
Immunodeficiency, combined, 313–314
In-hand classes, showing in, 236
Inbreeding, 316
Incised wounds, 490
Indians:
  blankets, 217
  Nez Percé, 25
  Plains, 14
Influenza, equine, 498–500
Insects and insect control, 186, 275,
    485–489
International Buckskin Horse Association,
    29, 91
Intestines:
  disorders, 353, 354, 472–474, 504–507
  large, 354
  small, 353–354
Investigative behavior, 163
Iodine, feeding of, 362
Iron:
  amounts in feeds, 445, 447, 449
  requirements, 363
  testing for, 363, 422–423
Issel, C. J., 468*n.*

Jack spavins, 128
Janus (horse), 32–33
Jay Farceur (horse), 77
Jigging horses, 258–259
Jobs in horse industry, 4–6
Jockey Club, 41–43, 55, 95, 273, 277, 344
Johnson, R. J., 441
Johnson, Thula, 457*n.*
Johnson, Virginia Weisel, 457*n.*
Johnson grass, 387
Joint ill (navel ill), 334, 495–496
Jones, William E., 30*n.*
Jordan, Robert, 561